# HOMO HIERARCHICUS

# HOMO HIERARCHICUS
## *The Caste System and Its Implications*

Complete Revised English Edition

## Louis Dumont

TRANSLATED BY MARK SAINSBURY, LOUIS DUMONT,
AND BASIA GULATI

THE UNIVERSITY OF CHICAGO PRESS
CHICAGO AND LONDON

Original French edition, *Homo hierarchicus: Le système des castes et ses implications*, © 1966 by Editions Gallimard
English translation © 1970 by George Weidenfeld and Nicolson Ltd. and by The University of Chicago
Appendices B, C, and D are reprinted from Louis Dumont, *Religion, Politics, and History in India: Collected Papers in Indian Sociology*, © 1970 by Ecole pratique des Hautes Etudes and Mouton & Co.
New Preface and Postface are translations from the TEL edition of *Homo hierarchicus*, © 1979 by S.P.A.D.E.M.
© 1980 by The University of Chicago
All rights reserved. Published 1980
Printed in the United States of America

87 86 85 84 83 82 81 80   54321

**Library of Congress Cataloging in Publication Data**

Dumont, Louis, 1911–
  Homo hierarchicus: the caste system and its implications.
  Bibliography: p.
  Includes index.
  1. Caste—India. I. Title.
HT720.D813   1980   305.5'0954   80-16480
ISBN 0-226-16962-6
ISBN 0-226-16963-4 (pbk.)

Louis Dumont, directeur d'etudes at the Ecole Practique des Hautes Etudes in Paris, received the Silver Medal from the French National Center of Scientific Research in 1967. His many publications include *From Mandeville to Marx*, also published by the University of Chicago Press.

# CONTENTS

# MAPS AND DIAGRAMS

# PREFACE TO THE COMPLETE
# ENGLISH EDITION

*The author is grateful to the University of Chicago Press for bringing out this edition, which is complete in two senses. First and foremost, it includes the three appendices (B, C, and D) that had been left out of the English edition and were, until now, found only in the French. It is gratifying to see the book thus regain its original stature, and it is important to me because, as I explain at length hereafter, each of those texts has marked a stage in the development of my research leading to the final work. Their omission obscured some of its main articulations and the general design and may well have contributed to misunderstandings.*

*This edition, which in the author's mind is definitive, also contains the following new preface, taking stock of the book's reception, and a new postface, dealing briefly with hierarchy in general. They are translated from the French 1979 ('Tel') edition.*

*The existing English text has been revised in certain details to the extent that technical constraints of production have allowed. I take the occasion to renew the expression of my gratitude to the original translator, Mark Sainsbury, whose toil and talent made a success of a difficult job. The text of the newly included appendices has been taken from* Religion, Politics, and History in India: Collected Papers in Indian Sociology *(Paris: Mouton, 1970), hereafter referred to as* Coll. Pap., *in which I had made them available.*

Twelve years after appearing in French and eight years after the publication of an English translation allowing all the specialists of the field to enter the discussion, this work, now reprinted, offers the occasion for a review. The body of the book remains unchanged for substantive as well as technical reasons. The new material is therefore concentrated in the new Preface and Postface.

In principle, our purpose here is to give a reading of the extensive discussion that has centred on *H.H.*, as I shall abbreviate the title, and of the subsequent development of the research. The non-specialist reader may have found strange or even shocking some particular viewpoint or statement found in the work. What are the opinions of the author's colleagues? Should the point be taken as scientifically established or as a gratuitous construct? Where does the matter stand today?

I

As we shall see, the task is not easy. To begin with, the reception accorded *H.H.* was highly complex. It was favourable but limited on the side of classical indology, very elaborate and very contra-dictory on the side of social anthropology, and practically non-existent on the side of sociology proper, where none of the major English-language journals reviewed it.[1] We might also distinguish the more favourable reactions of the French-speaking world from the statistically more hostile ones of the English-speaking world. It would be difficult to characterize the Indian reactions as a whole.

In sum, the discussion has largely been confined to social anthro-pology, as is quite natural. In the following remarks, our concern will be with that discussion, and our attention will be drawn almost exclusively to disagreements, objections, and negative opinions. This might give the impression that *H.H.* met nothing but disap-proval. This is not the case. Thus, we must first roughly charac-terize the book's reception. There have been favourable opinions, of which I shall cite two as exemplary.

J. H. Hutton, a former British official of the Indian Civil Service, who had become an anthropologist well known for his descriptions of the Naga of Assam, and who had been, in the end, a professor at Cambridge University, had written the latest work on the sub-ject twenty years before *H.H.*. Hutton was over eighty (and was to die the following year) when I sent him this book, in which his theory of caste is briefly dismissed (p. xlvi.). He promptly sent a note of congratulations, expressing regret that age kept him from immediately beginning a translation of the work, especially for Indians.

A few years later, I heard from a highly respected man whom I scarcely knew, Nirmal Kumar Bose – anthropologist, devoted ad-ministrator, and convinced Gandhiist (we recall that Gandhi had an egalitarian theory of castes, or at least of varnas) – younger than Hutton, but like him watched for by death. Professor Bose, having read the book in the English translation, sent word of his support in the form of a long review, written for his journal, *Man in India*, and published in a Calcutta newspaper by his friends, in which he expressed reservations only with respect to details.[2] *H.H.* can take pride in these two endorsements, and sometimes one would like to find more of the openmindedness shown by these two veterans in their perhaps more modern, but often less experienced, successors.

Most anthropological criticism of *H.H.* mixes praise and blame. Later we shall try to separate the arguments that are (more or less generally) accepted from the ones that are rejected, but what is distinctive is the mixture of opposite opinions addressing the work as a whole. It is not completely impossible to praise an author while condemning his work, and one also can, and often does, dissociate the theory from its application in order to favour one or the other.[3] Still, the work – condemned, not to say caricatured, here, extolled there (and sometimes meeting both reactions in the same spot) – has been granted an honourable place in the history of caste studies. Let us interpret this observation: all these paradoxes express the fact that the special study of India and, more broadly, the discipline of anthropology are deeply divided in their basic orientations.[4] A major factor in this division lies in the endemic materialist tendency, strongly reinforced by Marxism's hold over many minds. Here, French Marxist dogmatism has been slow to react. At first, serious authors silenced their preferences and surrendered. Eventually, it took an Africanist to give form – in fact, caricatural form – to the necessary refutation.[5]

Three facts govern both the level and the limits of what can be said here of *H.H.*'s place yesterday and today in the social anthropology of India. The scope of the controversy which *H.H.* has aroused calls for some explanation and makes simplification and selection necessary. Moreover, the field has evolved in the past ten years, and certain attitudes are outmoded. Finally, the author himself has moved away from Indian studies and he must take this into account. Let us take up these three points.

*H.H.* has been the subject of numerous reviews, often appearing as review articles, an unpublished public discussion at the 1971 Annual Conference of the American Anthropological Association in New York (No. 302), and two symposia.[6] The book has aroused emotions, a fact that has also contributed to the paradoxical nature of many of the reactions. This is scarcely surprising, for *H.H.* challenged certain attitudes, and its general orientation, as well as the orientation of the earlier *Contributions to Indian Sociology*, vols. 1–9 (1957–66), represented, in the eyes of many colleagues, not a constructive effort but an attack on their own conceptions and the conventions they considered well established. Thus, as a Britisher, for whom battle lines are readily drawn in intellectual debates, Edmund Leach – having first warned a large public of the difficulty of the work – chose to take spontaneous leadership of my 'opponents', writing that those who 'have not been persuaded by [my] earlier arguments will not alter their views now in response to this more sustained onslaught' (*South Asian Review* 4, no. 3 [April 1971]: 233). Again, recently, Owen Lynch has written a 'reply' to *H.H.* in which the book is presented as 'a direct attack on what Dumont considers the inadequacies, ethnocentricity, and distortions, of Anglo-American anthropology' (David 1977, p. 239). I observe that here the part is twice taken for the whole: *H.H.* is more than an attack, and English-language anthropology is more than Lynch's idea of it – I am thinking of E. E. Evans-Pritchard and a few others, for instance. In the Introduction to their symposium (JAS 1976, p. 579), R. W. Nicholas and J. F. Richards recall the 'bewilderment if not [the] derision' that greeted our programmatic statement of 1957, which was an English adaptation by David Pocock of my 1955 inaugural lecture.[7] They add that 'many scholars who remain in disagreement with Dumont over some matters have since come around to the general position established in that paper' (*ibid.*).

This leads me to the second point, the evolution that has taken place in the last ten years or more, going far beyond the domain of India; in anthropology, to some degree, the wind has changed, if I may borrow the expression from the title of a recent work. *The New Wind* (David 1977). In particular, for what concerns us here, certain ill humours have become subdued or transformed. Here are three examples of these changes. The same Edmund Leach who wrote in 1971 (p. 235) that the distinction presented in *H.H.* between status (hierarchical) and power (political) was a 'subtle and complicated proposition [that] is not revealed by the empirical data [and that] raises all sorts of practical and theoretical difficulties', in fact adopts this distinction when he writes in 1977 that in ancient Hinduism 'the brahman stood above the king, and the secular moral order of the kingship ... embracing the domain of politics and economics (*artha*) ... was not seen as the moral basis of society as a whole' (*Times Literary Supplement*, 14 January 1977, p. 22). In 1972 S. J. Tambiah amassed objections to the same view (*American Anthropologist* 74:832–35, esp. 833a). But he takes it up again on his own account in 1976 when he writes that, according to the Hindu formulation, 'moral authority was incarnated in the Brahman, temporal power in the king; that while spiritually the priest was superior, materially he was dependent on the king' (cf. my text below, App. C, p. 290) and he adopts my conclusion for South-East Asia (p. 215–16 below) when he adds that in South-East Asia there is a return – in spite of the influence of the Indian culture – to the 'prototypical situation of divine kingship' (*World Conqueror and World Renouncer* [Cambridge, 1976], p. 99). Of course, it remains to be seen whether these two 'opponents', having adopted my thesis for ancient India, continue to reject it for contemporary India.

Even *H.H.*'s most declared enemy has appreciably modified his language. In 1969 McKim Marriott introduced *H.H.* as containing 'a speculative sketch of a pair of models, strongly shaped by the author's personal ideology of social science and documented mainly with theoretical, textual, and philosophic allusions' (*American Anthropologist* 71 [1969] col. 1168a). In a 1976 correspondence he writes, 'We are pursuing further much the same sort of enterprise as Dumont undertook in the fifties, and are doing so similarly by bringing together contrastively some findings of anthropology ... with some findings of indology .... Like him we are weighing alternative formulations, and not yet speaking of exhaustive proofs. We share with Dumont ...' (*Journal of Asian Studies* 36:1 [November 1976]: 190). This example clearly differs from the preceding ones in that it indicates a radical change on the level of strategy.

Let it not be concluded from this that the theses offered in *H.H.* have finally been accepted. The situation is more complex; it is ambiguous. These modifications or evolutions simply invite us to detach ourselves from temporary attitudes and superficial reactions in order to concentrate on deeper and more durable traits.

I have mentioned a third fact, less important in itself, which bears on the author of these lines. Following the course of my own research, I have, over the course of the past years, moved away from Indian studies and turned back to the ideological system that characterizes modern civilization (*cf. From Mandeville to Marx*). In doing this, I have by and large lost contact with contemporary Indian research as a whole. I must therefore be careful not to act as though I had maintained the same familiarity as in 1962 – the last year of the systematic bibliographical analysis for *H.H.* –with a literature that has accumulated at an ever-increasing pace. In short, I must keep in mind a lessening of my competence and not simply avoid making diagnoses, but give up the idea of offering a picture of even the most important recent works. In compensation, I can see better than in 1965 or 1966 the link between certain attitudes of anthropologists and the surrounding ideology, can emphasize this aspect, and shall later consider in this spirit recent developments which refer back explicitly to *H.H.*

These three facts taken together compel us to limit our discussion to the main questions, single out, as much as possible, collective orientations rather than individual, sometimes ephemeral, reactions, and, when necessary, to record without discussion certain statements of position.


2

In the case of *H.H.* it is clear that the resistance to innovation has been strongly reinforced by the aversion to hierarchy prevailing in modern societies. One may find that I put too much emphasis on this point, but, to use a contemporary expression, hierarchy is at the heart of the 'unthought' (*l'impensé*) of modern ideology, and it would be unreasonable to expect the anthropologist to be exempt from this common reaction or to overcome it without a concerted effort and patient exercise. This situation explains not only the antipathy of some, but also the reservations and misunderstandings that are intermingled with positive opinions.

The book has rarely been considered on its own terms, as a sort of experiment (pp. xvii, 212). We confront a complex ensemble in which we recognize the presence of numerous phenomena described, in a first approximation, as 'hierarchical'. The experiment consists of putting these phenomena in the foreground and attempting to draw out their principle as the guiding principle of the whole ensemble. In the process, the various sorts of data fall into place remarkably well (*cf.* for a recapitulation CIS 1971, pp. 215–17), and, in parallel, the notion of hierarchy is refined by stages: values and rank (§7), the gradation principle of the elements relative to the ensemble (§31), and beginning only with section 34, the 'encompassing and encompassed'. Hierarchy is both clarified and brought to life for us by what is, in fact, a complex process, one that it has not been possible to indicate with as much precision as is desirable. On the one hand, there is the idea for which I am indebted to Raymond Apthorpe. It is the idea of the hierarchical relation as a relation between the encompassing and the encompassed (for all of this, see the Postface, p. 239). On the other hand, Indian society is seen to correspond to this idea; it appears in this light as the concrete manifestation of hierarchy, and thus teaches us to recognize hierarchy *in vivo* with its connexions and implications. In a word, it makes the idea *visible* to us. It is indeed true that *H.H.* includes no theory of hierarchy (Nur Yalman, *Man* 4, no. 1 [March 1969]: 124). The intent was to 'isolate' it, as they say in chemistry, and to do so by a process moving in two directions, consisting, so to speak, in universalizing India, while making our concepts concrete.

Very few have been willing to go along with the author in this approach. Thus, the conception of hierarchy in *H.H.* has been criticized independently of what it accomplishes in the book while constructing itself. Above all it was said that I had confused different things under this term – and, in fact, it was important to lose nothing – and yet people have not bothered to inquire whether, in the end, a single principle had been brought out. At bottom, the approach itself was rejected in the name of prevailing canons.

One may draw a sort of composite picture of *H.H.*'s unfavourable reception by Anglo-American anthropologists. It would be a tree called 'anthropological empiricism', a powerful tree, solidly rooted in empirical commonsense, but its trunk would rise far above its roots, reaching the altitude of scientism, and dividing, in our case, into four branches raised like so many gallows: condemnation for betrayal of empirical data; condemnation for an approach focussing on ideas and representations (and for French intellectualism); condemnation for the inclusion of ancient texts in the study of contemporary society; and finally and most important, condemnation for the distinction proposed in *H.H.*, and in fact central to it, between status and power, which is rejected chiefly, we may suppose, because political and economic power is a solid, universal, and 'infrastructural' given, and because it is scandalous to emancipate hierarchical status from it – as hierarchical status is hardly more than a fantasy, or at best an aspect of the social 'superstructure'.

The first condemnation is basic and more or less governs the others. Through my 'cavalier attitude toward the empirical data' (CIS 1971, p. 9), I am said to have, in general and from the start, forsaken empiricality-cum-empiricism, without which scientific knowledge is impossible. If I introduce a distinction here, and a seeming neologism, it is both as a claim to have been soundly empirical and as a challenge to the whims and pretensions of empiricism.[8]

Empiricality, as we know, prescribes personal experience and field inquiry; it also calls for a cautious approach, the collection of as much information as possible, and the questioning, when necessary, of accepted ideas. Empiricism, on the contrary, values so highly its own categories and the techniques implementing them that it authorizes radical cuts in the data and the more or less definitive adoption of limited viewpoints; it minimizes the importance of the cultural environment, and it has even begun to erode – but I cannot develop the point here – the primacy of fieldwork.[9] One may compare the writer and his critics from this point of view. Those who have no experience of India nonetheless pronounce categorical judgments on points where that experience is relevant. Thus Leach, however important his studies may be in other respects, knows India only at second hand; still, he opines that I steer away from 'the empirical jati ( = caste) which *we encounter* in twentieth-century India' in favour of an ancient configuration. I have italicized two words that are obviously to be taken figuratively (Leach 1971, p. 235). Among those who did fieldwork in India who radically criticize *H.H.*, I know of none who has subjected himself to an empirical discipline comparable to that reflected in the chronological list of my own studies (*cf.* the bibliography in JAS 1976, pp. 647–50). I shall mention only a few aspects of it here. To begin, there is the most complete description we have of an Indian group (*Sous-caste*, written between 1952 and 1954), covering all aspects of social life, from techniques to law and religion. If this monograph – of a type that is classic, but which at least in England, was already held in disfavour – had not remained the only one of its kind, we would have at our disposal today, given the number of enquiries completed in the interval, an ethnographic picture on the scale of the subcontinent, as a basis upon which to build. We do have works of other types, and, in certain respects, more advanced and highly detailed, but of limited scope; but we also have many brilliant elaborations that are like so many pyramids standing on their points. There is a great risk that the immense ethnographic wealth of India may finally disappear as Europe's has, without having been recorded as well as the available means permit. The blame will lie with empiricism and its overestimation of its own techniques as against the concrete culture. In anthropology, empiricism culminates in a scientism that tends, ultimately, to put us in the power of technocracy.

I have not exhausted the empirical complexity of my South-Indian ethnographic work, for the monograph just mentioned was lent support by a little comparative-regional study. This study led, on the one hand, to formulations later applied to a famous case, adjacent but external to the region, that of the Nayar (here, specialists have subsequently corrected my information in points of detail but have not cast doubt on the argument) and later proven more broadly generalizable on the level of India. On the other hand, it resulted in a general theory of marriage alliance (recently challenged by Harold W. Scheffler in *American Anthropologist* 79, no. 4 [December 1977]: 869–82). That was the first stage.

There followed a series of elaborations, of which the four main ones constitute the appendices of the present edition. The earliest, and most important in the sense that it provides the main framework for all my later work, both on India itself and beyond that setting, is the theory of renunciation. Beginning with a hypothesis formulated in 1955 (Dumont 1957, pp. 16–17), I used both the results of observation (*Sous-caste*) and, in a somewhat widened sense, the well-known institution, classic but still alive, of world renunciation, to propose a relatively unitary view of Indian religions and their history ('World Renunciation in Indian Religions', App. B).[10] The anthropological study of the present was thus applied, to be sure, in a complex and indirect manner, to the understanding of the historical past. Further, it appeared little by little that with the notion of the individual-outside-the-world (the renouncer), the comparison with the West was greatly facilitated, to the point of providing a comparative point of departure for the study of modern individualism.[11]

I must apologize to the nonspecialist reader for having left all this in the form of a twenty-five-page scholarly essay, but the necessary clarification has begun, for a few indologists have taken up the argument for themselves and have utilized it. Madeleine Biardeau, who developed it, is correct in saying that I have left to others the task of systematically bringing to light the impact of renunciation on society.[12]

The next study, 'The Conception of Kingship in Ancient India' (App. C), offers a second incursion into ancient India, this time concerning the conception of kingship. It is different from the first and, on the whole, has been quite poorly received. I should like to discuss it briefly. This text is, in fact, a fragment of a work on ancient Indian society.[13] The aim was to define Indian kingship *comparatively*, and to do this in an intellectual atmosphere distinguished by a pronounced tendency, among indologists as well as anthropologists, to make light of religious functions that, on the contrary, there is reason to attribute, generally or in principle, to the king (*cf.* n. 32g). Yet the conclusion, which states that the royal function in India has been secularized from an early date, was found suspicious, if not revolting. Later we shall discuss anthropologists' objections, but classical indologists seem not to have been convinced either. At the very least, Biardeau's opposition, succinct as it is, should be indicated, given, among other reasons, her incomparable familiarity with the epics. It cannot be considered in context here, but one may simply wonder whether the comparative perspective has not, in this case, given way to a purely Indian perspective that dissociates, as do others, representations from institutions.[14]

This study is basic to the next stage, where the sociologists' accepted notion of 'social stratification' is set in opposition to the idea of social hierarchy borrowed from India ('Caste, Racism, and "Stratification,"' App. A, esp. §E, p. 251). This essay now appears in several readers. The discussion continues, as is normal and desirable, and there is no reason to go over it again. We shall simply observe that, in sum, the main point is to give primacy to meaning (the hierarchy) over the mere external form (stratification). In this sense, this essay's dedication to Evans-Pritchard is not misplaced.

Appendix D, 'Nationalism and Communalism', focusing on an attempt to provide a comparative definition of the 'nation' as a modern concept, bears on recent history (and presupposes that of the nineteenth century; *cf.* 'The British in India').

All the works that have just been reviewed are basic to *H.H.* If the empiricists fail to see their relevance – as they think that one may delimit at will the field of each of one's undertakings – it seems to me, at least, that the empirical requirement of the widest possible information and of the recognition of the historical dimension has been met.

This is all very well, one will say, but that is not the point; the point is the book itself, and first of all the misuse in *H.H.* of ethnographic data. An extreme criticism from Gerald Berreman states that 'hierarchy' is simply a lure: the superior castes' conception of the social system and theirs alone has been espoused; the Brahmins have been heard, the Untouchables have not. No doubt most observers do not share this view, but it has the virtue of showing a naive faith in egalitarianism that is, in its pure form, a state of mind more subtly present in other critics. One can detect, in this case, the working of a widespread fallacy, which I would call 'the fallacy of equal traits.' My intention was not to claim that in India there has never been the slightest trace of equality as a tendency or even as a norm, nor to deny the differences between the larger or smaller regions (Berreman's study was undertaken in the Indian Himalayas), nor to fail to recognize more or less modern movements.[15] I meant to isolate the predominant ideological note of a social system in relation to its morphology. Now one frequently encounters the demand that all observed traits be put on the same plane, that all be accorded the same weight, that proportions be neglected, which is to say that egalitarianism should be projected into the object.[16] Whoever does not do so will stand accused of failing to account for the entire data, of offering a partial and distorted image of it.

One more misunderstanding seems to me attributable to the powerful action of our ideals and values in the building of our representations. It has sometimes been thought that *H.H.* praises or approves the caste system, whereas it seeks only to understand it. One critic has found it possible to write that I have presented 'the ideal Vedic society as the best of all possible worlds.' From the pen of no less an anthropologist than Leach (1971, p. 236), as whimsical as he may be on occasion, the fact must set us thinking. At this point, one remembers that Lévi-Strauss was able to compare 'totem' and 'caste' with subtlety without in the least thinking of hierarchy (*La pensée sauvage*, 1962, pp. 144–77).

Let us return to the question of the handling of ethnographic data. Various writers, of whom two are benevolent witnesses, find a marked separation between text and notes in *H.H.* In her generous preface to the Paladin edition (Granada Books, 1972), Mary Douglas writes that the etiquette of erudition has here been pushed to the extreme, that the concern for documentation and the discussion of conflicting views are sometimes tiring (pp. 11, 14). She would plainly have preferred a more independent, more openly personal exposé, and this accords with the dominant tendency in the contemporary literature. But I wished to recognize and integrate all that I took as established, to mark carefully the boundary between this zone of consensus and my attempts to go beyond it, and to justify differences and rejections. Here, as in *Sous-caste* and elsewhere, the orientation of the work is essentially collective. A nonspecialist was able to recognize this without apparent difficulty[17], thus casting light indirectly on one of the profession's current aberrations that strongly resembles a 'personality cult'.

T. N. Madan distinguishes between text and notes in a slightly different way; for him the notes are 'a supplementary work', the orientation of the work is essentially theoretical and deductive, and the author is 'concerned only secondarily with ascertaining the "fit" between [the model] and contemporary social reality', hence the 'devaluation of the ethnographic datum' of which some have complained (CIS 1971, p. 4). The good faith of the commentator is here beyond question, and yet I must protest energetically; the 'model' is given in order to account for 'contemporary social reality' entirely in the perspective governed by social anthropology. If another model does it more economically, this one must be rejected. I believe Madan here confuses the order of the exposition (see p. xlvii below) and the progress of the research. I state that I have always given the last word to observed reality, as indeed Madan acknowledges at several points (CIS 1971, p. 6). I think this is confirmed by the fact that, when necessary, I have emphasized the difficulties the argument contains and the antinomies it draws near, so that critics who wish to stress them often need only quote the text, as Tambiah (1972, col. 833a) has skill-fully done. There the issue bears on the status/power distinction and, in fact, the claimed devaluation of the empirical data is fo-cused on this crucial point. If one wishes, there is certainly deval-uation in the sense that not all the empirical data are situated at the same level of ideology. The objection really bears on the hierarchization of traits. We shall have to return later to this point.

From an empiricist point of view, one could not fail to protest with regard to *H.H.*, as was formerly done with regard to the pro-grammatic statement of the *Contributions* of 1957, the primacy given to ideas and values, the excessive recourse to abstractions, in brief, and according to the savory formula of one critic, the 'Gallic intemperate intellectualism' of the author, and also the introduc-tion of ancient texts to the study of contemporary society. These reproaches are a bit dated in the sense that the two aspects criti-cized have since been enfranchised by some, and, on occasion, by the critics themselves. I shall not, therefore, go back once more to first principles but only specify a few points. First to get rid of the reference to nationality. *H.H.* laid itself open to this criticism at two points: First, by its declared allegiance (pp. xlv–xlvi) to the French tradition of sociology. There as elsewhere, my intent was to identify the predominant feature and briefly characterize the general perspective. More important is the fact that the introduc-tion to the book, having to lead the reader from the common-sense viewpoint to the viewpoint of the work itself, readily takes *French* common sense as its point of departure. As modern ideology dif-fers, subtly if one likes, from one country to another, a foreign reader may have the impression here that the Introduction is not addressed to him. As soon as an author steps out of the rarified setting of the scientific discipline to greet the reader in somewhat concrete terms, he confronts the existence of *national variants* of modern ideology. There is nothing disturbing about the event; quite the contrary.[18] But the fact remains that *H.H.* would require a slightly different Introduction in English or in German, for instance.

What was clear for the writer in 1955 or 1957 has, to some degree, compelled recognition since then: an intransigent nomin-alism, for which only individuals exist, a summary materialism, or a functionalism, doubtless shaken, but which persists in closing off the historical dimension – none of these could find favour with one who proposed applying social anthropology to the study of a vast society historically the bearer of a great civilization. There is one point I should like to make once again. When, by chance, the discussion of these questions with empiricists does not bog down, but deepens, one can perceive the essential difference between the study of thinking and acting men and the study of behaviour, as would be made of insects, occasionally sprinkled with more or less epiphenomenal indigenous representations. The difference depends on the depth of the scholar's motivation: either he is ready to challenge himself in his own representations, the better to understand the other, or else he is reluctant to do this and, consequently, refers what he observes and experiences to a system of essentially immutable coordinates. The relation to the other is deepened by the consideration of ideas and values. The refusal to focus attention on ideologies is tantamount to the scholar's refusal to challenge himself in his research. It is true that this challenge can only be empirical and piecemeal; one challenges now one representation, whether familiar or scientific, that is found to obtrude, now, perhaps, another one. One cannot wipe out at once one's own consciousness, nor all the conceptual apparatus of the discipline, upon which its members depend to communicate with one another. It is this last point that appears more clearly today, as we shall see.

The 'intellectualism' of H.H. has been criticized for leading naturally to an unjustified use of scholarly Indian texts of ancient origin, sometimes described as 'esoteric'. Their use has been considered irrelevant, excessive, and irritating. On this point empiricist critics have been nearly unanimous. Here again, things have changed to the point that these complaints might well apply at present to some of the critics. I should like briefly to describe the use made of old texts in H.H. In a milieu dominated by present-day (synchronic) structuro-functionalist analysis – which, rejecting speculation on 'origins', excluded, in the same breath, history – the reintroduction of past states in any form whatsoever must have seemed like a 'mixture' of two things that should have been kept separate. But, with respect to H.H., it is inaccurate to speak of a 'reiterated mixture of Vedic ideas and contemporary facts' (Leach 1971, pp. 235–36). In the first place, the consideration of the past is clearly distinguished from that of the present. Two parts (Appendices B and C) relate essentially to the past. As for the text, it contains four short and precisely delimited explorations into the ancient texts, and in each case the relation to the present is explicitly established at the level, not of isolated details, but of the delineated ensemble (cf.§25.3–4 and particularly the concluding paragraph of §25.4; §32 and what immediately precedes and follows it; §57; and §65). It is only on pages 165–66 and 167–68 that one might speak of a 'mixture', but there our concern was with the fundamental Indian categories of the 'structure of social action' – to speak with Talcott Parsons. As to 'Vedic' ideas, only one deserves this name and we shall return to it shortly.

In view of certain recent developments, it seems appropriate for me to explain in detail how the relation between present and past is conceived and utilized in *H.H.* What is known of the past, on the plane of general and, more or less, preliminary information, is useful to the anthropologist. This is the first point, which can be cast in doubt by empiricists only because they underestimate the chanciness of direct observation and interpretation. The second point is Mauss's: the present has an advantage over the past. He said it often; the intensive study of the present by the anthropologist, because it is complete by definition – which excludes the arbitrary delimitations of empiricism that slice up the social domain – is incomparable for bringing to light relations, configurations, or structures in the social datum, in contrast to historical data, always fragmentary. Once such a configuration is isolated in the present – as a real and not a nominal system, as that of the empiricist – one may hope to find something of it in the past, and to use it to put in an intelligible order what often appears in the hands of classical indology, which is essentially philology, as a purely accidental collection.[19] Such has been my approach, and what is astonishing is that it has not been used earlier. The fruits had been ripe since the turn of the century, thanks to Mauss, the Sanskritist-cum-anthropologist, and the Durkheimian school, and – except for the absence of 'distinctive opposition', perhaps decisive – one may imagine that, had it not been for World War I, they would have been gathered thirty years earlier. What is more, the harvest has only begun.

I may be blamed, having introduced this apparent novelty, for not having specified the procedure I followed. I think the following two points can be verified: (1) I have always used ensembles, large or small, defined without arbitrariness, whose relation to the ensembles of the present is beyond question; (2) I have always considered representations in relation to *institutions*. Let me make this second point explicit. One may imagine an exegesis that would be based essentially on Brahmanic texts, the conceptions of educated men. This exegesis has sometimes been mistakenly attributed to me, while some scholars seem to approximate it today. The only texts I considered were texts dealing directly with social relations, and, in the past as in the present, the representations I took as basic related – I was going to say 'to social morphology'; let us rather say, to institutions in the broad sense of the term. Thus, renunciation is an institution, or, to select a more limited feature, the dichotomy of the Kallar temples into pure and impure gods – without any immediate Brahmanic influence (*Sous-caste*, p. 32 and *passim*) – is for me one such institution that does justice to Mr. Berreman's daydreaming. For it is not a literary matter, or a matter of pure representation, more or less gratuitous or exceptional; it is a basic feature of these people's religion, which is not in any way marginal.

This went so much without saying for me that I did not underscore it (just as I did not mention the Kallar fact in this book). In sum, the ideology that *H.H.* has tried to isolate is always seen in immediate relation with the most constant and most constraining social practice. This stands in complete contrast to the flights that 'symbolic analysis' has invited us to behold in the past several years in the same domain; the ethereal image that empiricist adversaries have tried to conjure from my book is the product of their imaginations.

There is, however, one point on which I have overstepped my programme – a central point. Present-day India has raised a problem for contemporary research, that of the general relation between the dominant caste and the Brahmanic caste at the local level (§74.2). It was clear that what we call 'dominant caste' in the village in fact reproduces at this level the royal function, which, with some exceptions, can no longer be observed. During an exploration of ancient India (App. C), I happened to find among some very old ritualists a formulation – which may, for once, be called 'Vedic' – of the relationship between the Brahmans and the king that perfectly solved the contemporary problem. I borrowed it from them, thus admitting a continuity or rather a permanence in this respect between the present and a very ancient period and bringing a feature borrowed from a distant past into the present. Doubtless this is one of the reasons for the scandal that was provoked. Still, it is true that anyone wanting to limit himself to the present may, if he likes, disregard the origin of the formulation (as I have said in CIS 1971, p. 68). What is exceptional about the case methodologically is that it is not ourselves, but ancient authors who, on a page of their treatises, have characterized the basic relation in question. Further, in this manner they refer us back from the innumerable castes of today to the four classical varnas, which are thus proven to be not only the historical basement of the caste ideology, but its implicit support. For this reason I have introduced them as early as the third chapter. If the varnas are a 'Vedic idea', I must plead guilty. But who could fail to see that they are much more than that, much more than Vedic and much more than an 'idea'? The resulting theory is complicated, doubtless, and goes beyond the synchronic plane, but, though it has 'irritated' some, it has yet to be replaced.

I have already mentioned that the use of texts is now accepted. Unfortunately, their use is often deficient. Leaving aside whimsicalities, to which I shall later allude, I shall take as an example a work that has every external appearance of being serious but in which the anthropologically normal relation of the present with the past is reversed for tendentious purposes. I refer to the long article by S. J. Tambiah entitled 'Dowry, Brideprice, and the Property Rights of Women in South Asia.'[20] The topic is not irrelevant to the caste system, but that is not our concern here. It is first of all surprising to see that where the question bears essentially on India, material recognized as marginal (from Ceylon and Burma) occupies half the work. Further, two observations may be made: the writer sets up his paradigms and deals with the Dharma texts *before* summarizing the present state of anthropological knowledge relative to contemporary India. Moreover, he places the marriage prestations under the exclusive aegis of *property* and inheritance. In fact, the second observation explains the first: the juridical texts, concerned above all with property, suit the author better than contemporary descriptions and analyses. Far from interpreting these Brahmanic texts in the light of popular custom directly apprehended, he prefers to take as his point of departure an 'intriguing' category like *sulka*, to apply a hypothetical reasoning ('as if') to it, and to observe that the interpretation thus constructed

'holds good for contemporary marriage payments as well' (pp.
86–87). He then, quite accurately, sums up contemporary studies,
but it is in order to lay their conclusions on the procrustean bed of
categories made beforehand. Where anthropology has shown an
*exchange* of prestations that is irreducible to the simple transmittal
of property and that valorizes affinal relations (I am thinking of my
own work), Tambiah reintroduces, with the aid of official jurists,
property and its transmission as the essential preoccupation (T. N.
Madan points out just this fact in CIS 9, no. 2 [1975]: 235–57).
The aim is, moreover, acknowledged by the authors in the preface:
'our aim is to by-pass, shortcut, even eliminate such arguments
[on questions of kinship] by calling attention to the nature of property relations' (p. ix). The texts, in short, serve to insure the
victory of materialism over the conclusions of conscientious anthropological work. If I dwell on the fact, it is because I myself
have studied these texts in the course of preparing an unpublished
essay on ancient India (see above, n. 13) and have touched on the
question in this book (n. 54c). Here, as elsewhere, the texts, in so
far as one can find a reflection of customs in them, 'substantialize'
things (see below, App. B, n. 14), and this appeals to an author
wishing to put a *substance*, property, in the place of that *relation
par excellence* which marriage, or rather intermarriage, is in India.
Must basic facts be recalled? Can one explain the considerable
sumptuary expenses that accompany marriage by reference to
property and inheritance?

Allusion has been made in the preceding paragraphs to the empiricists' fourth main criticism of *H.H.*: they reject the distinction
between status (hierarchical) and power (political) as proposed
therein. Let it pass for the relationship of king and Brahman in
ancient India, but is the relation in modern India between the
dominants and the Brahman who serves them radically different?
What is, perhaps, particularly inadmissible in the eyes of the
empiricist is that the theory contradicts itself and is thus impossible to refute, to 'falsify'. If the two functions oppose one another
on a major level as is claimed, one cannot accept that they should
intermingle and that power should be equivalent to purity at a
minor level. One demands that the relation remain the same
throughout – homogeneous or monolithic – or that it should not be
said to exist.

At this point, one thinks of McKim Marriott, who has actually proposed going beyond *H.H.* with the aid of monism (Marriott 1976a). For him dualism is Western, India is monist. Therefore, a monist perspective is more faithful to Indian culture. Let us avoid these very general propositions. Let us also avoid seeing a 'dualism' in every distinctive opposition, as the monist himself has certainly to make distinctions (he does so, and his distinctions are sometimes far from current, as for example *dharma/çarīra*, whose source he does not give). Let us ask a more limited question: to what degree does *H.H.*'s 'dualism', or its 'dualisms', represent the introduction of an element foreign to India? I see two basic 'dualisms' in the book. First of all, a methodological 'dualism' implicit in Evans-Pritchard's very simple presentation of the an-thropologist's work:

As ethnographer, he goes to live among a primitive people and learns their way of life. He learns to speak their language, to think in their concepts, and to feel in their values. He then lives this experience over again critically and interpretatively in the conceptual categories and values of his own culture and in terms of the general body of knowledge of his discipline. In other words, he translates from one culture into another. (*Social Anthropology* 1951, p. 61).

Does Marriott believe he can rid himself of this dualism? If so, his monism deserves the name of mysticism and his 'ethnosociol-ogy' is akin to theosophy. The claim to master the whole field of India's vast and complex literatures in the different disciplines (Marriott 1976a, pp. 193–94) and the incredible levity of Marriott and his disciples towards philological knowledge (the intermingling of unlike notions, etc.) tend in this direction. As some of his critics have remarked, Marriott passes directly from behaviour (trans-action) to signification; he 'intuits' meaning (Barnett, Fruzzetti, Ostor, in JAS 1976, p. 634–35).

The other 'dualism' of *H.H.* is the hierarchical dualism, the status/power distinction. Here Marriott has a good part of the pro-fession behind him, as we have seen earlier. The situation can be summed up in this way: if one seeks a simple representation of the society on the plane of values, one finds that the major, or 'maxi-mal', representation, the ultimate one (i.e., the opposition of pure and impure), although encompassing all the others, fails to account for them. At the secondary levels, the representation contradicts itself by becoming fused with its opposite. One asks for a consis-tent explanation or representation that takes account of the data without exception or omission. One finds that this condition is not fulfilled and concludes that the interpretation is not valid, that it has permitted itself excessive liberties.

Now, what is it, in the final analysis, that is demanded here? It is that a global ideology should cover without contradiction the entire field of its application, uniformly and without distinction of levels, and at the limit, that it should not leave in the observed object any irreducible residue, that is to say, that the 'dualism' of observer and observed, hence the anthropological situation itself, should be suppressed. But if it is shocking for some, as for the monist Marriott, that our absolute view (without relation to the observer) of the society or culture should be thus intimately bound to the existential situation, so to speak, of the observer, it is on the contrary satisfying to us, for it gives us the assurance that we have not made a leap beyond our mode of knowing, but, on the contrary, have preserved, with its limits, its authenticity.

In short, the demand expressed by the critics is for a 'true' ideology, that is, identical in its breadth and content to the reality as lived. This requirement is that of idealism, and it is surprising to see it formulated by the same critics who have reproached us in the name of empiricism for granting too much importance to ideas and values. At the most general level, what our conclusion means is that hierarchical ideology, like egalitarian ideology, is not perfectly realized in actuality, or, in other terms, does not allow direct consciousness of all that it implies. Our critics themselves would no doubt feel distressed at any contrary conclusion.

Let us return to the hierarchy of levels. I think India here teaches us a universal fact – and this also seems to me to show that we have treated it appropriately. In fact, it is only in our egalitarian ideology that reality appears on a single plane and as composed of equivalent atoms. We carry with us everywhere this flat and uniform view of reality and experience, thanks to the specialization that allows analytic planes of this type to be multiplied, all in principle homogeneous throughout their extent and independent from one another as to orientation and situation. Numerous criticisms, of which I have mentioned several, arise from the application of this viewpoint. On the contrary, sociology and the life sciences in general must recognize the organization of the data in hierarchized levels (*cf.* Dumont 1978).

3

After giving this response, perhaps overlong, to my critics, I should like to see what becomes of *H.H.* in contemporary research. I shall limit myself here to a few works that make more or less explicit reference to it in terms of leading ideas and conclusions, and shall try to distinguish the general lines.

In *H.H.* I have proposed to show in the caste system a devaluation of power in the common sociological sense of the term. This feature runs counter to modern thought, and one would expect to see it called into question. Susan Wadley has done just this, in the conclusion of her monograph on religion in one village of the gangetic plain.[21] One might merely observe that the 'power' she speaks of is not the same as that which I considered. This is clear when she writes; 'Brahmins are both the most powerful beings and the most pure beings' (p. 186). But we must complete the argument: Wadley prefers her notion of power to mine because it is truly indigenous, having been isolated by an analysis of religion, the domain in which one has the best opportunity to discover ultimate values. In order to avoid confusion here, I would call Wadley's 'power' by a different name, say potency (*puissance*).

It should first be said that we are indebted to Wadley for having given the first detailed picture of popular religion in this region, including the extensive literature, oral and fixed, related to it. She has chosen to focus her analysis on the notion of 'power', which she uses to define the supernatural, the gods. Two points must be made. We observe first that this is not a comparative definition, as 'power', or potency, is doubtless an attribute of the gods of all religions. Nor is it even a definition properly speaking, for we are told at the same time that 'power' is not a distinctive attribute of the gods; 'power' (potency) is scattered among all beings and things, on this earth as in other worlds, and it is, moreover, this trait that lets the author apply the notion to the society at large. No doubt this 'power' is not everywhere present in the same fashion or to the same degree, but the author makes no attempt to refine or qualify her definition. Such as it is, this definition, stated a priori, is surprising, for in this matter, what at first glance would characterize India is not the 'power' of the gods, but rather the continuity between the 'supernatural' and the natural, the fact that human beings (the bridegroom) or objects (the tools of labour) may, in certain situations, be the object of what we call a 'cult' (*pūjā*) similar to that offered to the gods.

What does this mean? We cannot discuss in detail here a work that, for its descriptions alone, merits our respect. Our concern is this concept, stated from the beginning, that the author believes expresses the essence of religion. Must we believe that it has no validity? In fairness to Wadley, I think it must be granted that she has perceived something. I think that she has perceived a continuity, a 'monism', as her teacher Marriott would say, an attitude that covers the whole field of realationships, something one would prefer to call, as a first approximation, a 'feeling of dependency'. That one can indicate the same thing by the terms 'feeling of dependency' or 'power' shows the gulf that can separate two interpretations. To return to our concern, it will be easily understood that the universality of such a feeling of dependency does not constitute an argument against the status/power relation of *H.H.*, which is situated in a wholly different sphere.

Another, very different, attempt to link closely status and power is offered by Tambiah. Among the 'timeless truths' about the caste system 'enshrined' in the treatises, he thinks he has disclosed two principles, or orders, of pure and impure; in addition to an 'inverse order' corresponding to status, he sees a 'direct order' corresponding to 'privilege and dominance', for example, 'access to women' (of the lower varnas) [22]. This last point has been taken up again by F. A. Marglin, who has stated that 'power is at the heart of the hierarchy of caste', while, at the same time, she has limited the power of which she speaks to 'certain privileges in terms of access to women, occupations, and wealth'. [23]

The authors that remain to be considered have in common the fact that they figure a movement of development beyond *H.H.*, which might be called a 'new wind', by broadening the meaning K. David has given to the expression as a title for a rather heterogeneous symposium. More exactly, these authors have, at different levels, combined or synthesized two distinct perspectives into an original and, in their eyes, better approach.

The relation to *H.H.* is purely external in the case of Marriott. True, in the curious correspondence quoted above (Marriott 1976a), he presented himself as the avenging heir of a predecessor who had ultimately taken the wrong tack, going beyond the dualism that he imputes to me by means of a monism in fact meta-anthropological. However, there is here nothing more, as the detail of the text shows, than a bypassing 'strategy', as Marriott might say. In reality, Marriott's former transactionalism – according to which the gradation of ranks results from points marked in the exchanges of food – has been combined with the analysis of culture, or of symbols and meanings, in the manner of David Schneider, thanks to a monist metaphysic that permits them to coincide like matter and idea. The empirical bond between representations and institutions is in large measure abandoned, and the scholar is free to draw as he likes from the vast thesaurus of Indian literature for the notions that suit him. He does this unstintingly, and in Marriott and certain of his followers one finds a syncretism of disparate notions, taken out of context, which goes far beyond the known feats of Hinduist popularization.[24] Here there is truly a 'mixture' of contemporary reality and fragments torn from the literature. Thus, for example, when Marvin Davis presents a highly ambitious picture in which the three basic tendencies called *guna* are represented now as active and now as suppressed in each of the four varnas, one is led to believe, in the absence of any contrary indication, that this picture seeks to reproduce a view that would be common to Bengali informants and various texts,[25] which is naturally improbable.

As for Kenneth David (in *The New Wind*; see n. 6), he starts from the idea that *H.H.*'s intellectualism, on the one hand, and empiricism or 'sociostructuralism', on the other, are reductive, take the part for the whole, and so forth. To go beyond them, he develops a level intermediate between ideology and behaviour, a level of what he calls 'normative schemata'. He finds three of these. In addition, he identifies 'codes of conduct' (between men and between men and gods) and, within the mode of conduct governing men of different castes, he finds two modes of relation, the 'obligatory' mode and the 'free' mode. The material thus atomized – it comes from the Tamils of Jaffna and is in itself quite interesting and rich in several respects – calls throughout for a hierarchization to give it unity, but in vain, for the aim of the operation is, precisely, to be able to juxtapose differences – between castes, between contexts, and so forth – by giving equal weight to each case or particular aspect. Equality is saved, but the unity of the culture and the society is sacrificed. It is, however, true that an experienced eye can catch a glimpse of this unity; as arbitrary as the method may sometimes be, the material is rich enough, and, on the whole, faithfully enough treated that one may see – counter to the author's intention – how it tends to order itself.

Another kind of combination or synthesis claims kinship with *H.H.* I am indebted to its three authors, Steve Barnett, Lina Fruzzetti, and Akos Ostor, for their valiant defence and illustration of *H.H.* in a symposium (JAS 1976, p. 627–46). Here I shall consider the series of four studies they have published together,[26] and particularly the fourth one, 'The cultural construction of the person in Bengal and Tamil Nadu', which forms the conclusion and is signed by the three authors. The authors claim to combine two perspectives, to borrow on the one hand from Dumont, on the other from David Schneider. As its title suggests, the study clearly does not give equal place to these two scholars; the first named receives, in fact, second place. Indeed, it is paradoxical that they should claim *H.H.* as an authority while striving to define the unity (of two regions) of India, starting from an individualist conception of society. For my part, I do not believe that the comparison of societies should be made in terms of those societies' conception of the human person, for to me this is something that is basic for some societies and not for others, even though every conception of society necessarily implies a certain manner of conceiving men.

Let us try to reconstruct our authors' argument in the abstract. The theory expressed in *H.H.*, and Dumont's theory generally, continues to distinguish between the domains of caste and kinship. (Schneider's attack on the idea of a kinship domain is well known.) The two concepts at issue, kinship and caste, refer ultimately to a partitioning effected by the anthropologist. In the very line of Dumont, who has, for example, rejected the notion of social stratification and attempted to go beyond the purely analytic notion of 'cross-cousin marriage', fidelity to the native viewpoint requires that this distinction be done away with, as it has no real basis in the mind of Indians themselves.

What are we to think of this demand? It is perhaps not unjustified in the absolute, but it is, so to speak, angelic, in the sense that it overlooks the need to preserve, at the level of major categories, a common language for the profession, an indispensable condition for an already badly eroded consensus. Kinship is, *pace* Schneider, a scientific category in the making. We saw earlier that our representations can be questioned only step by step. Yet here the attempt is to make a clean sweep of them. Our authors fail to keep both ends of the chain in hand at the same time – native conceptions, no doubt, but also a medium of our own conceptions that must be preserved if we do not wish to find tomorrow as many anthropologies as anthropologists. Once this a priori reservation has been made, it might be taken away, if the problem at hand was acute and the proposed solution convincing. In my estimation, this is not at all the case. We cannot go into detail here and must, therefore, leave the question open. Let us stress only that here again 'culture analysis' moves representations dangerously far away from institutions and behaviour. It is particularly marked in the second article on Bengal, where the subtle analysis of a series of concepts is quite unaccompanied by the customary ethnographic description, even of the immediately relevant circumstantial and ceremonial aspects. An ambitious analysis must be given a solid and complete descriptive basis. Shall we return to this method at last?

In sum and quite paradoxically, I have the feeling that *H.H.* is surviving about as well as can be expected in the existing state of the anthropological profession (Dumont 1978). This justifies the reprinting of the book. It is true that, though some of its major theses have been adopted for use here or there and are more or less accepted, and though the manifestations of hierarchy command attention now as they did before, the main idea, the idea of hierarchy separated from power, is generally rejected, and where it is not it is scarcely the better for it. In the last analysis, it is rejected in the name of commonsense prejudices and an atomizing empiricism. It has not been replaced, and its opponents have not come to agreement among themselves. At least, this is my reading of the situation. Given current orientations, it is doubtful whether the near future will be more favourable. Apart from its particular subject matter, let us add that the type of controversy involved here is doubtless a constituent feature of anthropology as situated in our world, so much so that one could hardly wish its extinction. The main question is whether cultural analysis, especially American, will persist in rejecting any connection with social forms, institutions, and behaviours, and in using ethnographic data in the broad sense of the term only very selectively, if at all, or whether sound global and empirical procedures will once again assert themselves.

The few attempts to go beyond *H.H.* that we have mentioned

have seemed unconvincing. Contrary to Marriott's claim to confine the book to a short-term perspective (Marriott 1976a, p. 193), I believe it can be seen in a longer perspective. It is, nevertheless, dependent on a certain state of classical indology and anthropology (and the social sciences generally). In time it will be surpassed, if all goes well. In the works cited may we already glimpse aspects of a possible advance over *H.H.*? Let us consider the book's limitations. It is bound to social forms. As such, it obviously covers only a part of Indian culture, not because it has intentionally been restricted in that direction, but because nothing of the culture, or of representations in particular, has been included, other than that which was immediately necessary with respect to social forms. All sorts of connections must yet appear, suggesting additional developments and internal reorganizations of the material. Here, though rejecting the arbitrary shortcuts that Marriott and his school propose, one may retain certain features that have been brought forth by the desire to be true to Indian sentiment. Thus, to speak of a 'feeling of dependence' is still an imperfect way to describe the habitus of the actor in the *pūjā*, yet it touches closely on one of the culture's main components. Again, the notion that what happens within one actor is by nature no different from what happens between two actors, shows a genuinely structuralist viewpoint (Marriott 1976b, p. 109; *cf.* at another level, my book, *Sous-caste*, p. 3) that should be implemented less mechanically than it has been up to the present. Even Marriott's 'monism', as an absence of the mind/matter dualism, constitutes in the first approximation an accurate perception of the Indian mind. The relation between such features, and many others, and the social morphology has yet to be worked out.

It should also be recalled that we have sought to establish only a global perspective. In short, we have done no more than set out in relation to each other the main forms or masses as they appear when attention is focused on a primary level that is basic and general. Assuming that the perspective remains the same, there is room for two kinds of developments that ought to modify, in some way, the general design: one would be a specific study of secondary levels relative to the primary level; the second, a study of regional patterns. On the first point, for example, I do not believe I have reduced the so-called economic phenomena to 'epiphenomena in a novel way' (David 1977, p. 221). To say this is to deeply misunderstand the notion of hierarchy; the inferior, the subordinate, certainly exists and at the same time is ideologically incapable of moving out of its limitation. To say that it is not the most important element for the global characterization of the system in no way precludes the study of what it becomes once it is subordinated – by comparison with our own views – in this way. Life is not limited to what ideology brings to the fore, but each of its situations is coloured, not to say structured, in varying degrees, with reference to the global ideology. Let us take another example. Wondering what has resulted in India from the nonvalorization – that is, in a sense, the nonmoralization – of the individual, Tambiah finds 'a . . . lively self-seeking . . . untutored by an abstract ethic of the collective good . . . in the uninhibited search for power and money' (1972, col. 835a). Here is a reputedly universal feature coloured, as the author indicates in passing, by distinctive characteristics.

As for the regional sphere, who will claim that the pattern of the Jat farmers is not quite far from the common model that has been presented and that its study may not lead to some reconsiderations? Tambiah thinks he will embarrass me by stressing that the South, more religious about impurity, does not fit into the varna theory, as it lacks the two intermediate varnas (1972, col. 832b). This raises the problem, let us say, of a Tamil pattern, with Jaffna, located north of Sri Lanka (Ceylon) and studied by David, offering yet a second-order modification. To be able to articulate all of this, I think the first step was to posit a general Indian formula. It was a necessary stage, but it was only a stage; more limited and specific studies that have thus been made, if not possible, at least surer and directly fruitful, will enrich, modify, and perhaps transform the global view.

Finally, one must here briefly mention the possibility for direct comparison between traditional societies. Chie Nakane for Japan and Francis L. Hsu for China have noted some important features that have their counterparts in India. One can conceive, ideally, if one cannot hope to see soon realized, a comparison between these three great civilizations that would, of course, be based on modern universalism but would be spared, in the detail, the detour through the very exceptional conceptions that characterize modern ideology in the history of mankind.[27]

## 4

In the preceding sections we have been concerned with *H.H.* as a whole or with its main design. Some more specific remarks, relative to a chapter or passage of the text, must still be made. These have been kept to a minimum and they vary in importance, proposing, in some cases, simple corrections of detail. The fact that they are accompanied by references to recent studies should not be interpreted as an attempt to bring the bibliography up to date. I have only mentioned a small number of works in order to let the reader find his way in the recent literature. On principle I have omitted localized monographs, although these often renew our knowledge of a region, notably, for India proper, studies by A. Béteille for Tamil Nadu, P. J. Hiebert for Andhra, R. S. Khare for Uttar Pradesh, T. N. Madan for Kashmir, H. Orenstein for Maharashtra, M. N. Srinivas for Karnataka, and to which we must add Nur Yalman's study of Sri Lanka, at once monographic and comparative.

For the general subject, we must mention David G. Mandelbaum's monumental work *Society in India*, 2 vols. (Berkeley: University of California Press, 1970) and also the large-scale symposium conducted by Milton Singer and Bernard S. Cohn, *Structure and Change in Indian Society* (Chicago: Aldine, 1968). We shall mention in passing a few collective works devoted to particular aspects of the society, which are rich in reference.

Now to follow the order of the book's numbered sections, indicating them by '§'.

§6, p. 18, line 39, I should have said 'a sort of romanticism'.

§11. In an article devoted to the sociological status of the term 'caste' and focused on Spanish America, Julian Pitt-Rivers has contributed some useful detail about the word's history in European languages, especially on its earliest history in the Iberian languages, where it is devoid of any connotation of status ('On the word "caste"', in T. O. Beidelman, ed., *The Translation of Culture* (London: Tavistock, 1971), pp. 231–56, esp. pp. 234–35, 251–52, n. 7).

§25. Das and Uberoi have indulged in a formal demolition of the concepts of the pure and impure in general. It is regrettable that this discussion was not opened ten years earlier, when an attempt was made in the *Contributions* to raise the problem in all its complexity for the profession (CIS 3 [1959], pp. 9–39). Much could be said about our authors' very ingenious challenge, and certainly something could be learned from it. But when these critics ask us to return to the opposition between the sacred and the profane (or 'non-sacred'), they seem to me to be treating very lightly the study referred to and turning their backs on a comparative view, as India shows us precisely the differentiation within what appears as the 'sacred' in other societies. (This is an approximate statement; for greater precision see the text mentioned.) What can India teach us chiefly, if not precisely the meaning of the pure and the impure? We feel something of the same kind of confusion when, at the other end of the platform, we see Mary Douglas, with all her characteristic imagination and sensitivity, evolve a general theory of pure and impure based on that which a Congolese tribe possesses of it in an infinitely weaker and less articulated form. If one concentrates no more on function but on meaning, then each sort of representation must be grasped where it is fully accentuated and elaborated, where it rises to predominance and not where it is kept, by the prevalence of other representations, in a rudimentary or residual state. I venture to say that this is more or less what Mauss said.

§25.2. The expression 'in a tribe' (p. 48, l. 25) has sometimes been taken to refer to Indian tribes. I might better have said 'a tribal society,' but the context, with the reference to Dobu, just preceding, and to Fiji, just following it, should have been enough to show that I was referring to a tribe in general, and not especially to a tribe in India.

§25.3–4. See the note below for §32, concerning the variation of impurity according to the status of the subject.

§31. The most detailed criticism of the concept of 'hierarchy' in *H.H.* is Pauline Kolenda's 'Seven Kinds of Hierarchy in *H.H.*' (JAS 1976, p. 581–96). Owen M. Lynch (in David 1977, pp. 258–59) follows suit, but with an unconditional and motivated rejection of the concept. In general, these criticisms have been answered at the beginning of §2 above (see also the postface). P. Kolenda seems not to have been aware that any concept, when given a basic place becomes endowed with a multitude of partial or secondary meanings as a direct consequence. She has proposed replacing the pure/impure opposition as encompassing value by the *dharma*, order and duty. But the *dharma*, as such, is not distinctive for the highest and the lowest statuses; like all the others they have their own *dharma*, nor is it as such used in all of life's circumstances. Here the argument has slipped away from an anthropological viewpoint to an intellectualist, or even textual viewpoint.

§32, pp. 70–71. Two writers think they have clarified a fact here described as 'incomprehensible' (p. 70). According to the classical texts, the duration of impurity (caused by the death of a parent) varies inversely with the status (of *varna*). Since 1965, Henry Orenstein has written a series of articles about the 'grammar of defilement', distinguishing various sorts of impurity, each provided with a different 'paradigm' regarding its variation in intensity or duration with the status of the major social categories called *varnas*. According to the author, the defilement created by the death of a parent is conceived as purely social and is for this reason weaker as the status of the group in question is higher. This view is confirmed by the fact that impurity likewise decreases within a group as the personal status of the subject rises. Orenstein has exploited in great detail the elaborate classifications of the texts where status differences are involved – although one can observe nothing of this sort in contemporary practice – in order to grasp the principles at work in the authors' minds (most recently, H. Orenstein, 'Logical Congruence in Hindu Sacred Law', CIS, n.s., 4 [December 1970], pp. 22–35, with bibliography). Tambiah has proposed a modification of Orenstein's vocabulary, and a classification of the sanctioned impurities according to the direction of their scale ('direct order' corresponding to a privilege of the superiors and 'inverse order' to a liability of the superiors), finding in this a parallel to, and even an organic link with, the intervarna unions (marriages) as classified by the texts, as in §57, p. 126 below. (S. J. Tambiah, 'From Varna to Caste through Mixed Unions', in J. Goody, ed., *The Character of Kinship* [Cambridge University Press, 1973], pp. 191–229).

§32, p. 71. On the theory of the 'mixing of varnas', it should be added that it allows classical authors to attribute, with reference to the varnas, a relative rank to the categories or groups that are supposed to result from their mixing (S. J. Tambiah, *ibid.*, p. 207).

§32, p. 72. 'The supremacy of the spiritual was never expressed politically.' We may add: except in an extreme development of certain sects, which is not pertinent here. For the sect, *cf.* §93.

§35, n. 35d (p. 82, note pp. 287–89). Brenda Beck thinks she has found, in Tamil Nadu in the Kongu country, the old division of castes of the left hand and castes of the right hand. In fact, it seems to be a modern regional use of the old distinction. Her book, *Peasant Society in Kongu, A Study of Right and Left Subcastes in South India* (Vancouver, 1972) has been discussed by G. Obeyesekere in *Man*, n.s., 10, no. 3 (September 1975), pp. 462–68; *cf.* my comments, Dumont 1978, p. 105.

§36–37. It is remarkable that the same kind of chart has been used to show the exchange of food both here (pp. 86–87), and, simultaneously and independently, in a study by McKim Marriott which introduces some new ethnographic details: 'Caste Ranking and Food Transaction, A Matrix Analysis', in Singer and Cohn, *Structure and Change* (see above, p. xxxviii). As I have mentioned, Marriott has since complemented his transactional theory, on which our comments (p. 91), for the most part, remain valid. *Cf.*, most recently, 'Hindu Transactions' (Marriott 1976b).

§54. The work of D. F. Pocock, *Kanbi and Patidar* (Oxford, 1972) is recognized as a classic on hypergamy. There is some progress in recognizing the importance of affinity in North India, as shown in the little symposium presented in CIS, n.s., 9, no. 2 (1975), and particularly in the article by T. N. Madan.

§62. See J. Michael Mahar, ed., *The Untouchables in Contemporary India* (Tucson: The University of Arizona Press, 1972), sixteen authors.

§64. On the exchange of food, see above, §36–37.

§73, and the chapter in general. Robert Eric Frykenberg, ed., *Land Control and Social Structure in Indian History* (Madison: University of Wisconsin, 1969), ten contributions.

§74. See the well-balanced synthesis of M. N. Srinivas: 'The Indian village: Myth and Reality', in J. H. M. Beattie and R. G. Lienhardt, eds., *Studies in Social Anthropology, Essays in Memory of E. E. Evans-Pritchard* (Oxford, 1975), pp. 41–85.

§75, pp. 165–66. While it is true to saȳ that the normative texts are silent on the values of the merchant, it should also be added – and has quite rightly been observed – that these texts offer a whole set of provisions relating to what we would call 'commercial law'.

§84.4. See, by the late Pierre Rolland, 'Le cérémonial d'exclusion de la caste dans l'Inde ancienne', in *Prof. K. A. Nilakanta Sastri Felicitation Volume* (Madras, 1971), pp. 487–97 [from a manuscript dated 1861].

§97. James Silverberg, ed., *Social Mobility in the Indian Caste*

*System: An Interdisciplinary Symposium*, Comparative Studies in Society and History, Supplement 3 (The Hague: Mouton, 1968), seven authors.

Writing today, I would add a section that might be '98. The place of things'. It would offer, so to speak, a summary in intaglio of all the preceding developments. It would bring together the conclusions regarding wealth – movable wealth in particular – the now too brief and scattered notes on the ideology of the gift, and other remarks such as the one bearing on 'extrinsic borrowing' (§94). Having more surely recognized, in the interval since the publication of *H.H.*, that the economic viewpoint predominating in modern ideology subordinates relations between men to relations between men and things (property, etc.; *cf. From Mandeville to Marx*), we see clearly the possibility of assembling the traditional Indian traits to form precisely the opposite of this configuration (*cf.* n. 42n): here relations to things are used for the expression of relations between men. This addition would complete and strengthen §75.

§102. C. J. Fuller renews the question with his field study, 'Kerala Christians and the Caste System', *Man*, n.s., 11, no. 1 (March 1976): 53–70.

§103. *Contributions to Indian Sociology*, n.s., 6 (December 1972) is devoted to Muslims.

§105. See Akbar S. Ahmed, *Millenium and Charisma among Pathans: A Critical Essay in Social Anthropology* (London, 1976), and discussion in *Current Anthropology* 18, no. 3 (September 1977): 514–18, also Jerome Rousseau, 'On Estates and Castes', *Dialectical Anthropology* 3, no. 1 (February 1978): 85–94.

§111. Milton Singer, ed., *Entrepreneurship and Modernization of Occupational Cultures in South Asia* (Durham: Duke University, 1973), eleven contributions and extensive discussion.

Bibliography: As we have said, systematic examination of the bibliography came to an end in 1962. For the present edition, we have simply brought up to date some of the references. Malcolm Crick has kindly corrected the reference to *Chips*, by Max Müller (four volumes instead of three), and has called attention to the relevance of two other texts by the same author, a letter to Risley about the 1886 *Ethnological Survey* published in *Chips*, vol. 1, (new edition, 1894), and an appendix entitled 'Philology vs. Ethnology', in *Biography of Words*, 1888.

*List of Abridged References*

CIS 1971    Symposium, T. N. Madan, ed., *Contributions to Indian Sociology*, n.s. 5 (December 1971): 1–81.

David 1977    Kenneth David, ed., *The New Wind: Changing Identities in South Asia* (The Hague: Mouton, 1977).

Dumont 1957    Louis Dumont, 'For a Sociology of India' [adapted by D. Pocock], *Contributions to Indian Sociology*, no. 1 (1957), pp. 7–22, and *Religion, Politics, and History in India: Collected Papers in Indian Sociology* (Paris: Mouton, 1970), no. 1.

Dumont 1978    Louis Dumont, 'La communautè anthropologique et l'idéologie', *L'Homme* 18, nos. 3–4 (July–December 1978): 83–110 [English translation in *Social Science Information* 18, no. 6 (1979): 785–817.

JAS 1971    Symposium, J. F. Richards and R. W. Nicholas, eds., *Journal of Asian Studies* 35, no. 4 (August 1976): 579–650.

Leach 1971    Edmund R. Leach, 'Hierarchical Man: Louis Dumont and His Critics', *South Asian Review* 4, no. 3 (April 1971): 233–37.

Marriott 1976a    Correspondence, McKim Marriott, 'Interpreting Indian Society: A Monistic Alternative to Dumont's Dualism', *Journal of Asian Studies* 36, no. 1 (November 1976): 189–95.

Marriott 1976b    McKim Marriott, 'Hindu Transactions: Diversity without Dualism,' in Bruce Kapferer, ed., *Transaction and Meaning*, A.S.A. Essays in Social Anthropology, vol. 1 (Philadelphia: ISHI, 1976).

Tambiah 1972    S. J. Tambiah, review of *Homo Hierarchicus*, American Anthropologist, 74, no. 4 (1972), pp. 832–35.

# PREFACE TO THE FIRST
# FRENCH EDITION

The study of the caste system is both useful for our knowledge of India, and is an important task of general sociology. Yet no French writer has devoted a book to it since the two important works of the turn of the century: one by the Sanskritist Senart (1896), the other by the sociologist Bouglé (1908). On the other hand, since the end of the Second World War the subject has been to some extent renewed by a new kind of research, namely, intensive studies by direct observation: many anthropologists, mostly Anglo-Saxon and Indian, have lived in Indian villages in order to examine the society of the castes. Thus, to someone who has specialized in the study of Indian society, and for several years pursued his research at the public expense, it appeared as a duty to provide the French reading public with a book on this subject, a book which should attempt, in the light of recent studies, to give a general view of the question.

I should perhaps at once warn the reader that he will find nothing here immediately relevant to the very urgent problems of contemporary India. As is well known, no sooner was India independent than she resolutely set out on the road towards modern economic development, yet she was at the same time determined to avoid sacrificing to this end the democracy established by the new constitution which must little by little permeate the whole society. This book is concerned with the traditional social organization of India from the point of view of theoretical comparison, and so the most it can do is help one to understand the immensity of the task which has been undertaken (Chapter 11).

In a work of this nature, everything depends in the last analysis on the theoretical orientation. On this point it is not enough to say that I owe everything, or almost everything, to the French tradition of sociology. For not only has it nurtured me, my ambition is to extend it. My debt to Bouglé will be obvious. Together with him, I would like to mention in particular Robert Hertz – less for his theory of 'double obsequies' or of the polarity of hands than for the spirit of his general method – and most of all Marcel Mauss.

Faithfulness to Mauss' profound inspiration seems increasingly to be a condition of success in our studies, his teaching the cardinal organizing principle of our research. If I seem to depart from him, a closer look should be taken: for if I really do so, this will be through my own inadequacy and not a deliberate departure. In my personal experience, modern acquisitions in this specialized discipline need to be ordered in a perspective based on Mauss' ideas, discernible at least to his most attentive pupils. In these days, seen from the outside, he often seems vague, and we must be more precise. Rather than concepts, he imparted an approach. I wish to continue this approach, introducing such concepts as are strictly necessary. Yet I would prefer to be accused of lack of precision rather than resort to contemporary jargon in which precision of detail is made precarious by the neglect of the fundamental problems on which the validity of a scientific language depends.

The task is not without difficulty. The book has been in preparation for a long time and but a short while ago still seemed to reflect only an intermediate and provisional stage of the research. The views of specialists on this topic are various indeed. Two relatively recent works available in French are at opposite poles. That by Hocart, published in French in 1939 thanks to Marcel Mauss, who also wrote a preface for it, is full of profound insights for a reader already reasonably well versed in the subject, but there is a danger that it might seriously mislead a novice. That by Hutton is excellent factually, but the theoretical side is inadequate and obsolete. Since 1950 there has been a relative abundance of publications, the fruit of the proliferation of field work. It is natural to devote as much space as possible to these. However, they are various and of very unequal worth, and they will often provide matter for debate. Beyond a certain point there are no generally accepted conclusions on which to rely; I shall have to establish my theses by discussing and even rejecting others. To avoid over-loading the exposition, it is divided into two parts: the text itself contains the body of the exposition, taking into account only the main problems and works, and the hurried reader may confine himself to this; the notes complete the text, providing some divergent views and bibliographical references which are not intended as exhaustive.

This divergence of views springs from the admittedly embryonic state of these studies. In my opinion, the lack of progress in this field, as in others, is due to the fact that the main effort has not been directed towards the proper aim of questioning our preconceived ideas. I have experienced this myself, even though I thought I was sufficiently aware of the danger from the outset. As far back as 1952, when I first had occasion to embark upon these issues, I set out on the following course: (1) I accepted Bouglé's theory as a starting-point and tried to extend it; (2) I brought the theory obtained in this way face to face with all the observed facts, thus, among other things, making it possible to profit from Hocart as fully as the facts allow. But the confrontation of theory with reality was not without difficulties. It was only at the time of the conferences of 1963-4* that I realized I had been checked, though at a somewhat different level, by the very obstacle which has hindered all researches on this topic and explains, still, the slow progress of the common endeavour. We shall see this obstacle specifically in what follows: it is our misunderstanding of hierarchy. Modern man is virtually incapable of fully recognizing it. For a start, he simply fails to notice it. If it does force itself on his attention he tends to eliminate it as an epiphenomenon. Should he finally accept it, as I did, he must still take pains to see it as it really is, without attributing imaginary properties to it. By contrast, all the difficulties vanish if we keep it firmly before our eyes, accustom ourselves to following its outlines and implications, and rediscover the universe in which it operates. Moreover, there are far-reaching consequences, affecting the place and general function of ideas and values – ideology – in social life, a relationship very different from what is ordinarily supposed.

Many things follow from this. In the first place, one is led in this way further and further and more and more exclusively in the direction of sociological analysis and discussion. On specific points, concrete examples will be given; for the sake of simplification, we shall sometimes confine consideration of an aspect of the system

* Cf. *Annuaire de l'E.P.H.E.*, 6th section, 1964-5, pp. 208-10. For an intermediate state of the question, see Dumont and Pocock, 'Caste', *Contributions to Indian Sociology*, II, 1958.

to one particular region. But, taking them in the round, we must to a large extent sacrifice the factual side of things as they are actually experienced. We cannot give the detailed ethnographic picture which perhaps the reader would like to have, though he is probably far from imagining how extremely complex it would be. For this one must refer to Hutton's regional descriptions (*cf.* 21) and the other works quoted.

In the second place, the focal point of the account is systematically shifted: in place of the isolation and the *separation* of the castes from one another, which have been found so prominent, we shall bring *hierarchy* to the forefront; the merits of this procedure remain to be judged. Moreover, an account which kept to the order of the research, describing first everything which follows from the ideology and then all the corresponding aspects of its context, would have been too long and too repetitive. We shall place confidence in the modern reader and make the exposition more complex and shorter. Once the structural principle of the system has been detected (Chapter 2), the reader will be asked to bear in mind in turn hierarchy, division of labour and separation (Chapters 3–6), and to read, as it were, on two planes at once, that of consciousness and that of external observation. To make it easier a sharp terminological distinction will be made between these two complementary components of social reality, one of which is present to the light of day, the other accompanying it as its vague yet vital shadow.

The reader is entitled to ask for more than this: if on our own admission many specialists are unready to effect the transformation we suggest, how should the reader follow us in a course that runs counter to the familiar ways of modern mentality? To help him in this, we shall, so to speak, begin with the end. In the Introduction our conclusions about hierarchy are used to sketch an account of the egalitarian ideology of modern men. Tocqueville contributes to this. In this way, without completely leaving his familiar universe, it is hoped that the reader will be put in a position not to misunderstand a quite different world. Continuing the Introduction, the first chapter gives a brief history of ideas about the castes, and the main attitudes of our predecessors are set out. As these attitudes are certainly known to the reader, criticism of them should help him to accept the perspective which is suggested here.

With the study of power and territory, of the royal function and dominance, and of rights over the land (Chapter 7) we tackle directly the basic implication of the system of ideas and values. From this the study of justice and caste administration (Chapter 8) follows naturally. Chapter 9 is devoted to the most important of the other concomitants and implications, starting with the institutions of renunciation and the sects. The last two chapters are addressed to comparison through two questions: first, that of the presence of castes among non-Hindus and outside India (Chapter 10) and second that of recent changes (Chapter 11) in so far as they proceed from the interaction between traditional India and the modern world. This leads, in conclusion, to a schematic overall comparison between egalitarian society and a society which is its opposite from the point of view of values and their immediate concomitants.

I have not set out to provide a *history* of the caste system, but I have not felt debarred from appealing to historical data whenever they can clarify and complement modern facts on important points. Without prejudging the question of knowing when the system as such first came into existence, the past, often the very remote past, can easily be seen to contain elements later to become an integral part of the system or even some of its foundations.

No doubt the work is heavier and more complex than might have been wished for a fairly wide public.† Whilst endeavouring to reach simple principles, one cannot without ceasing to be scientific fail to mention the uncertainties, nor above all can one escape the complexity of this subject, a complexity whose governing rule can become apparent only if it is scrupulously reconstructed. In short, whilst deductive argument is used as much as possible, the work as a whole remains semi-deductive, which is hardly surprising in the present state of the social sciences.

The chapters are divided into sections numbered by decimal notation (Chapter 4, sections 41, 42, etc., eventually sub-section 42.1). It has not been possible to give the notes in the form of a continuous commentary; they are designated by letters within each section (e.g. 41a).

A note on the transliteration of Indian words follows, and at the end of the volume there is a map showing the places or regions mentioned in the text.

† For a brief general account, see Dumont, *La Civilization Indienne et Nous. Esquisse de sociologie comparée*. Paris, A. Colin, 1964.

# BRIEF NOTE ON THE
# TRANSLITERATION OF INDIAN WORDS

All words which are properly Indian appear at least once in italics, transliterated in the conventional fashion, and their language of origin is indicated either in the text or the index. Some of such words also appear in roman type: some of the rules adopted for spelling are given below.

Words belonging to the *lingua franca* called 'Anglo-Indian' are written between quotation marks ('sahib', 'coolee').

The essential minimum *re* pronunciation and spelling is given below. For further details see, for example, for Indo-Aryan languages, the elementary Sanskrit grammar by Louis Renou (Paris, Adrien Maisonneuve, 1946).

| ITALICIZED TRANSLITERATION | PRONUNCIATION | SPELLING IN ROMAN TYPE |
|---|---|---|
| *c* | as in 'pa*tch*' | ch (an exception: for simplicity, *kacca* is rendered 'kacha' rather than the cumbrous 'kachcha'.) |
| *ś* | as in *sh*ock | sh |
| *u* | as in z*oo* | u |
| *j* | as in ba*dge* | j |

# INTRODUCTION

*...Democracy breaks the chain and severs
every link of it.*

Alexis de Tocqueville

## 1  Castes and ourselves

The caste system is so different from our own social system in its central ideology that the modern reader is doubtless rarely inclined to study it fully. If he is very ignorant of sociology, or of a very militant turn of mind, his interest may be confined to wanting the destruction or the disappearance of an institution which is a denial of the rights of man, and appears as an obstacle to the economic progress of five hundred million people. It is a remarkable fact that, quite apart from the Indians, no Westerner who has lived in India, whether the most fervent reformer or the most zealous missionary has ever, so far as is known, attempted or recommended the abolition pure and simple of the cast system, either because of an acute consciousness of the positive functions fulfilled by the system, as in the case of the Abbé Dubois, or simply because such a thing appeared too impracticable.

The reader, even on the assumption that he is more moderate in his opinions, cannot be expected to consider caste other than an aberration, and the very authors who have devoted books to it have more often tried to explain the system as an anomaly than understand it as an institution. This will be seen in the following chapter. If it was only a question of satisfying our curiosity and forming some idea of a social system which is as stable and powerful as it is opposed to our ethics and unamenable to our intellect, we would certainly not devote to it the effort of attention which the preparation of this book has required, and which I fear the reading of it may also require to some extent. More is necessary: the conviction that caste has something to teach us about ourselves. Indeed, this is the *long term* ambition of works of the type to which this book belongs, and it is necessary to stress this point in order to indicate

1

the nature and context of this endeavour. Ethnology, or more precisely social anthropology, would have only specialist interest if the subject of its study – 'primitive' or 'archaic' societies and the great civilizations of other countries – revealed a human kind quite different from ourselves. Anthropology, by the understanding it *gradually* affords of the most widely differing societies and cultures, gives proof of the unity of mankind. In doing so, it obviously reflects at least some light on our own sort of society. But this is not quite enough, and anthropology has the inherent and occasionally avowed aim of achieving this in a more systematic and radical way, that is, of putting modern society in perspective in relation to the societies which have preceded it or which co-exist with it, and of making in this way a direct and central contribution to our general education. No doubt we have not yet reached this point, but in this respect the study of a complex society, which has sustained a great civilization, is more advantageous than the study of simpler societies, socially and culturally less differentiated. Indian society in particular may be the more fruitful in that it is so different from our own: with this clear-cut case, one can hope to begin a comparison which in other cases will be more fine-drawn.

To anticipate in a few words: the castes teach us a fundamental social principle, hierarchy. We, in our modern society, have adopted the principle contrary to it, but it is not without value for understanding the nature, limits and conditions of realization of the moral and political egalitarianism to which we are attached. There is no question of reaching this point in the present work, which will stop in substance at the discovery of hierarchy, but this is the prospect to which the study is directed. There is one point to be made clear. The reader may, of course, refuse to leave the shelter of his own values; he may lay it down that for him man begins with the Declaration of the Rights of Man, and condemn outright anything which departs from it. In doing so he certainly limits himself, and we can question not only whether he is in fact 'modern', as he claims, but also whether he has the right to be so-called. In actual fact, there is nothing here like an attack, whether direct or oblique, on modern values, which seem in any case secure enough to have nothing to fear from our investigation. It is only a question of attempting to grasp other values *intellectually*. If one refused to do this, it would be useless to try to understand the caste system, and it would be impossible, in the end, to take an *anthropological* view of our own values.

It will be readily understood that the inquiry, defined in this way, forbids us to adopt certain facile approaches. If, like many contemporary sociologists, we were content with a label borrowed from our own societies, if we confined ourselves to considering the cast system as an extreme form of '*social stratification*', we could indeed record some interesting observations, but we would by definition have excluded all possibility of enriching our fundamental conceptions: the circuit which we have to travel, from ourselves to caste, and back again from caste to ourselves, would be closed immediately because we would never have left the starting-point. Another way of remaining shut in upon ourselves consists in assuming from the outset that ideas, beliefs and values – in a word, ideology – have a secondary place in social life, and can be explained by, or reduced to, other aspects of society. The principle of equality and the principle of hierarchy are facts, indeed they are among the most constraining facts, of political and social life. There is no space here to dwell upon the question of the place of ideology in social life: as far as methodology is concerned, all that follows, both in outline and in detail, aims to answer this question.[1a] The clear recognition of the importance of ideology has an apparently paradoxical consequence: in the case of India it leads us to make much of the literary heritage and the 'superior' civilization as well as of 'popular' culture. The adherents of a less radical sociology then accuse us of falling into 'culturology' or 'indology', and of losing sight of comparison, which, in their eyes, is sufficiently guaranteed by concepts like 'social stratification' and by the mere consideration of the *similarities* which allow phenomena taken from different types of society to be grouped together under a common label. But such an approach can only ever achieve the general, as opposed to the universal, and with respect to our goal of comparison it represents another short circuit. In sociological studies the universal can only be attained through the particular characteristics, different in each case, of each type of society. Why should we travel to India if not to try to discover how and in what respects Indian society or civilization, by its very particularity, represents a form of the universal? In the last analysis, it is by humbly inspecting the most minute particulars that the route to the universal is kept open. If one is prepared to devote all the time necessary to studying all

3

aspects of Indian culture, one has a chance, under certain conditions, of in the end transcending it, and of one day finding in it some truth for one's own use.

For the moment, our first aim is to come to understand the ideology of the caste system. This ideology is directly contradicted by the egalitarian theory which we hold. And it is impossible to understand the one whilst the other – modern ideology – is considered a universal truth, not simply *qua* a political and moral ideal – which is a declaration of faith beyond dispute – but *qua* an adequate expression of social life – which is a naïve judgment. This is why, to smooth the reader's path, I shall begin with the end, and use from the outset the results of the study in order to provoke a preliminary reflection on modern values. This is equivalent to a brief general introduction to sociology, which may be considered very elementary but which is nevertheless needed. The first issue is the relation between modern values and sociology, followed by the consideration of egalitarianism from a sociological point of view.

## 2 *The individual and sociology*

On the one hand, sociology is the product of modern society, or rather an integral part of it. It can escape this limitation only partially and by a deliberate effort. On the other hand, it is easy to find the key to our values. Our two cardinal ideals are called equality and liberty. They assume as their common principle, and as a valorized representation, the idea of the human *individual*: humanity is made up of men, and each man is conceived as presenting, in spite of and over and above his particularity, the essence of humanity. We shall return to this fundamental idea later. For the moment let us mention some of its obvious features. This individual is quasi-sacred, absolute; there is nothing over and above his legitimate demands; his rights are limited only by the identical rights of other individuals. He is a monad, in short, and every human group is made up of monads of this kind. Common sense finds no problem about the harmony between these monads. Thus is conceived the social class, or what is called at this level 'society', that is an association, and in some respects even a mere collection, of such monads. There is often claimed to be an antagonism between 'the individual' and 'the society', in which

4

the 'society' tends to appear as a non human residuum: the tyranny of numbers, an inevitable material evil running counter to the sole psychological and moral reality which is contained in the individual.

This sort of view, while forming an integral part of the current ideology of equality and liberty, is obviously very unsatisfactory for the observer of society. Yet it infiltrates even into the social sciences. Now the true function of sociology is quite other: it is precisely to make good the lacuna introduced by the individualistic mentality when it confuses the ideal with the actual. In fact, and this is our third point, while sociology as such is found in egalitarian society, while it is immersed in it, while it even expresses it – in a sense to be seen – it has its roots in something quite different: the apperception of the social nature of man. To the self-sufficient individual it opposes man as a social being; it considers each man no longer as a particular incarnation of abstract humanity, but as a more or less autonomous point of emergence of a particular collective humanity, of a *society*. To be real, this way of seeing things must, in the individualistic universe, take the form of an experience, almost a personal revelation, and this is why I speak of '*sociological apperception*'. Thus the young Marx wrote, with the exaggeration of a neophyte: 'It is society which thinks in me.'

It is not easy to communicate this sociological apperception to a free citizen of the modern State, who would be unfamiliar with it. But we may try to clarify it a little. Our idea of society remains superficial so long as we take it, as the word suggests, as a sort of association which the fully formed individual enters voluntarily and with a definite aim, as if by a contract. Think rather of the child, slowly brought to humanity by his upbringing in the family, by the apprenticeship of language and moral judgment, by the education which makes him share in the common patrimony – including, in our society, elements which were unknown to the whole of mankind less than a century ago. Where would be the humanity of this man, where his understanding, without this training or taming, properly speaking a creation, which every society imparts to its members, by whatever actual agency? This truth is so lost from sight that perhaps it is necessary to refer our contemporaries, even if well-read, to the stories of wolf-children, so that they may reflect that individual consciousness has its source in social training.[2a]

Similarly, the social is often considered exclusively as a matter

5

of the behaviour of individuals, individuals who are assumed to be fully formed in advance. In this regard, it is enough to observe that actual men do not *behave*: they *act* with an idea in their heads, perhaps that of conforming to custom. Man acts as a function of what he thinks, and while he has up to a certain point the ability to arrange his thoughts in his own way, to construct new categories, he does so starting from the categories which are given by society; their link with language should be sufficient reminder of this. It is an idiosyncratic psychological disposition that makes it hard for us to recognize this evidence clearly: when a hackneyed truth, hitherto foreign to me, becomes a truth of experience for me, I am apt to imagine that I have invented it. A common idea presents itself as a personal one when it becomes fully real. Novels are full of examples of this sort: we have a strange need to imagine that what happens to us is unique in order to recognize it as our own, whereas it is the bread and the tears of our particular collectivity or humanity. A strange confusion: there is indeed a person, an individual and unique experience, but it is in large part made up of common elements, and there is nothing destructive in recognizing this: tear from yourself the social material and you are left with nothing more than the potentiality for personal organization.[2b]

It is the prime merit of French sociology to have insisted, in virtue of its intellectualism, on the presence of society in the mind of each man.[2c] Durkheim has been reproached for having had recourse to notions of 'collective representations', and even more of 'collective consciousness' in order to express it. No doubt the second expression is misleading, even if it is ridiculous to see in it a justification for totalitarianism. But let me say outright that from the scientific point of view the drawbacks of these terms are nothing compared to the widespread view that the individual consciousness springs ready armed from the affirmation of self. This latter view is frequently found in current 'sociological' literature.

Let us note again that the sort of view I am criticizing, at least taken as the fully developed and pivotal view with which we are familiar, is really modern and of Christian ancestry. (It might even be suggested that it has appreciably increased its dominion over men's minds since, for example, the beginning of the nineteenth century.) Ancient philosophers, up to the Stoics, did not separate the collective aspects of man from the others: one was a man because one was a member of a city, as much a social as a political

6

organization. Admittedly Plato, in a superficial way, made the Republic the product solely of the division of labour. But Aristotle criticized him for this, and one can see in Plato himself, given the almost strictly hierarchical order which reigns in the *Republic*, that the true man there is man as a collective being, and not man as a particular being, even though the latter shares so closely in the former that his own advantage lies in seeing the exaltation of man as a collective being. Finally, one need only recall a famous example: why does Socrates, in *Crito*, refuse to flee, if not just because there is no moral life outside the city?

In modern society the apperception of man as a social being comes about spontaneously through certain experiences: of the army, a political party, any strongly united collectivity, and above all travel, which, rather like anthropological inquiry, enables one to see in others the modelling by society of features which one does not see at all, or else considers 'personal', when one is in one's own country. As far as teaching goes, this apperception should be the *a b c* of *sociology*, but I have already alluded to the fact that *sociology*, as the study of modern society alone, often dispenses with it. Here one must underline the merits of anthropology as a *sociological* discipline. Nowadays it is impossible to conceive of any anthropological work or teaching which does not bring about the apperception in question. The attraction, I would almost call it the fascination, which Marcel Mauss had for most of his pupils and listeners was due above all to this aspect of his teaching.

In this regard, I may perhaps be allowed to recall the following anecdote as a striking example. Towards the end of the year in which he was to take his diploma in ethnology, a fellow student, who was not going to make ethnology his career, told me that a strange thing had happened to him. He said something like this: 'The other day, while I was standing on the platform of a bus, I suddenly realized that I was not looking at my fellow passengers in the manner I used to; something had changed in my relation to them, in my position relative to them. There was no longer "myself and the others"; I was one of them. For a while I wondered what the reason was for this strange and sudden transformation. All at once I realized: it was Mauss' teaching.' The individual of yesterday had become aware of himself as a social being; he had perceived his personality as tied to the language, attitudes and gestures whose images were reflected by his

7

neighbours. This is the essential humanist aspect of the teaching of anthropology.

It must be added that the same goes for this apperception as for all fundamental ideas. It is not acquired completely in the first instance and once and for all: either it deepens and ramifies in us, or on the contrary it remains limited and becomes a sham. Starting from it we can understand that the perception of ourselves as individuals is not innate but learned. In the last analysis, it is laid down for us, imposed by the society in which we live. As Durkheim said, roughly, our own society obliges us to be free. As opposed to modern society, traditional societies, which know nothing of equality and liberty as values, which know nothing, in short, of the individual, have basically a collective idea of man, and our (residual) apperception of man as a social being is the sole link which unites us to them, and is the only angle from which we can come to understand them. This apperception is therefore the starting-point of any comparative sociology.

A reader with no idea of this apperception, or who, like the majority perhaps of philosophers today, does not recognize that it is founded in truth,[2d] would probably read the present work in vain. To start with we shall make use of it for two ends: first to focus on the individual as a sociological problem, and secondly, starting from equality as a modern value, to throw into relief in our own society its counterpart, hierarchy.

## 3 Individualism and holism

If sociological apperception comes about as a reaction to the individualistic view of man, then it follows immediately that the idea of the individual constitutes a sociological problem. Max Weber, in whom sociological apperception expressed itself in a very indirect fashion, such a romantic or modern philosopher was he, outlined a programme of work for us when he wrote in a footnote in *The Protestant Ethic* (German edition, p. 95, note 13; English translation Talcott Parsons, p. 222):

The expression 'individualism' includes the most heterogeneous things imaginable [. . .] a thorough analysis of these concepts in historical terms would at the present time [after Burckhardt] be highly valuable to science.

8

To start with, much imprecision and difficulty arise from failing to distinguish in the 'individual':

(1) *The empirical agent, present in every society*, in virtue of which he is the main raw material for any sociology.

(2) The rational being and *normative subject* of institutions; this is peculiar to us, as is shown by the values of equality and liberty: it is an idea that we have, the idea of an ideal.

For sociological comparison, only the individual in the full sense of the term must be taken as such, and another word should be used to designate the empirical aspect. One will thereby avoid inadvertently attributing the presence of the individual to societies in which he is not recognized, and also avoid making him a universal unit of comparison or element of reference. (Here some will object that all societies recognize the individual in some fashion; it is more probable that relatively simple societies show a lack of differentiation in this respect, which should be described and estimated with care.) On the contrary, as with every complex and concrete category, one should endeavour to reduce this analytically to universal elements or relationships which can serve as coordinates for comparative reference. In this approach, the first fact to emerge is that the individual is a value, or rather part of a configuration of values *sui generis*.

It is immediately obvious that there are two mutually opposed configurations of this kind: one is characteristic of traditional societies and the other of modern society. In the first, as in Plato's Republic, the stress is placed on the society as a whole, as collective Man; the ideal derives from the organization of society with respect to its ends (and not with respect to individual happiness); it is above all a matter of order, of hierarchy; each particular man in his place must contribute to the global order, and justice consists in ensuring that the proportions between social functions are adapted to the whole.

In modern society, on the contrary, the Human Being is regarded as the indivisible, 'elementary' man, both a biological being and a thinking subject. Each particular man in a sense incarnates the whole of mankind. He is the measure of all things (in a full and novel sense). The kingdom of ends coincides with each man's legitimate ends, and so the values are turned upside down. What is still called 'society' is the means, the life of each man is the end. Ontologically, the society no longer exists, it is no more than an irreducible datum, which must in no way thwart the demands of liberty and equality. Of course, the above is a description of values, a view of mind. With respect to *what happens in fact* in this society, observation often refers us to the first type of society. A society as conceived by individualism has never existed anywhere for the reason we have given, namely, that the individual lives on social ideas. An important consequence follows: the individual of the modern type is not opposed to the hierarchical type of society as part to whole (and this is true within the modern type of society where there is, properly speaking, no conceptual whole), but rather as an equal or *homologue*, for they both correspond to the essence of man. Let us apply Plato's (and Rousseau's) idea, the idea that there is a parallelism between the concept of the particular man and the concept of society: whilst Plato conceives the particular man as a society, a set of tendencies or faculties, in modern times the society or nation is conceived as a collective individual, which has its 'will' and its 'relations' like the elementary individual, but unlike him is not subject to social rules.

Any doubt that this distinction immediately clarifies the issue may be dispelled by referring to the confusion introduced by the two senses of the word 'individual' in the sociology of Durkheim and his followers, or again to the 'primitive communism' of Victorian or Marxist evolutionism, which confused absence of the individual with collective ownership.[3a]

When looking for the origins of sociology one should, therefore, above all focus on its principle or essence, that is, trace the history of sociological apperception in the modern world. In France it became especially apparent under the Restoration, as a reaction to the disillusionment brought about by the experience of Revolutionary dogmas and as an implication of the socialist programme of substituting deliberate organization for the arbitrariness of economic laws. However, it is to be found before this,[3b] for example in natural law, where it is a continually eroded legacy of the Middle Ages, or in Rousseau, who in these lines of the *Social Contract* indicates superbly the transition from man as a natural being to man as a social being:

He who would dare to institute a People must feel in himself the capacity to change human nature as it were, to transform each individual, by himself a complete and isolated whole, *into a piece of a greater whole*

*from which that individual may* [as a man] *receive his life and being.*
(Italics and gloss mine.)

The same apperception is present in an indirect form in Hegel's conception of the State, a conception which Marx rejected, thus returning to individualism pure and simple: a somewhat paradoxical attitude for a socialist.

A remark is required to encompass the ideology and its context: this individualistic tendency, which became established, generalized and popularized from the eighteenth century to the age of romanticism and beyond, was *in fact* accompanied by the modern development of the social division of labour, of what Durkheim has called organic solidarity. The ideal of the autonomy of each person became established among men who were dependent on one another for material things to a much greater extent than all their predecessors. Still more paradoxically, these men ended up by reifying their belief and imagining that the whole of *society* functioned in fact as they had thought the *political* domain they had created ought to function.[3c] A mistake for which the modern world, and in particular France and Germany, have paid dear. Compared to simpler societies it looks as if there had been an exchange of levels: at the level of fact, simpler societies juxtapose identical particular persons ('mechanical solidarity') and at the level of thought stress the collective totality; modern society, by contrast, acts as a whole and, at the theoretical level, thinks in terms of the individual.[3d] This accounts for the emergence of sociology as a special discipline, replacing an idea that was common to all in traditional society.

## 4  Rousseau on equality

Now we come to the modern feature which is most immediately opposed to the caste system: equality. The ideal of liberty and equality follows immediately from the conception of man as an individual. In effect, if the whole of humanity is deemed present in each man, then each man should be free and all men are equal. This is the foundation of the two great ideals of the modern age. By contrast, as soon as a collective end is adopted by several men, their liberty is limited and their equality brought into question.

It is striking to find out how recent and belated is the development of the idea of equality and its implications. In the eighteenth century it played only a secondary role, except in the works of Helvetius and Morelly. Even in the nineteenth century, among the precursors or fathers of socialism in France, the relative place of equality and liberty is variable. The difficulty of separating the concept of equality from associated ideas makes it all the less easy to give its history here. However, we shall try to isolate it, while retaining a minimum of historical perspective, by comparing its place in Rousseau and in Tocqueville, at an interval of eighty years.

Rousseau is often considered a rebel against inequality, but in reality his ideas remained very moderate and were to a large extent traditional. In the *Discourse on the origin of inequality*, Rousseau's prime merit is to distinguish between natural inequality, which is but a small thing, and moral inequality, or 'inequality of combination',[4a] which results from the exploitation of natural inequality for social ends. The man of nature, a brutish creature, endowed with a sense of pity but not knowing good from evil, and innocent of the differentiations on which reason and morality rest, is sometimes said to be free and even to be acquainted with equality (p. 199), which must no doubt be understood in the sense of absence of moral inequality (but would it not be better to say he is acquainted with neither of the two opposites?). It is explicitly stated that inequality is inevitable and that true equality consists in proportion (p. 216, note); thus one has here again something like Plato's ideal of distributive justice.

From the economic point of view, inequality is inevitable. From the political point of view, equality cannot be defined independently of liberty: equality in abjection, under the despotism which marks the extremity of the development of society, is not a virtue. In short, equality is only good when it is combined with liberty and when it consists in proportionality, that is, when it is applied reasonably (equity, perhaps, more than equality).

In the *Social Contract* (end of book I), equality is clearly defined as a political norm: 'The fundamental compact substitutes, for such physical inequality as nature may have set up between men, an equality which is moral and legitimate' (p. 19).

Whilst inequality is evil, it is nevertheless inevitable in certain domains. Whilst equality is good, it is above all an ideal which man introduces into political life, to compensate for the ineluctable fact of inequality. Rousseau would probably not have written that 'men are born free and with equal rights'. He only opened his

*Social Contract* with the famous phrase: 'Man *was* born free, and everywhere he is in chains' (my italics). One can see the transition: the Revolution was to attempt to put natural law into effect as positive law. One can see with Babeuf and the Conspiracy of Equals how the demands of equality swept away the limitations which the Philosophes found in the nature of man. These demands not only put equality before liberty but were even ready to hold liberty cheap in order to bring about an egalitarian utopia.

## 5 *Tocqueville on equality*

Let us move on to Tocqueville and his *Democracy in America* (1835–1840).[5a] Tocqueville contrasts the democracies of England, America and France according to the relative place which each gives to the two cardinal virtues. In England there is liberty with scarcely any equality. America has largely inherited liberty and has developed equality. The French Revolution took place entirely under the banner of equality. Tocqueville, rather like his teacher Montesquieu, has really an aristocratic conception of liberty, and perhaps he felt no freer as a citizen than he would have as a noble under the *Ancien Régime*. He defines democracy by the equality of conditions. (Note in passing that, again as in Montesquieu, we are here going beyond pure politics.) This for him is the 'germinal idea', the dominant and formative ideal and passion, whence he tries to deduce the characteristics of the society of the United States (taking into consideration geographical factors, laws and customs). Looking at France, Tocqueville sees equality developing from an early date. The remarkable pages should be read in which he shows how it was introduced in the Middle Ages by the Church (the clergy recruited from all classes), then encouraged by kings, with the result that finally, in the given conditions, all progress led to levelling.[5b] Tocqueville finds the fact so clearly inscribed in history that he does not hesitate to characterize it as providential, and there is no doubt that his advocacy of democracy, courageous at the outset and always lucid, had its roots here: it would be impossible to oppose the overriding tendency of the history of Christian countries. Tocqueville insisted at length, here and in *The Ancien Régime and the Revolution*, on the considerable degree of levelling in pre-Revolutionary France, a situation which rendered intolerable the remaining distinctions of estate and privileges in the laws, and called for their destruction. If Tocqueville is right, Revolutionary demands for liberty seem rather to have been the expression, mainly for the lower orders, of essentially egalitarian demands, the restriction of equality being felt as absence of liberty; but this is already an interpretation.

At the risk of straying a little from our main subject, a word must be said here on one of Tocqueville's very important ideas, which concerns the place of modern political ideology in relation to values as a whole. Tocqueville raised the question of the *realization* of the democratic ideal. Together with many Frenchmen of his time he wondered what the reason was for the disappointing course taken by events in France after 1789. Briefly, France was unable to achieve democracy in a satisfactory manner (and this is one of the origins of French socialism and of sociology in France). Tocqueville stated that in the United States, by contrast, democracy functioned properly. Looking for the reason for this disparity, he was not content to refer it to environment and history; he believed it was to be found in the quite different relationship in the two cases between politics and religion. From the beginning of his book he deplores the fact that in France there had been a divorce between religious men and those who loved liberty (Reeve, I, pp. 10–11), whilst he states that in the United States there was an alliance between the spirit of religion and the spirit of liberty (I, pp. 40–41). Here is his conclusion (II, p. 19):

For my own part I doubt whether man can support at the same time complete religious independence and entire public freedom. And I am inclined to think, that if faith be wanting in him, he must serve, and if he be free, he must believe.

Here is a thought so opposed to the French democratic tradition that it must shock many readers. Its only relevance here is to the general configuration of values in the democratic universe and comparison with the corresponding configuration in the hierarchical universe. Tocqueville sets a limit to (political) individualism, and again makes man *dependent* in real life. In more detail, there are two aspects. In the first place the domains of religion and politics are necessarily separated in democracies, and in two ways: on the one hand, religion must be made to relinquish political power, leaving politics to go its own way; on the other, it is wrong that the political domain should set itself up as a religion, as is often the tendency in France. (Tocqueville notes elsewhere that the French Revolution proceeded in the manner of a religious revolution, M. W. Patterson, trans., *De Tocqueville's L'Ancien Régime*, pp. 15, 158 ff.).

In America, religion is a distinct sphere, in which the priest is sovereign, but out of which he takes care never to go. Within its limits he is the master of the mind; beyond them he leaves men to themselves, and surrenders them to the independence and instability which belong to their nature and their age. (H. Reeve, trans., *Democracy in America*, II, p. 14.)

It will be noted that in the twentieth century France has succeeded somehow or other in achieving this separation. But this is not the whole of Tocqueville's idea: separation is not enough for him. In addition, he advocates that politics and religion be complementary, as he found them to be in the United States: 'If he be free, he must believe', meaning, so to speak, that the particular domain of politics, while setting itself up as the absolute within its own sphere, can be no viable substitute for the universal domain of religion – or, let us hasten to add, philosophy. To make this idea plausible, it is necessary either to consider it from the comparative angle, as might become possible after reading the present work, or else to reflect seriously upon the misfortunes of democracy in nineteenth-century France and twentieth-century Europe – which is hardly ever done.[5c] At the empirical level, it must be stated that the two democracies which have proved viable within the limits of their frontiers both appeal complementarily to another principle: in America in the way Tocqueville has indicated, and in England by preserving alongside modern values as much tradition as possible.

For us the most valuable thing in Tocqueville is his study of the egalitarian mentality, as contrasted with what he perceived of the hierarchical mentality in the France of the *Ancien Régime*, to which he was still closely attached despite his unreserved adherence to democracy. The first feature to emphasize is that the concept of the equality of men entails that of their similarity. This is a notion which, if not absolutely new, had become more widespread and had gained authority since the eighteenth century, as we see from Condorcet who believed strongly in equality of rights, but declared that inequality was to a certain extent useful in practice.

So long as equality is only an ideal requirement expressing the transition in values from man as a collective being to man as an individual, it does not entail the denial of innate differences. But if equality is conceived as rooted in man's very nature and denied only by an evil society, then, as there are no longer any rightful differences in condition or estate, or different sorts of men, they are all alike and even identical, as well as equal. This is what Tocqueville says: where inequality reigns, there are as many distinct humanities as there are social categories (Reeve, II, p. 12, *cf. A.R.*, Chapter 8), the reverse being true in egalitarian society (II, pp. 2, 3, 12). Tocqueville does not develop this point, he seems to take it for granted; like everybody else, he even seems to conflate the social form and the 'natural' or universal being. However, at one point he does make the distinction when he contrasts the way in which the equality of man and woman is conceived in the United States and in France: 'There are people in Europe who, confounding together the different characteristics of the sexes, would make of man and woman beings not only equal but alike' (II, p. 191). The Americans, for their part, consider both of them, 'though their lot is different . . . as beings of equal value' (II, p. 193). The distinction is even expressed between the social level, where the woman remains inferior, and the moral and intellectual level, where she is equal to the man (II, p. 194).

In general, however, we may grasp here, in Tocqueville himself, how the ideal is made immanent and reified, in the way characteristic of the modern democratic mentality. The fusion of equality and identity has become established at the level of common sense. This makes it possible to understand a serious and unexpected consequence of egalitarianism. In a universe in which men are conceived no longer as hierarchically ranked in various social or cultural species, but as essentially equal and identical, the difference of nature and status between communities is sometimes reasserted in a disastrous way: it is then conceived as proceeding from somatic characteristics – which is racism.[5d]

The whole of the second part of *Democracy in America*, which was published in 1840, is a concrete study of the implications in all domains of the equality of conditions. Tocqueville was able to make this meticulous, remarkable, and sometimes prophetic portrait of egalitarian society thanks to the fact that he regarded it with sympathy and curiosity, while still bearing in mind the aristocratic society in which, so to speak, he still participated. He saw the characteristics of the new society clearly, in contrast with those of the preceding one. It is thanks to this comparison, analogous to that implicit in the work of an anthropologist studying an unfamiliar society, that Tocqueville achieved a work of sociology, and one in a deeper sense than many by subsequent authors who were unable to detach themselves from egalitarian society.

This circumstance enables us to make use of Tocqueville, though as it were in the opposite direction: starting from egalitarian society and without leaving our own civilization, he can give us some insight into hierarchical society. It is enough to 'turn the picture round', as Tocqueville himself used to do. We shall be content here with quoting, almost in its entirety, a short chapter, which is one of the most telling in this connection, and has the advantage of being connected with a theme on which we have already touched.

## 6  Tocqueville on individualism

'Of individualism in democratic countries' (*Democracy in America*, II, part 2, Chapter 2, pp. 90–92):

*Individualism* is a novel expression, to which a novel idea has given birth. Our fathers were only acquainted with egotism. Egotism is a passionate and exaggerated love of self, which leads a man to connect everything with his own person, and to prefer himself to everything in the world. Individualism is a mature and calm feeling, which disposes each member of the community to sever himself from the mass of his fellow-creatures; and to draw apart with his family and his friends; so that, after he has thus formed a little circle of his own, he willingly leaves society at large to itself. . . .

Individualism is of democratic origin, and it threatens to spread in the same ratio as the equality of conditions.

Among aristocratic nations, as families remain for centuries in the same condition, often on the same spot, all generations become as it were contemporaneous. A man almost always knows his forefathers, and respects them: he thinks he already sees his remote descendants, and he loves them. He willingly imposes duties on himself towards the former and the latter; and he will frequently sacrifice his personal gratifications to those who went before and to those who will come after him. Aristocratic institutions have, moreover, the effect of closely binding every man to several of his fellow-citizens. As the classes of an aristocratic people are strongly marked and permanent, each of them is regarded by its own members as a sort of lesser country, more tangible and more cherished than the country at large. As in aristocratic communities all the citizens occupy fixed positions, one above the other, the result is that each of them always sees a man above himself whose patronage is necessary to him, and below himself another man whose cooperation he may claim. Men living in aristocratic ages are therefore almost always closely attached to something placed out of their own sphere, and they are often disposed to forget themselves. It is true that in those ages the notion of human fellowship is faint, and that men seldom think of sacrificing themselves for mankind; but they often sacrifice themselves for other men. In democratic ages, on the contrary, when the duties of each individual to the race are much more clear, devoted service to any one man becomes more rare; the bond of human affection is extended, but it is relaxed.

Amongst democratic nations new families are constantly springing up, others are constantly falling away, and all that remain change their condition; the woof of time is every instant broken, and the track of generations effaced. Those who went before are soon forgotten; of those who will come after no one has any idea: the interest of man is confined to those in close propinquity to himself. As each class approximates to other classes, and intermingles with them, its members become indifferent and as strangers to one another. Aristocracy had made a chain of all the members of the community, from the peasant to the king: democracy breaks that chain and severs every link of it. . . . They owe nothing to any man, they expect nothing from any man; they acquire the habit of always considering themselves as standing alone, and they are apt to imagine that their whole destiny is in their own hands. Thus not only does democracy make every man forget his ancestors, but it hides his descendants, and separates his contemporaries from him; it throws him back for ever upon himself alone, and threatens in the end to confine him entirely within the solitude of his own heart.

No doubt it will be understood why I have quoted at length from this admirable text. In part, it replies in advance to the question about individualism raised by Max Weber. It clearly contrasts modern universalism with traditional particularism, and at the same time two opposite views of time. It evokes on the one hand a romanticism which still persists nowadays, even in sociological circles, and on the other, over and above Western aristocracy, it evokes the caste system and its hierarchized interdependence. I have found no better introduction for the modern reader to the universe so different from our own into which I am going to lead him. There are many other passages which could be quoted to complement this one.

## 7  Necessity of hierarchy

There is a point however at which Tocqueville himself abandons us. It is not surprising to find that our contemporaries, who value equality, find scarcely anything to contrast it with except inequality. Even sociologists and philosophers seem to speak of 'hierarchy' reluctantly and with averted eyes, in the sense of the residual or inevitable inequalities of aptitude and function, or of the chain of command which is presupposed by any artificial organization of multiple activities, briefly 'power hierarchy'. However, that is not hierarchy proper, nor the deepest root of what is so called. Tocqueville, by contrast, certainly had the feeling of something else, but the artistocratic society whose memory he retained was not enough to enable him to make this feeling clear. Philosophers have a happier example in their own tradition, namely Plato's Republic, but they seem rather uncomfortable about it (*cf.* note 2d). On the sociological side, among so many platitudes about 'social stratification' the sociologist Talcott Parsons has the great merit of having brought fully to light the universal rationale of hierarchy:

We conceive *action* to be oriented to the attainment of goals, and hence to involve *selective* processes relative to goals. Seen in their relations to goals, then, all the components of systems of action and of the situations in which action takes place, are subject to the process of *evaluation* . . . . *Evaluation* in turn has, when it operates in the setting of *social* systems of action, two fundamental implications. First the units of systems, whether they be elementary unit acts or roles, collectivities, or personalities, must in the nature of the case be subject to *evaluation*. . . . But given the process of evaluation, the probability is that it will serve to differentiate entities *in a rank order*. . . . The second implication is the well-known one that it is a condition of the stability of social systems that there should be an *integration of the value-standards* of the component units to constitute a '*common value-system*'. . . . The existence of such a pattern system as a point of reference for the analysis of social phenomena is a central assumption which follows directly from the frame of reference of actions as applied to the analysis of social systems. (Talcott Parsons: 'A revised analytical approach to the theory of social stratification', first published in *Class, status and power*, edited by Reinhard

Bendix and Seymour M. Lipset, Glencoe, 1953.) (I have italicized certain words.)

In other words, man does not only think, he acts. He has not only ideas, but values. To adopt a value is to introduce hierarchy, and a certain consensus of values, a certain hierarchy of ideas, things and people, is indispensable to social life. This is quite independent of natural inequalities or the distribution of power. No doubt, in the majority of cases, hierarchy will be identified in some way with power, but there is no necessity for this, as the case of India will show. Moreover it is understandable and natural that hierarchy should encompass social agents and social categories. In relation to these more or less necessary requirements of social life, the ideal of equality, even if it is thought superior, is artificial. It expresses a human claim, which also entails the choice of certain ends. It represents a deliberate denial of a universal phenomenon in a restricted domain. We have no intention, any more than did Tocqueville, of throwing doubt on this ideal. But it is well to understand to what extent it runs contrary to the general tendencies of societies, and hence how far our society is exceptional, and how difficult it is to realize this ideal.

To return, after Tocqueville, to the question of the *realization* of democracy is certainly a much neglected and necessary task, but it is not our task here. I wanted only to mark the point after which Tocqueville fails to guide us, and the merit of the sociologist who succeeds here. Talcott Parsons does so because he combines the intellectualism of Durkheim (recognizing that action is dominated by representations or ideas) and the pragmatism of Max Weber (confronting, beyond the problem of the representation of the world, that of action in the world as represented). Returning to the more limited object of this book, we shall see that our modern denial of hierarchy is what chiefly hinders us in understanding the caste system.

# CHAPTER ONE

# HISTORY OF IDEAS

11 *Definition. The word 'caste'*

In view of what has been said, it is not surprising that a social system centred on hierarchy has given rise to the most various and curious discussions by modern Western writers. Here we shall see what can be learned from a general look at these modern attitudes. To fix our ideas we must have an initial definition. Let us take Bouglé's[11a] and say that the caste system divides the whole society into a large number of hereditary groups, distinguished from one another and connected together by three characteristics: *separation* in matters of marriage and contact, whether direct or indirect (food); *division* of labour, each group having, in theory or by tradition, a profession from which their members can depart only within certain limits; and finally *hierarchy*, which ranks the groups as relatively superior or inferior to one another. This definition indicates the main apparent characteristics of the system, and for the moment it will suffice for the discussion of the literature.

Beginning with the word which has served to designate the fact, 'caste' is of Portuguese and Spanish origin: '*casta*, properly something not mixed, from the Latin *castus*, chaste' (Littré's *Dictionary*). The word seems to have been used in the sense of race by the Spaniards, and to have been applied to India by the Portuguese in the middle of the fifteenth century.[11b] In English, there is a use (*cast*) in the sense of race in 1555, and the Indian sense is encountered at the beginning of the seventeenth century; the French spelling, *caste*, is scarcely found before 1800. In French, Littré records that the word was only inserted in the Dictionary of the Academy in 1740 and appears neither in Furetière nor Richelet. It was used in the technical sense at least from 1700.[11c]

In English, as in French, there was for a long time no distinction between caste and tribe, and a confusion with the ancient division of Indian society into four categories. Thus Littré writes: '1. Each of the tribes into which Indian society is divided. There are four castes. . . .' The derived sense of 'exclusive group', as in the expression 'caste spirit', is found in both languages (recorded in English from 1807, in French in Tocqueville for example: 'Its distinctive mark is birth', as opposed to 'aristocracy' which designates 'the chief men').[11d]

## 12  Main attitudes

A complete history of the Western conception of the castes of India would require a whole book, but one who is familiar with the subject matter is led to form an idea of the main attitudes which have been current, and a brief review of them can be given here. Three periods will be distinguished. The first is characterized by the predominance of an explanatory attitude: the caste system is surprising or shocking, and consequently an *explanation of its existence* is sought. In the second period, which begins a little before the twentieth century, the explanatory tendency is still present but attention to *description* predominates. Finally, the contemporary period, starting from 1945, is characterized by *intensive studies* by anthropologists in the field: description becomes more precise and more detailed, sociological considerations predominate and tend to replace research into origins.[12a]

For the moment we shall be concerned with the explanatory attitude. In the early period in which it dominates it is found in its most categorical and simple-minded forms. Naturally it is the contradiction between the egalitarian mentality and an extremely hierarchical ideology which leads to *explanation*. But to some extent the aristocratic mentality survived within the modern age, especially at its outset, as in the case of Tocqueville, for example. Thus there are some people who tend to find caste less mysterious and shocking, and who are better prepared, at least to some extent, to understand it. Three types of explanation may be distinguished. The most immediate attitude when faced with an incomprehensible social institution is to attribute its existence to the will of certain men: this is the voluntarist or artificialist explanation.[12b] The contrary attitude consists in trying to connect it with known features of the society with which we are familiar: caste then results from the extreme development of certain features; this is the explanation as a limiting case. The aristocratic attitude, to which hierarchy is not totally foreign, tends to this type of explanation. Finally, the third attitude consists in attributing the phenomenon to the more or less unique confluence of circumstances or factors; this is historical explanation. Each of these types contains in turn a great variety of theories, in relation to the historical situation and the main paths of development of indological and anthropological studies.

## 13 *Voluntarist explanation*

This tendency was necessarily very strong in this case, from the beginning almost to the present day, for two reasons. First, all societies were in the eighteenth century still thought to have been instituted by early legislators. Secondly, the religious aspect is very pronounced in the caste system, and the priests, the Brahmans, have a privileged place in it. Now, for the anti-clericalism of the philosophy of the Enlightenment, 'superstition' was an invention of priests, for their own benefit. This view was brilliantly confirmed here, and both the recourse to irrationality and the conscious – indeed rational – form of the indigenous doctrine were explained at one go: the first as deception, the second as a deliberate construction.

We shall consider only two examples of this tendency, both very characteristic. The Abbé Dubois had left France before the end of the eighteenth century, and he proved rather Voltairian when faced with pagan religion. But this father of anthropologists lived for long years among the population of Southern India (in Mysore), trying to understand this society and its religion, and finally giving an excellent description of it. He concludes that, whatever the drawbacks of the 'division into castes', its advantages carry the day; it constitutes 'the *chef-d'œuvre* of Indian legislation'. Indeed, according to the Abbé Dubois, this people left to itself would tend to barbarity.

Such an institution was probably the only means that the most clearsighted prudence could devise for maintaining a state of civilization amongst a people endowed with the peculiar characteristics of the Hindus.

Still in artificialist language, the Abbé Dubois records from the beginning of the book a fundamental feature of the system: the specialization of labour is oriented towards the needs of all.

They set out from the cardinal principle common to all ancient legislators, that no person should be useless to the commonwealth.[13a]

The 1824 supplement of the *Encyclopaedia Britannica* contains an article entitled 'caste' by James Mill. Let us recall this eminent man's importance: apart from the education he gave his son, his threefold achievement was to definitely establish utilitarianism, to define the East India Company's policy in the essential period of 'liberalism', and finally to mould the minds of Indians who had an English education, during the whole of the nineteenth century and beyond.[13b] James Mill's article is divided roughly into three parts, devoted respectively to the presumed origin of the system, description of it, and criticism of it. The institution is presented as having been fairly widespread in antiquity (Egypt, Greece, Iran). It is bound up both with the history of the division of labour and with conscious intervention: the transition from a pastoral to an agricultural life entailed a decisive development in the division of labour; moreover, in this distant epoch, an innovator – in short a legislator – attributed the new organization to the divine will; priests were put at the summit because superstitition was powerful then, and heredity was instituted to obviate the (purely imaginary) risk of the disappearance of the division of labour.

One can see that in this account, by contrast with that of the Abbé Dubois, the legislator has a residual role: division of labour comes about by itself. Thus one ends up with a duality which we shall find again in similar guise and which, it may be said, is still with us in a more general form, for contemporary sociology has still to reconcile technical and economic aspects on the one hand, with religious aspects on the other.

### 14   *Caste as the limiting case of known institutions*

Since the end of the seventeenth century the question of whether caste is in essence religious or simply 'social' has constantly arisen. We shall content ourselves with three milestones. The question was for a long time vital for the Catholic missionaries. For the high castes, such an opprobrium attached to the way of life of the Portuguese that certain Jesuits had the idea of denying all solidarity with them and with those missionaries who were occupied with the low castes, and of adopting Hindu customs. They would thus be able to convert people of high caste, and the others would follow. De Nobili, an Italian of noble birth active in Madura in the first half of the seventeenth century, in this way won the esteem of those Hindus most given to spirituality and obtained some success. On the Catholic side he was accused of having condoned superstition and of having betrayed the true faith. He replied that caste only represented an extreme form of those distinctions of rank and estate well known in the West, and consequently was essentially only a social, not a religious matter, and that he did not have to show himself more rigorous towards pagan habits than the first apostles of Christ, his role being not to reform customs but to open souls to revelation. Pope Gregory XV found in his favour, in letter if not in spirit, in a bull of 1624. But, as is known, the daring policy of the Jesuits, in China as well as in India, was later condemned by Rome (the notorious Quarrel of Rites).[14a]

Writing in the nineteenth century, the Sanskritist Max Müller raised the same question for similar ends, but in a different context. If caste is by nature religious, the English government of India, whose principle was never to interfere in matters over and above the immediate interests of civil order, was justified in respecting it. If on the other hand it is not, nothing stood in the way of a bolder policy, in so far as it was judged just and prudent. Now, contrary to what Hindus often imagine, caste has no place in the Veda, which, for the Hindus, contains all revelation. It follows that the government and the missionaries could do what they liked with caste.[14b] Like de Nobili before him, Max Müller, whose theory of the origin of caste is complex, admits that it is essentially a question of a particular form of distinctions relating to birth, social situation and degree of education, as are known in all societies. The contrast with Europe consists in the religious justification, added to the social rules for the greater profit of the Brahmans. Rather like the Abbé Dubois, Max Müller thinks that the institution is doubtless well adapted to the circumstances and that 'if it were destroyed overnight [very likely] more evil than good would ensue'.

The third item of our appraisal is this: nowadays Hindus often assert to Westerners that caste is a social and not a religious matter. It is clear that the motivation here is quite different: it is mainly a question of finding some justification for the institutions from a Western point of view, the point of view usually accepted by the educated Hindu.

In the twentieth century, Max Müller's and de Nobili's idea is found again more or less unchanged in the work of the sociologist Max Weber, for whom caste is a particular kind of status group (German *Stand*) or estate, in the sense of the three estates of the *Ancien Régime* in France. Similar, though even more vague, is the very widespread idea that caste is a limiting case of social class in the modern sense of the term. Thus for Kroeber, the American anthropologist, the caste is a class which is conscious of itself as distinct and which has closed itself in upon itself. Two points should be noticed: to the extent that social class tends to be defined by economic characteristics, an economic grouping is here confused with a status group; further, consciousness is reduced to an epiphenomenon, which allows the religious justification of caste to be eliminated as easily as was done by Max Müller. This is the theory of 'social stratification', which conflates all social distinctions stamped with inequality, and is in this sense socio-centric.[14c]

There is another point of contact between caste society and modern society which allows a continuity to be set up between the two. This is the division of labour or professional specialization, the more accessible to the Westerner in that he can take it, in part, as separate from religion. Even today, many modern laymen are seduced by the idea of considering caste as a special development of the guild. In this respect the latest systematic theory is Nesfield's (1885), which had the merit of offering an explanation of hierarchy. According to Nesfield the hierarchical order corresponds inversely to the order in which the corresponding specializations emerged, the most ancient professions being the lowest. Unfortunately this hypothesis scarcely agrees with the data. For instance, were priests the last to emerge? No, but they established their supremacy belatedly. Despite his willingness to consider caste as a purely secular fact, Nesfield in fact appeals to ceremonial functions. Thus fishermen are superior to hunters because the superior castes need water carriers, and these are more or less identical with fishermen. Further, the difficulty for such a theory resides in the explanation of endogamy. How did the guild come to forbid all outside marriage? According to Nesfield, endogamy was introduced by the priests, the Brahmans, for their benefit. Originally a professional grouping, the Brahmans were the first to turn themselves into a caste and this sort of thing became general by imitation. So religion is introduced after all, and one comes close to voluntarism: 'Among all castes there prevailed a twofold test of precedence, the industrial and the Brahmanic.' One wonders whether this eclectic solution, with the importance it gives to imitation, was not the result of Nesfield's collaboration with his indigenous assistant, Ambika Prasad.[14d]

It will be noticed that in every case in which caste is taken as an extreme form of something which exists in the West, the religious aspect of the system is considered secondary. This is necessarily so, for it is the aspect which, if better appreciated, would introduce a discontinuity. Where the discontinuity appears people resort to artificialism (Nesfield).

A more recent and altogether different theory, which is best expounded by Hutton, can be linked to the preceding ones. Caste is no longer likened to more or less Western institutions but to the institutions of so-called primitive peoples or simpler societies, and the importance of the religious aspect is better recognized. On the other hand, like the previous writers, Hutton atomizes: he extracts from the system a long list of 'factors' which are in part known or presumed features of simple societies, and sees the system as resulting from their more or less fortuitous confluence. Where previously we had the *limit* of an institution we now have a *combination* of distinct features, a combination which apparently springs from an historical accident; the theory is in this respect similar to those which follow.[14e]

15  *'Historical' explanations*

All the explanations assembled under this heading refer more or less explicitly to past events, corroborated or assumed, but they are of various kinds. Three types may be distinguished: the Indo-European or Dravidian theory, the racial theory, and finally the diffusionist theory. It is known that in the nineteenth century, scholarly interest in India was first directed to the Indo-European aspect and the most ancient period of Indian history, that accompanying and following the entry into India of a population of Indo-European language, a population known from its religious texts, the Vedas and related texts. It is therefore natural that there should be an Indo-European theory of caste, and Senart provided it in 1896. The date is relatively late, given that the main interest had already shifted to more recent periods and that India had already ceased to appear purely Indo-European. On the other hand, Senart's approach belongs to the twentieth century in that he begins with a precise description of the contemporary state of affairs in order to go back into the past, and he opens discussions which are still current. It is no less true that, preoccupied by explaining above all the exclusiveness of caste, he saw its prototype in an Indo-European kin grouping corresponding to the Roman *gens*.[15a]

Recently the racial theory of caste has certainly been the most widespread. Many reasons can be seen for this. On the ideological side, there has been a tendency to derive the whole culture of post-Vedic India from the mingling of the culture of the Indo-European invaders with that of the autochthonous populations. The racial theory derives the institution of castes from the encounter between the two populations: the invaders sought to preserve the purity of their blood by the creation of closed groups – notice voluntarism again – or by a more subtle but equivalent mechanism. This explanation appears almost obvious to the modern mentality, for which it is precisely the notion of race that corresponds to the notion of caste, however great the difference may be in reality.[15b] The result is the use of arguments by analogy with supposedly similar modern institutions (Whites and Blacks in the United States or South Africa). Thus one has, here again, the benefit of an apparent continuity with modern phenomena. The theory, which had the advantage of calling on the contribution of physical anthropology, was systematized by Risley, who claimed that he found a simple correlation between the order of the castes and the nasal index of their members. It has been discussed and modified up to the present day. Let us simply notice that, whatever its origins, to the extent that each caste constitutes more or less perfectly a demographically isolated unit, it is natural that the average physical characteristics of its members should differ from those of another caste.[15c]

Let us mention solely for the record a third type of explanation which derives from a form of cultural history which has enjoyed a certain vogue in anthropology, diffusionism. Such an explanation would consist in tracing the history of the phenomenon to a unique origin in terms of its geographical distribution. Hocart, to whom we are much indebted in another connection for our understanding of caste, sometimes seems to presuppose such an explanation in the often daring comparisons he suggests with other civilizations.[15d]

## 16   Composite explanations

We have noted in passing certain combinations among the various types of explanation. There are many others. Thus in Max Müller's view, there were at first two distinct races; then the priests and nobility were distinguished from each other, and were distinct from the common people. Thus arose the classical four estates or *varṇa* (*cf.* Chapter III). Finally the common people were distinguished according to their profession.[16a] The idea of combining the explanations was bound to suggest itself, for each at best accounts for only one aspect of the system: either its hereditary character and the clear-cut separation between different groups, or the division of labour, or hierarchy, or, much more rarely, the religious aspect. All try, in short, to derive the whole from the part. Moreover, all the theories which we have reviewed, except Hutton's and the artificialist theory, try to grasp caste in some immediate way by starting from our own civilization. No doubt there is basically no other point of departure, even if one effects the transition by the intermediary of so-called primitive societies; but the very clear-cut difference, so shocking to modern man, can be understood only by a more laborious and radical approach.

## 17   The period 1900–1945

While the previous types of explanation were being developed, the first half of the twentieth century was characterized by progress from the point of view of comparison, understanding and analysis, and by a better appreciation of the place of religion. Ghurye, Hutton, Hocart, all three having experience of caste society in varying degrees, made explicit comparisons.[17a] Hocart's whole aim was to remain faithful to the indigenous point of view and to restore to it its internal logic. He sometimes allowed himself to speculate, but he did so starting from an improved description in which the place of religion was fully recognized.[17b] At the beginning of the century, Bouglé analysed the system on the basis of the literature about it and, by contrast with the partial theories which he discussed, insisted on the presence of three characteristics (hierarchy, separation, interdependence). He too was tempted to associate each with a different cause, but in the end he based them all together on the opposition between the pure and the impure, and this will be our starting-point. Finally, Max Weber, apart from contributions to general sociology (distinction between economic class and status group, nature of the division of labour) achieved in his vast fresco of comparative religion the richest and most fine-drawn comparison between the Western and the Hindu universe. Given that the work drew only on secondary sources and that its central viewpoint was taken from European developments, it is a miracle of empathy and sociological imagination.[17c]

Among the features of the caste system, these writers had a tendency to emphasize separation above all (except Hocart who, by contrast, neglected it too much). Bouglé for example assumed a 'repulsion' which automatically kept the castes apart from one another.[17d] All said and done, even where the intention was to treat caste as part of a whole, the tendency to treat each caste as a small self-sufficient society was not completely overcome, and it will be encountered again in the subsequent period.

## 18 *After 1945*

The contemporary period, since the last war, is characterized by the predominance of field studies, of observation of restricted groups by professional anthropologists. It is a rich and various period, even if it has not yet produced anything comparable to Bouglé or Max Weber. The studies are of varying size and importance. They rarely take the caste system itself as their topic, but more often one of its aspects or a related aspect of the society. On the whole, sociological considerations and descriptions replace speculation about origins. Over and above the diversity of the works and tendencies, one can isolate a certain consensus on some points. It was very quickly realized that the category of the 'village' should not be overestimated, and the old notion of the self-sufficient 'village community' has been criticized. Much emphasis has been placed on the fact that each actual caste system very likely corresponded in the past to the territory of a small political unit, the 'little kingdom'. As will be seen (Chapter VII) the idea was not unknown, but in this period it has taken on a new prominence. Two concepts proposed by Professor Srinivas have been much employed. These are that of the 'dominant caste', that is the caste which dominates the village because it possesses the land, and that of 'Sanskritization', designating mainly the tendency of inferiors to imitate the Brahmans in the hope of improving their status.

There is a predilection for the study of modern phenomena, 'social change' and political facts. After a long period in which the changes were overestimated, this concern seems to me to lead today to the need for a more precise comparison between India and the West (Chapter XI). In this period, ancient literature has often been neglected, and there have even been protests against the propensity of previous writers to make use of the old Sanskrit texts.[18a] No doubt this should not be done indiscriminately, but there is a tendency to exaggerate both the contribution made by direct observation alone, and the distance between what it reveals and what is provided by ancient sources.

Finally, whilst there has been progress in the detailed consideration of the various aspects of the system, there still remain obstacles. Thus, as far as hierarchy is concerned (Chapter III), not to mention monographs, Stevenson marks progress over Blunt, and McKim Marriott progress over Stevenson,[18b] but even so there still persists a lack of understanding of hierarchy as such. The widespread fashion in this period for the theory of 'social stratification' has already been mentioned. Doubtless it represents an advance to the extent that it stresses differences of rank, but it also blocks all understanding of hierarchy (Appendix) and at the same time tends to ignore or exclude the other aspects of caste (division of labour, etc.). Just as previously the religious aspect of the system was often reduced to an epiphenomenon, so here one observes at least an attempt by anthropologists to reduce hierarchy to relations of power (K. Gough).[18c] The study of the system of division of labour in the village also shows an incapacity to grasp hierarchy in its true perspective. Wiser, a pioneer, had described it in detail for a Northern village as early as 1931, but counter to all the evidence he insisted on seeing it as a matter of 'reciprocity' amounting to equality. More recently Beidelman, in a work drawing only on secondary sources, rightly criticizes him on this point, but he, in turn, though seeing inequality, confuses it with 'exploitation'. Both failed to see that the system assures subsistence to each *proportionally to his status* (Chapter IV).

Finally, the refusal to take an over-all view, and the insistence, in a structural universe, on identifying *the* caste as the 'real group', as a substance or an individual, is perpetuated by certain authors. We shall shortly see how the problem is raised in full by Hutton. Recently Stevenson, in an article in the *Encyclopaedia Britannica*, suggests a subtle solution to Hutton's problem: to consider 'caste' as a more or less indefinable attribute of certain groups, thus making it secondary.[18d] Even more plainly, for Mrs Karvé the real group is the group which entered the system at a given time and is recognizable by its customs and the physical characteristics of its members. As this group is at the level of the subcaste, the caste itself, though identified by its name in Indian society, is reduced to being called a 'cluster': thus, a cluster of 'castes' (i.e. in ordinary terminology, a cluster of subcastes).[18e] The system is taken as a mere collection of 'blocks' and their arrangement is neglected. But this is an extreme and exceptional case; more characteristic of the period as a whole is the fact that direct observation does not put an end to views which are Westernistic, atomistic, materialistic, behaviouristic, and which lead, for example, to the confusion between caste and racism. One can expect some progress here, for the period of intensive research has not long begun, and has yet to yield its full harvest.

As a whole one sees that the inevitable sociocentricity of the first period made itself felt in the second and is not yet absent from the third. We have seen that its chief manifestations are: the reduction of the religious to the non-religious; the tendency to take the part for the whole, either *the* caste instead of the system, or one aspect (separation *or* hierarchy) instead of all the aspects together; finally, and especially at this time, the underestimation or the reduction of *hierarchy*, the failure to consider it or the incapacity to understand it. As was predictable from the contrast between our notions and those in question, and as will be seen more clearly in what follows, this is the stumbling block, the main obstacle to the understanding of the caste system.[18f]

CHAPTER TWO

# FROM SYSTEM TO STRUCTURE:
# THE PURE AND THE IMPURE

As we have seen, we are in danger of projecting our own prejudices onto the phenomenon we are studying, and we require a method based on our relationship to it. In a sense, this raises the question of the method of social anthropology in general; this preliminary discussion, kept to the minimum essential to our particular subject, is contained in the first three sections of this chapter, and precedes the statement of the ideological principle of the system – the opposition of the pure and the impure.

## 21 *Element and system*

How many castes are there in India? Can some of the main castes be listed, can they be counted? No doubt such questions occur to the reader. We will not try to answer them here since, as will become apparent later, they are largely meaningless. Let us try to show briefly why this is so. As will be seen, every actual caste system was more or less limited to a definite geographical area. So for the sake of simplification let us picture India as composed of an indefinite number of small territorial districts and as many actual caste systems, outside which marriage was impossible. To arrive at the total number of castes in India, should the number of castes in a system (supposing this is constant) be multiplied by the number of districts? Or should the similarities between one district and another be taken into account and, since there are Brahmans everywhere at the top of the hierarchy, should it be said that there is a 'caste' of Brahmans? This would be to ignore the extreme partitioning within this category (for it is a category – *varṇa* – and

33

not a caste). The same goes for the Untouchables at the foot of the ladder: several castes of them are present even in a single district. Barbers also are found everywhere, but they are internally partitioned and their hierarchical status is not the same in the north as in the south.

In practice, to enumerate the castes one must be content to see them from the outside: in a given linguistic area there is a large but not indefinite number of names of castes. They could be added up, but in doing so one would overlook an important aspect of the phenomenon: seen from the inside, the category corresponding to one of these names is subdivided at least once and often several times, and marriage, for example, takes place only within one of the subdivisions. In fact there is no end to this subdivision: what from afar seemed unified appears as partitioned at close quarters. Nevertheless, a regional list of castes seen from the outside is not meaningless, for this is more or less how the system appears to those who live in it from the point of view of the relationships between different castes (see n. 21c). Later, examples will be given of the caste composition of village populations.

The caste, unified from the outside, is divided within. More generally, a particular caste is a complex group, a successive inclusion of groups of diverse orders or levels, in which different functions (profession, endogamy, etc.) are attached to different levels. Finally, far more than a 'group' in the ordinary sense, the caste is a *state of mind*, a state of mind which is expressed by the emergence, in various situations, of groups of various orders generally called 'castes'. This is why the whole should not be seen by starting from the notion of the 'element', in terms of which it would be known through the number and nature of the constituent 'elements', but by starting from the notion of the 'system' in terms of which certain fixed principles govern the arrangement of fluid and fluctuating 'elements'. To be convinced of this one need only refer to one of the most recent exegeses of *caste*, that by J. H. Hutton. Having presented the definitions or descriptions proposed by various authors, he concludes:

The truth is that while a caste is a social unit in a quasi-organic system of society and throughout India is consistent enough to be immediately identifiable, the nature of the unit is variable enough to make a concise definition difficult. . . .[21a]

34

The mode of expression is awkward. Yet the admission of the difficulty contains its solution: if the element cannot be defined, then let us try to define the system, which is apparently constant and 'quasi-organic'. But Hutton notes the shortcomings of an atomistic conception without trying to replace it. It is characteristic that he makes no reference in this connection to Bouglé's *Essai* which, much earlier, had started from the system instead of the element. Moreover, in a regional volume of the 1931 *Census*, of which Hutton was the all-India Commissioner, an anonymous author had written precisely this: 'Modern science asserts that it is impossible to understand or appreciate any element in a structure unless its function as part of the whole be taken into account. . . . Our first duty, therefore, is to survey the system as a whole.'[21b]

But what is to be understood by 'system' of castes? The word assumes two different senses, an empirical sense and an ideological one. The set of actual castes which are found together in a definite territory may be spoken of as a geographically circumscribed system of castes. As we shall see, there are good reasons for thinking that in the past the caste system in fact existed in the form of such concrete wholes spatially juxtaposed and each corresponding to a small political unit. It is therefore useful to consider things in this way, but from the theoretical point of view it is neither sufficient nor primary, for these concrete wholes, once isolated, are seen to be alike and to rest on common principles. In this sense one can speak of *the* caste system as a pan-Indian institution. At this level, the caste system is above all a system of ideas and values, a formal, comprehensible, rational system, a system in the intellectual sense of the term. It is this aspect which led previous authors, like the Abbé Dubois, to consider caste as a conscious creation of legislators of times past.[21c] Our first task is to grasp this intellectual system, this ideology.

This approach has the disadvantage of greatly extending the subject matter. If we were content with the empirical approach the system would be conveniently limited to those groups called castes and to the corresponding individual or collective relationships, either within the caste or between members of different castes. This again can be understood either broadly or narrowly: there has been for some years a tendency to leave out of consideration the village network of specialization and interdependence between different castes, known as the '*jajmāni* system', as if it constituted a distinct reality and not an aspect of the caste system. Witness Hutton, who, no doubt carried away by his tendency to atomize, says not a word about it.[21d]

⟨On the contrary, the more one stresses the ideological aspect, the more difficult it is to isolate a special domain within the caste society in its entirety. For example, the idea of hierarchy, so important as far as caste is concerned, is not confined to it but penetrates the domain of kinship: it is not unreasonable to suppose that in the evolution of Hindu law, the father–son relationship has been modelled on the interdependence which obtains, in terms of castes, between a superior and an inferior person.[21e] For the sake of the exposition an arbitrary limit must be drawn, and this sort of fact, which extends beyond castes in the system of ideas concerning them, must be deferred to what we shall call the implications and concomitants of the system, of which the most important will be indicated later (Chapter IX).

## 22   The place of ideology

We have said that we shall be concerned first and foremost with a system of ideas and values. We have also in passing acknowledged territory or locality as an example of a factor which, while not figuring directly in the ideology, intervenes at the level of the concrete manifestations of the caste system. It is as well to throw some light on this duality. First let us note that the two kinds of aspects are perceived in different ways, so that the distinction between them expresses our position in relation to the object. On the one hand it is the indigenous theory which provides us with the name: when we say 'caste' we are more or less translating an indigenous concept (*jāt, jāti,* a word of Indo-European root but which is probably encountered everywhere); if we were to speak of 'social stratification' we would introduce the following arbitrary judgments: (1) that caste and social class are phenomena of the same nature; (2) that hierarchy is incomprehensible; (3) that in the Indian system the separation and the interdependence of groups are subordinated to this sort of obscure or shamefaced hierarchy.[22a] On the other hand, in so far as we are able to detect in the facts a dimension other than that contained in indigenous consciousness, this is thanks to comparison, thanks first and foremost to the implicit and inevitable comparison with our own society. This must be obvious.

We must therefore proceed in two phases: first take lessons from the Hindus, Hindus of today and of times past, in order to see things as they do. They see them very systematically and it is not impossible to isolate the principle behind their view. Indeed, we shall realize that they have largely done the work for us. Some eight centuries perhaps before Christ, tradition established an absolute distinction between power and hierarchical status, and this is a cardinal point which modern research has not been able to elucidate by its own means. Yet on certain points we shall take the liberty of completing and systematizing the indigenous or orthogenic theory of caste – not without employing empirical aspects in a secondary capacity – by postulating that men in society behave in a coherent and rational manner, especially in such an important matter, and that it is possible to recover the simple principle of their thought. Naturally we make these modifications at our own risk, the touchstone always being what the people themselves think and believe. There is nothing new in all this, of course: it is what the ethnologist or social anthropologist has always tried to do. But the itinerary is made longer and more complicated, but at the same time more certain, by the fact that we are dealing with a great and ancient civilization. It is only recently that the premature generalizations of sociology, in the restricted sense of the term, have offered specious short-cuts in this lengthy journey.

But ideology is not everything. Any concrete, localized, whole, when actually observed, is found to be decisively oriented by its ideology, and also to extend far beyond it. This poses the fundamental problem of these studies in general. Currently several solutions are offered: nowadays, ideology is often sacrificed to the empirical aspect, but sometimes the reverse is done, or else the two may be opposed absolutely to each other.[22b] We shall give some examples. Let us observe in passing that the fact is universal: if it reflected only the data, and reflected it completely, the system of ideas and values would cease to be capable of orienting action, it would cease to be itself (§7). In our case, in every concrete whole we find the formal principle at work, but we also find something else, a raw material which it orders and logically encompasses but which it does not explain, at least not immediately and for us. This is where we find the equivalent of what we call relations of force, political and economic phenomena, power, territory, property, etc. Those data which we can recover thanks to the notions we have of them in our own ideology may be called the (comparative) concomitants of the ideological system. Certain authors select them for study without noticing that the devaluation which they undergo in the present case alters them profoundly. The specialist steeped in modern ideology expects everything from these phenomena, but here they are bound by the iron shackles of a contrary ideology. To confine ourselves to these is – to take a local simile – to entrench oneself in an inferior caste. On the contrary they must, in our opinion, be set in their place and related to the ideology which they accompany in fact, it being understood that *it is only in relation to the totality thus reconstructed that the ideology takes on its true sociological significance.*

True, research has not advanced much in this direction and we cannot hope to get very far here, but at least the method is beyond doubt. Taken overall our object appears like an iceberg: only one part, the easier to describe, emerges into the light of consciousness, yet it is of a piece with another part, more obscure, but whose presence we know how to detect. The observed phenomenon has an ideological component and another which, without prejudging any ontological question, I shall call residual, in order to indicate the way in which it is ascertained. Once what happens on the plane of observation $O$, is related to a first plane of reference, the plane of ideology, $I$, it brings to light another component situated in the residual plane $R$: $(o = i + r)$. From observation and ideology we deduce by 'subtraction' the residual empirical component of each observed phenomenon. It goes without saying that we are liable to error in this sort of operation: in particular, we run the serious risk of being mistaken in the application of the ideology to a particular situation, especially at the beginning and if we overestimate our understanding of the system. Happily, the different phenomena or vectors are not independent of each other, and little by little we shall see emerging the first features of a general law of the relations between $I$ and $R$ in the system.[22c]

A word remains to be said about the exposition. It would be irksome first to describe the ideology and then take up each point again on the plane of observation. Although the $R$ or non-ideological plane is not dealt with directly until Chapter VII (Power and Territory) the corresponding component will be brought out *pari passu* in the treatment of the properly ideological aspects. For example, in the case of hierarchy (Chapter III) we shall begin with the ideology and then consider the observed datum and thus bring to light the residual component.

There is scarcely need to repeat that whilst the aspects called 'politico-economic' are thus considered secondary in relation to the ideology of caste, this is not the result of any prejudice but only of the necessity of giving a faithful picture of the system as it appears to us. It is not impossible, although it is hardly conceivable at present, that in the future the politico-economic aspects will be shown to be in reality the fundamental ones, and the ideology secondary. Only we are not there yet. For the moment it is a question of a comprehensive description, one which is both intelligible and all-embracing.

## 23 *The notion of structure*

Starting from our current view of hierarchy we tend at first to picture the caste system, or a concrete set of castes, as a linear order going from the highest to the lowest, a transitive non-cyclic order: each caste is lower than those which precede it and higher than those which follow it and they are all comprised between two extreme points. It will be objected that this is too simple a picture: in the middle region in particular it is often difficult to rank one of two given castes absolutely in relation to the other (*cf.* 35 ff.). Further, an order of this sort, should we have to content ourselves with it as a final datum, is scarcely convenient. Happily, things change if one considers the *principles* whereby the castes are ranked in a more or less exact order. Underlying this order is found a system of oppositions, a structure.

The word 'structure' is used today very broadly and variously. Let us briefly recall the strict sense in which it will be taken here, and the consequences as well as the conditions of this use. We owe the introduction of the strict concept of structure in anthropology to Claude Lévi-Strauss. It comes from phonology and, from the standpoint which interests us, it is necessary to refer back also to *Gestalttheorie*, or theory of form, and to phenomenology.[23a] The difficulty found in the consideration of systems in anthropology is rather like that recently pointed out in physics by Louis de Broglie:

[In quantum physics] . . . the individuality of the elementary particles is the more attenuated the more they are engaged in interaction. As, on the one hand, there is no completely isolated particle and as, on the other hand, the bonding of the particles into a system is practically never sufficiently complete for something of their individuality not to remain, it can be seen that reality seems in general to lie somewhere between the concept of autonomous individuality and the concept of a completely fused system.

The solution in our subject is to avoid a mixture and to speak either one or the other of two languages. This is possible because one corresponds well enough to modern mentality, the other to the mentality I shall call traditional because it is dominant in the societies which have preceded our own. According to one approach, a system is conceived as made up of objects each with its own essence, and it is in virtue of this essence, together with a definite law of interaction, that they act on one another: for example, physical bodies each have their own mass and act on each other to an extent determined by this mass and their relative position. This way of thinking, which separates the individual being from the relation, is essentially modern. No doubt it is found in other societies, but it is typical of modern societies in so far as it is fully developed and excludes the opposite way of thinking. According to the other approach, the 'elements' in themselves of which the system seems to be composed are disregarded, and only considered as the product of the network of relations; this network would then constitute the system. A phoneme has only the characteristics which oppose it to other phonemes, it is not some thing but only the other of others, thanks to which it signifies something. We shall speak of structure exclusively in this case, when the interdependence of the elements of a system is so great that they disappear without residue if an inventory is made of the relations between them: a system of relations, in short, not a system of elements. The passage from one mentality or state of mind to another, from the world of structure to the world of substance or conversely, is no doubt the major problem in the comparison of societies. Here we have the good fortune to find ourselves faced with a world which is structural to a very high degree. This deserves a moment's reflection, for it is the prime reason for the difficulty we have in understanding the world of caste. As soon as we hear of human groups which separate themselves, distinguish themselves, isolate themselves fiercely from one another, we believe we know what we have to deal with: very well, we think, we know about this, it is rather like what we do as individuals, these castes resemble our precious modern persons, they are just so many little societies shut in on themselves and juxtaposed as we are juxtaposed to our fellow men in modern society. Well, nothing is more false. The caste isolates itself by submission to the whole, like an arm which does not wish to marry its cells to those of the stomach. We shall see this more clearly hereafter, and also how it is to a large extent hierarchy which dictates separation. For the moment let us only say that while in our society the reference is to the elements, in this society it is to the whole.

This introduction of the idea of structure is the major event of our times in social anthropology and sociology. The very fashion for the term in its loosest senses in a way bears witness to this. After a long period dominated by a tendency which led to atomization, the essential problem for contemporary thought is to rediscover the meaning of wholes or systems, and structure provides the only logical form as yet available to this end. The convergence with electronic procedures and with modern mathematics (too long neglected by our educational system) is not due to chance. In social anthropology itself, the unique repercussion of Evans-Pritchard's monograph on the Nuer, published in 1939, is evidence to the same effect.[23b] In my opinion, this was due to the independent discovery of the notion, and its revelation to a professional milieu saturated with empiricism, by a profound and prudent analyst, moreover one steeped in French sociology. While Evans-Pritchard's discovery has particular value in so far as it is an independent development springing – so far as one knows – solely from the analysis of the political and lineage systems of the Nuer, his notion of structure is at first sight more limited and less radical than that borrowed by Lévi-Strauss from other disciplines. For Evans-Pritchard it is a question of the non-substantiality, the relativity of the various orders of groupings or distinctions, with respect to the situations in which they are seen in action. Actually, careful reading shows that Evans-Pritchard has really discovered on his own account the structural principle of the 'distinctive opposition' – which is conceptual – even if he expresses it for the most part in the language of oppositions of fact, of conflict. In this sense his 'structure' generally appears as tied to empirical circumstances. In a certain situation, group A and group B are opposed, each united against the other. In another situation, we see $A_1$ and $A_2$ face to face, segments of A which but a moment ago were not differentiated. And so on. . . . I have not mentioned this theory solely from a historical point of view or as a reminder of the progress which may be made by studying conceptual forms in the diverse social situations in which they prevail, but also for a practical reason. For it directly introduces the notion of *segmentation*, which we shall resort to later. In the caste system, as in the political system of the Nuer, which groups appear – or disappear – depends on the situation at hand. Sometimes we are concerned with one caste opposed (in fact or idea) to another, sometimes we see the same caste become *segmented* into subcastes (etc.). For this reason we shall employ the words 'segment' and 'segmentation' only to designate the division or subdivision of a group into *several groups of the same nature but smaller scale*.[23c] Segmentation is an aspect of structure as opposed to substance. Substantially, we reduce everything to a single plane of consideration: the individual man, or the nation, or the caste. Structurally, the caste appears in certain situations and disappears in others in favour of larger or smaller entities. Here there is not, as in our universe of the individual, a privileged level. In particular, we shall see that the various properties of caste are attached to different levels of the phenomenon.

## 24 *The fundamental opposition*

To return to caste. For the moment it is a question of the formal system. We shall try first to grasp its principles and then to reduce it to a structure. Though Hutton cannot serve as our starting-point, Hegel can, for he, as long ago as 1830, went further than many a more recent author. Hegel saw the principle of the system in abstract *difference* (and indeed *jāti*, caste, is also 'species' in the botanical or zoological sense). True, Hegel seems at first to bring caste close to the modern individual in the way we have criticized, but one very soon realizes that he ascribes this 'difference' to the whole and to hierarchy: it is a question of a differentiation of functions, which could not come from the outside, and culminates in the universal.[24a]

More recently, Bouglé says nothing very different, though his language is more precise. His *Essai*, dating from the beginning of the century, is still topical. The work has not made the mark it deserved for two reasons. First it was written in French, while few Indians read French; English is of necessity the main language of these studies.[24b] Secondly, the work was in advance of contemporary ideas, it moved away from the dominant empiricist and materialist tendencies of these studies, and as the author had acquired no direct knowledge of India it passed all the more easily for a manifestation of French intellectualism. Bouglé's *Essai* provides us with the best initial definition; it is indeed a work relying exclusively on secondary sources, though Bouglé was a sociologist of Durkheim's school who had devoted his thesis to egalitarian ideas, and who was careful to reduce things to their principles while omitting nothing essential. According to him, the caste system is composed of hereditary groups (the castes, except for the segmentary aspect which will be mentioned again later) which are both distinguished from one another and connected together in three ways:

(1) by gradation of status or hierarchy;
(2) by detailed rules aimed at ensuring their separation;
(3) by division of labour and the interdependence which results from it.[24c]

Bouglé sometimes tends to separate these three aspects from one another. However, it is obvious that all three are given together and that their separation is an analytic distinction introduced by the observer. Indeed, Bouglé himself recognizes this in certain passages of his book. The three 'principles' rest on one fundamental conception and are reducible to a single true principle, namely the opposition of the pure and the impure. This opposition underlies hierarchy, which is the superiority of the pure to the impure, underlies separation because the pure and the impure must be kept separate, and underlies the division of labour because pure and impure occupations must likewise be kept separate. *The whole is founded on the necessary and hierarchical coexistence of the two opposites.* One could speak of a 'synthetic *a priori*' opposition: it is unprofitable to atomize it into simple elements just to gratify our logic, and in any case it should not be analysed without being subsequently recomposed.

This fact is of extreme importance, since it transports us at once into a purely structural universe: it is the whole which governs the parts, and this whole is very rigorously conceived as based on an opposition. Moreover there is no other way of defining a whole as distinct from a simple collection, and if we have to a large extent forgotten this, it is because of the predominant tendency of our civilization to replace reference to the whole by reference to the simple, the independent, the self-sufficient, that is to say, the individual or substance. Here we have in our grasp the fact which enables us to understand the institution, to raise it from the rank of an antiquarian's curiosity to that of a form of humanity. This is properly the idea of caste.

But this point is far from being admitted. Before throwing some light, in the following section, on the nature of the pure and the impure, a brief account is called for of the doubts and objections of specialists, in which the reader will naturally be tempted to join. First of all, it must be understood that we are not inventing anything: as will be seen, preoccupation with the pure and the impure is constant in Hindu life. Observers, whatever their tendencies, are compelled to acknowledge it. All they can do today is to minimize the fact, for example by shifting it back into 'culture' considered as a more or less gratuitous additive to society. (*Cf.* note 21c, above.) This is in keeping with a general prejudice against ideology. A master of Sanskrit, Louis Renou, some years ago wrote tersely that the notion of impurity 'is at the basis, theoretically at least, of the caste society'. Hutton says somewhere that a religious theory can help us to understand caste but cannot account for its existence throughout history. He seems to imply that for this we would have to invoke economic factors.[24d] This type of attitude is very widespread but it hardly expresses more than the scepticism of modern man about the place of religion in social life, *pace* Hegel, Durkheim and Max Weber and the whole of ethnology. Besides, preoccupation with causes is so general that I must make clear that I do not claim that the opposition between pure and impure is the 'foundation' of society except in the intellectual sense of the term: it is by implicit reference to this opposition that the society of castes appears consistent and rational to those who live in it. In my opinion the fact is central, nothing more.

Over and above this general attitude, precise objections are, fortunately, already forthcoming. We shall consider two of them. According to the first, the distinction between pure and impure

44

does not account for all the distinctions or segmentations of caste. For Hsu, the criteria of rank vary regionally, and there are criteria other than purity,[24e] according to Hsu and Béteille, relative purity does not account for the territorial subdivision of castes. On the first point, it will be shown later that all the *criteria*, properly so-called, are reducible to the fundamental opposition, but it will also be found that alongside the criteria there are *factors* on the level of observation which complicate or warp the status rankings and segmentation. These factors, though extraneous to the ideology, are operative empirically, and they will be brought to light, as we have already said, by confronting the results of observation with the ideology. We have already encountered one such factor in the partitioning into small territorial units, each of which serves as a factual framework for the deployment of the ideological system, a state of affairs which must have existed in the past. This brings us to the second point. Under present conditions, one is confronted within a given caste by subdivisions of a territorial nature which, as Béteille says, are inexplicable in terms of relative purity.[24f] Let us be more precise to prevent misunderstanding: we do not claim that the fundamental opposition is the *cause* of all the distinctions of caste, we claim that it is their *form*: it would be very surprising to learn that where two territorial subdivisions of a Brahman caste are present nowadays in the same locality, one is not considered superior to the other; at the most, it may be that each claims to be superior. The requirement of hierarchy is so exacting that it expresses in a unique language phenomena which the observer can distinguish by, for example, linking them to different 'causes'. This fact, which is essential, will become clearer as we proceed. It is, as always, the relation between the ideological and the empirical aspects which is at stake. In this case, the ideology takes no account of the territorial factor, it ignores it and encompasses it. For the present let us only insist on the fact that this relation, far from being a matter of pure 'form', which would launch us on the search for a 'content', is constitutive. Or will it be claimed that purity has its source in territory?

There is a second objection, at least implicit in Hsu's observations, which looks much more awkward for the theory. It could be formulated by saying that the opposition between pure and impure varies so much from one group to another that it is impossible to regard it as the universal rationale of the system.

Indeed, not only are there great variations, at least in the intensity of the corresponding feeling, among the Hindus themselves (§§25·6; 35), but above all two sorts of facts appear crucial: on the one hand a sectarian group like the Lingayats (who may or may not be classified as Hindus depending on the definition adopted) can formally deny impurity, and on the other hand the Muslims and the Christians have nothing in their official religion other than the opposite of the notion, yet all, at first sight at least, certainly have castes. (For further details, see §§93·2, 104). Hence it is true that the ideology in which we see the conscious centre of caste can be lacking here or there *within the Indian world*, and observation of these cases is of the greatest interest, to show us to what extent and in what conditions institutions of this kind can survive the weakening or disappearance of their ideological aspect. (In point of fact intensive study is needed to throw light on this.) In short, one must distinguish the basic ideology present in the society at large, and which observed systems demand for their intelligibility, from what is encountered by way of ideology in each particular observation. One may say that the basic ideology is incontestably very widespread and powerful in most of the actual cases: it does not spring from the imagination of the inquirer, and it is not a purely literary or 'cultural' matter. The fact that it is lacking in extreme cases and that it is weakened in a large number of cases – increasingly so nowadays – poses a problem, and requires an inquiry of a finer degree of precision than we can reach here; but it does not throw doubt on the elementary level with which we must be content for the moment.

## 25  Pure and impure

25.1  *General view.* Here we propose to specify the nature of the opposition between pure and impure by successive approximations.[25a] At first sight, two main questions will probably come to mind: why is this distinction applied to hereditary groups? And, if it accounts for the contrast between Brahmans and Untouchables, can it account equally for the division of society into a large number of groups, themselves sometimes extremely subdivided? We will not answer these questions directly but will confine ourselves to some remarks in relation to them. It is generally agreed that the opposition is manifested in some macroscopic form in the

46

contrast between the two extreme categories: Brahmans and Un-touchables. The Brahmans, being in principle priests, occupy the supreme rank with respect to the whole set of castes. The Un-touchables, as very impure servants, are segregated outside the villages proper, in distinct hamlets (or at least distinct quarters). The Untouchables may not use the same wells as the others (barring recent local relaxations), access to Hindu temples was forbidden them up to the Gandhian reform, and they suffer from numerous other disabilities. (It must be said that the situation has been somewhat modified since the Gandhian agitation, and that independent India has declared Untouchability illegal; this is an important step, but it cannot transform overnight the traditional situation which concerns us here.) The term 'Untouchable' to designate the category is English rather than indigenous: the notion is present, but in common usage these people are designated by the name of the particular caste to which they belong. Euphem-isms are usually resorted to when the category is designated, the most recent, introduced by Gandhi, being 'Harijan', 'sons of Hari', that is, creatures of God (Vishnu).

Why, it may be asked, this separation of the Untouchables? May it be supposed, for example, that it is due to the nauseating smell of the skins they are accustomed to treat? Hygiene is often invoked to justify ideas about impurity. In reality, even though the notion may be found to contain hygienic associations, these cannot account for it, as it is a religious notion. I shall show in what follows that the immediate source of the notion is to be found in the temporary impurity which the Hindu of good caste contracts in relation to organic life. Starting from this, we shall see that it is specialization in impure tasks, in practice or in theory, which leads to the attribution of a massive and permanent impurity to some categories of people. Ancient literature confirms that temporary and permanent impurity are identical in nature. But one must not lose sight of the complementarity which exists between pure and impure, and also between the social groups in which these ideas are expressed. One can subsequently trace not only the multiple derivations of the notion, but also the multiplication of the criteria of distinction and the extreme portioning out, so to speak, of hierarchical status between a large number of groups. We will end by mentioning some variants and irregularities and by sketching a semantic comparison with our own notions.

25.2 *Temporary impurity and permanent impurity*. In large areas
of the world, death, birth and other events in personal or family
life are considered to harbour a danger which leads to the temporary seclusion of the affected persons, to prohibitions against contact,
etc. Although the notion of impurity is lacking and although these
dangerous situations are not distinguished from other situations,
it is believed in Dobu, for example, that a transgression of the
prohibition will lead to a skin disease; or again contact with
mourners can be dangerous for the same reason as contact with
the chief's head (Polynesia).[25b] Not all traces of notions of this
kind are absent from Catholicism. Thus Candlemas is the Feast
of the Purification of the Virgin, and even recently the newly-
delivered mother was actually excluded from the church for forty
days, at the end of which she would present herself carrying a
lighted candle and would be met at the church porch by the priest.
In so far as the notion of impurity is present, the bath is the most
widespread remedy for it. In India, persons affected by this kind
of event are impure for a prescribed period, and Indians themselves identify this impurity with that of the Untouchables. Thus
Professor P. V. Kane, the learned jurist to whom we owe that
monumental work, the *History of the Dharmaśāstra*, writes that a
man's nearest relatives and his best friend become untouchable
for him for a certain time as a result of these events (II, 1, p. 170).

If we compare more precisely what happens in the case of death
among the Hindus with what happens in a tribe, we see first that
among the Hindus the notion of impurity is distinct, different from
the notion of danger which corresponds elsewhere to the sacred
in general and not only to the impure. Then we notice another
difference: elsewhere one gets rid of the danger of the situation,
in one respect, by recourse to complementarity, which is conceived
as instantaneous and reciprocal: I bury your dead, you bury mine.
In India itself affinal relations are seen on occasion to undertake
certain functions of the kind, but in general the principal functions
are entrusted to specialists. As Hocart says, in the south of the
country the barber is the funeral priest and thus burdened with
impurity; in the whole of India except perhaps the Maratha
country the washerman takes care of washing the soiled linen at
times of birth and menstruation. In these cases the washerman
and the barber are specialists in impurity, who, in virtue of their
functions, find themselves living permanently in a state bordering

upon that which the people they serve enter temporarily: a state which these people get out of thanks to, among other things, a terminal bath. (It is true that these two specialists do not belong to the Untouchables proper.) Thus it is seen that, in the setting of the opposition between pure and impure, the religious division of labour goes hand in hand with the permanent attribution to certain professions of a certain level of impurity. From this it should not be inferred that the religious division of labour cannot arise in another setting. This is what Hocart has shown, though involuntarily, by comparing the caste system to the specialization of religious functions in Fiji. In Fiji, the system is centred on the chief, let us say the king, and the pure and the impure are not distinguished. In India, the king or his equivalent is indeed the main employer, but the Brahman, the priest, is superior to him, and correspondingly the pure and the impure are opposed. I have anticipated in order to show straight away how Hocart must be corrected on an important point.

Notice two further essential differences between the Indian and the tribal case. Elsewhere, the dangerous contact acts directly on the person involved, affecting his health for example, whereas with the Hindus it is a matter of impurity, that is, of fall in social status or risk of such a fall. This is quite different, although traces of the other conception can be found in India. Furthermore, in human relationships the relation between superiors (who are sacred elsewhere and pure in India) and inferiors is reversed: the tribal chief is taboo, i.e. dangerous for the common people, whereas the Brahman is vulnerable to pollution by an inferior.

25.3 *Historical data.* Normative literature, the literature of the *dharma* or religious law, has purification (*śuddhi*) as one of its main themes, the impurity resulting from birth and death being specially designated *āśauca*. According to *Hārīta*, the purity he calls external is of three kinds, bearing on the family (*kula*), objects of everyday use (*artha*), and the body (*śarīra*). For the body, the main thing is the morning attention to hygiene culminating in the daily bath. According to Manu there are twelve secretions or impurities, including excrement, saliva, and the lowly fate reserved for the left hand (in Tamil the 'hand of filth'). Objects are distinguished by the greater or lesser ease of their purification (a bronze vessel is merely cleaned, an earthenware one replaced) and their relative richness: silk is purer than cotton, gold than silver, than bronze, than copper. But above all one realizes that objects are not polluted simply by contact, but by the use to which they are put, by a sort of participation by the object, in being used, with the person. Thus nowadays a new garment or vessel can be received from anybody. It is said that his own bed, his garment, his wife, his child, his water-pot are pure from pollution for the person himself, but impure for others.[25c]

Family impurity is the most important: it is that of birth (*sūtaka*) and above all death. Birth only lastingly affects the mother and the new-born child. Death affects the relations collectively and it is a social rather than a physical matter, since the impurity essentially affects not the people in whose house someone dies, but the relations of the deceased wherever they may be. Moreover the effect varies according to the degree of kinship. The strength of these ideas can be realized in the light of the reforms proposed by Kane to counteract what he regards as being nowadays anachronistic and troublesome excesses. He suggests what he considers a sufficient maximum for mourning, namely: ten days' mourning and impurity for the father, the mother, the son, the wife or the husband, the chief mourner (if he is not one of the above); three days for the other members of the joint family; for the rest it would suffice to take a bath on hearing of the death within a year.

Note some further prescriptions which are evidence to the same effect: a menstruating (or pre-pubertal) woman may not mount her husband's funeral pyre, she must wait for four days and the final bath (she would have to bathe in any case before burning herself alive). A marriage ceremony must be postponed if a fairly close death occurs during the preparations for it, or if the mother is menstruating. It is sometimes said that one should not come near the fire nor breathe on the fire with one's mouth if one is impure. A verse of Manu (II, 27) clearly shows the nature of impurity: 'The pollution of semen and of the womb [that is to say, birth] is effaced for the twice-born by the sacraments of pregnancy, birth, tonsure and initiation.' (The 'twice-born' are the members of the categories who are entitled to initiation, a second birth.) It can be seen that impurity corresponds to the organic aspect of man. Religion generally speaks in the name of universal order; but in this case, though unaware in this form of what it is doing, by proscribing impurity it in fact sets up an opposition between religious and social man on the one hand, and nature on the other.

According to some authors, certain functions or professions involve absence of impurity, or immediate purification (*sadyaḥ*, 'the same day'). Thus the king is never impure, as he must not be reduced to idleness even temporarily; thus again the Brahman student is affected only by the death of very close relatives. The same applies to priests who are performing a ritual, and sometimes to humbler workers, no doubt in virtue of the task in which they are engaged. The case of the king is striking. One sees here that the Indians are realistic whereas, we are told, Chinese civil servants retire for at least twenty-seven months after a bereavement (*Enc. of Rel. a Ethics s.v.* Purification).

How, according to the texts as well as custom, is impurity to be remedied? Through the bath, water is the great purificatory agent. Yet it must be noticed that its virtue has certain limitations: when the pollution is particularly intense, at the death of a near relative for example, one must wait for the period prescribed for the duration of mourning before taking the terminal bath. Further, not all baths are equally efficacious: most strictly a bath in running water, fully clothed, is required, and certain especially sacred waters, like the Ganges, have the maximum purificatory or in any case religious power. Mauss' statement may be verified: water acts not simply in accordance with a magical mechanism but by reason of the spiritual presences which it contains or represents. As Mauss said further, water in general 'separates' different states of purity: one sometimes bathes *before* encountering an impurity. Fire on the other hand has scarcely any direct purificatory value, though it has connected functions (ordeal, ritual). Shaving, especially shaving the whole head, accompanies purificatory baths, as at the end of mourning; on the other hand, the ban on shaving during mourning and in other circumstances is a mark of an ascetic performance; further, a child's head of hair is sometimes dedicated to a god. Apart from minor measures (bleeding the little finger, chewing a chilli, touching iron) and water, the main purifying agents are the five products of the cow (urine, dung, etc.). These purificatory procedures are also employed in the case of what may be called caste pollution: one bathes after the market or work, one is reintegrated into the caste by a ceremonial bath. Moreover, there is an easy transition from purification to expiation (absorption of the products of the cow, bath in the Ganges).[25d]

25.4  *Historical data (concluded).* Thus the literature is explicit about impurity in personal life within a caste or social category – particularly that of the Brahmans. From this point of view, purification already appears as a perpetual necessity. The literature also shows the transition from this occasional or temporary impurity to the permanent impurity of certain human groups. The laws of Manu say (V, 85), 'When he has touched a *Caṇḍāla*, a menstruating woman, an outcaste, a woman who has just given birth, a corpse ... he purifies himself by bathing.' Here the three occasional impurities are identified with that of the 'outcaste' and the *Caṇḍāla*, who is none other than the old prototype of the Untouchable. There is another list in the same book at III, 239, 'A *Caṇḍāla*, a domestic pig, a cock, a dog, a menstruating woman and a eunuch must not look at Brahmans while they are eating', and the following verse adds that the same people likewise render certain sorts of ritual ineffective. We shall see that a man who is eating is particularly vulnerable to impurity; moreover the animals mentioned feed on refuse and filth which they find in the village and its outskirts. Here again, functional characteristics are thus equated with individual events as sources of impurity, and different sorts of impurity are identified. (The case of the eunuch remains to be explained.) So we find that Manu said the same thing as Kane says at the present day.

If the laws of Manu are difficult to date precisely, at least it is admitted that no part of them is later than the third century AD whilst certain elements could be very much older. So it can be seen that specialization in impurity at least, if not the caste system such as exists these days, is recorded from the beginning of our era. In the same text the *Caṇḍāla* is relegated to cremation grounds and lives on men's refuse. The collection of *Jātaka*, or previous lives of the Buddha, a text descriptive rather than normative in character, is also hard to date but is certainly earlier than the earliest date of Manu. This text gives a very similar picture of the *Caṇḍāla*. A Brahman who meets him on his way says to him: 'Fly away, crow of ill-omen.' The daughters of a merchant and a chaplain who were playing near the town gate have the misfortune to catch sight of a *Caṇḍāla*; they wash their eyes and the unfortunate one is beaten. Eating the left-overs of a *Caṇḍāla* results in exclusion for a Brahman, and a young Brahman who, suffering from hunger, shared the food of a *Caṇḍāla* goes off to die of despair in the forest. Another *Jātaka* shows that the king may not share the food of a daughter he has had by a slave. In all this it is clear, as R. Fick said long ago in his social exegesis of these texts, that the Brahmanic theory of pure and impure was not only in existence but was really applied in fact at least several centuries before the Christian era. These very clear facts are minimized when we are told that caste as we know it is more recent. This is true, but does not prevent the fundamental principles having been present for a long time.

In short, not only are the impurity of individual life and that of the Untouchable considered today as being of the same nature, but it was already so for the author of the Laws of Manu, and the *Jātakas* show that there was a very strong feeling of impurity among certain groups and that untouchability already existed to a considerable extent.

25.5 *Complementarity.* The above does not in the least mean that impurities of personal life are, in the world of caste, independent of caste pollution in their conception and elaboration. Quite the contrary: it is clear that the two are interdependent and it is at the least very probable that the development of caste must historically have been accompanied by the development of Brahmanic prescriptions relating to the impurities of organic life, whether personal or of the family. Thus one can observe a parallelism between the states which accompany the ceremonies of the ages of life, and even the main actions of everyday life, and caste ranking. A mourner not following the precepts and lacking the help of specialists would remain more or less untouchable. A menstruating woman may not cook for her family. Marriage on the contrary, the only *rite de passage*, it may be noted, which is not accompanied by any impurity, gives the impression, by the prestige which it radiates and many other traits, that in it the Hindu finds himself symbolically and temporarily raised from his condition and assimilated to the highest, that of prince or Brahman for a non-Brahman, that of god for a Brahman. In daily life, the long ceremony which the Brahman performs in the morning, and which combines cares of hygiene with prayer and the purificatory bath, is necessary for him to be in some way reborn to his condition of the highest purity and to make him fit to have his meal. When he eats he is in an extremely vulnerable state, and even if everything takes place without mishap he rises from his meal less pure than he sat down. If he works away from home, as in these days, he takes care to have a bath when he returns.

It is clear that the impurity of the Untouchable is conceptually inseparable from the purity of the Brahman. They must have been established together, or in any case have mutually reinforced each other, and we must get used to thinking of them together.[25e] In particular, untouchability will not truly disappear until the purity of the Brahman is itself radically devalued; this is not always noticed. It is remarkable that the essential development of the opposition between pure and impure in this connection bears on the cow. Cattle and especially the cow are, as is well known, the objects of true veneration. It was not the same in the Veda although the cow was much revered; as is natural among a pastoral people, cattle were not killed without rhyme or reason, but sacrificed animals were eaten and, at least sometimes, cows were sacrificed. Among Hindus, on the contrary, even the involuntary killing of a cow is a very serious crime, and one can see a relation between the transformation thus shown and the progress of ideas of non-violence.[25f] But there is also a social connection: the murder of a cow is assimilated to that of a Brahman, and we have seen that its products are powerful purificatory agents. Symmetrically, the Untouchables have the job of disposing of the dead cattle, of treating and working their skins, and this is unquestionably one of the main features of untouchability. It is noteworthy that in the Gangetic plain, for instance, by far the most numerous caste of Untouchables, which constitutes the greater part of the agricultural labour force, is that of the *Camār* or 'leather' people, while in the Tamil country the typical untouchable caste is that of the *paRaiyar* or 'those of the drum (*paRai*)' (from which we have 'pariah'), drum skins being of course impure, and the Untouchables consequently having the monopoly of village bands. Thus it is seen that the cow, the sort of half-animal, half-divine counterpart of the Brahman, effectively divides the highest from the lowest of men. Its sacred character has a social function. The development or the transformation of this character must historically have accompanied the genesis of Hindu society from Vedic society, a genesis which is related to the functional generalization of the opposition of pure and impure.

There remains at least one remark to be made about the situation of the Untouchables. Seeing them physically rejected from the villages and obliged to perform ignominious tasks, one is tempted to regard them as outside religious society. Although the principle which distinguishes them is religious, the basis of the opposition, in other words what they have in common with other men, would have to be sought in another domain: it would be a matter of fact pure and simple, of economic and political fact if you like. This is not quite accurate, and here we must get used to a form of thought which is foreign to us. We have already noticed that the execution of impure tasks by some is necessary to the maintenance of purity for others. The two poles are equally necessary, although unequal. Ethnographic literature would provide spectacular confirmation of this especially in the south: in village ceremonies the participation of the Untouchables is required, as musicians or even as priests. The conclusion is that the actual society is a totality made up of two unequal but complementary parts. The beliefs about transmigration point in the same direction.[25g]

25.6 *The multiplication of criteria and the segmentation of status.* We have until now studied the fundamental opposition in its main form inasmuch as it is exhibited in untouchability. Let us turn now to the second question raised at the beginning of this section: is it true that the opposition of the pure and the impure accounts not only for the segregation of the Untouchables but also for the fact that there is an almost indefinite number of distinct castes? Leaving until the next chapter the traditional division of society into four castes or *varṇa*, we shall exhibit two phenomena in parallel: the multiplication of the criteria of status, which all relate to the fundamental opposition, and the portioning out – we shall say by analogy the segmentation – of hierarchical status between a large number of groups.

We acknowledge that the elementary and universal foundation of impurity is in the organic aspects of human life and from this the impurity of certain specialists (washerman, barber in the case mentioned) is directly derived; in the veneration of the cow we have already encountered one criterion, which is evidently bound up with the distinction between pure and impure, but which is an ancient creation of Indian society and which, we have seen, is at work in the condition of the Untouchable. A whole series of other criteria have appeared in the same manner. Thus, very likely under the pressure of the ethics of renunciation as found in Buddhism and especially Jainism, a vegetarian diet was adopted by the majority of Brahmans and, either directly or through their agency, came to prevail as a practice superior to a meat diet, that is, as a mark of purity opposed to a mark of impurity. Note that so far superiority and superior purity are identical; it is in this sense that, ideologically, distinction of purity is the foundation of status. The distinction in diets is very important: it corresponds to a great rift in society (but we shall see that it is sometimes counter-balanced by other factors). Moreover it is valuable for the classi-fication of castes in yet another sense, for it is susceptible of segmentation: it is less impure to eat game than domestic pig, raised by lowly castes and fed on garbage, it is less impure to eat the meat of a herbivorous than a carnivorous animal, etc. Thus within the class of meat eaters numerous distinctions can be made.

Still other criteria are at work; Brahmans forbid divorce and the remarriage of widows, and they practise (or used to practise) infant marriage; on each of these points, castes which do not conform to the superior practice are considered inferior, and these are numerous. Should we say that this again is a question of purity? For the Brahmans the indissolubility of marriage has religious value, and the same holds in some measure for infant marriage (the girl must be pre-pubertal). It is by association with the Brah-mans that these practices take on the colour of purity. I have only listed some absolute criteria from among those most current. We shall also encounter relative criteria: who accepts such-and-such a kind of food from the caste in question? Is it or is it not served by such-and-such a specialist?

Now let us analyse how a rank is attributed to a caste in relation to the neighbouring ones. In general a caste will be recognized as inferior to some and superior to others. To settle its rank, a certain number of criteria will be used, and it will be observed that at least two criteria are indispensable. For example, one can imagine the members of the caste saying: 'We are vegetarians, which places us above X, Y, Z, who eat meat; but we allow the remarriage of widows, which places us below A, B, C, who forbid it.' It must be noticed that each of these two elementary judgments has the effect of dividing the set of castes under consideration into two parts, respectively superior and inferior: to say 'we are vegetarians' is to unite oneself with all the vegetarian castes and oppose oneself to all the others. Consequently, the caste is ranked by effecting a series of dichotomies of this kind, two at the minimum (supposing there exists a strict linear order of castes): one dichotomy which separates it from what is beneath it, and another from what is above, each at the same time uniting it with the corresponding complement in each case.

So it can well be imagined that it is difficult to grade all the castes of a given area in a fixed hierarchical order even though the fundamental principle is beyond question and universal in its operation. The complication springs from the multiplicity of concrete criteria and from the necessity of evaluating them in relation to each other. Each group will try to manipulate this situation to its advantage but other groups may be of a different opinion. We will encounter this question again in connection with hierarchy. For the moment we have tried to establish three points: (1) in people's consciousness all the criteria of distinction appear as so many different forms of the same principle; (2) all permit the operation of an overall dichotomy of the society; (3) this is really the hierarchical principle, of which the linear order of castes from A to Z is in any case only a by-product.

In what follows we shall make use of the statement that each elementary judgment relating to status unites the caste with all those which share the same feature, while opposing it to all the others. It can be seen that a fundamental opposition which is conceived as the essence of a whole series of concrete distinctions really underlies the hierarchical order. As a corollary it can also be seen that if one supposes that there is a large number of groups to be classified, a considerable demand for concrete criteria results, since for the linear and unambiguous ordering of $n$ groups, $n - 1$ criteria of distinction are required.

25.7 *Variants and anomalies.* After what has just been said it is not surprising to encounter regional differences and irregularities or anomalies. We have said that the barber owes his inferior rank in the south to his function as a funeral priest. And indeed, in the north, where he has not this function, he has a higher status,

appearing as a helper or servant of the Brahman in family ceremonies and serving as a messenger for auspicious events; a
special priest officiates in the funeral rites, called by antiphrasis
'Mahabrahman' or great Brahman, who is in fact an Untouchable
of a particular kind, inspiring such an aversion that care is taken
not to have the slightest relation with him beyond the circumstance
in which he is indispensable as representative of the deceased. To
be precise, I have spoken of the north in general thinking particularly of Uttar Pradesh. Immediately to the east, in Bihar, the
barber is said to be impure. Farther east in Bengal he is not
(Dalton, p. 324), and one may presume that there is a corresponding difference in his functions. More generally there are notable
differences in the intensity with which Untouchability is felt and
codified. The south is much more traditional than the north, and
it would even seem that it still feels religiously that which would
often be only etiquette elsewhere (for example in Uttar Pradesh),
but it is still necessary to make distinctions. Apart from the
marginal regions where the Brahman is less solidly implanted
(Bengal, Assam) it may be supposed that, prior to modern influences, Islam was influential. Thus in the Panjab, Untouchability
is relatively weak: it is only food touched by sweepers which may
not be eaten. Hindu families in Delhi would accept water from
the leather flask of a Muslim porter (it was said that the water was
purified by the air); in western Panjab, Hindus themselves would
make use of such a container (O'Malley, *Indian Caste Customs*,
p. 110). Moreover the use of leather for footwear would appear
to have been more common in regions under Muslim influence,
though neither the material nor the object in any other way lost
its degrading character. Thus Blunt reports that in certain castes
in Uttar Pradesh a transgressor incapable of paying a fine would
place the shoes of the members of the assembly on his head, thus
incurring a serious degradation (*Caste System*, p. 124). Note in
passing that it is not properly a question of impurity here (for
example, a bath would not be efficacious) but rather a question
of a means of bringing about a fall in status – or only in prestige? –
a more or less definitive opprobrium. Conversely, it is probable
that the Jains have particularly contributed to the reinforcement of
the requirement of separation from the organic world. Not only do
they observe very long periods of pollution – forty days for birth,
like the Hebrews and the Christians – but, at least for the monks,

the requirement of respect for life takes precedence over 'external' purity: the monk does not bathe so as not to kill 'the life of the water'.[25h] Elsewhere there is the inopportune zeal of neophytes: thus the Raj Gonds, a tribe which very likely turned Hindu when it managed to establish kingdoms in the Deccan (around the fifteenth century), are reputed to wash the wood used for cooking (O'Malley, p. 103). Elsewhere again one encounters the raw material of the belief rather than the belief itself. Thus a member of the caste of betel growers carefully preserves from 'impurity' the nursery where this creeping plant grows (Blunt, p. 294): here the notion is apparently that of a danger to the plant, rather as in societies in which the notion of impurity is not differentiated. Here is a very different example, an extract from a novel in Hindi, which has nothing to do with impurity. A student, the son of a city merchant, is overwhelmed with joy when he enters the room in which his wife has just given birth to a son. The feeling of the disproportion between himself and his happiness takes a character-istic form: he is seized with fear, he has not deserved this happiness. 'How should he, a sinner, take upon himself this divine grace for which *he has not prepared himself by any ascetic performance*', 'the mercy of God is unbounded' (my italics). Here, in conformity with a very ancient model, the necessity for a transition is felt if access to the sacred is to be obtained (Premchand, *Karmbhūmi*, p. 70). Examples of reversal are also encountered, where paradoxically it is the inferior who fears contact with the superior.[25i] In the follow-ing example one sees the resurgence of the primitive idea of direct (and not social) danger from certain contacts, but applied this time to contact between social categories: the Pallar Untouchables of a Tamil village (Tanjore district) believe that if a Brahman were to enter the Pallar hamlet he and all the Pallar would fall prey to illness and misery.[25j] All these facts testify to the existence of notions underlying, or connected with, that of impurity.

25.8 *Outline of a semantic comparison.* The opposition of pure and impure appears to us the very principle of hierarchy, to such a degree that it merges with the opposition of superior and inferior; moreover, it also governs separation. We have seen it lead at many levels to seclusion, isolation. The preoccupation with purity leads to the getting rid of the recurrent personal impurities of organic life, to organizing contact with purificatory agents and abolishing it with external agents of impurity, whether social or other. The ban on certain contacts corresponds to the idea of untouchability, and all sorts of rules govern food and marriage. It must be pointed out that, segmented though it is, the relative degree of a group's purity is jealously protected from contacts which would diminish it. It must also be noted that each group protects itself from the one below and not at all from the one above, and that the actual separation from the one above is the result only of the exclusiveness of the superiors. Those rules which are dominated by the preoccupation with separation from the impure have been deferred to later chapters, so as to treat first of everything which relates the particular group to the whole.

In concluding this section, an indication of the limits of the examination in which we have been engaged and an outline of a more complete account are called for. We have endeavoured to reconstruct an idea which is fundamental and hence extremely all-embracing or encompassing for the Hindu. To do this, we have refused to confuse it with our habitual ideas, for example to trace purity back to hygiene. We have isolated a predominant idea which is absolutely different from our own. This was indispensable for the understanding of the social system, but it was only the first step in the comparison of Western and Hindu ideologies, and a brief indication can be given of how this approach could be developed. A situation similar to that encountered in passing from one language to another is involved, when it is recognized that a given semantic field is divided differently. Edible plants are apt to be classified in English into fruits and vegetables, whilst Tamil opposes *kāy* (green fruit which has to be cooked or prepared for eating) and *paLam* (ripe fruit). But in our case there is a hierarchical relation between different levels. The notion of purity is rather like an immense umbrella, or as we shall say the mantle of Our Lady of Mercy, sheltering all sorts of things which we distinguish and which the Hindu himself does not confuse in all situations. It is as if different configurations of notions cover the same sector of the semantic universe. If need be one could speak of function in order to pass from one case to the other, say for example that the idea of purity has hygienic functions, but clearly this would be to fall back into sociocentricity. Let us confine ourselves to noting certain obvious overlaps. Apart from the immediate physical aspect (cleanliness, hygiene) the etiquette of purity corresponds in one way to what we call culture or civilization, the less punctilious castes being regarded as boorish by the more fastidious. In relation to the social organization, those who are pure are in one way the equivalent of what we call 'decent' or 'well-born' people. In relation to nature, we have indicated in passing how impurity marks the irruption of the biological into social life. Hence we find here a functional equivalent of that rift between man and nature which is so strongly in evidence in our own society and which seems to be unknown to, or even rejected by, Indian thought. Finally, the notion does not correspond solely to the prestigious, the beneficial, the auspicious (even though there are not only nuances but curious reversals): it is clear that in the general scale of values it tends to occupy a region which in our society derives directly from good and evil, but it introduces a relative rather than an absolute distinction: this offers an insight into the Hindu ethical universe.

## 26 Segmentation. Caste and subcaste

We have seen so far only one aspect of the structural nature of caste. Indeed, in attending to the general principles of the system we have been content to consider the caste as if it were one niche among others in a vast dovecote. Now the caste is not a niche or a block but is generally subdivided, at least at a primary level, into different subcastes, and there are often many further subdivisions. So much so that it has sometimes been suggested that the subcaste be considered the important group, the 'real' group. The Sanskrit scholar Senart was it seems the first to pose the problem. As has been said, Senart was concerned with starting from a precise idea of the modern state of affairs. He realized that it was not the caste but the subcaste which in reality bore some of the most important characteristics ordinarily attributed to caste: you do not marry just anywhere within your caste but usually only within your sub-caste, and it is also the subcaste and not the caste which has judicial institutions: it meets as an assembly covering a definite locality, and can excommunicate its members. Hence, Senart concluded, it was the subcaste, the endogamous unit and framework or organ of internal justice, which was the fundamental institution and which in all logic ought to be called scientifically the true caste.

Senart has had emulators, in the first rank of whom must be mentioned Professor Ghurye, doyen of sociology in India. Ghurye wrote in 1932: 'Stated generally, though it is the caste which is recognized by society at large, it is the subcaste which is regarded by the particular caste and individual', and he concluded, 'There is ample reason why, to get a sociologically correct idea of the institution, we should recognize subcastes as real castes'. It does not seem, however, that Ghurye really put his precept into practice, but someone has recently done so: Mrs Karvé insists strongly on her opposition to Ghurye on a neighbouring point: she holds that castes result from the aggregation of subcastes, rather than subcastes from the subdivision of castes, and more generally perhaps that castes result from the fusion of diverse groups, rather than the scission of pre-existing groups.[26a] She does not seem to have realized that she only develops Ghurye (and Senart) in giving reality to the subcaste as against the caste. The fact remains that she takes the terminological plunge and says 'caste' for the subcaste and 'caste-cluster' for the caste itself. This is a serious innovation, for it is tantamount to saying that there is no caste of washermen or dhobis but only washermen of such-and-such a kind (subcaste). This is evidently absurd so far as the overall system goes, and can only be justified from the limited viewpoint of an author interested exclusively in the origins, particular customs and racial composition of groups which doubtless constitute *the material* of which the system is made up at the empirical level, but certainly do not constitute the system itself.

Another school of thought is opposed to this one. Blunt, while insisting on endogamy in his definition of caste, rejects Senart's conclusion in virtue of two arguments: first, endogamy is less rigid at the level of the subcaste than at that of the caste (this is in Uttar Pradesh where intermarriage is sometimes tolerated in certain directions between different subcastes); secondly, one must adapt to the ideas of Hindu society. He insists, like Ghurye, on the relativity of the term. If one asks someone 'What is your caste?' (*jāti*) he may indicate either which of the four *varṇa* he belongs to (see Chapter III), or a caste title, or his caste, or his subcaste, or even the exogamous section (clan) to which he belongs. Note that this is strictly accurate: a matter of situation no doubt, but *jāti* ('caste') connotes above all birth, the hereditary group, and while it corresponds mostly to endogamy and to bilateral transmission it

FROM SYSTEM TO STRUCTURE

in no way excludes unilateral transmission and exogamy. It is what is called a reference group: I identify my nature by indicating the group to which I belong, and one must make clear at what level the question is asked. Two other authors recognize in a more precise fashion the structural nature of these groups. As Ketkar says: 'There are several stages of groups . . . the word "caste" is applied to groups at any stage. . . . A group is a caste or subcaste in comparison with smaller or larger' (p. 15). From a slightly different point of view that excellent and too little known author, O'Malley, says: 'Each division (of caste) has "social value" in relation to other divisions.' It is like reading Evans-Pritchard or his disciples (*cf.* above, §23), yet this was written by a former British administrator, the author of innumerable *District Gazeteers*, in a small general work published in 1932. Thanks to O'Malley, Ketkar, and the general observation of Blunt and even Ghurye, the careful reader will certainly have grasped the structural nature of these groups. This is indicated further in the fluctuation in anthropological usage noted by A. C. Mayer.[26b] In these conditions it is useless to claim to make a choice of level in order to define the 'real group', that is to say a sort of social substance existing independently of the system, like a modern individual. Besides, one could only succeed by attaching primary importance to certain features (endogamy, administration of justice, specific customs, etc.) which, in relation to the system, there is no reason to privilege. For example, where the caste is professional, it is so independently of its segmentation into subcastes; in the same way, a caste's rank, even if it depends on customs which are in fact those of its segments, is attributed not to these but to the caste itself. The situation can be summed up as Ghurye himself does in the passage quoted: seen from the outside, from the overall point of view or from that of another caste, it is the caste which appears; seen from the inside, it is segmented at least into subcastes and, in practice, into territorial fragments of the subcaste. The diverse characteristics of the caste are not borne by a 'group' at a unique level but by groups at different levels of segmentation.

This formulation is still imprecise, as is seen in our recourse to the words 'group' and 'segmentation' in senses which are too vague. Adrian C. Mayer has made the question one of the major themes of an important and substantial work, and thanks to him we can be more precise. He writes: 'There are two levels of definition for both the caste and subcaste. The first is in terms of their "total" population, and concerns the formal definition considered in most of the literature on caste. The second, on the other hand, is the level of the *effective* caste group and subcaste group; and here we step down to purely local relationships' [my italics].[26c] The relations between different castes are in practice contained within the village: a barber is employed as such, and not as a member of such-and-such a subcaste of the caste of barbers; the 'effective caste group' is thus the population of the caste in a single village. Relations within the caste are, on the contrary, mainly those within the subcaste: one leaves the village as a member of one's subcaste for marriage and justice: the 'effective subcaste group' corresponds to a region formed by a large or small number of villages, which may be much smaller than the area over which the whole subcaste is distributed (and which corresponds to the circle of recognized kin relations). One sees that Mayer, as we try to do here, carefully distinguishes between theory and practice, between ideology and that which is yielded by observation, without sacrificing one to the other. Likewise, and for this reason, he formulates more clearly than his predecessors the 'relativity' of levels, the segmentary character of the caste taken in all its forms and functions. One could sum up his analysis by saying that he shows us how the theory of caste is combined in fact, at the level of effective relations, with the territorial factor, and that this is due to the segmentary character of caste, permitting different functions to be attached to different levels of the phenomenon.[26d]

For the moment we rest content with the notion that there is continuity between the plane of the caste (and relations external to the caste) and that of the caste segments (and relations internal to the caste), and we defer till later further information about the subcaste.[26e]

# CHAPTER THREE

# HIERARCHY:
# THE THEORY OF THE 'VARNA'

## 31  *On hierarchy in general*

We have encountered hierarchy but we have not defined it. Hierarchy must be our starting-point for two connected reasons: first, it is none other than the conscious form of reference of the parts to the whole in the system; secondly, it is the aspect of the system which escapes modern writers.[31a]

For modern common sense, hierarchy is a ladder of *command* in which the lower rungs are encompassed in the higher ones in regular succession. 'Military hierarchy', the artificial construction of progressive subordination from commander-in-chief to private soldier, would serve as an example. Hence it is a question of systematically graduated authority. Now hierarchy in India certainly involves gradation, but is neither power nor authority; these must be distinguished. We can already do so within our own tradition. Thus the Shorter Oxford Dictionary says under *hierarchy*: '(1) Each of the three divisions of angels. . . . (2) Rule or dominion in holy things. . . . (3) An organized body of priests or clergy in successive orders or grades. (4) A body of persons or things ranked in grades, orders, or classes, one above another.'[31b] It can be seen that the original sense of the term concerned religious ranking. We shall keep to this sense here, making it somewhat more precise. We shall admit that, any idea of command being left aside, the religious way of seeing things requires a classification of beings according to their degree of dignity. Yet the presence of religion is not indispensable, for the same applies whenever the differentiated elements of a whole are judged in relation to that whole, even if the judgment is philosophical as in

Plato's Republic. So we shall define hierarchy as the *principle by which the elements of a whole are ranked in relation to the whole*, it being understood that in the majority of societies it is religion which provides the view of the whole, and that the ranking will thus be religious in nature. (The necessity for such a view was mentioned in the Introduction, §7.)

We are concerned in this case with concepts which have become totally foreign to us, for our egalitarian society adopts their opposites, as Tocqueville has shown us. In the modern age, hierarchy has become 'social stratification', that is, hierarchy which is shamefaced or non-conscious, or, as it were, repressed. The notion has become incomprehensible even to many of the Indian intelligentsia, brought up as they are in the European tradition and subjected to the influence of modern political ideas for more than a century.[31c] Consequently, it is not surprising that hierarchy should be the stumbling block for modern writers studying the caste system, as has been seen in the case of the earlier writers, and as will be seen in the case of the more recent.

Once hierarchy has been isolated as purely a matter of religious values, it naturally remains to be seen how it is connected with power,[31d] and how authority is to be defined. In the previous chapter, we linked the principle of hierarchy with the opposition between the pure and the impure. Now we cannot but recognize that this opposition, a purely religious one, tells us nothing about the place of power in the society. On this question, we must resort to a traditional Hindu theory which, while not dealing with caste (*jāti*) *stricto sensu*, yet has an intimate bearing on it, I mean the classical theory of the varnas. In any case, one cannot speak of the castes without mentioning the varnas, to which Hindus frequently attribute the castes themselves. Thus there are good reasons for studying the varnas, even in ancient India, and then specifying the relationship between varna and caste, especially from the angle of the relationship between hierarchy and power. This will enable us to consider some regional or local examples of caste ranking.

## 32  The theory of the varnas: power and priesthood

There is indeed in India a hierarchy other than that of the pure and the impure, namely, the traditional hierarchy of the four varnas, 'colours' or estates (in the sense the word had in France in the *Ancien Régime*), whereby four categories are distinguished: the highest is that of the Brahmans or priests, below them the Kshatriyas or warriors, then the Vaishyas, in modern usage mainly merchants, and finally the Shudras, the servants or have-nots. This is only a preliminary enumeration, and we shall have to specify the content of these categories in historical terms. There is in actual fact a fifth category, the Untouchables, who are left outside the classification. Now the relationship between the system of the varnas and that of the *jāti* or castes is complex. Indologists sometimes confuse the two, mainly because the classical literature is concerned almost entirely with the varnas. Following Senart, one must certainly keep the two distinct.[32a]

On the other hand, it seems that recent anthropological literature does not give the importance of the traditional schema its full due, even from the point of view of castes in the strict sense. There has been too great a tendency to consider the classification of the varnas as nothing but a survival without any relation to contemporary social reality, as Hocart observed.[32b] Nearer our own time, it has been recognized that the theory of the varnas has certain functions in the modern age (§33) but there has been little attempt to account for this fact. In this connection one must first draw attention to a similarity in the constitution of the hierarchy of the varnas and that of the castes.

Thanks to Hocart and, more precisely, to Dumézil, the hierarchy of the varnas can be seen not as a linear order, but as a series of successive dichotomies or inclusions. The set of the four varnas divides into two: the last category, that of the Shudras, is opposed to the block of the first three, whose members are 'twice-born' in the sense that they participate in initiation, second birth, and in the religious life in general. These twice-born in turn divide into two: the Vaishyas are opposed to the block formed by the Kshatriyas and the Brahmans, which in turn divides into two. I comment elsewhere on this last feature, as first encountered in the Vedic ritual commentaries called Brahmanas (800 BC? See Appendix C). Let me simply say here that the lot of the Shudras is to serve, and that the Vaishyas are the grazers of cattle and the farmers, the 'purveyors' of sacrifice, as Hocart says, who have been given dominion over the animals, whereas the Brahmans–Kshatriyas have been given dominion over 'all creatures'. We shall return to the solidarity between the two highest classes and the distinction between them: the Kshatriya may order a sacrifice as may the Vaishya, but only the Brahman may perform it. The king is thus deprived of any sacerdotal function. It can be seen that the series of dichotomies on which this hierarchy rests is formally somewhat similar to caste hierarchy, and it also is essentially religious; but it is less systematic and its principles are different.[32c]

It seems that this fourfold partition of later Vedic society can be regarded as resulting from the addition of a fourth category to the first three, these corresponding to the Indo-European tripartition of social functions (Dumézil) and to the triad found in the first books of the Rig-Véda: *brahman-ksatra-viś* or: the principle of priesthood, that of *imperium*, and the clans or people. The Shudras appear in a late hymn of the Rig-Véda and seem to correspond to aborigines (like the *dāsa* and *dasyu*) integrated into the society on pain of servitude.[32d] It must be noted that the Brahman is the priest, the Kshatriya the member of the class of kings, the Vaishya the farmer, the Shudra the unfree servant. This classification has remained identical in form throughout all the literature right up to modern times, though naturally with shifts and modifications in the contents of the categories. In particular, this is the only conceptual scheme which is made use of by the classical texts of Hinduism in order to characterize persons and their function in society, even though actual groups do appear otherwise in these texts, and sometimes have an ambiguous place in the scheme. In all likelihood these texts are contemporaneous with the development of castes in the strict sense of the word, yet they always refer castes to the varnas, and see them, as it were, as varnas. First and foremost, these texts were to mask the emergence, the factual accretion, of a fifth category, the Untouchables, each emulating the others in proclaiming that 'there is no fifth . . .'. Note that this amounts simply to applying the existing scheme: the Untouchables are outside the varnas just as the Shudras were outside the 'twice-born'.

It is worthwhile to follow Professor Kane[32e] and see how the classical texts define the duties and occupations of the varnas. For the Shudras, the matter is perfectly simple: their only task is to obey or serve without envy (*śuśrusām anusuyayā*, Manu I, 91). In contrast to these, the twice-born are vigorously characterized as alike in virtue of a threefold common duty: study, sacrifice, and gift (*adhyayanam ijyā dānam* Gaut. X, 3), that is: to study the sacred texts, offer sacrifices, and give to the Brahmans. They differ in their sources of income, which correspond to *optional* activities or occupations: in this field, the Brahman has the privilege of teaching, performing sacrifices, and receiving gifts, the Kshatriya of protecting all creatures, the Vaishya of living from the land, commerce, grazing and usury (Gaut., *ibid.*). Manu says the same in a scarcely different way: the Brahman's three ways of making a living are optional for him, but forbidden to the Kshatriya, the common duty (*dharma*) of the twice-born contrasts with what they do for a living (*ājīvanārtham*) (X, 76-7, 79). The Brahman is characterized by six actions (X, 75; I, 88) of which only three are common to the other twice-born (I, 88-90). The first verse, in which the six actions of the Brahman are enumerated, must be translated literally in order to understand how the Brahman's activity is complete, and forms a totality: this idea is expressed by the pairs of opposites 'make others study and study, makes others sacrifice and sacrifice, give and receive...' (repeated word for word in X, 75). It can be seen that the ancient conception has been preserved in its essentials: the order of increasing status comprises service, economic acitivity, political dominion, priesthood. At the same time, with imperturbable logic, the sources of income, so far as they are optional, are subordinated to the religious ends, even if this involves what we tend to consider a contradiction, namely that the Brahman, as compared to the other twice-born, is characterized by inessential (optional) activities, or even, so far as instruction and sacrifice is concerned, by service – albeit religious.

Apart from the implicit statement that the different sorts of twice-born are essentially homogeneous, the feature which most contrasts with the caste system is perhaps the stress laid on function rather than birth.

There are some details to be noticed in connection with the hierarchy of the varnas in classical Hinduism. The Brahman naturally has privileges, and these are listed in the literature. He is inviolable (the murder of a Brahman is, with the murder of a cow, the cardinal sin), and a number of punishments do not apply to him: he cannot be beaten, put in irons, fined, or expelled. The learned Brahman (*śrotriya*) is in theory exempt from taxes, and the

Brahman is specially favoured by the law about lost objects, which generally, when they are found, revert mainly to the king, and which only a Brahman finder may keep in part or whole; similarly, if a man dies intestate, only if he is a Brahman do his goods not accrue to the king (here one can see a certain mixing of the two functions).

It should be recalled that although the Brahman is characterized in the Vedic period by his sacrificial function, in the Hindu period, in harmony with the decline of sacrifice in favour of other rites, the Brahman is, above all, purity. Further, the Brahmanic varna became segmented, even in the classical period, and the priests in charge of public temples, the *devalaka*, were despised by their colleagues. Today the Brahman lineages are graded in virtue of the rank of the castes they serve as domestic priests (*Panjab Census Report*, 1911, I, 310), the highest being the learned Brahmans who do not serve at all.

Generally speaking, the hierarchy of the varnas is expressed in many ways by the differentiated treatment that each is accorded. The punishment of Brahmans just mentioned is an example of this. Whilst there is generally privilege or immunity, at the same time *noblesse oblige*, and a Brahman thief, for example, is punished more severely than his inferiors. Some points are difficult to interpret. Thus Manu lays down that a Shudra may not carry a Brahman's corpse (V, 104), which is incomprehensible from the point of view of purity. But above all, starting from the Dharmasutras of Gautama and Vasistha, one finds seemingly illogical injunctions, which later became very widespread. These are those which prescribe, all other things being equal, an increasing period of impurity for a decreasing status: in the case of death, close relations are impure for ten days for Brahmans, twelve for Kshatriyas, fifteen for Vaishyas and thirty for Shudras. Even nowadays, where orthodoxy prevails, the proportion goes in the same direction (the longest periods are often reduced). But, going by the nature of the system, we would expect the contrary, for impurity is more powerful than purity, and the higher the degree of purity to be regained, the more severe should be the effect of impurity. Either we have not yet managed to enter into the spirit of the system, or else the Brahmans have here transformed into a privilege what ought to be a greater incapacity. This view is reinforced by the fact that, while other prescriptions go in the same direction (for example, how far water must reach to purify someone, Manu II, 62), we find the gradation reversed in certain cases: thus in the case of stillbirth, Brihaspati (*Āśauca*, 34–5) prescribes respectively ten, seven, five and three days for the Brahmans and the following varnas. As we shall see (Chapter VIII), the same goes for expiations.

We have said that the classical texts described in terms of varna what must surely have been at that time a caste system in embryo. The word *jāti* does occur, but it is generally confused with varna (except in Yajñavalkya, II, 69, 206) and, according to Kane, the emphasis is on birth rather than function. Moreover, concrete names of reference groups are encountered, as in the case of the Chandala already mentioned, and so are names of other groups, either equivalent in status (placed outside the village, Manu, X, 36, 51) or else of distinctly superior status. Although from a very early epoch the Buddhist texts confirm the actual existence of despised castes and inferior occupations, the normative Hindu texts mostly present the groups they name as if they were products of crossing between varnas. This is the very detailed theory according to which the 'mixing of varnas' gave birth to mixed categories, inferior and more or less hierarchized. It is generally admitted that this theory was used to refer real *jāti* to the varnas. It is difficult to say how these groups come into the classification of the varnas. At least the lowest of them seem outside it, and yet it is repeated that 'there is no fifth (varna)', and there is a tendency to associate them with the Shudras. Already in Panini (500 BC) this produced a distinction among the Shudras, since one hears of 'excluded' (*niravasita*) Shudras. Later, expressions like 'the last', 'the outsiders' etc., increase,, and the word 'untouchable' (*aspṛśya*) is not quite unknown. The distinction which people had for so long refused to make in theory finally compelled recognition: the Shudras have acquired rights, they have become in fact members of the religious society, and those excluded are now the fifth, the Untouchables.[32f]

A point which must be emphasized in connection with the varnas is the conceptual relationship between Brahman and Kshatriya. This was established at an early date and is still operative today. It is a matter of an absolute distinction between priesthood and royalty. Comparatively speaking, the king has lost his religious prerogatives: he does not sacrifice, he has sacrifices performed. In theory, power is ultimately subordinate to priesthood, whereas in fact priesthood submits to power.[32g] Status and power, and consequently spiritual authority and temporal authority, are absolutely distinguished. The texts called the Brahmanas tell us this with extreme clarity, and, whatever has been said to the contrary notwithstanding, this relationship has never ceased to obtain and still does. For example, the obligation of the powerful and rich to give, as is prescribed in the texts, has not been a dead letter. On the contrary, sovereigns have always supported the Brahmans – and their equivalents in this respect – by endowments of land which, as the inscriptions show, may be under two different rubrics (donations to the temples, and the establishment of Brahman settlements). The difference with the West, let us say Catholic Christianity, seems to consist in the fact that in India there has never been spiritual *power*, i.e. a supreme spiritual authority, which was at the same time a temporal power. The supremacy of the spiritual was never expressed politically.

Thus in the theory of the varnas one finds that status and power[32h] are differentiated, just as the general consideration of hierarchy seemed to require (§31). This fact is older than the castes, and it is fundamental to them in the sense that it is only once this differentiation has been made that hierarchy can manifest itself in a pure form. We shall return to this fact in the following section. This is not all, for we must remember that these two entirely distinct principles are nevertheless united in their opposition to the other categories which constitute the society. As early as the Brahmanas, these are 'the two forces', represented by the men who, according to Manu, have been given dominion over 'all creatures'. In submitting to priesthood, royalty shares in it.

## 33   Caste and varna

We must try to indicate the main features of the relationship between *jāti*, caste, and varna, category or estate, or more precisely, the relationship between the caste system as it can be directly observed, and the classical theory of the varnas. This task is necessary if we remember that the classical authors scarcely speak of anything other than the varnas, and that even nowadays Hindus often speak of castes in the language of the varnas.

In the first place this transition is quite comprehensible, not only in virtue of the traditional prestige of the varnas, but also in view of the homology already mentioned between the two systems, both of which are structural, and both of which culminate in the Brahmans, either as a varna or as a particular caste or subcaste of Brahmans which may be regarded as the representative of the varna in a given territory (the highest if several are found there). In the second place, the varnas have the advantage of providing a model which is both universal throughout India, and very simple compared to the proliferation of castes, subcastes, etc. Consequently it is a model which can among other things facilitate the comparison between different regions, as Srinivas has pointed out.[33a] Something of the kind is found in Marx: on the one hand there is the antithesis between the bourgeoisie and the proletariat, as described in his political writings, and on the other the more complicated picture of social classes which emerges in his historical works. There is a tendency to sort the many castes in a given territory into the four classical categories (and the fifth, traditionally unnamed). However, there are regional peculiarities. Thus in the south there are scarcely any castes intermediate between Brahmans and Shudras; the warrior castes themselves are considered as part of the Shudras, and scarcely worry about this at all.

So this provides a very convenient form of classification, distinct from, or supplementary to, the criteria of purity whose complexity we have mentioned. Has its importance increased in modern times, with the improvements in transport, and, even more, with the registration of castes in the decennial Censuses made by the government in the last part of the nineteenth century, and that of 1901 which sought to achieve a status ranking for each province? Srinivas thinks so. Certainly many castes took advantage of these Census Reports to present claims aiming to make the public authority sanction a higher status than their real status, and these claims, sometimes vindicated in published memoranda,[33b] were expressed, with greater or lesser plausibility, in terms of the varnas. Here the varnas were an instrument for mobility, but to make a claim is one thing, and for it to be accepted is another. Furthermore, the circumstances were exceptional (cf. Chapter VII).

Far from being completely heterogeneous, the concepts of varna and *jāti* have interacted, and certain features of the osmosis between the two may be noticed. The notion of the varnas which prevails nowadays, even among anthropologists, is influenced by caste. Thus it is often said that the true Kshatriyas have been long extinct, and that the Rajputs, though having the function of the Kshatriyas in modern times, are not real Kshatriyas. It is thought that in ancient India the accession to the throne, and to the dignity of Kshatriya, by dynasties of a different origin, was an irregularity. This assumes that heredity is more important than function, which is true of caste but not of the varnas (above, §32). So far as the varnas are concerned, he who rules in a stable way, and places himself under the Brahman, is a Kshatriya. Moreover, these categories were not strictly endogamous either. Probably the Kshatriyas have always been rather lax in this matter. The particular place given to power in the system has had notable and lasting results: in the first place, the pattern of polygyny and meat diet, which does not correspond to the Brahmanic ideal, has been quietly preserved at this and lower levels until quite recently; in the second place, since the function is related to force,* it was easier to become king than Brahman: Kshatriya and Untouchable are the two levels on which it is easy to enter the caste society from outside.

Conversely, it is not enough to say that the caste system is influenced by the theory of the varnas. In the first place, the existence of the theory of the pure and the impure presupposes at least the relationship established in the varnas between priesthood and royalty (§32; cf. §25.1). It is correct to say that the opposition between pure and impure is a religious, even a ritualistic, matter. For this ideal type of hierarchy to emerge it was necessary that the mixture of status and power ordinarily encountered (everywhere else?) should be separated, but this was not enough: for pure hierarchy to develop without hindrance it was also necessary that power should be absolutely inferior to status. These are the two conditions that we find fulfilled early on, in the relationship between Brahman and Kshatriya.

In the second place, we shall maintain that the theory of castes resorts implicitly or obliquely to the varnas in order to complete its treatment of power. Indeed, in the theory of purity a vegetarian merchant ought logically to have precedence over a king who eats meat. But this is not the case, and to understand this fact it is necessary in particular to remember that the theory of the varnas,

---

* *Force* in French. *Pouvoir*, meaning legitimate force (§71), is translated as 'power'. – TR.

74

whilst it subordinates king to priest, power to status, establishes a solidarity between them which opposes them conjointly to the other social functions. This is a subtle and important point and requires special discussion.

## 34  Hierarchy and power

Most contemporary authors see things differently. In previous generations, with the exception of the aristocratic tendency which took for granted the existence of status ranking, hierarchy was often overlooked as the central feature of the system, but the better of the materialist writers tried to explain it in terms of other features (Nesfield). Only one contemporary writer, K. Gough Aberle, has in turn taken on this thankless task.[34a] Nowadays hierarchy, or rather the existence of an order of precedence, a status ranking, usually compels recognition, but it is seen only from the outside ('social stratification'), and leaves a residuum which is not reducible to the clear and supposedly basic notions of power and wealth. This unresolved duality, which has not even been properly characterized, hangs like a millstone round the neck of the contemporary literature.[34b]

Usually, those who study the status ranking of the castes of a definite region distinguish between what happens 'at the extremes' and what happens in the 'middle zone' of the ranking. The extremes, where the pure and the impure are in evidence, are said to be less important than the middle zone, where the operation of power is rightly recognized. Such authors conclude, in short, that their categories are sufficient for the understanding of the system: according to them, the distribution of power (and wealth) is in the last analysis congruent with (ritual) status, except, naturally, at the 'extremes', where questions are raised by the lowly place of the Untouchable, and particularly by the precedence taken by the priest over the master of the land. Emphasis is often placed on situations in which the priest is to a striking degree materially dependent on the masters of the land, but the more this is done, the more the claimed congruence is destroyed. In short, it is laid down as a principle that hierarchical status is of small importance when it does not simply validate an economico-political situation. To describe this attitude is enough to pass judgment on it: it raises the question of whether our task is to provide a semblance of confirmation for our sociocentric prejudices or to do scientific work. Here is an illustration:

There was a high degree of coincidence between politico-economic rank and the ritual ranking of caste. This is a reflection of the general rule that those who achieve wealth and political power tend to rise in the ritual scheme of ranking. It is what is meant by saying that the ranking system of caste-groups was validated by differential control over the productive resources of the village. But the correlation is not perfect, since at each end of the scale there is a *peculiar rigidity* in the system of caste . . . in between these two extremes, ritual rank tends to follow their economic rank in the village community.[34c]

I have italicized a particularly delightful expression: here a basic feature of the caste system is reduced to a 'peculiar rigidity' at the extremities of the social order. It will be understood why we prefer another approach.

For us, on the contrary, what happens at the extremes is essential. We must free ourselves from familiar ideas: we tend to put the essential at the centre and the rest at the periphery. Here, by contrast, because it is a question of hierarchy, and more generally of ideas, and of sociology, that which encompasses is more important than that which is encompassed, just as a whole is more important than its parts, or just as a given group's place in the whole governs its own organization. Our approach is quite unlike the preceding one and, as we have said, involves two stages: first we shall be concerned with the ideology, which easily accounts for the overall framework; secondly, finding the concrete factor, power, in the 'middle zone', a factor not immediately accounted for by the theory of purity, we shall consider it in its turn.[34d]

The controversy is exemplary from the epistemological point of view, for, by keeping to the level of power, one is prevented from understanding the essential characteristic of the Indian system. This characteristic is the subordination of power, which, as we shall shortly see, is both intellectually absolute and practically limited. The alternatives must be clearly stated: one may either start from conscious ideas and move from the whole to the parts, while bringing out the important and unnoticed fact that power in India became secular at a very early date; or else one starts from behaviour, in which case one can neither account for the whole nor finally build a bridge between Indian concepts and our own.

Two approaches to the question of the relationship between hierarchy and power have just been contrasted. For us, the question only arises for the present in connection with the relationship between varna and caste. Anticipating the study of actual observable status rankings, we admit in advance that they give power a place which is not allowed for by the theoretical hierarchy of the pure and the impure. At first sight it is an example of that 'residual' component which should normally be brought out by the confrontation of ideology with observation. Then we would have to take notice of it as accurately as possible and be content with that. However, when the king or a man of royal caste, an eater of meat, takes precedence over a vegetarian merchant or farmer, it is not that the hierarchy of relative purity is simply complemented – that one could accommodate – rather it is contradicted. Must it be said that the ideology is false in the 'median zone' of the status ladder, or should it be admitted that an extraneous factor counterbalances ideology at this point, once the extremes are located?

To start with it must be observed that, although very important, hierarchy or its concrete and incomplete form, status ranking, is not everything. It leaves out power and its distribution, but given the fact that it does not attack or negate power, should it not reflect power within itself in some manner? Otherwise, and in general, the ideology provides an orientation or ordering of the datum rather than a reproduction of it, and the act of becoming conscious of something in fact always means making a choice of one dimension in preference to others: one can only see certain relationships by becoming, temporarily at least, blind to others. Then this sort of complementarity can lead to a real contradiction when it is a matter of completely ordering the datum in accordance with a single principle. In our case, power exists in the society, and the Brahman who thinks in terms of hierarchy knows this perfectly well; yet hierarchy cannot give a place to power as such, without contradicting its own principle. Therefore it must give a place to power without saying so, and it is obliged to close its eyes to this point on pain of destroying itself. In other words, once the king is made subordinate to the priest, as the very existence of hierarchy presupposes, it must give him a place after the priest, and before the others, unless it is absolutely to deny his dignity and the usefulness of his function. Brahman authors have had a feeling of this sort, as can be seen from the way in which they consider royalty within the theory of the *dharma*. As Lingat shows in his fine work on the relationship between *dharma* and the law, the king tends in this tradition to appear as a quasi-providential instrument whereby the theoretical world of the dharma is linked with the real world here below. Although they lay down an absolute rule, these authors are keenly aware of its transcendant nature and of the impossibility of introducing it into the facts just as it is. Thanks to the king, and in particular to the king as the supreme judge, as the link between Brahmanic wisdom represented by his counsellors and the empirical world of men as they are, the dharma rules from on high, but does not have to govern, which would be fatal.

Thus it can be seen that there are internal reasons for the contradiction in question. The remaining task is to understand how it has been possible for this contradiction to be accepted, and it is here, in my opinion, that the theory of the varnas must be taken into consideration. Indeed this theory from the outset sees in the first two varnas 'the two forces' which, united in their particular way, must reign over the world; in this way it enables the prince to share to some extent in the absolute dignity whose servant he is. It should be observed, moreover, that there is no contradiction in the classical authors, for they speak only of the varnas, even when we may suppose that they have the caste society in mind. In this sense, it is we who distinguish a hierarchy of purity as a distinct social principle. In the minds of these authors, as soon as government or secular matters in general are involved, this view unceasingly relies for external support on the varnas. All the more reason for us to avoid incorrectly dissociating the two views, and to recognize their implicit connection as reflected in actual status rankings, when power in some way counterbalances purity *at secondary levels*, while remaining subordinate to it at the *primary or non-segmented level*.

As the mantle of Our Lady of Mercy shelters sinners of every kind in its voluminous folds, so the hierarchy of purity cloaks, among other differences, its own contrary. Here we have an example of the complementarity between that which encompasses and that which is encompassed, a complementarity which may seem a contradiction to the observer. Before becoming familiar with this phenomenon through concrete examples, it must be stressed that we have made a first step out of the dualism of the 'religious' and the 'politico-economic', of idealism and materialism, of form and content. Let us admit at once that the tendency we have criticized has been a considerable help to us: by its one-sided insistence on power it has made it impossible for us to overlook it.

It must be borne in mind that here we have only indicated the intrusion of power into the domain of hierarchy. A subsequent chapter is devoted to the description of power (Chapter VII).

## 35 Regional status ranking (1901 Census)

Now let us consider hierarchy as it is described and analysed in modern literature. Any sociological work in India, unless it is very specialized, must necessarily take hierarchy into account. But certain works study it more specifically. We shall consider first Risley's efforts to isolate it at the level of the 'Provinces', in the decennial census of 1901.[35a] It was a laudable undertaking, and while experience has shown up its drawbacks and limitations, it at least had the merit of throwing into relief the markedly different ways in which a universal principle was applied in different Provinces. The aim was to arrive at a classification of castes in accordance with an order of precedence established on the basis of native public opinion.

The following criteria were considered: the varna to which the caste in question belonged; whether or not the Brahmans accepted water from it; whether it was served by Brahmans of high status, by other Brahmans, or by its own priests; whether it practised infant marriage and forbade remarriage of widows; profession; whether or not it was served by the barber and other specialists; whether or not it had access to the precincts of certain temples; whether or not it was excluded from using the communal well, was relegated to a distinct quarter, was obliged to leave the road when a superior was encountered. It will be noticed that absolute or direct criteria (rules about marriage, profession) are mixed with relative or indirect criteria which introduce the attitude of another caste (Brahman, barber, etc.). In fact, other criteria have come in, and are recommended by an author like Ketkar: for example, one can rank the high castes in ascending order on the basis of whether the Brahman will accept water, fried food, or boiled food from them; and one can rank the low castes in descending order on the basis of whether their contact pollutes water, an earthenware receptacle, or a brass receptacle.[35b]

The main result was to confirm the massive difference between the north and the south (the provinces of Bombay and Madras). Whilst in the north the Brahmans accept water and certain delicacies from inferior castes (as a function of their occupation and diet), in the south, by contrast, the high castes take water from their own caste or even subcaste only, and, in Madras (to be precise, on the west coast, that is, in Malabar or present-day Kerala) the Untouchables pollute not only by contact but also just by proximity. It seems that as a whole impurity is felt more acutely in the south than in the north,[35c] but later we shall suggest a qualification concerning certain very severe rules in the south. One can also see the importance of criteria derived from rules about food and drink, which are especially strict. We shall study these rules in the chapter on separation; the rules of attenuated separation provide precise criteria of hierarchy.

The provincial commissions which drew up the lists of precedence did not make use of the same criteria, but we shall see by taking two examples, Bengal and Madras, that the main categories, variable in number, among which the lists divided the castes, were based on a series of hierarchical oppositions. Thus in Bengal there are first: (1) the Brahmans. The rest are divided into two: those from whom the Brahmans accept water, and those from whom they do not. The first of these categories is again divided into two: some are served by superior Brahmans, others only by inferior Brahmans; there is a further distinction of quite another kind among the former, and so we have: (2) the Rajputs (the royal or warrior caste) and assimilated castes; (3) the 'nine branches' of relatively pure serving castes. One can see that the distinction between (2) and (3) seems to be politico-economic, and we shall return to this problem. Then: (4) the castes from whom, like the preceding ones, the Brahmans accept water, but who have only inferior Brahmans as priests. The category below, from whom the Brahmans do not accept water, is divided: at the bottom are those who eat beef, at the top, those who do not eat it, these being divided in turn in a rather unclear way, hence: (5) 'the degraded, the sectarians'; (6) those who eat meat and fowl (a very numerous category, comprising half the total population); and finally the lowest: (7) those who eat beef, work leather, etc.

Madras was at this time a very large province, including to the north part of the Telugu-speaking lands (today Andhra Pradesh), Tamil country to the south, and to the west a district on the west coast. As has been said, the criterion of water cannot be used in this case. The main distinction is between those who pollute and those who do not pollute. Those who do not pollute can be divided according to varna: (1) Brahmans; (2) Kshatriyas, extinct; (3) Vaishyas, very few; (4) pure (*sat*) Shudras (about one-third of the total population). Those who pollute do so either by touching or without touching. The former, more or less the same as the impure Shudras, are divided into three categories according to what Brahmans are willing to be employed by them: these are the categories (5), (6) and (7), together less than one-third of the population. Among those who pollute from a distance (corresponding to the Untouchables in less strict districts), one category (8) does not eat beef, while at least three others do so: tribes (9), castes (10) representing one-seventh of the population, finally people who do not recognize the Brahmans (11), etc.

In both examples one can see the importance of reference to the Brahmans (whether they accept water; are or are not polluted, and in what manner; serve as priests or do not). This constitutes a relative or indirect criterion, which takes precedence over absolute criteria like diet or profession (the latter being relatively secondary at this level, as the aim was to rank the populations of very large regions using only a few categories).

Risley himself stressed the difficulty of obtaining consensus among the interested parties in the English Provinces of those days, provinces often covering a large area and heterogeneous in language. These classifications must be regarded as compromises aiming to combine different ranking-scales, each applying to smaller regions. Again, emphasis has recently been placed upon the difficulty of obtaining an unequivocal linear order, even for a small region, for middle-ranking castes. This difficulty has often been attributed to a change in modern times, but there is no certainty that things have not always been thus, and this is the second reason which detracts from Risley's contribution: in common with many others, he believed that hierarchy consisted in a linear order, and he did not see that this order was only the consequence, not to say the by-product, of a hierarchical opposition: a single opposition so far as its principle is concerned, but indefinitely diversified and segmented according to circumstance, region, etc.[35d]

A qualification should perhaps be introduced concerning certain features which seem at first sight to be particularly clear expressions of hierarchy. We have already, in passing, made the distinction between absolute criteria, drawn from the way of life of the caste, and relative criteria, based on the attitude that other castes have to it. There is a third kind, if not of criteria, at least of features, which may be distinguished, roughly, as *imposed features*; these are often accompanied by sanctions bearing on the inferior caste. It is such features which, in the literature on the subject, make the south, and especially Kerala, a sort of paradise of the ranking mania. Closer inspection shows that these features derive more from power than from the hierarchical principle. Take for example the scale of distances which the lowest castes were supposed to keep from the higher ones. By comparing apparently divergent sources it will be seen that this is a very systematic scale (one has only to arrange in a diagram the data assembled by Hutton, pp. 69–70). This was not a custom, but a genuine *regulation*. This should have been guessed, for how would a Nambudiri Brahman ever have noticed that a Pulayan had come closer than the prescribed ninety-six paces? Similarly, in the neighbouring district of Tinnevelly, I saw the marks of blows on the back of an Untouchable, blows which he had received for having crossed the village of a martial caste (the Maravar) wearing sandals. The inhabitants themselves wear leather sandals, blows have never removed impurity, and it is clear that the village was not polluted, but that the villagers had simply wanted to uphold a symbol of subjection. The same is probably true of most of the rules concerning clothing and of the sumptuary rules reviewed by Hutton (pp. 70–74). Naturally, regulations, royal or otherwise, may have registered and fixed customary features. Naturally also the criteria proper are themselves, in the last analysis, a product of the system. It is none the less necessary to distinguish between that which results rationally from the hierarchical principle and is admitted as a custom, and that which contradicts it and is imposed by power. If it is true, for example, as we have supposed, that the scale for each varna of the duration of mourning was arbitrarily inverted by the Brahmans, the principle of this feature is power, and not hierarchy, although it has been accepted for centuries as an expression of hierarchy. It will be objected that we are here attributing power to the Brahmans, but they do have some effective share in power in the domain of ritual, for example in the case of expiations.

## 36  A local example (Central India)

In order to take an accurate view of the way in which the hierarchical principle is expressed in the caste system, one must obviously study what happens at a given place among the actual castes which co-exist there. On the other hand, it will have been noticed that the rules which lay down for the members of each caste from whom they may or may not accept such and such a kind of food, or simply drinking-water, without degradation, are one of the most convenient manifestations of the hierarchical principle from the point of view of recording and observing. I say 'recording and observing', for it is not enough to list the rules which the witnesses recite. One must also know if and under what circumstances these presumptive rules are applied in practice. In the first period of inquiries into these questions, people were too often content to ask informants and reproduce the rules which they mentioned. But what can a rule like the following signify: 'I may, or may not, take water from X', if the witness cannot cite a single moment in his life when the question has really arisen for him? From this point of view, there are different kinds of food which, as McKim Marriott has rightly said,[36a] are suitable for different situations: ordinary everyday food based, according to region, on wheat cakes or boiled rice, is essentially for the family, and is accepted only by servants of a distinctly inferior rank, and so on this level is food for service. By contrast, food fried in butter (or certain equivalent foods) is the food of feasts: its greater purity, or rather, its greater resistance to impurity, enables a greater number of castes than in the preceding case to accept it, and it is thus suitable for banquets to which one invites neighbours; if these include superiors, it is advisable that the cook should himself be of high caste. Akin to this type are certain special preparations which can be called food for travelling; these too are relatively resistant to impurity in virtue of their composition and preparation, and they make it possible to eat in circumstances where it is preferable not to have to do any cooking. Finally, if one remunerates a superior – a Brahman, say – in food, this will be raw food which is immune from pollution and which he will cook himself (*sīdhā*); Marriott rightly calls this the food of gifts. Our aim here was not to study food in itself (see Chapter VI), but to throw just as much light on the question as is required in order to use the corresponding rules for the study of caste ranking.

A good study of this topic is available: Mayer's book about a village in Southern Malwa (Central India).[36b] Perhaps it is not perfect, but one must take into account the complexity of the phenomena and the difficulty of recording them correctly, which is what this writer has done. He cannot be reproached for not having pursued his analysis far enough, for it is open to the reader to do so. The village includes twenty-three castes, and their relationships will be studied under three headings: use of the same pipe, and the provision of ordinary food, called *kaccā*, and of perfect food, called *pakkā*. In the north-west of India, men of castes of similar status are wont to meet round a hookah (*hukkā*), which is smoked in turn. This would be inconceivable in the south in view of the contact between the lips, and hence saliva, and the mouthpiece of the pipe, even if a cloth or a hand is placed between. Here the pipe smoked is of clay without a tube (*cilam*), and a cloth is interposed between lips and mouthpiece. The pipe is shared among roughly the same castes as those from whom one accepts water, and there is considerable tolerance. The data are to be found in Figure 1b. Higher castes share the pipe with almost all castes excluding, apart from the Untouchables (F), only four other castes (Mayer's category 4, category E here) and, in a varying way, certain of the lower castes included (D). In some cases, a different cloth must be placed between the pipe and the lips of the smoker. Briefly, between twelve and sixteen castes smoke together; in the first place, this is very remarkable by comparison with other regions, and in the second it indicates a cleavage which is higher than that marked by Untouchability, and is obviously important. Let us also note that lower castes either do not share the pipe (these are Untouchables, and their exclusiveness is not exceptional), or else do so only with one or two castes immediately below (the two castes of my category E).

For the rest, and to see it more clearly, we must arrange Mayer's material in a hierarchical way. The facts about the food for feasts, pakka, are not essential, for it is not really used in its true function

84

in this locality. Indeed one reads that at a banquet the food was partly kacha and partly pakka: in such a case the pakka has no more than a gastronomic significance since all those who could eat pakka alone but not kacha could obviously not partake of it. There remains the ordinary food, kacha. There are two ways in which it may be considered here: from whom do I accept kacha, and who accepts it from me. The two are not necessarily connected, for I may be punctilious in my acceptance, and yet at the same time possess other characteristics which make others refuse kacha from me. The essential thing here is the common opinion which others have of me, and not my own opinion of them. Hence we shall take as the essential criterion for the order in which we shall rank the castes: *what castes accept kacha from the caste in question?* Thus we obtain the table (Fig. 1a) in which the caste under consideration is placed on the diagonal; the castes which take kacha from it are read vertically, forming a kind of ladder from left to right at the bottom of the diagram; the castes from which it accepts kacha are read horizontally.

The choice of our main criterion leads to a slight modification of the grouping proposed by Mayer, namely, to the division of category 2 into B and D. For the rest, his 3 corresponds to our C, his 4 becomes our E and his 5 our F (untouchables). Still considering only kacha, it will be seen from the table that the castes of category B have a peculiarity which distinguishes them from all the others: the other castes, except the very last, F, will accept (horizontally) kacha only from very superior castes. By contrast, the castes of category B form a compact rectangle in this respect: B1, B2, B3, B4, B5 eat the ordinary food together! Now B1 represents the Rajputs, the dominant caste, which, in this instance may be called the royal caste, and group B as a whole represents what Mayer calls as a result the 'allied castes'. The commensality of the group is even more remarkable because it includes 'serving' castes like the potters B4, who accept kacha from a caste outside the group, the carpenters, and especially the barbers, B5, who, as a necessary result of their domestic functions, accept it from four of the castes in category C, which are themselves very exclusive. This is in general an admission of inferiority, and one might expect to see the B castes dissociate themselves from B5 in order to preserve their status. This is far from the case, and one may even observe that an inferior caste, D3, makes no distinction between

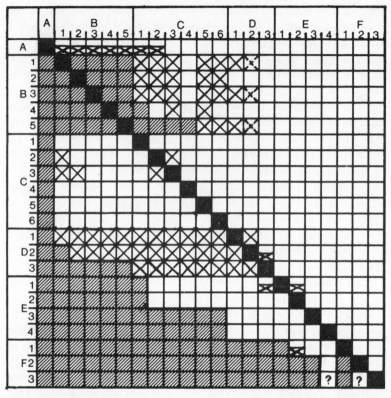

For each caste ( ■ ), the castes from whom it accepts such-and-such a food are read horizontally, those who accept the food from it are read vertically,

☐ kaccā food
⊠ pakkā food
⊟ pakkā food for some of the group
⊠ — dubious

| A | Brahmans | C 1 | Carpenter | E 1 | Bhilala |
|---|---|---|---|---|---|
| | | C 2 | Blacksmith | E 2 | Mina |
| B 1 | Rajput | C 3 | Farmer | E 3 | Nath |
| B 2 | Gosain | C 4 | Gardener | E 4 | Drummer |
| B 3 | Tobacco-curer | C 5 | Bairagi | | |
| B 4 | Potter | C 6 | Tailor | F 1 | Balai Balaji + Weaver |
| B 5 | Barber | | | F 2 | Tanner |
| | | D 1 | Dairyman | F 3 | Sweeper |
| | | D 2 | Oil-presser | | |
| | | D 3 | Goatherd | | |

Figure 1a.  Status ranking on the basis of exchange of food in a Malwa village (from the data in A.C. Mayer, *Caste and Kinship*, pp.33-40).

86

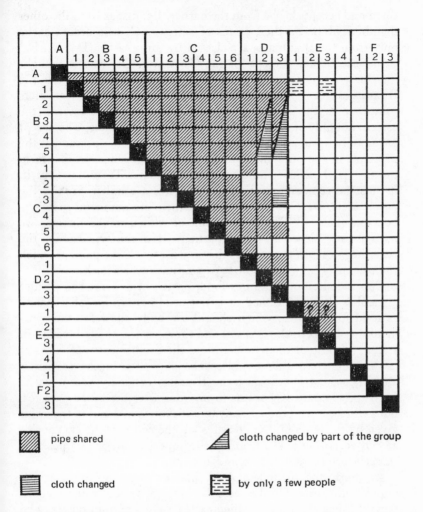

pipe shared

cloth changed by part of the group

cloth changed

by only a few people

Figure 1b.   Pipe sharing. The inferior castes with whom a given caste will share the pipe are read horizontally, starting from the caste in question ( ■ ). Same locality.

them and accepts kacha from the barber, B5, just as from the other members of B. Further, castes of category C, who accept kacha only from the Brahmans, are classed by three castes (D3, E1, E2) below the barber (except for the Carpenter, C1, who is thought inferior only by D3). Now the C castes are vegetarian, while the B castes eat meat. Hence in this case the promiscuity of meat eaters prevails over the separatism of vegetarians in public esteem (the esteem not only of inferiors, but even of the Brahmans, who accept pakka only up to and including C2). Here, to all appearances, the principle of the pure and the impure is in abeyance. In this form the fact is, I believe, unique up to this date. To understand it, it must be remembered that the B castes are united around the power caste, B1. (Moreover, some of them are dominant in neighbouring villages.) This is the point at which, in the manner we have already hinted at, power participates in purity, although the latter negates it in theory; in other words, this is the point at which the solidarity between the first two varnas reveals itself.

Consideration of the purer food, pakka, brings out two points: (1) as has been mentioned, it is not used here in its full capacity as food for festivals, which should normally allow for the commensality between the B castes and the C castes which are close in status; (2) The distinctive feature of the exclusiveness of C castes is that they refuse almost all pakka as well as kacha (which is absurd), whilst by contrast the B castes generally accept pakka from the C castes (C4 seems to be inferior to the other C castes, but I do not intend to make any modifications in detail to the order given by the author); the D castes, on the contrary, behave normally in accepting pakka from all the superior categories; pakka is scarcely used among the E and F castes.

In short, the main lesson of this investigation concerns the opposition of the B and C castes, whose behaviour must be seen together. Faced with the 'allied castes', allied around power, who here display exceptional carefreeness and solidarity, the C castes seem to exaggerate the reserve and self-containment of vegetarians, to such a degree that even the Brahmans scarcely take them seriously. We are told that the B castes are lavish and freely invite other castes to their family ceremonies, followed in this by the carpenters (C1). By contrast, the farmers (C3) are niggardly and scarcely invite any except members of their own caste; at the same time, they pose as puritans, and if they are invited they insist on receiving raw food and cooking it in their own homes. That it is a question of asserting themselves in face of the B castes is the more clear in that in other villages this same caste is part of the group of 'allies'.

We have seen how, in an actual situation, power may victoriously offset purity. In a less spectacular form this is a very widespread phenomenon. This is why we have been at pains to indicate above how the theory of varnas opens the road to this possibility.

## 37   Attribution or interaction?

Among recent works showing the increased interest in the manifestations of hierarchy, we shall here consider an inquiry by P. M. Mahar, and more especially the works of McKim Marriott.

Pauline Mahar chose to throw light on a different aspect from the one we have studied in Mayer's work. It is not a question of an observed form of interaction, and the technique is that of the interview. This is the first systematic attempt to extract, in terms of Stevenson's classifications, a scale of intercaste pollution in a village (see Chapter VI) and, on this basis, a status ranking of castes.[37a] On this last point, the result is much clearer than one would expect from the scepticism often professed by the specialists, especially in connection with the region in question (Western Uttar Pradesh): at least sixteen of the twenty-two castes in the village can be unambiguously classified into fifteen ranking categories, and the main divisions emerge clearly. The actual bearing of the linear order obtained in this way, which awaits the eventual addition of complementary studies, is unfortunately limited by the fact that we know nothing of the groups in question, except their names and hence their theoretical profession.

McKim Marriott's theoretical works on hierarchy are based on experience acquired in a village in the west of Uttar Pradesh. A detailed and still unpublished investigation led him to conclude that the full development of caste ranking, its full 'elaboration', depended on a certain number of conditions. In his first book, written in 1953, *Caste Ranking*, which has already been mentioned, he aimed to verify this hypothesis for five chosen regions of India, and concluded in particular that one of the necessary conditions for a precise and elaborated hierarchy was a high degree of interaction between castes in their relevant capacities.[37b] In 1959, this view was systematized in a very remarkable article 'Interactional and Attributional Theories of Caste Ranking',[37c] which must be summarized and discussed. This article marks a step forward in these studies and, without going into disagreements of detail, its positive aspects must be briefly indicated, and it must be said in what respects the view proposed by Marriott seems inadequate in terms of the approach set out here. The opposition between attribution and interaction is in part reminiscent of our summary distinction between absolute and relative criteria. For Marriott, the theory of attribution is that a caste's rank derives from the characteristics of its way of life, high or low according to the criteria of relative purity. Marriott criticizes this theory. He has no difficulty in showing that Stevenson, its main representative, provides an inadequate account (p. 93, cf. above, n. 25a). Without accepting all Marriott's arguments (pp. 94–6), it is clear that the 'attributional' theory is inadequate. Marriott contrasts it with the theory of interaction, which is his own, whereby 'castes are ranked according to the structure of interaction among them' (p. 96). This is an obscure expression, but it must be approved to the extent that it emphasizes not the caste in itself, but inter-caste relationships. Here Marriott shares in a salutary reaction (similar to Leach's, above, n. 21c) when he insists on two kinds of interaction: 'the ritualized giving and receiving of food, and the giving and receiving of ritual services'. In other words he provides an opportune reminder that interdependence and professional specialization are part of the caste system, and he insists, further, on exchanges of food. In fact Marriott seems to be following in the steps of Hocart, whom he does not quote, especially when he refers to the way in which the villagers themselves establish their judgments of superiority and inferiority, and when he reinstates the importance of the ritual services which the castes perform for one another. This sentence should be borne in mind: 'An occupation is a kind of behaviour rendered as a service by one caste for another caste' (p. 98). (I would say rather that it is a service performed for the whole by means of its castes.) It is certainly true also that impurity is something social rather than something innate (p. 98), and we have already made good use of the classification of foods suggested by Marriott.

But we cannot follow him when he claims to reduce status ranking to a matter of the relationship between the quantity and quality of services received and those rendered. On this basis, the king would have precedence over the Brahman, and curiously enough the author, set apart as he is from those we have criticized by his recognition of religion, is faced with the same difficulty as them: the difficulty of 'the extremes'. He readily returns to the 'attributional' theory to account for the place of the Brahman (it is true that he wants to find a complementary function for this theory). Similarly, when he tries to define a particular 'way of advancement' for each varna, he loses sight of hierarchy, which is still operative here: one could indeed isolate a 'Kshatriya model' alongside the Brahman model, but it is an underlying model, in some way shamefaced. The Vaishya model is even more so, to the point at which it eludes precise description.

However well founded the stress on interaction, both in itself and as a reaction to the one-sided 'attributional' view, we must admit in the last analysis that both are present: we have just seen how Marriott was tempted to encompass interaction in attribution. The principle of hierarchy is the *attribution* of a rank to each element *in relation to the whole*. Yet Marriott, concerned as he is with caste ranking, precisely fails to grasp both the hierarchical principle itself and also, it seems, the orientation towards the whole. Reading his first work, one wonders occasionally whether he was not tempted like others to reduce the hierarchical principle to the conditions presumed necessary for its manifestations. We can agree that hierarchy and division of labour are intimately connected, but by their relation to the whole. This implies some degree of separation, that is, attribution. 'Interaction' cannot replace the overall ideological orientation.

# CHAPTER FOUR

# THE DIVISION OF LABOUR

The caste system comprises the specialization and interdependence of the constituent groups. Specialization entails separation between these groups, but it is oriented towards the needs of the whole. This relationship to the whole, which must be repeatedly emphasized, links the division of labour with hierarchy. It also sharply distinguishes the Indian form of the social division of labour from the modern economic form, which is oriented towards individual profit and in which, at least in theory, the market is left to regulate the whole.

It has been mentioned that in the past attention was drawn to the professional aspect of caste, and that there was a tendency to explain castes in terms of the industrial (not the religious) division of labour, to suggest that they derived, for example, from trade guilds. We went on to say that, curiously enough, the literature of the 'fifties seems, by contrast, to have neglected this aspect, and in particular the form it takes in the village, often called the *jajmānī* system (§21, n. 21d). The attention given to other aspects of the system (pure and impure, etc.), while legitimate in itself, was accompanied by an arbitrary dichotomy between 'caste' and 'village': there was a tendency to consider the caste as a sort of separate substance, while the relations between castes were referred to their usual empirical setting, the village. This did not last: very quickly the interdependence between castes had to be accepted, and it no longer appeared as a phenomenon extraneous to the caste itself. But this initial inadequacy of social anthropology in this field seems to me to reveal the two main difficulties we shall find: the necessary shift from element to whole, and the relation between those aspects we tend to distinguish as religious and non-religious.

### 41 Caste and profession

There is a definite relationship between caste and profession. This is not simply identity. Thus within certain limits one may have recourse to a livelihood other than that which is traditional for the caste of which one is a member. Moreover, it is quite clear that the caste system is not purely and simply a professional system; the caste is not the same as a trade guild. This relationship has given rise to difficulties and misunderstandings, especially since, as has been seen in Chapter I, it was tempting to understand the system as a purely industrial one, in which the religious aspects were secondary.[41a] Much of the difficulty disappears if one admits, with Hocart, that caste and profession are linked through the intermediary of religion, which is obvious in the case of the ritual specialists like the barber and the washerman. For, if only the profession's status of relative purity is important, then one can understand how professions that are similar in this respect may replace or be added to the traditional profession for members of a caste, on condition that the newer professions are not less pure than the old. But there remains an important difficulty: only in certain cases does religion clearly account for the link between caste and profession. There are some religiously neutral professions which are followed by a number of different castes.[41b]

However, the fact remains that, in the general scale of relative purity, features which are deemed professional carry great weight compared with features not connected with profession. A caste bearing such a strong religious mark as that of the 'leather people' would gain nothing by introducing refinements into its other customary features: nowadays when it wants to end its infamy, it tries to put an end to the function which justifies this infamy.

The examples quoted by McKim Marriott need to be made more precise, but he is right on this point: the same activity is more polluting if it is the object of a specialization than if it is practised within the household. Comparing the relative status of two Bengal castes which are both given to fishing, Bh. Mukherjee remarks that, while the Kaibarta are farmers who fish for themselves, the Namasudra live by fishing, and he suggests that it is the sale of fish which makes the second inferior to the first. It may be suggested, rather, that it is fishing as a specialized activity as opposed to farming (and fishing for its own sake) which makes the difference. This is understandable: the specialized activity is directly related to the system, whereas the other is only one feature among others of the particular caste.[41c]

Considering the castes of what is today Uttar Pradesh, the most densely populated of the Indian States, corresponding to the western part of the Ganges Valley, Blunt (*Caste System*, p. 233) stated some time ago that, apart from a few exceptions (one tribe, the four kinds of superior Muslims, and sectarian castes) each caste could be made to correspond to an occupation, or group of connected occupations. He distinguished functional castes, traditionally associated with a profession which, according to him, preceded or caused their formation from others where the association is accidental but of long standing, as is the case with the *Ahīr* or cowherds, whose name connects them with the tribe called *Ābhīra* in the first centuries of the Christian era. Blunt classed the professions into twelve main groups: (1) agriculture is poorly defined. It is difficult to distinguish between those who hold land (I avoid the notion of ownership) and those who cultivate it, though there are some castes of landholders, like the *Rājpūt* ('sons of kings') and the *Bhuinhār* or *Bhūmihār* (from *bhūmi*, land); there are also some castes of specialists in certain crops (neither inclusive nor exclusive). (2) The agricultural workers, a rather vague category, with certain specialist functions and castes of tribal origin. (3) Pastoral occupations, where the traditional relationship is strict (the cowherds, above, are distinguished from those who care for sheep and goats). (4) The learned professions, with strict association and sometimes specialist functions. (5) Transport and peddling, where the association is strict and the functions always specialized. (6) Hunting (aboriginal tribes, etc.). (7) Fishing and navigation (a caste-marked profession, three castes). (8) Commerce and industry: (a) traditional but undefined functions, e.g. the *Baniyā* or merchant (Vaishya). (9) Commerce and industry: (*b*) specified functions, and (10) Trade in food and drink (9 and 10 are purely functional). (11) Jugglers and actors. (12) Specialized criminals and mendicants.

This classification is rather arbitrary, for it does not bring out those professional castes which bear the strongest religious mark. However, one fact stands out immediately: most of the occupations are distinctively religious, and, even more generally, they are precisely defined, the exceptions being commerce in general (to be distinguished from occupations connected with food which are often of religious relevance) and, above all, agriculture, particularly so far as labour is concerned. This must be remembered. Following on from Blunt, we shall see later to what extent the members of the caste practise or do not practise the profession theoretically assigned to them.

Whilst Blunt's inquiry bears on the caste's traditional profession independently of its name, Ghurye has taken the question linguistically.[41d] He noticed that caste names are very often the names of trades, but that these are not the only names: ethnic or tribal names, names of sects and names indicating still other features are also found. The same author adds that this does not hold for the names of subcastes, for these mark territorial rather than professional or other distinctions. One may conclude that profession is one of the differences, perhaps the most indicative difference, whereby a group seen from the outside, a caste, is designated. But this designation by profession is more exterior than real, more 'attributive' than effective, since not all the members of the caste necessarily follow this profession: it may even happen that subcastes are distinguished within a caste of this sort by the name of another profession. Thus according to Blunt the *Kahār* of Uttar Pradesh may be classified as fishermen, water bearers, servants of women; or again the *Khaṭik* as masons, rope-makers, fruiterers and sellers of bacon (*bekanvāle*). It may be thought that there are two distinct cases here. In one case the indicated profession carries with it a status difference which probably entails separation: it may be that the other *Khaṭik* no longer intermarry with their brothers who have become pork butchers. In the other case, profession can only have provided a label for a division whose real basis is something else. Let us take the details of profession which appear in the segmentation of the potter castes: apart from the distinction between pot-makers and tile-makers, must one really consider as having a bearing on profession the fact that some use oxen and others donkeys for transport, some a large wheel and some a small one, some a stone and others the hands for shaping (Bouglé, Ghurye)? One would think, rather, that these features have been used to distinguish groups which differ among themselves in other ways, to *express* differences.

Blunt made a special study of the changes in occupation. This is a delicate matter. Insofar as it is really a matter of occupation, it can be said roughly that there is only a scission at the level of the caste, or separation at the level of the subcaste, if there is an important difference in status between the old profession and the new.[41e] Blunt has attempted a statistical study, and has endeavoured to see, on the basis of the data provided by the official census, what proportion of the members of a caste with a recognized profession effectively follow this profession, and what percentage of people in a given profession belong to the castes for whom it is the traditional occupation. Agriculture is evidently the most important occupation, and 90 per cent of the farming castes follow it; so do 43 per cent of non-agricultural castes, as against 42·2 per cent of these who follow their own profession. Blunt invokes modern economic changes to explain the fact that traditionally non-agricultural castes have to such a large extent turned to agriculture. He accepts the widespread idea that the decline of ancient handicrafts (weaving) obliged the castes who lived from them to fall back on agriculture. No doubt this is in part correct: some crafts did die out and moreover there was an increase in the area under cultivation, notably as a result of increasing the extent of irrigation. But what proof have we that this was an entirely new situation? We would admit it to be so if we thought, like Blunt, that there must have been a time when caste and profession coincided exactly. But this is a gratuitous assumption. It must not be forgotten that agriculture – defined as vaguely as this it is more a kind of occupation than a true profession – is a religiously neutral occupation for the majority of castes (though there is a prejudice amongst high castes against using the plough in person), and is respectable from the non-religious point of view. Anyone who has direct or indirect access to the land – the important point – will see no disadvantage in profiting from it in any way open to him. It has been seen above that there is only a loose association between the agricultural professions and caste.[41f] Also, Blunt reports the diminishing but still considerable stability of certain trades which are mostly village specialities, and often bear the mark of religion: 76 per cent of sweepers follow their profession, 75 per cent of goldsmiths, more than 60 per cent of confectioners and grain parchers, 60 per cent of barbers and washermen, 50 per cent of carpenters, weavers, oil-pressers and potters. This is the more remarkable in that there are limited outlets for these professions and they have in some cases suffered from industrial competition (oil-pressers, weavers – but weaving has not died out). These facts evidently lead us back to the interdependence in the village between the farmers and the specialists, which we shall now consider. Provisionally, we may conclude from this preliminary review that the link between caste and profession is primarily a matter of status, that the important thing is the hereditary profession provided it is not contradicted by following too inferior a profession, and that the system has probably always carried with it some plasticity of this sort, whilst the village specialities, ritual or other, constitute its solid core.

The castes of specialists, or more exactly their regional and local groups, often show strict professional solidarity. In this respect they have been compared to our medieval corporations. Their privilege or monopoly is scarcely ever attacked, but they secure their position by preventing competition between their members, and supporting with solidarity those of their members in conflict with a patron (by boycotting the latter and even getting him boycotted by another caste).[41g]

## 42   The 'jajmānī' system

42.1   *General remarks.* It has become common practice to apply the term 'the *jajmānī* system' to the system corresponding to the prestations and counter-prestations by which the castes as a whole are bound together in the village, and which is more or less universal in India. To a large extent it is a question of natural as opposed to monetary economy. It is also a question of the closed economy of the Indian village in which essential goods and especially services are found, or used to be found, either on the spot or in the immediate vicinity: this fact corresponds, therefore, to what has long been called the 'village community',[42a] in the economic sense of the phrase.

Those who are part of this system do not always use the word *jajmānī* nor even the word *jajmān*. However, the latter is very widely used to designate the employer or patron with respect to the person he employs. Now this is an interesting word. It comes from the Sanskrit *yajamāna*, a participle having reflexive force and meaning 'sacrifier' (as opposed to 'sacrificer'): 'he who has a sacrifice performed'. It can be seen that etymologically the *jajmān* is the master of the house who employs a Brahman as a sacrificer.[42b] The religious connotation is important, and is still present today, although there is no longer any question of Vedic sacrifice. A Hindi dictionary gives for *jajmān* 'he who has religious (*dhārmik*) rites performed by Brahmans by giving them fees, etc.' (note the mention of the counter-prestation immediately evoked by the notion); for *jajmānī*: 'the privilege (*adhikār*) of performing the function of domestic priest (*purohit*), barber, *bārī* (a helper) on the occasion of a marriage, etc.'. Everything in this definition should be remembered: it is a question of family ritual, and above all, of marriage. It is a privilege to take part, even in the capacity of preparing the humble ceremonial materials, cups made from a leaf pinned together (the *bārī*). I have translated *adhikār* by privilege, but it is also responsibility, and a personal asset is involved: each family has its *purohit*, its barber, etc., and neither party is free to escape from this relationship, so much so that the *jajmānī* in the sense of such an obligation can, for example, stand as security for a loan of money (Blunt, p. 260). *Brit* is also used in the same sense. The words may vary or be absent, yet the notion is omnipresent. There are many words to designate the specialists, who are more like clients in their relation to a patron than employees in relation to an employer, since the relationship is a personal one: in Hindi, *prajā* (also 'creature, descendant, subject'), *paunī*, *kām karnevālā* (workman), etc. Incidentally, this whole vocabulary is mostly North Indian.

Whilst religious overtones are in the forefront, the word *jajmān* designates anyone who employs someone in conformity with the system, and the complementary word, let us take *prajā*, anyone thus employed. This applies not only to ceremonial tasks; all others are expressed *in the same language*.

What is the principle behind what is called the *jajmānī* system? In the first place it makes use of hereditary personal relationships to express the division of labour: each family has a family of specialists at its disposal for each specialized task. Secondly, it regulates prestations and counter-prestations in a way which accords with custom: for the usual tasks, repayment is in kind: it is not made individually for each particular prestation but is spread over the whole year, as is natural for a permanent relationship in an agricultural setting: a little food may be provided each day, and there is always the right to a fixed quantity of grain at harvest time, and finally there are obligatory presents (often of money) on the occasion of the main festivals of the year and, above all, at the major family ceremonies, which are advantageous occasions for the *prajā* of the house. A fact which underlines the limited but effective solidarity which is thus set up between *jajmān* and *prajā* is that in many regions those who are considered the main servants of the village enjoy an allotment of land from a communal fund set apart by their patrons.[42c]

It is here that the division of labour, which forms an integral part of the caste system, may be most clearly understood. As Hutton does not mention it, and as it will be more vividly grasped from a concrete example, we shall give a summary of the first unofficial monograph to be devoted to the 'system'. The institution was not unknown, although more often referred to under the title of 'village community', and Blunt accords it a place in his book.[42d] But an American missionary, Wiser, was the first to describe it in detail, as he observed it in a village in the west of Uttar Pradesh some time before 1930.

42.2 *An example*. Karimpur is a village of 754 inhabitants situated in the Doab between Gange and Jamna. There the Brahmans are the dominant caste in that they dispose of the greater part of the rights to the land; they are also the most numerous (forty-one families out of a total of 161 belonging to twenty-four different castes). Wiser has given a complete list of the prestations and counter-prestations. In the first place, the *kām karnevāle*, 'workers' and specialists enjoy a number of concessions. In particular, small areas of land are reserved for them, which they work rent-free. The Brahman whose job it is to light the bonfire at the festival of Holi has 2·33 acres, the florist has an orchard and a small patch, the carpenter, the sweeper, the oil-presser and the seamster, and the washerman have respectively 1·34, 1·15, 0·86 and 0·41 acres. This is not much, but it indicates the official function these people have in the village and such arrangements occur very widely. For the rest, we shall divide the relationships in question into several categories. The relationships are naturally permanent, personal (or inter-family) and hereditary. We shall distinguish dependents (A) from manufacturers and merchants (B). Each caste is arranged in descending order from 1 to 24.

*Category* A1: Dependents with permanent maintenance functions and fixed rights in grain. Twice a year at harvest-time, six specialists receive fixed quantities of threshed grain from each of their patrons. These are: the Brahman (1), the carpenter (8), the barber (9), the water carrier and palanquin bearer (10), the potter (14), the washerman (17). (The others if they come to the field receive an armful of each crop, a sort of charity which is never refused and which represents between 1·4 and 2·8 pounds of grain.)

*Category* A2: Dependants with ceremonial functions who draw customary payments on such occasions. At the times of the major festivals of the year, the clients of a household receive small presents, but certain specialists take an active part in the family ceremonies, which are remunerative occasions for them – especially marriages! Most of the people from the preceding list reappear in this category, the others (in italics) are new: Brahman (1); *genealogist* (2) who also serves as a messenger; *florist* (5); barber (9); water carrier (10); washerman (17); *basket-maker* (18); *sweeper* (20); *Mohammedan beggar* (21) with no precise function; *Mohammedan dancing-girl* (24).

These two categories between them correspond to the central nucleus of the system. By way of an example, some details about the functions and remunerations of the barber will be found in the footnote.[42e]

Next comes a category in which the personal relationship of dependence is still marked, more marked if possible than in the preceding categories. It includes not ritual or ceremonial specialists, but simply the agricultural labour force (excluding seasonal workers). Leaving aside two watchmen appointed by the State and taken from the lower castes, and also messengers and herdsmen, there remains a number of people paid daily or monthly. In effect, these are 'unfree'* workers who are subjected to an employer, work for others only with his permission, and often pay off their debts to their master by their work. Fourteen frequently work by the day, forty-four occasionally. Only three work by the month (for one meal daily and 5·6 rupees a month).

*Category* A3: Dependents constituting the agricultural labour force (the number of 'frequent', then 'occasional' workers is

---

* Note [1969]: I write 'unfree' in preference to 'tied', 'bond' labourers, etc., following D. and A. Thorner. This abstract and negative expression alone covers all relevant cases. (D. and A. Thorner, 'Employer–Labourer relationships in Agriculture', *Land and Labour in India*, Bombay, etc., Asia Publ. House, c. 1962, pp. 21–38 [from *Indian Journ. of Agric. Economics*, XII, 2, 1957, pp. 84–96].)

shown, arranged by caste, the subscript indicating the number of families in the caste).

Vegetable growers (6) 2 plus $10_{26}$; carpenters (8) 0 plus $6_8$; water carriers (10) 3 plus $13_{19}$; shepherds (11) 3 plus $1_6$; mat-makers (18) 3 plus $3_7$; leather workers (19) 4 plus $4_8$; (remember that these people, the Chamars, are the preponderant labour force in view of their numbers in the Ganges plain); sweepers (20) $1_8$ (one messenger, one guard); Mohammedan beggars (21) 1 plus $5_8$; cotton carder (23) $1_1$; 1 cowherd from another village is employed by the month.

Now we come to those I call the manufacturers and merchants. The personal relationship holds good for the first category.

*Category* B1: Manufacturing artisans paid in kind by a customary proportion of the commodity which they treat on behalf of their personal patron: grain parchers (12) and oil-pressers (16).

*Category* B2: Manufacturing artisans paid in money on a customary scale: gold and silver smiths (4); seamsters (13).

*Category* B3: Sellers of goods: vegetable growers (6); shepherds (11); tradesmen (15); Mohammedan glass-bangle sellers (22).

*Remarks*. Specialists of category A, like the ploughwright, can figure in B when it is a question of work to special order, over and above maintenance (of the plough): for example, building an ox-cart. Such work is paid for separately in each case. On the other hand, it will be noted that even in cases where there appears to be a sale, the price of the commodity is not a commercial one: thus milk costs a Brahman 1 anna but costs the others $1\frac{1}{2}$ annas: here again status, the fabric of personal relationships within the village, intervenes.

Wiser presents the system as being more or less symmetrical overall: a member of any given caste, except the lowest ones, has in turn the role of master and servant, and according to Wiser there would be exchange of services: for example, some artisan or other is employed by the Brahmans, and conversely, as head of a household, he employs a Brahman for his domestic ceremonies. It is true that we may thus speak of reciprocity, but it is hierarchical, a feature which Wiser, in his idealization of the system, curiously failed to see. However, he notes that the barber does not serve the sweepers. Even among the Brahmans there appears not only a status ranking but also a sharp distinction between the function of farmer and that of specialist. In effect, the Brahmans are divided into seven different ranks. Only three families (out of forty-one) serve as priests. The first, rank 1, serves those of rank 2 and 3; reciprocally, it is served, like the other two families of rank 1, by a priest from a neighbouring village, of superior status – in conformity with the rule which, it can be seen, here again upholds the general distinction between power and status. The second family of priests, rank 3, serves the Brahmans of lower rank (and 5 out of 34 of higher rank – an unexplained exception) and a small number of the non-Brahmans; the third, rank 6, serve the rest of the non-Brahmans (except sweepers and Mohammedans).[42f] Finally, it must be noted that some castes are served but do not serve. This is the case for Brahmans who are landowners and who do not act for others (thirty-six out of forty-one families); for the accountant (3); the rice grower (7) and for the commercial castes in general: gold and silver smiths (4); vegetable growers (6) (these in theory have their jajmans); shepherds (11) and tradesmen (15).

So it can be seen that, even if in the middle ranks the specialists serve one another reciprocally in their several capacities, the system is not on this account an egalitarian one: in the first place, rank is clearly marked, secondly, and above all, there are two strongly contrasted functions: that of patron and that of specialist client, and only those who have at their disposal the main source of wealth and power, the land, can really display the system in all its pomp. In short, it constitutes a device which guarantees them the services of the specialists, and conversely indirectly guarantees the subsistence of the specialists, by giving them limited but real rights over the products of the land and the affluence of their masters.

42.3 *Discussion.* This 'jajmani system' has given rise in recent years to an interesting discussion. This clearly illustrates the difficulty experienced in doing justice to hierarchy, and thereby at the same time challenges our most firmly anchored habits of thought. The universality of the system has been contested, though with little foundation.[42g] Otherwise, discussion has centred mainly on the appraisal of the system. We have said that Wiser idealized it a little in his interpretation. He saw in it not only security for the poor, but also, by stressing the middle orders, a sort of egalitarian harmony, which accords ill with the whole, but is somewhat reminiscent of the idyllic picture of the 'village community' painted by the romantic civil servants of the beginning of the nineteenth century.

Beidelman has given a comparative analysis of the system which has great documentary value, but suffers from the fact that the author, then a student, wrote it without direct experience of the institution.[42h] He rightly criticizes Wiser, as we have done here, but he goes much further: the system entails an inequality in the distribution of power, and thus represents a form of 'exploitation' and 'coercion'. The 'ritual' aspect is secondary, the politico-economic aspect, dominated by the relation to the land, essential. In short, to say hierarchy is to say 'exploitation'. This is dogmatic and blind materialism, so extreme that Gough, an author of similar tendencies but more experience, took the trouble to point out to Beidelman that he had exaggerated. Although he came to a contrary conclusion, Beidelman, like Wiser, failed to grasp hierarchy. To do so, one must pass to the consideration of Beidelman's critic, Orenstein.[42i] It is a radical criticism, and it attacks Beidelman for not seeing that the system does not consist only in the unequal distribution of the means of production, but also, and more particularly, in other aspects: it institutes an interdependence between those who dispose of these means and those who do not, an interdependence which is in the end to the advantage of the latter. The rich depend on the poor to a certain extent, thanks to the 'ritual' aspect. This is certainly correct. The system entails both inequality and, as Wiser said, some security for the lower orders. It is not necessary to follow Orenstein when he insists, as against the supposed 'exploitation', on the 'functional' aspect of the system as contributing to social cohesion.

At this point, the question of the relationship between the 'religious' and 'economic' aspects must be raised again. We left it open in connection with Hocart's religious interpretation and the difficulty facing its general application. Take, for example, the *Camār* or leather people: in theory, they are untouchable because they are in charge of dead cattle and the tanning of skins. In fact, they are a very numerous caste in the Gangetic plain, for the most part unfree agricultural workers, since tanning leather could provide a livelihood for only a small proportion of them. Should one say, as many do, that the 'ritual' theory is a rationalization of their 'exploitation'? An article by David Pocock is addressed to this question within the framework of the '*jajmānī* relationships'.[42l] Pocock introduces a distinction between what he calls religious specializations – the only ones, according to him, which are really *jajmānī* – and economic pseudo-specializations, which moreover he finally recognizes are expressed in the language of religious specialization. (Among pseudo-specializations he goes on to distinguish between the personal dependence of the unfree worker and the truly artisan handicrafts which are involved in the mercantile economy in varying degrees.) Doubtless this distinction is analytically useful, and there is some glimmer of it in Wiser's list, but if it is a question of the system as a whole, it seems to avoid the problem rather than solve it. If one wanted to introduce the economic point of view, one could take all the aspects into one's purview and try to express them in economic terms (one would posit, for example, that status is in fact expressed quantitatively in the 'price' of milk, religion in the relative remuneration of a Brahman, etc.). It is less easy to see how one could effectively distribute the facts among two such different categories as religion and economics. Pocock escapes this difficulty by distinguishing rather between what depends on local politico-economic conditions and what does not. For example, the relationship between landholders and unfree workers would depend on such conditions (but unfree workers are also the 'leather people', a general criterion).

The term 'primitive economy' is often used, though scarcely ever is a definition provided as a basis for the generalized application of such a specifically modern term to very different societies. Shall we define the economy by value and the market, as did Mauss, or by need and utility, as in *Notes and Queries*?[42k] The first sense would be too narrow, having application only to some professions. Nevertheless, it seems at first sight that the division of labour necessarily has an economic aspect. Were we to travel in our imagination to a threshing floor in traditional India, we would see there the farmer measuring one after the other the King's share, that of the person who is found to have a superior right over the land, then the shares of the Brahman who serves as domestic priest, the barber, and so on, until perhaps he reaches the untouchable ploughman. Would we not have the impression of a phenomenon where, as in a market, qualitatively different prestations are in fact measured in the same units, and thus reduced to a common element, an element which clearly extends beyond religion? One would then speak of the 'value' of the various prestations.

In my opinion, such a view would be a mistake, for in bringing the two phenomena together in this way, a vague exterior likeness is allowed to conceal profound differences between them. This fact did not escape Max Weber.[42l] In a market all buyers and all sellers are as such identical, each after his own profit, and needs are adjusted unconsciously, by the market mechanism. But this is not the case here: not only are the majority of the relationships personal, but this is so in virtue of an organization which is to some extent deliberate and oriented towards the satisfaction of the needs of all those who enter into the system of relationships. What is effectively measured here is, so to speak, interdependence. Whilst directly religious prestations and 'economic' prestations are mingled together, this takes place within the prescribed order, the religious order. The needs of each are conceived to be different, depending on caste, on hierarchy, but this fact should not disguise the entire system's *orientation towards the whole*.[42m] Thus we shall say that distribution on the threshing floor is essentially different from a market in that it takes place in virtue of the fact that everyone is interdependent. If we look closely we see the farmer part with a significant portion of his crop for the benefit of a whole series of different people, we shall feel in the end that we are not in the world of the modern economic individual, but in a sort of co-operative where the main aim is to ensure the subsistence of everyone in accordance with his social function, almost to the extent of sharing out the produce of each piece of land. In the one case, the reference is to the *individual* pursuing his own gain, in the other to the *hierarchical collectivity*. By adding to these contrasting cases the claims of modern socialism, we obtain three terms which can be arranged in a series:

(1) hierarchical collectivity; resources distributed more or less consciously;
(2) anarchic individualities: external and automatic regulation;
(3) regulated individualities (or) egalitarian collectivity: deliberate regulation.

In short, the caste system should be seen as less 'exploitative' than democratic society. If modern man does not see it this way, it is because he no longer conceives justice other than as equality. The conclusion to be drawn from this for the jajmani system is that it eludes what we call economics because it is founded on an implicit reference to the whole, which, in its nature, is religious or, if one prefers, a matter of ultimate values. What would otherwise be economic is subjected to this reference. The system consists in one uniform language to express what we distinguish, and this is not improper nor fraudulent, nor a superficial phenomenon, but rather the very essence of the thing. Here, as elsewhere, 'power' is encompassed, limited, referred to something else. Yet it is not absent, nor is it what it would be were it not encompassed in this way.[42n] Perhaps this constitutes a difficulty, but to push it to one side would be to give up hope of grasping what we are studying. Yet in the last analysis, what happens here has its counterpart in our own society. A painting by a famous artist sells for many thousands of pounds at a certain time because we have agreed in effect to reduce to the common denominator of economics all products and all goods, even those products which nowadays are increasingly acquiring religious value. It only remains for them to be declared the inalienable property of a certain group for their sale to be regarded as sacrilege.

## 43  Conclusion

Taking the jajmani system as the basic form of the division of labour in traditional India, let us try to summarize its characteristics.

There are, briefly, two kinds of castes: those who hold the land, and those who do not. In each village, the land is held by one (or several) castes. This is deliberately left vague, and a more precise account will be given later (Chapter VII). This caste is thus the 'dominant' caste, enjoying economic power, since it controls the means of subsistence, and political power, allowing for its subordinate position within larger territorial units, say, its subordination to the king whose function it reproduces at the level of the village. For such castes, the relation between caste and profession is vague. For in the last analysis, their function can be acquired by force: that which is reserved for the Kshatriya varna in the classical ideology is in practice shared among a large number of castes.

All the other castes are dependent. Roughly speaking, their members obtain direct or indirect access to the means of subsistence through personal relationships with the members of the dominant caste, in virtue of the functions which they are fit to perform and which the dominant caste requires. The link between caste and profession is weak in the case of the intermediary agricultural functions (farmers, share-croppers, tenants, etc.) and is strong in the case of specialist castes, for the most part religiously marked, and also in the case of unfree labour, generally untouchable.

Up to this point everyone is agreed. Everything usually said about power is true at this level, except that one must notice the personal aspect of the relationships and the whole set of accepted ideas. For example, these ideas impose rather strict limits on economic power, which we tend to consider on the modern model. But it is true that at this level religious values do not come to the fore, as is shown by the fact that almost any group whatsoever has, in favourable circumstances, been able to become the dominant caste in a given locality. Note that this feature accords with the devaluation of power, which is part of the theory of the varnas and is presupposed by the hierarchy of purity.

But all this is obviously only one aspect of the thing. Dominants and dependants live under the sway of a system of ideas in which the 'power' aspect we have isolated is in fact encompassed. The essential idea, from the present point of view, is the orientation towards the whole which, even if unconscious, determines the most minute attitudes because it governs specialization and interdependence. This orientation, which in the eyes of those who participate in it legitimizes their respective positions, appears as the opposite of an economic phenomenon in the strict sense. An economic phenomenon presupposes an individual subject; here on the contrary everything is directed to the whole, to the 'village community', if one likes, but then as part and parcel of a necessary order. This view of an ordered whole, in which each is assigned his place, is fundamentally religious. Within this overall view are located the various functions and specializations which seem to us to be very unequally religious in themselves. It is no accident that the specializations which are most marked in the accepted religious language are those in which the link between caste and profession is strongest, and, even nowadays, most stable. It is correct to say that these are most strictly jajmani, but at the same time one must not lose sight of the fact that they serve as a model for the others. Just as we have seen how the ideology of the pure and the impure serves to express all sorts of things, so here the universal form of the relation is given by the properly religious relation, as the etymological connotation of jajmani incidentally reminded us. One employs a Brahman, a geneologist, a barber, one employs similarly a carpenter, one employs an untouchable unfree labourer: each case is always, so to speak, on the same model. In other words, the 'religious' is here the universal mode of expression, and this is perfectly coherent if one knows that the overall orientation is religious, that the language of religion is the language of hierarchy, and that the hierarchy is necessarily, as we have seen, a matter of pure and impure.

In the last analysis, the division of labour shows not a more or less gratuitous juxtaposition of religious and non-religious or 'economic' tasks, but both the religious basis and the religious expression of interdependence. Better, it deduces interdependence from religion.

Let us hasten to add that this conclusion does not exhaust the problems and topics of study, even within the jajmani system. It simply helps to locate the true problems and get rid of a pseudo-problem.

Moreover, the jajmani system is not everything, and it is well to recall this in concluding this chapter. Even in the village money plays a role; this has long been the case but is increasingly so nowadays. In addition, there are other specializations, both large-scale (villages of weavers) and urban. I have neglected all this because it seemed to me that, in the present state of knowledge, the ordinary type of village, and the jajmani, contained the main lesson in connection with this aspect of the caste system.[43a]

# CHAPTER FIVE

# THE REGULATION OF MARRIAGE:
# SEPARATION AND HIERARCHY

It is generally agreed that caste is characterized by the obligation to marry within the group, by endogamy. Thus, at first sight, following most of the literature, the regulation of marriage is an expression of the principle of separation: castes separate themselves from one another by prohibiting marriage outside the group, just as they forbid contact and commensality between persons belonging to different groups. At a certain level of segmentation, the caste prescribes endogamy and thus ensures its own reproduction. One belongs to the caste, or rather the subcaste (etc.) of one's parents. In fact this view, no doubt satisfactory from a statistical point of view but theoretically too simple and too narrow, would give rise to numerous exceptions. Here as in other matters, we shall see the necessity for the principle of hierarchy: it in a sense encompasses the principle of separation. We shall first recall the importance of marriage in this society and the various rules which relate to it at the level of the caste and also in connection with kinship, then we shall summarize the common view, which stresses endogamy, and finally we shall attempt to reach a more general view. A few details will be added on the subdivisions of caste in relation to intermarriage, and the treatment of marriage from the point of view of the varnas in ancient Sanskrit literature will be recalled.

## 51  *Importance of marriage*

Marriage dominates the Hindu's social life, and plays a large part in his religion. The social importance of marriage can be seen from a number of features. It is the most prestigious family ceremony, and at the various social levels constitutes the main occasion on which the greatest number of members of the caste and other persons gather together. It is also the most expensive, and the marriage of a daughter in particular is known to be the main cause of debt among Indian peasants, so imperative are the dictates of prestige, even for the poor.[51a] For many castes, the celebration of a marriage is the occasion on which a Brahman priest is indispensable, as are the services of the barber, washerman and other castes (services which must be liberally remunerated). It is the occasion for a lengthy series of ceremonies and complicated prestations.[51b] Finally, it is naturally a matter which is strictly codified for each caste, certain customs having the value of positive hierarchical criteria, like infant marriage, prohibition of remarriage of widows and even the absence of divorce. By its nature, marriage constitutes to a large measure the link between the domain of caste and that of kinship, and the kinship rules relating to it are as elaborate as the others. It is not surprising to see that adultery is very severely punished when the occasion demands, especially when it takes place between different castes; nor that premarital sexual relations are forbidden – probably universally – for the castes, unlike the tribes.[51c]

What I translate as 'infant marriage' designates the fact of celebrating marriage long before cohabitation can begin, in fact at a very young age, especially for the girl. The custom is, or rather was, in force among Brahmans and the high castes generally, and was a sign of high status. I say 'was' because it is one of the features which have been fought by the reformers as being both repugnant to the modern mind and devoid of clear religious foundation. However, it is an ancient custom; in Dharma literature, it was essentially a question of getting the girl married before puberty, and for not obeying this commandment a father brought upon himself a supernatural sanction. The age of the girl at marriage became lower in the course of time. In modern eyes the most shocking result was the existence of young 'widows' who had never lived with their husbands.[51d]

Among the Brahmans marriage tends to be unique (monogamous) and indissoluble. I say 'it tends' because the duty to have a son makes an infertile union a legitimate ground for exceptions, and the man takes a second wife in such a case. As for indissolubility, it is expressed by the fact that divorce does not exist (at most there can be separation) and by the prohibition against remarriage of widows. It is not surprising to see the inferior marriage partner bearing the whole brunt of its indissolubility, and furthermore, the widow leads, or used to lead quite recently, a life of penitence. Among royal castes, things have a different aspect: there is hierarchized polygamy, but the remarriage of widows is likewise forbidden, and it is essentially these castes which must be connected with the practice of *satī* ('virtuous' spouse) whereby the main wife (at least) sacrificed herself on her husband's funeral pyre (a custom also sometimes practised by the Brahmans, and forbidden early on by the English).[51e]

It has sometimes been written that the castes in general forbade the remarriage of widows. Even as a rough approximation, this is very inaccurate: most castes, the overwhelming majority of the population, permit it, and a considerable part of the population even recognize divorce and marry girls after puberty, not before. But a distinction must be made: the true marriage, a woman's first marriage – *primary* marriage – is universally unique (but not indissoluble). The difference is between castes who forbid and castes who allow the woman, if her first marriage is ended by widowhood or divorce, to contract a kind of inferior marriage, which we shall call a *secondary* marriage.[51f] In direct opposition to the absence of the woman's secondary marriage, the custom of levirate – or it would be better to say quasi-levirate – is widespread; it allows the widow to marry (secondary marriage) the younger brother of her husband (the elder brother being generally excluded).[51g]

Little will be said here about kinship. The place of marriage in the explicit kinship system is very different in the south (the lands of Dravidian language) and the north (of Indo-Aryan language, with some simplification: Maratha country, of Indo-Aryan language, is transitional). In the former case, marriage is central, and the affinal relationships based on it are developed to the point of perfectly counterbalancing blood relationships. In the north, on the contrary, at first sight marriage seems to have a role almost as secondary as in our own culture. However, in the one case as in the other, there are exogamous groups, and whilst marriage between close relatives is forbidden in the north, this prohibition itself is extended and elaborated among the Brahmans, in theory if not always in practice, in a manner which looks like a way of going one better. In fact it has been shown in a detailed study that affinal relationships, or what we would call in the south marriage alliance relationships (alliance being an extended and permanent affinity), play an important part, although their direct expression is absent and, so to speak, repressed by 'Aryan' orthodoxy. In spite of the presence of another feature, hypergamy, which will be mentioned again later, and in spite of the prohibition against the marriage of close relatives, the ceremonial roles and prestations which are produced by marriage alliance in the south are certainly also present in the north. The Dravidian aspect is there made incomplete and non-conscious, but it underlies what actually takes place. Therefore it is inaccurate to claim that caste and kinship are two utterly distinct domains: they are united through the importance of marriage, an importance which is obvious in the case of caste and which, in the case of kinship, is from the structural point of view sometimes explicit and sometimes implicit.[51h]

## 52  Endogamy: the usual view and its limitations

For Western common sense, the 'caste' is above all a 'closed' group: permanent, exclusive and self-sufficient. A man of caste X marries a woman of caste X and the children belong to caste X. This fact is expressed in various ways, by saying that the group reproduces itself by itself from generation to generation, is 'endo-recruiting', etc. On analysis, it can be seen that two distinct features are here combined: one marries within the group (endogamy), or rather one is forbidden to marry outside; and descent (the transmission of group membership) depends on both parents. The first feature contrasts the caste with the tribe and with the majority of societies which tolerate marriage outside the group, even though it *generally* takes place within. The second feature contrasts the caste with the clan in which descent is (uni-)linear, whether in the paternal or maternal line. Clans, like castes, depend by definition on their regulation of marriage: clan – generally at any rate – is accompanied by exogamy, the obligation to marry outside; caste on the contrary, entails, in relation to its mode of descent, the obligation to marry within.[52a] Let us note in passing that, compared with a tribe which breaks down into clans, caste society represents a higher order of complexity, since each caste generally has its exogamous clans or their equivalent.

It is roughly true that the caste system defines endogamous groups, but it is, of course, a little too simple to be true. We must not forget, first and foremost, that whilst it looks in general self-sufficient for its reproduction, yet the caste is strictly dependent upon other castes from the hierarchical point of view and in virtue of the division of labour. It would be surprising if nothing in the caste's internal organization, in particular marriage, reflected these external features. Further, we have already seen that in general a subdivision of the same kind as the caste, a segment rather than the caste itself, is the unit of endogamy in the sense of the group outside which marriage is forbidden.[52b] Even so, there is often a tendency to believe that the system is more rigid than it really is: it is commonly fancied that any breach of the rule of endogamy would automatically lead to excommunication. Now it does happen in certain cases that a man X marries a woman Y and that the children are legitimate, and, even more often that a man X has children by a woman Y without either him or them being expelled from group X. Status is really the essential principle here: certain irregularities are penalized simply by a loss of status, and it is at bottom the need to maintain the group's status which governs endogamy. In short, castes are self-reproducing because this is a condition for the application of the hierarchical principle by which they are arranged in order. Now the hierarchical principle which ranks castes and their segments does not stop at the bounds of the unit of endogamy, it permeates it, in a more or less effective way, and endogamous marriage does not necessarily unite spouses of equal status. Finally, when we speak of endogamy or of a unit of endogamy we place ourselves at the level of the rule or law, of what ought to happen; but what happens in actual fact? In practice, one often marries not throughout the whole range of the unit of endogamy but only into a part of it, often a territorial part.[52c]

If one confined the regulation of Hindu marriage to endogamy pure and simple, one would have to admit a large number of exceptions. But it will be seen that most of the exceptions disappear if two general principles are introduced: (1) endogamy is a corollary of hierarchy, rather than a primary principle; (2) the first marriage must be distinguished from subsequent freer marriages and, *a fortiori*, from illegitimate unions.[52d]

## 53 *Hierarchy of marriages and conjugal unions*

Let us recall first of all that neither premarital sexual relations nor adultery are tolerated. Next, the only true and complete marriage whereby one moves from the category of an unmarried person to that of a married person is the first. But the ceremony which effects this transition is especially important for the woman, and one must distinguish the case of a male from that of a female. In the case of a woman we shall call the first marriage the *primary* marriage. Once this marriage has been contracted, either it is indissoluble even by the death of the spouse (superior castes) or else the woman may, after her husband's death or even after divorce, contract another union, legitimate, but infinitely less prestigious, involving much less ritual and expense, which we shall call *secondary* marriage. Secondary marriage, being of lower status, is freer, sometimes much freer, than primary marriage. In the case of a man his first marriage becomes the *principal* marriage only if it bears him children, preferably sons. But a man has the option, either in the case of the barrenness of the first marriage, or freely in other castes (royal, etc.), of taking other wives, either with *full rite* (necessary for the wife if she has not been married before) or with *secondary* rite (if the wife has already been married). Thus for a man there are supplementary or *subsidiary* marriages, with a corresponding hierarchy of wives.

Here there are good reasons to say there are two contrasting patterns: the Brahmanic pattern consisting of monogamy (except in cases of barrenness) and a 'royal' polygynous pattern (subsidiary wives may be of lower status than the principal one and the sons ranked accordingly). Polygyny is often sororal in the middle castes (naturally it is limited as elsewhere by economic reasons). It must be insisted that in all these cases it is a question of marriages, that is to say, of legitimate conjugal unions uniting not only individuals but, through them, families or small lineages. In addition, the married man who can afford it may have one or several concubines; such a relationship depends only on the parties concerned; the offspring are not legitimate, the sons do not inherit (or only a lesser share). In short, it is seen that in addition to our distinction of legitimacy (between marriages and other unions) another distinction, which is in the main a status or hierarchical distinction, must be applied, between primary and principal marriage on the one hand and other unions in general on the other.[53a]

A spectacular example of the usefulness of this distinction was given by Chambard in Malwa (Central India). He found, among a caste of middle rank, that there were 'woman fairs' in which the women were, at first sight, bought more or less freely from their possessors. This may seem astonishing in India (given that the famous 'marriage by purchase' has never existed anywhere any more than the no less famous 'marriage by capture'). We must reflect that it is only a matter of *secondary* marriages: the women concerned have first been married (primarily) with all the usual care and solemnity, and it is the husbands who can afterwards 'sell' them, or rather abandon them to someone else in exchange for a money payment. Extreme as it is, the case represents an example of the freedom of secondary marriage and does not affect what has been said about primary marriage, except to this extent: that it can be terminated in an unexpected way.[53b]

There is an important difference between the north and the south of the country. In the south, there is a clearly marked status difference between the two sorts of marriage and their issue whenever these are encountered in the same family. In the north on the contrary the difference is scarcely more than one of ritual and of the prestige of the spouses, and it is not passed on to their descendants.[53c]

The relative flexibility of the system can be seen in the case of illegitimate children, insufficiently known as it is. We may think that excommunication applied only to cases presenting flagrant difference of status, and that the treatment of illegitimate offspring was largely a function of environment and circumstances. The universal principle is that the illegitimate child has a status markedly inferior to that of the legitimate children. Circumstances play a part in determining the intensity and expression of the difference of status: will the child be relegated to an inferior position within the caste – a position which may or may not be transmitted to his descendants – or will all relations with the child, and perhaps with his father, be broken off, or will he be attached to his mother's caste, if it is inferior (the most common case)? In the absence of fixed principles, dominance or simply wealth, even locality, and finally the caste's situation, whether or not it is isolated from castes of neighbouring status, must have played a large part. This is how one can reasonably picture the situation, though there is some risk of hasty generalization, due to our slender information. At any rate, we can be sure that there was no shortage of bastards, especially in the houses or retinues of princes. This is already something with which to temper our prejudices about the rigidity of the system.[53d]

## 54   *Isogamy and hypergamy*

We have not finished with the multifarious manifestations of status in marriage. We must again distinguish two patterns. In the first, there must be equality of status between the spouses in the primary and principal marriage (it being understood that the woman can be of slightly inferior status in the man's subsidiary marriage – which again is already the case in a sense if the woman has already been married, that is, if the marriage is secondary for her). In this pattern the (principal) marriage will be called isogamous. In the present state of our knowledge, this pattern seems to be general for southern India where, let it be recalled, one often marries what we would call a close relative, in particular a maternal uncle's daughter. This pattern obviously requires that one be sure of the status of the family into which one marries, or into which one marries one's daughter. And this requires, and above all formerly required, that the unit of endogamy be confined to a limited area, where everyone can know one another directly or indirectly, and that there be sanctions against irregular practices and bastardy, so that the group's status is not endangered. In short, the isogamous pattern must have been accompanied by a high degree of fissiparity of groups within the caste.[54a]

The word hypergamy was introduced at the end of the last century to designate a different pattern which is sometimes encountered in the north of India, although it is not universal there.[54b] In this pattern, a slight status difference, a slight inferiority of the wife's family in relation to the husband's, is considered normal and does not in the least affect the offspring's status. Of course, this relates to the principal marriage, and in no way excludes endogamy. It is because in such a marriage the daughter marries into a superior family (she 'marries up') that it has, rightly or wrongly, been called 'hyper'gamous. Three remarks can be made: (1) the term 'hypergamous' is not used to designate all marriages or unions in which there is a status difference in the direction indicated, but more precisely the fact that such a difference is, within certain limits, neutralized normatively in the first marriage. The term even implies if not an obligation at least a strong recommendation for the girl's parents to find her a superior partner. (2) As the woman is in general considered inferior to the man, the pattern would seem natural to the people concerned. (3) More importantly, the pattern harmonizes best with the Brahmanic-classical and universal ideology of a girl's marriage being a 'gift of a maiden' (*kanyā dān*). The gift in general is an extremely meritorious action: one acquires merit by the gift of goods to the Brahmans, meaning that one thereby exchanges raw materials of no value for spiritual goods. Now the 'gift of a maiden' is a special form of gift, and it is meritorious on condition that no payment is received for the girl; here the girl is, on the whole, assimilated to a material good, and the giving of her is in fact accompanied by material gifts and by as lavish receptions as possible; in the hypergamous pattern the superior status of the bridegroom's family makes it more demanding about the prestations it receives with the girl, as if it would only accept marriage into an inferior family on condition of receiving hard cash; but this precisely squares with the pattern of the gift: one gives a daughter and goods to a superior in exchange, not in this case for spiritual merits, but for something similar, namely the prestige or consideration which results from intermarriage with him.[54c]

In this case, in contrast with the isogamous pattern, the endogamous unit tolerates notable differences of status within itself and even some degree of uncertainty in this respect, since one may take a wife either within an equal group or within a group to a certain extent inferior to one's own. This fact probably accounts for the existence of extremely large endogamous units, for example in the Gangetic plain, which would be inconceivable in the south.

One can formally distinguish between obligatory hypergamy and optional hypergamy, but our knowledge just enables us to see that perhaps the distinction does not in fact have much interest. Imagine a caste which is not segmented but which is composed of a number of clans, each covering a very large area. This is how the *Rājpūt* caste (or should one rather say the subcaste of Rajputs proper?) appears in the literature.[54d] If these clans are strictly hierarchized in relation to each other, as is theoretically the case, then one could not marry an equal since one must marry outside the clan, and given that one cannot marry a woman of superior status,[54e] hypergamy will be obligatory. In another pattern, of which there are many examples, it is not clans which are ranked but groups having the nature but not the name of subcastes, which, curiously enough, are distinguished by numbers. In this case one may marry within one of these groups (isogamously) as well as outside, and thus hypergamy is only optional. We shall see an example of this.

In the theoretical model of obligatory hypergamy, and to a lesser extent in the case of optional hypergamy, it was observed long ago that men would be supernumerary in the inferior part of the endogamous group, since the women will have married for preference into a superior group, and on the contrary the women would be supernumerary in the superior part, unless recourse were had to large-scale polygyny. The first difficulty was overcome by unions of inferior status with women of other castes, the second by the infanticide of daughters, which the British government fought with success. This situation is characteristic of the Rajputs: infanticide of daughters at the top of the ladder, breakdown of endogamy at the bottom, polygyny among the powerful.

## 55  Some examples

Let us now give some illustrations of the foregoing, starting with the distinction between primary and secondary marriages. This distinction accounts for an arrangement which would otherwise constitute an exception from the point of view of endogamy. In various groups, in order to secure for women great freedom of (secondary) marriage or of sexual unions in general, primary marriage is, or rather was, reduced to a mere ritual formality. Sometimes women are married in this way to a god, an object, a fruit, or a man who immediately disappears from their lives: in the south this was the case for the Devadasi or ritual prostitutes, in certain districts for the Basavi, girls devoted to giving their fathers a son, in Malabar (Kerala) for the Nayar girls, in order to maintain matrilineal filiation, and, as a remarkable fact, at the other end of the country, for the Newar girls of Nepal (for a purpose which is not quite clear). After such a marriage the Devadasi was allowed to prostitute herself, the Basavi and the

Nayar girls to have unions in which they play the social role normally devolving to the man (transmitting unilineal descent), and the Newar girls probably to have unions with men of inferior status.

The Nayar case is very remarkable and deserves brief mention.[55a] A girl of the highest status among the Nayars was first of all married with pomp to a Nambudiri Brahman, for whom she and her children would subsequently have to go into mourning. Whether or not there was cohabitation and a divorce ritual, this relationship ceased almost at once, and the girl then contracted secondary marriages with different men, of status at least equal to her own, either Nambudiri Brahmans or Nayars. The difficulty here is that the primary spouse is not an object but actually a man, and a man not only of very high caste, but also of very high varna: a Brahman, where the Nayars are considered Shudras. Here then a major misalliance features as the principal marriage! On closer inspection it is nothing of the kind: from the hierarchical point of view it would be a misalliance only for the Brahman, since for the girl the relation is, on the contrary, one of the most honorific (this is its *raison d'être*: to secure her a husband of the highest possible status). Now precisely what is a marriage for the girl and the Nayars is not one for the Nambudiri priests. Among them only the eldest son marries, a Nambudiri girl, of course, whilst the younger sons are treated in the way illegitimate sons are treated elsewhere: they do not inherit, and must be content with concubinage with Nayar women, the offspring of such unions being Nayars. As for the Nayar girl's primary marriage, for the Nambudiri who figures in it as the 'spouse' it is only a ritual in which he plays the part which devolves on the father in Nambudiri marriages (tying the *tāli* round the woman's neck), a *rite de passage* in which there is no husband. This is a crucial case. The notion that marriage is universally governed by the principle of endogamy is invalidated by this exception. Let us, on the contrary, posit that endogamy is the result, nowadays general, of the law whereby a caste refuses to take spouses of clearly inferior status, and conversely cannot get spouses of clearly superior status, although it would have no objection. Then the fact that the ceremony does not constitute a marriage for the Nambudiri is enough to make this comedy possible. One can see from this example why it is necessary to regard as primary the principle of hierarchy and not the principle of separation, or a so-called 'repulsion' in the manner of Bouglé.[55b] Let us observe further that, contrary to what the use of the same word by certain authors might suggest, the symbiosis of the Nambudiri and the Nayar has nothing to do with hypergamy: there is indeed a difference of status in the usual direction, but this difference is not neutralized; on the contrary it remains relevant in the highest degree, for it is the search for a social father (*pater*) and physiological fathers (*genitores*) of the highest status which is, together with the maintenance of matrilineal filiation in a patrilineal environment, at the root of the institution.[55c]

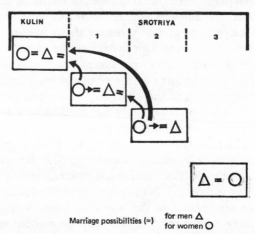

Marriage possibilities (=)   for men △
                             for women ○

Figure 2. Hypergamy among the Rarhi Brahmans in Bengal.

One can take as a relatively simple example of hypergamy the classic case of the Rarhi Brahmans of Bengal. They are divided into two subcastes, Kulin (literally 'of [good] lineage') and Srotriya. The Kulins, being superior, were so sought after as husbands for Srotriya girls that they used to marry up to several dozen of them, each time in exchange for substantial presents. Naturally they could not maintain so many wives, so the wives remained in their own families and simply received visits from their husbands (a situation similar to that of the Nayar girls who receive their secondary husbands, Nambudiri or otherwise, in their own homes). Moreover, the Kulin asked for a payment each time. The children were often brought up in their mother's family. The institution did not recover from the High Court judgment which decreed that husbands were obliged to maintain their wives. In detail: the Srotriya were segmented into three and the lowest subdivision was endogamous whilst the two higher ones gave their daughters in marriage to their superiors (to the exclusion of the inverse relation), namely, the first only to the Kulin – and its own members – the second to the Kulin, to members of the first division, and to its own members.[55d] Figure 2 shows that with equal numbers, and not taking into account the Kulins' polygyny, unmarried girls would accumulate among the Kulins, and unmarried men in the second division of the Srotriya. In this example, only the lowest subdivision is endogamous whereas the three others, one of which is first order in relation to the caste, the other two of second order, have optional hypergamous relationships. Such situations have led people to conclude that the caste was endogamous in a stricter sense than its segment, but this does not say enough: it is impossible to reduce the arrangement simply to a principle of endogamy: there is a tendency to secure husbands of high rank, and, when this is impossible, the group closes in on itself. We have insisted on the exchange of goods (a girl, as wife, and money in exchange for prestige).

We have mentioned the existence of a pattern in which the caste is segmented into units indicated by numbers. There are two cases. In the first, the higher group is indicated by a higher number, for example, the Agarwal (Vaishyas of Gujarat and the Panjab) have the 'twenty' (superior) and the 'ten' (inferior). The two divisions are endogamous. The numbers are to be understood as '20/20' (full status) and '10/20' (reduced status). As the second division corresponds to a degradation of full status, it is not surprising to find the same exogamous groups represented within the two divisions. The two modes of division, into 20 and 10 and into clans, are independent and their function is different (Blunt, p. 49).

The other pattern, the converse of the preceding one, is more widespread. Its meaning may be understood in Maharashtra, and it is very frequent in Uttar Pradesh. The clans of the Maratha caste are ranked into five levels of decreasing status, corresponding to the ascending numbers: five, seven, etc., ninety-six: the numerical increase is related to the fact that each level includes the previous ones: in theory there are ninety-six clans in all and the first five are included in the second seven (thus the second level in fact consists of two clans). Karvé pictures the whole in the form of concentric circles, in which the smaller are superior in status to the larger. These groups, being unnamed and probably relatively unstable, are by nature subcastes and not exogamous groups: one can in effect marry within the five clans, and women necessarily do so, for 'the five' accept wives from the inferior groups, but refuse to reciprocate.[55e]

The same arrangement of numbers is found again in Uttar Pradesh, although in this case, so far as we know, the less numerous are not included in the more numerous. Further, whilst the descriptions, already ancient, generally indicate hypergamy, they are often complex and confused.[55f] I shall take as an example the Sarjupari or Sarvariya Brahmans, which I have studied. This group will be called a caste or a subcaste depending on whether one considers the Brahmans as a varna or as being also a caste. They are localized in the eastern part of the State, their name indicating a locality, 'beyond (to the east of) the River Sarju (the Rapti)', though they are no longer confined to it nowadays. One hears repeatedly, and it has been printed, that they comprise 'the three and a half houses, the thirteen houses, and the one hundred and twenty-five thousand'. It is difficult to obtain a serious enumeration of the 'three and a half' and the 'thirteen'. The word 'house' seems to refer not to a clan, but to a localized patrilineal group, let us say a local lineage group and its descendants even if they have emigrated to another place. (The group, like others, has in addition another division, this being into two sections.) The inquiry confirms that status is in fact ascribed 'to such and such people of such and such a place', for instance to the 'Tivari of Rampur' (Tivari being one of the titles in use in the caste), and this is independent of the overall pattern quoted. This point is essential in many respects. In the first place, the caste is immense, having perhaps two million members. The superior section has very few members, and the inferior section, although comprising the overwhelming majority of the caste, still constitutes a (theoretical) unit of endogamy. The grouping within which one in fact marries is naturally much more restricted. Further, sustained attention is given to status only at the higher levels. A dozen titles are in use, which are evidently quite inadequate to distinguish someone's status. They are the usual titles in these regions: Tivari, Dube, etc. Besides, are we entitled here to speak of 'status'? The main concern is to prevent the reversal of a given relation of intermarriage, and the fact of giving a wife makes the group which gives inferior to the one which receives. The 'status' in question has no effect outside the relation of intermarriage; one would therefore rather speak of a certain sort of consideration or prestige, especially as this quality is extremely segmented, being ascribed in each case to a small local or regional group. In these conditions it is tempting to consider the overall pattern as a rationalization effected at a certain moment, which has subsequently worn thin and been more or less forgotten, and which gave a 'total' pattern for a prestige ladder which by its very nature tended to disintegrate. It is tempting to generalize, which would account for the diversity and confusion of the descriptions. For example, we find in a legendary account a king of Bengal, Ballal Sen, intervening to codify the order of precedence in certain castes. More importantly, here, as in the ideal, more or less Rajput pattern, mentioned above, status or its equivalent is attributed not to caste segments, but to *exogamous groups*. The difference with the Rajputs is that they claim to hierarchize entire clans whereas here only localized lineages are in question.[55g] This fact must be stressed: status is on the one hand attached to the caste and its segments (these latter being sometimes designated as quantitative aggregates of exogamous groups); on the other hand it is apportioned amongst local exogamous groups. In other words, within these enormous castes, in which hypergamy enables different statuses to be distinguished without the unity of the caste being impaired, status is ascribed not only to endogamous but also exogamous groups. This can explain the ease with which the native, preoccupied above all with status, can pass from one to the other, calling both of them, when occasion arises, by the term '*jāti*', 'birth' which designates, rather, the caste and its segments.[55h]

## 56 *Conclusion*

To sum up, from the point of view of Hindu India as a whole, endogamy is, in modern times, only an average and general result at one level or another of the principle of hierarchy. In effect:

(1) The separation or closure of one group with respect to those above results fundamentally from the closure of the other groups with respect to those below (Nayar).

(2) Apart from illegitimate unions, whose issue usually suffer

degradation of status rather than excommunication, marriages are strictly hierarchized, the primary marriage (for a woman) being strictly regulated but capable of being made fictitious, whilst the secondary marriage, where it exists, may be very free. The institutions tend to uphold the group's status but do not prevent as an addition the proliferation of inferior statuses.

(3) Hierarchy, in the form of hypergamy, penetrates to the very core of the institutions of marriage and kinship. Not only does it 'temper' the endogamy of the caste segment and transfer strict endogamy to a higher level (caste), but in certain cases (Rajput) it even produces a breakdown of endogamy at the group's lower limit.

It must be repeated that at the present time the specialists are not agreed on this interpretation. Yet the advance that such a view represents on those that are still currently accepted should be readily appreciated. For example, we now see the impossibility of claiming that caste and kinship are two absolutely watertight compartments. And above all, while unifying the domain under consideration, we obtain an infinitely truer picture of things than if we supposed that the men living in castes either automatically respected the most drastic rules or were excommunicated; moreover, this would contradict the spirit of the system, which is more concerned to classify human possibilities in an hierarchical order than to exclude or punish those who do not conform to its ideal. I am convinced that, seen in this light, many apparent oddities become comprehensible. Let us consider a complicated example of sub-caste ranking and relations in Uttar Pradesh, where such arrangements are not uncommon. It concerns the Dhanuk caste in the district of Cawnpore, according to the *Census* of 1911. Blunt and Hutton give the case as a curiosity.[56a] There are five subcastes whose relations vary from one part of the district to another. A reasonable hypothesis, given the environment, is to suppose a hypergamous pattern. We can then construct a diagram in which the horizontal order from right to left corresponds to a hypothetically decreasing status, and the vertical order, from top to bottom, to an increasing separation between subcastes. The numbers correspond to the order of enumeration (1: Laungbarsa, etc.).

It is seen that the order of the subcastes (horizontally) is variable for the lower numbers: 3 occupies a lower rank on the first line than on the following ones, 1 and 2 change their respective positions between the first two lines and the last two. These are the only arbitrary variations. This is not a serious matter, and these changes are explicable if one considers that, as the caste is small, the classification of subcastes must take into account differences in the behaviour of local groups.

To conclude, let us note that the most common modern change in this matter consists in marriage between different subcastes of

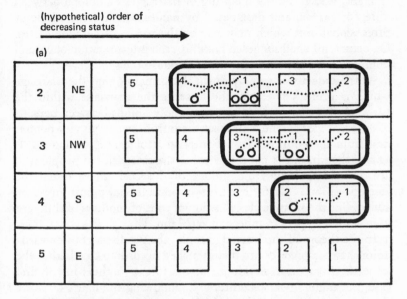

(a) : Number of segments (subcastes) not allowing intermarriage
········O : Girls may marry into another segment.
Figure 3. Segmentation in the Dhanuk caste, Kanpur District (U.P.).

the same caste (n. 112e). This is the better understood if one admits that endogamy is not only not attached *ne varietur* to a fixed level of segmentation, but also is more an implication of hierarchy than an independent principle.

## 57 *The classical theory: marriage and varna*

In general, the authors see in the classical theory either something very different from modern reality, not to say something arbitrary, or else a picture of a state of affairs infinitely more fluid, more flexible, than exists today. Now whilst the differences leap to the eye – in the first place it is a matter of varnas rather than jatis – yet it can be shown that the general view of the modern situation we have just formulated brings these ancient texts much closer to us. This is not to say they are devoid of difficulties. To keep to what is essential, and to try to grasp the spirit of these texts, we shall leave on one side the long enumerations of the people called 'mixed', said to be the offspring of marriages or unions between different varnas, and designated by names which seem ethnic or professional, but which may also be the names of genuine castes. On occasion I shall suggest a possibly rash interpretation of certain points in the light of modern knowledge.[57a]

At the outset one can lay down the principle that the marriage which is preferred, to say the least, is the marriage within the varna. As for marriages or more generally unions between persons of different varnas, the texts treat them from two main viewpoints: first from the point of view of marriage (for example Manu, III, 12 ff.), then from the point of view of the categories of people who are deemed to issue from unions of this sort, those called the 'mixed' (Manu, X, 6–39). Less important viewpoints must be added, like the relative classification of sons of mothers of different varnas with respect to inheritance (Manu, IX, 151 ff.).

In the theory of the 'mixed' people, the products of inter-varna unions, two categories are distinguished according to whether the father is of superior or inferior status to the mother: in the first case, the union is *anuloma* literally, 'following the hair', or as we should say 'with the grain', which means in conformity with the natural order (the woman being from a general point of view inferior to the man). In the opposite direction the union is 'brushed the wrong way' or 'against the grain', *pratiloma*. In both cases the offspring of such a union have inferior status (see below), but the natural order gives rise to offspring superior to those of unions which go against nature.[57b] It is not specified here whether this concerns marriage or just any sexual union. When they are concerned elsewhere with marriage, the authors ignore this distinction, but in practice they exclude *pratiloma* unions in connection with marriage. Only *anuloma* unions can count as marriages, although such marriages are not always approved. The point is confirmed by considerations relating to inheritance, in which only a man's sons by equal or inferior women are counted, since it is reasonable to identify right to inheritance with legitimacy.

On the topic of the regulation of marriage, the authors seem ambiguous and contradictory. On the one hand it is stated or implied that marriage should be between people of the same varna; on the other it is admitted (elsewhere) that not all children are born in this way and, even here, there are provisions for certain inter-varna unions as marriages. This is not a matter of a change occurring at the time of the writing of a particular text, for all the texts present this difficulty. Thus Gautama, who in connection with marriage prescribes endogamy of the varna, mentions elsewhere the existence of 'mixed' people. Likewise Yajñavalkya prescribes marriage within the varna or (for a man) in the varna immediately below only, but in his treatment of the 'mixed' people he mentions every possible *anuloma* combination. Manu has several successive verses which are characteristic (II, 12–15). The first recommends a twice-born to marry first of all a girl of his own varna and then, if driven by desire, girls from inferior varnas. The second indicates that a woman may marry either in her own varna or into a superior varna. The possibility of *pratiloma* marriage is thus removed. The last verse excludes a *Śūdrā* wife for a Brahman or a Kshatriya, giving as a reason that this would lead to the off-spring being degraded to the rank of *Śūdrā*. (Note that a little later (17) Manu condemns not only marriage but even sexual relations with a *Śūdrā* woman.) As usual all this is found again in other texts. By reference to contemporary observations or even directly with the help of other passages (Renou), one is tempted to understand that the principal wife, mother of children of full status, must be of the same status, but that one can add inferior, secondary wives, whose children will also be inferior. This corresponds pretty well to the hierarchy of sons, in which the principal son – the only one who is both legitimate and natural – born of an isogamous marriage is ranked above the secondary sons who are either legitimate or natural. The *Śūdrā* wife of a 'twice-born' is often referred to as a pleasure opposed to dharma (Vas., XVIII, 18), and it is not just a question of concubinage, for Vasistha knows of such a marriage (without *mantra* or Vedic formula) but does not approve of it (I, 25–6). There are direct references even to the ceremony of this type of marriage (Manu, III, 44): the *Śūdrā* woman shall touch only the edge of the husband's garment, etc. Now we have seen above that Manu prohibits this marriage for the first two varnas. We thus come to perceive a distinction between what is possible and what is commendable: the ideal is clear, practice adds inferior customs to it, and with respect to these the authors take attitudes which vary both from one to another and within the same text: thus Manu, apart from a word on the abhorred pratilomas, indicates both what is done and what it would be best not to do. (*Cf.* III, 155, where he excludes from the *śrāddha* the Brahman married to a *Śūdrā*.) One must thus recognize in these texts both the (religious) recommendations of dharma, and the properly juridical prescriptions, the two being linked and as it were dominated by the overriding and constant concern to rank marriages and unions, wives and children, in relation to each other. It can be clearly seen that marriages are ranked in three categories: (1) intra-varna marriage, indispensable to the twice-born for the maintenance of the status of the lineage (except for certain devices designed to regain it once lost) and the only one permissible for *Śūdrā* men; (2) for the 'twice-born', marriage to a woman of inferior twice-born category; (3) for the same, marriage to a *Śūdrā* woman which, although it exists, is not recommended. It can be understood that this last embarrasses the authors: in particular, is a twice-born really bound by a marriage without the recitation of *mantra*, or is this only a means of attaching the *Śūdrā* woman, who is really from this point of view little short of a concubine? This seems to be borne out by the ambiguity of the position of a *Śūdrā* woman's son from the point of view of legitimacy or inheritance. Sometimes Manu prescribes (IX, 152–3) that if a Brahman has one son each from wives from each of the four varnas the shares in the inheritance shall be respectively, in tenths, in descending order of the varnas, 4, 3, 2 and 1; that is, he transcribes the status hierarchy into proportions and implicitly assumes that the son of a *Śūdrā* woman is legitimate. Sometimes, on the contrary, he disqualifies him, only allowing him what his father was able to give him in his lifetime. In the hierarchy of secondary sons, some authors put the *Śūdrā* woman's son in the last, the thirteenth, place. In a more problematic way, one may wonder whether certain complications in these texts do not come from another source. Did there not exist, then as now, two different patterms: isogamous monogamy among the Brahmans, and graduated polygyny among the Kshatriyas? If this were the case, the hierarchical schema would require both the acceptance of Kshatriya customs, though as subordinate, and that the Brahman should not be refused a prerogative so abundantly enjoyed by the Kshatriya. This might be what has led to many difficulties. But we are not even at all sure of a close relation between these prescriptions and the practice of the period (what period?). Did not the Shastras translate caste practices into the language of the varnas? Here we could only try to reconstruct a part of the conceptual scheme presented by these texts.

# CHAPTER SIX

# RULES CONCERNING CONTACT AND FOOD

## 61  *Place within the whole*

In this chapter we shall conclude the study of those characteristics which, like endogamy, seem at a first approximation to spring from the different castes' separation from one another. However, there is one exception: justice, or more generally authority within the caste, will be relegated to a later chapter (Chapter VIII) because internal authority is difficult to separate from external authority, the latter being in turn closely bound up with power (Chapter VII).

At first sight one might be tempted to group together under the same rubric the rules concerning marriage, food, and direct and indirect physical contact, the rubric being that of rules of separation or prohibitions on 'contact' in the most general and loose sense of the term. This approach, which the literature tends to adopt, is mistaken. It has already been seen that so far as marriage is concerned, separation was implied by and encompassed in hierarchy, and did not constitute a distinct fundamental principle. Likewise, in discussing the concrete forms in which the principle of hierarchy is manifested, one was led to take food into account as well as other forms of indirect physical contact, and it has been seen in particular that the rules concerning food permit certain relations between castes. What would appear to Western man as springing from separation can nowhere be completely isolated from interrelations and hierarchy. The rules which we shall briefly review are only so elaborate because they allow some relationships while forbidding others, and because they are thus intimately connected with hierarchy and the division of labour.

Separation as a general principle is deeply embedded in our

minds, and we must rid ourselves of the excessive emphasis on it in the initial definition we used. In the last analysis, separation results from the organization of the whole. As we have already mentioned in passing, this is a particular case of a structural law: for a group placed in a whole, its relation to the whole takes precedence over or governs its assertion of its distinctness and its internal cohesion.[61a] Then again, at the other end as it were, each of the actual agencies involved in contact has its concrete characteristics which govern the details of the relevant rules. Likewise with food, which is especially important: we could profit little by considering it as a particular mode of indirect physical contact. Rules concerning food are closer, rather, to marriage rules, but here again one must be careful not to push the similarity too far.

After a few remarks about contact and untouchability, we shall be concerned mainly with food.

## 62 *Notes on contact and untouchability*

To speak of prohibitions on contact, even if by 'contact' is understood solely direct or indirect physical contact, excluding the case of food, is only a rather rough and external way of grouping together a number of facts. One must avoid isolating this aspect of caste relations and seeking a special principle to explain it. For then one would fall into a mechanistic approach, in the manner of the author of one of the most meticulous general works on this question. Stevenson tends to explain the importance attached to marriage and to food and drink by considering them as especially serious forms of contact. He distinguishes between external pollution, which can be eliminated by physical means (bath, cleaning in the case of an object), and internal pollution – such as may result from the absorption of foodstuffs, or sexual relations in the case of a woman – which, according to him, is more serious because these remedies cannot be applied. Only a fraction of the facts can be explained in this way. It may be that notions more or less similar to those assumed by this author are sometimes present, but his attempt amounts in the last analysis to the reduction of a very different world of beliefs and ideas to the specialized ideas of modern men about cleanliness and hygiene. The case of the woman is characteristic, for how is it possible to leave out of account everything to do with her status and her social role, which must be related to the alleged fact?[62a]

Actually, the facts to be considered here are strictly linked in the first place to the effective caste ranking and to the division of labour. As already said, we must here make ample room for McKim Marriott's 'interactional' approach. But these facts are also linked, in the second place, to the ideas on impurity in so far as they go beyond permanent caste impurity, and touch on impurity in personal life, or on the qualities of objects in relation to impurity. If it is borne in mind that hierarchy is not, in general, correctly appraised, that the theory of the pure and the impure is still in its infancy, and that the majority of investigators have little interest in all these religious aspects whereas the facts, in their regional diversity and in the infinite detail inherent in them, call for the most minute attention if they are to be correctly described, then it will be understood that we shall be content with a few brief remarks. The essential things were said when we dealt with the transition from temporary personal impurity to permanent caste impurity, with the multiplication of the criteria of hierarchy, and with status ranking.[62b]

When Ketkar, apparently thinking of Bengal, distinguishes the inferior castes in descending order according to whether their contact pollutes an earthen pot, a bronze pot, the courtyards of temples, and the place they inhabit,[62c] he seems at first sight to measure the intensity of pollution according to the nature of the intermediary in the contact. But it is not so simple. In the first two cases, it is said that the earthen pot in use by a Brahman – let us suppose – and touched by a person of sufficiently impure caste, must be replaced,[62d] and that a bronze pot under the same conditions must be washed. In the third and fourth cases we are told in fact that certain castes do not have the right to enter a temple courtyard (if pollution is definitely involved here, it must be possible for the courtyard to be freed from the impurity contracted in this way; there are examples of this in Kerala), and that Untouchables are not allowed to reside in the village, but live in a separate hamlet. In short, we saw elsewhere (§35) that Ketkar appeals to criteria which are convenient for a given region but which are heterogeneous, in order to provide a scale which divides the castes into broad status categories. So far as pollution through the intermediary of places is concerned, one can begin with the kitchen, the most vulnerable place in the house; this is clearly related to the vulnerability of food and of the eater, although the matter is more complicated, for the kitchen is also the location of certain spiritual beings (possibly essentially ancestors, as is known to be the case among certain tribes, *Contributions*, III, p. 38).

The scale of contacts prohibited or avoided as impure, relative to a given family or household, represents, in general terms, the fact of the graded interaction between castes, as experienced in real life. This is seen clearly in what is so far as I know the only precise inquiry into the matter: that by Pauline Mahar already mentioned.[62e] In fact this investigator, in her careful study of the status ranking of castes in a village, chose thirteen criteria of contact (including two relating to food) for her interview questionnaire. This was enough for her to obtain at one go a ranking not only of castes but also, complementarily, of the criteria or forms of contact, or at any rate part of them. It is very remarkable indeed that all the informants classed six of the thirteen forms of contact in a fixed order. They are (in order of increasing intensity of contact): (1) touching your children; (2) touching you; (3) smoking from your pipe (but not the same mouthpiece); (4) touching your brass utensils; (5) serving you fried food (pakka); (6) serving you boiled food (kacha). Further, five other criteria are placed very close to three of the above. In particular, touching a water vessel, entering the place where the cooking is done and touching an earthen pot are placed close to the level of the most intense pollution (that of the food called kacha).

Whatever the merits of such an inquiry, and whatever lessons may be learnt from it, it is limited in the sense that it states principles without studying their application: whether it is a matter of entering the kitchen or touching a pot, one would like to know under what circumstances the question really arises, and what is the relation between these prohibitions and the domestic services rendered by some castes and not by others. For example, to borrow from another context, no one really has to touch bronze vessels if the dirty crockery is regularly cleaned by a Kahar (a pure caste: water bearers); moreover, if a dog has meanwhile licked the dishes, no complication arises (Eastern U.P., personal observation). It is necessary to distinguish between general contact and specialized contact. For example, how is it that the washerman, who would otherwise come freely into the house, pollutes it when he comes to decorate it for a marriage? One suggestion is that he does not pollute the house in so far as he is an agent of purification, which he is when he comes to collect the dirty laundry, but that he does pollute it in this particular circumstance because he is then acting as a profane agent, supplying and installing the fabrics he has available.[62f] To throw light on such points, and on the relation between the principles, which at one time were much talked about, and reality as it is lived, we need intensive research conducted according to reasonable hypotheses.

Almost as much could be said about untouchability, despite recent contributions.[62g] Let us bring together some points which have already been made in other connections in order to make the limitations of our knowledge felt, while not going back on the principle (§25.1). We shall define untouchability in the way that is most current, by the segregation into distinct hamlets or quarters of the most impure categories. This feature is pan-Indian, as is the association with a religiously relevant function (quartering of dead cattle and consumption of the meat, leather tanning, role in incineration or cleaning of rubbish and excrement, pig rearing and consumption of pork). There is already a problem here: although the washerman has to do with a very serious impurity, he is not excluded from the village, nor is the barber where, as in the south, he has religious functions at funerals. Is this due to the personal aspect of their services, which they could not provide for their patrons if they themselves were untouchable? However, it will shortly be seen that the washerman is untouchable for the Untouchables in Uttar Pradesh.

Over and above these general aspects, regional differences compel recognition. At first sight, the south is much more rigorous than the north, and one feels that what in the south is felt religiously is to a large extent a matter of etiquette in the north. This judgment must be modified to some extent. It is true that in the south the sentiment of interdependence is more marked (musical functions of the Untouchables in family ceremonies and even more in the temples, even priestly functions in which interdependence is clearly marked),[62h] and it is not surprising to find that the south, in a complementary way, accentuates distance, and has gone to extremes in the imposition of incapacities on the very impure. Yet we have found precisely that the rules about gradations of distance in Kerala are imposed features rather than functional rules for

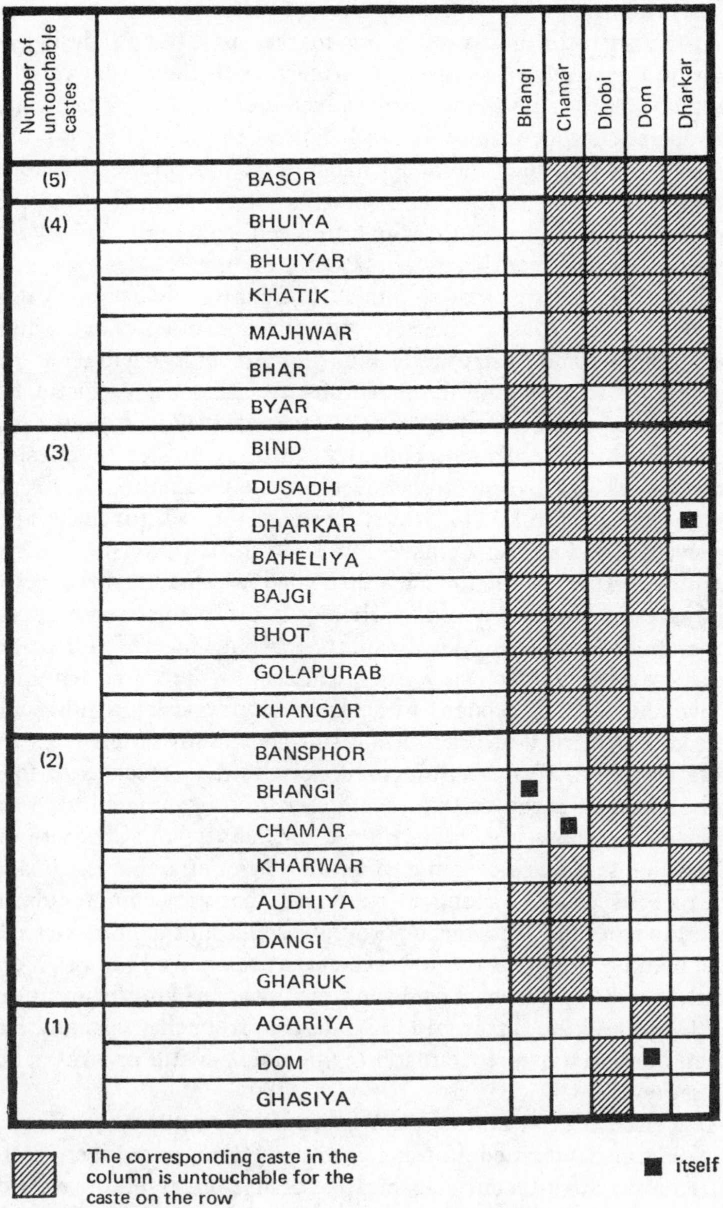

| Number of untouchable castes | | Bhangi | Chamar | Dhobi | Dom | Dharkar |
|---|---|---|---|---|---|---|
| (5) | BASOR | | ▨ | ▨ | ▨ | ▨ |
| (4) | BHUIYA | | ▨ | ▨ | ▨ | ▨ |
| | BHUIYAR | | ▨ | ▨ | ▨ | ▨ |
| | KHATIK | | ▨ | ▨ | ▨ | ▨ |
| | MAJHWAR | | ▨ | ▨ | ▨ | ▨ |
| | BHAR | ▨ | ▨ | ▨ | | ▨ |
| | BYAR | ▨ | ▨ | ▨ | | ▨ |
| (3) | BIND | | ▨ | ▨ | ▨ | |
| | DUSADH | | ▨ | ▨ | ▨ | |
| | DHARKAR | | | ▨ | ▨ | ■ |
| | BAHELIYA | ▨ | | ▨ | ▨ | |
| | BAJGI | ▨ | ▨ | | ▨ | |
| | BHOT | ▨ | ▨ | ▨ | | |
| | GOLAPURAB | ▨ | ▨ | ▨ | | |
| | KHANGAR | ▨ | ▨ | ▨ | | |
| (2) | BANSPHOR | | | ▨ | ▨ | |
| | BHANGI | ■ | ▨ | | | |
| | CHAMAR | | ■ | ▨ | | |
| | KHARWAR | | ▨ | ▨ | | ▨ |
| | AUDHIYA | ▨ | ▨ | | | |
| | DANGI | ▨ | ▨ | | | |
| | GHARUK | ▨ | ▨ | | | |
| (1) | AGARIYA | | | | | ▨ |
| | DOM | | | ▨ | ■ | |
| | GHASIYA | | | ▨ | | |

▨ The corresponding caste in the column is untouchable for the caste on the row

■ itself

Figure 4. Which of five untouchable castes are untouchable for twenty-five very low castes (Uttar Pradesh, cf. Blunt p.102).

preserving the purity of the superior persons. Also, while it is true that this sort of thing is much less marked in Uttar Pradesh – not only in the west, where the *Jāt* farmers, with their relatively less religious pattern have long been noticed, but even in the east where the society is much more hierarchical – at the same time we have pointed out that the funeral specialist, the Mahabrahman, inspires a truly religious horror there, and we shall borrow a chart of untouchability from Blunt, which by itself is enough to show that we are not dealing with a mere matter of etiquette.

Not only is there a sort of competition between Chamar (leather people), Dom (basket-makers with funeral functions), Dhobis (washermen) and still others, but they are untouchable for one another: it is as if pollutions of different origins were distinct in themselves. Only a few out of a total of twenty-five low and untouchable castes fail to consider the three castes in question untouchable, viz. respectively seven for the Chamar, eight for the Dom, nine for the Dhobi, whilst there are thirteen for the Bhangi or sweepers. So here we have the three most powerful kinds of impurity. Apart from the fact that Chamar women often act as midwives, the impurity of the Chamar is complementary with the veneration of the cow. With respect to twenty-five inferior castes, Blunt considers which of five typical castes (the four mentioned above and another related to the Dom) are regarded as untouchable. Conveniently ordered, the result is as follows: one (upstart) caste considers all five untouchable, six limit themselves to four, eight to three, seven to two (keeping as untouchable either Dom and Dhobi, as is the case with the Chamar, or Chamar and Bhangi), lastly three consider only one caste untouchable. Finally, it can be seen by looking at the chart that a certain regularity emerges from the apparent disorder, which is all the more remarkable because it holds for the whole of that extensive State. It is due partly to certain castes considering each other as kin, for example, the Doms and the castes said to be derived from them. In any case it can be seen that preoccupation with status is still present at the lowest level.[621]

It will have been noticed that Blunt, following the 1901 *Census* of the region, defined untouchability relative to a given caste, whereas we have taken it absolutely, or if one prefers in relation to unsegregated castes. Moreover, Blunt does not give precise criteria.

Concerning untouchability in general, the modern reader will no doubt ask some question such as: why are huge castes like the Chamar in Uttar Pradesh, representing the bulk of the agricultural labour force, unfree labour, considered untouchable? Is this not simply a 'rationalization' of their oppression and exploitation? First of all, we have no idea why the Chamar are more numerous than all the other Untouchables of the region put together. More scientifically, the question can be put in this way: what is the relation between the religious expression of the condition of the Untouchable and the general function of these castes as labourers close to agricultural serfdom? Without exhausting the significance of the fact, which will become somewhat clearer when we have dealt with dominance and power in general, it may be said simply that the overwhelming religious inferiority of these castes in effect expresses and encompasses their strict secular dependence on the dominant castes: the lowliest suffer the greatest subjection. Or again: the hierarchical solidarity between the two highest varnas is here reflected in the fact that those who are most oppressed materially are at the same time seen as supremely impure.

## 63   *Food in general*

The preparation and consumption of food is the subject of various rules, to which are linked those relating to water and the pipe. Blunt lists seven kinds of 'taboo' bearing on the following questions: with whom one eats, who prepares the food, what sort of food, what are the ritual observances, from whom one accepts water, with whom one shares a pipe, and finally what vessels one uses (Blunt, p. 88). Some of these rules are not directly connected with caste. By beginning with the more general aspects of beliefs and ideas concerning food, we may hope to find points of comparison with casteless societies and thus further our understanding. As in connection with impurity in general, we shall find that, especially so far as cooked food is concerned, India presents features which are found elsewhere, and also that these ideas are elaborated in India in a quite special way. For example, certain dairy products are used for the preparation of food which resists impurity, and this consequently allows relations between castes which would otherwise have been impossible with ordinary food. Let us take first of all an example from within kinship. In a hypergamous environment, as has been seen, a father *gives* his daughter in marriage and simultaneously *gives* material goods to a family of higher status. In one observed case, this is fully elaborated and food plays a twofold symbolic role.[63a] On the one hand, in conformity with the pattern of the gift, the bride's father makes it a point of honour not to receive anything in exchange, other than the reflected glory of his son-in-law's family, which will be of higher status than his own. It is said that the bride's father (or eldest brother) should not accept food, nor even water, from the bridegroom's family after the marriage. Food is here a minimal material gift, and its refusal is symbolic. It is a unilateral refusal, for the young husband eats freely at his father-in-law's when he stays there. But here we must go back to the marriage ceremony, where we shall find a detail which is very widespread in the region, even outside hypergamous marriage. The bride's family offers the bridegroom a morning collation, and the tradition is that the bridegroom does not accept until he has been entreated at length. Here the bridegroom's superior rank betrays itself: to agree to eat food with somewhat inferior people, the bridegroom claims a present. The demand is expected, but it may be extravagant, adding considerably to the prestations agreed beforehand, and may thus lead to lengthy bargaining.

It can be seen that commensality between affines is not immediately established and remains incomplete. May one assume that underlying these customs is the idea that families of different lineages, united by marriage, have a distinct essence, and that, at first, the same goes for their food? Other facts would have to be taken into consideration. But in this respect one cannot refrain from calling to mind parallels outside India: for example, among the Nuer the son-in-law does not at first accept food from his wife's family, but only after a certain time.[63b]

We come now to the rules concerning the consumption and preparation of ordinary food within the family. It is not only a question of avoiding contact with polluting agents (even of the same caste) but of general precautions. Among the Brahmans, the eater must be pure (he has bathed and his torso is bare) and he must be sheltered from any impure contact. He eats alone or in a small group in a pure 'square' (*caukā*) in the kitchen or a nearby part of the house carefully protected from intrusion. Any unforeseen contact, not only with a low caste man (sometimes going as far as his shadow) or an animal, but even with someone from the house (woman, child, man who is not purified for eating) would make the food unfit for consumption.[63c] It is thought that ordinary cooked food is particularly vulnerable, and so is the eater, who, the texts tell us, is in any case less pure when he finishes his meal than when he began. True, the rules are far less strict for non-Brahmans.[63d] The fact remains that one can scarcely ever eat side by side with any but one's equals, that the host does not generally eat with his guests, and that meals are not those pleasant conversational gatherings with which we are acquainted: they are technical operations which leave room for only a limited margin of freedom. Psychologically and linguistically there is a considerable accent on the 'eating'. So far as the preparation of the food goes, it is well known that, at least very generally, menstruating women do not take part. On solemn occasions at least, and for all castes, the cook must be as pure as the eater. The Brahman is naturally the preferred cook, and he is respected in this function, being addressed honorifically (as 'Pandit', etc.). We shall encounter a Brahman serving a lower caste who calls another to replace him in the mourning ritual, whereas he takes care of the cooking for a banquet himself.

It is not surprising that this everyday food whose cooking and eating requires so many precautions, and which is, like the eater himself, so vulnerable to impurity, cannot in general be passed from one caste to another. And however intimately the preoccupation with impurity may unite everything concerning food with the institution of castes, one can nevertheless try to understand why cooked food presents quite specific characteristics. Various hypotheses have been brought forward. It is obvious that Stevenson's mechanistic hypothesis already mentioned at best accounts only for a part of the complex: if food was a powerful agent of pollution simply in view of the fact that it is ingested and becomes an integral part of the eater, then neither the crucial difference between cooked and raw (a ripe fruit is eaten without any ado), nor the purification of the eater, would be comprehensible. Hutton, for his part, refers to animist notions, which were at one time used to explain the 'participation' between things or between man and objects, and he also refers particularly to the notion of 'soul-stuff'. This brings one nearer to a well-oriented comparison and to the ideas underlying customs, but the notion itself is questionable.[63e]

By way of comparison, some facts from Polynesia may be

mentioned. They are even more striking in that they relate to societies in which, while there is great emphasis on chieftainship and 'social stratification', the distinction between pure and impure does not exist, there being only the notion of 'forbidden sacred' (*tabu*). I am indebted to an unpublished course by Mauss on sin and expiation in Polynesia.[63f] Cooked food pollutes the forest. At funeral banquets the food was cooked separately for people of different ranks and different degrees of taboo. To eat the left-overs of an important taboo person would cause death. Taboo people were fed by others, and did not touch the food with their hands; people who had handled a corpse 'gnawed' (Mauss) the food with their teeth without touching it with their hands. Whilst food (*kai*) is likely to lead to sin and death, water (*wai*) dispelled these dangers (Fornander). In one sense, the fundamental sin is to cook, which desecrates things and destroys their essence (Mauss following Mariner Martin and Hocart for Tonga). To call someone by the name of a cooked food is a grave insult.

Many of these features are evocative of a very close parallel in India, and suggest a general interpretation. For one thing, food, once cooked, participates in the family who prepared it. It seems that it is appropriated like an object in use (pot, garment) but even more intimately – and without even entering the body, ingestion being only one part of the matter. This is perhaps because, by cooking, food is made to pass from the natural to the human world, and one may wonder whether there is not here something analogous to the 'marginal state' in *rites de passage*, when a person is no longer in one condition nor yet in another, and consequently exposed, open in some way, to evil influences. In India itself most of these *rites de passage* correspond to an impurity which expresses the irruption of the organic into social life; now there is something of the organic in our case, as with excretion, and, with the necessary difference, there is if not true impurity at least an exceptional permeability to impurity.[63g] Hence the preliminary bath which, however, is not enough, because, as we know, the pure is powerless in face of the impure and only the sacred vanquishes it (hence in what follows, the use of the products of the cow).

The general hierarchy of foodstuffs, which gives each caste's diet its hierarchical value (Blunt's 'food taboo', Stevenson's 'diet avoidances') is chiefly interesting for its main cleavages, which go back into history (veneration of the cow and untouchability of beef eaters, inferiorization of a meat diet and consumption of alcohol as compared to a vegetarian diet, *cf.* §65). But this classification of foods essentially refers back to the classification of men and to relationships between human groups, and is not a basic and independent fact resulting from a universal classification into pure and impure.[63h] In detail, interpretation is not easy: some say that the Brahmans' abstinence from tomatoes is due to the presence of seeds, a 'living' element, but Brahmans also abstain from onions and garlic. Further, there are many regional differences: there are Brahmans who do not eat meat but do eat fish (Bengal), and even some who sometimes eat meat but abstain completely from eggs (Eastern U.P.). These are features which only a regional history of the population would make comprehensible. From the present point of view all this constitutes a framework of absolute criteria which the castes use to differentiate themselves hierarchically from one another: thus Brahmans probably eat meat where competition from vegetarians did not make itself felt or else where these particular Brahmans have accepted a relatively inferior position.[63i]

## 64 *Food and drink (water) in caste relations*

64.1 *Commensality and connubium.* For a long time some degree of coincidence between commensality and intermarriage has been noticed: intermarriage in general presupposes that the two parties can eat together, and marriage is the chief occasion on which people of the same caste (or rather subcaste, etc.) gather together, so much so that among middle and low castes it often happens that marriages, together with funerals, are the occasions on which the group forms itself into an assembly and passes judgment on litigation or lays down rules. But people have been over-anxious to subordinate or reduce the one feature to the other. For Senart, commensality was both less strict and more subject to regional variation, and intermarriage was fundamental. Hutton, arguing from the fact that one can have a concubine from a relatively low caste without loss of status on condition that one does not accept the relevant food from her, reversed the priorities; but a concubine is precisely not a wife, and marriage is not reducible to sexual relations plus the sharing of food. Blunt, while bringing together the two aspects and the corresponding rules, gave historical primacy at least to marriage. Stevenson has pointed out that the circle of commensality does not coincide exactly with the circle of con-nubiality.[64a] Really the essential question, on which Blunt rightly insisted, is: who did the cooking? Previous authors seem to have taken 'commensality' in the restricted sense of 'possibility of eating in the same group', or as is sometimes said 'in the same line'. In a broader sense there is no doubt, at least for the north, that very different castes can eat the same food at the same time at banquets, by isolating themselves more or less from one another when their status is too different (*cf.* §36 (Mayer), §64.4).

In reality, accepting food and intermarrying are both important in their way, and strictly regulated. There is a parallel but not coincidence within the caste, but the main thing is that food, as opposed to marriage, corresponds to relations outside the caste as well as to relations within it. This will be seen presently; the account refers to northern India and particularly to Uttar Pradesh (western part of the Gangetic plain).

64.2 *Ordinary and 'perfect' food.* The restrictions on the transfer of food between castes vary according to the sort of food. There are none, it seems, for raw food, which McKim Marriott calls the food of gifts. The Brahman who performs a ritual service for an inferior caste often receives for example a small quantity of different sorts of food, something like the raw material of a meal, *sīdhā*, or provisions generally. The restrictions are greatest, by contrast, for ordinary or everyday cooked food, based, depending on the region, on boiled rice or wheat flour cakes cooked without fat (*capātī*). This in the Indo-Aryan language is imperfect food, *kaccā* (Hindi), vulnerable to impurity, and reserved, roughly speaking, for relatives or members of the endogamous group and servants of very inferior caste. Between these two extremes comes *pakkā* (Hindi), the 'perfect' food [64b] consisting of pancakes fried in butter (*pūrī*) accompanied by vegetables fried in the same way (notice the protective role of butter, a product of the cow), and also other dishes which are considered pure like parched grain, for example *lāvā*, rice burst in hot sand. Later we shall consider the combination of *ciurā*, rice crushed with a pestle after treatment, and *dahī*, yoghourt, which is at the same time pure, easy to keep, and liquid enough to make the *ciurā* with which it is mixed edible. This 'perfect' food, more costly, is used for festivals, inter-caste banquets, light meals, and on journeys.

Blunt shows the difference between the two kinds of food in Uttar Pradesh. He considers seventy-six castes. Among them, thirty-six forbid all *kaccā* not prepared by a member of the endogamous group (or by the guru, the spiritual master who is assimilated to the father), whilst ten castes only confine themselves to accepting *pakkā* when it is prepared by: a member of the caste, a guru, a confectioner,[64c] or a Kahar servant (water-bearer). Sixteen and thirteen castes respectively accept kacha and pakka only from, in addition to the above, Brahmans (and in some cases Rajputs). Finally and most importantly, whilst only eighteen castes accept kacha from castes other than the above, forty-five accept pakka under the same conditions. Thus it can be seen that the possibility of transfer of cooked food from one caste to another is considerably enlarged thanks to pakka.

64.3 *Water and the pipe.* Still speaking of Uttar Pradesh, the rules concerning water are similar to those concerning pakka. Yet distinctions must be made: 'A high caste man will allow a low caste man to fill his *lotā* (drinking vessel) for him: but he will not drink from the *lotā* of that low caste man.' (Blunt, *ibid.*, p. 98.) We see here again that a personal object shares the caste of its owner and user, and this explains how water, in itself an agent of purification, can, once as it were appropriated by one man, become a vehicle of impurity for another. Generally one drinks *à la régalade* without touching the receptacle with one's lips, and a Brahman can pour water for an Untouchable which the latter will drink in his hands. Further, the serving castes supply their masters with water: 'all castes will take water from Barhais (carpenters), Baris, Bharbhunjas, Halwais (parchers and confectioners), Kahars (water bearers) and Nais (barbers)'. This is important for the extent of the prohibitions: one can refuse water from some castes if others provide it as part of their service.[64d]

It is quite otherwise elsewhere: we have seen that on this point the authors of the 1901 *Census* were compelled to recognize a vast difference: a southern Brahman accepts water from no other caste (§35). Moreover it seems that the south does not have a generalized custom equivalent to pakka and that the castes there are much more closed in upon themselves.

In Uttar Pradesh, one scarcely ever smokes except with a member of the same caste. Notice that in fact the question is complex: the lips come into contact with the mouthpiece of the pipe (remedied by interposing both hands to form an intermediary receptacle – likewise if one shares a cigarette – or by interposing a cloth); and in the hookah or narguile the smoke is cooled in water. It has been seen that elsewhere there is greater freedom and that one smokes more or less, with precautions, with those with whom one drinks.[64e] Moreover, the hookah is not found everywhere (it is absent in large areas) and the same is true of the pipe generally.

64.4  *The factual aspect.* In fact the Census Reports, even when conscientious, are scarcely satisfactory on this point. Generally, informants of each caste were asked from whom they could or could not accept such-and-such a kind of food, or water. There is no doubt that not only the observer but also the informant was concerned with hierarchy and separation, and that the latter would readily reply to this sort of question. But what exactly does a denial like 'I do not accept kacha from a Chamar' signify, or even an assertion like 'I can accept kacha from a Brahman'? One would like to know whether the question arose in practice, whether the informant made use of this ability once in his life or more often. And there appear to be different sorts of circumstances in which the question can arise. Let us leave aside both circumstances of service, and modern relaxations (restaurants and cafés in the towns are still often kept by Brahmans). On short journeys a man of good caste will have only a light meal, and will wait until he gets home and has bathed before he takes a proper meal. In the case of a long journey the man or the household will do the cooking itself; thus Indian soldiers in the British army for a long time used to cook for themselves individually. The case of water is different, for one must obviously be able to accept it from at least some castes (a Kayastha of Uttar Pradesh for example excludes only the Untouchables and Muslims), and the question is much more relevant here. There remain the banquets at family festivals and in other circumstances. These are the occasions on which different castes really come together, and all steps are taken to make this possible, as we shall see.

In short, the circumstances and relations which accompany the consumption of food must be considered from a sociological point of view. This approach has been unobtrusively introduced into the account above, following McKim Marriott, in which everyday food and service food was distinguished from food for banquets and journeys. To take an example, a Kayastha informant (Gorakhpur district, U.P.) declared that *in theory* he 'will eat' kacha with any Kayasthas, and 'can eat' or 'habitually eats' it also with Brahmans and Kshattris. But *in practice* he never ate except with relatives. Finally he remembered having eaten once with a Kshattri, at the time of elections (N.B.: a modern circumstance). And the Brahmans? He had eaten with two families (one in his own village, the other elsewhere) on the occasion of family festivals, tonsure and initiation. (Naturally at funerals he had eaten the pakka food prepared for everyone with these same people.)

A word may be said here about banquets as the main occasion for commensality. Unfortunately the literature is not very extensive. We have already mentioned Mayer's data (§36) and have discovered that in this region of central India, pakka food is not used in a rational way. It is quite different in Rampur, Gorakhpur district, Uttar Pradesh (personal inquiry) where this form of sociability is well developed and where we shall see that such features as the cook's caste come into play. There the end of mourning is the occasion for a whole series of meals: sixteen Brahmans should eat before everyone else, and by this act they terminate the mourning for the family. The food is pakka, cooked by a Brahman, probably the family priest (*purohit*) (who in case of need will delegate another Brahman to direct the ritual proper), and served by Brahmans. However, the caste of the dead man's family has an influence: a Brahman of relatively high status will not agree to cook in the house of too low a caste (Teli) and the same house may have difficulty in gathering together the necessary number of Brahmans for the meal. Then comes a meal of rice (*bhāt*), taken by the members of the family, the relatives from outside (they bring presents of *dahī* and *ciurā* for the pakka banquet), and members of the endogamous group living locally (but certainly not necessarily all of them), and after them such mendicants, renouncers and itinerants as are present. Then there comes a truly intercaste meal, open to all those who have accompanied the mortal remains to the place of cremation. Pakka food is cooked by the Brahman, so as to permit the greatest possible number to consume it. However, superior castes may abstain (Kayasthas do not eat even in this way as guests of the Telis). Further, the susceptibilities of the different castes will be humoured by having several sittings in succession and by setting groups of nearby status apart from one another (several groups of Untouchables may thus eat separately).

Perhaps one can now see more clearly the extent to which the rules given in the Census Reports are theoretical: to a great extent (in ordinary circumstances) there is simply no commensality; and when the question really arises, general arrangements enable it to take place on a much larger scale than the rigour of the rules would lead one to suppose. The example quoted is perhaps particularly broad, as a result of the relative weakness of the feeling for the impure already mentioned, but it suggests that the views inherited from the period of extensive literature must be modified.

Apart from the fact that certain Brahmans refuse to share the common food and insist on being given their share raw and cooking it themselves, which can correspond, it must not be forgotten, to personal taste as much as to a certain affectation of purity,[64f] I have already alluded to the fact that not all representatives of the subcaste living in the same place always take part in the family banquets. It can happen that they take part in strangers' banquets.[64g] Further, the frontier of commensality in certain cases lies within the exogamous group itself: patrilineal kinsmen in the same village give vent to a quarrel by putting an end to commensality, and this is a recognized procedure.[64h] We are a long way from the theory according to which the commensal unit coincides with the unit of endogamy. Even if the case is exceptional, it teaches us not to take at cash value generalizations which really result from the questionnaires used; above all it teaches us that it is not so much the people concerned as the investigators who try to attach the various aspects of the system to one given level when, as has been seen, they are found at different levels.

## 65 On the history of vegetarianism

65.1 *From the Veda to Manu.* Vegetarianism has compelled the recognition of the whole of the Hindu population as the superior form of diet, and in contemporary India it constitutes one of the essential norms relating to food and status. Vegetarianism has often been attributed to the population which the Indo-Europeans found on their entry into the country. This is unlikely for several reasons. In the first place, vegetarianism is quite obviously not a 'primitive' feature but a fact of high civilization, unknown in less differentiated societies the world over and lacking profound roots, even in India, at the popular or tribal level. Then again, supposing that the pre-Indo-European population of India had actually been vegetarian, it would be hard to see how its vegetarianism would have been imposed on the invaders. Finally, only the Brahmans and not the Kshatriyas traditionally became vegetarian. In fact the texts tell quite another story, which Alsdorf has recently recounted in a short treatise. We shall summarize the main points: the evolution of living sacrifice and the consumption of meat from the Veda to Hinduism; the development of the idea of *ahiṃsā* ('non-violence', or rather absence of the will to kill) and of vegetarianism in Jainism and Buddhism; the relationship between the two series of facts; and a word will be said about the veneration of the cow.[65a]

Grazing played a large part in the life of the Vedic Indians, and it may be supposed that like many other pastoral peoples they killed cattle only when there were good reasons, sacrificial reasons, and only the meat of sacrificed animals was eaten. In other words, there was a religious attitude towards cattle, which is not surprising, and which is to be taken as the starting-point for what was later to become the veneration of the cow, the cow having been already extolled in Vedism as a cosmic symbol, the universal mother and source of food, etc. It was the 'sacred animal most preferred for sacrifice' (Alsdorf). The ritual treatises give voice to this state of affairs, and one sees the emergence of the notion of the five products of the cow, as a beneficial and purificatory mixture, which was later to triumph. At the same time, in the sutras of the domestic ritual and of the dharma, a cow is killed on certain ritual occasions: in ancestor worship, and to honour a distinguished guest (the guest is called *goghna*, 'cow killer', by the grammarian Panini); a bull is sacrificed in a specific sacrifice.[65b]

For the sake of simplicity let us pass to the Laws of Manu. The situation here is quite different, as Alsdorf has shown. Meat retains all its value in offerings to the ancestors (III, 247 ff.; a doubtful passage, 271, perhaps mentions cow's meat). In the fairly complicated regulations about food (V, 7 ff.), the permitted or prohibited kinds are listed; the link between sacrifice (or at least rudimentary consecration) and consumption of meat is stressed, and sacrifice and a meat diet is defended (30, 39). Yet on the other hand vegetarianism is praised in verse 53 in which abstention from meat is said to be equivalent to a hundred horse sacrifices. Equally, it is said that 'to kill in sacrifice is not to kill' (39), whereas a little later (44–55) *ahiṃsā* is praised. All in all, the new ideal makes itself felt sufficiently for the contradiction to be noticed and a compromise sought. Alsdorf quotes texts from the great epic which corroborate the situation found in Manu.

Later, at the time of the commentaries, vegetarianism had become established and references to sacrifice and the meat diet became embarrassing. One of the current procedures was employed: these customs, though conforming to the dharma, were declared to be no longer practised because they had become 'odious to the people' or again because they were unsuited to the present, degenerate, age of the world, the Kali age.[65c]

65.2 *The development of ahiṃsā.* How did it come about that these practices became odious to the people? What were the origins of *ahiṃsā*, already recognized in Manu, that is to say at around the beginning of the Christian era at the latest? What had happened since the end of the Vedic period? An extraordinary theoretical development had taken place, and at the same time the society had made the transition from varna to caste. Thus arose the renouncer type – a person who leaves social life to devote himself to his salvation – and the two great disciplines of salvation, Buddhism and Jainism. Let us indicate briefly the development concerning *ahiṃsā* and vegetarianism. *Ahiṃsā* is not unknown to our contemporaries, for Ghandhi used it as a political weapon and himself translated the term into English as 'non-violence'. One might prefer 'non-harming', but Madeleine Biardeau has given a more precise translation: 'absence of desire to kill'. This etymologically exact sense is also essential historically, as we shall find.[65d]

The term *ahiṃsā* and a certain reluctance about killing any living being, is already apparent in the Veda, where it may be a question only of the universal ambivalence of the act of sacrifice.[65e] Some passages of the Chandogya Upanishad are more precise: 'The wise man does no harm to any creature, except in the case of sacred rites . . .'. *Ahiṃsā* and four other qualities are the reward of the internal sacrifice[65f] which tends to replace Vedic sacrifice for those thinkers who are at that moment renouncers-in-the-making.

The chronological indications drawn by Alsdorf from the

Buddhist and Jain texts are very interesting. Buddha refused to endorse the prohibition on eating meat and fish: it was enough that the animal was not killed for the monk, or that this was believed in good faith to be so. In short, the renouncer has his own ideal and his own morality, but he has no tendency to impose it on the men-in-the-world. Even among the Jains it was only later that meat and alcohol were forbidden, and that concern for *ahiṃsā* assumed its truly extraordinary development. There are living things in water, and water must be boiled by someone else before being drunk by the monk.[65g] Generally speaking, whilst *ahiṃsā* played a reduced part in the monastic discipline of the Buddhists, among the Jains, on the contrary, it was very important, and closely linked with doctrine. The relationship between *ahiṃsā* and the doctrine of transmigration and retribution for actions has been much discussed; such a relationship seems inescapable, the more so if one admits that renunciation and belief in transmigration are intimately linked. In any case it is clear that *ahiṃsā* is above all the doing of the renouncer as 'an article in the programme which enjoins him to all possible abstentions in his behaviour so as to obtain the total detachment necessary for his salvation' (Biardeau).[65h]

In short, whilst these ideas are functional in renunciation, they are contradictory in Manu. This contrast suggests the conclusion that vegetarianism forced itself on Hindu society, having begun in the sects of the renouncers, among which are Jainism and Buddhism. No doubt these two disciplines of salvation are but the two main testimonies we have to a more extensive movement: *ahiṃsā* came from farther afield and was more widespread; it remains true that to all appearances it was the renouncer who carried it right through to its practical consequences for diet, and gave it to Hindu society as an example of a value higher than the Brahmanical values of sacrifice. But Alsdorf shuns this conclusion, strongly as it is suggested by his work. What reasons does he give? According to him, there was a general spiritual movement throughout India which simply found particularly favourable conditions in 'heresies'.[65i] He supports this view by the fact that the *ahiṃsā* of the Emperor Ashoka was not properly speaking Buddhist. Even if this was so – and this is a controversial point – it is not enough to show that Brahmanism was as 'non-violent' as Jainism, which is contradicted by the texts studied. No doubt it must be stated that vegetarianism was by its nature fit to be easily integrated into the ideas about pure and impure. For the vegetarian Hindu, to eat meat is to eat corpse. But it should not be forgotten either that modern popular Hinduism, like ancient Brahmanism, acknowledges the consumption of sacrificial meat. Alsdorf does not take this aspect into consideration. If he imagines, wrongly but in agreement with his predecessors, that vegetarianism (and *ahiṃsā*) can be understood as primitive features (*'ur-indische'*), it is doubtless mainly because he fails to take a sociological view of the situation – a situation which has reigned in India for more than a millennium – in which Brahmanism and the sects reacted on one another. After all, how many kinds of spiritual authority were there? Only two: the Brahman and his tradition, the renouncer and his sects. How many factors of initiative and invention? Only one, the renouncer, faced with whom the Brahman was such an effective factor of integration and aggregation that in the long run he almost completely absorbed his rivals. There was rivalry in public opinion between these two sorts of 'spirituality', and this by itself can contribute to the explanation of the efforts to go one better, the hardening of the doctrines as, penetrating into the social world proper, they were taken up by the Brahman on his own account.[65j] (Let us not forget that the Kshatriyas have traditionally remained meat eaters.) In short, the Brahman would have adopted vegetarianism so as not to be outdone by the renouncer *qua* spiritual leader.

Therefore nothing is more natural than to adopt Jacobi's view that *ahiṃsā* was originally confined to the renouncer and became general under the influence of Jainism and Buddhism. In fact the Arthashastra enjoins it only for the 'wanderer' (*pavivrājaka*, I, 3) and Megasthenes says much the same.[65k]

To return to Alsdorf in order to profit from his remarks on the origin of the veneration of the cow. The historical problem here is the transition from the Vedic situation (animal honoured and sacrificed) to the Hindu situation (animal venerated, its murder constituting a crime equal to the murder of a Brahman, and its products having a remarkable purificatory value). We have seen that the mixture of the five products was introduced early, and the stress on purity is to be expected; clearly the predominance of *ahiṃsā* must be recognized if the change is to be explained,[65l] but is it sufficient to account for the specific place of the animal and its assimilation with the Brahman? Here one has an inkling of an intensification similar to that in the case of vegetarianism, but doubtless a social circumstance must be taken into account: the opposition of pure and impure is applied in a social context in which the Brahman and the Untouchable are at opposite poles, the latter responsible for dead cattle and the former a paragon of purity, assimilated to the cow (*cf.* above, §25.4).

# CHAPTER SEVEN

# POWER AND TERRITORY

## 71  *Introduction*

We shall proceed as if we had finished with the ideology of caste; so, in conformity with our method, we shall now begin to set out what is actually encountered in caste society while not figuring directly in the ideology. Actually we have not exhausted that complex of conscious ideas called ideology, for the government of caste remains to be dealt with. But this cannot be done conveniently until we have shed light on the topics which are the subject of the present chapter.

Confining ourselves provisionally to social organization, what is really at issue? One can already reply *a priori*, from the viewpoint of our own society, that we have to look for everything the ideology seems to have neglected. This corresponds fairly well, as a first approximation, to what we call the politico-economic domain, as opposed to the domain of religion. The ideology has led us to describe certain aspects of the society and in this description we have already met certain features, elements or factors which are extraneous to the ideology itself. The ideology does not take cognisance of these as they are in themselves, but merely cloaks them, so to speak, in its all-embracing language.

From the outset, we have been obliged to refer to the fact that actual caste systems, in contrast to the theoretical model, were organized within a fixed territorial area, were so to speak contained within a spatial framework. We often encountered this feature again in what followed, in connection with segmentation and hierarchy and with the jajmani system, which, we have seen, functions within each village as a unit. So far as jajmani is concerned, we have insisted on the orientation of the division of labour towards the whole, and seen this as a fundamental fact, a fact which in the last analysis is religious in nature; but at the same time we have stated both that this interdependence combined non-religious as well as religious aspects, and that the pivot around which it is organized – the dominant caste – was implicit rather than clearly recognized. Finally, studying hierarchy in the strict sense and leaving aside the question of command or authority on account of the component of power it contains (for this reason it will be dealt with in the following chapter), limiting ourselves *in concreto*, that is, to status ranking, we have seen that power, devalued to the advantage of status at the overall level, surreptitiously makes itself the equal of status at the interstitial levels. It is true that this fact corresponds to the relationship established between priest and king in the theory of the varnas, but the latter definitely remains implicit in the ideology of caste as isolated here. From this point of view, we have, thus, already acknowledged that power exists and that it is located in a framework of ideas and values, confined within the limits of this framework but distorting it to some extent.[71a]

Territory, power, village dominance, result from the possession of the land. This we have already been compelled to recognize, and we must now deal directly with it. Having so far followed in Bouglé's footsteps, we shall now take much more advantage of recent research, for these are the questions to which it has given preference and on which there is a notable consensus of opinion among specialists. Consequently one can be very brief, the major concern being to restore this partial domain to its place in the whole. The change of level raises a problem of terminology. We must above all define what we mean by 'power'. It is exclusively political power that is in question, the political domain being defined as 'the monopoly of legitimate force within a given territory'. Power is thus legitimate force. Today the definition may seem very limited. It has the advantage of corresponding quite well to Indian notions: power is roughly the Vedic *kṣatra*, the principle of the Kshatriya varna (literally 'the people of empire'); it is force made legitimate by being subordinated hierarchically to the *brahman* and the Brahmans. So we shall deal successively with the territorial framework, the rights in land, the village with its dominants, and conclude with some remarks on the economic approach.

## 72  The territorial framework: the 'little kingdom'

Contemporary anthropological literature frequently stresses the fact that actual caste systems are – or rather were – contained within a territorial setting of rather small scale. Here social anthropologists found what they were at the same time mistakenly seeking at the level of the village (cf. §74): a social whole of limited extent, established within a definite territory, and self-sufficient; a small society not too unlike the tribe, the usual object of their study, and which did not belie the territorial conceptions which are bred in us by the existence of nations. Authors readily dilate on the necessity for a caste system to have a limited spatial extent, and on the consequences of this fact. Once the common ideology on which all these actual systems rest has been recognized, as it has been here, the fact of territorial fragmentation is doubtless important. It should be noticed that this fact is closely linked to the ideology. In effect: (1) the ideology ignores territory as such; (2) an ideology which had a place for territory, which valorized it, would obviously promote territorial, and hence political, unification; (3) caste ideology, as has sometimes been said, assumes and upholds political divisiveness (cf. Contributions, IV, p. 8).

The fact of territorial compartmentalization is not absolutely new. Jackson, among others, mentioned it in an early article of his quoted by Hutton. Nevertheless, it was Eric J. Miller who clearly expressed it, in a brief article on Malabar (in Kerala State) which appeared in 1954: 'a necessary correlate of a rigid caste system is a system of territorial segmentation'.[72a] In Malabar Miller found a small territorial unit, the nāḍ (a common name in the south) comprising a number of villages (dēsam). He stated that: 'For all the lower castes the chiefdom (nāḍ) was the limit of social relations within the caste, while their relations with other castes were largely confined to the village' (p. 416). Only the superior castes had an internal organization which extended throughout the nad and beyond, though not beyond the frontiers of the kingdoms. Only the Nambudiri Brahmans transcended political frontiers.[72b] Here is a relationship between hierarchy and territory which harmonizes well with the complementarity between the two. Miller added that the uniformity of culture was closely related to the lines of territorial segmentation, the level differing according to the caste.

Even reduced to the simplified notion that each 'little kingdom' had a caste system more or less different in actual fact from the neighbouring one, the matter has many aspects.[72c] We shall return to the king's authority in caste affairs. The fact has been stressed that the 'local hierarchies' of castes differ from one another. And indeed each chiefdom has its own population and history, from which arise differences which may be very marked not only in the number, name and function of the castes (or subcastes) present, but even in the development of different ranking criteria. In particular, much must have depended on the Brahmanic settlement, on the variety or varieties of Brahmans present – and earlier on the extent of the popularity attained by Jainism and Buddhism.[72d] Similarly it must be thought that in the 'little kingdom' the king or chief would have been able to enjoy considerable power, patronage and influence as against the Brahmans. Think of the commensality among the castes allied to the holders of power in a Malwa village (§36). This can help to explain how the features of the royal way of life (meat diet, polygyny), although devalued in relation to the Brahmanical model, have been able to survive and set an example to some castes for so long.[72e] By contrast, the disappearance of the king from vast regions under the Muslim domination must, as various authors have supposed, have increased the Brahman's influence, which then would have lacked any counter-balancing opposition (see below, Appendix D).

It has been mentioned above that whereas professional castes are often designated by the name of their trade, their subcastes usually take the names of the territory or locality. According to Karvé, each subcaste attached to a given area is of a different origin, and the caste is only a 'cluster' resulting from their purely external juxtaposition, as in the case of the potters of Maharashtra (cf. §26). But they are potters none the less.

Again according to Miller, British domination caused the disappearance of the traditional territorial compartments or, as Srinivas puts it, 'let the djinn out of the bottle', allowing among other things each sufficiently widespread caste to unite on a much broader territorial basis, in associations of which there are nowadays many examples (§113).[72f] It is beyond doubt that many castes or subcastes have taken advantage of the new circumstances to extend well beyond their former confines. Thus in Uttar Pradesh the Brahman castes cover a very wide area and often many of them co-exist in a given district; but if one pays close attention to the quantitative aspect of population, one finds in each case that by far the greater part of the group is concentrated in a few districts central to its present distribution, and that the areas thus defined no longer overlap. It is just as if each group had spread like a drop of oil, mingling peripherally with its neighbours. Although there is not necessarily a political unit in the strict sense in each case, this fact confirms the hypothesis that the composition of the settlements has recently become more complicated compared with a previous period of regional compartmentalization.

To conclude, there is one reservation to be made: one must not take too literally the theory arising from Miller's discovery. The compartmentalization of the little kingdom must have been at its height at periods of instability and political disintegration, although there was always some movement of warriors. But in India, such periods have been interspersed with times of political unification into large states, of spatial mobility at least for certain castes of government officials or merchants. The case of Kerala State is exceptional, and that of the neighbouring Tamil country, although much less a place of passage than the Gangetic plain, demonstrates by its political history and the composition of its present population that the isolation of small units was often disturbed. One must think rather of a *tendency* for regions to close in on themselves, a tendency sufficient to differentiate the regional systems, but not sufficient to shelter them from external influences and upheavals (one should think also of famines and repopulation). The history of this topic alone would require a whole book, and we can only hope to piece together some fragments of it.[72g]

## 73 *Rights, royal and other, over the land*

The question of the appropriation of the land, in the widest sense of the term, naturally arises in the present consideration of power and territory. Land is the most important possession, the only recognized wealth, and is also closely linked with power over men. At least this was the case until recently, and it generally is so in complex traditional societies.[73a]

It so happens that the question of rights over the land, whilst amply discussed in the nineteenth and twentieth centuries, has scarcely ever been related to the caste system. As certain aspects of the question have been mentioned elsewhere, and as it will be encountered again in the following section, we shall be very brief.[73b] Many questions have been discussed which are not independent of one another: in Hindu India, was the king the owner of the land? Was he, in ancient times, a god or a servant? Was there collective ownership, a kind of communism, in the 'village communities'? The concept of the king as a functionary appointed for public order is a rationalization resulting from the secularization of the royal function and the political domain, a secularization made much of in ancient literature. As far as the 'communities' go, to the extent that they existed they represented joint possession by the dominant caste or lineage (§74.1). To look for 'ownership' of the land is a false problem, since everything shows a complementarity between different rights bearing on the same object, for example, those of the 'community' and those of the king. Moreover it is remarkable that the majority of British administrators tackled this question in terms of the more or less philosophical general concepts of the West and not with the special concepts of English law, which would have been closer to the actual state of affairs in India.

Just as the distribution of grain on the threshing floor showed us a series of rights of very different origins being actually exercised over the harvest, so the sometimes lengthy chain of 'intermediaries' between the king and the farmer shows a superimposition of rights, which are not only interdependent but even susceptible of variation in detail. Only if the king were to give up his own right and to take care that all rights were united in the same hands, as was the case with certain religious donations, would something like ownership be created. But even in this case, alienation of rights was probably impossible in principle.

In short, far from a given piece of land being exlusively related to one person, individual or corporate, each piece of land was the object of different rights relating to different functions, expressed in the right to a share of the produce or to some due from the cultivator. The king's share in particular, far from representing a kind of salary for the maintenance of order, expressed an overall right over all land, but limited to this levy in each case. The interdependence of the castes is expressed here by the existence of complementary rights, where that of the king and that of the cultivator are only the main links in a chain which was sometimes complex.

In short the caste system is strongly contrasted to what we call land ownership. What takes place in this domain could almost have been deduced *a priori* from the general characteristics of the system. Given an object, the land, which in complex traditional societies in general is of the greatest importance and intimately linked with political power, one could have foreseen that the caste system would not relate it exclusively to an individual or a function, but rather to the whole set of functions comprised in the system. If something like customary rights are defined in practice, these will be fragmentary rights and mutually complementary; no doubt there will be an eminent right, but this will be a right subordinated to values and therefore subjugated to its function. Moreover, the system does not take cognisance of force, except when subjected to it: it is defenceless on this quarter, this is its Achilles heel. Not only royal favour, but violent interference can at any moment change the titulars, introduce new rights, modify what seemed to be stable rights (without so much as touching the principle of interdependence). The history of India must often have seen the dominants reduced to the state of tenants, tenants to dependants.[73c] This is how the caste system, by the fragmentation of 'rights' and by their insecurity, diminishes the importance that we are ready to accord to the appropriation of the land. A kind of collectivism is involved, but of a more subtle form than our predecessors imagined.

## 74  *The village*

The notion of dominance, or rather of the dominant caste, represents the most solid and useful acquisition of the studies of social anthropology in India. To appreciate it fully, the history of ideas about the Indian village must be briefly recalled.

74.1  *The 'village community'*. People have spoken for a long time of the 'village community', and the expression has taken on somewhat different meanings since the beginning of the nineteenth century. The first stage is that of the now famous descriptions by English administrators in the first thirty years of the century (Wilks, *Fifth Report*, Elphinstone, Metcalfe, etc.). They described the village as a 'little republic', self-sufficient, having its own functionaries, and surviving the ruin of empires.[74a] The stress is above all on political autonomy; India tends to appear as a worm whose segments are the villages. There are regional peculiarities in these descriptions (*Jāt* villages in the Delhi region described by Metcalfe), there are real general characteristics (*jajmānī*), and there is also a certain amount of idealization. This was the romantic period and the great administrators of this time, rather paternalist as we would say nowadays, wanted to defend the indigenous institutions against the claims of bureaucrats and utilitarians who urged reform. The idealization can be seen from the fact that the village's link with the central power (levy on the harvests by the king and his representatives, nature of the official village chiefdom where it exists) is minimized; and it can be seen even more clearly from the fact that the inegalitarian aspect goes unmentioned, perhaps because at that time it still seemed normal. In any case, the 'community' continued its career under the banner of equality.

In the Victorian period, 'village community' took on another meaning related to the supposed communism of primitive peoples or of Indo-European prehistory. Marx shifted the stress from political autonomy to economic autarchy. While he finally attributed ownership of the land to the king, so that only possession in common remained to the communities, he considered them as 'units of production' which were consequently subject to division of labour *sui generis*. Maine stops short at the search for vestiges of the Indo-European commune. It is remarkable that these two authors, relying on the same source, missed its most important feature. Indeed Marx quoted Campbell, and it was from him that Maine drew the essential part of his data before setting out for India. Now Campbell stated clearly that joint ownership was found among the dominants and was accompanied by the subjection of the other inhabitants.[74b] Marx overlooked this and Maine rejected it because he did not make use of his stay in the country to improve his ideas on this point. Here as elsewhere, European scholarship has been ill-fated. Where joint possession existed, it was related to two facts: kinship, or rather the lineage organization in the dominant group on the one hand, and on the other the structural unity of this group as against others who could have disputed or gradually eroded its position.

Finally, in the third period, Indian nationalists, relying on the descriptions and scruples of the British of the first period, constructed for themselves an idyllic picture of the village community as a secular and democratic institution – did it not have the assembly, the famous village panchayat? – which only the British domination ruined irremediably.

We shall encounter the question of the panchayat again in the next chapter. What lessons can be learnt from these various incarnations of the 'community'?In the first place, the elements of truth must be restored to their place in the setting of dominance, and the role of force and conquest, sources of instability, must be recognized. Further, the situation in the village is not independent of regional political circumstances: 'despotism' is often reflected to some degree in the village chiefdom, which not only represents local interests vis-à-vis the political power, but also the reverse. Finally, while recognizing that the 'village community' springs from a Western point of view which is inapplicable to India as a whole, because hierarchy and dominance are omnipresent, and the relation to the land less fundamental than has been supposed, one must also recognize considerable regional developments of communal solidarity (as among the *Jāt*), village exogamy (in the north), and village councils found for example in Tamil country in the Cola period.[74c]

74.2   *The dominant caste.* At the beginning of intensive studies in social anthropology, certain authors seem to have been attracted towards the 'village community': the village was considered at least as isolable, if not independent of environment, and the emphasis was placed on general characteristics rather than specific ones, on the territorial basis rather than the ideology of caste.[74d] It is scarcely too much to say that the introduction of the notion of 'dominant caste' had the chief merit of once again putting caste in the forefront and giving a more precise content to the vague idea of village 'solidarity', of, in short, extricating the Indian village from the sociological limbo in which it was still slumbering. Its second merit is to have isolated in the village the non-ideological aspect with which we are concerned here. We cannot observe a kingdom, but we have in the village a reduced version of it: the principle of the royal function. The word 'dominance' is well chosen in its opposition to 'status' – at least in the sense of those terms we have chosen here. Let us look closer. The term, borrowed from African anthropology ('dominant lineage' in a territorial group), was introduced by Srinivas. In an article on a village in

Mysore, published in 1955, he defined the dominant caste as follows:

A caste may be said to be 'dominant' when it preponderates numerically over the other castes, and when it also wields preponderant economic and political power. A large and powerful caste group can more easily be dominant if its position in the local caste hierarchy is not too low.[74e]

A rather vague definition, which must be discussed and made more precise. It is a fact that in the Indian village one (or more than one) caste had even recently the superior right over the land or the larger part of it. 'Superior right' is to be understood here in relation to the other villagers, for the king's right, itself higher than this one, lies above the level of the village. For example, the distinction has often been pointed out between occupants with full rights, those who possess the village land (whether originally or by conquest or allocation) and inferior or 'foreign' occupants, tolerated by the former (*Coll. Pap.* No. 6, n. 17, 20). We have noted before that the joint possession which, for Maine for example, gave the greatest strength to the 'village community' was in reality the joint possession by occupants of superior right, joint possession within the dominant caste or lineage. As Campbell emphasized (*ibid.*), the 'village community' is dependent on this group.

The numerical criterion introduced by Srinivas is somewhat surprising. Is it necessary for the caste which is dominant so far as the land goes also to be the most numerous in order to 'dominate' in general? One fact to be stated is that usually, when sufficient data are available, it can be seen that the most numerous castes in a village are, first, the dominant caste, and secondly the caste which provides the greatest part of the labour force and is usually untouchable, rather as if the castes in the closest relation to the land, either in theory and practice, had the greatest possibility of increasing in number. However, this would not be enough to introduce number as one of the criteria of dominance. Srinivas justifies it in an article on the dominant caste in the same village,[74f] in which he explains that the real status of one and the same caste in different villages can depend on the number of men it can put into the battle line, and that even Brahmans feel insecure where their numbers are rather small. This emergence of brute force does not cause much surprise. But it does not show that it is necessary for the caste which is powerful in land to be itself numerous, for such a caste easily attracts a clientele. Numbers also have a bearing in modern times, i.e. in elections, but here again the numbers can be made up by members of a clientele more surely than by the members of the dominant caste, among whom there would probably be rivalries or 'factions' once they are numerous. In the same article the author introduces a new criterion of dominance, the level of education: this arises from modern conditions and one might just as well introduce external relations, especially with the town, not to speak of entrepreneurship.

There comes a point when we shall no longer follow this author, for he seems not only to contradict himself, but also to throw overboard everything worth while in the concept. This is when he speaks of 'ritual dominance' in connection with the Brahmans who are neither numerous nor rich in land (*ibid.*, p. 2). One naturally thinks of symmetrical uses of the word 'status' by authors who, not content to speak of the status they call ritual, add 'secular status' to designate in fact dominance, power, etc. (*cf.* §34 and n. 34b). At this point there would no longer be any essential difference between 'status' and 'dominance', for these would designate two different aspects of the same thing. We prefer to maintain a fundamental distinction between the two, a distinction which, as we have seen, is built into the theory of the varnas itself, if not into that of the castes.[74g]

Mayer has enlarged the concept of dominance by considering in addition to the village two other levels, that of the little region and that of the little kingdom, where the dominants are not always the same, although there are certain links between them, at least in his example. A rather obvious proposition emerges from his analysis, as from those by Cohn,[74h] namely that there is a homology between the function of dominance at village level and the royal function at the level of a larger territory: the dominant caste reproduces the royal function at village level. Let us list its main characteristics: (1) relatively eminent right over the land; (2) as a result, power to grant land and to employ members of other castes either in agricultural capacities or as specialists, to build up a large clientele, not to say an armed force; (3) power of justice also: the notables of the dominant caste are often entrusted with the arbitration of differences in other castes or between different castes, and they can exact penalties for unimportant offences (§82); (4) generally speaking, monopoly of authority: if the village headman chosen by the State is not one of the dominant notables he can only be their pawn, unless he has unrivalled personal qualities; (5) the homology extends so far that the dominant caste is often a royal caste, a caste allied to royal castes (Mayer), or a caste with similar characteristics (meat diet, polygyny, etc.).[741] The relationship between the Brahman and the dominant caste is the same as that between the Brahman and the king. It is understood that the Brahmans can be dominant just as they can be kings; in this case they lose their caste characteristic with respect to other Brahmans who serve them as priests (*cf.* Wiser, 42.2).

74.3 *Factions.* A word must be said on a phenomenon which accompanies dominance and which, like it, is a question of fact and not at all of theory. Very commonly the Indian village is divided into 'factions'. People have long recognized the importance of quarrels, rivalries and legal wranglings in the Indian village. We quoted above Metcalfe's fear based on this fact (n. 74a). So far as India is concerned, we owe the name, and certainly the first systematic study of the phenomenon, to Oscar Lewis and his collaborators in a study near Delhi. The village is divided into more or less permanent rival groups of which the more powerful at least include a fraction of the dominant caste and at the same time a clientele recruited from dependent castes. The important point is obviously the scission of the dominant caste or lineage into two or more fragments which do not necessarily always follow lineal cleavages. The factions use every occasion of friction and litigation to confront each other; even if they do not incite them, it is probable that they considerably aggravate them. Lewis has given a very precise account of the membership and relations of these factions, which do not have only hostile relations but also those of sympathy and neutrality. One may wonder whether he has not somewhat reified the relations and made them rigid, when in reality they may be more fluctuating and often more ambiguous.[74j] Also, most importantly perhaps, his example, in which there are objective cleavages (the factions smoke separately), may well constitute a limiting case, as the *Jāṭ* peasantry in many ways represents a deviant type with respect to India in general. However, even if, as one is inclined to believe, things are in general more fluid and unstable, Lewis certainly put his finger on an important fact. The fact is confirmed by other works using the same concept, in particular that by Dhillon: after participating in the research just mentioned he studied a village in the Deccan in a similar way and brought out interesting differences (role of affinal kinship in the south).[74k] The overall fact is that within the village and within the dominant caste itself there is scission into units which spring from no traditional principle, and in which each man's adherence is mainly or to a large extent governed by his interests. In short we have here an important *empirical* addition to the groupings and divisions which spring from caste, lineal kinship, and local association. All kinds of questions arise. In particular, is this phenomenon bound up with the traditional organization in some way still not clear, or is it, as most authors are doubtless inclined to think, a modern fact, linked to recent changes brought about by the insertion of the village into a political and economic whole which has strongly affected it? It is clear that contemporary changes have multiplied the causes of friction, but this does not mean that the phenomenon itself is recent. Let us be content with one remark by way of transition to the following chapter. From the formal point of view, the fact seems to be linked to a characteristic of authority: as we shall see, in this system a man can only have uncontested authority with respect to people of dominated or inferior caste. Within a group of a given status, authority is more often plural than singular. It is a well-known fact that, apart from official functions, one rarely encounters a single chief or leader, authority and influence being more often shared among two or more elders.

## 75   The problem of economics

Can we go further, and, as a sequel to the political implications of the caste system, study its economic implications? I would like here to raise the question of the applicability to traditional India of the very category of economics, and the connected question of the place of wealth in moveables and chattels, money and commerce in Indian society. To raise the question is not to answer it, but it does arouse doubts and also indicates some topics for study.

First of all, one must remember the elementary but too often forgotten fact that, even in our society, it was only at the end of the eighteenth century that economics appeared as a distinct category, independent of politics.[75a] So far as India is concerned, a further fact, many of whose aspects are known and studied but which is often overlooked in itself, in its full generality and fundamental character, is that the British domination emancipated wealth in moveables and chattels by substituting for a political régime of the traditional type, a modern type of régime, one of whose fundamental tasks was to guarantee the security of property, a régime which, compared to the previous one, abdicated part of its power in favour of wealth. The transformation of land into a marketable commodity is only a part of this change. No doubt there is in India today a distinct sphere of activity which may properly be called economic, but it was the British government which made this possible.[75b] However, there are many authors who do not hesitate to speak of the economy in traditional India, without always saying how they define it. We have already encountered the difficulty in connection with the jajmani system, but it is not confined to this. Certain authors seem aware of the difficulty, for they do not separate politics from economics; unfortunately, what for them defines the 'politico-economic' domain is 'power' in the vaguest sense. Now 'power' is a notion which, while playing a central role in contemporary political science, is so obscure that it has scarcely justified this role. However, this procedure has one advantage, namely that we can find something in the Indian tradition which corresponds with the politico-economic domain, namely the domain of *artha*.[75c] In fact, throughout this chapter where we have said 'politics' we have assumed it to contain something like an implicit economic component. This is the case with dominance which consists in 'wealth', possession of landed interests, as well as political power. But the main characteristic of this society, like many other traditional societies, is that the two aspects are bound together in the same phenomenon, no distinction being made between them. One can say that just as religion in a way encompasses politics, so politics encompasses economics within itself. The difference is that the politico-economic domain is separated, named, in a subordinate position as against religion, whilst economics remains undifferentiated within politics. Indeed, one can study kingship in the Hindu texts, even if it receives less careful treatment than priesthood. But if we go one step further and raise the question of the merchant, the normative texts are silent. Thus we are reduced to putting a question of pure fact: to what extent was the merchant's wealth guaranteed by royal power, or, on the contrary, at its mercy? Various periods in history must then be explored to try to see what happened in this respect. The task is difficult. From a rapid inquiry, it seems to be the case that the situation varied greatly from one period or region to another.[75d] It was only in periods of political unification and large and fairly well policed kingdoms that the king was able to concern himself with the kingdom's prosperity and promote trade for his own interests. Such fluctuations are to be expected, since the ideology is silent on the question.

So it was no idle question whether one can speak of economics in traditional India. The main 'economic' implication of the caste system is, as it were, the very uncertainty which has just been indicated. However, this is only a part of what can be surmised. It seems that Max Weber was right to see a specific link between trade and certain sects, especially Jainism, and that economic history is in this sense indebted to the history of the heresies, which will be touched on in Chapter IX.

# CHAPTER EIGHT

# CASTE GOVERNMENT: JUSTICE AND AUTHORITY

## 81 *From power to authority*

Most of the castes have organs of government; and even those which have not exercise authority over their members in a diffused and unformalized way, and can, for example, excommunicate or banish one of their members. But this is not the whole story: not only may conflicts between different castes require the recognition of a higher authority, but castes frequently have recourse to people of superior caste to settle their internal conflicts, and we shall even see that excommunication required official approval. When, in a village, members of a dominated or dependent caste come to ask a notable of the dominant caste to settle a difference, they recognize his authority as arbiter or judge. Thus we pass here from power to authority. If force becomes legitimate by submitting to Brahmanic ideals, and thus becomes power, then as can be seen from our example power is invested with judicial authority by those subjected to it. Thus acknowledged, and in some way internalized by its subjects, power becomes equal, in a specific sphere, to authority *par excellence*, i.e. religious authority: just as the Brahmans have authority in religious matters, so the dominants have authority in judicial matters. Hence we observe the (secondary) equivalence between the two opposed principles of status and power that we have already encountered in the case of status ranking. These are the reasons why we were obliged to speak of power and dominance before speaking of authority within the caste.

So far as justice is concerned the classical texts are very clear: the king, advised by Brahman specialists in the dharma, metes out justice in full sovereignty. It may be said that legislative authority belongs to the Brahmans, judicial authority, administration of justice, to the king. Generally speaking, the royal function appears in the Dharmashastras as the almost miraculous solution to a formidable problem, the pivot which permits the attachment and coupling together of two otherwise irreconcilable universes: force and the law, ideal and fact.[81a] Thanks to the king in particular the Brahman transcends the administration of this world. The king's essential function being to preserve the system of the varnas by preventing them mixing, he quite naturally had authority over the castes. The twofold nature of authority is encountered again in a striking way in connection with judicial sanctions. Whilst the king would decree a penalty, the Brahmans would prescribe – sometimes for the same action – an expiation. The distinction is not always clear, and there has been at the very least some blurring between the two. We shall come across expiation again in modern times for the most serious religious faults. So far as the government of castes is concerned, another classical feature must be recognized: the texts put the king under an obligation to take full account of the manners and customs of established groups, lineages, corporations, etc., and even, notably, of the customs of heretics. Likewise nowadays the dominants settle litigation according to the customs of each particular caste.

Thus before studying internal caste government in detail, it is as well to see to what extent the castes are, or were, ruled from the outside, by the king or by an acknowledged religious authority. As the royal function is reflected at the level of the village, we shall move from royal jurisdiction to that of the dominant caste in the village, but here we shall have to discuss the existence of a semi-mythical being, the so-called 'village assembly', as an agent of justice. We shall conclude by trying to characterize authority in general.

## 82  Supreme authority in caste affairs

The king being judge *par excellence*, the supreme judge, he can be pictured traditionally as keeping serious matters for himself and as settling in appeal any suit judged by another court, whether customary or otherwise. Conversely, he could refer back cases submitted to him to such a customary court. He was normally assisted by a committee of Brahman experts in dharma, and he could delegate his authority to one of them.[82a]

There are examples of the king intervening directly in the caste hierarchy to refashion it or to fix the respective rank of different castes or subcastes (this latter case especially where hypergamy is the rule (§55)).[82b] The king could sometimes even promote a caste, or move someone from one caste to another. For Uttar Pradesh, Nesfield reports several legendary traditions of the individual or collective 'manufacture' of Brahmans. The king's role in excommunication and reintegration of an excommunicate is important and better confirmed. The king could excommunicate not only a person (in Cochin his decision was necessary), but even a whole group, as is shown by Baroda, and an arresting example given by O'Malley for Orissa. Royal sanction was often necessary for the reintegration of an excommunicate, and this prerogative passed to the Moghul sovereigns and even, for a short time, to the English government. It should be noticed that a large proportion of the examples come from distant regions or mountainous districts where caste was relatively fluid and where the traditional organization was maintained, a situation contrasting with that in the plains in the north, where the Mohammedan conquest had deprived the Hindus of their own sovereigns and, as Ibbetson has pointed out for Panjab, had left them to the influence of the Brahmans alone.

Alongside royal control, there are examples of religious control: in Kashmir, the Dharma Sabha assembled in the royal temple and judged caste matters, to the extent of decreeing exclusion. A Brahman, a 'guru' or a member of a sect, often helps or even replaces the caste's court, the *pañcāyat*. It is not surprising to see that religion has a hand in the matter of the murder of a cow or of reintegration, in which it is a question of decreeing an expiation which has a purificatory aspect. It should simply be remarked that the sect appears here as well as the Brahman.[82c]

We may note with Hutton that these functions were lucrative (Manipur), and the continuity between former royal justice and today's official justice should be pointed out. Whatever novelties were introduced by British justice, it was no novelty in so far as being official justice; however, it would have been novel if the caste or village had really been self-sufficient until that time, as is so often supposed. Even the petitions which flooded the authorities of the Census and which were aimed at obtaining government recognition of a desired status for a given group, testify in their way to the prerogatives of power in this domain.[82d]

One should picture to oneself the king's judicial functions as distributed along the chain of territorial subordination and spreading out from him to his local representatives, or remaining attached to the local kings or chiefs subjugated by him. Thus there is continuity, from the sovereign to the local and regional chiefs, and to the village dominants, as O'Malley has shown. The masters of the land in a small region dispensed justice in the manner of local seigneurs, and collected not only fines but also dues on marriages, etc. These functions, where they were recognized by the British, have endured, for example in the case of the Zamindars of Uttar Pradesh until the abolition of the Zamindari system in 1951.

## 83  The 'village panchayat'

Works on modern Indian history are apt to speak of the village council or assembly, usually referred to as the 'village panchayat'. We shall return to the word 'panchayat' (§84.1). Let us simply say for the moment that traditionally it may designate any assembly for the purposes of justice or arbitration, whatever its size; in short it is a customary court in a very broad sense and, in the case of the caste assembly, an executive and even legislative organ. The expression 'village panchayat' is scarcely ever defined, but, especially in twentieth-century Indian literature, a link has been established between it and the notion of 'village community' which we have criticized. In the terms of a very widespread belief, the 'village community' had more or less universally the 'village panchayat' as its organ. The economist Vera Anstey formulates the belief in a characteristic way:

It has long been recognized . . . that one of the worst results of British rule has been the decline in the status and powers of village panchayats. These bodies formerly controlled village life and formed a strong social bond amongst the masses.[83a]

The same idea is to be found in all, or almost all, the literature. People believed so strongly in this institution that they set out to look for it. The investigators of the 1911 *Census*, urged to study it, had to acknowledge its absence in vast regions of India. Blunt tells us that it did not exist in the plain of Uttar Pradesh, and the

*Census* of Bombay goes so far as to say that it is all a myth.[83b] How is this to be explained? Some will say that the panchayat certainly existed: if one can find no trace of it, it is because it was destroyed by British domination, and how otherwise could one explain the fact that the existence of the institution is vouched for at certain points? There is another explanation, which to be fully convincing would require an historical study of all the literature on the question. What happened is itself instructive: a belief has come to constitute its object. The belief sees ancient and eternal India as a 'democracy of villages', and in order to be democracies the 'communities' necessarily had to have a representative organ. They have been given it.[83c] How? By assembling, in complete innocence, heterogeneous facts around certain accurate data so as to obtain the desired degree of consistency and generality. We shall briefly show how this has been possible.

In the first place, a good part of the literature in question ignores the best documented panchayats, the caste panchayats, and thereby introduces a vagueness into the sense of 'village panchayat', as if one were to speak of rural justice. In the second place, whenever experts are brought together under the aegis of the dominants to arbitrate or judge differences within the village, for example within a dominated caste, or between different castes, one can speak, in a sense already made more precise, of village panchayat. Now this sense is, I think, the one that predominates in the writings of Munro and Elphinstone, which have been constantly quoted. These great administrators of the early nineteenth century were concerned so far as possible to have differences at the level of the village settled by panchayats, so that they did not all come before the official seat of justice.[83d]

In the third place, it should be noticed that where people met in assembly to settle the common business of the 'village', whether it was a question of collecting taxes or of the administration of the village in general, it was *first and foremost* a matter for the dominant caste. Consequently, it would be better to speak in this sense of the assembly or panchayat of the dominants, rather than of the village panchayat. Whether the meeting was sometimes public, or whether the dominants secured, according to local tradition or circumstances, the collaboration of representatives of the dominated, is relatively secondary from the point of view of the effective power of decision. Finally, in the fourth place, one must not picture to oneself the functioning of village administration, in particular the greater or lesser extent to which its functions are articulated and formalized, as independent of the royal or central power.[83e] Everything we know tends to show that on the contrary all this depended, and still depends today, on the establishment of a satisfactory relationship with the central power. Perhaps it can now be seen how it has been possible, by confusing various sorts of deliberative meetings and by taking advantage of the idealization of the 'village community', to construct a mysterious being of which it can be said both that it has been encountered and that it does not exist. Also there are rare but very remarkable historical documents, like the minutes engraved in stone of the assembly and special commissions of the village of Uttaramerur in the Cola kingdom in the twelfth century, and such monuments further our understanding of how patriotic ideals, struggling against foreign domination, were able to erect the ennobling picture of a village democracy which only foundered in modern times.[83f]

Leaving on one side village administration and considering only justice, we conclude that on the eve of the British conquest, and excepting exceptional cases, there was no village panchayat as a permanent institution, distinct from caste panchayats. There was a panchayat of the dominant caste of the village, and there were meetings of *ad hoc* arbitrators or judges, of a temporary nature. Only encouragement and recognition on the part of the government could bring into existence true village panchayats.

## 84 *Internal caste government*

84.1 '*Panchayat*': *word and object.* The supreme authority within the caste is, where it exists, the caste assembly (or more exactly the assembly of a fragment of the caste). This assembly is often called 'panchayat' in the literature, and probably is also often so called in fact. But the meaning of the word is much wider than this. The word *pañcāyat* is formed from *pañc* (Indo-Ayrian), meaning 'five', and thus immediately evokes the idea of a small committee rather than a large assembly. This is why Blunt supposes, in the case of Uttar Pradesh, that it designates rather the committee directing the assembly, which sometimes numbers just five members. In reality the word designates a meeting of some notables, 'four or five' as we should say.[84a] Such a committee is appealed to not only to direct the assembly (U.P.) but very often to settle a dispute. Moreover certain groups distinguish very precisely the different kinds of meeting, committee or assembly (*cf.* my *Sous-caste*, p. 268). The caste assembly is, in virtue of the authority with which it is invested, the most solemn meeting of the kind. These meetings are not only judicial, for on the one hand they may simply arbitrate, and on the other the caste assembly may have administrative or executive functions, and even legislative ones, to the extent that it can modify custom, decide for example to cease to tolerate remarriage of widows, or to modify the rules of intermarriage.

The word *pañcāyat* ought to evoke for us first and foremost this *plural authority*, guardian of custom and concord, appealed to in particular to settle conflicts, whether by arbitration or by passing judgment against what is contrary to custom. It is formed in essence by a small nucleus of notables or specialists, possibly joined by more or less active spectators. While bearing in mind that for the people concerned there is continuity between all such meetings, from the most modest and ephemeral to the one which exercises the supreme authority within the caste, we must nevertheless make distinctions. In particular we must especially distinguish the case where different castes are involved, for example in the arbitration of an intra-caste difference by the dominants of the place.

There is a relative paucity of recent literature on the caste assembly and the intra-caste panchayat in general. Therefore to start with we shall summarize the account of the caste assembly given by Blunt for Uttar Pradesh following the *Census* of 1911. We shall generalize as the occasion demands.[84b]

84.2 *The caste assembly (U.P., etc.).* Blunt distinguishes three cases according to whether the caste has no assembly, has a permanent assembly (that is, an assembly with a permanent membership) or has a non-permanent assembly. The first case is often encountered among superior castes, the castes of the 'twice-born', of the three superior varnas. Authority is diffuse, it is 'public opinion' which excommunicates or boycotts, and moreover does so effectively. The case of what Blunt calls the non-permanent panchayat is that in which the assembly only meets at the request of a guilty party, after he has been excluded by his community without any formal decision: he then appeals against this collective attitude before the assembly, so as to obtain his reinstatement conditional to a punishment to be decided. Actually, such meetings seem to be exceptional, and in the case of only a few castes can one be sure they take place; in short this is a type intermediate between the previous one and the following one. By contrast, the 'permanent panchayat' is attested for one hundred and four castes in the region, of which eighty-eight are either professional (sixty-six) or low (twenty-two). This point should be noted.

In this case the assembly or panchayat possesses one or more permanent dignitaries, who are responsible for bringing infringements to its notice and convening it when the need arises (p. 106). These people are always members of the committee. Most of the time there is a chief, hereditary or elected, generally for life, who is the president of the assembly (*sarpañc*, etc.), and there may also be other more or less specialized dignitaries, or simply several members of the committee, themselves hereditary or elected, called *pañc*, literally '(one of the) five'. The existence of a single president or chief is doubtless not indispensable. In other regions there may not be one, even in a very articulate and active organization (*Sous-caste*; Srinivas, 'Joint Family Dispute': two notables take turns to preside).

The assembly is sometimes specially convened, and it may also, perhaps more often, meet at the request of a plaintiff on the occasion of one of the banquets which mark family ceremonies (marriages, funerals) and where the members of the fraternity are present in large numbers, or again on the occasion of one of the great regional pilgrimages, where even several fraternities, corresponding to several assemblies, may meet and discuss reforms to be made in the subcaste's customs.

The group which meets in official assembly is often called, as Blunt says, *birādarī* or 'fraternity', and every head of a family has the right to speak in it; in Uttar Pradesh the assembly is generally directed by a committee, which often has five members; more rarely the panchayat is formed of chosen representatives. We have already insisted on the fact that the assembly generally corresponds in the north at least to a territorial fragment of the subcaste. The subcaste is in effect a theoretical more than an effective unit: one *may* marry anywhere within the subcaste (or more generally of some such subdivision of the caste, which can be lower level: sub-subcaste, for example); but in effect one marries only within a smaller group, territorially limited, which is the 'effective' group with respect to relations within the caste (Mayer, above 36), and which meets in assembly. This is a purely empirical matter, and this group does not constitute a unit among others of the same nature which together would constitute the subcaste; these groups do not know each other well. This is what Blunt calls an 'independent local section'.[84c] The territorial extent of the assembly being a purely empirical matter, it is subject to great variation. For example, the assembly of a caste of specialists like the washermen, who are dispersed on account of having only a small number of families in each village, would cover a larger area than that of a caste of farmers, densely settled in a small region. Thus it is not too surprising to find in Mysore an assembly of washermen with an immense area of jurisdiction (two districts?, Srinivas, 'Caste Dispute'). In addition, in Uttar Pradesh itself, and certainly if one generalizes, the assembly studied by Blunt is after all only the largest, most official and most powerful of panchayats which can effectively meet. Gough mentions that in the south (Tanjore) there are panchayats of castes of tenants limited to a single village, the dominant caste exercising strict control over the relations between castes in the village (in Marriott, ed., *Village India*, pp. 44 ff.); this would probably not exclude assemblies covering a wider area. One can have panchayats at several levels, whether it is a question of a territorially segregated caste (*Sous-caste*) or a dominant caste in a given area (Jats: Lewis), and, in exceptional cases, one level may be represented at another.[84d] In Panjab, successive circumscriptions are designated by the number of villages which they are deemed to include.[84e]

84.3 *Jurisdiction, procedure*. It has already been mentioned that the jurisdiction of the assembly goes beyond the domain of internal justice. It can decree rules and exercise a controlling function.[84f] It also defends the professional interests of the group against third parties, like a kind of privilege. Blunt found relatively little regulation of techniques, and he attributes this fact to recent changes. In return, the assembly watches jealously over the maintenance of jajmani relations, both punishing a member who attempts to take someone else's patron or who has been patently remiss in his professional duties, and boycotting the patron who, without sufficient reason in the caste's eyes, attempts to put an end to the services of one of its members or replace him by another: the group here is solidly united – one of the rare cases in which it is – behind one of its members whose professional rights are threatened. Sometimes the reciprocity of services is in dispute, sometimes the privileges of the caste itself are attacked and it defends them indirectly by putting an end to one of its other services. In order to make a person of another caste see reason, it may even happen that one caste counts on the support of another. Thus respectively in the following three examples (Blunt, pp. 243–6):

The Barbers boycott dancing girls who refused to dance for their marriages.

In Gorakhpur, a planter tried to end the trade of the Chamars, who, he believed, were poisoning the cattle (as they are often suspected of doing); he ordered his tenants to lacerate the hide of every animal which died of no apparent cause. The Chamars retorted by ordering their women to stop serving as mid-wives; the planter gave in.

In Ahmedabad (Gujerat), a banker who was having his house re-roofed had a quarrel with a confectioner. The confectioners came to an agreement with the tile makers who refused to provide the banker with tiles.

According to the Abbé Dubois, this caste solidarity operated even against the power of the State.[84g] Nowadays, solidarity sometimes works in the opposite direction, and in opposition to custom: for putting an end to activities considered dishonourable (§17).

From the purely internal point of view, it is certain that the assembly and even more generally the panchayat has 'some measure of judicial power, and investigates and punishes offences against custom' (Blunt, p. 104). But the very facts quoted by Blunt show that certain cases are civil rather than penal, and are for settling disputes between members of the group; recent literature is insistent on this point. It could almost be said that the task of the panchayats is above all to settle conflicts, whether by arbitration or by passing sentence (*cf.* Gough in Marriott, ed., *Village India*, pp. 44–5). However, this would not be enough, for it is beyond doubt that the caste 'will . . . keep all its members within the bounds of duty'. Following the Abbé Dubois, O'Malley has insisted on this in very felicitous language.[84h] Caste justice definitely has two aspects, a point we shall return to later.

Blunt gives a list of offences known to the assemblies. His examples mostly concern commensality, marriage and morals (divorce, adultery, concubinage), trade, and Hindu crimes (murder of a cow). Apart from the fact that where for example marriage is concerned it is often a matter of differences rather than offences, it is perhaps a mistake to try to define the jurisdiction of caste panchayats theoretically: given the existence of official courts, it hinges rather on what happens in practice: the traditional assemblies are naturally concerned, first and foremost, with everything that does not come before the official courts, but in addition Blunt says that '*panchayats* seldom encroach on the jurisdiction of the magistrate' (p. 116). In general this is very variable, and much less clear-cut (§85). The limitation of the panchayat's competence by the existence of other courts is much more practical than theoretical.

We cannot go into the details of the procedure, with the oath, the ordeal and more generally the religious sanctions which support it.[84i] It will simply be said that, when sufficiently well known, the procedure does not seem to justify Hutton's rather condescending judgment that it is extremely simple, informal and 'untrammelled by the law of evidence'. In U.P. Blunt indicates the influence of modern official courts, but there are also differences and variable rules of evidence and of mode of decision (unanimity or vote, often unanimity in the council and majority in the assembly).

From what is known from other sources, it may be wondered whether the formal vote is more than something recently borrowed from Western ways. Writing about local elections, Mayer describes the dislike of the division produced by voting with raised hands: all kinds of deals and compromises are arranged behind the scenes, but on the surface the election is unanimous. The author recalls 'the ideal pattern of the panchayat which should take none but unanimous decisions, whether truly or overtly', and this applies perfectly to the caste panchayat. Lewis also mentions 'the traditional method of reaching a unanimous verdict'.[84j]

The influence of modern official courts on the panchayat is known, but one must also think of the influence of royal jurisdiction in the past, which in U.P. has left its mark on the name of the dignitaries of the assembly.[84k]


84.4 *Excommunication.* The most severe penalty which can be pronounced by the caste assembly – conditional perhaps on the approval of the supreme authority – is exclusion. It is also the most interesting sociologically, 'a kind of social excommunication. ... It renders him dead to the world', as the Abbé Dubois said (I, p. 36; Beauchamp, p. 38). In reality there are differences, and authors draw distinctions; the Abbé Dubois distinguishes more or less radical cases of exclusion, reintegration ranging from being easy to being impossible, as for someone who has eaten cow's meat (p. 37–8, 43; Beauchamp, 38–9, 43).[84l] Likewise for Srinivas ('Caste Dispute') exclusion may be final – for a Brahman who has cohabited with a Paria woman – or temporary, until reintegration. According to O'Malley, exclusion is either for life, or for a defined period, or until expiation, *prayaścitta*, has been made (p. 75); he adds that the sentence of temporary excommunication is not always applied, but sometimes commuted on condition that the guilty party makes amends.[84m]

Blunt quotes a number of examples, but without many details, and there are few which are described in full, perhaps because excommunication is rare nowadays. However, there are perhaps still other distinctions to be made. Thus Hutton, who makes the above distinction, identifies the cessation of commensality (prohibition of pipe and water, which comes to the same thing) with the cessation of specialized services (p. 93). But there are surely cases, especially in U.P., where the one does not entail the other. And indeed the question arises of knowing whether the assembly, which incontestably has the power to reject one of its members, has authority over the servants. The reply to this question is certainly in the affirmative in the case of the dominant caste, but in other cases one may wonder whether total excommunication does not require the sanction of an authority outside the caste. In point of fact, Dubois attributes it to the 'guru or failing him the tribal chiefs', and he considers that excommunication pronounced by kinsmen, that is the local group, is not final; it has been seen above how the king may intervene (§82). Failing such a sanction, commensality may cease, and yet the servants continue to serve the guilty party.[84n]

Thus there are degrees, and alongside true excommunication, final or temporary, one could mention a kind of boycott which is not accompanied by decisive sanctions.

The person concerned often suffers excommunication with little apparent complaint, but when the question of marrying his children arises he makes great efforts to obtain his reintegration, and theirs at the same time; thus the dispute reported by Srinivas ('Caste Dispute') is bound up with the marriage of the son of a woman of doubtful status (*cf. Sous-caste*, p. 311).[840]

As for reintegration, it has been seen that it often requires the sanction of religious and even royal authority. It in effect entails rites which are both expiations (*prayaścitta*) and purifications (pilgrimage to the Ganges, treatment by the five products of the cow), and it is symbolized by a meal offered by the guilty party to the assembly (and often to Brahmans). This formality of the meal for the fraternity has become general as a total or partial punishment for less important offences. In general in caste justice, the expiation is closely bound up with the punishment proper; this is natural if, as we shall see, it is above all a matter of preventing or remedying a loss of status.

## 84.5 *General character of caste jurisdiction*

The jurisdiction of caste panchayats is conceived as extending to any matter in which the men of the caste consider that the interests or reputation of the caste require action to be taken against a member of the caste (Hutton, *op. cit.*, p. 89).

Such a way of putting the matter takes account of the basic nature of excommunication: a man made impure by serious contacts with impure substances or people, jeopardizes by what Hutton calls 'contagion' the status not only of his family but of his whole group: thus he must be separated from the rest, just as a gangrenous limb is amputated; it is a safeguard as well as a punishment.[84p] It is correct to speak of 'reputation', and there are some things on which one could turn a blind eye if it were not for the fact that disapproving neighbours keep their eyes open. Also the rigor of the decision is less a function of the caste's own 'territorial concentration' (*ibid.*) than of the fact that it lives in more or less close contact both with castes of rival status and with more or less exacting superiors.[84q] One can thus explain how it is that being struck with a slipper or having worms in a wound may be punishable: these are minor offences against the status of the group. One can also understand the fact which the Abbé Dubois (II, 461; Beauchamp, 658-9) found striking, that serious crimes against one's fellow men and public order, like murder or theft, not jeopardizing the caste's status, can appear much less serious than an infringement of the rules about food.

But all this only represents one aspect of the caste panchayat's judicial or quasi-judicial activity; very often it is concerned to settle such differences between its members as are not immediately relevant to the status of the group, and it does so, as we and contemporary authors have insisted, with much flexibility and patience in order to reach *conciliation*. Should one say, to make this aspect tally with the account quoted above, that good relations between its members is one of the caste's interests? This would obviously be inadequate. The structural approach, once again, enables us to go further. Caste justice is Janus faced: one face is turned towards the exterior, and this is penal justice; the other is turned towards the interior, and this is justice by arbitration, by conciliation, tending both to re-establish harmony within the group and *maintain the authority of the panchayat*. Indeed, it is noticeable that this authority, though strong when it is a matter of preserving the group's status, is weak in the other case. Solemn phrases are often quoted like 'the voice of the panchayat is the voice of God' or 'the king of the caste is the caste'; in this context they take on a precise sense, the first as the expression of a pious wish in relation to the twofold aspect mentioned: the panchayat which defends our status must also be obeyed in other matters; the second as an implicit recognition of the fact that authority within the caste is to a large extent derived from royal authority and outside authority in general (§85). In short, the caste tries, or tried, to be its own king.

For the moment let us stress the weaker aspects of the panchayat. In the first place, as we have said, a large number of the higher castes do not have an assembly; secondly, there are great variations in the activity and authority of the assemblies or more generally the panchayats where they exist, even within the same social level and the same region. It is true that the present situation, in which people complain of the panchayat's ineffectiveness, is usually attributed by the people concerned to recent decadence, and observers ascribe this to modern influences (to the British domination, as above, etc.). This is quite likely, but it is doubtless not the whole truth: there are good reasons for thinking that the panchayat's authority has always depended on outside circumstances. In any case, it is tempting to maintain that the conciliatory character of the panchayat is the sign of its wisdom, in particular in that it is aware of its relative weakness with respect to everything which is not concerned with the group's status.[84r]

## 85  *Relations between jurisdictions: authority in general*

Contemporary observation shows that there are three main organs of justice: the caste panchayat, the panchayat of the dominant caste, and the official courts. To begin with, what is the relationship between the first two and the last? In Tanjore, according to Gough, the Brahmans, who are dominant, have even recently been able to prevent inter-caste matters within the village from coming before the police, even in criminal cases; by contrast, some of the internal affairs of the Brahmans, who have no caste panchayat, came at least for a time before official justice. Srinivas is categorical in the case of Mysore: it is considered a bad thing to bring matters before official justice rather than before the dominants, and is felt to be an attack on the solidarity of the village. For Malwa, Mayer, referring to this statement, declares on the contrary that there is no sign of such a reluctance. For the Delhi region, Lewis mentions the existence of many official actions at law between factions, serious matters being settled in this way. This is understandable to the extent that land rights were at stake, which are guaranteed only by the State. Among the Kallar, Dumont shows that the State got hold of criminal cases with limited success (in one case, official justice having been misled, the caste assembly met and the guilty party was judged, *cf.* Carstairs); the police are readily appealed to in intra-caste matters, and having recourse to the courts indicates determination to destroy the adversary, as opposed to the arbitration which is sought within the caste. According to Bailey (Orissa) the State has deprived the village of its right to judge the criminal. One caste remains outside the local community (the 'distillers of Ganjam') and resorts only to the official courts. According to Beals (Mysore), it is only very recently that people have started to resort to State justice.

What now is the relationship, in traditional justice, between the caste panchayat and recourse to justice at the hands of the dominants? Do a caste's internal affairs come before the one or the other? In the case of a unicaste population (Kallar) the only caste present (with the exception of servants) is dominant: the two jurisdictions merge. Gough seems to indicate that matters remain internal to the caste; it would be normal for there to be the possibility of appeal to the dominants, who moreover have jurisdiction if there is a disturbance of order in the village. According to Srinivas, clients normally have recourse to their patrons (in a joint family dispute) or turn to them in appeal; the justice of the dominants is on the spot and better in touch with the circumstances than caste jurisdiction, covering too wide an area. Conversely, in Mayer, few disputes are brought before the dominants. Lewis mentions a complex situation (the Jats have faction panchayats and clan panchayats). In Bailey's study the caste panchayat, very widespread, seems non-existent by comparison with what he calls the village panchayat.

In short, there is great diversity, doubtless relating to local circumstances and history. However, it can be said that traditional justice, apart from the fact that it is an expression of dominance, tends more to arbitration and reconciliation, and that official justice serves as an instrument of chicanerie and intrigue.[85a]

Can we generalize and present some conclusions on authority in the caste system? We first studied hierarchy, then political power, so that in the present chapter we could appreciate the combination of the two in command or authority, this combination being most readily understood at the level of justice. Naturally the domain of authority is found to contain the dichotomy, operative throughout the society, between religion and its opposite: religious authority is in the hands of the Brahmans, with the notable addition of representatives of the sects (Chapter IX). Temporal authority is in the hands of the king, supreme judge and, more generally, the executive instrument of the law of dharma. Hence there are classically two sorts of sanction: punishments decreed by royal justice, and expiations imposed by the Brahmans. At the level of the village, the dominants quite naturally reproduce the royal function in miniature. Not only do they have power over the dominated, the latter recognize their authority to the extent of having recourse to them to settle internal disputes.

The distribution of authority between different castes is thus relatively simple and well known. The question of authority within a given social level is more intricate. The effective subcaste group has its elders, often its assembly, perhaps its president, but the predominant idea is that of collective or plural authority; on a small basis, the caste group in a village also has its influential people who exercise some authority over their equals. Even so there must be enough members and, in this case, especially if it is a question of the dominant caste, we encounter a remarkable phenomenon, which has often been noted and which we have mentioned in connection with factions: this sort of authority or influence is plural rather than singular. As a general rule, there is no single chief, explicit or otherwise, but several more or less rival leaders. The elder of a lineage has a pre-eminent dignity, but precisely for this reason he is often somewhat out of touch with everyday affairs, with the dealings and intrigues where a younger man may be more at home. This is not all, and a considerable fragmentation of authority has been found more or less everywhere. Is this a modern phenomenon, resulting from recent disorganizing influences? One would sooner believe that modernization has only accentuated the fact, for it has a structural explanation: it can be seen as an implication of hierarchy. The principle of hierarchy, completed by dominance, results in authority over a given caste being concentrated in the hands of castes which are superior to it either directly or in so far as they are dominant. Equally, by implication, it is difficult to constitute authority among people of the same status. However great the inclination to dependence, and despite the authority which emanates from kinship and lineage, a man's authority cannot spread very far among his equals. Most probably only relationships with the outside, in particular with external power, provide a real basis of authority on this level. One can see what wishful thinking there is in the adage 'the king of the caste is the caste'. Here comes the case of the 'village headman' chosen by the State, although his authority is real only if certain local conditions are fulfilled, that is to say, if he appears to the dominants as the link between them and political power. There are naturally more complex forms of influence, especially in modern times with the new forms of political, professional, and economic relationships between the village and the outside world.[85b]

# CHAPTER NINE

# CONCOMITANTS AND IMPLICATIONS

## 91 *Introduction*

In this chapter we shall recall, or point out, some features which in fact go hand in hand with the social system we have tried to review, leaving open the question of whether to regard these concomitants as implications. At the level of social organization the first sort of implication or concomitant of the ideological system is the 'politico-economic' one; such aspects were specified in Chapter VII and were described as enclosed more or less logically in the fundamental system of ideas. Here we shall be concerned with other aspects of a rather varied kind. The following will be considered: first, a social institution which transcends the society: renunciation, and the social form governed by renunciation, the sect. Second, the cultural implications: tolerance, imitation, the concept of time. Third, some diachronic implications concerning social groups themselves. Ideas do indeed have implications for actual events; hierarchy implies a tendency for status groups to divide by scission. Unfortunately research in this field is not very far advanced, which is why I shall be content to indicate certain relationships, factual or ideological, with the hope that future research may recognize here the 'dynamic' or kinetic side of the system of groups, whose static side I have described.[91a]

## 92 *Renunciation*

The most striking concomitant is that there exists in the society of castes itself, and alongside the caste system, an institution which contradicts it. By renunciation, a man can become dead to the social world, escape the network of strict interdependence which we have described, and become to himself his own end as in the social theory of the West, except that he is cut off from the social life proper. This is why I have called this person, this renouncer, an individual-outside-the-world.

This way of seeing things is suggested by an overall view of Indian religions. I have tried to show (see below, Appendix B) that by introducing a single dichotomy, namely the distinction between man-in-the-world and individual-outside-the-world, one could attain a unified and ordered view of the proliferation of religious and contemplative movements in India, and at the same time understand their chronological development. Having referred the reader to this work, we shall here simply make a few remarks about the relationship between the caste system and renunciation.[92a]

It has been objected that the renouncer leaves his place in society, he symbolically dies to the world; this much is granted. But he lives from alms, and he preaches to the man-in-the-world. *Ergo* he does not in fact escape complementarity, he does not *really* leave society; consequently, how can he develop an independent way of thinking, an individualistic way of thinking? The answer is simple: that this occurs must simply be stated as a fact, even if it means that in this case what agents imagine is more important than what the outside observer describes as really happening, that ideas are more important than behaviour. Moreover, the objection rests on a misunderstanding: to leave society is to renounce the existing role which one is given by society (as member of such-and-such a caste, father of a family, etc.) and to adopt a universal role which has no equivalent in the society; it does not involve ceasing to have any actual relationship with its members. Naturally enough, from the point of view of the sociologist the renouncer is *in* the society in the sense that society shapes his relationships as well as the others'; but the renouncer is a man who leaves his social role in order to adopt a role that is both universal and personal; this is the crucial fact, both from the subjective and the objective point of view.

Now, if we bring together the society on the one hand and the renouncer on the other, we have a whole containing an equilibrium between quite different things: on the one hand a world of strict interdependence, in which the individual is ignored, and, on the other hand, an institution which puts an end to interdependence and inaugurates the individual. In the last analysis, the overall system does not neglect the individual, as the description of the caste system alone would lead one to believe. It may be doubted whether the caste system could have existed and endured independently of its contradictory, renunciation. The point is important for comparison with the West: we are not dealing with a solid opposition, as if in the one case there was nothing but the individual, in the other nothing but collective man. For India has both, distributed in a particular way. Then we have only to discover man as a collective being in Western society, which is not so difficult, in order to formulate the comparison not as an opposition between A and B but as a *difference in the distribution and emphasis of the parts of* (A + B).

One can perceive the complementarity between caste society and the renouncer by referring back to their historical origin. Vedic society may be called relatively individualistic by comparison with caste society. At the end of the Vedic period, in the Upanishads, one can see the development of philosophical speculation bearing first and foremost on the universal being. This speculation emanates from some Brahmans and Kshatriyas who withdrew in order to devote themselves to it. From this point the historical transition can be represented schematically as a twofold movement: on the one hand society, under the aegis of the Brahmans, was to become more and more settled into categories of strict interdependence, having the pure and the impure as their axis; on the other hand the individualistic philosopher of the previous age was to become the renouncer, Hindu or heterodox.

For certain anthropologists, this is all a matter of 'culture' rather than society. Now the distinction we have introduced enables us to avoid gross errors, and great difficulties, in understanding the contemporary Hindu; furthermore, we are still only beginning to discern how the values of caste suffer relativization under the influence of the sects led by renouncers since long ago. In writing recently: 'The order of the castes is respected even if it seems a profane matter in the light of sectarian truth', I was thinking quite specifically of the assertions of a villager of Uttar Pradesh. In this book I have insisted on the religious nature and texture of conceptions of caste, and this was above all necessary *for us*, to enable us to understand them while starting from our own very different social concepts. Having done this, it should then be indispensable to show how, to what extent and in what forms, these concepts have in India itself lost their absolute, religious character, in which lay their origin and their coherence, have been depreciated by the blossoming of superior religious forms – superior from the Indian point of view – even while the caste system remained in force, becoming more rigid and partitioned as the form of organization of life in the world. Unfortunately, this *relativization* of the fundamental caste values by the action of disciplines of salvation offering a religion for the individual is still difficult to grasp precisely in the present state of studies; we shall touch on it in connection only with sects in the following section, and later to the extent to which other religions act in the manner of the sects (104 ff.).

It is far from possible to consider renunciation as a 'purely cultural' institution, for it has produced a type of social group of the greatest importance: the sect. The sect has all the characteristics of that prominent subject of Anglo-Saxon anthropology, the 'corporate group', characterized by having rights over things and a chief. We have already come across the sect or its representatives, and it is high time to shed some light on its nature.

93 *The sect and its relation to the caste system: example of the* Lingāyat

I have briefly indicated elsewhere the interaction between renunciation and wordly Hinduism in the field of religious forms (See Appendix B, §2 ff.). One may observe an analogous phenomenon, so far as social groups are concerned, between sect and caste. Indian religious groupings which are readily characterized in terms of renunciation are conveniently called 'sects', without prejudging their similarity to what are called by this name in Christianity. The Indian sect is a religious grouping constituted primarily by renouncers, initiates of the same discipline of salvation, and secondarily by their lay sympathizers any of whom may have one of the renouncers as a spiritual master or guru. Taking the word in its widest sense, one may include Buddhism and Jainism among the sects. In theory, for the man-in-the-world adherence to a sect is an individual matter, superimposed on caste observances, though not obliterating them, and the sect respects these observances even though it relativizes them and criticizes worldly religion from the point of view of individualistic religion. Moreover, the sect, springing from renunciation, has the power to recruit irrespective of caste.

One can see that in theory caste membership and sect membership operate at different levels. The two could conflict only if the sect made itself exclusive not only *vis-à-vis* other sects, but also *vis-à-vis* caste values, and forced its members-in-the-world to despise these values. It will be understood that such an attitude is contrary to the spirit of the whole; if by chance this attitude did arise it left a mark only in exceptional cases (but see below). Much more noticeable is in the first place a tendency for sect to come to resemble caste: only suppose that adherence to a sect is handed down from father to son, and the possibility arises within the caste group of a division corresponding to the sect, whether the sect is the ground, or perhaps simply the sign, of the division. The two sections may appear as subcastes, and they do not always forbid intermarriage between one another, as is shown in Gujerat in the case of some merchant castes, part 'Hindu', part Jain.[93a] Sectarian adherence may, in the same way as profession, serve to differentiate a particular caste. In all this, sect only adds a criterion for or ground of distinction to those already known to the caste; it is not a case of 'sectarian castes' proper.

It also happens that the sect degenerates into a caste. Let us suppose that a group of renouncers perpetuates itself, by admitting women and conjugal unions, and by recognizing as its own its members' children: here we have a group which resembles a new caste except that it admits recruitment from outside. Let this cease and it is a genuine caste. The characteristic of a sectarian caste of this sort is that the children are initiated as members of the sect; at least a rudiment of the discipline of salvation becomes hereditary in this way. Such castes are known in Northern India, for example the Sadhs of Uttar Pradesh. In other cases, a sectarian caste may recruit within itself celibate renouncers (Gosains of U.P.),[93b] and even perhaps priests at an intermediate level, priests who will replace Brahmans in the service of the caste and may be of other castes of the same obedience, or again they may be in charge of certain temples. Thus one can conceive, in the limiting case, the possibility of a whole small localized system of castes in which the sect has replaced Brahmanism. There exists at least one system of this kind which is relatively well known, and we shall take it as an example.

The *Viraśaiva*, 'heroic Shaivites', also called *Lingāyat* for carrying on them a small linga, emblem of Shiva, are a sect whose social development is particularly rich and distinctive. They are mostly concentrated in the present State of Mysore, and in its northern districts (Dharwar) they constitute a considerable part of the population. From the social point of view, this is a case of a sort of distinct caste system, but for one important exception: the sect here becomes the equivalent of a huge reference group: one is in the region a Lingayat *or* a Hindu.[93c]

Three main social levels can be distinguished: (1) the superior level comprising two 'castes', the *jangama* or priests and certain merchants called *banjiga*, who admit hypergamous relations among themselves (the priests can take a wife from among the merchants without reciprocity);[93d] (2) the intermediate level comprising some seventy professional 'castes' all endogamous; these two levels taken together include all the Lingayats in the strict sense, characterized by wearing the linga and strict vegetarianism; (3) finally the inferior level corresponding to the impure or untouchable castes of Hinduism; these groups are not vegetarians, and, nowadays in any case, they are not counted as Lingayat in the strict sense although Lingayat priests officiate for them (but refuse to share their food, while they do so in the case of Lingayats proper; one sees that the Hindu rules of commensality are contradicted to a large extent).

Two sorts of religious functionaries are recruited within the Jangama 'caste'. First, the Jangamas in the strict sense, priests who officiate for the members of the sect as the Brahmans do for the Hindus.[93e] They live in 'maths' or monasteries – each village has its own – and are each attached to one of the five great maths which correspond to the five legendary masters of the sect. These priests are also the 'gurus' or spiritual masters of the lay members, who are thus indirectly linked to the five monasteries. Many of these features – monasteries, function of guru – are reminiscent of renunciation, but the sect also has renouncers proper, the *virakta*, 'those detached from passions', who have their own monasteries, and whose main business, as much in their personal life as in their propaganda for the laics,[93f] is the practice and development of *bhakti*, devout love of the deity. In accordance with bhakti, the philosophy of the sect is a form of qualified monism: at the highest point in his ascent, the believer attains close union with his Lord, not a blurred fusion with the divine.

Bhandarkar has stressed the parallelism between this organization and the Brahmanical organization, and between the ritual of the Virashaivas and that of the orthodox Brahmans (*Smārta*). What seems most characteristic is the proliferation of *rites de passage*: initiation into the sect (a kind of 'baptism'), choice of a guru, entry into the priesthood.[93g] Just as clear, and more basic, is the aspect of renunciation on which Farquhar has insisted. According to him this aspect is of Jain influence, the sect having originally been – in the twelfth century or a little earlier – a Shaivite movement of reconquest directed against Jainism. This would account for the vegetarianism, which is found at least nowadays.

Worship is by everyone individually, and is addressed to Shiva alone but under two aspects: in the form of the miniature linga which everyone carries on his person, and in the form of the guru or the priest who is called 'Jangama', i.e. 'walking' linga. The sect presents other noteworthy features. In the first place impurity, even the impurity which we have called immediate or personal, such as is occasioned by death, etc., is denied, and the equality of all men proclaimed. 'Where the linga is found, they say, there also is found the throne of the deity', says the Abbé Dubois. Thus people have been led to suppose (Enthoven among others) that the movement was originally directed against caste. Now the origins of the sect, from its own texts and inscriptions, are still not firmly established, and in the present state of knowledge the surmise is futile. Indeed, the denial of impurity and social hierarchy is quite natural for the renouncer because he transcends the social world. Therefore it is enough to suppose that the renouncers taught the men-in-the-world their own truth as the absolute truth, without having intended to do away with the other aspects of caste, being content to degrade it in this way from a religious fact to a purely social fact.[93h] The movement would then have settled down into a kind of reformed Brahmanism thanks to its success in the region (adherence of members of different castes) and thanks to the pressure of the surrounding Hinduism.

The disappearance of the notion of impurity, which we have taken as the ideological basis of the castes, and the presence of groups strongly resembling castes, raises a serious problem for the approach we have chosen. Roughly speaking, either we cannot speak of castes in connection with the Lingayat groups, or else we must discover what features replace impurity in this case in the function we have assigned it. We can in the first place note the fact of the predominant Hindu environment, which we shall encounter again when dealing with Muslims and Christians (§§102–4). Hinduism and Virashaivism are closely mingled, their adherents often live together in the same village, often nowadays as rivals, and share the services of the same specialists. But there is another aspect. One can observe that the small and more or less incomplete caste system formed by the Lingayats is grouped under the aegis of the sect and in virtue of this depends closely on renunciation, either directly or through the medium of the sect's own priests. This is a special feature, as this is not so in Hindu castes. It may be wondered whether this complementarity between caste and renunciation does not in some manner replace the complementarity of the pure and the impure. In other words, only the presence of renouncers dedicated to bhakti and, beneath them, of priests sharing the doctrine and the dignity of the renouncers, can preserve the Lingayats from impurity; at the same time, it tends to maintain the division into castes, this being in fact part of the definition of the Jangama priests.[931]

## 94 *Tolerance and imitation*

People have often noted what has been called the tolerance of Indians or Hindus. It is easy to see what this feature corresponds to in social life. Many castes, who may differ in their customs and habits, live side by side, agreed on the code which ranks them and separates them. They will assign a rank, where we in the West would approve or exclude. It may be supposed that the more loosely society is integrated, the greater is the permitted variation, but what happens here is more radical. In the hierarchical scheme a group's acknowledged differentness whereby it is contrasted with other groups becomes the very principle whereby it is integrated into society. If you eat beef, you must accept being classed among the Untouchables, and on this condition your practice will be tolerated. It would only create a scandal were you to insist on your practice being recognized as indifferent, or on coming into physical contact with vegetarians. More than an orthodoxy, Hinduism is an 'orthopraxy' (Staal). This feature is important in relations with renouncers, their 'disciplines of salvation' and their sects.[94a]

Caste hierarchy entails another feature which is connected with tolerance thus defined. No doubt the tendency to imitate, and in particular to imitate superiors, is encountered more or less everywhere. But in India it is carried to an extreme that is probably unique. In contemporary works it is often spoken of as 'Sanskritization', that is, imitation of the Brahmans, adoption of features which are Brahmanical or associated with the Brahmans. Everything has been said both for and against this linguistic term. Its vogue is no doubt due to the fact that it connotes both the strength of the tendency to imitate and also the main direction of the tendency. Among other drawbacks it takes the place of explanation and isolates imitation of the first *varṇa* from imitation of the second, or imitation of the prestigious foreigner (nowadays 'Westernization'), both of which are also present. Finally, the term does not tell us exactly in what imitation consists, nor how it is that all Hindus are not completely 'Sanskritized' if the tendency has been at work for millenia.[94b]

We shall encounter the phenomenon again a little later in connection with its diachronic consequences. What is borrowed is more a social sign than a feature which would be relevant to religion, craftsmanship, or whatever. This is why we shall speak in this case of *extrinsic* borrowing. The borrowing assigns a meaning to the element borrowed, and usually the original functional feature does not disappear: the new (prestigious) one is superimposed on it. As there is in general structural homogeneity between the popular level and the scholarly level, borrowing from the latter only adds a duplicate case. Moreover, there are two main poles of imitation: not only the Brahman but also the king,[94c] and this accounts both for the imitation of foreigners if they are dominant in secular matters, and for the fact that, with or without the help of prohibitions and adverse factors, Sanskritization remains to be accomplished in many fields. It must have intensified in the Muslim period and, on a par with Westernization, in modern times: while the upper strata become modern, the lower strata tend to become 'Sanskritized'.[94d]

## 95 *Diachronic implications: aggregation*

If any aspect of the social or cultural history of India is considered over a sufficiently long period, the same phenomenon will always be encountered: the number of categories, groups, or elements increases by successive aggregations or accretions. This fact should be linked with tolerance and imitation, and more generally with hierarchy and complementarity: one ranks rather than excludes, and complementarity permits both the loosest and broadest integration of extraneous elements. In fact the process takes various forms, which must be distinguished. But all tend to ensure a certain permanence of form by integration of the extraneous element.

So far as social groups are concerned, we have already encountered the case of (serving) castes, apparently formed of heterogeneous groups which have become subcastes (Karvé). Further, there are two main avenues whereby a foreign group could enter a territorial set of castes. One is at the level of the Untouchable: even nowadays one can observe groups who are in the process of transition from tribe to untouchable caste; it is only inaccurate to say that this occurs without modification of the customs and beliefs of such a group,[95a] because, while it may preserve most of its own features, it is clear at the same time that as a whole it is greatly affected by the acceptance of heteronomy quite apart from the borrowings which occur under these conditions. The other possible avenue into a caste system is at the level of dominance: force enables large or small kingdoms to be conquered, and people often speak of the conversion of the invaders.[95b] Directly or indirectly, the same used to be the case for the village. In short the result was a superior right over the land, which forced former rights into an inferior position. This is one of the causes of the piling up of rights over the land, rights which the cultivator had to satisfy.

For the large social categories, the historical process is readily summarized: the three functions of Indo-European times give way to the four varnas of the Vedic period, probably by aggregation in the fourth position of some of the aborigines. The Untouchables then formed a fifth category, for a long time not recognized in theory (*cf.* §32). Finally, with the partial social integration of the Untouchables achieved nowadays by the Gandhist reforms which give them the right to enter Hindu temples ('Temple Entry Acts'), there appeared a sixth category. In effect the non-Hindus, Christians, Muslims, etc., who were until then merged with the Untouchables, are now distinct from them in that they remain excluded from the temples.

From the point of view of culture, imitation, or rather extrinsic borrowing, that is borrowing from superiors of certain features as social signs and not as functional features, gives rise in the simplest cases to a superimposition of features; examples have been given of this. But if intellectual phenomena are in question, this extrinsic borrowing certainly entails some intrinsic modification.[95c] Thus in the nineteenth century, Neo-Hinduism was born as a response on the part of intellectuals to the social and political challenge of the West. In fact, while wanting to save Hinduism, something quite different was created; whilst appearances are preserved there is a profound misunderstanding regarding both the living religion of the people and Western values themselves. In a word, Hinduism was not touched; all that happened was that new sects were created.[95d] There is every reason to think that the Brahmans long ago reacted in a similar way to the 'heresies' of Jainism and Buddhism. Vegetarianism was functional in these sects and their renouncers enjoyed great prestige. The Brahmans, threatened with being outclassed as spiritual leaders, were goaded into emulation, and borrowed vegetarianism; it is even likely that the rivalry between renouncers and Brahmans by itself intensified the practice of vegetarianism. The fact remains that the vegetarian diet became a fundamental Brahmanical feature.[95e] No doubt this is not a case of merely extrinsic borrowing, since the horror of meat is in harmony with ideas about impurity. Yet we have given reasons for thinking that this supposed borrowing is primarily an episode in the process of Hinduism's reabsorption of 'heresies'. Now this is the very type of Indian historical process which is recognized from outside as 'stagnation'. There was stagnation in this sense because the intrinsic was made subordinate to the extrinsic, that is to say, in the last analysis, on account of the presence of hierarchy in its pure form. If this view is correct, it teaches us something fundamental, namely that hierarchy in actual fact culminated in its contrary, the renouncer!

## 96  *Stability and change*

One must note briefly a strict implication of the system which is of the greatest importance. This is its relationship to time. Traditional society in general is seen as stable, it eliminates 'lived' time by means of the myth, which transfers 'lived' reality to the plane of the eternity of thought, and also by means of *rites de passage*, which regulate the flow of time into a series of stable states, like stretches of water connected by ritual lock-gates.[96a] The myths refer to the time of the origins of everything, which is properly the absence of time, and, compared with the atemporal model, nothing occurs in time except degeneration.

This property of traditional societies is at a maximum in this case, where it is extravagantly expressed: the four ages (*yuga*) mark the progressive degeneration of the world, and the present age, the *Kali* age, is separated by three successive transitions from the divine age. The notion of *kalivarjya* or 'prohibition in the Kali age' is used in the treatises to explain the discontinuance of customs recorded in the ancient texts, that is, the extent of the departure from the Veda.[96b] Thus for the traditional Hindu mentality, nothing changes so far as values are concerned. Perhaps everything changes, but only by departing from the models and hence losing significance.

The indifference to time, to happening, to history, in Indian literature and civilization in general, makes the historian's task very hard and probably places a premium on the sociological perspective even for the study of Indian history. But under these conditions, is there a history of India in a sense comparable to that in which there is a history of Christian civilization, or even of China? One can see the extent of the questions raised by the feature with which we are concerned. We shall not expand here on this point, which has been discussed elsewhere. I wrote recently: 'If history is the movement whereby a society reveals itself for what it is, there are in a sense as many qualitatively different histories as there are societies (or: types of society).' In fact, the search for fundamental constants in Indian civilization – renunciation, specific place of royalty, hierarchy with its implications mentioned here – yields correspondingly a certain idea, a certain form, of historical development.[96c]

I must be content to draw attention to a single aspect of the matter. In traditional India, significance is attached exclusively to the immutable model of the society and the truth, the model of the *dharma*; as a result everything else, devoid of sense, can change at will. The temporal is indeed subordinated to the spiritual and enclosed in it. But the king is not submitted to the priest, artha to dharma, except in the relevant respect. Hence anything may happen on what we call the political plane, either in contradiction to the dharma or, more importantly, while the dharma is sufficiently respected. Not the slightest value or intellectual interest is attached for example to the stability of dynasties: there is nothing in the texts on this point. If someone stronger imposes his rule by doubtful methods, one can imagine that if he lavishly endows the Brahmans and 'toes the line' he will not lack henchmen. This indifference is, at bottom, due to the fact that artha is held in check by dharma as by a yoke immune to corruption: no risk of contamination. From the present point of view, the history of India rests on this tacit agreement, this complicity, between force – whether exerted by a Kshatriya or someone else – and the priests. It is largely here that the long, edifying discourses of the Epics take on their full sense: this pact had to be stamped upon the 'royalty', a pact disastrous for their possible ambitions.

In short, in virtue of the encompassing of the *Kṣatra* in the *Brahman*, and of the devaluation of *artha* in relation to *dharma*, India was condemned to political instability. This must be remembered when India is seen to lay itself wide open to modern political ideas. It is tempting to generalize: is not the stability of a society the stability of its values, modification being possible only outside this sphere? It will rightly be objected that the hypothesis thus expressed is not easy to verify, and above all that the great problems are that of changes in values and that of change as a value. Nevertheless there must be a relation between the stability of the norms and the course of events, between what is thought and what happens.

## 97 *Group kinetics: scission, aggregation, social mobility*

Corresponding to the synchronic structural aspect of the morphology there is a diachronic aspect and this can in part be deduced from the former. We have touched on it by the way, but, at the risk of repetition, it is worth collecting together those scattered notes. We saw in Chapter II and afterwards that different characteristics are linked to groups of different levels. Thus, whilst status is mainly attributed from outside, say to an entire professional caste in a given area, it is a segment of this caste, say the actual territorial section of a subcaste, which is the unit of endogamy and which meets in assembly. The corresponding diachronic aspect may be foreseen: not only will there be a twofold tendency to scission and (to fusion or rather) to aggregation of groups, but even scission and aggregation will operate at different levels. Only, one must beware that when we pass to the diachronic aspect, we pass from pure structure to something more complex, namely the whole formed partly by structural properties and partly by the empirical concomitants present in every actual situation. Further, by comparison with our modern societies, one has been led to discuss the mobility of groups if not of individuals along the supposedly linear order of castes, and there is good reason to consider things from this point of view as well.

Bouglé postulated a reciprocal 'repulsion' whereby groups would be separated from each other like particles charged with electricity of the same sign, and would probably explain their fissiparity in this way. In reality, we have seen that separation seems to be to a large extent implied by a high degree of hierarchy: it is because each is jealous of his status that he protects himself from ill-advised contacts and marriages. The intensity of the hierarchical field acting on the castes would lead one to suppose that the endogamous group would have a strong tendency to separate by scission. Indeed it ought to split whenever a danger to its status appears within it, and excommunication constitutes a limiting case where the danger is great and is concentrated in one person or a few people. It could be the same should a progressive part of the group think it could gain status by breaking its ties with another more conservative part. But as the status which is recognized overall relates to the whole caste, it is not enough for a group to make itself into a distinct subcaste; it must do more and become another caste, either by forming a new caste or by joining up with an existing one. For this, there must be places available in the system, either on the spot or, traditionally, not far away. Now the positions in the system which provide a livelihood are traditionally of two sorts: professional specializations and agricultural occupations. More precisely, one can either become dominant (by force, we have seen that this was the most important form of social mobility), or else find a position, agricultural or specialized, near the dominants. Let us note again, still at the empirical level, that only dominance (or to a lesser extent a close enough relation to dominance) permits the deployment of all the liberality and display necessary for the coveted status to be effectively recognized. It has not been recognized that the system of groups is bifurcated towards the top and that its codified branch (status) is necessarily less open to change than its non-codified branch (dominance); the result is that the importance of Brahmanization or 'Sanskritization' of customs for the sake of social climbing has probably been much exaggerated in recent years. On the one hand, anthropologists have had modern facts in mind – we shall return to these in the last chapter – and not traditional facts; on the other hand and above all, they have often lost sight of the fact that to claim a status is one thing, and for it to be recognized is another. The example of status ranking taken from Mayer (§36) showed us that puritanical exaggeration alone did not in this case counterbalance dominance. Hence let us repeat once more: it was among the dominants, prepared to use force and obliged to procure themselves a clientele, that mobility was very probably at its greatest in the traditional system. Dominance over a large territory could even open the gate to the Kshatriya varna. Moreover, there are cases throughout India of castes associated with power and the army, who practise theft and brigandage when circumstances demand, and this confirms that brute force is all-powerful at the level of naked fact.

At the level of the endogamous group, scission is the most important, and fusion proper is probably rare. (But among low castes there may be aggregation of people excluded from high castes.)[97a] Blunt catalogued fissions on the basis of his records for U.P. His information must be treated with care. Where there are distinct subcastes, one must if possible differentiate between the sign of this distinction, its rationalization, on the one hand, and, on the other, its substance and the ground of a more or less recent scission which may have created it. So one must distinguish between legends about prestigious origins – a frequent stereotype among low castes which is in keeping with the idea of the progressive degeneration of everything – and those facts which are close to the observer (hence modern) and well attested. Thus there is no reason to see a change of residence behind all the territorial names of subcastes. By contrast, many of the scissions of subcastes attributed by Blunt to a change of occupation or to the Brahmanization of customs (ban on remarriage of widows and adoption of a vegetarian diet) seem genuine. Scission due to interruption of intermarriage with bastard lineages, which Blunt delicately calls a change connected with impurity, is as likely to be a fact as a convenient rationalization.[97b] Scissions are also said to be due to 'increased prosperity', to disagreements, and to a sectarian difference or the partial conversion of the group to another religion. In this last case, it must be established that it was not on the contrary a case of different groups becoming joined by aggregation to the same caste (below). In general, the constitution of a new subcaste by scission is already a movement, within the caste, in the sense that the result is to modify the status, in one direction or the other, of the members of one of the subcastes which result from the scission. Let us stress that the moving principle of scission is a hierarchical one: in every case, this is not a simple hypothetical 'repulsion' which divides a subcaste into two; in the case of profession for example, scission occurs only if the new profession entails a notable change of status as compared with the old one, in one direction or the other. One must still beware of conceiving all this as occurring automatically: circumstances are probably a determining factor in most cases.

Scission can go further, and be completed by fusion. A change of occupation, especially in a case where this entails a fall in status, can lead to the appearance of a new caste (but here again, beware or rationalizations!). Still according to Blunt, a subcaste which has broken from its caste may be affiliated to an existing caste: 'Such was probably the method by which functional castes were formed.' Likewise Nesfield attributed professional castes to the coming together of distinct groups, and quite recently Mrs Karvé has strongly insisted on this.[97c] She has brought new facts to bear, showing that different populations have come together within one of the positions in the system of groups. Thus the caste of potters in Maharashtra is made up of subcastes each of which is established in a more or less exclusive territory; they have different origins and, according to this author, have nothing in common other than the common status, which society attributes to them, of potter – which, contrary to this author, is a far from negligible point. One must thus give fusion a place at the level of the caste, like scission at the level of the subcaste (or rather of the theoretical or real unit of endogamy). Muslim domination, and then British domination, have probably altered certain aspects of social mobility, and it is best to defer to the following chapter the discussion of truly modern facts.

CHAPTER TEN

# COMPARISON: ARE THERE CASTES AMONG NON-HINDUS AND OUTSIDE INDIA?

## 101  *Introduction*

There remains the task of comparison, to which this and the following chapter are devoted. First and foremost, it is our turn to answer the question: Are there castes outside India? People often speak of castes in Japan or Madagascar, and sometimes even in the United States. Compared with these very broad uses of the term, ours, at least up to now, may seem very narrow. We have tried to understand the inner connections of the specifically Indian form in which ideas and values, social groups and social facts, are bound together in a structural whole. But it may be objected that if we insist on speaking of caste only in the presence of this configuration, we make it impossible to use the term for the classification of social groups. Some would even say that we are confining ourselves to Indology and making comparison impossible. To this it may be replied that there is no absolute need for purposes of classification to use a concrete term like 'caste', and that abstract terms or neologisms should be used as paradigms rather than impoverish the content of the term 'caste' by extending its use in an arbitrary manner. But there is more: we have, after all, linked caste to Hindu beliefs about the pure and the impure. If it was confirmed that elsewhere there existed groups in other respects similar, but lacking this link with religious beliefs, then should not these beliefs be considered purely accidental? Even within properly Indian religions, we have already encountered the case of a sect like the Lingayat, who do not recognize impurity but who are divided into groups that must indeed be called castes.

201

We believed we could explain this, but what should be said about the Muslims and the Christians? If they have castes, as is usually admitted, without adhering to the corresponding Hindu ideas, does not their case demonstrate, in India itself, that the link between the two aspects among the Hindus is fortuitous?

We shall begin by examining this question, before turning to the more general problem of comparison outside India. This will consist only of bringing certain issues into focus from a theoretical point of view: we shall use the foregoing study to bring out those characteristics of the system which are basic to comparison, and we shall contrast this with current ideas of 'social stratification'. This will pave the way for summarily setting in perspective the apparently similar facts found outside India.

## 102  Christians and caste

Compared with the Muslims, Christians are less numerous and the Christian population is to a lesser extent distinguished into different groups and dispersed through the actual social ladder. Incidentally, we are much less well-informed than we would wish. The first question that arises, and which is far from easy, is the place accorded to Christians by the Hindu majority in Indian society. We shall take first the case of the European, and then the case of Indian converts.

The case of the European brings a paradox to the surface. Even though it is common knowledge that he indulges in beef and alcohol, as was very likely the case with British civil servants, he is not nowadays treated purely and simply as an Untouchable. Why? There are strong reasons for thinking that this is because Hindus have become used to showing submission and deference to British power, as previously to Muslim power. A letter from a missionary notes how much easier was the situation of the missionaries in the Tamil country in the nineteenth century than that of their predecessors in the period prior to the establishment of British domination. They 'enjoy great liberty in their way of life, food and clothing'. These advantages had their counterpart: governments were the object both of a 'hypocritical and forced respect' and of an 'inner and real contempt', and these attitudes were not welcome to the missionaries.[102a]

The case of converts seems slightly different, for one can assume that they spontaneously refrain from adopting a way of life which would upset the Hindus of their caste. To the extent that adherence to Christianity presents itself as adherence to a sect involving certain dogmas but respecting social customs, it does not necessarily entail tension. It is only when there are customs which the Christian no longer accepts, or in virtue of the fact that his frequentations no longer respect the Hindu limits, or perhaps in virtue of the fact of a decree by the responsible authority of the caste, that converts may be excluded from the connubium or even excommunicated. After what has been said previously, one would expect differences between social levels: the situation should be serious for a Brahman, indifferent for an Untouchable. Ill-informed as one is, one can yet see a great variety in the reactions of Hindus. It may also be assumed that the indirect association with power which results from adherence to a religion imported by Europeans, and still represented by them, was, in certain situations, able to counterbalance the negative aspects of conversion. Moreover, converts are especially numerous among inferior castes, and this may explain why conversion has not always occasioned the scission of the endogamous group, even though this may have been the usual case.[102b] It is beyond doubt that the Untouchables, in accepting conversion, were often responding to the appeal of an egalitarian religion preached by the powerful; but in actual fact their social situation was not improved by it, either in the Hindu milieu, nor even, as we shall see, in the Christian milieu.[102c]

The case of Kerala, where the Christians constitute a considerable part of the population, would be a good example of their internal subdivision into groups strongly resembling castes, but we have scarcely anything save generalities on this topic. The Syrian Christians, whose legendary origin goes back to Thomas, Christ's disciple, are divided, as a result of colonial history, into several persuasions which, while authorizing commensality with each other, are mostly endogamous. Even the Catholics, of more recent origin, are divided into four distinct groups or castes. Christians originating from the Untouchables seem to have their own churches.[102d]

To bring home the strength with which the caste system has operated in the Christian setting, I shall summarize a relatively well-known case, that of the Catholic missions in the Tamil country, mainly that of Madura.[102e] This is an extreme case in that the region is especially strict so far as caste is concerned. The effect of caste was to impose unexpected social divisions on the missionaries. These divisions naturally resulted at first from the Hindu milieu itself, as soon as the missionaries tried to gain converts at various levels in the caste hierarchy, but later persisted within the local Christian communities once they were formed.

Robert de Nobili settled at Madura in the beginning of the seventeenth century. He adopted Indian customs, made himself out to be a renouncer of noble birth, and dissociated himself completely from the Portuguese and the Fathers who administered the coastal fishing communities, the Paravar or 'Paravas' converted by St Francis Xavier. He sought in this way to escape the opprobrium in which the high caste Hindus held his colleagues on account of their customs and frequentations. He succeeded in getting initiated into the Hindu texts, in arousing curiosity and interest, and in converting Nayakkars – people of the king's caste – and Brahmans.[102f] From this time forth, missionaries were divided into two categories: 'missionary-Brahmans' or '-Sannyasis' who lived like members of superior castes and were active among them, and 'missionary-Pandarams' who worked among the Shudras and the Untouchables.[102g] Some notion of complementarity between these two categories is perceptible in the missionaries' letters: the presence of 'superior' colleagues is useful for the work of 'inferior' missionaries.[102h] But in the case of the latter the division between Shudras and Untouchables asserted itself: missionaries could remain in contact with the former only on condition that they did not go into the houses of the Parias. The separation between the two categories made itself felt in worship, the Parias being present at the same service, but keeping to a distinct building.[102i] Although Rome, at least at first, was disposed to approve adaptation or accommodation to the social customs of higher civilizations (apart from superstition and idolatry), she did not fail to be particularly sensitive to this discrimination between Christians in the holy place itself. Not without difficulty, it became possible to shelter them under one roof in distinct parts of the church, either by means of a wall or at least a separating barrier.[102j] Missionaries were under an obligation to visit the houses of the Parias, especially for giving them the last sacraments (decree of the Legate, 1704), and this gave rise to great difficulties, the missionaries asserting that this measure would lead to the desertion of the Shudras. It was finally resolved to have, in addition to the 'Pandarams' (the missionaries called Brahmans or Sannyasis had by then disappeared), special missionaries for the Parias; but it was quickly realized that this led to a dichotomy in the sacerdotal hierarchy itself and amounted to giving in to caste spirit. It was therefore necessary to revert to the original policy and, at the cost of a difficult struggle, to force the Shudras once again into the minimum of Christian fraternity.[102k]

In conclusion, we see in this case that the great separations of the caste system survived conversion. This is the same, naturally, for many customs. For example, the practice of bathing after funerals, although attacked by the Church, shows at least a fragmentary survival of the feeling of impurity. Adherence to a monotheistic and egalitarian religion is not enough, even after several generations, to lead to the disappearance of the fundamental attitudes on which the caste system is based. There is all the less cause for surprise if one realizes how slow transformations of this kind are, and also that Christians are generally in the minority in a Hindu environment. In short, this shows the vitality of caste attitudes: they have survived a partial change in the set of beliefs, and an imported religious belief, whose ideological implications remain little developed, has been impotent against them.[102l]

## 103 Caste among the Muslims

Like Christianity, Islam is a monotheistic religion and infused with egalitarianism. While the case of the Muslims is thus similar in principle to that of the Christians, it differs from it by the duration, character, and importance of the impact of Islam on India – especially in the north – and even by the number of its followers: Muslims are not an infinitesimal minority, but a massive minority, and were so especially before the political division between India and Pakistan. We are not as well-informed as we would wish on the relations between the Muslims and the caste system. But the important political events which have affected the two communities this century provide a frame of reference in which to set the questions that particularly interest us here. In another study I allowed that the increasing alteration in the relations between the two communities in the nineteenth and twentieth centuries was deeply rooted in two facts: the social heterogeneity of the two communities, and the effect on their relations of the fall of Muslim political power.[103a] It is in short a question of two societies which were strangers to one another in virtue of the opposition of their values, although living cheek by jowl in fact, their association resting on a sort of tacit and reciprocal compromise. For their part the Hindus had to adjust themselves for long periods and over huge regions to political masters who did not recognize Brahmanic values, and they did not treat even the most humble Muslim villagers as Untouchables. In fact the Muslims occupied a superior position in society than that which would have resulted from the application of Hindu values alone. Why was this, unless because these values were counterbalanced by a factor of quite a different nature, I mean force, illegitimate from the Hindu point of view, but organized? On their side, the Muslims had made and went on making concessions to co-existence, in a way which no doubt varied according to environment and period, but which was no less genuine.[103b] This co-existence has certainly had a profound effect on the two communities: it is very likely that the loss of political power by the Hindus contributed to a shift in the equilibrium of religion and politics amongst them, and thus probably altered Hinduism to a notable degree.[103c] In the opposite camp, the influence of caste certainly made itself felt among the Muslims, as we shall see. At first sight one might see in this an aspect of the cultural osmosis between the two societies. But, if it is true that ultimate values were not affected, which is shown by the political movement, this would still be an inadequate view: the society was certainly affected on both sides, but at a lower level than that of its overall identity and of the values on which the latter is based. The case is thus of great sociological interest, and one would like to know more about it.

For a start it is not surprising to find little information, even in anthropological works, on the place which the Hindus made for the Muslims in their social hierarchy: theories are here deficient in the face of brute facts.[103d] Muslims were and are divided into a large number of groups of graded status, which from this point of view represent a kind of replica of the Hindu system. On this point, we shall summarize briefly what is provided by the literature, confining our attention to the State of Uttar Pradesh as it was before the population shifts which followed the partition of the sub-continent.[103e] Muslims are divided first of all into two categories: the Ashraf or nobles, supposedly the descendants of immigrants, and divided into four kinds; and the common people, whose Indian origin is acknowledged, and who are distributed into a large number of groups which are very similar to castes (respectively 2·5 and more than 4 millions in 1911). The Ashraf belong to four 'tribes' or rather 'groups of tribes supposedly of the same blood' (Blunt). The first two of these, in theory of Arab origin, have honorific names: Saiyad and Shaikh, while the following two have ethnic names: Pathan (that is, roughly, Afghans) and Mughul. The first represent a slow immigration, in small groups, of religious people, corresponding more or less to the literate Brahmans; the Saiyids are the descendants of the daughter of the prophet, Fatima, and Ali, but the Shaikhs are very numerous compared to the Saiyids (1,300,000 against 250,000 in 1911) and it is admitted that their ranks have been swollen by influx from other categories. Mughuls and Pathans (60,000 and 960,000) correspond rather to the Hindu Kshatriyas, and at the very time of the census the number of Pathans was perceptibly swelling by many converted Rajputs declaring themselves such. It can be seen that these categories are not entirely closed, yet one should distinguish between the assertions of the people concerned and the opinion of them held by those groups to which they claim to belong. Among the Ashraf there is no (absolute) endogamous grouping in the sense which we have given the term. There is however a marked preference for marriage within a very small group, the biādharī (translated 'marriage circle'; it is known that a Muslim may marry even his first cousin in the paternal line, his father's brother's daughter); beyond this five levels of status are distinguished; beyond this again marriage is not impossible, which would contradict the religious law, but it is sanctioned by a fall of status, and in this case it is generally the wife who is of inferior status. It can be seen that whilst there is some social mobility, the principle of the superiority of unions which preserve status is nevertheless present. In short, the Ashraf are contaminated by caste spirit although they have not completely succumbed to it. Commensality is liberal among the Ashraf. Roughly speaking, whilst there are differences of custom among the Muslims, prohibition of commensality never appears except between Muslims and Hindus or between Muslims whose status is widely different (Ashraf and non-Ashraf).

Among the non-Ashraf, three levels of status can be distinguished: (1) the converts of superior caste, who are mainly Rajputs – except for those who have been admitted into the Ashraf; (2) a large number of professional groups corresponding to the artisan castes of the Hindus, the most numerous being the *Julāhā*, theoretically weavers; (3) converted Untouchables who have preserved their functions. These groups indeed seem to be endogamous in the Hindu sense of the term, and quite a large number of Hindu customs which they have preserved have been mentioned, some to do with marriage. However, Muslim marriage is essentially a contract, and the rules concerning marriage are certainly modified to a great extent by the influence of Islamic rules.

### 104 *The case of the Pathan of Swat*

In a brilliant work on the Pathan of Swat, Barth provides a limiting case.[104a] There are no Hindus in this remote valley of the High Indus (formerly 'North-West Frontier'), except for certain unimportant elements. Yet the population is divided into groups which strongly resemble castes. These groups are linked together by something equivalent to a jajmani system, they are ranked by status, and a high proportion of marriages are endogamous. The influence of the Hindu model is obvious, and the lowest castes are considered impure (barber, washerman, etc.). But Barth does not stop here: for him it is a cultural matter, and his theme is rather to display the local function of these borrowed features. On the other hand, he thinks it sociologically indispensable to give caste a very broad definition, to dissociate it from its justification in Hindu culture. His conclusion is consequently that here is a caste system which is not based on ritual but on the division of labour and on the opposition in the political domain between the masters of the land and the rest. In his analysis, he identifies caste with the principle of hierarchy alone. He refers endogamy to the kinship system, professional specialization to the economic 'system', dominance to the political 'system', and he studies the congruence between these different 'systems'.

For the sake of brevity, we shall remark only on the ambiguous and basically contradictory nature of the procedure followed. If Hindu influence accounts for the presence of a good number of the features of the social system, it is paradoxical at the same time to leave it out of account and postulate that caste *must* be defined in general terms. In the preface to the volume containing Barth's study, E. R. Leach certainly saw this, for he asserted that one could not here separate structure (in the sense mainly of social organization) from culture (*ibid.*, p. 5). This touches on a general question which springs from a literal interpretation of the distinction between sociological analysis and cultural history. To put it briefly, it is postulated that all social systems, whatever their history, have the same kind and same degree of consistency, and are thus susceptible of a structural-functional analysis *with the same chance of success*.[104b] Now in my opinion experience belies this assertion. Although it is relatively easy to isolate structures, in the strict sense of the term, in the case of relatively stable and isolated systems, it can be very difficult in the case of systems which are known from other sources to be culturally hybrid, and to have been subjected relatively recently to influences and transformations. There is a certain *plasticity* in the interrelation of social facts which we will never learn to appraise if we totally separate cultural history from sociological analysis in those cases where they need to be brought together.

Moreover, in the case in question, Barth, curiously enough, was led to exaggerate the similarity with Hindu India on certain points.[104c] From our point of view, the relationship between two sub-sets of features should be reversed: it is not a question of a caste system but of a system of patronage and clientele which has assimilated caste-like and (if I may venture the term) Hocartian 'liturgies'. In saying this, we in addition make the blending comprehensible, for it is based on the fact that the two parent systems have in common what Barth calls the principle of 'role summation', which I would call conversely the *lack of differentiation* of the political and economic levels.

## 105 *Caste among non-Hindus: conclusion*

Let us now try to summarize our observations, including the case of the Lingayat (93) whom for this purpose we shall characterize as non-Hindu in so far as they do not subscribe to the religion of the pure and the impure. (It is agreed that they can also be included in Hinduism, by contrast to religions of foreign origin, on condition that renunciation *and all its developments* is so included.) We have already concluded so far as the Pathans are concerned that they do not have a caste system, but the case is instructive in that it shows us the direction Muslims tend to take once they escape from strict cohabitation with Hindus. Lingayat and Muslims present a system of groups which seems like a replica of the adjacent, and so to say circumambiant, Hindu system. The same perhaps goes for the Christians in Kerala, but what we have especially considered among the Christians is rather different, namely the manifestation of overall distinctions (between Brahmans and Shudras, Shudras and Untouchables) within a local Christian community.

There is a parallelism between the case of the Lingayat and that of the Muslims: on the one hand the Hindu ideological justification is lacking, or at least much weakened and contradicted in theory (denial of impurity among the Lingayat, equality of believers among the Muslims), and on the other hand the system of groups is subjected to alterations (no strict endogamy in the Ashraf categories of U.P., no disjunction between status and power among the Lingayat, everywhere a relaxation of commensality). Therefore we must recognize that these communities have at the very least *something of caste despite the modification in their ideas or values.* Caste is weakened or incomplete, but not lacking altogether.

The reason for this fact is seen in the proximity of the Hindu environment, which predominates both generally and regionally. All the facts seem to point in the same direction, whether it is a question of the attitude of Christian converts, or the different pattern found in Swat, or of the paradox of the Lingayat – only an apparent paradox, since it is understood in this particular case that the renouncer, even though he denies the ideological foundation of the caste system, has no alternative to offer. One is therefore led to see the caste system as an Indian institution having its full coherence and vitality in the Hindu environment, but continuing its existence, in more or less attenuated forms, in groups adhering to other religions. In other words, *in the Indian environment,* the ideological features may be missing at certain points or in certain regions, although other features constitutive of caste are present. A non-Hindu group cannot be regarded as independent of the environment in which it is set, as really constituting a society by itself, however strongly its own values push it in this direction.[105a] Light can be cast on this complex situation, this situation of sociological tension, first by returning to the probably exemplary drama of the divorce between Hindus and Muslims, and then by reflecting on the functional perfection of the caste system.

In the light of the political developments in the last hundred years, which I have tried to summarize elsewhere (See Appendix D), Hindus and Muslims form two distinct societies from the point of view of ultimate values. Moreover, these societies are, and to a greater extent were, associated with one another, interacting through this association. Therefore, such an *association* by definition escapes the domain of values and the relatively simple sociological descriptions based on them: we are faced with a *reunion* of men *divided* into two groups, who devalorize each other's values and who are nevertheless associated. This association, quite inadequately studied, has no doubt had a profound effect on Hindu society and has created a Muslim society of a quite special type, a hybrid type which we are scarcely in a position to characterize, except by saying that, lying beneath the ultimate or Islamic values are other values presupposed by actual behaviour. If we hardly know how to characterize the situation, it is quite simply because sociology is little advanced: where the place of ultimate values is not properly recognized, how could one expect a satisfactory description of phenomena of a higher order of complexity and tenuity?

However, we can make one more remark. How would it have been possible to avoid this complication, this internal tension among Muslims in India, who are indeed mostly (though this is irrelevant) descendants of converted Indians? It could have been avoided if Islam – or Christianity, or Virashaivism – had offered or imposed an alternative social system to the caste system. Now this is precisely what they have not done. This is why one can speak of 'Hindu influence' over these groups, or of the permanence of 'psychological dispositions' to the extent that each Muslim, Christian or Lingayat has something of the Hindu in him. What stands out here is the functional value of this very elaborate and complete type of *social order* which we have described. Everything happens, or happened, as if the foreign religions had brought a message similar to that which the Hindu could find by adhering to a sect, a message which only made the social order relative, without abolishing or replacing it. This is particularly clear in the case of Christianity; it did not transfer its followers into a new society, but confined itself to struggling, not without difficulty, against the aspects of the caste system it found especially shocking, without claiming to replace the system any more than the Vira-shaiva renouncers claimed to do.

## 106  *Fundamental characteristics for comparison*

In order to take an overall point of view, let us retrace our steps. Starting with Bouglé's definition and with the opposition of the pure and the impure as the ideological principle common to the three immediately apparent aspects of the caste system, we first of all made a bet. We bet on hierarchy as the fundamental conscious aspect. We thus learnt to come to know hierarchy in an unmixed form, as an ideal type so to speak, and the subsequent analysis showed the choice to be a good one and enabled us to test the consistency of the system. As a second step we tried to restore to within this encompassing conscious form, which we compared to the mantle of Our Lady of Mercy, everything it contains and conceals and which gives it its true sociological significance. This was first and foremost a matter of power, or dominance, whose true and complete relationship with status and with hierarchy we learnt to recognize. Power is subordinate to status in its direct relationship to it, and it is surreptitiously assimilated to status in a secondary capacity in opposition to everything else. This configuration has seemed to us to take into account the whole set of observed facts.

If we now want to characterize the caste system in a comparative way and by a single principle, which should we choose? We could stop at the opposition between pure and impure, considered not only in itself but in its universal function, or again we could take hierarchy which, in terms of ideology we have seen in a form unadulterated by any foreign element. But in this way we would remain within the ideology, and we could only say of other societies that they have got, or rather have not got, these features, and that in these societies they are replaced by other features in a fashion which would be difficult to specify. The relationship between status and power is more suitable as a comparative characteristic because it encompasses both a central feature of the ideology and its empirical counterpart. All societies in some way display the raw material of this relationship, even if they organize it differently.

Thus one could almost say of our own society that it takes the opposite choice and subordinates status to power: it is egalitarian as far as ideology goes, and to a large extent puts power in the forefront, at least if contemporary political science is to be believed.

Here, moreover, the hierarchical disjunction in question has seemed to us to provide an explanation, a causal one in this case, of many of the system's features. The decisive step in its historical establishment was probably when the Brahmans were attributed the monopoly of religious functions as against the king. From this flowed two fundamental facts: the existence of the pure type of hierarchy, completely separated from that with which hierarchy is usually mixed, namely power; and the form of this hierarchy, namely the opposition between pure and impure. To make this last point explicit: the primacy of the priest introduced a ritualist point of view, directed to *access* to the sacred more than to the sacred itself, and effecting in this point of view the disjunction of the pure and the impure, while at the same time putting the profane as it were in parentheses. The opposition of purity is thus the *necessary* ideological form of the ideal type of hierarchy.

In the division of labour also, we have acknowledged a non-ideological residuum. The division of labour in fact gravitates around the function of dominance. This nucleus is given, and the ideology encompasses it but could not have created it. This is exactly the aspect on which Hocart insisted, with Fiji as his starting-point. But he failed to see how the Indian system encompasses this small universe, despoiled of its sacredness, within a larger one, governed not by the king but the priest. So Hocart is here included in an enlarged and simplified version of Bouglé. We ventured to say in passing that the preceding considerations suggest after all a view about the historical origin of the system. It can be supposed that pre-Aryan India had Hocart-style chiefdoms with 'lineages' specialized in the services which the *taboo* person of the chief commanded. The disjunction between status and power, which was after all Indo-European, led to the transformation of the 'Hocartian' system into a caste system. This historical hypothesis is not unreasonable in the present state of knowledge, but it is only a by-product of our work. More important is the point that the caste system can be characterized for the purpose of comparison – partially, no doubt, but adequately – by the disjunction we have described between status and power. We shall say that there is caste only where this characteristic is present, and we shall request that any society lacking this characteristic, even if it is made up of permanent and closed status groups, be classified under another label.

107  *The school of 'social stratification': caste and racism*

The foregoing is far removed from a very widespread view in contemporary sociology. People speak of the 'system of social stratification' of some society starting from a twofold postulate: (1) that one can isolate or abstract such a 'system' from the overall society; (2) that such a 'system' can be characterized by features taken exclusively from the morphology of groups, without considering the ideology which in every case underlies behaviour. Thus, the word 'caste' is used to designate any permanent and closed status group. Then 'castes' can be found more or less everywhere, even in modern society, in South Africa and in the United States; indeed, according to this criterion, the American 'colour bar' can be assimilated to a caste phenomenon. It is hard to imagine a greater misinterpretation. In Appendix A I show that racism really represents a contradictory resurgence in egalitarian society of what finds direct expression as hierarchy in caste society.[107a] The tendency in question has quite simply failed to recognize the nature, function and universality of hierarchy, as is shown by the term 'stratification' taken from the natural sciences. This term in the last analysis denotes the adoption of an egalitarian point of view for the consideration not only of the *residuum of hierarchy* which remains in egalitarian society, but even of *actual hierarchy* where it is present. Naïve egalitarianism, prejudice against other ideologies, and the claim to build a science of society straight away on this basis: these are the elements of smug sociocentricity. Let us emphasize this last point. The worst fault of this kind of superficial sociology is to give the impression that the basic search is over when it has only just begun, as this work, it is hoped, will have shown. Caste is assumed to be known once the term is used in a general classification. In so doing, the development of science is sacrificed to the convenience of immediate discourse, whereas sociology is still endeavouring to know what it is talking about.[107b] As against sociocentric misunderstandings, which often reduce sociology (of modern society) to a conformist catechism, social anthropology opens the way to a true comparative sociology.

## 108  Castes outside India?

Let us suppose that the reader, having referred to the Appendix, agrees that it is a misinterpretation to speak of caste in egalitarian society. He will perhaps still urge that similar facts encountered in traditional societies, as in Madagascar and Japan, be grouped under the same term. Without going into details, there are two distinctions to be introduced. The first point will be readily granted: to be able to speak of caste there must be a *system* of castes in the sense that the set of castes includes all the members of the society. It is one thing for a society to have what tends to be called a caste of Untouchables (Japan), of blacksmith-musicians, of parias or itinerant foreigners, or even for a society to mingle the 'castes' and the clans (Madagascar); it is quite another thing for it to be entirely constituted by a set of castes. For there to be caste, the entire society must without remainder be made up of a set of castes.[108a]

This is not all, and I shall ask once again that reference be made to the principle we have brought to light. In order to decide whether one can speak of a caste system in a society, one must ask: are status and power completely dissociated, can one find the equivalent of the Brahman/Kshatriya relationship? This question, though it may appear improper, has the virtue of immediately fixing a limit to Indian influence in South-East Asia. Important as this influence has been from the cultural and even social point of view, it would seem, roughly speaking, that *nowhere* in Indo-China and Indonesia has the king been dispossessed of his religious prerogatives. This may tally both with the autochthonous society and with the fact that Buddhism, where it was dominant, in fact favoured the king to the detriment of the Brahman. In any case the fact is there, unshakeable.[108b]

An even more revealing case, because closer in all respects to the case of India, is that of Ceylon. All authors speak of castes in Ceylon while pointing out their mild nature compared to India. In general, the whole social organization, especially among the Sinhalese, is found striking for the breadth of options left to each man or, as Ryan calls it, the 'loose integration' of the society.

It has been mentioned that Tambiah defended Hocart's theory of castes against our criticisms. This theory is indeed correct *for Ceylon*. In fact many works, especially Pieiris' on the later Kandian kingdom,[108c] describe an extremely fully worked out 'liturgy' centred on the king, and markedly bureaucratic in nature, at first sight different from the Indian system as we know it today. It is known that there are only a very few Brahmans, temple priests, among the Sinhalese (and even among the Tamils of Ceylon); Buddhism is predominant. In a word, Ceylon has all the characteristics of caste, except for its vigour, and for the crucial disjunction on which I have insisted: the king there has remained the centre both of group religion (as opposed to individualistic religion, the discipline of Buddhist salvation) and of political and economic life.[108d]

We see therefore that the supremacy of the priest is an Indian fact which has remained unexportable: India has exported quasi-caste rather than caste proper. After its influence, as before, these countries knew only the strictly royal 'liturgies' described by Hocart. This fact reinforces our analysis and even our historical hypothesis.

# CHAPTER ELEVEN

# COMPARISON (CONCLUDED):
# THE CONTEMPORARY TREND

## 111  *The problem*

What is the caste system becoming nowadays? This is the question to which most of this chapter will be devoted. Having summarized an authoritative description of the observed changes and a recent discussion of their nature, I shall try to throw light on the question by an overall comparison between caste society and egalitarian society, and this will serve as my general conclusion.

There is no shortage of literature dealing with what it calls 'social change'. It is out of the question to consider it as a whole here, for that would require a separate book, so rich and various is this literature, and above all, so much does it require commentaries, critical discussions and value distinctions. To put it plainly, this literature is usually very unsatisfactory, it generally overestimates change, and the task of the critic is not only to show this, but to explain why this is so.[111a] We must therefore restrict ourselves to a set of general questions concerning modern changes in relation to the caste system.

Even so, a brief preliminary discussion is necessary in order to outline the problem which the notion of change raises for the structuralist, and to avoid misunderstandings. An imposing list could be drawn up of well-confirmed phenomena which as a first approximation will be taken as changes occurring *within* Indian society from 1780 to the present day. Let us take agriculture and land rights, and briefly list the points, most of which are well established, introducing times and places as the need arises. There was an increase in the population, and a state of scarcity of labour in relation to cultivable land changed into a state of scarcity of land in relation to the available labour force. Ownership of land was created, and the position of certain social categories in relation to land rights was drastically changed. The State's annual levy ('Land Revenue', not exactly a tax) became high and inexorable. The circulation of money increased, and rapid means of communication and large-scale transport were set up. The importance of mercantile economy as compared with natural economy increased considerably. Food crops and commercial crops grew in importance in view of the national and international market. Moneylenders grew prosperous and secured the expulsion of peasant farmers for their benefit, until this was curbed by law. Here, it seems, is a sufficiently solid set of facts to make it indisputable that changes have occurred.

The difficulty begins with the appraisal of these facts. The modern mind believes in change and is quite ready to exaggerate its extent. Further, the word 'society' does not designate quite the same thing for the holders of different tendencies in Sociology, or for the sociologist, the economist, and the historian. We shall see that social anthropologists are divided at present as to the nature of the social change that occurred, whether it is purely quantitative or really qualitative, regressive or progressive. One thing is certain: the society as an overall framework has not changed. The castes are still present, and untouchability still effective, although it has been declared illegal. All the specialists are agreed about this. Therefore, as a first approximation, there has been change *in* the society and not change *of* the society. This fact emerges clearly by contrast with Karl Marx's definitive assertions of the ruin of society and his predictions of the end of hereditary division of labour:

England has broken down the entire framework of Indian Society, without any symptoms of reconstitution yet appearing (*N.Y. Daily Tribune*, 25 June 1853; 'On Colonialism', p. 33).

Modern industry, resulting from the railway system, will dissolve the hereditary division of labour, upon which rest the Indian castes (*ibid.*, 8 August 1853; *ibid.*, p. 80).

Given our way of thinking, we must face the fact that the anticipated links between technico-economic change and social change did not operate, and that caste society managed to digest what was thought must make it burst asunder. This is the main fact which even the very common overestimation of change has not managed to conceal.[111b]

But can we stop here? There is a problem, since as will be seen later, social anthropologists are divided into two tendencies: some cling to modern facts and see almost nothing but change, while others try to grasp the traditional society 'structurally' or 'functionally' and see only stability, and even reinforcement. Evidently these rival and limited points of view must be combined. To do so, a comparison between caste society and the modern type of society must be initiated. In this way it will be possible to describe their interaction, that is, to follow and measure change in a more certain and precise way than under the vague and tendentious label of 'social change'.

The matter can be seen in another light. To say that there has been no change *of* the society is roughly to say that there has been no revolution or overall reform: a form of organization does not change, it is replaced by another; a structure is present or absent, *it does not change*. If we are entitled to state that *so far* the changes that have occurred have not *visibly* altered what we have taken to be the heart, the living nucleus of the society, who can say but that these changes have not built up their corrosive action in the dark, and that the caste order will not one day collapse like a piece of furniture gnawed from within by termites? Who can say even whether the ideas and values have not already been profoundly altered, and that only the coarseness of our notions and methods of investigation and the *absence of any precise idea of the former state of the system*, say at the beginning of the Mughul domination, prevents us from seeing this? The question that arises at this point is that of knowing more precisely about the plasticity of social systems and the possible variability in the *actual* relationship between the ideology and the other aspects. As it is basically only by comparison that we know the non-ideological aspects of a social system, it is to comparison that these considerations lead us. We have thus left on one side the narrowness of our initial position (changes *in* and *of* society) and raise the question of changes *in relation to* the caste system.

It is enough to raise the question to see that it is not absolutely unanswerable even in the present state of knowledge. No doubt the Indians' ideas of the decadence of their society have subjective roots, but perhaps they are not all imaginary. The hybrid aspect of the culture of the Gangetic plain compared to that of the Deccan already tells a story, and chance observations show revealing features, like the foundering of an aesthetic style since the beginning of the nineteenth century.[111c] The theoretical model we have started to set up enables us, by comparison with observed states of affairs, to form an idea of the extent to which the system has broken some of its moorings, not only in the cases of the Lingayat or the Muslims, but for example in a well-known fact like the relative weakness of ideas about impurity in the north, a weakness probably occasioned by the ascendancy of the sects and the impact of Islam.

## 112  Recent changes as portrayed by Ghurye

Sociologists and anthropologists do not share the wishful thinking found in other quarters, which has it that the castes are in the process of weakening under modern influences and will one day simply disappear. Whilst their ideas are somewhat imprecise in general, a very interesting disagreement has recently sprung up among them. To understand it better, we shall go back to the general account of changes in relation to the caste organization, given in 1932 and completed in 1952 by Professor Ghurye.[112a] This account is important in itself, as coming from an Indian author, and even more as the starting-point of a tendency, for Professor Ghurye influenced more than a generation of research in India as Head of the active Department of Sociology in the University of Bombay.

It is not very easy to summarize Ghurye, for his treatment is rather discursive; it is contained in two chapters, completed in the 1952 edition, of which one, entitled 'Caste and British Rule', contains a judgment on British domination, while the other, 'Caste and Nationalism', is aimed at stirring up minds in the University. From subtle detail, which is sometimes contradictory or equivocal – one must not let oneself be carried away from reality by incomplete views, yet a certain fondness for Brahmanism is discernible – there finally emerges a guiding idea. In what follows I shall regroup some scattered details.

Ghurye had the great merit of drawing attention to otherwise little known aspects of social movements, mainly to the activities and claims of the so-called non-Brahman movement. This was inaugurated by the florist Phule in Poona in about the middle of the nineteenth century, and was later illustrated, still in the lands of the Maratha, by the Maharajah of Kolhapur. It developed into the twentieth century, with the concession of privileges of representation and employment to minorities and to castes considered backward (Montagu–Chelmsford declaration of 1917), especially in the south (Justice Party and later the Dravidian Association – *draviḍa kaLagam*). The same goes for the Untouchable movement.

Ghurye points out that hierarchy is attacked by the non-Brahman movement (p. 193), notions concerning impurity being much weakened (p. 209) and the rules concerning food and drink considerably relaxed, especially in the towns. The freedom of the new professions means that the caste no longer prescribes occupation. As a counterpart, endogamy continues to hold sway with undiminished force save for certain differences of nuance (p. 186).[112b]

Pre-eminently characteristic of the period is urban growth, and there again caste asserts itself. Castes group themselves by quarters, they have reserved houses, and this not without benevolent motives; they create their co-operatives, banks, maternity homes and general hospitals (p. 201), and their associations (pp. 189–91). All this represents new forms of solidarity and caste 'consciousness', and one can speak of 'caste patriotism'.

Emphasis must be placed on the caste associations or *sabhā*. They are becoming more widespread and 'comprise all the members of the caste speaking the same language' whereas the caste panchayat covered a smaller area (confined, according to Ghurye, to the limits of the village or town). Their functions consist in serving the general interests of the caste and its status in the hierarchy, in providing study grants, and in helping its poor members, and sometimes in legislating on certain customs. The author notes that the same objectives were formerly mostly pursued by temporary groupings set up with a precise aim in view.[112c] To return to urban caste (p. 193), it can be seen to serve its members in the competition in which they are engaged, especially for obtaining remunerative posts and jobs, which are relatively few in number. He concludes:

The community-aspect of caste has thus been made more comprehensive, extensive and permanent. More and more of an individual's interests are being catered for by caste; the feeling of caste-solidarity is now so strong that it is truly described as caste patriotism (p. 192).[112d]

The author idealizes the past, but he vigorously stresses *competition* as a modern fact when he writes (*ibid.*): 'Conflict of claims and opposition has thus replaced the old harmony of demand and acceptance.' Ghurye warns against gradualness in the reform of connubium. Modernization consists mainly in marriage between different subcastes of the same caste; it may be imagined that the barriers between neighbouring castes will also be lifted, but the result would be disastrous, for one would end up by aggregating a multitude of small groups into a few large blocks, which would be mutually hostile and exclusive to a dangerous degree.

In short Ghurye, although not expressing it with all the clarity one would have wished, has put his finger on an essential phenomenon, which may be called the substantialization of caste. In fact a number of the features quoted together indicate the transition from a fluid, structural universe in which the emphasis is on interdependence and in which there is no privileged level, no firm units, to a universe of impenetrable blocks, self-sufficient, essentially identical and in competition with one another, a universe in which the caste appears as a collective *individual* (in the sense we have given to this word), as a substance.[112e]

The author is sometimes led astray by what might well be called his Brahmanic 'patriotism'. This can be seen in his idealization of the past, and in many passages[112f] like the one where he deplores the fact that some castes have ceased to employ Brahmans as priests: 'Even the apex ... the priesthood of the Brahman ... the great bond of social solidarity in this finely divided society, is being loosened by caste after caste.' One comes to assume that if Ghurye deplores caste 'patriotism', it is as much out of fondness for an idealized past as out of hostility towards caste; it seems that he believes in the possibility of a transformation which would end caste while preserving Brahmanism and interdependence. Although a keener observer, he is scarcely more realistic than Gandhi about the relation between the future and the past. I mention this point because his attitude is shared by others, and because this exclusively Brahmanical attitude has in India coloured the whole political tendency that is called liberal.[112g] Anti-Brahman schemings, although they have a demagogic and somewhat violent side, are a positive aspect in the struggle against caste. No doubt it takes little courage on the part of a foreigner to say this, but it must be said all the same, and it must be added that it follows that Madras State, with its Dravidian Association or Associations, is probably further advanced on the road to the disappearance of castes than all the other states in India. [I should add that a recent visit to Madras has done much to shatter my naïve confidence in this respect (1969).] Above all, it will be concluded that the road to their abolition is likely to lie in caste actions, and that only the content of a caste action indicates whether it militates for or against caste. Not to recognize this is to remain within the traditional Indian way of thinking. Nothing is more deplorable than the failure of Ambedkar and of the Untouchable movement, for it is clear today, contrary to Gandhi's opinion, that the Untouchables will not be finally emancipated save by themselves: *the good will* of their politician superiors cannot be enough.

## 113 Complements

It is convenient to group here some of the judgments of the Bombay school which, in their modesty and moderation, bear witness to Ghurye's positive influence and show true penetration. In an article of 1955, I. P. Desai and Damle take up the inventory of changing features and stable features, in order to insist on the limitations of change and on the fact that it does not alter the system as a whole. They stress that it is above all a question of tolerated variations in behaviour, which do not touch the traditional ideology. The idea is taken up again by Kapadia reviewing opinion studies among students (1962): the adaptations concerning commensality and intermarriage are not based on a voluntary rejection of the traditional rules: factors which favour marriage between different castes – a very rare occurrence – are not resisted, but there is no 'social acceptance' of this type of marriage. The inquiries among students are revealing, especially B. V. Shah's in Baroda, the most precise and sincere.[113a] It shows in effect that young men belonging to high castes and to the most moderniz d strata of society, subjected at university to the full impact of Western ideas, are essentially conservative. Only a tiny minority declared themselves opposed – in theory – to the joint family and traditional marriage. The majority confined their desire for innovation to this or that modification in details of the traditional system. Whether one should praise their wisdom or deplore their pusillanimity, their opinions show that individualistic values have ceased to be a challenge to caste. The intellectual acquisitions no longer bring with them an overall moral condemnation of the system.[113b] Caste values envelop and encompass modern ferments. The desire for security and the old loyalties carry the day against whims for independence. One could find no better demonstration to date of how powerless are modern education and social and political transformations to overthrow the traditional system. A recent author gives voice to this situation. He speaks of the 'equilibrium' and 'reconciliation' which is on the way to being effected between the two universes. 'In the life of an individual, there may be an attempt to better his traditional status with the means of modern education, and in the family, while some members may uphold traditional roles, other members of the family may venture out into the new occupations.'[113c] In fact there is more than an 'equilibrium' here; for the new is subordinated to the old: for the individual, education is the means, the traditional rank the end, and the family, thanks to being traditionally a joint family, *encompasses* both old and new. (It goes without saying that by thus incorporating change the family must itself be modified to some extent, but this is a much more difficult aspect to detect.)

It seems that one can generalize and apply the foregoing remarks about education and the modern professions to all the assumed factors of modernization. Thus it might be applied to urbanization, of which it is said that it does not occasion 'the social changes necessary to economic development' (Sachin Chaudhuri). Finding that life in the towns often remained rural in content and spirit, Desai and Damle have even spoken of 'fake urbanization'. More recently, R. D. Lambert has questioned the idea that change spreads from the town to the village. Apart from great metropolises and recent artificial conurbations, like the steel towns, industry adapts itself to the traditional environment more than it transforms it.[113d]

All these facts should not be considered as absolutely negative, or surprising. It is quite natural that new and old should combine. The facts in question take on their real bearing only in relation to those ideas according to which modernization should have shattered caste society from the outset. These ideas came from modern men who, aware of the incompatibility between the two sets of values, assumed that everything accompanying modern values in Western society must automatically be an effective destructive factor against traditional Indian values. However, it is found that the interaction between the two types of society takes other paths.

## 114    Is caste reinforcing itself?

In an article published in 1957 and in other writings, Srinivas carries on from his master Ghurye and is more pessimistic.[114a] He insists from the outset of his article on the fact made clear by Miller: the modern epoch has seen castes lose their limited territorial basis (the 'little kingdom') and spread freely beyond: 'The djinn has been let out of the bottle.' In what follows, he shows the role caste has played in politics since Independence, basing his account partly on specialized works. He concludes (to quote a striking passage from another work):

> In general it may be confidently said that the last hundred years has seen a great increase in caste solidarity, and the concomitant decrease of a sense of interdependence between different castes living in a region (*Report of the Seminar on Casteism and Removal of Untouchability*).

This is not to be taken literally. The 'increase in solidarity' refers mostly to the disappearance of political barriers and the progress of communication, leading to a greater *spatial extension* of actual caste groups. And the 'concomitance' presupposes a purely theoretical constancy of the sum of solidarities at a given instant (likewise in A. R. Desai, *Contrib.* VII, p. 33). In reality the *sabhā* or caste associations generally rarely intervene in the everyday life of the village. The author quotes Bailey as showing that the increase in external relations weakened the integration of the village. But Bailey does not have in mind caste 'solidarities' outside the village, but the fact that – in the case he studied – *dominated castes*, and not the dominant caste, profited from the modern politico-economic system.[114b]

According to the same author, there has been in addition an increase in 'tensions'[114c] between different castes (anti-Brahman movement in the south, competition among the educated for the relatively few modern employments). These 'tensions' are interpreted as marking a reinforcement of caste solidarities. Here, within the progressives' point of view, the prejudice in favour of the Brahmans which we have already encountered again comes to the surface: the anti-Brahman movement is felt as bad in itself, whereas it is quite clearly an index of a weakening of the system as such. Again, we are told that the fact of having new fields of activity (politics and especially elections) reinforces the 'power' of the caste (Srinivas, *Mod. India*, p. 23). N. K. Bose judiciously pointed out that this is only one aspect of the matter, adding that in the economic field caste has been seriously weakened by the intrusion of a system of production and economic relations which is foreign to it.[114d]

In short, Srinivas had the merit of following Ghurye in recalling that caste was not in the process of disappearing. He saw it adapting in the most flexible way to new conditions, and extending its field of activity. He interpreted this as a reinforcement of the individual caste. Moreover, he has at least implicitly presented the fact as a reinforcement of the *system*. Now the system does not only consist of solidarities – it would be necessary to know precisely what degree of solidarity it entails properly speaking, and whether the very increase of solidarity does not weaken it – the system also entails interdependence, which Srinivas admits has been weakened, and also hierarchy, against which the anti-Brahman movement was directed.

Studying the very special conditions in East Africa, where until quite recently people from Gujerat exiled themselves temporarily to 'make money' in business, David Pocock has written that he found castes but not the caste system: 'Castes exist . . . but the caste system is no more.' While understanding his intention, one may wonder whether the components of a system can survive it as such. More subtly, the same investigator found in East Africa that hierarchy was replaced by a new, non-structural, sense of difference. In short, like Ghurye he had the feeling of a transition from structure to substance, and this is how the quoted witticism must be interpreted.[114e]

## 115 *From interdependence to competition*

In some brief remarks, E. R. Leach has questioned Srinivas' conclusion about the system. Caste is based on interdependence to the exclusion of competition and 'once it acts in a competitive way' it acts against caste tradition. If interdependence is replaced by competition, caste is dead. Bailey develops this idea in a recent article.[115a] He claims that in the village itself the system is altered by the fact that enrichment outside is possible, and by the fact that the low castes thus come to reject their position as clients *vis-à-vis* their patrons, and set themselves up in competition with them. Bailey draws this conclusion from his own experience (*cf.* n. 114b). This may be an exaggerated claim, and one must not generalize too quickly.

In short, according to Bailey, there has already been a transition from an 'organic' system to a 'segmentary' system. The expression 'segmentary' means something like what Durkheim called mechanical (solidarity); in our language we would say that there has been a transition from a structure to the juxtaposition of substances. There remain groups that one continues to call 'castes'; but they are set in a different system. According to Bailey, this is even clearer when a State as a whole is considered; the enlargement of the territorial framework has led the castes which were only 'categories', as opposed to subcastes, to become real 'groups', by among other things the creation of caste associations (*sabhā*, etc.), interest groups in competition with one another, thus making the castes into 'political units'. In this case the caste is not a status group, and so another word is needed to refer to it.

Competition, already mentioned by Ghurye, is also mentioned in Leach and Bailey, but in this case it is interpreted as the sign of a transformation of the system. It is a question of competition *between different castes* on the politico-economic plane, for competition itself is not unknown in the traditional system.[115b] One indeed seems to be present at the transition, in one part of the field of activity, from the world of caste to the modern world.

### 116 *Provisional conclusion*

Two conclusions may be drawn from this confrontation of views. In the first place, the substitution of competition for interdependence is only one aspect of the phenomenon, the behavioural aspect. It could just as well be said that the caste seems to accept equality[116a] or that from the ideological point of view, structure seems to yield to substance, each caste becoming an individual confronting other individuals. At this point it can be seen that there is

HOMO HIERARCHICUS

some truth in the modern accounts which we have rejected, like Kroeber's (caste as the limit of class), or Karvé's (caste as a *sui generis* block in the construction of society).[116b] In other words, the modernization of caste seems to transform it into what modern men spontaneously see in it. There is nothing astonishing about this, since in both cases it is a question of a transition, intellectual or empirical, from one universe to the other.

But one must not lose sight of the fact that this alleged modification, however genuine it may be, remains incomplete. It bears on the politico-economic domain of social life. In order to estimate its overall significance, we still need to know what position this particular domain occupies within the whole. Now in the traditional perspective, the essential perspective here, this domain neither governs the rest of social life, nor is it autonomous or exterior with respect to it; on the contrary, the politico-economic domain is encompassed in an overall religious setting. This remains true even when there is a weakening of the opposition between pure and impure, the opposition we have considered as the ideological core of the system. Here resides the secret of the caste system's plasticity, and the ambiguous nature of the undoubted changes. Everything happens as if the system tolerated change only within one of its secondary spheres. This fact would lead us to dismiss equally both of the opinions in question: we would conclude that the facts they adduce display neither reinforcement nor any essential transformation of the system, but only a change involving its minor areas. To see if things are really thus, the embryonic comparison suggested by Leach must be developed. Failing this, we would either, like Srinivas, be aware only of the continuance and reinforcement of the old in new forms, or, like Bailey, of the substitution of the modern for the ancient: we would not be able to localize or even describe the changes.

117 *Attempt at an inventory*

One can start by listing the main general changes which are to a greater or lesser degree relevant to the caste system, both on the ideological plane and on the empirical plane.

On the ideological plane, the major fact is the insertion of an egalitarian sub-set at the juridical and political level, without a corresponding voluntary modification of the overall hierarchical

228

framework.[117a] One finds also a thrust towards reform which, in connection with the previous feature, includes modernization of religion – neo-Hinduism – and also a limited effort to reform customs (especially Untouchability). On an intermediate plane, mainly empirical but carrying ideological overtones, there exists what I shall call a foreign royal model: the ruling British were in fact the object of imitation ('Westernization') just like the orthodox kings, in spite of the fact that they did not themselves adopt the Brahmanic values, though they took care to run counter to them as little as possible. Finally there are three solid facts on the empirical plane: the emergence and development of modern professions, usually neutral from the religious point of view, and urban development; territorial unification and new spatial mobility; emancipation of economics and development of the market economy.

These features are diverse in nature, some deliberate or pre-supposing acceptance, passive or active, by at least a part of the population; others imposed from outside or even resulting directly and as if unconsciously from Western domination, with its own techniques and values. One cannot help but feel that they must have affected the caste system to different extents and in various ways.

One can also try to classify the types of interaction to which such factors have given rise. Let us distinguish them into three: rejection, mixture, in which traditional and modern features exist happily side by side, and combination, which unites them intimately in new forms of a hybrid nature and ambiguous orientation. It will doubtless be readily agreed that caste society reacted to the very cautious British rule by a minimum of *rejection*. However, at the ideological level, it is said that the mutiny of 1857 was a violent reaction against an imaginary threat of subversion of the social order.

*Mixture*, on the contrary, is ubiquitous and seems at first sight to be the general form of reaction, in keeping with what was said above (§95) about the capacity of this society for integration or aggregation. At the overall level, the subordination and isolation of what could be called the politico-economic 'pocket' relative to the prime values permits the insertion of the modern egalitarian sub-set. Likewise the freedom of the new professions coexists with the maintenance of religiously relevant professional constraints (stability of ritual specialities in the village); again, competition on the largest territorial level coexists with interdependence at the level of the village, spatial mobility with the maintenance of the essential characteristics of marriage, Westernization with 'Sanskritization', freedom concerning food on the occasion of visits to the town with the maintenance of the rules in the house. The pressure for reform was at first a limited phenomenon without much practical effect; only the Arya Samaj really had a mass audience in the Panjab and Uttar Pradesh, but even in this case the will for reform remained rather utopian: the Untouchables were advised to give up their degrading occupations, and where they tried this they discovered by experience that the advice was in vain, and also that it was in general useless to try to escape their condition by 'Sanskritization'.[117b] Similarly, few castes have obtained the recognition in their environment of the exorbitant claims which they saw fit to make at the time of the Census Reports. So far as the economy is concerned, while innovation has easily become included in the system, the mercantile or capitalist mentality has on the whole failed to supersede the traditional mentality of prestige and conspicuous and unproductive expenditure.

*Combination* has hardly as yet been systematically studied in itself. However, it is in evidence in the abundant literature concerning the relations between the traditional society and modern politics: the role of caste in elections, and a large part of political life in general, carries with it an aspect of skilful manipulation of new conditions for the traditional ends of clientele and patronage.[117c] The conflict between Hindus and Muslims, which ended in the partition of the country, corresponds to a political form ('communalism') whereby the traditional regime, in which religion predominates, is interbred with the nation (see Appendix D).

One small but characteristic fact is the use of modern courts to obtain traditional privileges. Thus in the Tamil country there are interminable suits about who takes the first rank, or a given rank, in the honorific distributions which follow the celebration of festivals in the great temples. The State of Madras also provides an example of a very interesting type of reaction (unfortunately I have been unable to pursue its development since 1950). This is how the conservative circles of this very traditionalist region responded to the movement and measures aimed to grant the

Untouchables the right to enter the Brahmanic temples: there was at first resistance against the Gandhist movement, but the reform was more or less generally imposed, and laws ('Temple Entry Acts') were passed in various states (in Madras in 1947). Then a sort of puritan reaction by vegetarians established itself in Madras, which flourished after Independence; prohibition on sacrificing animals in the immediate vicinity of the great temples, as the meat-eating castes were wont to do; prohibition by certain municipalities (Dindigul) on butchering, even by Muslims; finally in September 1950 the vote by the Madras Assembly (the State was not yet divided between Tamil- and Telugu-speaking peoples) prohibiting by law animal sacrifices in general (and so even in the private worship of a locality, a caste or kinship group). As the majority of the population was given to such sacrifices, one cannot see either how such a law can really be applied, or how it could have been adopted if democracy had functioned normally.[117d] But the reason for all these measures is clear: from the moment the Untouchables enter the temples, the purity of the high castes and their very idea of worship and god is jeopardized: so the only solution is the forcible reform of the Untouchables, so that they would cease to be abettors of impurity. The aim is even exceeded, and there is a tendency to impose vegetarianism on everybody. This is a considerable event: the traditional hierarchical tolerance gives way to a modern mentality, and this is a totalitarian mentality: hierarchical structure is replaced by a single rigid substance. The fact is extremely significant: egalitarianism, leaving the limited zone in which it is well tolerated, causes a profound modification and brings the threat of religious totalitarianism.

The above account, incomplete as it is, introduces the comparative point of view, too often neglected, and makes felt the need for a general comparison.

118 *Hierarchical society and egalitarian society: a summary comparative diagram*

The foregoing, especially the last section, commits us to a consideration of modern change from the point of view of the interaction between India and the West, and to a consideration of this interaction itself in terms of a comparison between the two types of society. The aim is to construct an overall comparative model from this point of view, and this is a welcome task, as it obliges us to complete what had been left unfinished. In effect, we have constantly brought into play explicit or implicit comparison with the modern Western type of society: it was observed that the object of explicit and valorized ideas in the one case was, by contrast, subordinated or unrecognized in the other. So we must now set the two types face to face, in the form of a picture which encompasses but does not confuse the ideology and the non-ideological residuum in each case. We shall try to do so in the form of a diagram, inevitably very approximate, a kind of mnemonic in which we shall condense what we have learnt into shorthand form, so as to be able to take in at a glance the configuration of the whole. The terms we have used will figure in the diagram, but less importance should be attached to their exact specification than to their power of condensation and their *position* in the diagram (Fig. 5).

The basic overall opposition concerns the object of the main ideas and orientations: on the left-hand side (1), society taken as a whole ('holism'), on the right-hand side (2) the individual ('individualism'). Rather than make this figure in the diagram itself, we shall write above (1) 'HOMO MAJOR' to designate man as a collective being, man as society, and above (2) 'HOMO MINOR' for man as an individual.[118a]

In order to put the particular aspects of this fundamental opposition approximately in their place, I shall refer back to what has previously appeared as the fundamental characteristic of the caste system for comparison: the hierarchical disjunction between status and power, which will be represented by a horizontal line separating diagram (1): the upper part is HIERARCHY, and the lower part the politico-economic domain, etc.[118b] This procedure agrees with our concern to distinguish fundamental values and ideas from everything else, the ideological from the non-ideological, or rather the more conscious or more valorized from the less conscious or valorized. The horizontal line can be taken as a threshold of consciousness. We shall call what comes above *Substantive*, hereafter *S*, and what comes below, *adjective*, *a*, which can be taken as the main 'concomitants and implications' of the valorized ideas.[118c]

For the sake of comparison, one should likewise draw, in (2), a horizontal axis which ought to distinguish fundamental ideas

(S2) from their implications (a2). HIERARCHY has already been placed at the centre of S1, to which must be added immediately below: *interdependence* and *separation*, in the sense which has been seen. Correspondingly in S2: EQUALITY goes with the corresponding sphere of activity, which predominates in modern society: *economics*, and also *politics* in the sense in which it is predominantly conceived in this society (*cf.* §119, *in fine*). In a1 we have inscribed: *politico-economic domain*, and for present purposes we have refrained

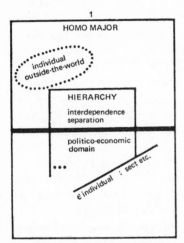
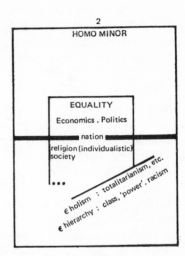

Fig. 5 Comparative diagram

from adding the other features which have been isolated. To find out what comes in a2, let us look for elements which both correspond more or less to what we have put in (1): (S1 + a1), and also occupy a position corresponding to a1, that is, are to some extent present in ideas without being really in the forefront.[118d] It comes to something like: *nation, individualistic religion, society*. The place of these elements is very various. The nation, as a 'collective political individual', has a right to figure in S2 but it is negated in an ideological form, internationalism, which was important at least for a period,[118e] and this is why we have given it its particular position. One must indeed look, comparatively, for what religion becomes here: one finds that it is subordinated to the individual (and that it can moreover change into philosophy).

As for society, it certainly deserves its residual place: it is no more than a juxtaposition of individuals, which in theory is the subject for a specialized science. Considering the relation $S2/a2$ it can be seen that it is, like $S1/a1$, a relation of complementarity (to eject hierarchy from $S$ is to relegate society and religion to $a$), but is also a relation whereby the individual directly implies the nation and individualistic religion.

Here certain major ideas and facts have been put into place and compared. To complete the diagram, one can try to recognize in each case the existence of features corresponding to what is brought to light by the values of the other: is there something like the individual in 1, like holism and hierarchy in 2? We have found in India the individual-outside-the-world, the renouncer, both exterior to and superior to the society proper. Yet he operates in the society through the sect, which we are here obliged to sacrifice to some extent.[118f] Conversely, in 2, in hypernationalism and totalitarianism the whole asserts itself against individualistic atomization, and there are residues of hierarchy more or less everywhere: in social class, annexed to the notion of 'power', and finally in racism. There is nothing to insert in 2 in the position corresponding to that which the renouncer occupies in 1: society is indeed transcended in religions or philosophies, but in various ways which, in the last analysis, are individualistic.

Let us insist on this point: the diagram at which we have arrived is only a useful memory-prop for comparison. It is quite the opposite of an abstract formula from which one could draw 'theoretical' results without recourse to concrete data. Perhaps the reader who has followed us so far will find it disappointingly meagre and will regret that we have not drawn this skeleton in more detail, or clothed it with flesh. In this case, let him reproach us for having produced a diagram which perhaps should never have gone beyond the experimental stage, for its unfinished aspect is in my opinion essential, and I think I would run counter to the spirit of the inquiry were I to excise the latent question marks with which it is bristling.[118g]

## 119  Conclusion

Such as it is, this diagram brings together two apparently incommensurable social types while rigorously preserving their differences. Our concluding comments will consider it in both directions: from right to left in order to consider India's reaction to the impact of the West, and from left to right to return to our starting point.

For the study of interaction, we have here a general framework, usually lacked by studies of 'social change'. But this framework makes no claim to replace such studies, so that we end, as it were, with prolegomena. The diagram permits the recovery or discovery of three general facts:

(1) As, in the caste system, profession is linked to status only by its religious aspects, and for the rest hinges on power, it has been possible for new neutral and urban professions to emerge, while the professions really relevant to the system (village speci-alities) were only slightly affected. At most it is likely that the jajmani has become restricted to properly religious and personal services and has let escape some professions which it covered previously.

(2) In the caste system the politico-economic aspects are rela-tively secondary and isolated. Hence there is a permeability to novelty in this domain, and these borrowings are relatively harm-less for *S*. The British government's Indian policy, consisting of not meddling in the domain of religion and the traditional social order (n. 112d), while introducing the minimum of reforms and novelties on the politico-economic plane, harmonized remarkably well with this configuration. It is a configuration whose negative aspects are immediately noticeable: the reactions of princes were not endorsed by the society, the Brahmans did not turn the 1857 mutiny into a holy war. The rise of non-landed capital, of mer-chants and usurers, did not arouse any but local reactions; the usurer is even well esteemed when he is not too aggressive.

(3) Finally and above all, an unnoticed fact, the presence of the individual-outside-the-world and his immemorial action was truly decisive for the permeability of Indian society to individualistic ways of thought. Let us recall the effect of the renouncer on the worldly mentality (introduction of the religion of choice and love, relativization of group religion, subjective morality). The general mentality was thereby penetrated with elements contrary to those which result from hierarchy from long before the Western (or even Mughul) impact. The Westerner, in so far as he was concerned with quite other things than power in the most obvious sense of

the word, appeared not only as a heathen prince, but also as a sort of sannyasi of an unusual type, for his preoccupation with truth, his unselfishness as expressed even in a modest ideal like 'scholarship', or again his humanitarian concern or his concern with social progress and with moral discipline in general evoke for the Hindu masses, and even more used in the nineteenth century to evoke, characteristics unique to the renouncers. Think also of the men who provided the reply to the Western challenge. Gandhi is an obvious example. Ram Mohan Roy expressed the awakening of religion to politico-social awareness as a sannyasi returning to the world. Further, British domination very likely reactivated renunciation as an attitude of mind, because it was only through it that the Indian could accept the new spirit. Vinoba Bhave is a renouncer who chose to draw on the traditional worldly mentality in order to carry out agrarian reform.

In short, the society was open to Western influence for two main reasons: the domain to which it confined itself was relatively neutral from the point of view of values, and the spirit in which it was active was not absolutely unknown.

Let us now consider the comparative diagram in the other direction, not to see how man as member of a caste appears to man as an individual – which, briefly, was the subject of this book – nor to see to what extent comparing them can help us to understand the contemporary history of India – on which a few words have just been said – but this time to ask ourselves what man as a member of a caste can teach us about man as an individual, about ourselves. Thus we return to our starting-point. It will be remembered that in the Introduction a hypothetical answer to this question was advanced in order to induce in the reader a sociological perspective, by raising the problem of the individual and by showing, with the help of Rousseau, Tocqueville, Durkheim and Talcott Parsons, that the theory of man as an individual being is, in our own culture, limited or encompassed as soon as his social nature is effectively and more or less explicitly recognized.

But from this point of view, the completion of our present task only sketches for us a new task: to reverse the perspective and throw light on egalitarian society by comparison with hierarchical society of the pure type, in a work which could be called *Homo Aequalis*. For the moment, I shall only attempt, from what has already been said here, and from the conclusions of other studies, to define this task briefly.

From a certain moment in Western history, men saw themselves as individuals. It matters little that this did not occur all at once, although one may hope to trace the genesis of man as an individual starting from man as a collective being in the traditional type of society. But men did not cease to be social beings the day they conceived themselves in a contrary fashion, and this situation is expressed in many ways. First of all, what a man imagines thereby becomes real from a certain point of view: the society in which man is conceived (essentially) as an individual is not, or not quite, what it was before. At the same time, the new Substantive introduced into social life does not modify it totally. It has already been remarked at the outset that this ideally autonomous man was in actual fact the most dependent of his kind, tightly enclosed in an unprecedented extension of the division of labour. Likewise, we have fallen in with Tocqueville's view that individualistic democracy is only viable if it is encompassed in a more extensive ideology of a traditional sort – of a religious, or perhaps other, type. There is another way of seeing this: if all societies present the same 'features' while modifying them profoundly according to the way they treat them (n. 118d), the constitution of a new individualistic 'Substantive' results in the appearance of an 'adjective' which accompanies it as its necessary counterpart, whose content should be predictable by means of comparison.

In a very imprecise way, this is true, in the present state of things. But all the same it is something to know that hierarchy is a universal necessity, and that it will become manifest in some way, in covert, shamefaced or pathological forms in relation to the opposed ideals in force. In the United States, the most extreme individualistic environment, the abolition of slavery was followed in a few decades by the emergence of racism, by a strange but explicable alchemy; difference in social status is denied, only for discrimination on somatic grounds to emerge (see Appendix A). In the same way one may hope to explain the phenomena of totalitarianism, not indeed by means of formulae, but in terms of an analysis which fits the facts as closely as possible.

To conclude with a more precise example. I shall take it from a work in which I tried to specify the place of the individual in modern political theory.[119a] Three political thinkers, Hobbes,

Rousseau and Hegel, can be brought together, all three being important, paradoxical and frequently detested. The usual accounts do not sufficiently bring out their basic common denominator, and they obscure the continuity between Hobbes and his two successors. By contrast, this is very clear in the perspective of our comparison: these three philosophers are united, and opposed to the majority of their contemporaries, by the fact that, starting from an apparently or really extremely individualistic position, they reversed it as they went along in order to force the individual to make himself, or to recognize himself as, a social man – in the form of a citizen, that is, of course, on the political plane; it is this circumstance which hides the true nature of the fact. All three have the distinction of having gone beyond the modern ideology in order to harmonize it with social reality, and this is why they often give offence. Whereas for the liberals the domain of politics is a special domain governed by abstract norms, whose relation to the overall social domain is not the object of systematic investigation, Hobbes, Rousseau and Hegel, by contrast, think of the whole society in political language, that is to say in a language which is, as opposed to the social language, the language of the modern individual. This was, of course, an impossible task, but it was imposed on those minds by their epoch; their greatness consists in not having shirked it. One can see why these philosophies were potentially dangerous, and one can reproach their authors for it only if one prefers mediocrity to intelligence. The reader is now in a position to see why there is room for a radical rethinking, in comparative terms, of questions of this kind, and that *Homo hierarchicus* can help *Homo aequalis* to complete the consciousness he has of himself.

# POSTFACE
# TOWARD A THEORY OF HIERARCHY

We shall here turn away from India, or rather we shall take what India has taught us about the opposition between the encompassing and the encompassed as a point of departure, trying to clarify it somewhat. If we cannot present a theory of hierarchy, we can at least move towards the formulation of such a theory.

It is appropriate to keep in mind our aversion to hierarchy. Not only does this aversion explain our difficulty in deepening our understanding of hierarchy, but we are facing a kind of taboo, an unmistakable censure, and caution requires the adoption of a circumspect approach, the avoidance of any provocative statements or premature judgments. At any rate this is what I thought, and, being left alone as I was, I chose to move forward slowly and let the brief grow heavier, the ground settle, the horizon grow more distinct.

Similarly here, as I am unable to offer a sustained study, I prefer to refrain from making external references and forgo any tempting allusions to, or excursions into, biology, esthetics, or to mathematics and mysticism. I shall limit myself to a concise presentation of what I consider has been gained from my studies subsequent to *H.H.*, referring only to the ones that have been published.[1] Once again, my purpose is to contribute a stone to a building with which, sooner or later, others will have to be concerned and not to establish a personal domain.

I believe that hierarchy is not, essentially, a chain of superimposed commands, nor even a chain of beings of decreasing dignity, nor yet a taxonomic tree, but a relation that can succinctly be called 'the encompassing of the contrary'.

The best example I have found is biblical. It is the story of the creation of Eve from Adam's rib, in the first book of Genesis, chapter 2. God creates Adam first, the undifferentiated man, the prototype of 'mankind'. In a second stage, he extracts a different being from this first Adam. Adam and Eve stand face to face, prototypes of the two sexes. In this strange operation, on the one hand, Adam has changed identity; from being undifferentiated, he has become a male. On the other hand, a being has appeared who is both a member of the human species and different from the main representative of this species. In his entirety, Adam – or 'man' in our language – is two things in one: the representative of the species mankind and the prototype of the male individuals of this species. On a first level, man and woman are identical; on a second level, woman is opposite or the contrary of man. These two relations characterize the hierarchical relation, which cannot be better symbolized than by the material encompassing of the future Eve in the body of the first Adam. This hierarchical relation is, very generally, that between a whole (or a set) and an element of this whole (or set): the element belongs to the set and is in this sense consubstantial or identical with it; at the same time, the element is distinct from the set or stands in opposition to it. This is what I mean by the expression 'the encompassing of the contrary'.

The matter of Adam and Eve is so surprising, so contrary to contemporary ideas, that a brief commentary may be useful. Let us first consider it linguistically. French and English use the same word to designate 'Man' (representative of the race, first level) and 'man' (opposed to 'woman', second level). Thus, these languages render 'woman' inferior, and we know that necessity plays no role here, as neighbouring languages, German, for instance, have two different words. But this arrangement is interesting because it fuses together the two levels and refers immediately back to 'the encompassing'. Nor is this type of arrangement an exception; it occurs frequently in vocabularies. I have taken only a schema from the text of Genesis. The text indicates the unity of the couple, 'they will be one flesh' (24). This is important, for it is to say that only by reference to the first level can there be unity at the second. This is the heart of the matter, the point which the contemporary mind – and I would say the modern mind in general – tries with all its strength, and in vain, to blur. You may well declare the two sexes equal, but the more you manage to make them equal, the more you will destroy the unity between them (in the couple or the family), because *the principle of this unity is outside them and because, as such, it necessarily hierarchizes them with respect to one another.* I should immediately add that this is only an incomplete truth. The same hierarchical principle that in some way subordinates one level to another at the same time introduces a multiplicity of levels, letting the situation reverse itself. The mother of the family (an Indian family, for example), inferior though she may be made by her sex in some respects nonetheless dominates the relationships within the family. One might say, from an egalitarian viewpoint, that traditional societies are made bearable by these reversals. The egalitarian mind loses sight of this because it is unable to concern itself with more than a single level. If it is forced to consider several levels, it builds them on the same pattern.

But enough about Adam and Eve, let us return to the problem, now in the abstract. I am indebted to Raymond Apthorpe for the idea of the encompassing/encompassed relation. It goes back to the time when, at Oxford, I supervised his doctoral thesis, highly original but unpublished.[2] Regarding the various possible logical relations between two classes, Apthorpe completed the presentation of Stebbing and of Euler, in the form of circles holding different relative positions, by introducing the consideration of the universe of discourse. He distinguished four cases, of which I shall use only two. Additionally, his purpose was to make forms of interaction correspond immediately to these logical types, which fall outside my purpose. In the hierarchical case, according to Apthorpe, one category (the superior) includes the other (the inferior), which in turn excludes the first.

Let us consider a universe of discourse, represented by a rectangle divided into two classes or categories with no remainder or overlap. There are two possible cases. In the first case, the rectangle is divided into juxtaposed parts, giving two smaller rectangles, A and B (Figure 1). Together, the two classes A and B exhaust the universe of discourse. They may be said to be complementary with respect to this universe, or again, contradictory, in the sense that each excludes the other and there is no third possibility. From the first viewpoint, one considers the universe of discourse in its composition (structural perspective). From the second viewpoint, one considers either one of the two classes and its logical relation to the other, or if one prefers, one considers the relation between the two classes, the universe of discourse being only implied in the background of the relation (substantial perspective).

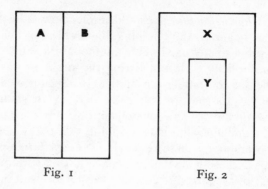

Fig. 1                    Fig. 2

In the second case, the case of hierarchy, class X is coextensive with the universe of discourse, and the other is set within the first as a rectangle Y contained in X: Y belongs to X and at the same time differs from it, as Eve does with respect to Adam (Figure 2). I think the clearest formulation is gained by separating and combining two levels. At the superior level there is unity; at the inferior level there is distinction, there is, as in the first case, complementariness or contradiction. Hierarchy consists in the combination of these two propositions concerning different levels. In hierarchy thus defined, complementariness or contradiction is contained in a unity of superior order. But as soon as we intermingle the two levels, we have a logical scandal, because there is identity and contradiction at the same time. No doubt this fact has contributed to the movement of modern thought away from the idea of hierarchy, to the neutralization or repression of this idea in the modern mind. At the same time, it evokes a formidable neighbour, the Hegelian undertaking that consists of transforming obstacle into instrument, in using contradiction as a base for superior understanding. We shall take this opportunity to compare the two models.

On the one hand we have 'structure', on the other, 'dialectic'. The followers of 'dialectic' readily consider 'structure' to be sterile. It is true that the distinctive opposition 'produces' nothing, nor does the hierarchical opposition that I shall ask to have joined with it. They are static; our oppositions, complementarinesses, and polarities are not surpassed through a 'development'. However, there is certainly a temporal process corresponding to them, that of *differentiation*, which may have far-reaching effects, for

example, when among living beings the organs of sexual reproduction belong to different individuals, as in the case of Adam and
Eve. It is thus a manifest error to suppose that diachrony and
'dialectic' mean the same thing. It is, however, true that differentiation does not change the global setting, given once and for all;
in a hierarchical schema the parts that nest one side the other may
increase in number without changing the law.

The Hegelian schema based on contradiction works quite differently. By the negation and the negation of the negation, a totality
without precedent can be produced synthetically. In fact, in Hegel's
thought the deepest motive is to produce a differentiated totality
from an undifferentiated substance, that is, a totality from a substance. In the hierarchical schema, on the contrary, the totality
preexists and there is no substance. The main point for our comparison is that in both cases there are two levels, one transcending
the other. For Hegel, transcendence is produced synthetically,
instead of preexisting, and this is the philosopher's essential aim –
even if the matter stands otherwise on the level of the absolute
spirit.

Hierarchical opposition as defined here, the relation between
encompassing and encompassed or between ensemble and element,
is to my mind just as indispensable to structural thought as the
distinctive opposition or relation of complementariness of older
standing. Actually, it is surprising that so little note has hitherto
been taken of it, or rather it would be surprising if we did not know
what a mighty force is set against this recognition.

I have tried to show this necessity in an article about dualist
classifications and the topic – classic since Hertz – of the opposition between right and left ('L'Homme', pp. 101–9). We observe
that this opposition has been treated as just any polarity by glossing
over the *reference to totality* that is a constituent element of it;
right and left exist only with respect to the human body (my right
is my reflection's left). The problem of 'the preeminence of the
right hand' is a false problem, or at least it is wrongly put. The
implicit reference to the whole of our body has as its necessary consequence the preeminence of one of the hands over the other. The
hands cannot be equal in any situation because they are always seen
in relation to a whole defining and organizing them.

This means that the relative *value* of the hands, determined by their relation to the whole of which they are a part, is inherent in their distinction; it means that the relative value of the hands cannot be dissociated from their distinction as if there were, on the one side, an idea of simple polarity, and on the other, a value that would be superadded to it. The same is true of dualism generally, for example, of tribal organization by moieties: here again, differentiation means differentiation of values. Unlike the mere distinctive relation, hierarchical relation includes the dimension of value.

But this is still simplistic, and we are obliged to complicate the picture further. We have said earlier, 'Hierarchy consists in the combination of these two propositions concerning different levels'. This proposition presupposes a second one: 'Hierarchy assumes the distinction of [two] levels.' In a sense it is this distinction itself. As moderns, we tend to put everything on the same plane. If it were possible, we would have nothing to do with hierarchy. When we introduce it, we must not forget that it is intrinsically two-dimensional. As soon as we posit a relation of superior to inferior, we must become accustomed to specifying at what level this hierarchical relation itself is situated. It cannot be true from one end of experience to the other (only artificial hierarchies make this claim), for this would be to deny the hierarchical dimension itself, which requires situations to be distinguished by value. Hierarchy thus offers the possibility of reversal: that which at a superior level was superior may become inferior at an inferior level. The left can become the right in what might be called a 'left situation', and again, in the complex complementarity that unites them, each of two moieties may appear alternately superior and inferior.

One may wonder what becomes of all this in the egalitarian ideology. We moderns have not stopped making value judgments; we give unequal values to people, things, and situations. One may wonder how we have managed to free ourselves as much as possible from hierarchy, and from the opposition between ensemble and element that is something like its formal principle. One method used is precisely the absolute distinction that lets *facts* be considered independently of *values*. One also observes that the encompassing of the contrary occurs frequently, though it does not appear as such. At any rate, it is what comes out of my inquiry on economic thought, for example (*cf. From Mandeville to Marx*, index, s.v. hierarchy, instances of encompassing). One observes that every time a notion gains importance, it acquires the capacity to encompass its contrary. To give only a few examples, it is in this way that goods encompass services in classical political economy, that work encompasses exchange for Adam Smith, that production encompasses consumption for Marx, all in the very sense that Adam encompasses Eve, and in a slightly different sense, that, for Hegel, the State encompasses 'civil society' or the system of needs. Given the essentially antihierarchical aim of all these writers, these examples should suffice to show that it is not easy to do without the opposition in question.

Perhaps sociology has only a single law, which we may call 'Parsons law', even if Talcott Parsons and his colleagues have not expressed it in this way, far too crude for them. It is that each social subsystem is governed in the first place by the system to which it belongs; the words 'subsystem' and 'system' have a quite relative meaning here (*cf.* Talcott Parsons, Robert F. Bales, Edward A. Shils, *Working Papers in the Theory of Action* [Glencoe, 1953]). It would not be hard to find the counterpart of this proposition in other fields. It is true that the definition of the 'system' at different levels, hence the recognition of 'levels' and their hierarchy, presents its own problems. Nevertheless, it is not difficult to find simple illustrations of this principle, which tells us, in short, that in order to grasp a given level, we must see it in relation to the superior level, that is, we must *transcend it.* On the contrary, it can scarcely be doubted that the principal and constant effort of modern thought has been and is now directed against *transcendence* in all its forms, as has been said of Hegel in passing. The fact that 'the law of Parsons' has been isolated, against the major current of modern ideology, gives it its seal of authenticity.

In short, whether what is in question is the need to restore value to ideas, or the need to recognize the presence of transcendence at the heart of social life, the encompassing of the contrary, or, what amounts to the same thing, the orientation to the whole, commands attention as a challenge to the main trend of modern ideology.

# APPENDIX A

CASTE, RACISM AND 'STRATIFICATION'
REFLECTIONS OF A SOCIAL
ANTHROPOLOGIST*

*To E. E. Evans-Pritchard*


In a recent article Professor Raymond Aron writes about sociology: 'what there exists of a critical, comparative, pluralist theory is slight'.[1] This in indeed the feeling one has when, after studying the caste system in India, one turns to comparing it with other social systems and to seeing, in particular, how it has been accommodated within the theory of 'social stratification' as developed in America. To begin with, the problem can be put in very simple terms: is it permissible, or is it not, to speak of 'castes' outside India? More particularly, may the term be applied to the division between Whites and Negroes in the southern states of the United States of America? To this question a positive answer has been given by some American sociologists[2] – in accordance with the common use of the word – while most anthropologists with Indian experience would probably answer it in the negative.[3] Ideally, this question might appear as a matter of mere terminological choice: either we accept the former alternative and adopt a very broad definition, and as a result we may have to distinguish sub-types, as some authors who have opposed the 'racial caste' (U.S.A.) to

* This is an English version of a paper first published in French in *Cahiers Internationaux de Sociologie*, Paris XXIX, 1960, pp. 91–112. The text is taken from *Contributions to Indian Sociology*, V, 1961. The following reflections have sprung mainly from the preparation of an article on 'caste' for the *Vocabulary of Social Sciences* (Unesco). The question of the proximate extensions of the term 'caste', for instance to societies of South-East Asia, is left out. Only a remote extension is considered which appears to require that sociological and anthropological approaches be confronted, even if in a somewhat hasty and temporary manner.

the 'cultural caste' (India); or we refuse any extension of the term and apply it exclusively to the Indian type precisely defined, and in this case other terms will be necessary to designate the other types. But in actual fact, a certain usage has been established, and perhaps it is only by criticizing its already manifest implications that a way can be opened to a better comparative view. I shall, therefore, begin by criticizing the usage which predominates in America in the hope of showing how social anthropology can assist sociology in this matter. Two aspects will particularly require attention: what idea the authors in question have formed of the Indian system, and which place they give to the concept of 'caste' in relation to neighbouring concepts such as 'class' and to the broad heading of 'social stratification' under which they often group such facts. Thereafter I shall tentatively outline the framework of a true comparison.

A   *Caste as an extreme case of class: Kroeber*

A definition of caste given by Kroeber is rightly regarded as classical, for the whole sociological trend with which I am concerned here links up with it.

In his article on 'Caste' in the *Encyclopoedia of Social Sciences* (Vol. iii, 1930, 254b–257a), he enumerates the characteristics of caste (endogamy, heredity, relative rank) and goes on to say: '*Castes, therefore, are a special form of social classes*, which in tendency at least are present in every society. Castes differ from social classes, however, in that they have emerged into social consciousness to the point that custom and law attempt their rigid and permanent separation from one another. *Social classes are the generic soil from which caste systems have at various times and places independently grown up* . . .' (my italics).

By 'caste systems' he means in what follows, apart from India, medieval Europe and medieval Japan. He implicitly admits, however, that the last two cases are imperfect: either the caste organization extends to only a part of the society, or, as in the Japanese 'quasi-caste system', the division of labour and the integration with religion remain vague.

For us, the essential point here is that 'caste' is considered as an extreme case of 'class'. Why? Probably in the first place because of the 'universality of anthropology', as Lloyd Warner says while accepting Kroeber's definition.[4] In the second place, because 'caste' is at once rigid and relatively rare, whereas 'class' is more flexible, vaguer and relatively very widespread. But the problem is only deferred, for in such a perspective it should be necessary to define 'class', which is much more difficult than to define 'caste'. Never mind, 'class', after all, is familiar to us, while 'caste' is strange. . . . We are landed at the core of the sociocentricity within which the whole school of authors under discussion develops. Actually, if one were prepared to make light of the relative frequency with which the supposed 'class' occurs, and if one were solely concerned with conceptual clarity, the terms could just as well be reversed, and one could start from the Indian caste system, which offers in a clear and crystalline form what is elsewhere diluted and blurred in many ways. The definition quoted reduces a society's consciousness of itself to an epiphenomenon – although some importance is attached to it: 'They have emerged into social consciousness.' The case shows that to do this is to condemn oneself to obscurity.

B    *Distinction between caste, estate, and class*

The oneness of the human species, however, does not demand the arbitrary reduction of diversity to unity, it only demands that it should be possible to pass from one particularity to another, and that no effort should be spared in order to elaborate a common language in which each particularity can be adequately described. The first step to that end consists in recognizing differences.

Before Kroeber gave his definition, Max Weber had made an absolute distinction between 'class' and *Stand*, 'status-group', or 'estate' in the sense of pre-revolutionary France – as between economy on the one hand and 'honour' and 'social intercourse' on the other.[5] His definition of class as an economic group has been criticized, but it has the merit of not being too vague. Allowing that social classes as commonly referred to in our societies have these two aspects, the analytical distinction is none the less indispensable from a comparative point of view, as we shall see. In Max Weber as in Kroeber, caste represents an extreme case; but this time it is the status-group which becomes a caste when its separation is secured not only through convention and laws, but also ritually (impurity through contact). Is this transition from status-group to caste conceived as genetic or only logical? One notes in passing that, in the passage of *Wirtschaft und Gesellschaft* which I have in view here, Weber thinks that individual castes develop some measure of distinct cults and gods – a mistake of Western common sense which believes that whatever can be distinguished must be different. Into the genesis of caste, Weber introduces a second component, namely a reputedly ethnic difference. From this point of view, castes would be closed communities (*Gemeinschaften*), endogamous and believing their members to be of the same blood, which would put themselves in society (*vergesellschaftet*) one with the other. On the whole, caste would be the outcome of a conjunction between status-group and ethnic community. At this juncture a difficulty appears. For it seems that Weber maintains the difference between *Gesellschaft* and *Gemeinschaft*: on the one hand the *Vergesellschaftung* of a reputedly ethnic group, a 'Paria people', tolerated only for the indispensable economic services it performs, like the Jews in medieval Europe, on the other the *Gemeinschaft* made up of status-groups or, in the extreme case, of castes. If I am not mistaken, the difficulty emerges in the concluding sentence, which has to reconcile the two by means of an artificial transition from the one to the other: 'Eine umgreifende *Vergesellschaftung* die ethnisch geschiedenen Gemeinschaften zu einem spezifischen, politischen *Gemeinschaftshandeln* zusammenschliesst' (my italics), or, freely translated, 'the *societalization* of ethnically distinct communities embraces them to the point of uniting them, on the level of political action, in a *community* of a new kind'. The particular group then acknowledges a hierarchy of honour and at the same time its ethnic difference becomes a difference of function (warriors, priests, etc.). However remarkable the conjunction here achieved between hierarchy, ethnic difference and division of labour may be, one may wonder whether Weber's failure is not due to the fact that to a hierarchical view he added 'ethnic' considerations through which he wanted to link up widespread ideas on the racial origin of the caste system with the exceptional situation of certain minority communities like Jews or Gypsies in Western societies.

What remains is the distinction, as analytical as one could wish, between economic group and status-group. In the latter category, one can then distinguish more clearly, as Sorokin did,[6] between 'order' or 'estate' and caste. As an instance, the clergy in prerevolutionary France did not renew itself from within, it was an open 'estate'.

## c 'Caste' in the U.S.A.

At first sight there is a paradox in the works of the two most notable authors who have applied the term 'caste' to the separation between White and Negroes in the U.S.A. While their purpose is to oppose the 'colour line' to class distinctions, they both accept the idea that caste is a particular and extreme form of class, not a distinct phenomenon. We have seen that Lloyd Warner accepts Kroeber's idea of continuity; however he immediately insists, as early as his article of 1936, that whilst Whites and Negroes make up two 'castes', the two groups are stratified into classes according to a common principle, so that the Negroes of the upper class are superior from the point of view of class to the small Whites, while at the same time being inferior to them from the point of view of 'caste'.[7] Gunnar Myrdal also states that 'caste may thus in a sense be viewed as the extreme form of absolutely rigid class', in this sense 'caste' constitutes 'a harsh deviation from the ordinary American social structure and the American Creed'.[8] The expression '*harsh* deviation' is necessary here to correct the idea of continuity posited in the preceding sentence. In other words, the supposed essential identity between class and caste appears to be rooted in the fact that, once equality is accepted as the norm, any form of inequality appears to be the same as any other because of their common deviation from the norm. We shall see presently that this is fully conscious, elaborately justified in Myrdal. But if, from the standpoint of comparative sociology, one purports to describe these forms of inequality in themselves and if, moreover, one finds that many societies have a norm of inequality, then the presumed unity between class on the one hand and the American form of discrimination on the other becomes meaningless, as our authors themselves sufficiently witness.

The use of the term 'caste' for the American situation is justified by our two authors in very different ways. For Myrdal, the choice of a term is a purely practical matter. One should take a word of common usage – and not try to escape from the value judgments implicit in such a choice. Of the three available terms, 'class' is not suitable, 'race' would give an objective appearance to subjective justifications and prejudices, so there remains only 'caste' which is already used in this sense, and which can be used, in a monographic manner, without any obligation to consider how far it means the same thing in India and in the U.S.A.[9] In point of fact, the pejorative coloration of the word by no means displeases Myrdal. While the word 'race' embodies a false justification, the word 'caste' carries a condemnation. This is in accordance with American values as defined by the author in the following pages. The American ideology is egalitarian to the extreme. The 'American Creed' demands free competition, which from the point of view of social stratification represents a combination of two basic norms, equality and liberty, but accepts inequality as a result of competition.[10] From this one deduces the 'meaning' of differences of social status in this particular country, one conceives classes as the 'results of the restriction of free competition', while 'caste', with its draconian limitations of free competition, directly negates the American Creed, creates a contradiction in the conscience of every White, survives only because of a whole system of prejudices, and should disappear altogether.

All this is fine, and the militant attitude in which Gunnar Myrdal sees the sole possibility of true objectivity could hardly be more solidly based. In particular, he has the merit of showing that it is in relation to values (a relation not expressed by Kroeber and Warner) that the assumed continuity of class and caste can be best understood. But was it really necessary in all this to use the word 'caste' without scientific guarantee?[11] Would the argument have lost in efficacy if it had been expressed only in terms of 'discrimination', 'segregation', etc.? Even if it had, ought one to risk obscuring comparison in order to promote action? Gunnar Myrdal does not care for comparison. Further, does he not eschew comparative theory, in so far as he achieves his objectivity only when he can personally share the values of the society he is studying?

Unlike Myrdal, Lloyd Warner thinks that 'caste' can be used of the Southern U.S.A. in the same sense as it is used of India. This is seen from a 'comparative study' by Warner and Allison Davis,[12] in which the results of their American study are summarized, 'caste' defined, and two or three pages devoted to the Indian side. This Indian summary, though based on good authors, is not very convincing. The variability of the system in time and space is insisted upon to the point of stating that: 'It is not correct to speak of an Indian caste system since there is a variety of systems there.'

In general, caste here is conceived as a variety of class, differing from it in that it forbids mobility either up or down. The central argument runs as follows: in the Southern States, in addition to the disabilities imposed upon the Negroes and the impossibility for them to 'pass', there is between Whites and Negroes neither marriage nor commensality; the same is true in India between different castes. It is the same kind of social phenomenon. 'Therefore, for the comparative sociologist and social anthropologist they are forms of behaviour which must have the same term applied to them' (p. 233).

This formula has the virtue of stating the problem clearly, so that if we do not agree with Warner we can easily say why. A first reason, which might receive ready acceptance, is that under the label of 'behaviour pattern' or 'social phenomena' Warner confuses two different things, namely a collection of particular features (endogamy, mobility and commensality prohibition, etc.) and a whole social system, 'caste' in the case of India obviously meaning 'the caste system'. It is not asked whether the sum of the features under consideration is enough (to the exclusion of all the features left out of consideration) to define the social system: in fact there is no question of a system but only of a certain number of features of the Indian caste system which, according to the author, would be sufficient to define the system. There is really here a *choice* which there is no necessity to follow.[13]

Let me try to indicate the reasons against the proposed choice. It is generally admitted, at any rate in social anthropology, that particular features must be seen in their relations with other particular features. There follows, to my mind, a radical consequence – that a particular feature, if taken not in itself but in its concrete position within a system (what is sometimes called its 'function'), can have a totally different meaning according to the position it occupies. That is to say, from a sociological standpoint it is *actually different*. Thus as regards the endogamy of a group: it is not sufficient to say that the group is 'closed', for this very closure is perhaps not, sociologically speaking, the same thing in all cases; in itself it is the same thing, but in itself it is simply not a sociological fact, as it is not, in the first place, a conscious fact. One is led inevitably to the ideology, overlooked in the behaviouristic sociology of Warner and others, which implicitly posits that, among the particular features to be seen in relation to each other, ideological features do not have the same status as the others. Nevertheless a great part of the effort of Durkheim (and of Max Weber as well) bore on the necessity of recognizing in them the same objectivity as in other aspects of social life. Of course this is not to claim that ideology is necessarily the ultimate reality of social facts and delivers their 'explanation', but only that it is the condition of their existence.

The case of endogamy shows very clearly how social facts are distorted through a certain approach. Warner and Allison treat it as a fact of behaviour and not as a fact of values. As such it would be the same as the factual endogamy of a tribe having no prejudice against intermarriage with another tribe, but which given circumstances alone prevent from practising it. If, on the contrary, endogamy is a fact of values, we are not justified in separating it in the analysis from other facts of values, and particularly – though not solely – from the justifications of it the people give. It is only by neglecting this that racial discrimination and the caste system can be confused. But, one might say, is it not possible that analysis may reveal a close kinship between social facts outwardly similar and ideologically different? The possibility can be readily admitted, but only to insist the more vigorously that we are as yet very far indeed from having reached that point, and that the task for the moment is to take social facts as they are given, without imposing upon them a discrimination scientifically as unwarrantable as is, in American society, the discrimination which these authors attack. The main point is that the refusal to allow their legitimate place to facts of consciousness makes true sociological comparison impossible, because it carries with it a sociocentric attitude. In order to see one's own society from without, one must become conscious of its values and their implications. Difficult as this always is, it becomes impossible if values are neglected. This is confirmed here from the fact that, in Warner's conceptual scheme, the continuity between class and caste proceeds, as we have seen, from an unsuspected relation to the egalitarian norm, whilst it is presented as a matter of behaviour.

The criticism of the 'Caste School of Race Relations' has been remarkably carried out by Oliver C. Cox.[14] From the same sources as Warner, Cox, with admirable insight, has evolved a picture of the caste system which is infinitely truer than that with which Warner was satisfied. It is true that one cannot everywhere agree with Cox, but we must remember that he was working at second and even at third hand (for instance from Bouglé). Even the limits of Cox's understanding show up precisely our most rooted Western prejudices. He is insufficient mainly in what regards the religious moorings of the system (purity and impurity); because for the Westerner society exists independently of religion and he hardly imagines that it could be otherwise. On the other hand, Cox sees that one should not speak of the individual caste but of the system (pp. 3–4), and that it is not a matter of racial ideology: '... Although the individual is born heir to his caste, his identification with it is assumed to be based upon some sort of psychological and moral heritage which does not go back to any fundamental somatic determinant' (p. 5).

Elsewhere he writes (p. 14): 'Social inequality is the keynote of the system ... there is a fundamental creed or presumption (of inequality) ... antithesis of the Stoic doctrine of human equality. ...' We see here how Cox strikes on important and incontrovertible points whenever he wishes to emphasize the difference between India and America. I will not enlarge on his criticism of Warner and his school; we have already seen that he makes the essential point: the Indian system is a coherent social system based on the principle of inequality, while the American 'colour bar' contradicts the egalitarian system within which it occurs and of which it is a kind of disease.[15]

The use of the word 'caste' to designate American racial segregation has led some authors, in an effort to recognize at the same time the ideological difference, to make a secondary distinction. Already in 1937 John Dollard was writing: 'American caste is pinned not to cultural but to biological factors.'[16] In 1941, in an article called 'Intermarriage in Caste Society' in which he was considering, besides India, the Natchez and the society of the Southern United States, Kingsley Davis asked: how is marriage between different units possible in these societies, while stratification into castes is closely dependent on caste endogamy? His answer was, in the main, that a distinction must be made between a 'racial caste system' in which hybrids present an acute problem, and a 'non-racial caste system' where this is not so. In India, hypergamy as defined by Blunt for the north of India, i.e. marriage between a man of an upper subcaste and a woman of a lower sub-caste within the same caste can be understood in particular as a factor of 'vertical solidarity' and as allowing for the exchange of prestige in return for goods (p. 386). (The last point actually marks an essential aspect of true hypergamy, in which the status or prestige of the husband as well as the sons is not affected by the relatively inferior status of the wife or mother.) Another difference between the two kinds of 'caste systems' is that the 'racial' systems rather oppose two groups only, whereas the other systems distinguish a great number of 'strata'. Finally, K. Davis remarks that the hypothesis of the racial origin of the Indian caste system is not proven and that at any rate it is not racial today (n. 22). It is strange that all this did not lead Davis to reflect upon the inappropriateness of using the same word to denote so widely different facts. For him caste, whatever its content may be, is 'an extreme form of stratification', as for others it was an extreme case of class. This brings us to the question of the nature of this category of 'stratification'.

D  *'Social stratification'*

Though the expression deserves attention in view of the prolifera-tion of studies published under this title in the United States and the theoretical discussions to which it has given rise, it does not in effect introduce anything new on the point with which we are here concerned. We meet again the same attitude of mind we have already encountered, but here it runs up against difficulties. As Pfautz acknowledges in his critical bibliography of works published between 1945 and 1952, it is essentially a matter of 'class'.[17] However, Weber's distinction has made its way in the world: one can distinguish types of social stratification according to whether the basis of inequality is power, or prestige, or a combination of both, and classes are usually conceived of as implying a hierarchy of power (political as well as economic), castes and 'estates' a hierarchy of prestige (pp. 392–3). One notes however that the community studies of Warner and others conclude that the status hierarchy is a matter of prestige and not of power. Let us stress here the use of the word 'hierarchy', which appears to be intro-duced in order to allow different species to be distinguished within the genus 'stratification'. But here are two strikingly different concepts: should the quasi-geological impassibility suggested by the latter give way to the consideration of values?

A theoretical controversy in the columns of the *American Sociological Review* is very interesting for the light it throws on the preoccupations and implicit postulates of some sociologists.[18] The starting-point was an article published in 1945 by Kingsley Davis and Wilbert E. Moore. Davis had, three years earlier, given basic definitions for the study of stratification (*status*, *stratum*, etc.). Here the authors raised the question of the 'function' of stratification. How is it that such palpable inequalities as those referred to under the name of social classes are encountered in a society whose acknowledged norm is equality? Davis and Moore formulate the hypothesis that it is the result of a mechanism comparable to that of the market: inequality of rewards is necessary in a differentiated society in order that the more difficult or important occupations, those demanding a long training in special skills or involving heavy responsibilities, can be effectively carried out. Buckley objected that Davis and Moore had confused true stratification and pure and simple differentiation: the problem of stratification is not, or is not only, one of knowing how individuals potentially equal at the start find themselves in unequal positions ('achieved inequality'), but of discovering how inequality is maintained, since terms like stratum or stratification are generally taken as implying permanent, hereditary, 'ascribed' inequality. In a rejoinder to Buckley, Davis admitted the difference of points of view; he added that the critic's animosity seemed to him to be directed against the attempt to explain inequality functionally. In my opinion, Davis was right in raising the question of inequality; he was wrong, as Buckley seems to imply, in raising it where inequality is weakest instead of tackling it where it is strongest and most articulate. But in so doing he remained within the tradition we have observed here, which always implicitly refers itself to equality as the norm, as this controversy and the very use of the term 'inequality' show.

In a recent article Dennis H. Wrong sums up the debate. He points out the limitations of Davis's and Moore's theory and quotes from a work of the former a passage which again shows his pursuit of the functional necessity of stratification, as illustrated for instance by the fact that sweepers tend to have an inferior status in all societies (he is thinking of India).[19] In the end, Wrong asks for studies on certain relations between the egalitarian ideal and other aspects of society, such as the undesirable consequences of extreme equality or mobility (p. 780). It appears that equality and in-equality are considered here as opposite tendencies to be studied on the functional level. Referring to the Utopians, Wrong recalls the difficulty of 'making the leap from history into freedom' (p. 775).

Something has happened then in this branch of American sociology. With the multiplication of studies on social classes, one has been led to introduce values and that value-charged word, 'hierarchy'; one has been led to search for the functions (and dysfunctions) of what our societies valorize as well as of what they do not valorize ('in-equality') and which had been called for that reason by a neutral and even pejorative term, 'stratification'. What is in fact set against the egalitarian norm is not, as the term suggests, a kind of residue, a precipitate, a geological legacy, but actual forces, factors or functions. These are negated by the norm, but they nevertheless exist; to express them, the term 'stratifica-tion' is altogether inadequate. Nelson N. Foote wrote in a preface to a series of studies: 'The dialectical theme of American history . . . has been a counterpoint of the principles of hierarchy and equality.'[20] The 'problem' of social classes, or of 'social stratifica-tion' as it appears to our sociologists springs from the contradiction between the egalitarian ideal, accepted by all these scholars as by the society to which they belong, and an array of facts showing that difference, differentiation, tends even among us to assume a hierarchical aspect, and to become permanent or hereditary inequality, or discrimination. As Raymond Aron says: 'At the heart of the problem of classes I perceive the antinomy between the fact of differentiation and the ideal of equality.'[21] There are here realities which are made obscure to us by the fact that our values and the forms of our consciousness reject or ignore them. (This is probably still more so for Americans.) In order to under-stand them better, it is advantageous to turn to those societies which on the contrary approve and emphasize them. In so doing we shall move from 'stratification' to hierarchy.

E  *Hierarchy in India*

It is impossible to describe the caste system in detail here. Rather, after briefly recalling its main features, I shall isolate more or less arbitrarily the aspect which concerns us. Bouglé's definition can be the starting-point: the society is divided into a large number of permanent groups which are at once specialized, hierarchized and separated (in matter of marriage, food, physical contact) in relation to each other.[22] It is sufficient to add that the common basis of these three features is the opposition of pure and impure, an opposition of a hierarchical nature which implies separation and, on the professional level, specialization of the occupations relevant to the opposition; that this basic opposition can segment itself without limit; finally, if one likes, that the conceptual reality of the system lies in this opposition, and not in the groups which it opposes – this accounts for the structural character of these groups, caste and subcaste being the same thing seen from different points of view.

It has been acknowledged that hierarchy is thus rendered perfectly univocal in principle.[23] Unfortunately, there has sometimes been a tendency to obscure the issue by speaking of not only religious (or 'ritual') status, but also 'secular' (or 'social') status based upon power, wealth, etc. which Indians would also take into consideration. Naturally Indians do not confuse a rich man with a poor man but, as specialists seem to become increasingly aware, it is necessary to distinguish between two very different things: the scale of statuses (called 'religious') which I name hierarchy and which is absolutely distinct from the fact of power; and the distribution of power, economic and political, which is very important in practice but is distinct from, and subordinate to, hierarchy. It will be asked then how power and hierarchy are related to each other. Precisely, Indian society answers this question in a very explicit manner.[24] Hierarchy culminates in the Brahman, or priest; it is the Brahman who consecrates the king's power, which otherwise depends entirely on force (this results from the dichotomy). From very early times, the relationships between Brahman and king or Kshatriya are fixed. While the Brahman is spiritually or absolutely supreme, he is materially dependent; whilst the king is materially the master, he is spiritually subordinate. A similar relation distinguishes one from the other the two superior 'human ends', *dharma* (action conforming to) universal order and *artha* (action conforming to) selfish interest, which are also hierarchized in such a way that the latter is legitimate only within the limits set by the former. Again, the theory of the *gift* made to Brahmans, a pre-eminently meritorious action, can be regarded as establishing a means of transformation of material goods into values (*cf.* hypergamy, mentioned above, p. 248: one gets prestige from the gift of a girl to superiors).

This disjunction of power and status illustrates perfectly Weber's analytical distinction; its interest for comparison is great, for it presents an unmixed form, it realizes an 'ideal type'. Two features stand out: first, in India, any totality is expressed in the form of a hierarchical enumeration of its components (thus of the state or kingdom for example), hierarchy marks the conceptual integration of a whole, it is, so to say, its intellectual cement. Secondly, if we are to generalize, it can be supposed that hierarchy, in the sense that we are using the word here, and in accord with its etymology, never attaches itself to power as such, but always to religious functions, because religion is the form that the universally true assumes in these societies. For example, when the king has the supreme rank, as is generally the case, it is very likely not by reason of his power but by reason of the religious nature of his function. From the point of view of rank at any rate, it is the opposite to what one most often supposes, namely that power is the essential which then attracts to itself religious dignities or finds in them support and justification.

One may see in the hierarchical principle, as it appears in India in its pure state, a fundamental feature of complex societies other than our own, and a principle of their unity; not their material, but their conceptual or symbolic unity. That is the essential 'function' of hierarchy: it expresses the unity of such a society whilst connecting it to what appears to it to be universal, namely a conception of the cosmic order, whether or not it includes a God, or a king as mediator. If one likes, hierarchy integrates the society by reference to its values. Apart from the general reluctance which searching for social functions at this level is likely to encounter, it will be objected that there are societies without hierarchy, or else societies in which hierarchy does not play the part described above. It is true for example that tribes, while they are not entirely devoid of inequalities, may have neither a king nor, say, a secret society with successive grades. But that applies to relatively simple societies, with few people, and where the division of labour is little developed.

F *The modern revolution*

There remain the societies of the modern Western type, which go so far as to inscribe the principle of equality in their constitutions. It is indeed true that, if values and not behaviour alone are considered, a profound gap has to be acknowledged between the two kinds. What has happened? Is it possible to take a simple view of it? The societies of the past, most societies, have believed themselves to be based in the order of things, natural as well as social; they thought they were copying or designing their very conventions after the principles of life and the world. Modern society wants to be 'rational', to break away from nature in order to set up an autonomous human order. To that end, it is enough to take the true measure of man and from it deduce the human order. No gap between the ideal and the real: like an engineer's blueprint, the representation will create the actuality. At this point society, the old mediator between man in his particularity and nature, disappears. There are but human individuals, and the problem is how to make them all fit together. Man will now draw from himself an order which is sure to satisfy him. As the source of this rationality, Hobbes posits not an ideal, always open to question, but the most general passion, the common generator of human actions, the most assured human reality. The individual becomes the measure of all things, the source of all 'rationality'; the egalitarian principle is the outcome of this attitude, for it conforms to reason, being the simplest view of the matter, while it most directly negates the old hierarchies.[25]

As against the societies which believed themselves to be natural, here is the society which wants itself to be rational. Whilst the 'natural' society was hierarchized, finding its rationality in setting itself as a whole within a vaster whole, and was unaware of the 'individual', the 'rational' society on the other hand, recognizing only the individual, i.e. seeing universality, or reason, only in the particular man, places itself under the standard of equality and is unaware of itself as a hierarchized whole. In a sense, the 'leap from history into freedom' has already been made, and we live in a realized Utopia.

Between these two types which it is convenient to contrast directly, there should probably be located an intermediary type, in which nature and convention are distinguished and social conventions are susceptible of being judged by reference to an ideal model accessible to reason alone. But whatever may be the transitions which make for the evolution of the second type from the first, it is in the modern revolution which separates the two types, really the two leaves of the same diptych, that the central problem of comparative sociology most probably lies: how can we describe in the same language two 'choices' so diametrically opposed to each other, how can we take into account at once the revolution in values which has transformed modern societies as well as the 'unity of anthropology'? Certainly this cannot be done by refusing to acknowledge the change and reducing everything to 'behaviour', nor by extending the obscurity from one side to the other, as we should by talking of 'social stratification' in general. But we remark that where one of the leaves of the diptych is obscure and blurred, the other is clear and distinct; use can be made of what is conscious in one of the two types of society in order to decipher what is not conscious in the other.

G  *From hierarchy to discrimination*

One can attempt, in broad terms, to apply this comparative perspective to the American racist phenomenon. It is obvious on the one hand that society did not completely cease to be society, as a hierarchized whole, on the day it willed itself to be simply a collection of individuals. In particular, the tendency to make hierarchical distinctions continued. On the other hand, racism is more often than not understood to be a modern phenomenon. (Economic causes of its emergence have sometimes been sought, whilst much closer and more probable ideological connections were neglected.) The simplest hypothesis therefore is to assume that racism fulfils an old function under a new form. It is as if it were representing in an egalitarian society a resurgence of what was differently and more directly and naturally expressed in a hierarchical society. Make distinction illegitimate, and you get discrimination; suppress the former modes of distinction and you have a racist ideology. Can this view be made more precise and confirmed? Societies of the past knew a hierarchy of status bringing with it privileges and disabilities, amongst others the total juridical disability of slavery. Now the history of the United States tells us just this, that racial discrimination succeeded the slavery of the Negro people once the latter was abolished. (One is tempted to wonder why this all important transition has not been more systematically studied, from a sociological point of view, than it seems to have been, but perhaps one's ignorance is the answer.[26]) The distinction between master and slave was succeeded by discrimination by White against Black. To ask why racism appears is already to have in part answered the question: the essence of the distinction was juridical; by suppressing it the transformation of its racial attribute into racist substance was encouraged. For things to have been otherwise the distinction itself should have been overcome.

In general, racism certainly has more complex roots. Besides the internal difference of status, traditional societies knew an external difference, itself coloured by hierarchy, between the 'we' and the others. It was normally social and cultural. For the Greeks as for others, foreigners were barbarians, strangers to the civilization and society of the 'we'; for that reason they could be enslaved. In the modern Western world not only are citizens free and equal before the law, but a transition develops, at least in popular mentality, from the moral principle of equality to the belief in the basic identity of all men, because they are no longer taken as samples of a culture, a society or a social group, but as *individuals* existing in and for themselves.[27] In other words, the recognition of a cultural difference can no longer ethnocentrically justify inequality. But it is observed that in certain circumstances, which it would be necessary to describe, a hierarchical difference continues to be posited, which is this time attached to somatic characteristics, physiognomy, colour of the skin, 'blood'. No doubt, these were at all times marks of distinction, but they have now become the essence of it. How is this to be explained? It is perhaps apposite to recall that we are heirs to a dualistic religion and philosophy: the distinction between matter and spirit, body and soul, permeates our entire culture and especially the popular mentality. Everything looks as if the egalitarian-identitarian mentality was situated within this dualism, as if once equality and identity bear on the individual *souls*, distinction could only be effected with regard to the *bodies*. What is more, discrimination is collective, it is as if only physical characteristics were essentially collective where everything mental tends to be primarily individual.

(Thus mental differences are attributed to physical types). Is this far-fetched? It is only emphasizing the Christian ancestry of modern individualism and egalitarianism: the individual has only fellow-men (even his enemies are considered, not only as objects, but also as subjects), and he believes in the fundamental equality of all men taken severally; at the same time, for him, the collective inferiority of a category of men, when it is in his interest to state it, is expressed and justified in terms of what physically differentiates them from himself and people of his group. To sum up, the proclamation of equality has burst asunder a mode of distinction centred upon the social, but in which physical, cultural and social characteristics were indiscriminately mixed. To reaffirm inequality, the underlying dualism demanded that physical characteristics be brought to the fore. While in India heredity is an attribute of status, the racist attributes status to 'race'.

All this may be regarded as an arbitrary view of the abstract intellect. Yet, the hypothesis is confirmed at least in part in Myrdal's work. Dealing with the American facts, this author discovers a close connection between egalitarianism and racism. To begin with, he notes in the philosophy of the enlightenment the tendency to minimize innate differences; then, generally everywhere and especially in America, the essentially moral doctrine of the 'natural rights' of man rests on a biological egalitarianism: all men are 'created equal'. The period 1830–1860 sees the development of an ideology for the defence of slavery: slavery being condemned in the name of natural equality, its champions argue against this the doctrine of the inequality of races; later the argument is used to justify discrimination, which becomes established from the moment when, about 1877, the North gives up enforcing assimilation. The author's conclusions are worth pondering upon: 'The dogma of racial inequality may, in a sense, be regarded as a strange fruit of the Enlightenment. . . . The race dogma is nearly the only way out for a people so moralistically egalitarian, if it is not prepared to live up to its faith. A nation less fervently committed to democracy could probably live happily in a caste system . . . race prejudice is, in a sense, a function (a perversion) of egalitarianism'.[28]

If this is so, it is permissible to doubt whether, in the fight against racism in general, the mere recall of the egalitarian ideal, however solemn it may be, and even though accompanied by a scientific criticism of racist prejudices, will be really efficient. It would be better to prevent the passage from the moral principle of equality to the notion that all men are identical. One feels sure that equality can, in our day, be combined with the recognition of differences, so long as such differences are morally neutral. People must be provided with the means for conceptualizing differences. The diffusion of the pluralistic notions of culture, society, etc., affording a counterweight and setting bounds to individualism, is the obvious thing.[29] Finally, if the tendency to hierarchize still exists, if the affirmation of the modern ideal is not sufficient to make it disappear but, on the contrary, by a complicated mechanism, can on occasion make it ferocious and morbid, the antagonisms and interests which exploit it should not be lost sight of – but this is beyond our subject.

Cutting short here the attempt to define racism comparatively, I should like to recall, albeit too briefly, a structural relation which is essential to the possible developments of comparison. Equality and hierarchy are not, in fact, opposed to each other in the mechanical way which the exclusive consideration of values might lead one to suppose: the pole of the opposition which is not valorized is none the less present, each implies the other and is supported by it. Talcott Parsons draws attention, at the very beginning of his study, to the fact that distinction of statuses carries with it and presupposes equality within each status (*op. cit.*, p. 1). Conversely, where equality is affirmed, it is within a group which is hierarchized in relation to others, as in the Greek cities or, in the modern world, in British democracy and imperialism, the latter being tinged with hierarchy (e.g., incipient racism in India in the second half of the nineteenth century).[30] It is this structural relation that the egalitarian ideal tends to destroy, the result of its action being what is most often studied under the name of 'social stratification'. In the first place the relation is inverted: equality contains inequalities instead of being contained in a hierarchy. In the second place a whole series of transformations happen which can perhaps be summarized by saying that hierarchy is repressed, made non-conscious: it is replaced by a manifold network of inequalities, matters of fact instead of right, of quantity and gradualness instead of quality and discontinuity. Hence, in part, the well-known difficulty of defining social classes.

H  *Conclusion*

To conclude in general terms, comparative sociology requires concepts which take into account the values that different societies have, so to speak, chosen for themselves. A consequence of this choice of values is that certain aspects of social reality are clearly and consciously elaborated, whilst others are left in the dark. In order to express what a given society does not express, the sociologist cannot invent concepts, for when he attempts to do so he only manages, as in the case of 'social stratification', to translate in a way at once pretentious and obscure the prejudices of his own society. He must therefore have recourse to societies which have expressed those same aspects. A general theory of 'inequality', if it is deemed necessary, must be centred upon those societies which give it a meaning and not upon those which, while presenting certain forms of it, have chosen to disavow it. It must be a theory of hierarchy in its valorized, or simple and direct forms, as well as in its non-valorized or devalorized, or complex, hybrid, covert forms. (Let us note, following Talcott Parsons,[31] that such a theory is only one particular way of considering the total social system.) In so doing one will of course in no way impose upon one society the values of another, but only endeavour to set mutually 'in perspective'[32] the various types of societies. One will try to see each society in the light not only of itself but of the others. From the point of view of social anthropology at any rate, this appears to be not only the formula for an objective comparison, but even the condition for understanding each particular society.

# APPENDIX B

## WORLD RENUNCIATION IN
## INDIAN RELIGIONS

Our greatest debt to Sir James Frazer and the British school of anthropology is probably for having pulled down hedges separating 'primitive' religions, the religions of antiquity and contemporary folk-religion. The Golden Bough stands as a monument in the name of 'the human species'.[1]

This assumption of unity is still fundamental to the development of social anthropology even though the evolutionary theory with which it was originally associated has been rejected. The phrase 'social anthropology' itself may come from Frazer. At all events, it was the name he chose when he inaugurated his chair at Liverpool in 1908. True, there have been many changes in the last fifty years. Anthropology has turned from its early intellectualist approach towards sociology.[2] It has developed monographic studies which might seem a far cry from Frazer's comparative studies. Yet we have become increasingly aware that comparison does not, as was sometimes suggested, merely consist of typological classification following upon the accumulation of factual monographs. In fact comparison and monograph are intimately linked, each descriptive work depending to a great extent on the contemporary state of comparison and contributing to it in return. Also, even at

First published in *Contributions to Indian Sociology*, IV, 1960. Criticism: A. K. Saran, *Eastern Anthropologist*, XV-1, 1962, pp. 53–68; my reply, *Coll. Pap.*, pp. 142, 159–61; J. F. Staal, *Journ. of the Amer. Oriental Soc.*, 81, 1961, pp. 147–49; J. C. Heesterman, *Bijdragen tot de Taal*, 119–3, 1963, pp. 244ff.; M. Biardeau, *Revue historique*, 475, 1965, pp. 53ff.

This is a slightly expanded version of the Frazer Lecture given at Oxford on 30 October 1958. Notes have been added. I am thankful for several observations and suggestions, especially from F. J. Staal. The French text was published in *Archives de Sociologie des Religions*, no. 7, janvier–juin 1959, pp. 45–69. I am much indebted to D. F. Pocock and R. G. Lienhardt for the translation.

the level of precise analysis and particularly in the sphere of religion, striking similarities constantly emerge among peoples who live far apart and belong to different civilizations. Even though beside descriptive work the comparison of religions has advanced little since Frazer's day, his ideal is still pointing the road, as indeed it should.

Thus in the way of homage to the memory of Frazer, a specialized worker of today may perhaps attempt to map out a particular field in a manner oriented to comparison. Since the foundation of anthropology and its conversion to sociology we have at least learned one thing: that apparent diversity can be simplified and ordered through the gradual elucidation of systems of relations. Therefore I shall try to speak the language of relations as far as possible.

It might well be thought a rash undertaking to try to offer a general view of the religions of India, within the limits of this lecture. It is true that their immense literatures have been the object for a century and a half of admirable study. To speak mainly of the West, humanist curiosity, philological discipline and sometimes even genius have devoted themselves to the reconstitution and understanding of an alien mentality, and the results of these labours have been summed up many times. However, taking Hinduism alone, it is still difficult to set its principal traits in order. Its complexity and internal diversity seems to resist the attempt. We are told that the grossest superstitions flourish side by side with the most sublime speculations, that the most varied beliefs and rituals are mixed with one another, while Brahmanic orthodoxy coexists[3] with a host of diverse sects. In the face of this, it is understandable if some have sought clarification by looking at the data as essentially heterogeneous. Some have identified Hinduism with Brahmanic literature and dismissed popular religious practice as a 'demonolatry' different in nature and origin.[4] Others, by comfortably adopting one of the most persuasive philosophical tendencies, neglect both the place of this particular philosophy within the whole and the truly religious development surrounding it. Or again, in modern India, we are occasionally offered a Hinduism which has been passed through the sieve of reform, impoverished and altered almost beyond recognition.

Of all these dichotomies, and in different forms, the confrontation with Christianity is a determining factor. Scientific comparison on the contrary[5] does not operate with such arbitrary distinctions.

It aims at recognizing similarities and, more important still, differences. It is found, at least implicitly, in all serious works on the subject, and has shown certain dominant themes in Indian religions, as compared to Christianity. Of these probably everybody has become aware. But there are two difficulties: the first appears as soon as one tries to formulate clearly what one has more or less confusedly perceived; the second arises from the fact that these dominant themes are broken here and there, as a river is lost in the sand: these disappearances must be located and understood.

There is another fact apparently favouring a unitary definition of Hinduism and even of Buddhist and Jain religions: the diverse and often opposed tendencies that we know have, in the course of time, reacted one upon the other. A characteristic aspect of this interaction in the progressive integration or, as I prefer to call it, aggregation by orthodox tendencies of elements introduced by the heterodox.[6] Indian society and religion on the one hand have produced a rich growth of movements considered heretical to a certain extent, and on the other hand they have tended to absorb formerly heretical inventions. This double movement, which we must try to understand, presupposes a common basis and we do at least know the social aspect of this basis: a sect cannot survive on Indian soil if it denies caste,[7] and it has long been recognized that Buddha himself, if he transcended caste, did not attack or reform it.

As a first step towards a general view of Hinduism and of postvedic religions in general, I shall try to bring together from a sociological vantage point the main findings of Indology. As a matter of fact, the direct study of a small Hindu group led me to abstract certain principles which, it then appeared, could be more widely applied. I shall start from them, and through them try to relate to the society and to each other the great complexes, movements or tendencies which classical Indology has revealed.[8] In my opinion, it is in relation to society that we are able to consider religion itself – and not philosophy under the name of religion – without cutting it off from speculation when it extends over into it. Rather than attempt to apply to India our own distinction between religion and philosophy, which is, as long experience has shown, a difficult enterprise, I shall use another distinction, an Indian one. In general, by distinguishing different levels of experience and thought, I hope to clarify some complexities and to remove some apparent contradictions.

I have previously suggested that the secret of Hinduism may be found in the dialogue between the renouncer and the man-in-the-world.[9] Rather than demonstrate the dichotomy upon which this suggestion rests, we shall take it here as a postulate which will be justified if it allows us to take a simple and consistent view of the whole both in its present shape and in its historical development. We shall see, I think, that on analysis the central role played by the idea, or, better, the *institution* of renunciation emerges more and more clearly.

## I  OBSERVED HINDUISM AND BRAHMANISM

At the outset we can assume that there are two kinds of men in Hindu India, those that live in the world and those that have renounced it, and begin by considering things at the level of life in the world. Starting from the observation of the common people we shall compare its results with the ideas, and practices, of orthodoxy.

In the first place it is known that the fundamental institution is caste:[10] the caste system is based upon a hierarchical opposition of the pure and the impure, it is essentially religious. Observation goes to show that belief in gods does not transcend this fundamental opposition of caste. The people are polytheistic in their practice, and caste values are a basic element in a belief which is directed towards a multiple divinity, a totality of interdependent gods. Put in another way, we can say that the gods have no reality except in relation with others; an individual divinity in isolation is as unreal as an individual human being. Everything is founded upon the complementarity of the pure and the impure, of the superior and the inferior.

Secondly, observation shows the importance of the institutionalized possession of a man by a god (or several gods). At least in those instances which are most clear-cut two religious functions balance each other: while the priest presents to the gods the offerings of men, the gods descend on one man, become incarnate in him and, using him as their oracle, inform and direct other men.

A third complementarity emerges from the study of village cults, it is the complementarity of function between a god and a goddess. While the god watches over the village land or supplies, the goddess rules the collective health of the group, i.e. particularly epidemics.

What becomes of these complementarities at the Brahmanic

level? That between god and goddess is in general absent from consciousness although, as is well known, divine couples are frequent, the great gods having very often one or two female companions.[11] It will be noted that while the idea of a couple is present in the background, the individual divinity tends to emerge in the foreground, sometimes and chiefly the god, but sometimes the goddess.

We do not find the oracle at the Brahmanic level, where he is replaced by the diviner-astrologer. Certainly we read that at the time of the cult the officiant is identified with the god, and this seems indispensable, but he does not prophesy, the god does not speak through his mouth.[12]

Although the Brahmanic treatises know of impurity they naturally have nothing to do with 'impure gods'. Theirs is a vegetarian world where meat-eating is a sign of impurity and inferiority and therefore has no place in the divine attributes. The 'carnivorous' trait then is absent from the theory, but we cannot say that it is not found in practice: the goddess in fact demands blood sacrifice and is nevertheless supreme in her domain.[13] Summarily the same thing happens in the matter of caste complementarity: while the theory insists upon both hierarchy and separation, it tends to leave implicit the fact of interdependence.

Generally speaking, we can say that the complementarities of common religious practice become blurred and indistinct when we move to the level of Brahmanic practice, where however they can still be detected. In Brahmanic theory they tend to disappear altogether. In so far as this theory represents religious consciousness, we find consciousness ignoring the relations that underlie practice. Of the two complementary poles it tends to choose one and reject the other. Without ridding itself of the multiplicity and the contradictions of the divine, it tries to give a reality to the individual gods. It gives a substantialistic theory of what is in fact a structural practice.

This can also be seen with regard to the hierarchy of values in the Dharmashastras. There are three 'human ends', *dharma*, *artha*, and *kāma*, duty, profit, and pleasure. All three are (necessary and) lawful, but they are so graded in a hierarchy that an inferior ideal may be pursued only as far as a superior one does not intervene: *dharma*, conformity to the world order, is more important than *artha*, power and wealth, which, in turn, is above *kāma*, immediate enjoyment. These three ideas are conceived as distinct substances, but let us consider, apart from their hierarchical aspect, what other relations exist between them. The analogy with the hierarchy of *varṇa* is apparent: *dharma* corresponds to the Brahman or priest, *artha* to the king or kshatriya, the temporal power, and *kāma* to the others. This is not all, and one can go further with the help of Talcott Parsons' method of structural analysis. First, *kāma* is opposed to the two others as an action flowing immediately from affective impulses is opposed to an action submitted to intellectual or moral considerations. Then, while *dharma* is moral universalism, *artha* is calculating egotism, something after the manner of 'rational action' in our economic theory – but extended to politics, since here wealth is little more than an attribute of power. While *artha* is opposed to *kāma* as deferred satisfaction to immediate satisfaction, *dharma* is opposed to both as ultimate ends are to particular ends, the sacred to the profane. In the language of Parsons, *kāma* is expressive action, *artha* instrumental action, *dharma* moral action. The trilogy gives an exhaustive classification of the types of action and is based upon a system of oppositions.[14]

This example shows clearly that, however much the Brahmanic theory of life in the world substantializes things, in reality it is a matter of relations. This is a most important point, for, if we were exclusively to consider the classical literature, the mentality of the man-in-the-world would escape us. This is not only because it is very different from our own, but also because it is disguised in the literature in many ways, and above all by its being impregnated with the very different thought of the renouncer.

To say that the world of caste is a world of relations is to say that the particular caste and the particular man have no substance: they exist empirically, but they have no reality in thought, no Being. The fact is after all not new and has long been recognized, but all too commonly one speaks as if one had forgotten it, while observation and analysis continually reassert it. I regard it as fundamental and would therefore firmly posit, at the risk of being crude, that on the level of life in the world the individual *is* not.[15] It is for this reason that any attempt to generalize must start from relations and not from individual elements. It is also why for the Hindus themselves, from the moment they take a substantialistic point of view, everything, including the gods, is unreal: illusionism is here in germ, and its popularity, together with that of monism, cannot surprise us. If this is admitted, then the problem is to understand how it comes about that there is still something else in Hindu India, another kind of thought, namely a kind of thought which conceives of the individual as being.

## 2 THE CHOICE OF SALVATION: THE RENOUNCER

What is before us so far is a religious organization of society, which shapes it according to the universal order and submits temporal power to the rule of religion. There is no transcendent sanction: only the notion of this very order, conformity with which takes on the value of a duty, *dharma*.[16] This has often been recognized as the core of the religion of the Hindu living in the world. Still, even if we add the belief in a multiple divinity, this is not the whole of Hindu religion by far.

In the first place we must consider a complex of notions connected with survival and salvation which deeply mark Hindu religious life. They are common to the majority of religious movements and sects which have appeared in India. Two closely linked ideas are in the foreground, transmigration or the flow of existences, *saṃsāra*, and the moral principle determining the successive existences, *karman*, or retribution for actions. These ideas are immediately related to the belief that it is possible to escape from the chain of existences and to attain liberation, *mokṣa*. The nature of liberation and the ways and techniques for achieving it occupy a major place in speculative thought. Asceticism, not only as a way of salvation, but as a general orientation, the tendency towards a negation of the world – ultramundaneity – have deeply imbued Hinduism. This has rightly received emphasis, but it is difficult to attribute the ultramundane tendency directly to the Brahmans as, implicitly or explicitly, Albert Schweitzer and even Max Weber have done.[17] We must in fact make a distinction. The Brahmans, as priests superior to all other men, are settled in the world comfortably enough. On the other hand, it is well known that classically whoever seeks liberation must leave the world and adopt an entirely different mode of life. This is an institution, *saṃnyāsa*, renunciation, in fact a social state apart from society proper.[18] The ultramundane tendency does not only hover in the minds of men in the world, it is present, incarnate in the emaciated figure of the renouncer, the *saṃnyāsin*, with his begging bowl, his staff and orange dress. We may imagine the reaction to this creature of the typical Brahman whom we may think of as he is early represented in a carving on the north gate at Sanchi (Vessantara Jataka), a round bellied figure, expressing an inimitable blend of arrogance and avidity.

In fact, to the three ends of life – religious duty, profit and pleasure – , the literature of *dharma*, which expresses worldly orthodoxy, sometimes superimposes a supreme end: liberation. This bringing together of all four masks the heterogeneity between the three legitimate and necessary worldly ends and the negation of the world which, although optional, is fatal to the other three once it is adopted. Another example, which is central to our discussion, is the place given to renunciation itself. It is often represented as the last stage in the life of the Brahman, who is successively novice, householder, hermit and sanyasi. The artificiality of this theory has been noted, for it also juxtaposes obligatory stages (novice, householder) and optional stages (that of hermit, *vānaprastha*, is even archaic). It seems as though the intention here has been on the one hand to represent *saṃnyāsa* merely as a moment in the life of the Brahman, reserving renunciation more or less to the Brahman class, and on the other hand to delay renunciation until the latest possible period of man's life, after his worldly obligations (the perpetuation of the ancestors, etc.) have been accomplished. In short, over and above the habitual orthodox tendency to aggregate, there seems here to be an attempt to limit renunciation in its relation to wordly conditions and, finally, a subdued hostility to renunciation itself.[19]

The man-in-the-world's adoption of notions which are essentially those of the renouncer should not conceal from us the difference between the two conditions and the two kinds of thought. La Vallée Poussin has emphasized this difference for Buddhism by distinguishing between the Buddhism of the laity, a religion, and the Buddhism of the monk, a 'discipline of salvation', which he clearly defined.[20]

The renouncer leaves the world behind in order to devote himself to his own liberation. He submits himself to his chosen master, or he may even enter a monastic community, but essentially he depends upon no one but himself, he is alone.

In leaving the world he finds himself invested with an individuality which he apparently finds uncomfortable since all his efforts tend to its extinction or its transcendence. He thinks as an individual, and this is the distinctive trait which opposes him to the man-in-the-world and brings him closer to the western thinker. But while for us the individual is in the world, here he is found only outside the world, at least in principle; also the relation between thought and action is different, for the speculation of the sanyasi has primarily a practical end. Moreover, and this feature is essential to our purpose, the renouncer does not deny the religion of the man-in-the-world. As La Vallée Poussin has said 'he is not sceptical, he freely admits all the traditional and popular mythology . . . his aspiration is directed beyond the worlds, it is something hyper-cosmical (*lokottara*)'. Here then lies the possibility of aggregation: the discipline of the renouncer by its very tolerance of worldly religion becomes additional to it. An individual religion based upon choice is added on to the religion of the group.

To consider Indian ideas from the point of view of the individual-in-the-world, which is the spontaneous western point of view, is to run the risk of obscuring and limiting them. We do better to remember that these ideas have two facets, one for the man-in-the-world, who is not an individual, and the other for the renouncer, who is an individual-outside-the-world. In fact the man-in-the-world, and particularly the Brahman, is given the credit for ideas which he may have adopted but not invented. Such ideas are much more relevant and they clearly belong primarily to the thought of the renouncer. Is it really too adventurous to say that the agent of development in Indian religion and speculation, the 'creator of values', has been the renouncer? The Brahman, as a scholar, has mainly preserved, aggregated, and combined; he may well have created and developed special branches of knowledge. Not only the founding of sects and their maintenance, but the major ideas, the 'inventions' are due to the renouncer whose unique position gave him a sort of monopoly for putting everything in question. Obviously I cannot demonstrate this thesis here. All I can hope to do is to show that it is useful to distinguish two 'ideal types', which in fact combine more and more in the course of time, in order to understand this combination itself and some of the major themes.[21]

Let us return to the idea of transmigration and retribution for actions. Max Weber, with many others, has insisted upon the justification it gives to the caste system. He considers it one of the most coherent answers to the problem of evil. Certainly people commonly explain present misfortunes as the consequence of evil actions committed in a former existence. But it would be a confusion of levels, I think, to follow this author to the point where he finds in these notions one of the rare 'dogmatic beliefs' of Hinduism. They belong much more to the speculative plane. First of all it is clear that transmigration issues into liberation, and that the two ideas determine each other and are inseparable.[22] This indicates that we are dealing with the thought of the sanyasi. In the West transmigration is often regarded as a pessimistic view of life since it seems to render any one particular life unreal. But as we have already seen, the unreality of caste and the individual in the world is given immediately. Transmigration does not therefore create it, it only represents or explains it. Further, when we find true pessimism, as with Buddha, it is in opposition to deliverance, it is a pessimism from the point of view of the renouncer, not of the man in the world.

One would rather say that the individual becomes real through transmigration, which takes him through all the unreal stages of the system. As the same thing happens to the renouncer – he becomes an individual – we could say that transmigration not only transcribes the caste system imaginatively, but also establishes the relation between the renouncer, as an individual man, and the phantom-like men who have remained in the world and support him. Transmigration is the idea that the renouncer, turned towards liberation, has of the world he has left behind. Rather than a pessimistic view, transmigration appears as a bold design lending to the men-in-the-world some reality taken from that which the renouncer has found for himself.

Within the framework of worldly religion, the moral determinism governing the retribution of action looks very intellectual indeed. It directs us more precisely to the historical origin of these ideas, which I shall now briefly consider. They appear before the formation of the caste system proper,[23] they are an early product of that extraordinary post-vedic and pre-hindu development which goes on from the first Upanishads to the Bhagavadgita, the golden age of speculation in which emerge, from discovery to discovery, all the major tendencies of Indian thought. Rich and diverse as this movement appears, it is the work of renouncers, and the various conclusions reached seem governed by the logic of renunciation. It is a critical movement, it begins with the reduction of vedic polytheism to the power of sacrifice, and the first Upanishads proclaim the identity of the individual Self and the universal Being. The extraordinary intellectual and spiritual effervescence which followed has been often noted, and Miss Silburn, in a fine book which appeared recently, shows us anew the milieus of renouncers, ascetics (*śramaṇa*), itinerants (*parivrajaka*), and others.[24] As opposed to 'eternalists', the 'nihilists', materialists or evolutionists, are known to us from the refutations of rival schools, even though they established no roots. Transmigration based on retribution had already appeared and seems to have occupied a prominent place in these discussions. The Buddha, who had learnt much from the nihilists, took the 'middle way': denying the existence of any kind of absolute with which man, being devoid of essence, might identify himself, he nevertheless held firmly on to transmigration.[25] It is easy to see why: without transmigration the liberation or extinction (*nirvāṇa*) which he recommends would lose all meaning, and with it would be lost the free choice, the free action of man. The whole situation is extremely significant and to my mind confirms the preceding analysis. Let us note two things only: on the one hand, Buddhism truly expresses the place of the individual in Indian society; on the other the extreme philosophies, which denied either transmigration or the possibility of freedom from it, that is to say those that rejected the Indian combination of society and the renouncer, have not survived for long.

The Buddhist point of view was not the only conclusion of the movement following upon the discovery of the identity of the Self and Being, of *ātman* and *brahman*. L. Silburn, who sees in transmigration-retribution one of the first stages of this movement, describes it as a march from monism and immanence to transcendence and dualism (p. 118). To contemplation pure and simple, to a discipline (*yoga*) of concentration succeeds a yoga of discrimination, an effort to reach, beyond the *ātman*, the tiny man (*puruṣa*) concealed in the inner heart, leading finally to the dualism of the *sāmkhya* system and to the personal God or Lord with whom the individual communicates by love (*bhakti*). This process seems to correspond to the progressive building up of the individuality of the thinker, i.e. of the renouncer.[26]

I shall return to *bhakti* and to the sects through which the renouncer has completed and modified religion. To be complete one should also mark the major stages in the process of aggregation to orthodoxy of sanyasic values. To mention only one important point, vegetarianism and non-violence seem likely to have been imitated by the Brahmans from the great heresies as prestigious ideals. Hinduism proper is complete only after it has reconquered India from Buddhism and Jainism.

So far then we have group religion on the one hand, the 'disciplines of salvation' on the other, and finally their interaction, the main features of which I have tried to indicate. Such are the principal factors of religion in traditional India, and it is on this basis that the great number of particular developments have taken place. But we have still only reached what I might call the restricted formula of this religion. In order to attain its generalized or complete formula, another tendency, to a great extent heterogeneous, remains to be considered.

## 3  COMPARISON: THE PLACE OF THE TANTRAS

We can compare our restricted formula on one point with a theoretical view of primitive religion. From Durkheimian sociology, one expects to find an alternation in time corresponding to the distinction between sacred and profane. In the last resort everything rests upon the sacred, but the profane must, at the same time, have recourse to it and protect itself from it. The everyday order of things in particular is founded *indirectly* upon the absolute order. It is shaken up, contradicted and renewed at one and the same time in festivals where the sacred irrupts for a limited period and reverses the ordinary norms of conduct, replacing separation by communion and interdiction by licence. The Hinduism of the restricted formula shows little of this. There is of course the popular festival of Holi, but it is not found in the South, where one can observe village life for a whole year and note the relative absence of the excess and unbridled joy commonly associated with the idea of a festival. This can be understood without bringing in the puritanical tendency upon which Max Weber rightly insists. For what is characteristic of the Indian order, with a division of labour based upon the fundamental religious values, is a complete differentiation between the spiritual and the temporal. This allows society, in relegating the temporal to a subordinate position, and in contradistinction to simpler societies, to found itself *directly* upon the absolute order. Since this is the case, naturally we find neither reciprocal alternations in the handling of impurity, in essentials the business of specialists, nor a complete reversal of values during festivals. I should go so far as to say that even the latter is replaced by a division of labour. For in fact, the everyday order, which becomes here the permanent order in the world, is in effect relativised, but only in the values of the sanyasi. In him, as the extramundane individual, a special kind of sacredness is reserved. With his negation of the world and his asceticism, he represents that very reversal of values which we expected to find in festivals. Put in another way we could say that he is the safety valve for the Brahmanic order, which can give a permanent place to the transcendent, while remaining out of the range of its attacks. By means of this compromise the Brahman rules over the world in peace, as a rather monotonous immanence.

If this is true it is, nevertheless, only a part of the truth: there is also a large branch of Hinduism where I believe we can see the rejection of ascetic renunciation and also, in its place, that reversal of values we looked for earlier. This is Tantrism. An essential rite in the tantric cult, the *pañcatattva*, consists of the sacramental enjoyment of all that is forbidden or despised in ordinary life: meat and fish, alcohol, sexual intercourse. To quote a text of the Kula or Kaula:[27]

For the adepts let that be drink which should not be drunk and that food which should not be eaten, and that which should not be the object of intercourse – let it be so.

The rejection of asceticism is expressed in the rehabilitation of enjoyment, *bhoga*. But it is characteristic that *yoga*, or the discipline of liberation, is preserved at the same time, and that the doctrine claims to transcend the opposition of *yoga*, discipline, and *bhoga*, enjoyment. 'Either the *yogī* is not a *bhogī* (enjoyer), or the *bhogī* knows not *yoga* [we are lost in contradiction], that is why the *kaula* doctrine, whose essence is of *bhoga* and *yoga*, is superior to all . . .'. In the clear concision of Sanskrit:

> *yogī cennaiva bhogī syād bhogī cennaiva yogavit*|
> *bhogayogātmakam kaulam tasmāt sarvādhikam priye*||

We see that while rejecting renunciation, Tantrism accepts ideas which derive from it. Far from making a *tabula rasa*, it builds upon what has been acquired through renunciation and has become at least a sort of universal language in India. In particular we are now, for ever, at the level of the religion of the individual. Not only do our texts speak of yoga but also of liberation:

The pleasure born of wine, of meat, of woman is salvation (*mokṣa*) for him who knows, for the non-initiate it is a fall (*pātakam*).

It seems that Tantrism had its *avadhūta*, equivalent to the sanyasis, and also did not ignore transmigration. The same text however admirably shows the heterogeneity of Kula Tantrism and how it transcends these notions, particularly the opposition between transmigration and liberation. The verse follows immediately upon the reconciliation of discipline and enjoyment:

Evidently, in the *kula* doctrine, enjoyment becomes yoga (*bhogo yogāyate*), sin becomes good action, transmigration becomes liberation (*saṃsāra mokṣāyate*).[28]

I have referred to what is often called the extreme form of Tantrism, which the Indians call left-hand Tantrism to distinguish it from the more conformist right-hand Tantrism. (Incidentally we find acknowledged in these expressions the incompatibility between reversal cults and the restricted formula). But the left-hand form is for us the pure one. It is true that there are attenuations, substitutions and sublimations; it is true that the left-hand practices appear, in Tantrism itself, perhaps increasingly through the centuries, mixed and combined with right-hand practices, to produce a system finally in which right-hand forms predominate, but which preserves nevertheless its distinctiveness.[29]

Even though Tantrism is in principle open to all without distinction of caste or sex, it is not, taken as a whole, a sect. It is, rather, a tendency which has affected all movements including Buddhism. The rite to which I have referred is a *śākta* rite and the Shaktas, with their elaborate initiations, come closer to being a sect. However, from the ritual alone and apart from speculation, Shaktism looks as an esoteric religion for people in the world rather than a sect founded upon renunciation.[30]

The *śākta* are the worshippers of *śakti*, the supreme goddess who incarnates the energy of the male god(s). We can distinguish a properly religious aspect and a philosophical aspect. On the religious side there is first of all the notion of the sexual couple: the couple is identical with the All, and is represented in the act of love. Here one kind of complementarity we encountered in common religion is acknowledged. From this point, it seems natural that the cult of the female principle is at the heart of Shaktism as a religion: once the couple is regarded as essential, by virtue of the principle of reversal the woman, inferior in life, becomes dominant in the cult. There is ritual intercourse, a woman or a girl is worshipped, and the *pudendum muliebre* is drawn as centre for the *pañcatattva* rite.

On the philosophical side, we are reminded of the dualism of the *sāṃkhya* system with its 'spirit', male (*puruṣa*), inactive, and its 'nature' (*prakṛti*), feminine and active. Historically this dualism appears as a conclusion of the great speculative movement mentioned earlier. Spirit in isolation transcends the world, it has as its complement a material principle conceived as feminine. The remarkable feature here, as compared with occidental dualism, is the attribution of activity and energy to the material principle, while spirit is conceived as passive. In the West it is the reverse, as witness the fact that Newton could not conceive of attraction or gravitation as a property of matter, but felt obliged to see in it the operation of spirit: the notion of force seemed incompatible with that of matter.[31] It seems possible to see a relation between the character of spirit, active for us, passive for the Indians, and the situation of the thinking man, here man-in-the-world who is active even when he constructs a philosophical system, and there man-outside-the-world, a contemplative spirit, passive in relation to the world in that all his activity tends to a reabsorption or involution instead of a creation or evolution.

Regarding the place of Tantrism in general in religion, we should recall at least its importance in orthodox ritual: the ritual in Brahmanic temples is essentially tantric, whether we consider the cult of images, the magic formulas, the theory of gestures or written symbols. The magical side of Brahmanism, which is considerable, is vedic and tantric. While the restricted formula earlier described can give no place to magic, tantrism offers a direct hold upon the supernatural. But there is considerably more in it than a simple resurgence of crude magic: I hope to have shown that we are faced with a truly fundamental variant of Hinduism, in which renunciation is replaced by reversal. While constituting and codifying Hindu ritual, while mixing intimately with other currents, and without ever forming a sect in the proper sense (see below), the movement has kept an esoteric side. Also, by its very nature it is in contact with folk religion and can give expression to some aspects of it which the restricted formula would exclude, such as the complementarity of sex, and blood sacrifices to the Goddess.

## 4 DEVOTION AND POSSESSION

Another major tendency integral to Hinduism is *bhakti*, devotion, which has considerably contributed to the proliferation of sects. Here the divine is no longer a multiplicity of gods as in ordinary religion, it is a unique and personal God, the Lord, Ishvara, with whom the devotee may identify himself, in whom he may participate. 'Participation' is in fact the original meaning of the word *bhakti*. There seems to be a linguistic correspondence between the devotee, bhakta, and Bhagavan, the Blessed Lord, or better He whose plenitude is open to participation.[32] Love, a total devotion to the Lord, suffices for salvation. Divine grace answers the appeal of the pure and humble heart. This is a revolutionary doctrine since it transcends both caste and renunciation and opens an easy road to salvation for all without distinction, as Burnouf pointed out more than a century ago.

As distinct from Tantrism, this, in my opinion, is a sanyasic development, an invention of the renouncer. This religion of love supposes two perfectly individualized terms; in order to conceive of a personal Lord there must also be a believer who sees himself as an individual. Historically, devotion appears in the development recalled above (2, *in fine*), since after one Upanishad the Bhagavad Gita reveals it and has remained as its Bible. Complex as the poem is and diverse as are the commentaries upon it, one can nevertheless perceive in it the very development which brought forth the *bhakti*. It expounds in order three paths to union or disciplines of salvation: through acts, through knowledge and through devotion. The first two correspond respectively to life in the world and to renunciation, but they are modified and even transmuted by the intervention of the third. There is no doubt about the preeminence of devotion, for the discovery of this alone makes possible the attainment of salvation through action. The central point is that, thanks to love, renunciation is transcended by being internalized; in order to escape the determinism of actions, inactivity is no longer necessary, detachment and disinterestedness are sufficient: one can leave the world from within, and God himself is not bound by his acts, for he only acts out of love. Devotion has come to take the place of deliverance. By transferring his conquests from the plane of knowledge to that of affectivity, the renouncer makes a gift of them to everybody: by loving submission, by identifying themselves unreservedly with the Lord, everybody can become free individuals. There is probably no need to emphasize the amplitude of this revelation. One would ask rather how it comes about that this new religion, so far from putting an end to other religious forms, has remained only one tendency among others. The perspective in which we have looked at it here, together with what remains to be said, may help us to understand the fact.[33]

The *bhakti* of the Gita is speculative and intellectual like the climate in which it was conceived. Its effusion is measured and ecstasy is absent from it. The Hindu bhakti proper, which we meet with later in the Tamil hymns and classically in Sanskrit in the Bhagavata Purana, the *bhakti* which tells us in the latter text that she was born in the South, is on the contrary highly emotional.

Bhakti in this work is a surging emotion which chokes the speech, makes the tears flow and the hair thrill with pleasurable excitement, and often leads to hysterical laughing and weeping by turns, to sudden fainting fits and to long trances of unconsciousness . . . (Farquhar, *Outline*, p. 230).

This mystic ecstasy puts us in mind of what we have called possession, which so far we have not encountered at the learned level. Even some of the recommended means for achieving this condition recall the situations where possession is habitually produced in village festivals: 'we are told that it is produced by gazing at the images of Krishna, singing his praises, remembering him in meditation, keeping company with his devotees . . .' (*ibid.*). It is true that 'meditation' also recalls the ritual identification of the priest with the god (above n. 12), and also that the *bhakta* does not prophesy as does the possessed. Yet it remains that both possession, a functional feature of folk religion, and *bhakti*, a characteristic of many sects, rest upon a common psychological condition, and that bhakti takes up in more or less sublimated form an aspect of common religion ignored by Brahmanic orthodoxy. We must remember that possession by a god is in popular religion one of the circumstances in which the divine resolves itself into an individuality. Even though it underwent a thorough intellectual elaboration, identification with a god was given in immediate experience.[34]

## 5 THE SECT

Another characteristic of Hinduism is the coexistence of a large number of sects, each one having a more or less particular cult and doctrine. What are these sects and what is their place? The first and foremost feature to be emphasized is the intimate connection between sect and the institution of renunciation. Practically all the sects have been founded by sanyasis and the greater part include, apart from worldly adherents, a sanyasi order constituting the nucleus of the sect. The link between both sides is provided by the ancient institution of the spiritual master or *guru*. Instead of the renouncer alone having his *guru*, he in his turn serves as *guru* to whoever wishes it. The institution is thus most remarkably enlarged or democratized. Probably a majority of Indian heads of families, of all castes – even Muslims – have chosen a *guru* who has initiated them by whispering a *mantra* in their ears, and who, in principle, visits them once a year. At least that is what I found in my field work in U.P. Of course there is scope here for degradation, but by this channel the religion and thought of the sects, that is of the renouncer, penetrate to the great mass of men-of-the-world.

A second feature of the sect is that, unlike orthodox Brahmanism, it is not essentially syncretic but holds to one doctrine, the principle of its unity. Often in fact it is monotheist in the true sense: it is not content with pushing the other gods, the gods of others, into the background, but denies them straightaway. Also, as is well known, the sect, whatever its dominant inspiration, transcends caste and, at least in principle, is open to all, as is appropriate in a creation of the renouncer. Here we can compare orthodox Brahmanism and the sect. On the one hand there is a multiplicity of gods (or a speculative pantheism), syncretism and considerable tolerance in the domain of belief, tolerance that is of the *object* of religion, which contrasts with the strict exclusivism as regards the *subjects* of religion, the people who can be admitted amongst the faithful. The sect, on the other hand, is inclusive as regards the subjects, the faithful, but strict and exclusive as regards the god or belief, the object of religion. Indian multiplicity then has its limits, it only bears upon one of the two poles that make a religion. Abstractly considered sect and Brahmanism appear as two variants of a disposition balancing multiplicity and unity, inclusion and exclusion.

One is thus just justified in looking at sects as non-Brahmanic formations. Yet, if from the outside it seems a matter of either-or, from the inside the sect appears to its lay members as a religion for the individual superimposed upon common religion, even if this latter is relativized to the point that Brahmanism is viewed simply as the order, or disorder, of the day-to-day world. The caste order continues to be respected, even if, in the light of sectarian truth, it is seen as a profane concern. Although one may come very close to monotheism, the attitude *vis-à-vis* the world remains that of the renouncer.

From the position we have reached, we can see that the developments of renunciation, with all their riches, are contained after all within narrow limits which they were unable to go beyond. Of the success of renunciation, in the place assigned to it by society, Buddhism is a witness. Situated outside the world but linked to it, the renouncer is impotent against it; if he ventures in that direction his ideas become ephemeral. On the contrary there is a positive dialectic between his 'discipline' and the religion of the world. But all the prestige and fecundity of renunciation end up by offering to the man-in-the-world a choice of religions for the individual. At the end of the movement – achieved very early, with *bhakti* –, the renouncer is in fact absorbed, whether he invents a religion of love open to all, whether he becomes the spiritual head of worldly people, rich or poor, or whether he remains a Brahman while becoming a sanyasi, as with Ramanuja. At this point, if to every one the path of spiritual adventure is as open as ever, socially the circle is closed. The two kinds of thought, the two ideal types I set out to distinguish, mingle at the mercy of various milieux and temperaments, and some men who in spirit are sanyasis live in the world. Incidentally if we leave renunciation on one side and only consider the fact of a religion of individual choice being superimposed upon group religion, something similar is found in classical antiquity: Greeks went to Eleusis for initiation.

To sum up, Hinduism, the religion of caste and of renunciation, has developed by integrating – in Brahmanism – and by tolerating – in the sects – the products of the renouncer's thoughts and mysticism. The most important aspect is the addition to group religion of individual religion, even in Tantrism which in place of renunciation introduced, as a fundamental variation and according to an elementary formula, the sacred reversal. The devotional cults have on the one hand inherited individuation from the sanyasi, and on the other they are in touch with a basic aspect of popular religion. Otherwise and in general, what popular religion displays in structural form is found again, partly, substantialized and disjointed, in Brahmanism, partly in Shaktism and in Bhakti.

In Hinduism and before it, India has effected a whole series of distinctions which are not those to which we are accustomed. So far from being fanciful exoticisms, the complications of Indian religions only appear to us as such because we happen to practise different ones. They seem to flow logically from an initial position or, as it were, an initial choice, which can perhaps be summed up as follows: that the society must submit and entirely conform to the absolute order, that consequently the temporal, and hence the human, will be subordinate, and that, while there is no room here for the individual, whoever wants to become one may leave society proper.

At this point a series of comparisons with the Christian West becomes possible. To note only one, by way of conclusion, may we not see in what in the West is sometimes naively called the relation between the individual and society a counterpart of the Indian dichotomy between the man-in-the-world and the renouncer? While man to the ancient Greek philosophers was still social man, the modern Christian development has led to a kind of splitting up of this concept. I mean that the stress has been set upon the *individual-in-the-world* (a concept which would appear contradictory from the Indian point of view) while the social aspect was left obscure, and reappeared as a problem: the problem of order, or of the convergence of individual wills has emerged with gathering strength. The need for a sociology, and the difficulties encountered in its conception and its development constitute a complication which is perhaps the reverse of those India has experienced as a result of having deliberately placed the individual outside the world.

# APPENDIX C

## THE CONCEPTION OF KINGSHIP IN
## ANCIENT INDIA

There is an abundant modern literature dealing with kingship, and political organization in general, in ancient India. This study is an attempt to sum it up, and set the findings of classical philologists and historians in a comparative, sociological perspective. It is restricted to the conception of kingship as distinct from its actualities, first because there are good sociological reasons for beginning in that manner, and also because practically the former aspect is better known at present than the latter.

If, to be called historical, a study has to be aimed primarily at detecting changes between one period and another, then this study should not be called historical, for, on the contrary, it is concerned in the first place with something permanent. Just as actual happenings or 'behaviour' are understood within an appropriate conceptual framework, I also think that actual historical changes cannot be understood, or even identified, before one has gained some general idea of 'what it is all about'. On one point, I shall submit that the supposition of an important, but entirely imaginary historical event can profitably be replaced by the understanding of a relation of extremely remarkable permanence.

First published in *Contributions to Indian Sociology*, VI, 1962. This paper contains the main part of two University Lectures given in London, at the School of Oriental and African Studies, in October 1961, with the sub-title: 'An Anthropologist's View'. A development dealing with the non-monarchical states is left out, while a few footnotes are added. I am thankful to Mrs. E. von Fürer-Haimendorf for her revision of the text.

THE RULER AND THE PRIEST FROM THE BRAHMANAS
ONWARDS

1 *Brahman and kṣatra in the Brahmanas*

We must start from the classification of society into four *varṇa*.
First Hocart, and still more precisely than Hocart, Dumézil have
shown that the hierarchical enumeration of the four *varṇa* was
based on a series of oppositions, the principle of which was religious.[1] The first three classes, respectively priests, princes and
herdsmen-husbandmen, are taken together as twice-born or as
those bestowing gifts, offering sacrifices and studying (the Veda)
as opposed to the fourth class, the *śūdra*, who are devoid of any
direct relation to religion, and whose sole task is to serve the former
without envy (Manu, I, 88–91).

Among the three kinds of twice-born, the first two are opposed
to the third, for to the latter the Lord of creatures has made over
only the cattle, to the former all creatures (Manu, IX, 327). It is
worth noting that this particular opposition is the least frequent
of all in the texts. On the contrary, the solidarity of the first two
categories, priests and princes, vis-à-vis the rest, and at the same
time their distinction and their relative hierarchy are abundantly
documented from the Brahmanas onwards. Before entering into
this, however, I shall stress the importance of Hocart's and Dumézil's observation: the possibility of replacing a linear hierarchical order by a system of oppositions, which in fact underlies
it, applies not only to the *varṇa* scheme but to the modern system
of castes (*jāti*) as well; in this the two systems are homologous,
which explains how it is that people pass so easily from the latter
to the former. As to the principle of the oppositions, if it is religious
in both cases, there is however a difference. In the matter of caste
the opposition is essentially between purity and impurity and it is
susceptible of indefinite segmentation.

Rather than of the first two classes, the Brahmanas (the texts
called *brāhmaṇa*) treat of their principles, resp. *brahman* and *kṣatra*
(both neuter). They go together, they are often designated as 'the
two forces', and they are to be united. Similarly in Manu (IX, 322)
Kshatriyas and Brahmans cannot prosper separately but only in
close association. But, as soon as this necessary union has been
stated, the hierarchical distinction between 'the two forces' mani-

fests itself (*Pañcaviṃśa Br.*, XII, ii, 9); the *brahman* does not fall under the jurisdiction of the *kṣatra*, the *brahman* being the source, or rather the womb, from which the *kṣatra* springs, is superior; the *brahman* could exist without the *kṣatra*, not conversely. For, while both the Brahman and the Kshatriya can offer the sacrifice, only the Brahman can operate it. The *Aitareya Brāhmaṇa* (VII, 19 sq.) gives a striking formula to this when it groups behind the *brahman* those who eat the oblation, and behind the *kṣatra* those who do not, not only the Kshatriyas, but implicity at any rate the Vaishyas and Shudras as well. Let us stress with Dumézil that the opposition we find here is not between two particular *varṇa* but between the Brahmans on the one hand, and all the rest on the other; this opposition separates into two the whole series of the *varṇa*-s. Similarly, we have seen that the pair Brahman-Kshatriya opposes itself, not so much to the sole Vaishya, but rather to all the rest. The fact is general, not only for the *varṇa*-s but for the castes as well, and it is essential. Regarding sacrifice, the *Aitareya Brāhmaṇa* draws the logical consequence: the king must, through appropriate rites, be identified with a Brahman during the performance of the sacrifice, and be made to leave this identification at the end of the ceremony.

Other passages illustrate the necessary solidarity, distinction and hierarchy of the two functions: [2] in the *aśvamedha* there are two lute players, one, a Brahman, plays by day, the other, a Kshatriya, by night (*Śat. Br.*, XIII, 1, 5, 2 sq.); elsewhere the Brahman seems to put himself beyond the authority of the king: 'Here is your king, o people; Soma is the king of us, Brahmans' [3] (*Śat. Br.*, V, 3, 3, 12, *vājapeya*), or 'the priest makes the king weaker than himself, and thus he [the king] will be stronger than his enemies' (*Śat. Br.*, V, 8, 4, 15, *cf. Ait. Br.*, VIII, 9).

## 2 King and chaplain

The relation between the spiritual principle and the principle of *imperium* is fully seen in an institution which embodies it in a personal form and commands perhaps in a great measure the abstract formulation. It is not enough for the king to employ Brahmans for the public ritual, he must also have a permanent, personal relationship with one particular Brahman, his *purohita*, literally 'the one placed in front'. We translate *purohita* as chaplain, but we must bear in mind the idea of a spiritual delegation or vanguard, almost of a *major ego*. The gods do not eat the offerings of a king devoid of a *purohita* (*Ait. Br.*, VIII, 24), so that the *purohita* presides, as *hotṛ* or *brahman* priest, i.e. as sacrificer or controller, to royal sacrifices. Moreover, the king depends on him for all the actions of his life, for these would not succeed without him. The *purohita* is to the king as thought is to will, as Mitra is to Varuna (*Śat. Br.*, IV, 1, 4, 1 sq.). The relationship is as close as a marriage (*Ait. Br.*, VIII, 27). As the Rig Veda has already said: 'He lives prosperous in his mansion, to him the earth bestows all its gifts, to him the people obeys by itself, the king in whose place the Brahman goes first' (IV, 50, 8, transl. Dumézil). Temporal authority is guaranteed through the personal relationship in which it gives preeminence over itself to spiritual authority incarnated in the *purohita*.

### 3   The Brahman as dependent in fact

Concretely, the relation between the functions of priest and king has a double aspect. While spiritually, absolutely, the priest is superior, as we have just seen, he is at the same time, from a temporal or material point of view, subject and dependent. And conversely the king, if spiritually subordinate, is materially the master. The former, ideological aspect of the relation is not unknown in the West on the level of values, but it takes on in this case a particular form, largely because the spiritual element here is embodied in a person. It is obvious that the second, the 'practical' aspect is important in fact. It is the combination of both aspects which actually constitutes the situation, a relation of mutual but asymmetrical dependence. And it is remarkable that our brahmanical authors have not reserved their attention for the former aspect. They proclaim: 'In truth, there are two kinds of gods, for, indeed, the gods are the gods, and the Brahmans who have studied and who teach the sacred lore are the human gods' (*Śat. Br.*, II, 2, 2, 6, transl. Eggeling). On the other hand they also occasionally recognize that the function of *purohita* is the livelihood of the Brahmans, that the king protects the Brahmans and the law (*Ait. Br.*, VIII, 17), that the chaplain walks behind the king, among his suite, and that king and *purohita* may come into conflict, so that it is useful for the Brahman to keep to himself a certain formula at the king's consecration in view of possible reprisals (*Pañcaviṃśa Br.*, XII, 8, 6; XVIII, 19, 8; etc.).

Still more remarkable is the characterization, in one passage of the *Ait. Br.* (VII, 29), of the three other *varṇa* from the view-point of royal power. The representative of a Brahmans' lineage, intent on recovering the patronage of a king, draws a dark picture of the condition of the other classes which, he says, only the proper distinction of sacrificial foods separates from the royal lineage. The Brahman is represented as 'one who receives gifts, one who drinks [*soma*], one who searches for food, to be moved at pleasure'; the Vaishya is 'tributary to another, food of another, to be oppressed at pleasure'; the Shudra 'servant of another, to be rejected, to be killed, at pleasure.' In modern times, this remarkable description has often been taken as contradicting the numerous affirmations of Brahmanical preeminence. Some scholars have sought to explain the discrepancy they perceived by attributing the two kinds of statements to different environments, or times. Actually, the difference lies in the point from which the situation is viewed and the dependency of the Brahman in relation to royal power or, one would almost say, to mere force, accompanies the fact that his preeminence is located on a different plane. In approximate, Western, terms, the situation arises because the distinction between spiritual and temporal is carried out in an absolute fashion. We have to do with the two opposite faces, the two complementary aspects of the real concrete relationship. We can say this with some assurance, as we can observe, in the Indian villages of today, a similar relation between the Brahmans and the dominant caste. The caste which we call dominant because it enjoys the main rights in the soil reproduces the royal function at the village level. It is noteworthy that the Brahmans, already in the remote period of the Brahmanas, if they more often proclaimed their spiritual preeminence, were also at the same time conscious of being temporally dependent. This double relation thus appears to be anterior to the caste system proper, and yet on analysis it appears as its essential characteristic, a feature not met anywhere else. This struck James Mill, and W. W. Hunter has expressed it in a remarkable manner:

from very ancient times, the leaders of the Brahmana caste recognized that if they were to exercise spiritual supremacy, they must renounce earthly pomp. In arrogating the priestly function, they gave up all claim to the royal office. They were divinely appointed to be the guides of nations and the councillors of kings, but they could not be kings themselves.[4]

## 4   *Comparative significance of the fact*

This complex and characteristic relation between priesthood and kingship, Brahmanas and Kshatriyas, is fundamental in itself and in its implications, and a brief reflection will be useful for locating it in a comparative perspective. The fact has surprised modern authors, most of whom, without clearly conceiving it, tried to explain it as the result of a hypothetical struggle between the two classes, and interpreted in that sense certain legends to which we shall return hereafter. They wrote of a struggle for the first rank (Lassen), or for 'the presidency, even spiritual' of the society (Dumézil), or, conversely, of a struggle for 'practical power' (*Vedic Index*). They are not all of one mind; however, among the different tendencies, one is the persistent rationalist and 'anticlerical' mentality according to which the priests are suspected of having 'usurped' something (James Mill). While the idea that there has been a struggle between Brahmans and Kshatriyas at one or another period of ancient Indian history is found in the works of indologists, it flourishes still more freely in second hand considerations. This shows that here we encounter a deep-rooted inclination of western minds when confronted with the Indian institution, as for instance when the guarded pronouncements of Hopkins were interpreted by the sociologist O. C. Cox in a rigid and affirmative fashion.[5]

Let us take a different path and look at the relation between king and priest, not as a contingent trait for which a conjectural historical struggle might account, but as a necessary institution. The first obstacle we encounter lies in the way we conceive the hierarchy of a society. As we live in an egalitarian society, we tend to conceive of hierarchy as a scale of commanding powers – as in an army – rather than as a gradation of statuses. One may note *en passant* that the combination of the two aspects seems to have been anything but easy in a number of societies, for there are many instances of sovereigns whose eminent dignity was coupled with idleness. The Indian case is one in which the two aspects are absolutely separated, and this apparently was the first reason for surprise.

Further, the very word hierarchy, and its history, should recall that the gradation of status is rooted in religion: the first rank normally goes, not to power, but to religion, simply because for those societies religion represents what Hegel has called the Universal, i.e. absolute truth, in other words because hierarchy integrates the society in relation to its ultimate values.

This is borne out, I think, by the exceptional place of Indian society in a comparison bearing on kingship. In most of the societies in which kingship is found, it is a magico-religious as well as a political function. This is common-place. In Ancient Egyptian or Sumerian kingship, or in the kingship of the Chinese empire for instance, the supreme religious functions were vested in the Sovereign, he was the Priest *par excellence* and those who were called the priests were only ritual specialists subordinate to him. Comparing this with the Indian situation, there seems to be a simple alternative: either the king exerts the religious functions which are generally his, and *then* he is the head of the hierarchy for this very reason, and exerts at the same time political power, or, and this is the Indian case, the king depends on the priests for the religious functions, he cannot be his own sacrificer, instead he 'puts in front' of himself a priest, the *purohita*, and *then* he looses the hierarchical preeminence in favour of the priests, retaining for himself power only.

This is, I think, the point which most modern philologists have failed to grasp, and they can hardly be blamed, since contemporary anthropologists too have sometimes thought that the rank of the king depended more on his exercise of power than on his religious qualifications.

Through this dissociation, the function of the king in India has been *secularized*. It is from this point that a differentiation has occurred, the separation within the religious universe of a sphere or realm opposed to the religious, and roughly corresponding to what we call the political. As opposed to the realm of values and norms it is the realm of force. As opposed to the *dharma* or universal order of the Brahman, it is the realm of interest or advantage, *artha*. We shall follow some developments in which the implications of this fundamental fact become apparent. All these can, in my view, be traced back to this initial step. In other words, they would have been impossible if the king had not from the beginning left the highest religious functions to the priest.

Incidentally, one might ask whether the king, while not having the first role in the brahmanical, the so to say official ritual, did not nevertheless retain something of the magico-religious aspects which adhere to his function and person everywhere else. We shall see that the texts answer this question positively.

But to return to supposed evolutions or changes, we may say, speaking comparatively, that in India the king has lost his religious prerogatives. It is not impossible that this happened through a process which would have taken place in the vedic period. If the Brahmans may be said to have 'usurped' anything, it would be that, and that only. On the contrary, from the time of the Brahmanas until now, the stability of the formula shows that neither the Brahman nor the king have arrogated anything belonging to the other. It happened that certain Brahmans became kings, at first sight blending in their person the two functions. (But this is only an appearance, since in actual fact there is no reason to suppose that a Brahman king did not employ a Brahman priest to perform the sacrifice on his behalf.) But in the matter of principle, the Brahmans as such have never claimed political power. Even nowadays, they are content essentially with guaranteeing spiritual merits to acts which are materially profitable to themselves and of which the *gift* is the prototype. To give to Brahmans is basically to exchange material goods against a spiritual good, i.e. merits. In its particular way the gift embodies the very relationship with which we are dealing.

5    *Legendary conflicts*

The legends of the classical period which tell of conflicts between Brahmans and Kshatriyas do not, in my view, reflect a struggle for supremacy between the two classes. On the contrary, in general they confirm what has just been said, for, far from putting in question the relation between the two, they take it as established. For instance when the Kshatriya *Viśvāmitra* tries to appropriate the magic cow of the Brahman *Vasiṣṭha*, he is driven to acknowledge that brute force is powerless against the magico-religious force which defends the right of the Brahman, and he finally decides to transform himself into a Brahman through austerities. But, you might say, what about the Brahman *Paraśurāma* exterminating the Kshatriyas? It is certainly true that this does not conform to the traditional ideal of the Brahman, but in the story it is very clear that *Paraśurāma* does not try to substitute himself for the Kshatriyas and to rule in their place. As we shall see more precisely later on, the principle of their dominion is not questioned.

Actually, the two episodes are part of the same cycle. Some degree of symmetry between the two cases does not seem to have attracted attention. Both *Viśvāmitra* and *Paraśurāma* display a mixture of brahmanical and royal features. The legend explains it mainly as the result of an ill-advised exchange of magic foods between the mother of the one and the grandmother of the other, following the intermarriage of a Bhrigu Brahman (*rcīka*) and the Kshatriya lineage of *Viśvāmitra*. Incidentally, this intervarna union has an ancient equivalent in the *Aitareya Br.*, where the adoption of *Śunaḥśepa* by *Viśvāmitra* had similar results.

The most likely object of the conflicts which we can presume from the texts would be the privileges and immunities of the Brahmans, starting from the Atharva Veda which already tries to protect the very wife of the priest from the concupiscence of powerful people. This is the theme of the bad kings whose excesses lead them to ruin, a theme found even in the Arthashastra, although there it takes on a philosophical rather than a social aspect. In particular the mythical stories of the kings of the moon dynasty, *Purūravas* and *Nahuṣa*, may well have served as didactic fables for the Brahmanical education of Kshatriyas.

In two cases the very principle of hierarchy is attacked. One is a mere discussion, where *Arjuna* puts the problem quite clearly: why should force not make itself supreme, as this would mean simply drawing the logical consequence from what actually happens, and make a law of what is already a fact? It would be a matter simply of crushing the pretensions of the priests, dependent as they are on the prince. Nothing less than a long discourse of *Vāyu* is necessary to bring the arrogant to a better appreciation of values. In the myth of *Veṇa* the affair is not discussed, but enacted, the impossibility is not merely demonstrated but experienced. We are in the first age of the world. *Veṇa*, as ruler, pretends to arrogate the religious privileges of the Brahmans, to identify himself, in their stead, with the sacrifice and the gods. In the ensuing catastrophe he is put to death by the sages, and they produce from his body, first his wicked genius, and then *Pṛthu*, the first consecrated king and the model of a king. *Pṛthu*, by submitting perfectly to brahmanical values, inaugurates plenty. In opposition to the confusion represented by *Veṇa*, *Pṛthu* represents the necessary distinction of functions.

In one element of the cycle of *Viśvāmitra*, the Brahman perhaps tries to usurp kingship, I am referring to the legend of *Satyavrata* in which Pargiter saw a Kshatriya ballad reflecting real occurrences. *Vasiṣṭha*, the king's chaplain, does not prevent the prince Satya-vrata from being unjustly banished for twelve years, and during that time he acts as a kind of regent. No rain falls. In the end, *Viśvāmitra* places *Satyavrata* on the throne again 'in spite of the gods and of *Vasiṣṭha*'. The drought is most probably a sanction against usurpation, and this is not particular to this tale. The feature will be found again, and here itself the myth of *Pṛthu* also leads us to the magico-religious relations between society and nature.[6]

## ORIGIN MYTHS AND THEORIES OF KINGSHIP

### 6 *The state of the question*

The ancient literature provides a number of myths or legends relating to the origin of kingship. These tales have, exceptionally, been the object of some kind of comparative treatment. In some of these texts modern scholars have found undoubted analogies with modern western theories of the social and political contract. This was very agreeable to some Indian scholars who, during a period when their country was struggling for independence, were carried away by their enthusiasm and national self-respect. The fact has been recently analysed very lucidly by R. S. Sharma. Indian scholars were irked, on the one hand, by the dominant stress western scholarship laid on the religious side of the Indian heritage, and they were pleased to find an opportunity to throw the non-religious aspects into relief. On the other hand their modern education as well as the new political climate in their country had imbued them with a deep respect for modern political philosophies. They were thus tempted to present the former in the language of the latter and sometimes went so far as to proclaim that ancient India had surpassed the Greeks and at least equalled the moderns. Such superficial views have been criticized aptly by more balanced and perceptive Indian scholars (Ghoshal, Kane, etc.). But in India the matter has become classical, without much effort being made to understand the really surprising convergences with western thought or locate the current which led to them within the vast and complex whole of Indian ideas.

To begin we can take Professor P. V. Kane as our guide. Two currents are found which sometimes intermingle. In the one kingship is in some manner a divine institution – although it would not be apposite to speak of a 'divine right' of kingship (D. R. Bhandarkar). This tendency is obviously ancient, 'primitive'. In the classical, and even to some extent in the Vedic texts, the king is identified with the one or other god by virtue of his nature and some of his functions. This should not surprise unless one were to imagine, rightly or wrongly, that logically the Brahman would have reserved identifications of that kind to himself. In the two most notable texts of the Mahabharata, the legend of *Manu* and the myth of *Pṛthu*, the supreme god gives a king to mankind at the request either of men or of the gods, in order to put an end to a state of anarchy and degeneracy.

In the other current, kingship has an entirely different character: it is based on, or it has its origin in, a 'contract' between the future subjects and the future king. The clearest exposition is found in Buddhist canonic literature in *pāli*, in the *Dīgha Nikāya*, and is taken up again in the *Mahāvastu*. Let us note that, in the corresponding Hindu version, the legend of *Manu* in the Mahabharata, as well as the Arthashastra, this contractual view does not in the least exclude the divine or quasi-divine quality of the king. What strikes one immediately here in contrast to the other trends is the quite profane notion of kingship: the king is just someone who is put in charge of the maintenance of public order, in exchange for which service his subjects leave to him a part of the crops they harvest. It is this lay, specialized aspect which, in the first place, brings this 'contract' near the political speculations of the modern West. In order to grasp the genesis of this state of mind, let us start from its opposite, i.e. from magico-religious kingship as revealed by ethnology.[7]

## 7   *The king of plenty: Pṛthu*

While *Manu*, the first king of convention, is placed in the present age of the world, the *kali yuga*, *Pṛthu*, the first consecrated king, is referred to the first age, *kṛta yuga*. According to the Epics and the

Puranas, the rishis produce his shining body from the corpse of *Vena*, but unlike *Vena*, and although he participates in the nature of the gods, being *naradeva*, he immediately demonstrates his submission to brahmanical values. Once praised and consecrated, he gets hold of the earth, the cow of plenty, and distributes its produce in a manner at once generous and hierarchical (Dumézil). The earth is often called *prthivī* after him, and so also are the (*pārtha*) oblations which in the ritual precede and follow the royal consecration and aim at producing plenty. The social order and the generosity of nature go together. While the efficiency of the king is linked with the will of his subjects, at the same time 'he can give so much only because he has, from the start, everything in his possession and discretion' (Dumézil, p. 61) in the name of or at any rate for the benefit of all. On the plane of the gods, *Prthu* recalls Soma, himself a king, who presides over vegetation, Soma, the life-giving sap which, as here the milk of the cow-earth, ensures the perpetuation of all beings.

It might be thought that the cosmic quality of *Prthu* is only an isolated feature, a survival, perhaps, in the classical period, from a world of archaic notions and beliefs. But this is not so, for one can follow up in the literature the persistence of such notions, particularly in relation to rain, and to the earth. A Brahmana associates rain and law; rain and order, disorder and drought go together (*Śat. Br.*, XI, 1, 6, 24). Later, in the legend of *Triśanku* (or Satyavrata, above) as in that of *Devāpi*, the rule of an illegitimate sovereign is signalled by drought. In the Jatakas, the king is rainmaker, and there is an appropriate royal ritual. On the other hand, even in the Smriti, unexpectedly in connexion with rights in the soil, the king is often conceived of as married to the earth, as the earth's husband. The name of the king as such (*Pārthiva*) refers indirectly to *Prthu*. The Vishnu Purana designates the reign of the younger instead of the older brother, *Devāpi*, by the same term which serves for the marriage of a younger brother before that of an older brother (*parivettr̥*), a marriage which is condemned. Furthermore, the earth, when it is about to be given by the king (*Ait. Br.*, VIII, 21), or when deprived of its normal master, as when *Paraśurāma* confides it to *Kaśyapa*, complains bitterly or disappears into the depths. In the latter event, as the Kshatriyas have been exterminated, their descendants must be discovered and put on the throne before the order of things can be restored.

I think we may conclude that, while the *kṣatra*, or the king, has been dispossessed of religious functions proper, or of the 'official' religious functions, there are at the same time, at the core of the idea of kingship, elementary notions of a magico-religious nature not 'usurped' by the Brahman. Below the orthodox brahmanical level, another emerges on which, certainly in contact with popular mentality, the king has kept the magico-religious character universally inherent in his person and function. In that universe, there can be no question of a 'contract' between king and subjects. For such a thing to be at all conceivable, kingship had first to be secularized. This fundamental transformation has been realized, as we have said, in the brahmanical definition of the relation *brahman-kṣatra*. In that sense, this definition is the necessary basis of what may be called conventional kingship as opposed to magico-religious kingship.[8]

## 8  *Conventional kingship: the Mahasammata, Manu*

The first and most categorical exposition of conventional kingship, that of the *Dīgha Nikāya*, is very remarkable. Though it appears in the end as an attempt to explain the four *varṇa* in a heretical manner, largely through fanciful etymologies, it consists almost entirely of a long tale, starting from the primaeval chaos, which presents a kind of gradual genesis of mankind through increasing differentiation and degeneracy. Men come finally, in order to preserve property, to elect one of themselves as Mahasammata or 'Great Elect', he who will be charged with the maintenance of the social order and as retribution will receive a part of the crops. This is presented as the origin of the 'Circle of Kshatriyas'. Scholars recognize in this story a golden age – but it should be remarked that at that stage the living beings are not yet men – and a complex process of progressive decay, marked by increasing differentiation and immorality – the differentiation of the sexes in particular – and by increasingly hard conditions of living. When people begin to behave too badly, the paddy, once plucked, ceases to grow again spontaneously; then private property appears and, accompanying it, theft. Chastisement becomes necessary, although it is only summarily indicated in the form of censure and banishment.

This Genesis is not only a-brahmanical, but a-religious; although one purpose of the story is to place the Kshatriya above the

Brahman, no advantage is taken of the magico-religious aspects of kingship, on the contrary they are shunned – and in this the brahmanical view is basically accepted, or implied. But secularization is carried further than in the brahmanical view of *kṣatra*; we can say that it is extended to the *brahman* itself, in so far as (group-) religion is banished from the tale and ultimate values only appear in individual morality. Here the tale bears the stamp of heresy. As Buddhism and Jainism have often been regarded as kshatriya reactions against brahmanical supremacy, I would remark that, to appreciate to what extent this is true, it is essential to note that this supposed reaction has been effected through renunciation, and not within the social order itself; in other words it occurred on a level transcending society. One observation will demonstrate the direct impact of renunciation. Probably the most striking aspect of the story is the fact that society, or polity, as in the modern theories of contract, is given as a mere aggregate of individual men. I have tried elsewhere to show that the individual in that sense appears in India only through the man who abandons life in the social world, the renouncer, and it is plain that the Buddha as well as the buddhist monks are renouncers (see Appendix B). It is significant that it is a text of renouncers which first introduces this individualized picture of society, which might otherwise look very strange in the Indian context. This is confirmed if we compare our buddhist tale with the corresponding Hindu legend, the legend of *Manu* in the Mahabharata. Manu, when he is offered kingship, begins by refusing, because he is afraid of the sins of men. He consents only when men promise to give the king a share of their crops and of their merits, but to keep their demerits entirely for themselves. It is not enough to say that here the 'contract' extends to the spiritual or moral domain. It would rather seem to consist not in the agreement to share, but in the stipulation that demerits will not be shared. From an agreement between individuals, we have passed to an interdependence which is so close that the very identity of the moral subjects is blurred or attenuated.

However different the spirit of the two texts may be, it is not difficult to understand how the Brahmans have been able to take up the buddhist schema in part: a further step in the secularization of the Kshatriya was in no way disagreeable to them. Perhaps for this reason, the idea enjoyed extraordinary favour and the dharma texts vie with each other in repeating the formula which balances public order, or the 'protection' afforded by the king, and the prestations the king receives, which consist first of all in a share, mostly of one sixth, of the harvested crops. Certainly, the idea bears a relation to actual practice; at the same time I think it represents a rationalization of it: because the king received a part of the crops and was responsible for police and justice it has been possible to connect these two aspects while excluding all others. But for this to be possible one condition had to be fulfilled, namely that kingship be considered from a specialized, 'rational' point of view – in the modern sense – that it be completely severed from the magico-religious cosmos to which it generally adheres. From our sources, this seems to have developed in two stages: I have tried to show that the first stage was attained very early, within orthodox brahmanism, in the relation between *brahman* and *kṣatra*; the second stage appears to have been the work of a current which was non-brahmanical in its orientation, the thought of individualists, *i.e.* of renouncers.

The remarkable fact is that a rough parallel can be drawn between this process of secularization and the movement which has given birth, in the modern West at any rate, to the theories of the social or political contract. For Spinoza, the real question was to wrench the domain of politics from religion and fanaticism; for Hobbes, to lay the foundations of the State not on ideals – or values – by their nature always open to discussion, but on the most general and undeniable factual realities. It is probable that the similarity in orientation, regarding the relation between kingship or the State and religion or absolute values accounts to a large extent for the similarity in the speculations, however different the backgrounds. Once the cosmic links commanding the hierarchy of society are cut off – and provided at the same time that the speculations about the Ideal State, as in ancient Greece, are excluded – society is reduced to a collection of individuals, and it is only from their individual will that a legitimate power can be derived. It is certainly noteworthy that buddhist thought discovered this so early, even if in a summary form. But this is only a part of the Indian process of secularization: it has not only produced a distant but striking counterpart to the western theories of contract, it has also, more generally, tended to constitute a domain which, to an extent we shall have to gauge, corresponds to what we call the political domain in the western tradition.[9]

## 9 Daṇḍa: legitimate force

In conventional or 'rational' kingship, where the king is in charge of the protection of people and things, he exercises his function with the help of chastisement or punishment, *daṇḍa*, in the proper sense, the stick. Without the primary meaning being ever forgotten, the word has a whole series of connotations: it means punishment, the power to punish, and even a kind of immanent power of justice; in this last meaning it appears more or less identical with *dharma* itself. Finally the word evokes the notion of legal or legitimate force, one is tempted to say of the 'monopoly of legitimate force' in which Westerners often see one of the characteristics of the political domain. For instance, in the Arthashastra, *daṇḍa* designates the army, also called *bala* 'force'. And *daṇḍanīti*, lit. 'the conduct of punishment', or of force, designates not only justice, but the science of government, politics in general. On the whole, here is a concept which covers at least an important aspect of what we call political phenomena.

The long eulogy of punishment, *daṇḍa*, in Manu is interesting. At the beginning of the chapter dealing with the king, it follows immediately upon the exposition of the creation of the king and of his divine nature (VII, 13–34). It deals throughout with the duty of the king to administer penal justice. First the necessity of punishment is vigorously insisted upon: in its absence the stronger would roast the weaker, the crows would eat, the dogs would lick the sacrificial offerings, nowhere would there be *svāmya*, mastery or ownership, inferior and superior would be confused; also, it is said, all beings, including the gods, deliver their benefits only through fear of punishment. The first theme is very widespread: it is often said that when punishment is absent, as during an interregnum, men fall under the 'law of fishes', what we call the 'law of the jungle'. So in the Mahabharata: 'if there was on earth no king bearing the stick of punishment, the stronger would roast the weaker as fishes on a spike', or in another variant, 'would devour them as fishes in water' (XII, 67, 16). This kind of view seems a little surprising in the Smriti. True, it is used in the literature of dharma to extol judicial functions. Yet, it is not a normative view, but something like a conclusion drawn from the empirical observation of human conduct. As for Hobbes, it is a matter, not of what should be, but of what actually is, less of the ideal, or *dharma*, than of the hard reality of conflicting interests, *artha*. Here there might well be a borrowing by dharma literature from the literature of politics.

But let us follow the praise of punishment in Manu. It must be administered indefatigably and without mistake, for error is here as fatal as absence and both lead to the corruption of the *varṇa*-s, the breach of dams (or 'bunds') and the war of all against all. It follows that the king must fear his own power, he is advised at length on the procedure to avoid injustice, as injustice would destroy him. Finally punishment is personified, the king is its guide, its power is superior to that of the king and it recoils against him as soon as he strays from justice. On the whole, legitimate force in the form of judiciary authority is here invited to acknowledge that its legitimacy can spring only from universal Law. The political aspect is reintegrated into *dharma*, as being merely its instrument.

10  *Artha: interested action*

A second concept which corresponds partly to the idea of the 'political' is *artha*, most closely perhaps 'aiming at' (in French '*la visée*'). The habitual translation, 'interest', has the advantage of marking at once that economic and political are here undifferentiated; *artha* denotes the principle of rational action directed to egoistic ends, if one likes the 'well considered acquisition'. I must recall that *artha* is given in the trilogy (*trivarga*) of human ends (*puruṣārtha*). Some modern Indian authors have a tendency to interpret these notions in the western terms of rational action as corresponding to ends (*dharma*) and means (*artha*). I think this is unjustifiable; at best it puts an undue stress on an aspect which in the Indian view is quite accessory. In fact, here we are dealing with a classification of types of action based on a series of oppositions. In particular, *dharma* is (action in conformity with) the universal norm, and hence disinterested, while *artha* is (action in conformity with) interest, without regard to the universal norm. As the supremacy of *dharma* is beyond question, one may ask how the recognition of *artha*, which implies its negation, is at all possible. The answer to this lies in the hierarchy of these 'ends': *artha* is recognized only in the second place, we may say in matters indifferent to *dharma*, *artha* finally remains contained within the all-embracing *dharma*, confined within *dharma* prescribed limits. The situation is parallel to that of *kṣatra* in relation to *brahman*: the same secularization takes place, entailing the same subordination; *artha*, like *kṣatra*, is severed from the whole of being, made in some way autonomous, special, or, as we would say in our modern language, 'rational'. This is the point where the way opens which leads on either towards the conventional or as it were constabulary type of kingship, or to the amoralism occasionally displayed by the theorist of the Artha-shastra – the often stressed parallelism with Machiavelli is by no means meaningless.

It is not a negligible result of the views I advocate here that they at the same time stress the secularization India has realized in this domain, and the recognition of its limits. For, if the notions of interest and of force recall western speculations, it should not be forgotten that the context is fundamentally different. Being nega-tion of *dharma* in a society which continues to be ruled by *dharma*, the political sphere is severed from the realm of values. It is not in the political sphere that the society finds its unity, but in the social regime of castes (Bouglé). The system of government has no universal value, it is not the State in the modern sense of the term, and as we shall see, the state is identical with the king. Force and interest work only for strife and instability, but these conditions may thrive without anything essential being put in question; much to the contrary, social unity implies and entertains political division.

Let us also note that, as we are dealing with a classification of types of action, action is here considered from the viewpoint of the actor: apart from *dharma*, the other criteria, immediate satisfaction or pleasure (*kāma*), and interest (*artha*) place us in the subjective perspective of the actor; *artha* in particular identifies us, that is any people speaking of *artha*, with the king. This is best seen from the only classical treatise of *artha*, the Arthashastra of Kautilya. Before turning to it, I must point out that the subjective, or quasi-individualist, perspective and the negation of (brahmanical) *dharma*, both implicit in *artha*, inevitably bring the *artha* theorist close to the renouncer. Both kinds of thought, however different in them-selves, contribute to the 'secularizing' current (*cf.* above, §8).[10]

KINGSHIP IN THE ARTHASHASTRA

11    *The definition of political science as based on danda or artha*

Kautilya (*Kauṭilya*), as he defines his discipline in two passages of his work, establishes in fact an equivalence between *daṇḍanīti* and *arthaśāstra*. At the beginning of his treatise, he defines as follows the last of what he calls the four sciences:

> *daṇḍa* is the instrument of the prosperity of [the other three sciences:] philosophy, religion and economics; the conduct of *daṇḍa* is *daṇḍanīti*, which aims at acquiring what is not acquired, which guards what is acquired, increases what is guarded, and distributes what is increased to the worthy (I, 4, 4–6).[11]

While the beginning of this passage might evoke political order as based on legitimate force, the second part, which defines *daṇḍanīti*, apart from a reference to justice or equity when it is prescribed that distribution should be made according to merit, introduces on the contrary a quite different order of ideas and refers to 'acquisition' and to 'increase'. We may remember here that *daṇḍa* designates also the army (*cf.* §14); from the next definition, it seems clear that the reference is first to the acquisition of land. On the whole, *daṇḍa* would here be force and *daṇḍanīti* the exercise of force externally as well as internally. We come now to the second definition, given at the end of the work, of *artha* and *arthaśāstra* (XV, 1, 1–2):

> *artha*, that is the subsistence of men, in other terms the land (earth) supplied with men;[12] the *śāstra* which treats of the means of acquiring and guarding (or: making to grow, Jayaswal), that is the *arthaśāstra*.

It is also briefly stated at the beginning (I, 1) that the treatises of *artha* deal with the acquisition and guard (or fructification) of the land. The notion of acquisition is perfectly in order in this definition, and we may conclude that the former shows a kind of osmosis between the notions of *daṇḍa* and *artha*. Taken together, the two would result in something like: 'the exercise of force for the pursuit of interest and the maintenance of order'.

On the whole, if we look here for an equivalent of our concept of 'politics' or 'political', we find two concepts, closely and subtly combined: legitimate force (the army as well as justice and the police), which corresponds to the objective function of the prince, and the interest to acquire which corresponds to his subjective ends. This is not all, for this second concept refers to economic as well as to political aspects.

## 12   *Economics-and-politics*

If we look closely at the second definition, we shall find that it does present for us a transition from the economic to the political level. It does this in a very peculiar way: *artha*, it says, is the subsistence of men [this is, for us, economics], and it goes on: it is the land supplied with men [politics]. In economics, the actors or agents are the men, and land is, implicitly, their principal means of subsistence. In politics, the agent is the Prince, and, *from his point of view*, men as well as land are means. Politics appear here as a superior kind of economics in so far as, thanks to power, it includes among its means men; politics is economics *par excellence*, and it bears upon the land with its complement of men, with the men who so to speak garnish it.

This may seem to be in contradiction with some elements in the context, and it will be useful to consider a few more of Kautilya's definitions and the spirit they betray. There is actually a distinct word which I have translated as 'economics' in the first definition, and which designates one of the four sciences, distinct, that is to say, from *daṇḍanīti*. This is *vārtā*, where the radical corresponds to what I have translated above as subsistence, *vṛtti*. The enumeration of the four sciences is very remarkable indeed. In the first place, philosophy, or logic, *ānvīkṣakī*, is proclaimed the critical judge of all, including what is *dharma* or opposed to *dharma*, and this subordination of religion to critical reason is rare enough to be emphasized. It is a landmark of the secularization on which I have insisted above. But philosophy will also judge of what is profitable (*artha*) and unprofitable in economics (*vārtā*): *arthānarthau vārtāyām* – and we see here the equation of *artha* and *vārtā*. After philosophy has been extolled, religion, *dharma*, is exalted as it would be in a dharma treatise – but it has been relegated to second rank! Then, in the third place, preceding the definition I have given of *daṇḍanīti* which is completed by the recommendation to keep a measure in administering punishment, only a brief passage is devoted to *vārtā*: '*vārtā* is agriculture, cattle breeding, and trade,[13] it is useful as providing grains, cattle and money, raw materials and *corvée* (unpaid labour) [here, by analogy with passages where the same enumeration occurs, it is probable that we should supply a few implied words and read: 'as providing (the prestations due to the king which consists of) grains', etc.]; through it the king, with the help of the treasure and the army, imposes his will on his own and on the opposite party' (I, 4, 1–3). We see that *vārtā* is an empirical activity, certainly indispensable, but one which, perhaps because it is made up of several different pursuits, has no principle and is not properly a science. It is not autonomous, but only a necessary condition for the exercise of political functions. The impression one gets from Manu is very similar; there *vārtā* is learned, not from masters as the other disciplines, but from the common people (VII, 43). If we call *vārtā* the economic activity of the common people, we could almost state the *artha*, as the acquisitive activity of the Prince, is a compound of *vārtā* and *daṇḍa*, power; these two terms, distinguished in the enumeration of the four sciences, are in some measure blended in the notion of *artha*, and even in Kautilya's book itself, to whose picture of the economic activities of the king we now turn.

## 13    *Economic activities of the king*

Immediately after Book I which deals with the education of the Prince, Book II of the Arthashastra, by far the longest, making up nearly one fourth of the work which comprises 15 books, expounds the revenues of the king or, if one prefers, of the state. The main place is given to what has to be called the royal concerns, industries of production and transformation administered by state functionaries. Taxes proper play a relatively small role if we measure importance by the space allotted to them: apart from some brief passages, only chapter 35 is devoted to the collection of taxes in the countryside. But it is often difficult to distinguish taxes from the profits derived from economic pursuits; for instance, if the Prince decides not to exploit his monopoly on mines or salt production, he rents them, and the dues which the farmer has to pay are often called taxes by modern translators or commentators. In fact, the taxes, as we conceive them, are likely to have represented only a small part of the royal income. Regarding the variety of royal concerns, one is tempted to speak, sometimes of monopolies, sometimes of royal manufactures, but in the end it would seem that the royal monopoly extended in principle to everything, and that the subjects could have independent activities only when the king allowed them to do so, either quite deliberately, or, as it is likely, following the custom or a situation of fact which he finds advantageous to comply with. If we take trade as an instance, we see the royal officers levying all kinds of duties on behalf of the king on the transportation and sale of commodities, and, furthermore, the king claims to control prices to a large extent. There is a Superintendent for Trade as there is one for Mines or Metallurgy. He directs the distribution of royal commodities through duly controlled employees, or, on occasion, through duly taxed merchants, and he seems to be the master to decide whether a given good will be taken charge of by the state system of distribution or left out to be dealt with by free trade.

There are frequent difficulties and uncertainties in the interpretation of the text, but the general picture nevertheless is not doubtful. Rather than speaking of monopolies, or distinguishing a public sector in the economy, one should think of a manor. There is certainly a difference in scale, but apart from that, is it not the manorial combination of a right in the land and a power over men, which we encounter here?[14] I am not implying that the system expounded in the Arthashastra is in any sense feudal, but only, and essentially, that it belongs to that vast group of phenomena where economics and politics are not differentiated. This explains the accumulation of technical detail regarding all kinds of industries in the general sense, including agriculture, the breeding of cattle and horses, the capture and rearing of elephants, as well as industries in the narrower sense of the word. Here, as in the articulation of the concepts themselves, politics, economics, and even technics are left undifferentiated. The taverns, a royal monopoly, may serve as illustration. They are in the first place profitable establishments, but they are also the workshops of police informants; at the same time, according to the general principle that the king and the police should restore stolen property to the owner, the manager is responsible for the property, and in particular the jewels, of the drinking customers.

But, it will be asked, what is the relation between the system expounded in the Arthashastra and what actually happened in ancient India? Although most Indian authors insist that the Arthashastra really belongs to the Maurya period, the work is not dated with any certainty; some regard it either as the ideal view of a theorist – which it is no doubt in part, as is shown by the careful and precise definitions, some of which I have drawn attention to – or even a kind of conventional description. However, I think we may assume that the practical preoccupations of the author did not allow him to wander too far from what he knew of the actuality of his time. Although I have occasionally, for convenience, referred to items of the description as actual happenings, I have, above all, dealt with the conceptual framework. For instance, some will certainly be inclined to doubt whether the hold of the king on economic activities has ever in fact been as complete as that portrayed by Kautilya. But here, this is not my main concern, my main concern is that, beyond all the uncertainties of the facts, the author did actually conceive the things as he did, within the perspective of *artha*. From his point of view, what we call economic and political phenomena were in the relation, or the condition, I have stated. To pass from ideas to facts, our inquiry should be supplemented in the first place by a long and painstaking study of the inscriptions. Let me say in passing that, although much work has already been done, a vast field is still open to scholarship in the publication and systematic exploitation of this kind of sources. For the present, we can say that, in its widest sense, the picture we get from the Arthashastra is probably closer to the actuality of life than the one from the *dharma* literature with the exception of the administration of justice. In the Arthashastra, the Prince is the economic actor *par excellence*. This contradicts the conventionalist thesis of kingship as a constabulary function, a thesis we have already been inclined to consider as a kind of rationalization of the practice. In the Arthashastra, the king exerts a complete hold on everything, and in the first place on the soil. His share of the crops (so often called *bhāga*), far from appearing as mere retribution for his service in protecting the agriculturists, is closely analogous to the share (*vibhāga*) he levies on the produce of the mines he leases out by virtue of a right of ownership (which is not open to question anywhere in the literature). This goes to show that the king really had a right in the cultivated soil, and was not a mere 'protector' as the Smriti would have us believe. But this conclusion on a much debated point has of course to be checked against more direct evidence.

14  *The political aspect: the seven elements of the kingdom*

The sixth book of the Arthashastra, a very short one, is almost entirely concerned with a definition of the kingdom as made up of seven limbs or natural elements (*prakṛti*): *svāmi – amātya – jana-pada – durgā – kośa – daṇḍa – mitrāni prakṛtayaḥ*: 1) the master; 2) the companion(s); 3) the country; 4) the stronghold or fortified town; 5) the treasury; 6) the army; 7) the ally.

This definition is found again in the Smriti, with variants regarding the names given to some elements and the order of enumeration. Obviously the order is meaningful and must be interpreted as having a hierarchical value. This is shown by the discussions, in the form of alternatives, found in Book VIII, as for instance: 'Which is the more serious, a difficulty regarding the master [first term] or a difficulty regarding the ministers [second term]?' That is: supposing that the two occur at the same time, which is to be remedied first? Let us note the form of alternatives, expressing a problematic action, quite in keeping with what we have said regarding the point of view of *artha*, and which recalls Machiavelli's discussions and, nearer to us, T. Parsons' theory of action. We verify in each case that the conclusion is always the one implied by the order of enumeration: a difficulty bearing on the master is more serious than one bearing on his ministers, etc., each element in the enumeration is more important, more fundamental, than the one which follows it. It is often so – but sometimes the reverse also applies – with Indian enumerations in general. The number 7 also indicates a totality; in this hierarchical enumeration of the components of a whole, a procedure which is basically religious is applied to the realm of politics.

Let us follow the enumeration: first comes the master, we might almost say the lord (or, more doubtfully, the owner). The word king, *rājan*, is relatively rare in the work. Yet it is once said that the kingdom is, in summary, the king himself. The second term, *amātya*, designates the members of the royal household among whom the king chooses his high functionaries and councillors (*mantrin*). The country, *janapada*, is sometimes in other texts *rāṣṭra*, the kingdom, or even *janāḥ*, the people. D. R. Bhandarkar has shown, from the enumeration of the characteristics of this element, that it connotes at the same time territory and population (as we had above 'the land with its supply of men'). The French word '*pays*', and the English word 'country' keep this double connotation. Here again, we encounter a state of undifferentiation, compared with modern western ideas, where the notion of territory itself looms large.[15] The *janapada* is (be it also, or only?) a territorial unit, divided in Kautilya into four parts.

The fortified town, *durgā*, in Manu *pura*, is described elsewhere (II, 2) as the capital, either of the kingdom, or perhaps of each constituent *janapada* or district. According to Jayaswal, the pair *paurajānapada* 'inhabitants of town and country' would have referred to a system of assemblies; the hypothesis has not been retained. The army is called by the same name as punishment, *daṇḍa*; elsewhere in the same text it is called *bala* 'force'.

The last term, the ally or friend, would seem not to belong here, as it is obviously external to the kingdom. Actually it is a sign of the importance given in India to a relationship as a factor or supporting prop of the particular being. This is the sort of situation which can lead one to understand how far we are here removed from the modern western mind for which the 'individual' exists by itself and which, in the present context, would conceive of the State, defined in itself, as 'having external relations'.

On three points, namely hierarchy, territory-cum-population, and the external relation conceived as a part of the real being, a description of a modern Indian group, drawn entirely from observation – I am referring to my own monograph on a South-Indian subcaste – happens to have stressed a situation exactly similar to that given in the Arthashastra. That cannot be attributed to mere chance.[16]

CONCLUSION

I have tried to set in a global and comparative perspective some well-known data about the way kingship was conceived in ancient India. This led me to emphasize two main events or stages. The first event, which really sets the scene for Indian history, is the secularization of kingship laid down in the *brahman-kṣatra* relationship. It invites us to revise some current notions about the relation between hierarchy and power. The second event is more complex. It has appeared to us under two forms: on the one hand in the idea of contractual kingship, apparently emanating from renouncers, on the other in the theory of *artha*, not unconnected with the renouncers' individualism and their negation of brahmanical values, but constituting a politico-economic domain. In the dominant tradition, this domain is *relatively* autonomous with regard to absolute values. In so far as it is autonomous, there is a rough parallel at this stage with the modern western development, leading to a generalizing hypothesis: that such a domain as we know it necessarily emerges in opposition to and separation from the all-embracing domain of religion and ultimate values and that the basis of such a development is the recognition of the individual.[17]

Certainly, the similarities with the West are the more striking, when the wide differences in the context are kept in mind: difference in the point of departure as recalled above, difference in the genesis and situation of the individual (only implicitly referred to in this paper; compare Appendix B, §2 with Appendix A, §F), difference also in the final result: in India the autonomy of the domain remains relative, and within it economics and politics remain undifferentiated. It would seem that, here as regarding religion (see Appendix B, n. 26), the difference with the West lies less in the development itself, or its principle, than in the fact that, on the Indian side, the development took place *within* the given framework without altering it or emancipating itself from it. I should like to anticipate another study and say that in the West, the political sphere, having become absolutely autonomous in relation to religion, has built itself up into an absolute: comparatively, the modern 'nation' embodies its own absolute values. This is what did not happen in India. It could not happen, I suppose, as long as the polico-economic realm was only relatively autonomous, and this in turn could not be otherwise while the individual remained, in essence, outside the social world.

I shall not engage here on the wide question of Indian history, to which we hope to return, but only note a welcome paradox. Here, as with religion, while primarily concerned with permanent characteristics, I have been led to recognize an historical development, I mean a development which is not only chronological, but meaningful in the Indian set-up as compared with the Western. Furthermore, while far from assuming at the start that Indian history should be reducible to Western schemas (*cf. Coll. Pap.*, p. 17), I end with a parallelism. This is in strong contrast with the approach of some modern historians. They follow Marx on all but one point: where – quite rightly from his point of view – he saw stagnation they want to find movement, even if only that of physical change instead of meaningful change. They appear to attempt to vindicate India's reality in Western terms. I think it is better to try and curb our terms to India's reality. The search for meaning reveals development, the search for changes does not produce history.

I should like to conclude by drawing attention to some of the limitations of this attempt and their reasons. I have not considered factual happenings, as distinct from ideas, as in the main the inscriptions can reveal them. But, apart from questions of fact, I have been obliged to leave out many aspects of the matter for a quite different reason, which may cause some surprise. It is because they show the need for a more satisfactory sociological formulation of the Western phenomena themselves than those at present available, at least to my knowledge. At first sight, it would seem that our side of the picture is known better, and that all the effort has to be directed towards the Indian side. But, if this is in a sense true, it is also a fact that our institutions and forms of thought have rarely been formulated in comparative terms. Actually, it is only because the Indian situation is so clear-cut and logical on some points that one is emboldened to put forward the beginning of a comparative view. But one is very soon made to acknowledge that, to proceed any further, one should begin with sweeping one's own doorsteps. The comparative task imposes itself, whether in religion we discuss the type of ultramundaneity and the place of monachism in Christianity; whether, even here, we touch on the assumed struggle between 'temporal' and 'spiritual' agencies, or, to refer to a notion widely used at present, when we speak of 'feudalism' (which should be analysed into clearly defined features). The time has perhaps come when the mirror anthropologists direct at other societies should be turned back by them on ourselves, when we should try and formulate our own institutions in comparative language, i.e. a language modified by what we have learnt of different societies, however incomplete. About the difficulty of the task there is no doubt. But it might well be the royal road for the advancement of sociological understanding.

# APPENDIX D

## NATIONALISM AND COMMUNALISM

*Introduction*

I propose to discuss here one of the major facts of the political history of India in the 20th century: the growing estrangement between Hindus and Muslims, which culminated in the partition of 1947 and its sequel of massacres and huge population transfers. The cause of partition can be looked for in the configuration of wills in the period immediately preceding it. The view is commonly held, especially in India, that the opposition between the two religious communities, or their representatives, had been increasing since the beginning of the century, mainly due to the British will to divide in order to rule, or to keep ruling. I believe however that the roots of the conflict lie much deeper, and I shall try to establish in regard to this major example that 'social change' in contemporary India can be understood as a combination of the old and the new, on the basis of a comparison between the traditional and the modern types of society. In the present case the main task will be to reach a comparative definition of the modern concept of the 'nation' in two directions: its relation to religion or absolute values, and its territorial aspect.

The opposition to each other of religious communities is commonly designated as 'communalism'. Communalism may be defined as:

that ideology which emphasizes as the social, political and economic unit the group of adherents of each religion, and emphasizes the distinction, even the antagonism, between such groups.

This text reproduces the constructive part of the essay in *Contributions to Indian Sociology*, VII, 1964, pp. 30–70. At the beginning, a critical discussion (pp. 30–47) is left out and replaced by a short Introduction. The notes keep their original numbers.

Wilfred C. Smith, from whom this definition is borrowed (*Modern Islām in India*, Lahore, 1943, p. 185), makes more precise the relation with religion and nationalism in an observation which will serve as our point of departure:

The Muslim middle-class could even be said to be substituting communalism for religion, in precisely the sense in which nationalism in the Western capitalist world can be said to have taken the place of religion (*ibid.*, p. 214).

I

Although parallel, 'nationalism' and 'communalism' present some asymmetry in their meaning. Nationalism refers to the nation either as a tendency inspired by its existence or as the aspiration to build up a nation. Communalism supposes the existence of a community, a group of adherents to the same religion, but it gets the edge of its meaning through the parallelism with the other term: it is something like nationalism, in which the nation, so to speak, is replaced by the community. In other words, communalism is the affirmation of the religious community as a political group. Its hybrid character is implied in the very coining of the word. There is even an implicit contradiction between the two, as if the allegiance that should normally go to the nation were given by the communalist to his community instead.

The nation, in the restricted sense of a modern political group possessed of certain characteristics, is generally defined *within the modern framework of political ideas* as a group of people united in accordance with their own will and having certain attributes in common (territory, history, and others which are optional).[15] Obviously for our present purposes we shall have to look at it against a wider background, to attempt to give a comparative definition of it or at least to recognize some of its comparative characteristics. What is generally implied in the definition will have to be made explicit, at least in part, by reference to the society as a whole and to other kinds of societies.

Our point of departure is as follows. Communalism, on the one hand, differs from nationalism in the place that religion seems to play in it, while on the other, the religious element that enters into its composition seems to be but a shadow of religion, i.e. religion taken not as the essence and guide of life in all spheres, but only as a sign of the distinction of one human, at least virtually political, group against others.

The first implication here is that a nation is not built on the common religion of a group of people. Still, there are examples of nations in the strict sense of the term which have a state religion, and, abstractly, it is not unconceivable that all members of a nation may have the same religion. The similarity of religious beliefs may even be cited among the factors which make for the cultural homogeneity of a given nation. Hence, it is clear that the exclusion of religion as the basis of the nation is not an empirical, but a normative affair. Why is it so? It is frequently said that in modern society as compared with older, traditional societies, social and political life, and the state in particular, have been 'secularized'. This means that in modern society the sphere of religion has been restricted in such a way that for one political organization falls outside it, is *autonomous*, in other terms has its own values and is supreme in its domain.[16] This is one aspect of the modern revolution which opposes the modern nation to most comparable political entities of the past, Hindu, Islamic or otherwise. It is possible to escape a difficulty and avoid speaking unnecessarily of the religion or worship of the nation by substituting for 'religion' the consideration of the ultimate values bearing on social life or on its different aspects. From this point of view, the systems of ultimate values are of two types: in the first, all spheres of life come immediately and formally under the same values; in the second, certain spheres have their own values, special but, by definition, absolute within their sphere. Moreover, the first type corresponds to group-religion; in the second religion is attached to the individual person.

It will be objected that certain nations possess an official religion. In the United Kingdom the relation between the state and the official religion is very close, the sovereign being the head of both. But precisely this survival is possible only because of a double thorough-going distinction, between religion and politics, and between the state and the nation: there is no religion of the nation seeing that, on the contrary, the state guarantees to every member of the nation the freedom to practise the religion of his choice (or none). The two distinctions are solidary, and we have here (a part of) a nexus, as it is only the religion of the individual that may allow the political sphere to escape from its authority.

To understand this transformation, and appreciate the full

meaning of 'the individual' here, we must once more return to the modern revolution in values, which is crucial for comparison between modern and traditional societies. The universality, the rationality which attached to religion as ruling the social order in accordance with the ultimate nature of things has been transferred to man as an individual and as the measure of all things.[17] The nation is the political group conceived as a collection of individuals[18] and, at the same time, in relation to other nations, the political individual.[19] It is therefore incompatible with the religion of the old type.

It is easy to contrast the kind of political group thus characterized, in relation to religion and ultimate values, with more or less corresponding political entities of the traditional kind. To refer, for commodity, to the ancient Indian kingdom (see Appendix C), order is not based on the autonomy of the particular man, but on the interdependence of particular men and kinds of men. There is, strictly speaking, no 'body politic', the only political subject being the king, and at that, not without important reservations: the king rules, but the *dharma* is sovereign. There is no autonomy of the political sphere, for religion once removed, there remains only a domain, economic as well as political, where no law, no universal command rules, but only technics and force.

How is communalism located between these two extremes? In communalism elements of both worlds are mixed, and modified by their combination. The main trend is perhaps modern. A community's consciousness of being different from others, as an individual is different from others, and its will to live united as against others as well as its capacity, which will be better seen later in the case of Pakistan, to reflect itself in a given territory, make communalism resemble nationalism. At the same time, the adherence to group-religion distinguishes it sharply. The critical feature is that group-religion claims to constitute the particularity of the group, while the accession of the individual demands that group-religion should be replaced by individual religion.

Thus communalism appears as a hybrid, or intermediary, perhaps a transitory phenomenon. It seems natural enough that such mixed forms should appear in the zone of transition between the two systems we have contrasted, if we take into consideration the profound change which separates them, and if we think of the difference of environment between the European society that has given birth to the nation and the countries that are now trying to adopt it. But even with us, the disentanglement of the state as an organization independent from religion has been anything but easy and immediate; it has entailed in some cases wars of religion,[20] although the opposed confessions were infinitely closer to each other than Hinduism and Islam.

It seems, from the present reflection, that those wars signalled the same transition which has produced communalism in India, and that there is thus some parallelism between the two phenomena. They might be called 'infantile diseases' of the nation, but the term would be wrong, as it implies that transitions are pathological phenomena, and, furthermore, that the nation is necessarily the end-product of the transformation. The assumption is not warranted in the contemporary case, the more so as the nation in the strict sense of the word has perhaps ceased to be dominant in the world of today. Communalism in itself is ambiguous. It can finally appear either as a genuine transition to the nation, or as an attempt on the part of religion to oppose the transformation by allowing for the external appearances of a modern state. It is a kind of political Janus, looking both backwards and forwards.

To conclude, the example of communalism shows that the nation does not arise from a nexus of solidarities without any relation to values, as some authors implicitly suppose. One system of values excludes the nation, another admits of no other political group. I submit: 1) that the understanding of a phenomenon of 'change' of this kind demands comparison between the traditional and the modern social universes; 2) that this comparison requires religion – or ultimate values in general, even when they do not look like religion – to be recognized as constitutive of human society.

After this attempt at distinguishing one aspect of the nation comparatively, and before treating another aspect of it similarly, we shall return to our concrete case.


II

A sober assessment of the causes of the political division between Hindus and Muslims was offered by an Indian professor of Political Science, Beni Prasad, in the first part of a short book published just after his death in 1945, *India's Hindu-Muslim Questions*.[21] In addition to factors which we have already encountered, he has the merit of bringing forth some others which are essential for the sociologist. There are four main points. In the first place, during the period of Muslim domination, 'general social fusion' could not take place. There were reciprocal influences and a cultural fusion only. Secondly, the Hindus, and later on the Muslims, in order to reaffirm their religion, or their culture, in the face of the Christian and Western challenge had to resort to their past glories and reform religion through revivalism. This appeal on the one hand to the Upanishads, the Veda or the Gita, on the other, later, to the Koran and the beginnings of Islam, further estranged the two communities. Thirdly, the difficult transition to a democratic ideology was left entirely in the hands of the middle classes, where rivalry developed between members of the two communities 'for the few available posts'; the Muslims, being relatively late in the development, were led to fear that the transfer of power might result in a 'Hindu Raj'. Fourthly, the institution of separate electorates accentuated the division. On the whole, two factors are stressed as predominant: religious revivalism and separate electorates (pp. 48, 52). This brief summary is insufficient, especially as regards the intricacies of representation and government under British rule. As for us, there is no question here of claiming to give a complete enumeration of the causal factors and to assess their relative importance. This would probably be premature, and in any case would require the historian's training. My concern is only to arrive at a reasonable picture, with the sociological factors approximately in their place. And I believe that if we add the consequences of the loss of power by the Muslims, the picture will be there. With the help of Beni Prasad and other authors, we shall only stress some points and discuss some others. In doing so, a number of questions for future research will crop up.

1   *Lasting social heterogeneity of the two communities*

This is the basic point, which Nirad C. Chaudhuri also has put at the centre of his consideration. It is obvious enough, and it is generally forgotten only because religion is not taken as constitutive of society. But its recognition also requires some analytical acumen, seeing that the symbiosis of the two communities in their lower social levels, particularly in North-Indian villages, would seem to show the contrary.[22] Indeed, a sociology of interaction would be likely to miss the problem and find sudden bursts of hostility and riots hard to explain. Not so if we are careful to distinguish all along between what happens and what should ideally happen in conformity with the people's values and norms. Following the Muslim conquest, the two communities have been drawn together on the level of fact. In relation to their respective values, this is expressed by the fact that the Muslims leave infidels alive – even abolish, from Akbar to Aurangzeb, the capitation tax on them, and that Hindus accept rulers who cannot be transformed into Kshatriyas, as they refuse to recognize the supremacy of Brahmans. This may account for the 'rancorous' Hindu and particularly Brahman feeling, on which Chaudhuri perhaps over-insisted. The crucial point is that coexistence has produced no general ideological synthesis. Whatever may be the truth about Akbar's moves in this direction – an obscure question – only partial syntheses occurred (Kabir, the Sikhs, etc.). This can be readily understood. On the Hindu side, each movement was caught in the traditional pattern; it became a sect superimposed upon the Hinduism of caste instead of superseding it (Appendix B, §5); only through the sect could Hinduism pass over to monotheism. On the Muslim side, the orthodoxy, the articulate monotheism of Islam was constantly reaffirmed from two sources: the revealed book upon which the tradition is based, and contact with the Muslim world outside (Wahhabi movement, Khilafat agitation in a time of easier communications). B. Prasad thought with others that Hinduism became more rigid in the Muslim period as a consequence of its being deprived of its normal temporal powers.[23]

The Hindu social system put itself on the defensive and tightened itself more than ever before. Priestcraft appropriated the authority which the State had so far exercised in a more flexible manner in social affairs (p. 15).

If not documented, this is a valuable suggestion as to a very likely process, and future research may confirm it as an important aspect of Indian social history.

Regarding the two communities, we should understand that the *modus vivendi* that they attained was, in relation to their respective values, a kind of compromise which depended for its maintenance on the continuance of Muslim power. It has often been noticed, and sometimes wondered at, that Muslims in the 20th century lived in a state of fear (fear of Hindu aggression, fear of Hindu political domination). But Muslims had been living in fear from a much earlier time (in Bengal the first part of the 19th century). And this is understandable, for in so far as they felt that the force sustaining them was being removed without their being immediately and completely crushed, they could not but have a deep feeling of insecurity. This of course was not true of all Muslims everywhere and at the same time. In particular, the relationships with Hindus were different for Muslims of the upper and of the lower categories.

As for the lower Muslims, who rubbed shoulders with Hindus in the villages and themselves had castes or quasi-castes, the very form of their cohabitation with the Hindus expresses a compromise. Their houses are located among respectable Hindu castes notwithstanding their distinctive mores and their reputed dietary habits. As regards especially the latter, it is clear that the Muslim had to make concessions to the stronger feelings of his Hindu neighbour.[24] Looked at from the Hindu point of view, this situation is seen as due to an equilibrium between religion and power, as if these Muslims had been lifted above their expected position by a kind of thread which was tied ultimately to the wrists of the Muslim rulers. The astute Tilak perceived this situation when he saw in British power a chance for the reaffirmation of Hindu values as binding on all, and spread his cow-protecting societies. On the other hand, Islamic instructors do not seem to have been very active in bringing these people to be more orthodox as long as the power lasted or even later, while there has been a propaganda in this direction at least since partition. What is remarkable, and fortunate, is rather the inertia of the system. The cultural symbiosis has receded, and is still receding, by a slow process which has been favoured on both sides, and which may be traced ultimately to the change of power and to other factors mentioned below. But we do understand that, once the power prop was removed, riots could very easily be provoked and unexpectedly flare up. Similarly, on a far larger scale, the announcement of partition must have appeared to the people as a complete vacancy of power, and an invitation to put an end to their mutual compromise and reach a new order by their own means.

The case is sociologically illuminating. We learn that people who lived together for centuries do not really constitute a society if their values have not fused. We note that, contrary to what is often admitted, power does not automatically find its 'expression' in terms of values, and that the coexistence was empirically accepted without being legitimized, and was therefore, together with the cultural symbiosis, at the mercy of a change of power.

## 2  Change in the distribution and nature of power

British conquest brought a change in power which struck the upper Muslims directly and indirectly. Either immediately, or later and progressively, they lost practically all their means of livelihood, along with political power itself. At the same time, by the substitution of the 'rule of law' to the arbitrary will of the prince, wealth – in the first place movable wealth and by way of consequence immovable as well – was emancipated from political power, and economic power was made independent and secure. To realize the general importance of this change, one must imagine the abject dependence on the ruler in which the merchant had until then found himself, at least in Mughal India and, to some extent, in Hindu India as well.[25] While the Muslims were thrown down from their position of power and affluence, the Hindu merchants and moneymen were promoted to a powerful position.

In his classic and dramatic description of the decadence of the upper class Muslims of Bengal, W. W. Hunter has mainly referred to the first of these two aspects: how they lost their quasi-monopoly of employment in the upper posts of the army and the administration, and later in the judiciary, and how they were slowly evicted from their dominant position in relation to land.[26] On this point the ascension of the Hindus is mentioned, and in general this second aspect is implied when Hunter sums up the economic decadence:

One hundred and seventy years ago it was almost impossible for a well-born Musalman to become poor; at present it is almost impossible for him to continue rich (p. 158).

and still more so when he adds: 'The greatest wrong which we did to the Musalman aristocracy was by defining their rights' (p. 164). He notes an ethnographic detail which is revealing:

During the last forty years they have separated from the Hindus by differences of dress, of salutation, and other exterior distinctions, such as they never dreamed necessary in the day of their supremacy (p. 181).

In the courts, the decisive blow came when, following the official choice of English education, English replaced Persian as the official language (1835). Muslims did not take to English and were consequently replaced by Hindus. We may note immediately that following this a petition signed by 8,000 Muslims of Calcutta declared that the evident object of the Government was the conversion of the natives, a statement which will be years later abundantly used in the preparation of the Mutiny.[27] As the Hindus, with the same flexibility as before, hastened to adapt themselves to the new political order, the Muslims were outdistanced not only in economic pursuits, but also in administration and the professions. Hunter paints them as brooding in sullen isolation. However, these high Muslims of Bengal did not take part in the Mutiny; on the contrary, there were early signs of a change of attitude in Bengal, as we see from Bimanbehari Majumdar's excellent and, indeed, important book on the political movement in the province.[28] Here as usual Bengal shows the lead. In 1868, slightly before Sir Syed Ahmed Khan entered upon his campaign, Abdul Latif declared that the Muslims were now ready to turn to English education. In 1882–83 the National Muhammadan Association (founded in 1855) demanded special privileges to compensate for their inferiority, and Mahomed Yusuf asked for separate representation of the minority (whether Hindu or Muslim) in local self-government:

In such cases when there is party spirit and angry feeling between the two classes of people it is necessary to reserve power for the representation of the minority (p. 398).

Sisirkumar Ghosh, on the other hand, condemned special privileges as weakening to the country (p. 340, from *Amrita Bazar Patrika* of 26 October 1882). We even read that Pearychand opposed separate representation as early as 1852 (p. 213). Thus such privileges were in the air long before the time when the British are sometimes said to have invented them, and regarding the Muslims alone, the idea seems to have accompanied their first awakening to modern conditions, naturally enough on the part of people who were more than others used to relying upon the political power.

This brings to mind a point of history. The British contemporary feeling that Muslims were the main inspirators of the Mutiny is understandable; this supposition is now out of fashion without having ever been conclusively refuted. At any rate, the comparison between Hunter's picture of the 'Wahhabi' movement and its stronghold in Patna with the Bihari documents suggests that this was one of the main instigating centres[29] (two others being Lucknow and Delhi). I have alluded to the Muslim origin of the propaganda, and this is confirmed by the proclamations issued by the rebels in several places. In general, the hypothesis is quite in line with the nature of the movement – more the last rebellion of the old powers than the first sign of national awakening, as propaganda would now make us believe.

## 3   *The separative effect of* 'revivalism'

To realize graphically the relevance of B. Prasad's second point, we can try to imagine for a moment that the events have not developed as they have. Let us suppose that at an early stage, led by far-sighted leaders, Hindus and Muslims have decided to subordinate everything to their necessary union against British domination, to drop their religious differences and establish in a brotherly spirit a purely secular nationalist platform on the basis of what they have in common and what they desire in common, i.e. to reform the society according to modern principles and develop the economy for the welfare and freedom of all. Let us further suppose that in course of time this policy is faithfully followed and has taken roots. Reforms have developed, Muslims and Hindus freely intermarry, untouchability is only a memory, religion having changed and become a purely personal affair; the colonial power has not been able to withdraw for long the benefits of heavy industrialization; perhaps independence has not yet been attained, but it is well on the way. There have been no cow-protecting societies, no satyagraha, the forms of the movement have been the ordinary forms of political agitation and national demands in the West, not excluding terrorism and some military operations.

This imaginary picture, in part more in accordance with materialist views, immediately conjures up the relevance of religious ideas, and shows how heavily group-consciousness draws on the picture the group is able to form of its own past. We are led to understand how fundamentally the political action of Tilak and Gandhi was based on the intellectual synthesis that was prepared in the 19th century and which is often called neo-hinduism. Unfortunately it

324

is impossible here to retrace the development from Ram Mohan Roy to Vivekananda, in which all the subsequent political movement on the Hindu side is rooted. Let us only characterize it schematically by saying that it is a synthesis in response to a Western challenge which is still more political and social than religious: an integration of the new social and political values within a reformed traditional, and at least outwardly, religious view; a reaffirmation of supposed Hindu values on a new level. The major fact for us here is that this integration and internalization of modern Western views, which was conscious of being a victorious reaffirmation of traditional Hindu values, was a preliminary condition of an active political struggle against foreign domination on the part of Hindus. One is led to speak of 'Hindu Nationalism', an expression which, were it not self-contradictory, would well describe the common ground between tendencies as different as those of Tilak and Gandhi.[30] This was obviously not destined to make for union between Hindus and Muslims. Moreover the Muslims also tried, later than the Hindus, to reinterpret their Scripture and tradition in order to find room for innovations.

The example of Bankim Chandra Chatterji shows best the limits reached by the Hindu intelligentsia in its effort to build up nationalism. B. Majumdar tells us how the word 'national' captivated the imagination of youthful Bengal in the sixties (p. 412). Here is a Bengali of great intellectual power and sincerity who has read Mill and Comte (in the light of the idea of *dharma*), who has no patience with empty political demands, and who is consciously working at building up nationalism for the times to come. His patriotism is a lofty ideal inspired by the love of humanity at large; in *Ananda Math* the hero is advised not to fight the Europeans from whom the country will learn for its revival. His *Bande Mataram* embodies a conscious effort – perhaps unique – to transmute into patriotism the apperception of the super-human or super-individual. The poem is sociological: the country is the life in the body of the inhabitants (p. 418), the goddess is identified with the country, with the people. But the subsequent history of the song, which could not be kept as a national anthem, illustrates the narrow limits that even Bankim's enlightened effort could not transcend. As B. Majumdar remarks, his patriotism remains 'intensely provincial' and we should add 'communal'. There is no place for the Muslims in a patriotism whose images are the Hindu goddesses. The distance is great, and most instructive, between the ambition and the fulfilment of this courageous spirit. Bankim had to build on existing sentiments, and he could have found no ground for exalting Hindu-Muslim unity at the national level. Only a common and hard struggle against the British could have forged such sentiments.

## 4   The undertones of Congress nationalism; Britain

The ideological basis of the national political movement, as laid out in the preceding century, is encompassed within a reaffirmation of traditional values. Similarly, to this day the political sphere in actual Indian life appears as one of several boughs carefully grafted on to a huge Indian tree. Moreover, the most influential leader of the period under study has spectacularly combined religion and politics. On the other hand, the tendency of many modern writers is to forget these facts and to accuse the Muslims of having introduced religion into politics on their own account. Clearly, the whole movement constituted by the Congress and the League has to be taken as a single whole. The two movements are complementary in the sense that the attitudes of the greater and older body did determine in some measure those of the other, the more so as the majority could rely on numbers to solve certain questions in practice, while the minority could not and had to be articulate on the same matters. Thus it is that the question of the place of religion in the Congress movement up to independence is forced upon us.

It is a delicate question to handle, especially for a non-Indian writer. But it has ceased to be vital: history or science can claim it as its own, and its discussion can hardly be even remotely harmful in our days. Scientifically it is a matter of research for the historian, for it involves the consideration of data much more difficult to document and assess than program and ideology. A book such as Sanjana's, although courageous and very useful, and even apparently convincing on some points, has to be taken as having opened avenues for more complete and detached research, for it is obviously too polemical to be relied upon without check.[31] I shall be content with trying to throw light on the problem by concentrating on some crucial issues.

It hardly needs to be recalled that, regarding the broad overt phenomena, the Congress appears essentially as a purely national movement. The Constitution of independent India is after all the touchstone in this respect. Similarly, in the whole history of the Congress there is no trace of communalism proper. Quite to the contrary, the dominant tendency has been to refuse to take into consideration on the political level the religious distinctions found in Indian society. The question appears only when one leaves the level of principles for that of facts, and asks whether this attitude, which can be taken as mere political modernism, did or did not correspond to particular political interests, did or did not in the first place mirror a tendency to identify the Indian nation with the dominant high-caste Hindus. This question is obviously very difficult because its answer requires that not only the conscious declarations of the party, but also its different tendencies, now successful and now defeated, should be transcended. It would require a sociological view of the Congress as a whole.

If we look at the actual agitation of the Congress through the initial phases of its history, we must first observe that, as in the case of Bankim, from the moment the supposedly purely nationalist leaders wanted to enlist the energies of the people immediately, they were naturally led to mobilize its actual deeper collective emotions, that is, they had to appeal to religion in the name of the nation-to-come. (This they could do thanks to the 19th century rehabilitation of hinduism, which had reconciled the intellectuals with the people's religion in general if not with all its aspects). If this is so, then the momentous decision was taken when Tilak overpowered Ranade (and at the same time virtually Ram Mohan Roy, Bankim and even Vivekananda), when, that is, instead of creating an Indian nation through reforms, the aim had become that of building up with every available weapon an uncompromising opposition to the foreigners. Rigorously, Tilak's tendency can perhaps not be called a communalism, in so far as it was directed in the first place against the British, but it necessarily bred communalism in the simultaneously antagonized Muslim partner. Furthermore, in so far as the establishment of a national ideology requires from traditional societies a fundamental change in the system of values, the policy of Tilak, if supposed purely nationalist in its aims, was self-defeating, for the means were to determine the end-result irrespective of the intentions. On the same supposition, the apprentice-sorcerer would have raised a flood that his descendants could not stop, he would have sowed the seed of the blood harvest of

1947. If importance is attached to the means – clearly known – as well as to the ends – sometimes doubtful – we must say with N. C. Chaudhuri that the nationalism of the Congress had become something else.

In the case of Gandhi the question is different, and much more difficult to answer. To assess the respective place in his action of religion and politics is a problem which goes beyond Hindu-Muslim relations and requires a consideration of all the aspects of his action. It demands special research, which is so extended and delicate that the personality of the researcher, rather than the datum, may in the end weigh more heavily on the result. But a previous remark offers, I think, a preliminary clue. Gandhi's position between Tilak and Gokhale is highly characteristic; it looks likely that, as the reformists before him, Gandhi was conscious of the contradiction involved in a caste society demanding anything like 'home-rule', and it may be said that he blended the reformist and the extremist approach in so far as he insisted that India should show her capacity to reform herself even while asking to be left alone. This synthesis is linked with the perfect integration of nationalist aspirations within the hindu-jain framework of 'non-violence', and also with the two main aspects of Gandhi's public personality: a political representative for the British, a sanyasi for the Hindu people. Further on I can offer only guesses.[32] It is reasonable to suppose that Gandhi's objective was also double: to attain independence and to save Hinduism. In order to attain both ends it was necessary to show the beginning of reform, but reform was, in fact if not consciously, subordinated to independence. This is a second guess, and it can go some way towards explaining Gandhi's extraordinary tactics, as, for example, his manner of suddenly calling off a movement, which baffled even Jawaharlal Nehru. Gandhi did not only want to show to the British, but also to persuade himself, that India was in the process of reforming herself; he must have had some doubts on this score, and his doubts became overwhelming when circumstances showed him the country as unregenerated. A revealing instance of Gandhi's conception of reform as having absolutely to take place *within* Hinduism occurred when, in Poona in 1931, he fasted to exact from Ambedkar his renunciation of a separate electorate for the Untouchables. This showed that the right to dispose of oneself could be opposed to England, not to Hinduism.

It is true that Gandhi did not oppose a separate electorate for the

Muslims. It can be granted that those Congressmen who did so the most effectively were not religious- but liberal-minded; and yet if we speak of the Congress as a whole, we have to blend the diverse motivations and say that its refusal of such measures was tinged with communal motives, or might have appeared so to Muslims. The only way for the Congress as such to appear non-communal in fact would have been to recognize the actual cleavages in the country, and not to pretend to a monopoly, as a purely national organization, of the representation of all categories of Indians. But it would then have appeared as endorsing communalism. There is here a complementarity between the level of principle and that of fact, and the fatal misunderstanding could have been escaped or broken only by splitting the organization in two: an organ of national struggle, and a party for internal politics. The blend goes back to Tilak's victorious attack on Ranade's Social Reform commission, i.e. to the choice of the anti-foreign struggle as against reform. We thus come to the hypothetical conclusion that the liberal political theory served the interest of the struggle against domination and, inextricably mixed up with it, the will to power of one party. Only a Congress much more intent on reform and accepting to this end the country's real cleavages would have been entirely free from communal tinge, but then it would have subordinated and, at least in its own view, delayed independence. This is not by way of suggesting that another course might have been possible, which was unlikely given the social and economic circumstances, but only of trying to make clear, on the political level, the connections between orientation, principles and facts, and the implications of the interaction between the different social groups involved.

As to the contribution that British policy may have brought to disunion, it is enough to have reduced the question to its real proportions, and therefore only a few remarks will be made. The main affair is that of separate electorates, special representation, and compensatory privileges in general. The idea, we have seen, had long been in the air. And it cannot but be acknowledged that the moment a minority or a category of people suffering under a long heritage of social and economic discrimination asks for safeguards and compensatory privileges, the democratic principle entails that these should be granted, either permanently or until the heritage of the past has been sufficiently counterbalanced. This is so true that independent India has maintained such devices, although there is a widely felt feeling that they entail serious disadvantages and do not very well serve their purpose. It is widely admitted that the Montagu-Chelmsford declaration has stirred into a new life minorities and underprivileged classes all over the country, and it is also widely thought that separate electorates and special representation have heightened separatist and fractional group-consciousness. This was inevitable, and the real question is whether those measures made, beneath the obvious rifts, for deeper unity, and for progress. The Simon Commission denied that 'if communal representation was abolished communal tension would disappear', and its Report adds that the true cause of Hindu-Muslim rivalry 'is the struggle for political power and for the opportunities which political power confers'.[33] As we have seen, modern authors concur on this being one factor, and it is for the historian to measure its relative impact. Another statement of the Simon Commission may be quoted for its objectivity, which in the circumstances is not devoid of merit:

Whatever may be its shortcomings and however distasteful some of its manifestations, it [the Congress Party] appears to be the one force in Indian society to-day that may perhaps contain within itself the power to overcome the deep and dangerous cleavages that threaten its peace.

III

In the more common view, the two communities are seen as united parts of the same society, so that their growing disagreement and the final partition look very unlikely events and must be attributed to an external cause and/or a series of accidental events. We have seen that both communities were in fact deeply divided among themselves by a series of historical causes. These causes were not independent but reinforced each other, and their effect could not but grow as the struggle for independence intensified and as the transfer of power by the British was enlarged by steps and promised to become total. We have thus made the development more understandable, but regarding the final event we have only made it less unlikely. We have by no means answered a question such as: Was partition inevitable? Or, more precisely: The events until, say, 1938 being given, could India in the long run have lived normally as an independent State without partition? I shall not answer this question directly, but, returning to the comparative model and developing another part of it, I shall point out a remarkable congruence between the model and the event. This comparison results, I believe, in tipping the balance of likelihood in the direction opposite to that most often assumed.

The question bears on the place of territory in the modern nation or state. The notion of a common territory appears so necessary in the modern consciousness of political identity that it is most unlikely that things might have taken another turn. There is at least one other type of explanation, based on the criss-crossing of the wills and moves of the different parties in the years of the final development, a mixture, that is, of voluntaristic and accidental explanation. At first sight such an explanation and a structural understanding might seem not to contradict, but to supplement each other. But are we not entitled to something more than the 'series of event' type of explanation when we are confronted, not with temporary states of things or with unstable equilibriums, but with a stable equilibrium of a system, if it can be demonstrated that no other state of stable equilibrium is possible? Here it can be objected that the division of India has not lasted long enough to be considered as stable, and that it is only a compromise, possibly an unstable situation, given the fact that Pakistan has hardly yet found its internal balance. On this question also I believe that the following is relevant.

We start with asking whence comes the importance of territory in the nation. It is the only element, with the will of the population itself, whose presence is generally considered as a *sine qua non* of the realization of a nation, while other elements, a common history (most recommended), a common culture, a common language, are more or less frequently found, but are not indispensable. It will perhaps be alleged that territory is almost synonymous with the political domain, and that to say that the nation has territory is the same as to say that it is a political group. This is not so, for we must as usual distinguish between the empirical presence of a territory – co-terminous with any human group of the required size – and the place of territory *as such* in the very consciousness the group has of itself. 'France' is not, for the French, only a collection of people or a collective individuality: this image is complemented by an image of a territory of a certain shape. The stress on the unity of the latter is such that the Revolution insisted in the indivisibility of the Republic, and that after the loss of Alsace-Lorraine in 1871 its deputies continued to sit in the Chamber until the next elections on the ground that a deputy represented constitutionally the people as a whole, and not the particular circonscription which had elected him. We also notice that sovereignty has for long not been territorial. Sir Henry Sumner Maine stressed this point most strongly.[34] According to him the notion that prevailed in Europe after the barbarian invasions was *tribe-sovereignty*, the alternative being the idea of *universal dominion*. (Such notions were not foreign to ancient India.) He adds that the idea of territorial sovereignty was a tardy offshoot of feudalism. Rousseau vigorously insists on the '*domaine réel*' as constitutive of the State; he subtly links private property (in land) with territorial sovereignty. According to him it is only within the territorially sovereign State that property is guaranteed, and he marks the distinction between the expressions 'King of the Persians' and 'King of France'.[35] This is an important point which, admittedly, would require further study.

At any rate, the modern nation is characterized in the first place by a People (a group of people possessed of a common will) as the political subject, and a territory as its inalienable attribute. Apart from the continuous tract of country symbolizing the unity of the collectivity (which may have no king), it forms the basis of the real sovereignty of the People as a corporation, and the relation between People and territory mirrors the distinction between soul and body or man and nature. If we now compare this with the old Hindu kingdom as we can fancy it from the dharma literature and, for the relevant part, from the Arthashastra, what do we find? The king rules in the name of dharma over the 'country', or more precisely over an entity which should be taken as population-cum-territory (*janapada*). This is not a mere linguistic matter, for, as we have seen previously, both men and land are equally means for the king's ends (Appendix C, §12). In brief the king in his official function mediates between the universal order or *dharma* and the empirical object, the population-cum-territory. I would suppose that this particularly clear formula holds in some manner for all 'traditional kingdoms'.

By comparison with the republican nation, we find that the replacement of the king, as sovereign, by the People entails a differentiation between people and territory. What here takes the place of dharma is the law, but the law being the will of the People we need not distinguish between People and law. Dharma is actually replaced by the People as a collective individual mirroring itself in its territory. The political sovereign has been promoted: it was a mediator between values and means, it has become the incarnation of values. What is ruled, instead of population-cum-territory, is a collection of individuals and their properties. The mediator between the population as sovereign (the People) and as subject (a collection of individuals) is found in the principles of liberty and equality.

But we are here directly concerned only with territory. The major fact that the comparison brings forth in this respect is the *differentiation between population and territory, territory becoming, in a secondary capacity, and as a necessary attribute of the People, part of the cognitive and normative aspect of the system.* In other terms, territory is a necessary factor of the individuation which is here part of the very essence of the system.

Let us now return to India and the final phase of events ending in partition. In 1937 the Muslim League was beaten in the elections, and the Congress, through the formation of homogeneous cabinets and the inauguration of its Muslim mass contact campaign, exacerbated the communalist feeling among Muslims. The major trend in Muslim League policy in the years that followed, apart from reorganization, use of the traditional religious leaders, and standing aloof of the extreme nationalist attitude of the Congress, was its adoption of the motto of Pakistan, i.e. of the Muslims having somewhere their own territories. The next elections in January 1946 were a triumph for the Muslim League and this, as the basis of Jinnah's intransigence in the negotiations of the following years, was a main factor of partition. Is it not clear that what happened is that the Muslim League had come upon the only term which could distinctly express for the Muslim masses their feeling of separateness and their desire to escape from an increasingly irksome coexistence with their Hindu neighbours and live as a separate people; or, to use a part of a formula of Smith, their 'striving towards freedom . . . in . . . terms that they can understand'? Was it really so, or was the success of territorial separation inspired by religious motives? Although it had been pointed out that orthodox opinion then and later on voiced the opposition of Islamic tradition to the 'territorial state',[36] we must also remember how in the 19th century some Muslims left the country of the infidels; we are not in a position to exclude either the traditional or the modern motivation; on the contrary, it is much safer to assume that their association accounts for the sudden and resounding success of the Muslim League.

In other words, partition was probably inevitable as a lesser evil in so far as the feeling of the Muslims of being socially distinct was disregarded by the leaders of the nationalist Congress. The attempt was made to coerce India into the abstract framework of modern political theory instead of recognizing its duality and trying to build the union of the two communities, at least for a long intermediary period, on their very separateness. This is probably what Beni Prasad meant when he said that the State was not necessarily to be uni-national (p. 82). The objection that arises from the actual coexistence in Bharat at the present time of Muslims and Hindus is valueless, as it disregards the existence of Pakistan as one element in the whole situation.

To conclude,[37] what has been attempted here is to try and understand a particular but important political phenomenon as an aspect of the *interaction* of traditional society and the historical legacy on the one hand, and British domination and modern Western ideals and norms on the other. To spot the broad features of this interaction and the difficulties encountered in the emergence, to this day incomplete, of nations and nationalism, we have compared in their political aspect the two social universes thus confronted. It has been shown that elements such as People and territory, normatively stressed on one side, are found *as empirical and undifferentiated datum* on the other. The orientation to ultimate values shows a more drastic and complex difference. On the traditional side, the ultimate values are found in the conformity of each element to the role assigned to it in the whole of Being as such; in the modern society, they are found in the concrete human indivisible element, which is taken as an end in itself, and as the source of all norms, rationality and order: in other words, the Individual. As history shows, the transition is difficult, and has given rise to intermediary forms.

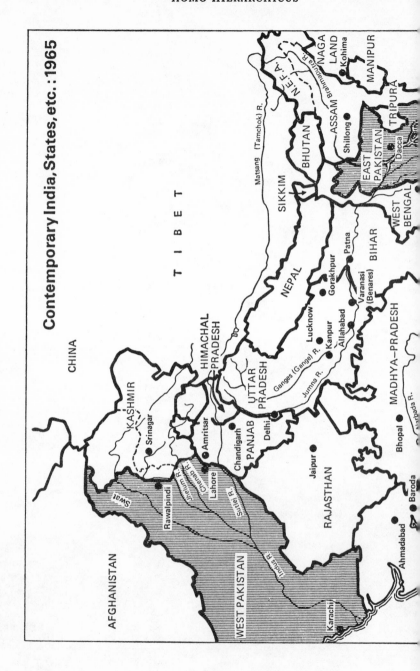

Contemporary India, States, etc.: 1965

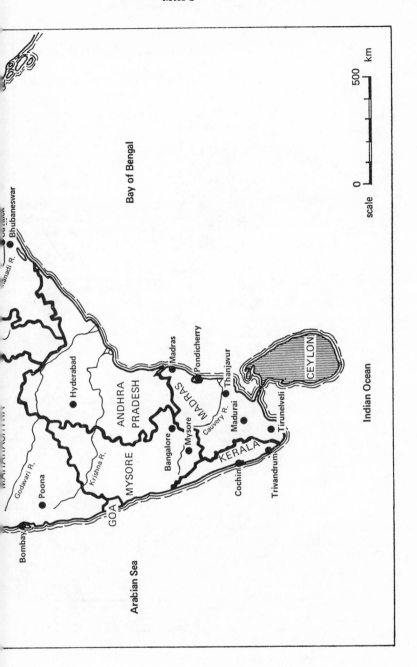

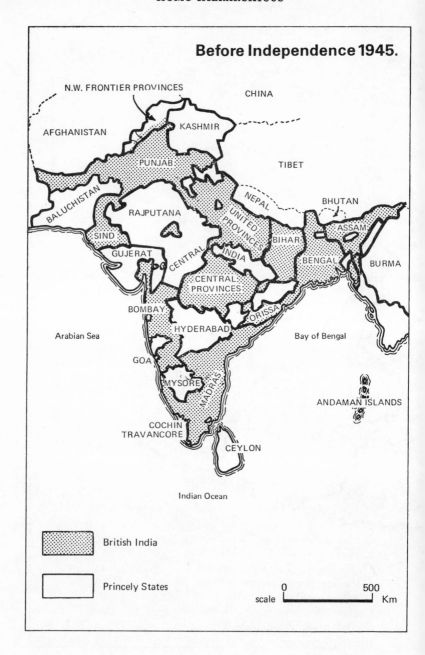

## Before Independence 1945.

N.W. FRONTIER PROVINCES

CHINA

AFGHANISTAN

KASHMIR

PUNJAB

TIBET

BALUCHISTAN

RAJPUTANA

NEPAL

BHUTAN

UNITED PROVINCES

SIND

ASSAM

GUJERAT

CENTRAL INDIA

BIHAR

BENGAL

BURMA

CENTRAL PROVINCES

BOMBAY

ORISSA

Arabian Sea

HYDERABAD

Bay of Bengal

GOA

MYSORE

MADRAS

ANDAMAN ISLANDS

COCHIN
TRAVANCORE

CEYLON

Indian Ocean

British India

Princely States

0        500
scale              Km

# NOTES

PREFACE TO THE COMPLETE ENGLISH EDITION (pp. xi–xliii)

1  The first two French reviews from classical indologists were exceptionally understanding and generous: M. Dambuyant, in the *Journal de psychologie* 65th year, No. 1 (1968), pp. 105–9; [Ch. Malamoud] in *Bulletin critique du livre français*, No. 70584, June 1967. The silence from sociologists obviously is comparable to the hostile trend among anthropologists (see below). The *Sociological Bulletin* of Bombay published a long abstract by J. Boel, March 1968, pp. 103–18. See also below, n. 5.

2  Letter from J. H. Hutton of 20 January 1967. This letter and the other documents mentioned form a record on file at the Centre d'Etudes de l'Inde et de l'Asie du Sud, E.H.E.S.S., where they can be consulted. See the obituary notice for Hutton by C. von Fürer-Haimendorf in the *Proceedings of the Royal Anthropological Institute* for 1968, pp. 66–77. Nirmal Kumar Bose, 'New Attempt to Understand Caste System', *The Sunday Hindustan Standard* (Calcutta), 13 June 1974.

3  Thus an anonymous critic – probably an anthropologist – of the *Times Literary Supplement* concludes that the book 'brilliantly displays the apparent irrationalities, contradictions, and ambiguities embodied in the caste institutions, as parts of a consistent system', yet fails to see any reason to revise his opinion of the theory that, in fact, permitted it to be done, and which he summarily dismisses (*Times Literary Supplement*, 31 August 1967, p. 784).

4  *Cf.* my essay, 'La Communauté anthropologique et l'idéologie', *L'Homme*, July–December 1978, pp. 83–110 (Engl. trans., see Dumont 1978).

5  Claude Meillassoux, 'Y a-t-il des castes aux Indes?' *Cahiers internationaux de sociologie* (1973), pp. 5–29. When sending his article to me, the author courteously invited me to enter into a

discussion. I replied that his initial refusal to recognize a historical dimension in my works alone justified my abstention (*cf.* Index, *s.v.* history). For a refutation of this critic from a viewpoint similar to his, see the contribution by Barnett *et al.*, 'Hierarchy Purified', to the symposium in *Journal of Asian Studies* 35, No. 4 (August 1976), especially pp. 641–44. In the United States, we can see an attempt at synthesis; see the contribution of Barnett in Janet L. Dolgin *et al.*, eds., *Symbolic Anthropology* (New York, 1977), and the Introduction to the collection.

6  *Contributions to Indian Sociology*, n.s., 5 (December 1971): 1–81, under the editorship of T. N. Madan, nine contributions by ten authors and my own response, 'On Putative Hierarchy' (pp. 58–78). The bibliography (pp. 79–81) lists most of the previous reviews. To fill in from 1971 to the present, one can add, besides the following two titles, the new reviews by S. J. Tambiah in *American Anthropologist* 74 (1972): 832–35, and S. A. Tyler in *American Anthropologist* 75 (April 1973): 381–85. Another symposium is *Journal of Asian Studies* 35, No. 4 (August 1976): 579–650, Introduction by J. F. Richards and Ralph W. Nicholas, four contributions by six authors. Finally, *H.H.* is discussed at length by Owen Lynch and the editor in Kenneth David, ed., *The New Wind: Changing Identities in South Asia* (The Hague: Mouton, 1977). (The book contains the proceedings of a section of the 1973 International Congress in Chicago.) The review of this symposium by N. J. Allen in the *Journal of Indian Philosophy*, 6 (1978): 189–93 is again relevant. For convenience, the above symposia are indicated hereafter by 'CIS 1971' and 'JAS 1976'; references to works by authors appear in the usual form, that is, 'David 1977', and only the references thus abridged are listed at the end of the preface.

7  'For a Sociology of India'; see Dumont 1957.

8  Clearly two words are needed. In French, there is only *empirisme*, but I took advantage of a remark of Lachelier to introduce '*empiricisme*' (*cf.* André Lalande, *Vocabulaire technique et critique de la philosophie* [Paris, 1926], *s.v.*). In English, I promise to make do with 'empirical' as far as I can.

9  I have contrasted the 'classifying' approach with its arbitrary divisions and the 'typifying' approach with its global grasp and comparison in 'Caste, a Phenomenon of Social Structure or an Aspect of Indian Culture', in A. V. S. de Reuck and Julie Knight, eds., *Ciba Foundation Symposium on Caste and Race* (London: Churchill, 1967), pp. 28–38.

10  A brief indication of the theme can be found in an article by N. K. Bose, in which he speaks, regarding renunciation, of 'individual

liberty' ('Caste in India', *Man in India* 31, Nos. 3–4 [July–December 1945], pp. 107–123, esp. p. 114).

11 The fruitfulness of the point of view will fully appear only with its application to the evolution of Christian ideology from Jesus Christ to Calvin.

12 'The ideal that he [the renouncer] proposes has fertilized through and through the society that he had left behind' (Madeleine Biardeau and Charles Malamoud, *Le Sacrifice dans l'Inde ancienne* (Paris, 1976), p. 86, n. 1. Another recent reference: Frits Staal, *Exploring Mysticism* (Penguin Books, 1975), pp. 104–5.

13 The study was undertaken at the request of the editors of *L'Inde classique* for inclusion in a third volume, to be published, of that textbook. I saw there a chance to show the contribution that antropology could make to history. Later, the project was abandoned, but I had had time to review the literature (which was not in vain and permits me to have an opinion on other historical questions) and to submit to Louis Renou this text, which he accepted, adding that he found in it a new way of looking at some 'well-worn' questions. (His letter is in the file at the C.E.I.A.S.)

14 Biardeau and Malamoud, *Le Sacrifice*, pp. 30–31, 84–86; see the general argument, p. 153. In any case, this is an important work. See also the reservations of J. D. M. Derrett, 'Rajadharma', JAS 1976, pp. 597–609. I think that the late Robert Linget had his own reservations. One hopes for the publication of the lectures on Buddhist kingship, of which he must have left the text.

15 See Gerald D. Berreman, 'The Brahmanical View of Caste', in CIS 1971, pp. 16–23, esp. p. 23. For the professions of equality among the Untouchables and their limits, one can refer to a serious inquiry like Michael Moffatt's *An Untouchable Community in South India: Structure and Consensus* (Princeton: Princeton University Press, 1979).

16 Because barbers shave one another, someone would like to conclude that 'equality and reciprocity' have the same importance as does hierarchy in the system (CIS 1971, p. 39).

17 Paul Thibaud on 'La Conception moderne de l'Individu', in *Esprit*, February 1978, p. 4: 'a manner of telling which materials one is working with, the better to lay oneself open to complements and criticism'.

18 For an example of continuity between common ideology and anthropological theory, see my *Introduction à deux théories*, 1971, and the review by Maurice Freedman in *Man*, 1972, p. 654.

19 This point of view is not articulated in *H.H.* itself, but see Appendix B, end of introduction and all of Section 1. See also

Dumont 1957, p. 15; *Dravidien et Kariera*, pp. 23–24; *Daedalus*, Spring 1975, pp. 161–62.

20 The article fills two-thirds (pp. 59–166) of Jack Goody and S. J. Tambiah, *Bridewealth and Dowry*, Cambridge Papers in Social Anthropology, No. 7 (Cambridge: Cambridge University Press, 1973).

21 Susan Snow Wadley, *Shakti: Power in the Conceptual Structure of Karimpur Religion*, University of Chicago Studies in Anthropology (Chicago: University of Chicago Press, 1975).

22 S. J. Tambiah, 'From Varna to Caste through Mixed Unions', in Jack Goody, ed., *The Character of Kinship* (Cambridge, 1973), pp. 191–229, esp. 224. *Cf.* below, p. xl.

23 F. A. Marglin, 'Power, Purity, and Pollution', in *Contributions to Indian Sociology*, n.s. 11, No. 2 (July–December 1977): 245–70.

24 Most recently, McKim Marriott, 'Hindu Transactions: Diversity without Dualism', in Bruce Kapferer, ed., A.S.A. Essays in social anthropology *Transaction and Meaning*, (Philadelphia: Institute for the Study of Human Issues, 1976).

25 This is but one example among many: Marvin David, 'A philosophy of Hindu Rank from Rural West Bengal,' *Journal of Asian Studies* 36, No. 1 (November 1976): 5–24, esp. p. 12.

26 S. Barnett *et al.*, 'Problems of Kinship and Caste in Two Regions of India', *Contributions to Indian Sociology*, n.s. 10, No. 1 (January–June 1976): 63–182.

27 *Cf.* 'On the Comparative Understanding of Non-modern Civilizations', *Daedalus* (Spring 1975), p. 170, and, on the place of modern universalism, Dumont 1978, p. 92.

INTRODUCTION (pp. 1–20)

1a The word 'ideology' commonly designates a more or less social set of ideas and values. Thus one can speak of the ideology of a society, and also of the ideologies of more restricted groups such as a social class or a movement, or again of partial ideologies bearing on a single aspect of the social system such as kinship. It is obvious that there is a basic ideology, a kind of germinal ideology tied to common language and hence to the linguistic group or the global society. There are certainly variations – sometimes contradictions – according to social milieu, for example social class, but they are expressed in the same language: proletarians and capitalists speak French in France, otherwise they could not oppose their ideas, and in general they have much more in common with one another, compared to a Hindu, say, than they might think. The sociologist needs a term to designate the global ideology, and he cannot accept the special usage whereby ideology is limited to social classes and given a purely negative sense, thus discrediting ideas or 'representations' in general for the sake of partisan aims. For the inextricable difficulties which result from such a usage in the sociology of knowledge, *cf.* W. Stark's *Sociology of Knowledge*, 1958, Chapter 2, and R. M. MacIver, *Web of Government*, 1943, p. 454, n. 54.

The question of the place or function of the ideology in society as a whole is to be left open as far as ontology is concerned, although it is crucial methodologically. Very briefly (*cf.* Chapter II, §22):

(1) The distinction between the ideological (or conscious) aspects and the others is required methodologically in virtue of the fact that these are not both known in the same manner.

(2) Methodologically, the initial postulate is that the ideology is *central* with respect to the social reality as a whole (man acts

consciously and we have *direct* access to the conscious aspect of his action).

(3) It is not the *whole* of social reality, and the final goal of the study is the difficult task of placing the ideological aspects in position relative to what may be called the non-ideological aspects. All that may be assumed *a priori* is that there is normally a relationship of complementarity between the two, a relationship which is variable.

It will be observed on the one hand that this procedure is the only one eventually to acknowledge that the initial postulate is contradicted by the facts, and, on the other hand, that it frees itself both from idealism and from materialism by giving both all the scope which they can claim scientifically, by giving them, that is, the opportunity to produce proof. For an example of a considerable difference both in the place and the internal coherence of a partial ideology, see the comparison of kinship terminology between Northern and Southern India in 'Marriage, III', *Contributions to Indian sociology*, IX (sect. II, *in fine*).

2a *Cf.* L. Malson, *Les enfants sauvages, mythe et réalité*, 1964. 'Must it be "admitted that men are not men outside the social setting"?' wonders a journalist in a review of this book (Y.R., *Le Monde*, May 6, 1964, p. 12).

2b This short discussion by no means claims to exhaust the sociality of man. For example it is well known that 'personal organization' is itself not independent of relationships with other persons occupying defined roles. But what could be more strange than this declaration attributed to a contemporary novelist: 'The only way to cease to be alone is to cease to think' (*Le Monde*, November 25, 1964, p. 13). This is indeed that 'false signification' of the self which Arthur Rimbaud complained of at the time he was writing to Izambard (May, 1871): 'It is wrong to say: I am thinking. One should say: I am being thought.'

2c Thus already in Bonald. See A. Koyré's summary in his *Études d'histoire de la pensée philosophique*, 1961, pp. 117–34.

2d Philosophers have a natural tendency to identify the social environment in which the philosophical tradition has developed with mankind as a whole, and to relegate other cultures to a sort of sub-humanity. In this respect, one can even note a certain regression. For Hegel and Marx, the discovery of other civilizations or so-called 'primitive' societies was an object of interest. It no longer is for the political philosophers in the tradition of either of these authors. These questions, instead of being reopened, and freed from an obsolete evolutionism by the progress of knowledge, are purely and simply left on one side. Correspondingly, the contribution of Durkheim and Max Weber is ignored, and the political history of the last one hundred and fifty years is not the subject of any deep reflection, despite the problems with which it is laden. Here there is a remarkable convergence of tendencies which in other respects are very different, and a paradoxical restriction of the Western tradition. Not to mention Sartre, a marxist like Marcuse, a hegelo-kantian like Eric Weil, and even the much lamented Alexandre Koyré confine themselves strictly within the universe of the individual and consequently adopt a condescending or hostile attitude towards the sociological approach. *Cf.* H. Marcuse's *Reason and Revolution*, 1960; Weil's *Philosophie politique*, 1956, where what he calls 'society' is the civil society pure and simple; Koyré's unexpected conclusion to the work already cited on Bonald, and also his indirect and almost surreptitious way of presenting hierarchy in Plato's Republic (*Introduction à la lecture de Platon*, 1962, pp. 131 ff.; L. C. Rosenfield, trans., *Discovering Plato*, pp. 90 ff.). In the last case one must perhaps take into account the date of these publications (1945–1946); one seems to see in the first how a promising reflection on totalitarianism, starting from Bonald's sound sociological thesis, has abruptly turned into a solemn reaffirmation of the democratic *ideal*. (No doubt the above is very incomplete; notably, the problems of political philosophy arise in a very different fashion in England, *cf.* the two volumes edited by P. Laslett and W. G. Runciman: *Philosophy, Politics and Society*, 1962.)

3a On Victorian evolutionism, see notes in *La civilisation indienne et nous*, Chapter 2, and 'The Individual . . .', in *Essays in honour of D. P. Mukerji*, 1967. The assimilation noted above is formally invalid in virtue of the fact that our notion of property proceeds from the individual. Regarding Durkheimian sociology, here is a characteristic passage from Mauss whose ambiguities should be made clear in the light of our distinction: on the subject of 'systems of total prestations', in an article on joking relationships (*Annuaire de l'École Pratique des Hautes Études, V$^e$ Section*, 1928, p. 4, note) he writes: 'The reader may perhaps be astonished at these last remarks. He may believe that we definitely abandon the ideas of Morgan . . . and those attributed to Durkheim regarding primitive communism and the confusion of individuals [= of men] within the community. But there is nothing contradictory here. Even the societies in which the notion of the rights and duties of the individual is supposed to be lacking attribute to him [= attribute to each man] a quite precise place in the camp, to the left, to the right, etc. . . . *This is a proof that* the individual [= the particular man] counts, but it is also a proof that *he counts exclusively as a* *socially determined being.* Nevertheless, it remains true that Morgan, and following him Durkheim, exaggerated the amorphy of the clan and that, as Mr. Malinowski remarks to me, they did not take sufficiently into account the idea of reciprocity.' (Italics mine.)

*Cf.* also what Mauss says about the nation (*L'année sociologique*, 3rd series, 1953–1954, pp. 7–68; also *Proceedings of the Aristotelian Society*, N.S., XX, 1920, pp. 242–252). One rereads with curiosity the Introduction with which Georges Davy opens his short *Sociologie politique*. It is striking to discover that such a highly qualified author does not manage to rid himself of the false dualism between individual and society and in the end places the individualistic and sociological views in uneasy juxtaposition. Hence a theme like 'Influence of social life on the material, intellectual and moral life of the human being', and its development in: G. Davy, *Éléments de sociologie*, I: *Sociologie politique*, 2nd ed., 1950, esp. pp. 6, 9.

3b *Cf.* 'The modern conception of the individual: Notes on its genesis', *Contributions to Indian sociology*, VII.

3c Typical in this respect is the disappearance of the (social) division of labour in Marx's communist 'society'.

3d This formulation is too simple, as is shown by caste society where the division of labour is oriented to the whole. It is the 'rationalization' of each compartment of activity in itself which characterizes the modern development of the division of labour. In his thesis on *Les idées égalitaires*, pp. 140–148, C. Bouglé noted the 'paradox' of social heterogeneity giving rise to egalitarian individualism (according to him, Faguet and Simmel: 'By virtue of the fact that the individual is something quite particular, he becomes equal to any other').

4a *Œuvres complètes*, G. D. H. Cole, trans., *Social Contract and Discourses*, p. 202.

5a In *Œuvres complètes*; as is *L'Ancien Régime et la Révolution* (1952–53). (English translations are respectively: Henry Reeve, *Democracy in America*, London, 1875; M. W. Patterson, *De Tocqueville's L'Ancien Régime*, Oxford, 1933. Subsequent references are to the English versions, roman numerals indicating volume number.)

5b To appreciate the historical insight with which Tocqueville depicts equality, one can compare Bouglé's positivist analysis (*op. cit.*) in which the following are envisaged successively as factors in equality: the quantity of social units, their quality (homogeneity and heterogeneity, see above, note 3d), the complexity of societies (differentiation of roles and specialization of groupings), and social unification. Bouglé discusses the idealist thesis (p. 240), but he thinks it is rather, on the contrary, the social morphology which brings to light certain ideas and values. In reality, the problem is not only of the birth of egalitarianism, but of the end of hierarchy, pure or qualified: a change of values.

5c Such a reflection evidently ought to consider the *whole* of the history of the modern democratic universe, including on the one hand the wars, and on the other the Second Empire, the Third Reich or the Stalinist régime. Sometimes Rousseau is reproached for having opened the way to Jacobinism and totalitarianism by his dogma of the general will. Rather, Rousseau has the merit of having seen the contradiction created when individualism is erected into a religion: totalitarianism is the nemesis of abstract democracy.

5d *Cf.* Appendix. For Bouglé (*op. cit.*, p. 26), equality entails likeness but not identity. Aristotle had already indicated the strict relationship between equality and 'perfect likeness', difference and inequality, whilst distinguishing equality of proportion from equality pure and simple (*Politics*, 1279 *a* 9, 1332 *b* 15 ff., 1332 *a* 28).

CHAPTER I   HISTORY OF IDEAS (pp. 21–32)

11a C. Bouglé, *Essais sur le régime des castes*, p. 4; English translation of the introduction in *Contributions to Indian Sociology*, II, 1958.

11b According to H. A. Rose, 'Caste' (*Encyclopaedia Britannica*, 1945 edition, IV, *s.v.*, pp. 976–86) '(the word) was used by the earlier Portuguese travellers in the sense of tribe or even race, being often applied to the lowest Indian classes in contradistinction to their overlords'. Regarding the etymology of the word 'caste' in the Iberian languages, *cf.* J. Pitt-Rivers, 'On the Word Caste', publication forthcoming, 1970. O'Malley (*Indian Caste Customs*, Cambridge Univ. Press, 1932, p. 1) quotes a decree of the Holy Council of Goa of 1567 (hierarchy, ban on sharing food or drink with an inferior), *cf.* Hutton, *Caste in India, its Nature, Function, and Origins*, Cambridge Univ. Press, 1946, p. 42; for further details, Yule and Burnell, *Hobson-Jobson*, 1903, *s.v.* Darwin uses the word caste of insects (Ketkar, *History of Caste*, vol. I, p. 12, following Murray's *Dictionary on Historical Principles*).

11c Père Martin's letter in Bertrand, ed., *Lettres édifiantes et curieuses de la nouvelle Mission du Maduré, Choix*, 3rd ed., VIII, Paris 1835, p. 68.

11d Tocqueville, *L'Ancien Régime*, trans. M. W. Patterson, Oxford, 1933, p. 88.

12a A history of the definitions which writers have offered will not be given here. The definitions are naturally related to the attitudes which we are trying to isolate. In connection with the explanatory tendency, and above all in the first period, the definitions are often incomplete, omitting one or other of the three main characteristics (*cf.* Bouglé, pp. 4–6). The same is often the case after Bouglé as we shall see in connection with a similar particular point (see Hutton for some historically important definitions or descriptions, pp. 42–4; also, for the school of 'social stratification', see Appendix). There is unquestionable progress in that incomplete definitions are becoming increasingly unacceptable, *cf.* general works like: Kingsley Davis, *The Population of India and Pakistan*, Princeton Univ. Press, 1951 (caste is defined by six characteristics); or Talcott Parsons, *The Structure of Social Action*, The Free Press of Glencoe (1949), 1961 (excellent account of castes and Hinduism, summarizing Max Weber, on pp. 552–63). Recently, Bailey defined the caste as a system of social stratification (groups which are exclusive, exhaustive and ranked in an order) having the following particular characteristics: (1) the groups are closed; (2) the interrelations are organized on the principle of 'summation of roles'; (3) they co-operate and do not compete ('Closed Social Stratification in India', *European Journal of Sociology*, IV, No. 1, 1963, p. 121).

12b This type is distinguished by Blunt (*The Caste System of Northern India*, 1931, pp. 11–12) as that in which the caste is both of great antiquity and the 'artificial product of the Brahmanical priestly order'. He contrasts it with the theory of historical origin.

13a Abbé J. Dubois, *Hindu Manners, Customs and Ceremonies*, pp. 28–30 (trans. Henry K. Beauchamp, Oxford, 1906). Compare pp. 44, 98–9, 105 (where the institution is said to have degenerated since its origin, a traditional idea in India as well as the West) and 275–6 (the veneration in which the Brahmans are held is profitable to them). The literature of the *dharma* (religious duty), such as the 'Laws of Manu', is couched in terms of a kind of 'legislation'.

13b The article is signed 'F.F.', but the author is identified (I, XXXVIII) and is generally known. For the part he played, *cf.* E. Halévy, *La Formation du Radicalisme philosophique*, II; E. Stokes, *The English Utilitarians and India*. Thereafter English writers often mentioned, and indeed deplored, the influence Mill exerted through his *History of British India* on young generations of Indians (1st ed., 1817; a similar view about castes: I, pp. 106 ff.).

14a For details and sources, see below §104.1.

14b F. Max Müller, *Chips from a German Workshop*, 1867, II, pp. 297–356, esp. pp. 301 ff., 308, 318, 346–50. John Murdoch, in *Caste, its Supposed Origin* (1887) gives a missionary viewpoint which was probably fairly widespread. He takes up Max Müller's arguments, develops the attack on caste and demands that the government ignore it for the purposes of identification of persons and taking of censuses. Earlier, B. A. Irving, in a work which is often very penetrating (*The Theory and Practice of Caste*, 1853), had taken the view of de Nobili and a Protestant missionary, Schwartz: caste is essentially a social matter, Christian influence will modify it, distinctions of rank are natural and necessary (pp. 4, 119 ff.).

Cf. also *Essays on Caste*, 1851, by missionaries.

14c Max Weber, *Wirtschaft und Gesellschaft*, II, 635–7. Kroeber, 'Caste', in the *Encyclopaedia of Social Sciences*. For further details on these theories, see also Appendix.

14d John C. Nesfield, *Brief View of the Caste System of the North-Western Provinces and Oudh*, 1885. On the introduction of endogamy, see pp. 89, 99, 116. Cf. the discussion by Bouglé, *Essais sur le régime des castes*, pp. 39–51. Nesfield's theory is like Mill's (mentioned above) in being dualistic. Similarly, according to Ibbetson, *Census Report, Panjab*, 1883, §§334 ff., profession is the primary basis of the system, and the dominance of the priests the decisive factor: 'The dominance of one special occupation gave abnormal importance to all distinctions of occupation' (§335). In addition to the way in which birth replaced the sacerdotal function as the criterion of membership among the Brahmans, Ibbetson takes note of a subsequent twofold differentiation, both political (distinction between *dominants* and subjects, in which Ibbetson heralds a recent development, see Chapter VII), and 'artificial' (criteria of purity, etc.). Discussions in Sarat Chandra Roy, 'Caste, Race and Religion in India', and K. P. Chattopadhyay, 'History of Indian Social Organization'. One still reads quite recently: 'The material needs of the society at a certain stage of its development led to the emergence of the institution, while it was stabilized by the ideological basis of society prevailing at the time' (Ramkrishna Mukherjee, *The Dynamics of a Rural Society*, p. 75).

14e J. H. Hutton, *Caste in India*, pp. 164–5.

15a Émile Senart, *Les Castes dans l'Inde: Les faits et le système*, 1894; discussion in Bouglé, *op. cit.* For theories of the pre-Aryan or Dravidian origin of caste, cf. Hutton, *Caste*, pp. 152 ff.

15b Cf. Appendix, §C.

15c For a bibliography, see Georges Olivier, *L'anthropologie des Tamouls du sud de l'Inde*, 1961. Risley's theory is first formulated in *The Tribes and Castes of Bengal: Ethnographical Glossary*, 1891, p. xxxiv; then in *The People of India*, p. 273; cf. Hutton, *Caste*, pp. 118–19, and Olivier, p. 30. Among the writers who adopt this theory in a more or less modified form are Ghurye, *Caste and Race in India*, 1931, Chapter 5 and p. 143; D. N. Majumdar, *Races and Cultures of India*, pp. 280–4, 291 ff., 306.

15d Hocart, *Caste, A Comparative Study*, London, 1950, *passim*.

16a Max Müller, *Chips*, pp. 320 ff.

17a Ghurye, *Caste and Race in India*, etc.; Hutton, *Caste in India*; Hocart, *Caste*.

17b It is difficult to do Hocart justice in a small space. In addition to his preoccupation with origins, touched by a hint of diffusionism, there remains in his work a narrow framework of Indo-European comparison, and he minimizes certain features (endogamy) for the sake of this comparison. In spite of this, our debt to Hocart outweighs any possible reproach. He best distinguishes two fundamental points: that to be faithful to the indigenous viewpoint, we must keep religion in the forefront, and that we can reach the essence of institutions only by comparison. This must be emphasized, especially as Hocart's insight is not always adequately expressed in his work. See the critical essay in *Contributions*, II. We shall return to Hocart, see §32 and Chapters IV and VII.

17c Max Weber, *The Religion of India. The Sociology of Hinduism and Buddhism*, trans. Hans H. Gerth and Don Martindale Glencoe, 1958; on class and caste, see Appendix; on the division of labour, note 42l.

17d Bouglé, pp. 25 ff., etc.

18a *Cf.* esp. M. N. Srinivas, 'Varna and Caste', *Caste in Modern India*, pp. 63–9, and *Caste, A Trend Report*, pp. 137–8.

18b E. A. H. Blunt, *Caste System*, 1931 (this very careful regional description ignores hierarchy when it comes to principles); H. N. C. Stevenson, 'Status Evaluation in the Hindu Caste System', 1954; McKim Marriott, 'Interactional and Attributional Theories of Caste Ranking', 1959.

18c E. K. Gough, 'Criteria of Caste Ranking in South India', 1959. In Marriott, *Caste Ranking*, empirical determinants are studied as factors in the *development* of the hierarchical principle (see §36 and Chapter III generally).

18d Stevenson, 'Caste', in *Encyclopaedia Britannica*, 1961, IV, pp. 973–82 (also in 'Status Evaluation'). For this writer, the caste is not a real group, and consequently it is characterized by a certain arrangement of groups distinguished analytically by the sociologist and considered real: endogamous group, commensal group, etc. The result is a complicated description in which the stress is transferred from the indigenous categories to those of the observer, with no hope of synthesis.

18e I. Karvé, *Hindu Society. An Interpretation*, 1961 (see below, §26.1).

18f It would be interesting to find out if the failure to recognize hierarchy varies according to the origin of the investigator,. Indians forgetting it less easily, for example, than Americans. Among recent writers, Francis L. Hsu has perhaps given the most emphasis to hierarchy, contrasting it with the case of China and the United States (*Clan, Caste and Club*, 1963, pp. 180 ff.).

## CHAPTER II   FROM SYSTEM TO STRUCTURE (pages 33–64)

21a Hutton, *Caste in India, Its Nature, Function, and Origins*, Cambridge, 1946, pp. 44–5.

21b 'Some Thoughts on the Caste System', *Census of India*, 1931, XVIII, United Provinces, Part I, Report, p. 541, §2.

21c On the system in the empirical sense, the sense in which it is geographically circumscribed, *cf.* for example, David G. Mandelbaum, 'Concepts and Methods in the Study of Caste' in *Economic Weekly*, 1959, p. 145. The concrete diversity is already evident between one vast region and another. To form an idea of the sets of castes at this level, see the three short pictures of regional populations in Hutton, *Caste*, Part I.

The two senses of 'system' we have distinguished are juxtaposed by F. G. Bailey in a single sentence: 'Both these facts are aspects of the caste. system [Pan-Indian sense], and each block itself [i.e. each chieftainship or traditional territorial unit] constituted a caste system [empirical sense]' ('Closed Social Stratification in India', *European Journal of Sociology*, IV, No. 1, 1963, p. 108). However, the same author had protested energetically against the idea of India as a sociological unity. ('For a Sociology of India?', *Contributions*, III, pp. 88, 101). It is true that he speaks in this article of *the* system, meaning roughly the pattern common to actual systems, and that he prefers to omit ideology in the definition of the system (p. 116). This is a curious procedure, if one considers that Indians feel very strongly that it is the ideology which gives them a unity over and above all regional differences; our distinguished colleague M. N. Srinivas has often insisted on this point, in his monograph on the Coorgs and elsewhere. Bailey adopts this view because he regards ideology as belonging to 'culture', sociology being concerned only with 'structure', that is, social morphology. This *petitio principii* is fairly widespread. To the extent that this approach aims to grasp the essence of society by rejecting ideas and values as irrelevant, it must naturally be rejected.

However, Barth has written in a similar vein that 'if one wants the concept of caste to be useful for sociological analysis, its definition must be based on structural criteria, and not on particular features of Hindu philosophy', which leads Leach to wonder whether 'it is best to consider caste as a cultural or structural phenomenon'. He concludes with Barth that it is structural, but against him that the Indian system is structurally *sui generis*. The distinction seems to vary even within Leach's own text; we shall not adopt it, but we may agree that the caste system is indeed 'structurally' different, while adding that it is also, and this is no accident, 'culturally' different. It will be shown later (§104) that the Swat system described by Barth is, contrary to what this author supposes, but in accordance with Leach's view, culturally influenced by the caste system but structurally different from it (E. R. Leach, ed., *Aspects of Caste*, pp. 2–5, etc.). Answering Leach's question from a methodological point of view, it may be said that the so-called 'structural' approach, that is the theory of caste as a form of social stratification, has precisely the drawback that Bailey (*European Journal of Sociology*, p. 116) attributes to the definition of caste in religious terms: it assumes that the discovery of caste has been completed, and halts basic research; on the contrary, if progress is to be made in understanding, and consequently in comparison, the ideology must be taken into consideration; I hope that the results of the present work may illustrate this approach.

21d The neglect or underestimation of the *jajmānī* (whether called this or not) is striking in works like: Stevenson, 'Status Evaluation', 1954; Srinivas, *Coorgs*, 1952; Bailey, *Caste and the Economic Frontier*, 1957.

21e On hierarchy in kinship, see §§53 ff. Following the historical process which thus brought about the diminution of the *patria potestas*, the interdependence between father and son in the joint Hindu family is stressed in the legal doctrine which predominates in modern times, that of the Mitakshara (*cf.* 'The notion of *sapiṇḍa* in ancient India', forthcoming).

22a As we go along we shall discover the justness of Leach's remark: the stress on 'social stratification' also obscures those aspects unconnected with hierarchy, and begs the question of the nature of the phenomenon: 'The tendency to stress the "status-group" component of caste prejudges the whole question as to what is the essential sociological nature of the Indian phenomenon' (*Aspects of Caste*, p. 1).

22b An author with no direct experience claims to raise the question in a few pages. E. W. Pohlman, 'Evidence of disparity between the Hindu practice of caste and the ideal type', *American Sociological Review*, 116 (1951), pp. 375–9. David Pocock and I, as co-authors of *Contributions to Indian Sociology*, were accused by F. G. Bailey of reducing everything to ideology (*Contributions*, III, pp. 88 ff.; our reply, IV, pp. 82 ff.). In the article already quoted (*European Journal of Sociology*, IV, No. 1), Bailey expresses himself less crudely, but his procedure is scarcely one which encourages discussion. He uses in two different ways our article in *Contributions*, II, devoted to Bouglé. On pages 109–10 he in effect turns to his own account, in a preliminary way, a definition which is purely and simply that given by Bouglé: 'I have broadly classified caste activities under the headings of segregation, interdependence, hierarchy.' The source of this definition is not given, Bouglé's name is not mentioned. A little later, on pages 114–16, Bailey attributes to us a 'definition of caste by religion'. To this end he extracts a number of quotations (of which the last was from Bouglé) which must certainly seem to make up an inept 'definition'. The critic neglected to mention that they were taken from a 'commented summary' of Bouglé (*Contributions*, II, pp. 31–44); the aim of this article was to make Bouglé's theory more widely known, while expanding it slightly. Bailey is willing to allow our view of the pure and the impure some coherence, but he adds that 'it is a hindrance in that it obscures the political and economic tasks performed by the Indian system of social stratification'. Now it so happens that the commentary on Bouglé was followed immediately by an essay on Hocart entitled precisely: 'A. M. Hocart, or Religion and Power.' In short, possibly influenced by logical positivism, Bailey goes his way alone; he even seems indifferent to the continuity between his successive publications. Previously he insisted that a definition of caste should cover racism, as found in the U.S.A. or South Africa (*Contributions*, III, p. 97); now, not only does he find such a definition inadequate (p. 113), he even requires that, for scientific purposes, modern Indian 'caste' associations be called by another name (below, §115). In this we would agree, but does it not imply *a fortiori* that something quite other than castes are involved in the case of America?

22c It may be objected that I am greatly oversimplifying a complex situation. The distinction is between the conscious and non-conscious aspects, and this is a relative and not an absolute distinction. This is true; for example, the politico-economic aspects are indeed not wholly absent from the consciousness of the people concerned. They are even written about, in the literature of the *artha*, although this is admittedly quite slender compared with the religious literature of the *dharma*. But just as in the literature taken overall these aspects are subordinated to the religious ones, so they are practically excluded from that constellation of strongly marked and interconnected ideas and values which form the ideology (or perhaps the main or predominant ideology) of the social system. There is certainly room for inaccuracies and inadequacies in such a definition of the conscious nucleus of the system; but a sociologist should be aware of this predominance of certain ideas, and it seems possible in practice to make a fruitful and non-arbitrary distinction between the two components.

23a This gives the gist of 'Is there a structure underlying the order of castes?', an unpublished paper read before the Association of Social Anthropologists, London, January 1952. Main references: Lévi-Strauss, *Anthropologie structurale*; Troubetzkoy, *Principes de phonologie*; Köhler, *Gestaltpsychology*; Goldstein, *Der Aufbau des Organismus*; Merleau-Ponty, *The Structure of Behaviour*, trans. A. L. Fisher, London, 1965. The quotation from Louis de Broglie comes from *Continu et Discontinu en Physique moderne*, 1941, p. 116.

Our concept of 'structure' differs from that of Radcliffe-Brown, among others. He defined 'social structure' as the sum of relations existing in a given society between the 'individual human beings' who, according to him, compose it (*Structure and Function in Primitive Society*, 1952, pp. 194, 190, 180). He readily resorted to a biological metaphor: in relation to the social whole, the individuals are like the cells of an organism, and the life of the organism shows the integration of its cells (*ibid.*, pp. 178–9, etc.); the 'whole' is something which lives, which 'functions'. It is true that for Radcliffe-Brown the notion of 'function' corresponds to the physiology of the overall system, the notion of 'structure' to its morphology. But at the same time, the notion of 'structure' should bridge the whole gap separating the individuals from the social whole as a functioning entity, and for this reason it remains very imprecise.

23b E. E. Evans-Pritchard, *The Nuer*, Oxford, 1940, pp. 136–7:

A man is a member of a political group in virtue of his non-membership of other groups of the same kind. . . . But a man does not see himself as a member of that same group in so far as he is a member of a segment of it which stands outside of and is opposed to other segments of it.

Few English works fail to quote this book in some connection. Doubtless other reasons than the one mentioned here can be found for this. It is remarkable that English empiricism has reacted, even within the theory of lineages and in works directly

354

inspired by *The Nuer*, by putting less emphasis on segmentation than on the '*corporate*' character of the groups, there being *solidarity* between all their members in virtue of their common interests. (Addition 1980: For more detail see my preface to the French trans. of *The Nuer* [Paris, *c.* 1968]; for English trans. by M. and J. Douglas see J. H. M. Beattie and R. G. Lienhardt, eds., *Studies in Social Anthropology: Essays in Memory of E. E. Evans-Pritchard* [Oxford, 1975], pp. 328–42.)

23c We shall say, for example, that a caste is *segmented* into subcastes, or, should the occasion arise, that it is *divided* into clans, that is to say, more precisely, that it can be considered as made up of groups of a different kind called clans. We shall also not speak of segmentation from the purely territorial point of view, although territory may be an attribute of the segments.

24a Hegel, *Lectures on the Philosophy of History*:

> In China there prevailed equality among all individuals. . . . The next degree of progress results in the manifestation of differentiation. . . . These differences are the castes. . . . But in India . . . the differences which prevail are only those of occupation, of caste. . . . The first and essential function is that which aims at the completely general, of which man becomes aware first in religion and then in science. . . . The highest caste will therefore be the one which produces the divine and is a manifestation of it: the caste of Brahmans. . . . Necessarily, one caste presupposes another, and castes are formed only as a result, generally speaking, of life in common. . . . Classes cannot be brought together from without; they are developed only from within.

Trans. J. Sibree, pp. 151–3. (Changes have been made to bring the English closer to the French translation by Gibelin which Dumont quotes.—TR.)

24b Célestin Bouglé, *Essais sur le régime des castes* (Paris, 1908). (Addition 1980: English trans., with an introduction, by D. F. Pocock [Cambridge: Cambridge University Press, 1971].)

24c Bouglé's three basic principles are not all alike in nature, and do not operate at quite the same level: hierarchy orders the castes as a whole and provides the ideological reference to the whole; separation, also indisputably ideological and normative, seems at first sight and if taken alone, on the contrary to isolate each group from the whole. Finally, the division of labour, as it also in principle isolates each caste within a function, seems to be ideologically similar to separation. It is mainly at the level of empirical observation that one clearly sees the interdependence and the orientation towards the whole that it involves. In other words, the interdependence of the castes is less conscious than their separation and hierarchy. This probably explains the fact that some authors (empiricist authors, paradoxically enough) have sometimes treated this feature as more or less external, as a concomitant rather than a component of the system. Yet it is obvious that there is a strict connection between hierarchy and interdependence: they are like two facets of the reference to the whole, the one more conscious, the other less conscious. These differences between the three principles isolated by Bouglé may explain why he sometimes reasoned as if he were dealing with three independent features.

24d Louis Renou, *L'Hindouisme*, 1951, p. 79; Hutton, review of Hocart, *Man*, 1951, No. 235. 'But this ritual theory alone does not explain caste as seen in Indian society over the last thousand or two thousand years, even though it may add much to our understanding of it.' In what follows an explanatory factor is implied: 'considerations of personal advantage'.

The evolution of the views on this question of an author as little concerned with religion as Bailey (see above, n. 22b) shows how important are these notions, minimized by the Westerner, to the man in the field. They force Bailey to recognize that the 'religious theory' of caste is well founded, even though he indicates his preference for the theory of 'social stratification'.

24e These criticisms relate to the 'commented summary' of Bouglé by David Pocock in *Contributions*, II, which is discussed at length by Francis L. K. Hsu in his large-scale comparison of the societies of India, China and the United States (*Caste, Clan and Club*, Princeton, 1963, pp. 128–33). The present account, more explicit and complete, should in itself answer Hsu's objections, of which only the most important are mentioned above. Here is another: Hsu claims that the explanation is too broad; the opposition between pure and impure is encountered elsewhere, but does not result in a system of the Indian type. My reply is: (1) even if this were the case, it would not show that our analysis was false, to the extent that, extending Bouglé's analysis slightly, we were only concerned to derive the Indian *theory* of the castes from a single principle: it could be that the same principle is applied differently in the two cases; (2) actually, as will be seen later, there seems to be no confirmation for Hsu's assertion: where the opposition between pure and impure exists in some guise outside India, it is never applied to the society as a whole. It is hoped that some light will be shed on how and why the opposition developed as it did in India (*cf.* §25.3 and especially §32).

24f Béteille's criticism is incidental to another discussion. ('A Note on the Referents of Caste', *European Journal of Sociology*, V, 1964, pp. 130–4). He takes the example of the Vadama (Smarta) Brahmans of Madras and their segmentation. Although he does not stress the point, the distinctions between 'temple priests' (*devalaka* in Sanskrit), 'priests of non-Brahmans' and 'landowning Brahmans' carry connotations of status. In a given locality, the same is probably true of distinctions of sect, or between sectarians and non-sectarians. There remains the territorial distinction. It may be that Brahmans of a single territorial kind are found in a given place, and Béteille is right to say that status has nothing to do with this subdivision: it is a matter of the territorial frame within which alone the hierarchy of the pure and the impure functions: there is no segmentation properly speaking, except in Bailey's spatial sense which we and Béteille both reject. But from the moment when, in a given locality and as a result of possibly recent spatial mobility and geographical extension, two territorial subdivisions are represented, they tend to become hierarchized. For the sake of simplicity, I have assumed with Béteille that the territories, and the cardinal points themselves, have no relative status. Actually, nowadays as well as in classical literature, the pure and the impure hierarchize the elements of space.

25a Stevenson has written the most fully worked out modern work on the question in general. 'Status evaluation in the Indian Caste System' (*Journal of the Royal Anthropological Institute*, LXXXIV, 1954, pp. 45–65). This account departs from it considerably. Some details will be found in Dumont and Pocock, 'Pure and Impure', *Contributions*, III (with a criticism of Stevenson's theses).

25b Anthropologists are familiar with facts of this kind, which are very widespread. Roy Fortune reminded me in conversation of how different is the situation in India.

25c There is however a case which contradicts what is said in the text. It concerns the Andhra country. Fishman mentions in his *Culture Change*, p. 140, the custom of the Komati merchants, who require cloth woven by the Mala Untouchables to be purified by being soaked before being offered to customers who are not Untouchables. The author adds that this fact at present benefits the non-untouchable competitors of these weavers.

Only a passing word has been said about impurity relating to objects. For further details see Stevenson, *op. cit*. It is true that animate beings and inanimate things are traditionally brought under an elaborate classification; but in my opinion this is a systematization springing from the classification of men from the same point of view (and also partly from immediate or organic impurity, and partly from the expression of Brahmanic customs and precepts in the language of purity). *Cf.* on the theory of purity in Manu, Ketkar, *History of Caste in India*, 1909, I, 116 ff. (*cf.* Chapter VI of the present work).

25d If one is looking for the Vedic antecedents of Brahmanic practices, one will naturally find them at the level of the ritual of sacrifice, both because this is what the Vedic texts tell us about, and because a religion of sacrifice necessarily involves purifications. Thus 'bathing, and cutting the hair and beard, figure as lustrative practices before or after a rite, and more rarely fall under a prohibition aimed to prevent the depletion of strength' (Renou, *Inde classique*, p. 352). This shows the continuity in technique. By referring to Hubert and Mauss, 'Essai sur le sacrifice' one can find the whole theory of *dīkṣā* or ascetic performance preparatory to sacrifice, which is, among other things, a purification. (On corresponding modern words in the south, see *Contributions*, III, p. 16.) For example, the hair and nails are cut 'in order to become pure' (p. 49 ref.), which is of interest in connection with the modern barber. It is said of the sacrifier of soma who consecrates himself in this way: 'He must have no relations with men of impure castes, nor with women; he does not answer when addressed, he is not touched' (*ibid.*, pp. 49–50). Here, one fancies, is a Hindu Brahman in the making. It is curious to find not only that the sacrifier refrains from eating meat (he fasts, almost completely), but also that the sacrificer, he who puts the sacrificial animal to death and who is euphemistically called the 'appeaser' (*śamitar*), is, if a Brahman, 'a Brahman of inferior rank, for he bears the sin of having killed a sacred being' (pp. 68–9). (In his translation of *Sacrifice: Its Nature and Function* by Henri Hubert and Marcel Mauss, London, 1964, W. D. Halls coins the word 'sacrifier' to translate *sacrifiant*. I have followed this usage. Halls defines a sacrifier as 'the subject to whom the benefits of sacrifice accrue . . . or who undergoes its effect'.—TR.) Perhaps this is only a contradiction inherent in sacrifice in general, and not the beginning of an aversion to violence and meat. Nevertheless, as opposed to the Bouphonia in Athens, a status is attributed to a class of men in virtue of their function. (*Cf.* J. C. Heesterman's new interpretation, according to which the seed of later developments was sown in the Vedic period: 'Brahmin, Ritual and Renouncer', *Wiener Zeitschrift*, VIII, 1964.)

25e The polarity between Brahmans and Untouchables should help us to understand how distant this case is from racism. The notion of interior purity has already been encountered in the Shastras. Ketkar, a Brahman from Maharashtra, has written that the

Brahmans have an exalted idea of the purity of their blood, but that it is not the same idea as that which anthropologists understand by these words: 'The racial purity is only a part of the purity to a Brāhmaṇa. . . . [This] is acquired by generations of pure conduct, which consists of doing actions that are pure, eating pure food, by increasing his own personal sacredness, by the study of the Vedas, and by marriage only with people who have kept pure conduct. Their abstaining from marriage with other castes does not come so much from their pride of birth, but is due more to their pride of purity, which would be contaminated by less sacred connections.' (*The History of Caste in India*, I, p. 120, n.). The idea of race does not govern separation; rather it is the ideal of separation, purity, which governs among other things the separation which is elsewhere distinguished as 'race'.

25f We shall consider this question again in connection with vegetarianism and *ahiṃsā*, §65.

25g *Cf. Sous-caste*, index, *s.v. Intouchables*, and more generally, pp. 365–71; *Contributions*, III, pp. 33–5 (ref.).

The theory of transmigration connects successive existences on the basis of the merit or demerit acquired in each, and so makes them interdependent. People often, at least proverbially, attribute their present misfortunes to supposed past faults. Ketkar mentions a Mahar (Untouchable from Maharashtra) who, though illiterate, knew many lines by devotional poets like Tukaram and Namdev by heart, and was acquainted with the theories of transmigration. He believed that although he was a Mahar in his present life on account of sins committed in his former life or lives, his keen desire to learn Sanskrit and to read the Gita and the Puranas showed that he would be a Brahman in his next life (*op. cit.*, I, p. 115).

25h *Encyclopaedia of Religion and Ethics*, *s.v.* 'Purification'. It may be recalled that Jainism is a sect parallel to Buddhism, but still represented in India today. (*Cf.* V. A. Sangave, *Jaina Community, A Social Survey*, Bombay, 1959.) Actually, in connection with the duration of impurity, the Jains in Gujerat seem to be in competition with the Nagar Brahmans, a very instructive situation, for it is precisely of a type with the one postulated above to explain the spreading of vegetarianism starting from the sects, in particular the Jains. (The last point is so important that I could not bring myself to omit it, although the reference on which it is based escapes me, at the time of going to press. It probably comes from a work by Alice Margaret Stevenson but I am unable to check this or give further details.)

25i *Cf.* for example Bouglé, *Essais sur le régime des castes*, pp. 205 ff.;

359

Hutton, p. 58 (following Buchanan and M. S. Aiyangar); Srinivas, *Coorgs*, p. 28. Bouglé saw these relatively exceptional facts as the sign of a tendency towards mutual 'repulsion'. Knowledge about them is scanty and their interpretation is a delicate matter.

25j E. K. Gough, in Leach, ed., *Aspects of Caste*, pp. 49–50.

26a Senart, *Les Castes dans l'Inde*, Paris, 1894; Ghurye also writes (*Caste and Race in India*, 1932, p. 19):

> To regard endogamy as the chief characteristic of a caste is to treat all so-called subcastes as the real castes. Gait advanced (*Encyclopaedia of Religion and Ethics*, II, 234) two reasons against this procedure . . . it would be 'contrary to the native feeling on the subject'. . . . As regards the Indian sentiment against making a subcaste into a caste, it must be pointed out that, at best, this is the representation of only one side of the problem, for if, to confine ourselves to the Maratha country, a Saraswat Brahman is known to the outsiders as a Saraswat, to a Saraswat he is better known either as a Shenvi or as a Sashtikar or Pednekar. Stated generally, though it is the caste which is recognized by the society at large, it is the subcaste which is regarded by the particular caste and individual.

Irawati Karvé, *Hindu Society, An Interpretation*, especially pp. 16, 19 (*caste-clusters*), 28–9. The idea that the castes were constituted by aggregation or accretion rather than by scission is not new, *cf.* for example Blunt, *Caste System*, p. 50: 'In earlier days, accretion was probably the usual process'; and p. 225, the case of the Bhangis of Uttar Pradesh: the name was only a professional label (sweepers or scavengers) uniting, apparently as one caste, groups which were in reality different castes: Helas, Lal Begis, etc. (from Crooke).

26b Blunt, *op. cit.*, Chapter 1, pp. 6–8, §§7–8: 'A caste is an endogamous group, or collection of endogamous groups, bearing a common name . . .' (definition developed from Gait, *Encyclopaedia of Religion and Ethics, s.v.*). According to Hutton, Senart is right, but Hindu usage must nevertheless be followed.

Ketkar, *The History of Caste in India*, I, 15; he adds: 'The words "caste" and "subcaste" are not absolute but comparative in signification. The larger group will be called a caste, while the smaller group will be called a subcaste.' O'Malley, *Indian Caste Customs*, p. 21 (see also the beginning). A C. Mayer, *Caste and Kinship in Central India: a Village and its Region*, London, Routledge, 1960, p. 3.

26c Mayer, *op. cit.*, p. 151. This monograph is the first to deal with a settlement in 'multicaste' villages (as opposed to unicaste villages which, apart from the servant castes, contain only one caste, as in my *Sous-caste*, for example) and at the same time to go beyond the framework of the village (by contrast with many monographs). The author is thus enabled to take a more comprehensive view (see his introduction, pp. 3–10). Blunt (*Caste System*, p. 10) had already clearly distinguished between what is the nominal caste, and the effective group; *zāt* (or *jāt*) is the caste 'as a whole', whereas *birādarı* or *bhāīband*, 'fraternity', is the 'group of caste brethren who live in a particular neighbourhood and act together for caste purposes .... quantitatively considered, (it) is a mere fraction of the *zāt*; qualitatively considered, it is the *zāt* in action'.

26d The author is very cautious about generalizing; he observes that definite functions are not attached *ne varietur* to a fixed level of segmentation (p. 160). We can agree with Mayer in saying, roughly, that relations within the village are relations between different castes (except for relations within the local group of the subcaste, which are agnatic relations in this case), whereas relations within the caste are always relations within the subcaste (except for rare relations between different subcastes of the same caste), and unite people from several villages. The work contains precious information in this connection (for example, p. 49: the rules of commensality apply within a given village, and any visitors will comply with them). But, as is shown by the exceptions mentioned between brackets (let us add that people from a neighbouring village may be employed), there is no homology between the mode of action of the territorial *factor* and that of the *principle* of caste, at once absolute and segmented. In one passage (p. 9) Mayer, interpreting Blunt, seems to say that caste and sub-caste, having different attributes, are groups of different kinds. Actually these attributes, some external, the others internal, are complementary. I would rather say that there are not two groups, but that the 'real group' which some have sought to discover is constituted by the complicated configuration of the 'caste', the 'subcaste' (etc.), as qualified by the territorial factor. I am not a member of two different groups, I am a member of one complex group which has different aspects and functions at different levels.

26e For a regional picture of the pullulation of caste sub-divisions and the nature of their names see, for example, Blunt, pp. 38 ff. It relates to present-day Uttar Pradesh; the author has grouped together the segments (subcastes) and the exogamous divisions (clans).

CHAPTER III   HIERARCHY; THEORY OF THE 'VARNA' (pages 65–91)

31a   We take hierarchy as our starting point both because we are starting from the whole and not the parts, and because we are starting from that which is more conscious (hierarchy) rather than that which is less conscious (division of labour). Compared with other aspects of the same level, hierarchy is in this sense the most fundamental. This primacy implies a relationship to ourselves, and is thus, at bottom, more a matter of methodology than ontology. We aim to go beyond existing views which appear inadequate, rather than attain a definitive statement of the truth of the matter, which would require, in particular, comparison with societies other than our own.

31b   The *Shorter Oxford English Dictionary* is more logical on this point than the positivist *Littré* (*s.v.*): '(1) the orders of the various degrees of ecclesiastical estate; (2) the order and subordination of the different choirs of angels; (3) by extension, subordination of powers, authorities, ranks.' The *Grand Larousse* quotes Bossuet: 'The holy subordination of ecclesiastical powers, in the image of celestial hierarchies.' *Cf.* also *Grande Encyclopédie*, *s.v.* (applied by extension, as early as the time of the Byzantine Empire, to government and social organization as a whole).

31c   Here is an example of lack of understanding on the part of modern Indian authors. In a studious work, K. M. Kapadia (*Marriage and Family in India*, p. 159, beginning of Chapter VIII) finds that the ancient texts rank the purposes of marriage hierarchically as follows: religious duty (*dharma*), progeny (*prajā*), pleasure (*rati*). He takes it that 'sex . . . is the least desirable aim of marriage', and he adds: 'Marriage was desired not so much for sex or for progeny as for obtaining a partner for the fulfilment of one's religious duties'. It is very questionable to interpret duty as excluding progeny, and there is a complete misunderstanding. As so often, this list indicates a hierarchized totality, in which the lowest item (pleasure) is both limited and consecrated by its association with the superior purposes. Obviously duty includes progeny, as progeny presupposes pleasure. Pleasure is not 'less desirable', it is desirable in its subordinate place. As interpreted by modern individualists, the datum is atomized, because they lose sight of the need felt by the authors of the ancient texts: to order everything rationally in relation to the supreme and permanent ends.

Add a good measure of sociocentricity, and you have these lines by Kardiner (*The Individual and His Society*, p. 447): 'The absence of such [social] mobility, as exists in caste systems, ought theoretically to augment anxiety about achievement of prestige; but practically this anxiety eventually disappears and is replaced by attitudes of resignation and submission.'

31d For the distinction between hierarchy and distribution of power see Parsons, 'A Revised Theoretical Approach to the Theory of Social Stratification', p. 95 (quotation above, §7) and also pp. 108, 128 and note 1, p. 665.

32a Senart (trans. Ross), pp. 114–19. Senart, whose starting point is the modern caste, may be regarded as the initiator of the modern tendency to undervalue the varnas. For him, these (classical) varnas represent an arbitrary expression in an older (Vedic) language of a reality which had become basically different. At the same period Oldenberg, more open to ethnology in general, is less clear-cut (see his critique of Senart's work in the light of Fick). Max Weber, in *The Religion of India. The Sociology of Hinduism and Buddhism*, Glencoe, 1958, still often translates *varṇa* by 'caste'.

32b 'This, we are constantly told, bears no resemblance to reality . . . the four-caste system (*sic*) is a pure figment' (Hocart, *Caste*, pp. 23–4).

32c For details and references, see Appendix C. The arrangement is equivalent to that noted in the case of the castes; thus the Brahmans and Kshatriyas taken together are opposed to the rest in that they preside over the society.

32d In order to give a racial explanation of the system of varnas, play has sometimes been made with the primary sense of *varṇa*, colour, and with the fact that the aborigines are described in the Veda as being dark-skinned. This explains only the distinction between the twice-born and the Shudras, and not the threefold division of the former. See Hocart, *Caste*, pp. 27 ff.; Srinivas ('Varna and Caste') and others consider the varnas as given hereditary groups to which certain functions would have been reserved. However, it can be seen from the outset to be a matter of function, a necessity, so to speak, for social organization which governs the identity of persons. Ketkar convincingly shows the importance, in this case especially, of attributive status (*op. cit.*, pp. 45 ff.). According to Manu (I, 28–9) these functions were 'allotted at the first creation'.

32e P. V. Kane, *History of Dharmaśāstra (Ancient and Mediaeval, Religious and Civil Law)*, II, No. 1, pp. 19–179, etc.

32f It is certain that, as in the case of the Shudras, modifications came about in the status of people attached to the class of Vaishyas; they should be identified and their history traced with reference to the general movement which has been briefly indicated. In a recent work, R. S. Sharma attempts to trace the evolution so far as the Shudras alone are concerned (*Shudras in Ancient India*). This is a substantial work, conscientious and well documented. But apart from the fact that the author endeavours to find change at all costs, where probably there is none (it seems gratuitous to regard the Shudras as members of Indo-European society whose status would have been degraded, when on the contrary aggregation of some of the indigenous population is more likely), he is wrong in the main because he studies the category as if it existed by itself independently of the whole – another instance of the mistake we have so often encountered. On the contrary, it should be obvious that the following is necessarily essential to the evolution of the status of the Shudras: the actual emergence of a fifth category, long unrecognized in theory, which eventually replaced the Shudras as the excluded category, the Shudras having been excluded in the system of the varnas just as the Untouchables are excluded in the caste system. One will retain mainly an attractive view of the period of the Laws of Manu. According to Sharma, the Shudras were on the ascendant in this period and acquired new rights, yet at the same time their incapacities were reasserted in the doctrine to the point of caricature. If this phenomenon were corroborated, it would have to be more strictly linked to the competition between Hinduism and the more or less heretical sects, for the Shudras were assimilated to the heretics sufficiently clearly to suggest that they were deeply indebted to them for their promotion.

32g I have discussed this point elsewhere (Appendix C, §1) from the point of view of its implications for the 'political' domain, but it was essential to mention it briefly here. The extent to which the comparative perspective is lacking in these studies can be seen by reading in a work by a master of Vedic studies that there had been a 'usurpation of sacerdotal offices by the layman' (Renou and Filliozat, *Inde Classique*, I, 375). To suppose that the king is generally or essentially a lay person is to have a strange idea of royalty. It is true that anthropologists do much the same thing in a more subtle way; thus it is one of the tendencies of the classic *African Political Systems* (Evans-Pritchard and Fortes, eds., Introduction) to reduce the religious functions of the king to his political functions.

32h The differentiation between status and power enables us to place the development in India in relation to simpler societies and to draw together some of its characteristic aspects. Hocart, as has been said, compared the system to chieftainship in Fiji, where some degree of religious division of labour is encountered, centred on the chief. For India, the distinction under consideration needs to be added, and Hocart (power) must be introduced into Bouglé (status). Compared with a tribe with moities, whether totemic or not, it can be said roughly that in Fiji chieftainship replaces complementarity by division of labour, and correlatively emphasizes the distinction between the sacred and the profane. As compared with chieftainship (in Fiji), the caste system both differentiates status and power (king and priest), and also in practice replaces the opposition between sacred and profane by the opposition between pure and impure. Roughly speaking, the sacred is differentiated into pure and impure, which up to then were identified with one another, but it must be immediately remembered that whilst in the case of chieftainship, and in other cases, states which correspond to that of impurity in the caste system are dangerous in themselves, they are not dangerous, but only *socially degrading*, in the caste system (see above, §25.1; *Contributions*, III, pp. 29 ff.). Moreover, as is natural in a world in which differentiation has been carried further, the division of labour is more developed, and more important, in India than in Fiji. But above all one must bear in mind the correlation between two phenomena: (1) the replacement of the king by the priest on the topmost rung of the status ladder; (2) the introduction of the opposition between pure and impure, with the innovations it entails. This opposition represents a ritualistic point of view: it originated historically in Vedic ritual and spread to the whole of social life, and it represents access to the sacred rather than the sacred itself. It is natural that such a point of view should be the work of the priest, and a logical connection between the two phenomena can be perceived.

It is quite natural that the distinction between priesthood and royalty, between status and power, while allowing the expression of hierarchy in a pure form, should permit the progress of differentiation in religious matters.

In an unexpected way we thus arrive at a plausible hypothesis about the origin of the system; pre-Aryan India would have had a system similar to that in Fiji, as Hocart suggested; Brahmanism, starting with Vedic development, and subordinating king to priest, would have encompassed it in a strict hierarchy, at the same time developing it and making it more precise.

33a Srinivas, 'Varna and Caste' (reprinted in *Caste in Modern India*). He insists on the fact that the varnas provide a common reference, and thus a means of comparison, for actual localized caste systems. But how would this be possible if, as he also claims, two quite heterogeneous things are involved? According to Gait, the varnas represent the 'external view' of the social organization (*Census of India*, 1911, India Report, p. 366, quoted by Blunt, *Caste System*, p. 8). One sometimes still finds the idea that the castes were the product of the subdivision of the varnas (A. R. Desai, *Social Background*, p. 223).

33b For example, the interesting pamphlet mentioned by Weber: A. C. Das, *The Gandhavaniks of Bengal*, Calcutta, 1903.

34a An example of what we have called the aristocratic tendency: 'Ranks and degrees, order and regularity, are essential to the well-being of every community. The regulations of caste are nothing else than these, carried to an excess of refinement' (B. A. Irving, *The Theory and Practice of Caste*, 1857, p. 4).

Kathleen Gough Aberle, in her article 'Criteria of Caste Ranking in South India' (*Man in India*, XXXIX, No. 2, 1959, pp. 115–26), tries to reduce caste ranking in Kerala (Malabar) to what she calls 'relationships of servitude', in the extremely broad sense of personal dependence extending from a quasi-feudal relationship to servitude proper. This hypothesis does not account for the superiority of the Nambudiri Brahman over the king, whether or not Kshatriya. In this sense, the dualism which is discussed later on in that same work is also present here. However, Miller had shown, for the same region, that whilst the princes were confined to limited territories, only the Brahman transcended these divisions and unified them ('Caste and Territory in Malabar', *American Anthropologist*, LVI, No. 3, 1954, pp. 410–20), which may be regarded as symbolic: the ranking which Gough calls 'ritual', far from being simply the expression of relationships of force, modifies and limits the impact of these relationships.

Ramkrishna Mukherjee, in *The Dynamics of a Rural Society*, tried to demonstrate a kind of statistical conguence between the caste system and three major economic classes which he distinguished in Bengal. Two of the classes in question are considered to have resulted from the British domination. However, were there not castes before this? By contrast, see the clear recognition of the subordination of the phenomena of class to those of caste in Marian Smith, 'Structured and Unstructured Class Societies' (*American Anthropologist*, LV, No. 2, 1953, p. 304): 'Indian society is structured in terms of caste but not in terms of class.'

34b This duality can be seen in terminological usage. These authors constantly speak of 'ritual status' and 'secular status', whereas from the indigenous point of view, and in the strong sense of the word, there is only one status, i.e. 'ritual' status. M. N. Srinivas has given us at least the concept of the 'dominant caste', which is useful provided it is well defined: the dominant caste to a greater or lesser extent reproduces the royal function on a smaller territorial scale, and 'dominance' is opposed to 'status', as fact is to right, or the dominant caste is to the caste of the local Brahmans (*cf.* §74.2).

34c This relates to a remote village in Orissa, where land is very cheap: F. G. Bailey, *Caste and the Economic Frontier*, pp. 266–67. Notice especially the inversion of the usual sense of 'validate'. In the text we have spoken only of 'power' (legitimate force, closely linked to control of the land). Wealth in movables and chattels is quite another matter, as it was first emancipated by British rule (see §§75, 117; Appendix D, §2; and 'The British in India', p. 1113).

34d (Note 1980): For the idea, derived from Raymond Apthorpe, of hierarchy as 'encompassing' relationship, see the Postface to the present edition.

35a H. Risley, *Census of India*, 1901, Calcutta, Govt. Printing, 1903, I, pp. 537 ff.; II, App. 2.

35b Ketkar, *The History of Caste in India*, I, pp. 23 ff. (with further details).

35c Or, to put it another way, the hierarchical principle is put to work in a much more precise fashion in the south. This is confirmed by McKim Marriott, *Caste Ranking*, which will be mentioned again later (§37). In it, he studies the degree of 'elaboration' of status ranking in five regions of India and isolates five different types, ranging from the very uncouth types of the Indus and Bengal, where the castes are divided into only two or three 'blocks', to the 'unilinear' type of Kerala. Marriott's comparative work, despite its ample documentation, calls for certain reservations about the definition of regions and the statistical aspect, *cf.* Cohn's review in *Journal of the American Oriental Society*, LXXXII, No. 3, 1962, pp. 425–30. For the dichotomy which he finds in his Coromandel type (Madras), see the subsequent note.

35d As Mandelbaum wrote very clearly in a passage in which he had comparison in mind: 'What is quite constant is a set of criteria for ranking; what varies is the interpretation given in a specific instance to a particular combination of characteristics' ('The World and the World View of the *Kota*', McKim Marriott, ed., *Village India*, p. 241).

Let us briefly mention a curious feature of Southern India, the division into castes of the left hand and castes of the right hand, described and discussed by Hutton in his recent book (pp. 9, 59 ff., 143; Dubois should be added to his bibliography), and also by Hocart (*Kings and Councillors*, pp. 267 ff.), Weber (*The Religion of India. The Sociology of Hinduism and Buddhism*, Glencoe, 1958, p. 296) and McKim Marriott (note 35c).

The phenomenon has practically disappeared (historical documents in T. V. Mahalingam, *South Indian Polity*, 1955, pp. 91, 173, 189–90), with the result that there is nowadays no question of observing it. (Note 1980: This was a rash statement, for Brenda Beck has found such a division in the Kongu country; yet the pattern may well be different from the traditional one. For references see the notice above, p. xl.) Let us mention some features. The division cuts across the hierarchical order; for example, of the two main untouchable Tamil castes, the Paraiyar were of the right hand, the Sakkiliyar of the left. Squabbles about ritual privileges drew the attention of the first modern observers. Certain castes were themselves divided into the right hand and the left hand. Finally, whilst all the artisans were of the left hand, the Brahmans, kings, and 'several castes of Shudras' (Dubois, p. 25) were neutral, and in the position of arbiters. Leaving on one side speculation about origins (dualistic organization, patrilinearity and matrilinearity, etc.), let us simply bring together what is known on this point and what is known regarding right and left generally. The first association to suggest itself is with the king sitting in council, with the persons attending distributed partly on his right hand and partly on his left (Hocart, *Caste*, p. 66; Dumont, *Sous-caste*, p. 288; Sardesai, *New History of the Marathas*, I, pp. 223–4 (Shivaji and his ministers); for ancient Ceylon, Geiger, *Culture in Mediaeval Ceylon*, p. 139 (army on the right, civilians on the left); classical literature: *Śukranītisāra* and *Mānasollāsa* quoted by B. P. Mazumdar, *Socio-Economic History of Northern India*, p. 21. Local differences are likely in this field, as is the alternating setting, one to the right and one to the left, of castes of similar status (or pure and bastard of the same group, or affinal lineages). This hypothesis does not depart from indigenous attitudes, as is shown by comparison with the legend about origins reported by Thurston: a king, before judging a difference between artisans (Kammalar) and farmers (Vellalar), has them placed 'on opposite sides' (III, 117).

Other associations are probable or possible: artisans are opposed to Brahmans, and there is evidence that among them women invert right and left in their dress (Thurston, *ibid.*); Tantric or bloody forms of worship, said to be of the left hand, are opposed to the dominant forms of worship or transcend the castes by a ritual reversal: a woman of the Madiga caste (untouchable) incarnates the goddess and purifies the proud Reddi and the rich Komati, her saliva purifies (Thurston, IV, 292). Finally, there are traces of an alliance of commensality like that brought to light by Mayer (see below): Kammalar and Beri Chetti (arbiters of the left hand) (Thurston, III, 113).

36a McKim Marriott, 'Interactional and Attributional Theories of Caste Ranking' (*Man in India*, XXXIX, No. 2, 1959, p. 97). The article from which this 'interactional' classification of foods is taken is considered below, §37.

36b Mayer, *Caste and Kinship*, pp. 33–40 ff. The picture given here results from an analysis of the material presented by Mayer. His categories have been refashioned as little as possible, and any changes clearly indicated.

37a Pauline M. Mahar, 'A Multiple Scaling Technique for Caste Ranking' (*Man in India*, XXXIX, No. 2, 1959, pp. 127–47). The inquiry was carried out and made use of with great skill and dexterity. Eighteen people of both sexes, belonging to eleven different castes, were asked to answer thirteen questions about each of the other twenty-one castes in the village. The presentation of this very detailed inquiry would have benefited by a brief introductory account of the village and its castes.

37b Marriott, *Caste Ranking*. The four conditions stated are: (1) a large enough number of castes in a small territory (each village); (2) a high degree of interaction between the castes in their relevant capacities; (3) congruence of individual actions with respect to members of a given caste; (4) sufficient isolation from neighbouring territories having a different system.

37c In 'Interactional and Attributional Theories of Caste Ranking'.

CHAPTER IV   THE DIVISION OF LABOUR (pages 92–108)

41a We can be very brief in dealing with the general aspects of the relationship between caste and profession, as these have been fully discussed in the early literature. In this connection, the reader is referred, for example, to Chapter 1 of Bouglé's *Essays*. At the end of this chapter, Bouglé writes: 'In the Hindu civilization it is above all religious views, rather than economic tendencies, which determine the rank of each group' (p. 50). This cautious remark is more or less our point of departure. Neither will ancient data be adduced on this point. After briefly recalling how the general problem has been posed since Bouglé, we shall, to try and solve it, go straight to the village system as laid bare by intensive research.

41b On relative purity as a relevant aspect of profession, *cf.* O'Malley, *Indian Caste Customs*, p. 122. It should be remembered that for Hocart, and in conformity with the custom in Southern India and

Ceylon, the barber is the funeral priest, and that his status is higher in the north, where he does not have such functions. The washerman is impure mainly on account of the clothes or linen soiled by childbirth or menstruation: one cannot wash these garments oneself (except in Maharashtra, for some unknown reason). On the barber and the washerman, see the dictionaries: Risley (*nāpit*, *dhobā*), Ibbetson (*nāī*); for the impurity of death in the north, see the case of the Mahabrahman (Blunt, p. 248; Brahmans called Gayawals of Gaya, sacred place of the dead, in Vidyarthi, 'The Extensions of an Indian Priestly Class'; see also 'Dom' in Crooke and Risley. Hocart tried to extend the explanation by presenting the potter as a priest (which he sometimes is in effect), and the artisans as being above all makers of holy images; he generalized this by insisting on the magico-religious aspect of any craft (p. 152, etc.); *cf.* Hutton, p. 164. The 'worship of implements and weapons' (Blunt, p. 294) is also mentioned as very widespread, each profession honouring its implements on a certain date of the year, often on the festival of Dasahra ('the ten days' in the north) or its equivalent (*ayudhapūjā*), in the month of September–October. But, quite apart from the fact that the word 'worship' is misleading, it will be observed that these manifestations are a group affair, and not a matter of its relation to the whole. There is indeed every sort of variation among the specialities, and at the limit complete absence of religious content. We shall return to this in §42.3.

41C Marriott, 'Interactional and Attributional Theories of Caste Ranking', pp. 94–5; Bh. Mukherjee, 'Caste-Ranking among Rajbanshis in North Bengal', p. 208. The same reasoning can be generalized to apply to impure commodities or those whose consumption leads to inferiority: their provision by professionals is more polluting than their consumption itself. For example the 'toddy-tappers' who supply fermented palm juice are made more inferior by this than one is by drinking the toddy. (Srinivas says that these people are impure because only low castes drink, 'The Social System of a Mysore Village', in Marriott, ed., *Village India*, p. 21). Moreover, our information is still quite insufficient: I learnt incidentally from a toddy-tapper of Tinnevelly district (south of Madras State) that he sees his disgrace in the calluses produced on parts of his body by the chafing of the trunks of the palm-trees he climbs. Marriott also remarks that the relative values of the various professional impurities are little known. One may even suspect rationalizations, for example when the low status of the oil-presser is attributed in the literature to the fact that in crushing the grain he takes life. This appears unlikely, at least at present; similarly for the plough, n. 41f. Intensive studies as carried out nowadays would improve our information on these aspects, if only they were more oriented towards them.

41d Ghurye, *Caste and Race in India*, Chapter 2.

41e On changes (formation of a new caste, affiliation to an existing caste, formation of new subcastes), see Blunt, *op. cit.*, pp. 236–8, 52. Only some of the many alleged cases seem well-established, and then status is in the foreground; in the other cases one cannot always be sure that profession alone is at issue. Note that on the second point Blunt explicitly mentions a case in which a caste was formed by the aggregation of groups of different origins, each becoming a subcaste. We shall take up the question again in general in connection with the diachronic aspects (Chapter IX). To quote the 1931 Census Report (I, 1, p. 399, from Cox, *Caste, Class and Race*, p. 61): 'There is [today] a tendency . . . to relax the rule of pollution by touch in the case of members of the untouchable castes who do not pursue *untouchable avocations.*'

41f The dharma literature contains rules concerning lucrative occupations for the superior varnas, especially for the Brahmans. There are wide provisions for cases of unavoidable circumstances (calamity, *āpad-dharma*). Concerning the Brahmans' prejudice against using the plough in person, *cf.* Manu, X, 84: the plough wounds the earth and the creatures which live in it. This is so surprising that one may take it as a rationalization: what is really a prejudice about occupation is expressed in terms of 'non-violence', betraying Jain influence (§65.2).

41g On professional solidarity, *cf.* Blunt, pp. 244–6 (and 143, which is connected with the following paragraph). For example, in Ahmedabad a banker who was having his house re-roofed had a quarrel with a confectioner; the confectioners' guild got the tilers to refuse to supply him with tiles, *cf.* Hopkins, *India, Old and New*, p. 194 (Enquiry in Ahmedabad, 1896).

42a For example, Marx calls the 'village communities' 'wholes of production', *Produktionsganze* (*cf.* my *La civilisation indienne et nous*, pp. 79–80).

42b The distinction between sacrifier and sacrificer, in French *sacrifiant/sacrificateur*, is taken from Hubert and Mauss, as translated by W. D. Halls (a sacrifier is 'the subject to whom the benefits of sacrifice accrue . . . or who undergoes its effect'). Nesfield (p. 48) writes 'yajaman' for someone who employs a genealogist (*bhāṭ*), who is himself identified with the sacrificing priest. The word *yājya* in Sanskrit has a sense close to that of *yajamāna*: in the Harivamsha, a sequence of the Epic (V, 733), the relation between the king and his spiritual master is given as:

*yājya-upādhyāya* (*sambandhād*): '(from the relation subsisting between) the person in whose behalf sacrifice is to be performed and the spiritual preceptor' (following Muir, *Sanskrit Texts*, I, 377). The following definitions are taken from the *Bṛhat hindī koś*, Banaras, Saṃvat 2013.

42c What was said earlier about solidarity in specialist castes applies here: the caste assembly ensures that the right of every one of its members over each patron is respected, *cf.* Blunt, pp. 243 ff.

42d The classical descriptions of the 'village community', having in Maharashtra for example twelve *bālutedār* or functionaries, were already dealing in fact with what is here called *jajmānī*. The British administrators sometimes had the details recorded: see Gooddine's detailed study, *Report on the Village Communities of the Deccan*, Bombay, 1852. Blunt, *Caste System*, pp. 242 ff., mentions the term, prior to Wiser, *The Hindu Jajmani System*, Lucknow, 1958, 1st ed., 1936. The merit of this small book is that it gives the details of the system in the form of a monograph, at a time when that type of intensive study was rare and attention was being diverted from these basic realities. As it stands, it is still the only one of its kind, although monographs have chapters devoted to this aspect of the caste system (n. 42i).

Wiser's village is different from the one Mayer studied (quoted above, §36) in that both the role of the dominant caste and that of the caste of highest status, which in the previous case were filled by Rajputs and Brahmans, are here held by the Brahmans alone. This is not an uncommon case, especially in wealthy areas (*cf.* E. K. Gough for Tanjore, Madras State, in 'Caste in a Tanjore Village', E. R. Leach, ed., *Aspects of Caste*). This constitutes an exception to the distinction of roles only at the level of the caste, for we shall see that the two roles are distinguished within the caste which is both foremost and dominant.

42e It will be noted that the only barber, helped by his son, could not serve all the families; some were served by two barbers from outside; the same for the washerman. This is not a rare occurrence, for there is nothing absolute about the village framework, and it often happens that the specialists' areas straddle more than one village. The barber receives from each patron at the spring harvest seven pounds of barley, fourteen of corn; at the autumn harvest, between seven and ten and a half pounds of corn on the cob, one load of millet (sorghum) (that is, seven pounds of grain and the fodder) and seven pounds of unhusked rice. From those who are not farmers he receives simply ten pounds of grain each year. What are the corresponding services? The important patrons, the village elders, are shaved twice a week, the thirty-six other Brahman patrons and the Kayastha once a week, and the others when convenient to the barber. He shaves armpits and cuts fingernails once a week, toenails once a fortnight; he cuts hair once a month, and for certain occasions. The barber also has important functions in family ceremonies. At the time of a marriage he and his wife have business to do intermittently for a fortnight. Apart from a share in the meals, they receive one rupee on eight different occasions and a new garment. Likewise in the case of birth, first haircut or tonsure, and initiation. No payment is made at mourning, although the barber has functions to perform. He shares in the terminal meals on the tenth and thirteenth day. Note that there, as generally in the north but unlike the south, the barber is an esteemed specialist. He is the messenger for good tidings, whereas Untouchables bring relatives the news of a death. However, and this is a paradoxical feature, it is the barber who brings the cremation fire to the burial-ground.

42f Apart from the relationship between the rank of the Brahmans relative to each other, and the rank of the castes they serve, there are Hindus of such low status that they are served neither by the Brahman nor by the barber. (This fact has been noted elsewhere, *cf.* for example, Gough, in Leach, *Aspects*, p. 24.) Here it is only the case for the scavenger (sweeper and cesspool cleaner). It is rather surprising to see that the other Untouchables, the *Camār* or leather people, enjoy these services here. It happens that these lowly castes specialize their barber and their washerman in a status inferior to their own (Gough, *ibid.*).

42g There is an unintended irony in Harper's article entitled 'Two Systems of Economic Exchange in Village India' (*American Anthropologist*, LXI, 1959, pp. 760–78). Harper challenges the term *jajmānī* and the notion it designates, in so far as it is pan-Indian, on the basis of his observations in Mysore. Yet he declares that the master or employer is there called *yejmanru*, which is nothing but a Dravidianized form of *jajmān* (*cf.* the Tamil *ejamāN*). Harper believed he had discovered a quite different system, to which he gave the name of the region, the Malnad. In fact, this is in all probability only a variant, built up into a different pattern by the exaggeration of particular features. In Malnad, the dominant caste is that of the Havik Brahmans, who make their living from the very lucrative production of areca nuts (which are chewed throughout India, usually with a betel leaf, and are produced only in certain regions). Taking the usual place of a food crop, this commercial crop obviously led to servants being paid in money. From this, the relationships may take on a more contractual form (which the author exploits excessively). Thus, when the village barber died without heir, the Haviks found a young barber elsewhere; by written contract they gave him 600 rupees for his marriage, in return for which he was committed to serve them for five years. It will be noted that this 'contract' was of a rather special nature. During this period, the barber, as elsewhere, was paid in grain by members of other castes who cultivate rice. Subsequently, the Brahmans paid him, but in money. We are told that in the discussions on this subject, the Brahmans every time unwillingly accepted the conditions laid down by the barber 'rather than choose ... to engage ... a new barber' (as they had been obliged to do after the death of the previous one). But should one not see there an unwillingness to deal contractually in this sort of business? Elsewhere, the author admits that the Untouchables are unfree workers (he speaks of 'permanent indentureship'). Like others, this author goes awry through his desire to attribute the primary role to relations which he can characterize as economic.

42h T. O. Beidelman, *A Comparative Analysis of the Jajmani System*, Locust Valley, N.Y., 1959.

42i E. K. Gough, 'The Hindu Jajmani System' (*Economic Development and Cultural Change*, IX, No. I, Oct. 1960, pp. 83 ff.); *cf.* D. Pocock (below, 42j); H. Orenstein, 'Exploitation and Function in the Interpretation of Jajmani' (*Southwestern Journal of Anthropology*, XVIII, No. 4, 1962, pp. 302–15).

N. K. Bose has likewise recognized the combination of inequality with 'economic adjustment' ('Caste in India', *Man in India*, XXXI, 1951, pp. 108–9).

Among recent publications, apart from chapters in monographs (Lewis, Chapter 2; Mayer; Majumdar, *Caste and Communication in an Indian Village*, Chapter 3) one can mention: Opler and Singh, 'The Division of Labour in an Indian Village', 1948; N. P. Gist, 'Occupational Differentiation in South India'; N. S. Reddy, 'Functional Relations of Lohars in a North Indian Village'; F. Barth, 'Ecological Relationships of Ethnic Groups in Swat, North Pakistan'; N. Patnaik, 'Service Relationship between Barbers and Villagers in a Small Village in Rampur'.

42j Pocock, 'Notes on Jajmani Relationships' (*Contributions*, VI, 1962, pp. 78–95).

42k Mauss, *Manuel d'Ethnographie*, 1947; *Notes and Queries on Anthropology*, London, Royal Anthrop. Inst., 6th ed., 1951, p. 158.

42l In *The Theory of Social and Economic Organisation*, trans. Henderson and Parsons, Max Weber classified the various types of the division of labour. The market economy corresponds to the type having autocephalous and autonomous elements: the agent acts of himself and in his own interest. In the Indian village, by contrast, the elements are autocephalous but heteronomous: they provide for the needs of the members of the group (p. 228), and a little later this type is called a 'demiurgic liturgy'. Marx had already emphasized two points in a rather similar way: the produce is for the immediate consumption of the community and does not become merchandise; and 'The law that regulates the division of labour in the community acts with the irresistible authority of a law of Nature' (*Capital*, Eng. trans. Moscow, 1954, I, sec. 4, Chapter 14, p. 358).

42m *Cf.* Wiser, p. 42: 'The jajman when he makes a cash payment thinks not in terms of value for value received, but that the payment together with certain concessions [of land, etc.] will give the "kam karnewala" his livelihood.'

42n Here one may recall a view that was at one time very widespread: that caste brought to a halt the division of labour, having previously promoted it (for example, James Mill in his article 'Caste' in the *Encyclopaedia Britannica*, quoted in §13). What Weber calls 'heteronomy' is involved. From a slightly different point of view, how is the fact that there exist specialist trades to be reconciled with the fact that, very generally, Indians consider a relation to an object only as a symbol of a relation to a person? In a specialized technique, the relation to the object is the affair of one particular caste, whilst relations between castes are interpersonal. For example, there are castes renowned for their agricultural talents. Ideally or by attribution, functions are specialized in accordance with people's abilities, and, if I am not mistaken, specialization itself (even that of the Brahman, if one takes the sectarian influence into account) is felt as a limitation.

43a A study is required of the singular, not to say aberrant situation of five important specialized crafts, sometimes grouped in a single caste (in the south: the *Pāñcāla*, comprising goldsmiths, braziers, carpenters, stonemasons and blacksmiths, *cf.* Hutton, p. 10). Among other things, they are 'castes of the left hand', call themselves the equals of the Brahmans and intermarry between themselves. Unfortunately, no intensive study is yet available (but see Srinivas' brief indications especially in 'The Social System of a Mysore Village', pp. 7, 23–5), and the older literature (Thurston, *Castes and Tribes, s.v.*) needs careful interpretation. For the classical Hindu literature, see G. Dumézil, 'Métiers et classes fonctionnelles chez divers peuples Indo-Européens', (*Annales, Économies, Sociétés, Civilisations*, 13e année, No. 4, Oct.–Dec.

1958), pp. 718–19. Pocock has recently advanced an interpretation (*loc. cit.*).

CHAPTER V   THE REGULATION OF MARRIAGE (pages 109–129)

51a The contrast with neighbouring populations, who are tribal or who have become Buddhist, is striking: in these cases funerals, or rather mourning and ancestor worship, have the greatest social importance, *cf.* B. Pignède, *Les Gurungs*, 1966, and the monographs by Hutton and others on the Nagas. Concerning Hindu marriage, *cf.* Dumont, *Sous-caste*, pp. 215, 225.

51b The dictionaries of 'Tribes and Castes' are full of descriptions of the ceremonies (*cf.* most recently Brenda Beck on one part of Tamil country, unpublished thesis for B.Litt. at Oxford). For the prestations, *cf.* Dumont, *loc. cit.*

51c O'Malley (*Indian Caste Customs*, p. 95) recalls the case mentioned by Buchanan in Malabar (adultery between a Nambudiri Brahman and a woman of the Shanan caste – toddy-tappers, very inferior: the man was blinded, the close relations of the woman killed or sold), and other cases in Bihar and Nepal.

51d On the different theories, indigenous or otherwise, which try to explain the custom, *cf.* Blunt, *Caste System*, pp. 75 ff. For the Dharma literature, see Kane, *History of Dharmaśāstra*, II, No. 1, pp. 443 ff., and Jolly, *Hindu Law and Custom*, trans. B. Ghosh, Calcutta, 1928, §17. It will simply be observed here: (1) that the custom is related to the place of the daughter, as opposed to the son, in the family, and the place of the woman in kinship, as will become somewhat clearer in what follows; (2) the progressive lowering of the age must be related not only to hypergamy (§54), but also to the prestige value of the custom, which would engender rivalry and outbidding. With a view to reform, the British brought pressure to bear by law (*Child Marriage Restraint Act*, called the *Sarda Act*, 1929, having little influence) and above all by persuasion. Thus the Rajputs, the royal caste of Northern India, founded an association in 1888 with a view to reform (limitation of expenditure in keeping with revenue, fixing of the minimum age at 18 for the man, 14 for the woman, finally, prohibition of polygamy, O'Malley, *Indian Caste Customs*, pp. 98–9). Later, modern associations (*cf.* §113) often similarly fixed age limits.

51e On the *satī* (Anglo-Indian 'suttee'), forbidden by Lord Bentinck in 1829 with the approval of enlightened Indian opinion, *cf.* E. Thompson, *Suttee*, 1928; Kane, *History of Dharmaśāstra*, II, 1, pp. 624 ff.

51f Marriage distinctions, *infra* §53. Distribution of practices in Uttar Pradesh, see Blunt, p. 64.

51g The levirate in the strict sense is the widow's *obligation* to marry the husband's younger brother, but it seems to have become increasingly common to enlarge the sense of the word by distinguishing between obligatory and optional levirate. Here there is never any obligation, *cf.* O'Malley, *Indian Caste Customs*, p. 93. This practice of inferior castes (*cf.* Blunt, *loc. cit.*) must be distinguished from the classical *niyoga* whereby if the husband dies childless, his younger brother would give him a son by cohabiting with his wife, a practice much discussed and regulated by the classics (Manu is contradictory on this subject, and this formerly accepted practice is sometimes said to be improper in the present age of the world, the Kali age; *cf.* the quotation from *Parāśara* in Nesfield, p. 53, and Kane, *op. cit.*, II, 1, pp. 599 ff.).

51h More details on marriage, both as such and in the context of kinship, will be found in existing works, notably Blunt, *Caste System*, pp. 43, 60 ff. On affinity in the south and north, refer to my works, *Hierarchy* and *Sous-Caste*; *Le Deuil à Rampur*; 'Marriage III, North India in Relation to South India' (*Contributions*, IX). On the Brahmanic prohibition on *sapiṇḍa* relations, a very extended but not very functional one, *cf.* 'Marriage III'. Leach has upheld the heterogeneity of the domains of kinship and caste (*Aspects*, pp. 7–8).

52a Every attempt to derive caste from clan, or to 'explain' caste in terms of clan, is thus in vain, even if, within the caste system, where both are found, we sometimes believe we are witnessing the one being transformed into the other.

52b If its full force is to be preserved, the notion of endogamy must be ascribed to the group within which one can marry anywhere (segment), and not to the larger group (caste) which can in the broad sense be called 'endogamous'; we shall call the first the 'unit of endogamy'. This is said without prejudice to exogamy, which on the contrary is ascribed to the largest group into which marriage is forbidden (for example, the exogamous clan, and not the lineages of which the clan is composed, is the unit of exogamy). Among marriage prohibitions, a distinction is required between exogamy, which affects all the members of a group in some way or other, and interdictions bearing on close relatives (incest, etc.) which vary for each person according to his particular kinship relations.

52c For the relationship between law and fact, see Mayer, *Caste and Kinship*, *cf.* above, §26.

52d Because the general literature is mainly oriented towards endogamy, the attempt at systematization which follows, though it relies on established facts, as will be seen, is more personal and hypothetical than one would have wished.

53a On the hierarchy of marriages and conjugal unions, see my 'Marriage, II', *Contributions*, VII, or in French 'Mariage Nayar'.

53b J. L. Chambard, 'Mariages secondaires et foires aux femmes en Inde Centrale' (*L'Homme*, I, No. 2, May–Aug., 1961, pp. 51–88).

53c See n. 53a and Dumont, 'Le mariage secondaire dans l'Inde du nord'; Blunt, *Caste System*, pp. 72 ff., mentions that secondary marriage is often confined to the husband's brother, etc. (*cf.* levirate above); see Williams, *Oudh* (Census of 1869, I, p. 93); Elliot, *Supplement to the Glossary of Indian Terms*, I, p. 5.

53d In the north bastards are often called, among other things, *dhakṛā* (Blunt, pp. 49, 53: mixed castes) and *golā* (*ibid.*, applied to the Rajputs). O'Malley (*Indian Caste Customs*, pp. 94–5) mentions that in Orissa, at the marriages of kings and rich landowners, the bride was accompanied by many bridesmaids (up to fifty) who were sent with her as a present; from this a distinct caste resulted, called Shagirdpesha. The presence in princely houses of a more or less numerous retinue of people of degraded status, men-at-arms, male and female servants, concubines, is probably general. In connection with the Rajputs in Uttar Pradesh, Crooke (*Tribes and Castes*, IV, p. 221) noted the distinction between 'two classes of different social rank: one the offspring of wives of legitimate descent, married in the orthodox way: the other the descendants of irregular connections with low caste women'. *Cf.* J. Tod, *Annals and Antiquities of Rajasthan*, III, Chapter 4 (1920 edition, I, pp. 207–9). For an example of liaisons with Untouchables, *cf.* Srinivas, 'Caste Dispute', *Eastern Anthropologist*, VII, p. 157, in which the treatment is different for men and women; a polluted earthenware pot is thrown away (parallel to the case of the woman), whereas a bronze one is cleansed (the case of the man). It will be noted that this also corresponds to a general preference for a difference of status in which the man is superior to the woman rather than the converse.

54a *Cf. Hierarchy*, 1st part; *Sous-caste*, pp. 141 ff., 265 ff.

54b See *Contributions*, VII, pp. 86 ff. Blunt says of Uttar Pradesh: 'Indeed, amongst all Hindus there is probably a tendency towards hypergamy.' I observed myself (Gorakhpur district) that even among castes who do not actually practise it, hypergamy is influential as a conscious model, a language. *Cf.* for the Maratha country, which in this respect seems to represent the transition from the north (hypergamy) to the south (cross-cousin marriage), Karvé, *Kinship Organization in India*, p. 156.

54c On this point we shall not follow O'Malley, *Indian Caste Customs*, p. 9, who speaks of 'marriage market', 'bridegroom price' in the high hypergamous castes, and 'bride price' in the low castes. The region is Bengal, for which no intensive study is available, but it may be supposed that there, as elsewhere, there is an *exchange* of prestations, in which the tangible prestations dominate in one or the other direction.

This is the place for a word about the classical list in ancient literature of the eight forms of marriage (Kane, *History of Dharma-śāstra*, II, 1, p. 516). It is hard to know what to make of this list until one realizes that it essentially contrasts marriage as gift to marriage as purchase. Briefly, I believe what is at issue is a theory of the prestations among the orthodox and the others. In the Brahmanical theory marriage is a gift, and the prestations, presents or payments, must accompany exclusively the wife, they must go from the wife's family to the husband's. As we shall see, this theory has to a large extent become fact. By contrast with this conception, the Brahmans have concocted a notion of marriage by purchase. Of course, such marriage has never existed anywhere, but the notion serves to express the fact, found among less elevated castes, of bilateral instead of unilateral prestations. The Brahmanic authors of the Shastras are here similar to modern anthropologists who, quite without justification in India, often speak of 'bride price' or 'bridegroom price' when they see that payments in one direction or the other predominate.

54d Mayer (*Caste and Kinship*, pp. 154–5) distinguishes three different subcastes in Malwa. Cole makes no mention of this in 'The Rajput clans of Rajputana' (*Census of India*, 1931, XXVII (App.), pp. 134–41), perhaps hampered by the official nature of the publication. Rivers, quite logically, regarded hypergamy as a custom of Rajput origin ('The Origin of Hypergamy', *Journal of the Bihar and Orissa Research Society*, VIII, 1921, p. 15).

54e Hypogamy is the converse of hypergamy. The difference in status is neutralized in the opposite direction (the woman superior to the man). This pattern is not wholly unknown, but no detailed data are available. It would mainly be a question of Bengal, but the indications are obscure and rather contradictory (*cf.* Risley, *Tribes and Castes*, s.v., Kaibartta). For other explanations of the preference for hypergamy, *cf.* Nesfield, p. 55, and the following note.

55a For further details, see 'Marriage II', *Contributions*, VII. The nature of the *tāli* rite (primary marriage) and of the *sambandham* (secondary marriage) among the Nayar has long been discussed. To simplify the exposition, I present in positive terms in the text a hypothesis which is not, at the moment, generally accepted. *Cf.* the different theory advanced by Nur Yalman, 'On the Purity of Women in the Castes of Ceylon and Malabar' (*Journal of the Royal Anthropological Institute*, XCIII, Part I, Jan.–June 1963, pp. 25–58), and the brief discussion in *Contributions*, VII, p. 81, n. 3. This juggling away of the primary marriage has a remarkable parallel in the case of the man: a bachelor who marries a widow is first married to a tree, which is then cut down (O'Malley, *Indian Caste Customs*, p. 93).

55b It is not claimed that separation, or even 'repulsion', may not be present somewhere, even perhaps as an independent factor. What is sought here is a universal formula, a rule without exceptions.

55c One should likewise distinguish from hypergamy and hypogamy the rare cases of marrying above the caste with a view to gaining status (*Census*, 1911, I, 1, p. 378 (Gait)).

55d Following Risley, taken up by Hutton, *Caste*, pp. 47–8 (and see his bibliography; the picture is somewhat different according to Bhattacharya, *Hindu Castes and Sects*, 1896, pp. 37 ff.); Karvé, *Kinship Organization in India*, p. 116.

55e Karvé, *Kinship Organisation in India*, pp. 157–8.

55f In Uttar Pradesh the Khattris are $2\frac{1}{2}$, 4, 12, and 52 (Blunt, p. 46), the Sanadh Brahmans are given as '$3\frac{1}{2}$ and 10', the Sarasvati Brahmans, who are hypergamous at least in Panjab, are 5, 8, 12, 52; the Kanaujiya Brahmans, rather confused, have among others a division into 6, 5 (?'*pañcādari*'), and 'bastards' (*cf.* Crooke, *Tribes and Castes*, III, 124; Elliot, *Memoirs*, I, 146; J. Wilson, *Indian Caste*, p. 152). For the Sarvariya, see Crooke, IV, pp. 293 ff., and Buchanan in Martin, *Eastern India*, II, pp. 451–2.

In Uttar Pradesh, hypergamy combined with a sort of spatial hierarchization (from west to east) produces a curious phenomenon. To quote Blunt (p. 46):

> In two successive Census reports (1901 and 1911), it is shown clearly, firstly, that the bulk of persons living in districts other than that in which they were born are women; secondly, that the migration of these women is due to their marriage: and thirdly, that the general trend of this migration is from east to west. As the lower branches [segments] of a widespread caste, generally speaking, live in the east of the Provinces, and the higher in the west, the conclusion that hypergamy has something to do with the nature of the 'marriage' migration appears sound.

55g Whilst Blunt (p. 46) indicates that the relative rank of Rajput clans is carefully determined, he adds that it varies from district to district. Hence it is probably *local groups* of clans that are involved, whose relative status probably depends on relations of intermarriage as much as the latter depend on it.

55h On the hypergamy of the Patidars of Gujerat, see Pocock, 'The Hypergamy of the Patidars'.

56a Census report 1911, XV, United Provinces, Part I, Report, p. 366; Blunt, *Caste System*, p. 128; Hutton, *Caste in India*, p. 46. Apart from the fact that Hutton's résumé is in part approximate, and even Blunt's inaccurate on one point, Hutton is hampered by his tendency to consider hypergamy as an exceptional fact, a transition between reciprocal intermarriage and the complete cessation of intermarriage. The Dhanuk are a service caste.

57a The basic reference is as usual to Kane (*History of Dharmaśāstra*, II, 1, pp. 51 ff.). See also Kapadia, *Hindu Kinship*, and *Marriage and Family in India*.

57b There is a noticeable structural difference between *anuloma* and *pratiloma* marriages (as abstract possibilities). *Anuloma* marriage, when men take wives from an inferior category (varna, or for the sake of generalization, caste), could jeopardize the status of the group (or lineage), and so one may count on the group forbidding or limiting it. *Pratiloma* marriage by contrast may appear to be advantageous to the groups or lineages who intermarry: the patrilineage could find its status elevated thereby, and the lineage which 'gives the woman' would not suffer directly so far as status goes and might find material advantage. Is this one reason for the attitude of the classical authors?

CHAPTER VI   RULES CONCERNING CONTACT AND FOOD
   (pages 130–151)

61a Bales and his associates provide evidence for this property in their experiments with small groups: R. F. Bales and P. E. Slater, 'Role Differentiation in small Decision Making Groups', 1956. As in the family, two types of 'leaders' emerge: one responsible for the group's external relations ('instrumental' function), the other for relations within the group ('expressive' function). Something of the kind is also found in the case of the complementarity in Tamil villages between the god Aiyanar (responsible for the soil) and the goddess of epidemics (group's collective health) see my article 'Définition structurale d'un dieu populaire tamoul', 1953 (but I did not draw this conclusion there). Or again there is an analogy with moral virtues in an Andalusian village: masculine authority (directed towards the region and the nation), and feminine modesty (*vergüenza*), the virtue of the family and intimacy (J. Pitt-Rivers, *The People of the Sierra*, 1954, p. 158). Similar again is the case of the popular religion of Tarascon-sur-Rhône, in which Saint Martha represents the Christian religion, hence the link with the outside, whilst the Tarasque which she vanquished in the legend represents local values, the community being linked with the outside world through their relationship; here again the conclusion is inescapable according to my analysis: *La Tarasque*, Paris, 1951.

62a Stevenson, 'Status Evaluation', *cf.* above, n. 25a. Nur Yalman, in his article, 'On the Purity of Women in the Castes of Ceylon and Malabar', shows a much more adequate insight in the case of women (already quoted in n. 55a).

62b See above respectively §25 (1–3, 6) and §§35–7.

62c Ketkar, *The History of Caste in India*, I, p. 24. According to Murphy, *In the Minds of Men*, pp. 63–4, a scale of social distance by Radhakamal Mukerjee gives the following degrees of social avoidance (in ascending order): '(1) against sitting on a common floor; (2) against interdining; (3) against admission in the kitchen; (4) against touching metal pots; (5) against touching earthen pots; (6) against mixing in social festivals; (7) against admittance in the interior of the house; (8) against any kind of physical contact.' This is not always very clear (the order of (1) and (2); for (6) rules are in any case relaxed for pilgrimages; precise sense of (8)?).

62d Stevenson thinks that the earthen pot, being porous, is more difficult to purify than the bronze pot. It is also inexpensive and easily replaced. Sometimes all the crockery is renewed at certain festivals. Use must be emphasized: a new pot can be touched by anyone (*cf.* §25.3).

62e Pauline M. Mahar, 'A Multiple Scaling Technique for Caste Ranking' (*Man in India*, XXXIX, No. 2, 1959, pp. 127–47), *cf.* n. 37a. There is regrettable lack of detail about two criteria which were the subject of disagreements among the informants, of which one was the eleventh: 'Can you take water from his hand?', which has such a large place in the literature (see §64.3).

62f The example is taken from Srinivas' *Coorgs*, the discussion from *Contributions*, III, p. 20. Minutiae of classification: 'Among the castes served by the barber, a distinction may be drawn based on the question whether the barber pares the nails or not; among the latter, whether he pares the toenails or not' (Ketkar, *op. cit.*, I, p. 26).

62g Among the best of these works is a collection of articles on the Chamar of a village in Eastern U.P. by Bernard S. Cohn. See also among others, G. S. Bhatt, 'The Chamar of Lucknow' (*Eastern Anthropologist*, VIII, No. I, 1954, pp. 27–41), and S.

Fuchs, *The Children of Hari*, Vienna, 1950, and 'The Scavengers of Nimar District in Madhya Pradesh' (*Journal of the Bombay Branch of the Royal Asiatic Society*, XXVII, No. I, 1951, pp. 86–98).

In an unpublished work quoted by Berreman, *Hindus of the Himalayas*, p. 212, Cohn writes that when the Thakur or 'landlord' (the dominant Rajput of the locality) says that a Chamar is untouchable, he means by this that he cannot accept food or water from him, and that vessels and cooked food are made impure by his touch. One reads in Bailey, *Caste and the Economic Frontier*, pp. 123, 126, that Untouchables in this region of Orissa may not husk rice. This fact seems to constitute an exception to the invulnerability of raw foods (and new objects, but *cf.* n. 25c); the employment of Untouchables by high castes is thereby reduced, husking being probably often the job of untouchable women (Chamar women in my observation in Eastern U.P.), *cf.* Wiser, *op. cit.*, p. 33.

62h In view of the state of knowledge, I draw a rough contrast between north and south. For the south, musical functions, Dumont, *Sous-caste*, p. 354; interdependence in general, Srinivas, *Coorgs*, especially p. 199; Mala and Madiga Untouchables are priests of the village goddess, *cf.* Whitehead, *The Village Gods of South India*, 1916, and Elmore, *Dravidian Gods in Modern Hinduism*, 1915, index, *s.v.*

62i In a village in the Gorakhpur district, the Chamar may not touch the Dom; they state that they may not receive food or water from the other Untouchables, or from Dhobi and Muslims (personal inquiry).

63a Eastern Uttar Pradesh, Sarvariya Brahmans, *cf.* 'Marriage III', *Contributions*, IX. In this chapter I frequently refer, for points on which the existing literature is less explicit, to a study of mine still in the process of publication. I hope this will be excused.

63b Evans-Pritchard, *Kinship and Marriage among the Nuer*, pp. 99 ff.

63c In the same inquiry, a small fact shows how certain aspects have there become pure etiquette: following a death in his family, a Brahman boy aged about ten stayed with neighbours of the same caste. Just as the men of the house sat down to take their meal, the child mischievously touched one of the plates. The diners got up and were on the point of abandoning their meal when one of them remarked that there were no witnesses apart from the child. And so they had their meal. The child told the story to his mother who ordered him not to breathe a word of it to anyone. For a maximum of rigour and elaboration, see the example of the Nagar Brahmans (natives of Gujerat) in Blunt, *op. cit.*, p. 97.

63d The Pramalai Kallar are rather unorthodox people from the Brahmanic point of view. The general rules have become much relaxed in their everyday life, which gives the impression of being at a profane level. But customary precautions can be found among them also, by considering the priests. These are common people but they are acquainted with the dangers involved in dealing with the sacred: they refuse to take part in banquets not held at their own house (danger from utensils and the woman cook being impure) and, in the days before an elaborate ritual, they must eat the prescribed food without touching it with their hands, or make do with milk, sugar and fruits (*Sous-caste*, p. 343).

63e Stevenson, *op. cit.*, Hutton, *Caste*, p. 161 ff. Crawley mentioned that certain human qualities were transmitted by food, and even by eating together (*The Mystic Rose*, 4th ed. 1932, pp. 129 ff.).

63f Course at the Collège de France, taking as its starting point an unpublished work by Robert Hertz, 1936, etc.; from listeners' notes. Cooking is done on heated stones.

63g One eats with the right hand. In the south, great stress is placed on the impurity of saliva, and so on remnants of food and the leaf which is used as a plate (*cf. Sous-caste*). In the texts, all parts of the cow are said to be sacred except the mouth (Kane, *History of Dharmaśāstra*, II, 2, p. 775). For further details, see the article, 'Pure and Impure', in *Contributions*, III.

63h Here one must agree with Marriott and give precedence to 'interaction' rather than 'attribution'.

63i A classification of foods would require some consideration of the food involved in ascetic penance (or rather, the various sorts of ascetic performance, n. 63d for example). Apart from privation and purity, primitive and more or less despised or forgotten foods are involved, for example in the numerous *vrat*, held above all by women, which are a kind of vigil observed in accordance with a vow (U.P. personal inquiry).

64a Senart, *Les Castes*, p. 39; Hutton, *Caste*, p. 62; Blunt, *Caste System*, p. 89. Stevenson, *op. cit.*, pp. 52 ff., mentions various facts, notably: one accepts certain foods from some superior castes (but for Blunt this is not a matter of commensality); there are prohibitions within the endogamous group (e.g. §63); but this belongs to another level. An example of a case in which connubiality and commensality do not go hand in hand: Risley mentions that in the Agarwal caste (Vaishyas of the north-west who are very strict about food) the members of different sects intermarry but do not eat together (*People of India*, p. 153).

64b See above §36 (Mayer) and §37 (Marriott); *kaccā* and *pakkā* mean literally raw and cooked, but this is not the sense here. The derivative sense is applied very broadly, and indicates in the one case precariousness, imperfection, and in the other solidity, perfection (one more notion tinged with hierarchy). The importance of (clarified) butter explains the emotion periodically engendered by the risk, or the fact, of its adulteration (H. Sumner Maine, 'India', in Humphrey Ward, *The Reign of Queen Victoria*, I, p. 447; Lord Ronaldshay, *India, a Bird's-Eye View*, 1924, pp. 209 ff., *cf.* below n. 82c).

64c Just as parched grain usually requires the oven of the parcher or Bharbhunja, so confectionery (the purest is made with milk and sugar without the addition of flour) is made by the Halwai.

64d On the subject of the Untouchables' disqualification from using the wells of other castes, it will be noted that nowadays the rural development administration (Community Development, etc.) sinks special wells for the Untouchables. It is certainly convenient to have a well on the spot. At a place where enlightened influence had resulted in the Untouchables being granted access to a nearby well, this step was equivalent to a setback in the struggle against untouchability (personal observation). One thinks of the segregationist motto: American blacks should be 'separate but equal'.

64e *Cf.* §36. Shore, *Notes*, I, 533, says: 'Many tribes [*sc.* castes] will allow a man to smoke through his hands from the bowl (chillum) which contains the tobacco, who would not allow the same person to touch that part of the hookah which contains the water.'

64f This attitude is reminiscent of the classical notion that it is improper to eat together unless special precautions are taken, Kane, *History of Dharmaśāstra*, IV, p. 493, *cf. ibid.*, II, p. 759, concerning the *śrāddha* (mourning banquet) among the Rigvedin Brahmans of Western India.

64g The Chamar of both subcastes in Rampur can eat *kaccā* together on condition that it has been cooked by men (personal observation).

64h I cannot assert that the rift was lasting. A similar fact in Gujerat, but in this case linked to status, is found in Pocock, 'The Hypergamy ...', p. 196.

65a L. Alsdorf, *Beiträge zur Geschichte von Vegetarismus und Rinderverehrung in Indien*, Mayence, 1962. Here as elsewhere my historical notes are aimed only to shed light on past and present in terms of one another, on particular points. For the general framework, see my essay on renunciation (Appendix B).

65b Alsdorf, pp. 63 ff., 18; Kane, *History of Dharmaśāstra*, III, p. 628, and II, pp. 2, 772 ff. Meat is mentioned in the *madhuparka*, hospitality rite; by contrast it does not figure in the morning and evening sacrifice to fire (*Āśval. Gṛhya S.* etc., *cf.* Kane, II, pp. 545

and 681). Alsdorf excludes the coincidence of sacrifice with consumption of meat from Vedism because he only finds it in evidence later (in the Smitri, in which there occurs an element of defence against the assaults of *ahiṃsā*). But the contrary is very likely the case, as is shown by *Aitareya Brāhmaṇa* 6, 8 (Kane, p. 773); ox, goat and ram are the sacrificial animals, as opposed to other species whose flesh must not be consumed.

The epithet *aghnyā*, 'not to be killed'(?), applied to the cow in the Veda, creates a difficulty. Alsdorf sides with an interpretation by H. P. Schmidt, which the latter subsequently abandoned, and which is indeed attractive in relation to the mentality of sacrifice; *aghnyā* would mean 'that which cannot be killed, reserved for sacrifice', 'to kill' being contrasted with 'to sacrifice' as in Manu, V, 39 (and see below). In order to understand this contrast, it should be recalled that in one of the constructions of the verb 'to sacrifice', *yajati*, one 'honours' a divinity (accusative) by means of a victim (instrumental) for the sake of N. (dative): this is a long way from 'killing'. Another interpretation, contemporaneous with the preceding one, is that by Kane and by W. Norman Brown ('The Sanctity of the Cow', 1957; in French, *Annales*, 1964) who assume that only cows with no economic value were sacrificed, and that only the others were called *aghnyā* (page refs. to French version: 646–8 and 663–4, ref.). Alsdorf points out (p. 68) that this would be to assume that 'the most valuable animals were systematically purloined from the Gods'.

65c Bloody sacrifice 'odious to the people': Mitakshara on Yajn, II, p. 117 (sacrifice of a barren cow, offering of a bull to the guest), Medhatithi on Manu, IV, p. 176 (sacrifice of the bull and eating of beef). Kali age: Krtyakalpataru (Alsdorf, pp. 43 ff.).

65d More precisely, Gandhi unites western non-violence (Tolstoy, etc.) with Indian *ahiṃsā* (Gandhi was born in an environment where there was very marked Jain influence). The root *hiṃs-* corresponds to the desiderative verb derived from *han-*, 'to strike, to kill'. *Cf.* M. Biardeau, *Théorie de la connaissance*, pp. 105 n. 1, 106, 149, and 'L'Inde et l'histoire', p. 53. It is surprising to see how small is the place given to such a powerful idea as *ahiṃsā* in certain classical accounts of Hindu religion. *L'Inde classique* by Renou, Filliozat *et al.* devotes only three or four passages to it, and not one single paragraph (1, 1204 food in Brahmanism; 11, 2247 trades and 2450, 2485 Jainist vows).

65e *Cf.* Kane, p. 779 n. 1864 and p. 775. Hubert and Mauss insisted on the name of the sacrificer (*śamitar* 'appeaser') and on the fact that the victim is suffocated to death outside the sacrificial area proper (*Sacrifice*, pp. 32–3). J. C. Heesterman has recently revised

386

the classical picture of Vedic sacrifice and attempted to trace the characteristic features of the subsequent epoch back to the Veda ('Brahmin, Ritual and Renouncer', *Wiener Zeitschrift für die Kunde Süd- und Ostasiens*, VIII, 1964, pp. 1–31).

65f *Cf.* Rhys Davids, *Encyclopaedia of Religion and Ethics*, *s.v.* *ahiṃsā*. The translation follows Kane, p. 775.

65g Alsdorf, pp. 6–14 (these examples and others). There are two ways of interpreting this. From the developments he admits, Alsdorf seems to extract the idea that vegetarianism was imposed there from the outside rather than being in force *ab initio*. On the contrary, we see it as established from the beginning, but in a form modified by the deeply felt distinction between the laic and the monk, the man in the world and the renouncer. Subsequently, the spread of the ideal among the laity themselves was to make the renouncer's vegetarianism more absolute.

65h M. Biardeau, 'L'Inde et l'histoire', p. 53. On transmigration *cf.* Crooke, 'Hinduism' (*Encyclopaedia of Religion and Ethics*, *s.v.*, 694a). Kane objects (II, 2, p. 776) that there was a chronological lag between the belief in transmigration and the entry of *ahiṃsā* into the literature of the dharma, but this is to underestimate the latter's conservative nature and to indirectly confirm that *ahiṃsā* has its origins elsewhere, see Appendix B (renunciation and transmigration).

65i Alsdorf, p. 49, '. . . Eine gemeinindische Geistesbewegung, die freilich bei ihnen besonders günstige Vorbedingungen traf . . .'; Ashoka: p. 53. For his part D. D. Kosambi recognized the historical emergence of vegetarianism, but he gives a materialistic explanation of it (transition from grazing to agriculture): 'Early Stages of the Caste System in Northern India' (*Journal of the Bombay Branch of the Royal Asiatic Society*, XXII, 1946, pp. 33–48).

65j Elsewhere (n. 25h) we have referred to the present puritan rivalry between Nagara Brahmans and their Jain neighbours in Gujerat. N. K. Dutt has written that vegetarianism 'might not have succeeded at all' had it not been for Jainism and Buddhism (*Origin and Growth of Caste in India*, 1931, I, p. 204).

65k Jolly, edition of the Arthashastra, 1923, intro., p. 25. Megasthenes (*cf.* Kane, II, p. 777) believed that the first caste, that of the philosophers, was divided into Brahmans and 'Sarmans' (*śramana*, ascetics), and said that its members abstained from animal food and sexual relations, and after thirty-seven years would start to eat animal flesh. Kane very plausibly suggested that the Brahmans in this case were Brahmanical students or *brahmacārin*, bachelors, whose subsequent transition to the condition of master of the house, at an advanced age, conforms with what we know; it was natural to assimilate them to renouncers.

651 Reference has been made to the Vedic situation (§65.1, and n. 65b) and W. Norman Brown's recent article on the subject was mentioned. Less recently, Crooke, 'The Veneration of the Cow in India', *Folklore*, XXII, 1912, pp. 275–306 (comparative references at the beginning; butter as a substitute for animal victims, p. 303). On the role of *ahiṃsā, cf.* Alsdorf, p. 68; Norman Brown, p. 660 (French version).

## CHAPTER VII   POWER AND TERRITORY (pages 152–166)

71a Let us again stress the point that all our difficulties and controversies hinge around a simple dilemma. Either power must be accommodated within the theory of caste, as here, or else the theory of caste must be brought under the notion of power and 'politico-economic' relations. Thus F. G. Bailey, 'Closed Social Stratification in India' (*European Journal of Sociology*, IV, No. 1, 1963, p. 118) thinks caste can be located within the political domain: 'Caste, in other words, is not a principle by which politico-economic groups are recruited, nor does it organize relations *between* political groups: but it is an organizing principle *within* such groups.' It is a matter of approach: at the empirical level, territory effectively encompasses the castes, as will be recalled shortly; at the conceptual level, representations or ideas encompass what is not directly represented, as we have tried to make clear. The fact remains that the empirical approach is a misconstruction of Indian civilization: it amounts to assimilating *dharma* to *artha*, see Appendix C, §10.

72a Eric J. Miller, 'Caste and Territory in Malabar' (*American Anthropologist*, LVI, No. 3, 1954), p. 410; *cf.* Bailey, 'Closed Social Stratification in India' (*European Journal of Sociology*, IV, No. 1, 1963), p. 123; Jackson, 'Note on the History of the Caste System', 1907, quoted by Hutton, *Caste*, p. 104: 'What we should expect if each of the old tribal kingdoms had its own sections of priests, traders, artisans, etc.' There is a parallel comment in Enthoven: with respect to the origin of caste 'no mean influence must be allotted to function, religion and political boundaries', (*Encyclopaedia of Religion and Ethics, s.v.* Lingayats, VII, p. 70a). *Cf.* Gait: 'In former times ... the members of a caste in each such principality usually married only amongst themselves, and so formed a separate subcaste' (*Encyclopaedia of Religion and Ethics, s.v.* Caste, III, p. 232b).

72b *Cf.* Srinivas (*India's Villages*, 1955, p. 8): 'The Brahman, by virtue of his ritual position, is both part of and not part of, the village' (*cf.* his *Caste in Modern India*, p. 15).

72c We have seen above that Marriott postulates the necessity for a territorial cleavage between different systems as a condition for fully developed status ranking (n. 37b); we have also seen that Mayer studied the combination of the ideology with the territorial or spatial factor (§36, *in fine*). B. S. Cohn has also insisted on the 'little kingdom' ('Law and Change', etc.).

72d Stevenson, *op. cit.*, p. 49, §2; Pocock, in 'Difference in East Africa: a Study of Caste and Religion in Modern Indian Society' (*Southwestern Journal of Anthropology*, XIII, No. 4, 1957, p. 290), mentions that one of the conditions for establishing a local hierarchy is the presence of a local Brahman caste which serves as a model for ritual behaviour (*cf. Contributions*, I, p. 32). For the regional differences (above, §35) see Hutton's work, and O'Malley, *Indian Caste Customs*, p. 166.

72e Read, for example, the Abbé Dubois: 'Subcastes which are despised in one district are often greatly esteemed in another, according as they conduct themselves with greater propriety or follow more important callings. Thus the caste to which the ruler of a country belongs, however low it may be considered elsewhere, ranks among the highest in the ruler's own dominions, and every member of it derives some reflection of dignity from its chief' (*Hindu Manners*, p. 23).

It was pointed out long ago that the subdivisions of a large number of castes are called by the names of Rajput clans (Blunt, pp. 38 ff.). Blunt mentions that in a few cases this may be a matter of filiation, but that the castes concerned are mainly 'functional' castes or castes of inferior servants, who very likely bear the name of the Rajput clan to which their ancestors were attached as artisans or dependents.

72f Srinivas, *Caste in Modern India*, p. 16. For Kerala itself, M. S. A. Rao has indicated the role played by religious reform among the Iravas in the territorial unification of the castes ('Caste in Kerala' *Sociological Bulletin*, IV, No. 2, 1955, p. 125).

72g Apart from Miller and Srinivas ('The Dominant Caste') for the south (and the historical literature), see B. S. Cohn, 'Political Systems in Eighteenth Century India: The Banaras Region' (*Journal of the American Oriental Society*, LXXXII, No. 3, July–Sept. 1962, pp. 312–20). Cohn noted (p. 315) that in the chain whereby the local dominants were subordinated to the king of Benares, and he in turn to the Nawab of Oudh, different governmental functions were attached to different levels of power. Here, as in the case of caste in general, there is a structural aspect, already encountered in Miller, which should make one wary of too rigid a notion of the 'little kingdom' and its isolation. See also A. M. Shah, 'Political System in Eighteenth Century Gujarat' (*Enquiry*, Delhi, I, No. 1, 1964, pp. 83–95).

73a The true emancipation of wealth in movables and chattels is quite modern, *cf.* §75.

73b Dumont, *La civilisation indienne et nous*, pp. 22–4; *Contributions*, VIII, pp. 94–7. As the royal function can hardly be observed nowadays, there is a paucity of anthropological literature on this topic, which is why the main aspects of this function are here envisaged separately. A picture of the whole would require that the extensive modern historical literature be brought into focus from a sociological point of view. (For the first chapter of such a work, see Appendix C.) The inscriptions are almost the sole source for the study of land rights except for recent times, and they remain to be studied completely and systematically. Currently, people often speak of 'feudalism' in connection with the superimposition of rights, the chain of dependence we have mentioned. If, following Max Weber, we take the contract of fealty to be an essential element of the feudal system, its total absence here means that one must avoid using this word: we shall speak of benefice rather than fief, of relationships of subordination rather than vassalage.

73c This point was admirably brought to light in Baden-Powell's classic work, which is rather neglected nowadays: *The Land Systems of British India*, Oxford, 1892, 3 vols.

74a R. C. Dutt brings together a series of these descriptions, *Economic History of India*, I, pp. 118, 141, 346, 386. For a more detailed discussion, see Dumont, *La civilisation indienne et nous*, pp. 36 ff.; D. Thorner, 'Marx on India and the Asiatic Modes of Production', and Dumont, 'The Village Community', both in *Contributions*, IX. Contemporary anthropologists themselves have sometimes undiscerningly revived old descriptions. Thus Bailey opens a work on Orissa with that by Metcalfe. Now elsewhere Bailey denied the sociological unity of India (*Contributions*, III, pp. 88 ff.). Had he referred to Metcalfe's report, he would have seen that it concerned exclusively the Delhi region, as Percival Spear carefully noted, while insisting on the social heterogeneity of these villages (*Twilight of the Mughuls*, pp. 117 ff.). What immediately precedes and follows Metcalfe's famous description, and which is rarely mentioned, is worth noting. The minute is dated 1830. The aim (as in the *Fifth Report*) was to oppose the possible application of the individual system of land tax called 'ryotwari settlement'. Metcalfe explained that he had a high opinion of this system, but nevertheless would not advise that it be universally applied in the north. 'The reason is that I admire the structure of the village communities, and am apprehensive that direct engagement for Revenue with each separate landholder or cultivator in a village might tend to destroy its constitution.' Why? 'The community is, I suspect, easily subverted . . . by any internal disturbance; litigation, above all things, I should think, would tend to destroy it' (Minute in *Report from Select Committee*, 1832, Evidence, III, Revenue, App. No. 84, pp. 328 ff.).

74b George Campbell, *Modern India*, 1852, p. 85: 'Where the democratic element prevailed . . . the proprietary members [of the community] were all equal, and considered themselves masters of the village, of all the lands attached to it, and of the other inhabitants . . .' See 'The Village Community from Munro to Maine', now in *Coll. Pap.*, No. 6. Durkheim displays a very similar attitude in a review in which he claims to rectify what is really Baden-Powell's substantial contribution, so much did such minds require the 'community' to be primitive, and not historical and structural ('B. H. Baden-Powell, *The Indian Village Community* (London, 1896'), *Année sociologique*, I, 1897, pp. 359–62).

74c Shelvankar gave a moderate and discerning historical résumé in his *The Problem of India*, London, 1940. For the Cola period, *cf.* n. 83f. We may add the cases in which the village appears as a unit from a limited point of view, for instance that of the rules of commensality (Mayer, *Caste and Kinship*, see above, §36; and 'Local Government Election in a Malwa Village', *Eastern Anthropologist*, XI, 1958, pp. 193–4).

74d 'Village Studies' in *Contributions*, I (bibliography), and the discussion on the place of the territorial factor, *ibid.*, III, pp. 92 ff., IV, p. 88. Among others one may add: S. C. Dube, *Indian Village* 1955; K. S. Mathur, 'Village Studies in India' (*Man in India*, XXXIX, No. I, 1959, pp. 45–52); I. Singh, 'A Sikh Village' (M. Singer, ed., *Traditional India*, 1959, pp. 273–97); Karvé and Damle, *Group Relations in Village Community*, 1963. The predilection of anthropologists for the village is partly explicable by the search for a complete and small enough group, more or less equivalent to the 'tribe', for the intensive study of a complex society. It was early recognized that whilst the village could be isolated for certain studies it did not by itself constitute a society in the strong sense of the word. *Dixit* Srinivas (*India's Villages*, 1955, p. 11): 'The completely self-sufficient village republic is a myth', which is not to say that the village was not in the past to a large extent independent of the outside world for subsistence and essential services. *Cf.* Opler, 'The Extensions of an Indian Village' (*Journal of Asian Studies*, XVI, 1957, pp. 5–10).

74e The category 'Landholders, Military and Dominant' is found in Baines, *Ethnography* (*Castes and Tribes*), 1912, §33, p. 42. The quotation from Srinivas is from 'The Social System of a Mysore Village' (Marriott, ed., *Village India*), p. 18.

74f The question of rank has been left aside here, having been explained elsewhere. Dominance, open to direct or indirect force, leads to a derivative respectability which is that of the Kshatriya.

M. N. Srinivas, 'The Dominant Caste in Rampura' (*American Anthropologist*, LXI, 1959), pp. 4–5. The criterion of number has been disputed, notably by A. C. Mayer, 'The Dominant Caste in a Region of Central India' (*Southwestern Journal of Anthropology*, XIV, 1958), p. 425.

74g The extension of the term 'dominance' to the religious level seems even less defensible than the extension of 'status' to the non-religious level. Whereas on the present view it is absolutely necessary to distinguish clearly, in the very terminology, between these two levels, we have noted that in certain conditions power surreptitiously becomes the equal of status. In such cases one could speak of indirect or derivative status (where the authors under discussion say 'secular status'), and say for example (previous note) that dominance entails a certain superiority of derivative status.

74h Mayer, *op. cit.*; Cohn, 'Law and Change' (*Economic Development and Cultural Change*, VIII, No. 1, 1959, pp. 79–93).

74i On all these points, see the contributions collected in Park and Tinker, eds., *Leadership and Political Institutions*, 1959, especially Hitchcock's 'Leadership in a North Indian Village: Two Case Studies', pp. 395–414.

74j Oscar Lewis, *Village Life in North India*, 1958, Chapter 4 (and earlier, Lewis and Dhillon, *Group Dynamics in a North-Indian Village. A Study of Factions*, Delhi, 1954). Such matters and attitudes being generally and necessarily rather secret, there is a risk of the statements one can obtain being extorted, and the data being often contradictory. It is open to doubt whether Lewis's large team, working without much discretion for a relatively short time, was really in a position to obtain a reasonably exact picture of such evasive facts. (Note 1969: Pitt-Rivers has called my attention to the fact that, prior to its introduction to Indian studies by O. Lewis, the word 'faction' was current in the analyses of North American Indian tribes.)

74k H. S. Dhillon (*et al.*), *Leadership and Groups in a South Indian Village*, 1955; see also Firth (*et al.*), 'Factions in Indian and

Overseas Indian Societies' (*British Journal of Sociology*, VIII, 1957); Beals and Siegel, 'Pervasive Factionalism' (*American Anthropologist*, LXII, 1960, pp. 394–417), (Namhalli, Mysore); McCormack, 'Factionalism in a Mysore Village' (Park and Tinker, ed., *Leadership*, 1959, pp. 438–44); Inayat Ullah, 'Caste, Patti and Factions in the Life of a Punjab Village' (*Sociologus*, VIII, No. 2, 1953, pp. 170–86); Park and Tinker, *Leadership and Political Institutions*.

75a The transition from the Physiocrats to Adam Smith and from Adam Smith to Townsend and Malthus is characteristic in this respect. *Cf.* Karl Polanyi, *Origins of Our Time: The Great Transformation*, London, 1946, pp. 76–7:

> A self-regulating market demands nothing less than the institutional separation of society into an economic and a political sphere. . . . True, no society can exist without a system of some kind which ensures order in the production and distribution of goods. But that does not imply the existence of separate economic institutions; normally, the economic order is merely a function of the social order. Neither under tribal, nor under feudal, nor under mercantile conditions was there . . . a separate economic system in society. Nineteenth-century society, in which economic activity was isolated and imputed to a distinctive economic motive, was a singular departure.

75b A few selected references can give an idea of the subjection of the merchant and the insecurity of wealth at the advent of British power. François Bernier is very explicit about the conditions in Delhi in the seventeenth century: the rich hid their wealth, the artisans (goldsmiths) were whipped by order of the nobles (*Voyages*, 1830, I, pp. 149, 221–6, 311–12, 319). Let us also note, rather tangentially, that the Mughul administration regularly used to torture governors of Provinces, who were always suspected of deceiving the Treasury about the tax returns (Spear, *Twilight of the Mughuls*).

The Abbé Dubois mentions the insecurity of wealth in movables and chattels in the face of despotism and force in Mysore (*Hindu Manners*, I, pp. 34–5; II, pp. 659 ff.). Shall we say that this was a feature of Muslim governments? Refer to the exactions of the Marathas in the territories under their administration, and reflect on this passage by Elphinstone concerning the heart of the Maratha country itself: 'The insecurity of property has rendered them so careless of the future, as to lavish on a marriage or other ceremony, the savings of years of parsimony . . . the effects . . are felt in the debts and embarrassments, in which the whole of the agricultural population is plunged' (*Report on the Territories*, 1838, p. 7). We see from this passage that Elphinstone was greatly struck by the insecurity, as well as by the irrational economic behaviour, of the Maratha peasants. Was this partly the result of constant wars? But precisely such a state of affairs reigned in the history of all regions of India for long periods. A more or less legendary conflict between kings and merchants is chronicled by Das, *The Vaisya Caste. I. The Gandhavaniks of Bengal*, pp. 99 ff., quoted with details in Max Weber, *Religion of India*, p. 88.

75c On *artha* and its 'economic' component, see Appendix C, §12.

75d *Cf.* D. D. Kosambi's *An Introduction to the Study of Indian History*, 1956, pp. 162 ff., for conclusions on the variations in the circulation of money. It may be found surprising that I have not included a résumé or discussion of the broad historical canvas painted by Max Weber in his *Religion of India* concerning the category of the Vaishyas, and including a description of the protracted conflict between patrimonial power supported by the priests, and the wealthy class of merchants or 'bourgeois' in the process of making good (pp. 77 ff.). To speak plainly, however incompetent the present author may be to judge this brilliant historical reconstruction, and however ingenious and penetrating Weber's interpretation may often be, it seems to me that the set of hypotheses introduced is excessive compared to the data used, and that this is to some extent a piece of fiction (it is true that Weber gives only general indications of his sources). More precisely, Weber interprets the data within the framework of general ideas taken from the West and, especially, from the European Middle Ages. Certainly, he in the end shows profound differences, but by presupposing similar dynamics. We have sketched above how the question could be tackled more radically.

CHAPTER VIII   CASTE GOVERNMENT (pages 167–183)

81a On this point and in general see R. Lingat's authoritative work, *Les Sources du Droit dans le système-traditionnel de l'Inde*, translated into English by J. D. M. Derrett (see Bibliography).

82a We have T. V. Gune's *The Judicial System of the Marathas*, 1953, to thank for what is known about justice under the Maratha dynasty. Let us mention in passing that the governmental system of the Maratha kings, or rather of their Brahman Mayors of the Palace, whilst in part influenced by the Mughuls, seems in other respects to have issued from a desire for Hindu revival on the part of Hindu scholars.

82b We shall be very brief. The substance of the excellent third

chapter in O'Malley's *Indian Caste Customs* (he had served in
Orissa, where the chiefs of the Feudatory States had preserved
these functions) is to be found in Hutton, *Caste*, pp. 82–6. The
Census of 1911 has been generally useful in this chapter: it included caste government on its agenda, and was used by O'Malley
and, for Uttar Pradesh, Blunt (pp. 127 ff.). One must place on one
side the case in which the king acts as the chief of his own caste,
even beyond the territory of his kingdom (thus the Maharaja of
Cashmere had authority over the Rajputs of neighbouring 'British' districts).

82c  See Blunt, pp. 118, 122, 127 (*dharmādhikarī*, headman or person
responsible for the dharma in Himalayan districts). Kane mentions
cases in the reign of Shivaji in which differences were settled by
the Brahmans and by the Shankaracarya, chief of the Vedanta
sect (*History of Dharmaśāstra*, II, 2, p. 971). The affair of
the adulteration of butter in Calcutta in 1917 reported by Lord
Ronaldshay (pp. 209–13, summarized in O'Malley, *Indian Caste
Customs*, p. 121) shows the combination of the role of the government, the Brahmans and the interested castes, and also the punishment given by the caste to the guilty parties (excommunication)
together with the expiation prescribed by the Brahmans for all
those who had unwittingly consumed the butter in question.

82d  There are limits to royal authority in these matters. It is sometimes
said that public opinion did not always follow the royal decision:
'The Sarasvat Brahmans in Maharashtra . . . succeeded in proving
their claims to Brahmanship in the Peshwa's Court; but since
public opinion was against them, they did not get the status equal
to that of other Brahman castes' (Ketkar, *The History of Caste
in India*, I, p. 22).

83a  O'Malley, ed., *Modern India and the West*, 1941, p. 263.

83b  Blunt, *op. cit.*, p. 147, n. 1; J. Matthai, *Village Government in
British India*, 1915, p. 19; Tinker, *The Foundations of Local
Self-Government in India, Pakistan and Burma*, 1954, p. 94; all
these authors quote the Census of Bombay State for 1911: 'The
myth has probably arisen from the fact that a village is generally
if not invariably formed by several families of one caste', that is
to say that a caste panchayat in a village has been called a village
panchayat. This is the case for a simple 'unicaste' population –
apart from the usual serving and untouchable castes.

83c  The *Report of the Study Team on Nyaya Panchayats* (judicial
panchayats), an official publication of 1962, often quoting R. K.
Mookerji, *Local Government in Ancient India*, says among other
things: 'The genesis of the panchayats has to be sought in the
democratic institutions . . . developed by the ancient autonomous

village communities . . .' 'The village assembly wielded supreme authority in the village.' 'One of the most important functions of the old village assemblies was the administration of justice', etc. (pp. 6, 7, 9).

83d The shift in sense is obvious in R. C. Dutt's interpretation of these texts (*Economic History*, I, esp. pp. 151, 321, 351). I am obliged to be very cursory here, and to keep to the main theme. For Elphinstone's region, see the following footnote.

Coupland is one of the few recent authors to make these distinctions in a general work: 'In Southern India it was an ancient custom for the headman of the village to convoke a committee of elders, known as a *panchayat*, to give an arbitral decision on a dispute between villagers.' (Note): 'These *panchayats* must be distinguished from the more common form, the caste *panchayat*, consisting of members of one caste only and dealing only with caste questions' (*India, a Restatement*, 1945, p. 76).

83e Thanks to Gune (*The Judicial System of the Marathas*, 1953, pp. 58–61) we have a precise picture of the village council or *gota* under the government of the Peshwa. Its members were of three kinds: (1) the Watandars, administrators and servants of the village, lead by the village headman or Patel, appointed by the government and responsible for collecting Revenue (the Patel could mete out justice and be helped in this; we have already said that the authority of such a headman is real only if he belongs to the dominant caste or is acknowledged by it); (2) the Mirasdars or dominants; (3) the Uparis, guests or clients who were not entitled to speak or vote. This is a distinct case: dominance, and the close link with royal power, are evident. For elucidation on the dominants and the Patel, see the extract from Robertson's report (*ibid.*, pp. 384 ff.). It will be noted that the *gota* fell into disuse and its judicial functions were taken over by the panchayats (*ibid.*, pp. 39 ff., 55, etc.). For the link between local and royal justice, see §84.

83f Uttaramerur is quoted everywhere, *cf.* K. A. Nilakanta Sastri, *The* Colas, 1955, index, *s.v.*, or *Studies in* Cola *History and Administration*, 1932; Appadorai, *Economic Conditions in Southern India*, 1936. In the work cited, Tinker brings many issues into focus. In particular he writes:

> The Hindu caste system . . . through the authority of the caste panchayat accustomed a man to regard himself first as a member of a hereditary caste group, and only second as a dweller in a particular area. . . . (p. 17) (the village council, the panchayat) was rarely representative of the village as a whole: it might be drawn from the members of

the founding families or from the Brahmans and superior cultivators (p. 19). Although Indian village government has never been 'democratic' in western terms, there was a sense in which the whole body of the villagers took their part in affairs. The old panchayat, whether as a caste tribunal [N.B.] or as a judicial or administrative body, normally conducted its deliberations in the presence of all those who cared to attend. The onlookers although having no direct share in the proceedings formed a sort of 'chorus'. . . (p. 20).

Here we are at last back again in India!

In recent anthropological literature, the 'village panchayat' is sometimes said to exist, but still with surprising vagueness. Lewis speaks of such a panchayat in the surroundings of Delhi, but he admits that it was dominated by the Jats; it seems indeed to be a case of a panchayat of the dominant caste. (Nor must it be forgotten that nowadays village panchayats have been created by law, and are called 'statutory' or official panchayats.) Beals categorically asserts their existence (Mysore State) and refers to ancient sources (in Marriott, ed., *Village India*, p. 89). In the same State, Srinivas is only acquainted with caste panchayats, of which one, that of the dominant caste, could be taken for a village panchayat in the broad sense ('The Social System of a Mysore Village', *ibid*., p. 18 ff., etc.). Bailey, for a remote region of Orissa, speaks at length of the village panchayat, claiming it existed prior to the British administration, but without enlarging on its organization (*Caste and the Economic Frontier*, pp. 107, 191 ff., and Chapter 12).

84a  The majority of recent authors implicitly or explicitly define the panchayat as a meeting of notables or elders, whether in the case of the caste panchayat (Carstairs in Srinivas, ed., *India's Villages*, p. 68 – Bhils of Udaipur – 'responsible caste fellows'); Gough in Marriott, ed., *Village India*, pp. 44–5: 'elect their own leaders') or more generally, Lewis, *Village Life in Northern India*, p. 26: 'a group of recognized leaders who meet . . .'; Srinivas in Marriott, *Village India*, p. 18, does not offer a definition but speaks all along of the elders; Mayer, 'The Dominant Caste in a Region of Central India', pp. 408–9: 'arbitrators', 'headmen', 'leaders'; Bailey, *Caste and the Economic Frontier*: village 'council'. On internal caste government, *Data on Caste, Orissa*, 1960, edited by N. K. Bose, came to my notice too late for me to be able to use it.

84b  Blunt, *op. cit*., pp. 104–31, summarized by Hutton, pp. 86–96. M. N. Srinivas has produced several studies: 'A Joint Family Dispute in a Mysore Village' (*Journal of the M.S. University of Baroda*, I, 1952, pp. 7–31); 'A Caste Dispute among Washermen of Mysore' (*Eastern Anthropologist*, VII, No. 3–4, 1954, pp. 149–68); 'The Case of the Potter and the Priest' (*Man in India*, XXXIX, No. 3, 1959, pp. 190–209); these three articles have recently been republished: *The Study of Disputes*, University of Delhi, n.d. (roneo). See also my *Sous-caste*, pp. 284–312 (very detailed; I refer to it only for certain points), and B. S. Cohn, 'Law and Change' (the strict and community-spirited organization of the Chamars). Lewis, *Village Life in North India*, would have much to say ('faction' panchayats, etc.) but unfortunately does not go into details. Other authors afford cursory notes; thus for Udaipur, Carstairs mentions the presence of 'scores of unrelated informal panchayats' (p. 37).

84c As exceptions, Blunt mentions mainly the barbers, who have a proper caste panchayat, and the Rajputs, who have territorial assemblies of members of the same (exogamous) clan. According to Lewis (pp. 135, 144–5), it would seem that the Jats also have clan panchayats; some ambiguity arises from the fact that this is a case of a dominant clan of a whole group of villages.

84d Village, group of villages and *nāḍu* among the Panikkar (Thurston, *Castes and Tribes*, *s.v.*) and the Iluvar (O'Malley, p. 40; Hutton, pp. 87–8).

84e Lewis, *Village Life in North India*, pp. 29–30, *cf.* Marriott, 'Village Structure and the Panjab Government: A Restatement' (*American Anthropologist*, LV, No. 1, 1953), p. 141; O'Malley, p. 40.

84f Blunt, p. 104; O'Malley, p. 43; Lewis: quasi legislative function and (p. 29) permission for holding a festival (no doubt the maximum extent of community discipline).

84g 'On the other hand, caste authority is often a check against abuses which the despotic rulers of the country are too apt to indulge in. Sometimes one may see, as the result of a caste order, the tradesmen and merchants of a whole district closing their shops, the labourers abandoning their fields, or the artisans leaving their workshops, all because of some petty insult or of some petty extortion suffered by some member of their caste; and the aggrieved people will remain obstinately in this state of opposition until the injury has been atoned for and those responsible for it punished' (Dubois, I, trans. Beauchamp, p. 33; *cf.* Gandhi's passive disobedience).

84h The phrase comes from Bailey, *Caste and the Economic Frontier*, p. 195. 'For the majority of Hindus, caste is the sphere within which morality operates. That morality may in some respects seem strange to European thoughts, but there is no question of the real value of caste in inculcating and maintaining principles of self-restraint. It is chiefly caste which checks vice and keeps up the standard of propriety, particularly among the lower castes. Take away the caste honour of the low caste man, and you destroy the basis of his virtues. As pointed out by the abbé Dubois ... the shame which would reflect on a whole caste if the faults of one of its individual members went unpunished guarantees that the caste will execute justice, defend its own honour, and keep all its members within the bounds of duty' (O'Malley, pp. 178–9). Perhaps, 'ethics' would be better than 'morality'.

84i On the oath and ordeal, see *Sous-caste*; Gune, *Judicial System*, etc. The assembly often met near a temple: Srinivas, 'Dispute among Washermen'; Gough, in Marriott, ed., *Village India*; *Sous-caste*.

84j Mayer, 'Local Government Election', *Eastern Anthropologist*, XI, p. 201; Lewis, p. 27; *cf.* Mayer, 'Associations in Fiji Indian Rural Society' (*American Anthropologist*, LVIII, 1956, pp. 97–108). This feature is well known today. It is more a question of tacit than explicit unanimity, of absence of protest, contradiction, or assertions of difference. Thus in Mysore it is said that 'The elders approved of the verdict' (Srinivas, 'Dispute among Washermen', p. 168). The existence of a difference prevents common worship (*Sous-caste*, etc.) and paralyses the panchayat itself: this is the great contemporary grievance. Certainly the overall fact is essential, and is connected with the very nature of these seats of authority and their conciliatory rather than coercive character. *Cf.* Y. V. S. Nath, 'Bhils of Ratanmal', *Economic Weekly*, 4 Dec. 1954, p. 1360: 'What is aimed at is, not so much to fix the blame on one of the parties to the dispute, but to effect a compromise', another point on which all observers are agreed.

84k On the first point, Srinivas, 'Dispute among Washermen'; on the second, *Sous-caste*, pp. 287 ff.

84l The following fact perhaps suggests that there has been some evolution in this respect; the Hindus forcibly converted to Islam by the Moplahs at the time of the 1921 revolt were reintegrated simply by the application of the five products of the cow (O'Malley, p. 84). It is not said whether they had been forced to eat beef.

84m Likewise, *Sous-caste*, p. 310, *cf.* p. 298: this is another instance of the desire for conciliation, on condition that the court's authority is recognized.

84n It can be seen also that the effectiveness of excommunication requires the confiscation of goods: following Molony, O'Malley quotes the case of a rich man who could not even be convicted: he bribed false witnesses to establish his innocence. The guilty party may also move to another place: where the caste has no assembly, a young Brahman can continue to live in a distant village with an untouchable girl, the couple working in the fields (eastern U.P., personal observation).

84o Other cases of social death have much in common with excommunication, itself often symbolized by funeral ceremonies (as among the Nambudiri): for example, the man who renounces the world (see Appendix B, n. 18), and people who, brought dying to the Ganges to die in sanctity, survive after having been immersed in the river and having had water and mud from the river bed put in their mouth. There were colonies of these outcastes in the suburbs of Calcutta. Their loss of status is attributed to their having been thrown back by the goddess Ganges (O'Malley, *Indian Caste Customs*, p. 85). In fact the rite had apparently brought these people into the category of the dead, the socially dead who were having a physical respite, like the renouncer.

84p Not only the guilty party but his close relatives may be excommunicated. This is because the subject or bearer of status is less the individual than the family, and beyond this the whole group. Yet individuals may impair this status by their actions and they must be prevented from so doing. To recall one of Mayer's remarks: the status not only of the fraternity but of the whole caste is defended by the assembly of the fraternity.

84q *Cf.* the very un-Brahmanical nature of justice in a territorially segregated caste (no emphasis on the murder of the cow, etc.: *Sous-caste, loc. cit.*).

84r I have compared the importance of the panchayat among the (Pramalai) Kallar with its non-existence among the (Kondaiyam Kottai) Maravar. Intensive inquiry among the former revealed that the panchayat's authority is connected with religion, and, above all, with royalty (*Sous-caste*, p. 296 and pp. 151–2).

85a Gough, in Marriott, *Village India*, pp. 44–5; Srinivas, *ibid.*, pp. 18–19; Mayer, *Caste*, p. 174, and 'Dominant Caste', pp. 408–9; Lewis, *Village Life in North India*, pp. 135 ff.; Dumont, *loc. cit.*; Carstairs, in Srinivas, *India's Villages*, p. 69; Bailey, *Caste and the Economic Frontier*, pp. 209, 185, 203, 208–9 (distillers); Beals, in Marriott, *Village India*, p. 89.

85b Some good studies and several illustrations of the points mentioned here will be found in Park and Tinker, *Leadership and Political Institutions*. Among the Pramalai Kallar, it was found that the investiture given by the king of Madura to a lineage chief established the authority of this delegated 'king' among his own people, and also the authority of internal justice. Internal authority is here a reflection of the king's authority (*Sous-caste*, pp. 138 ff.).

CHAPTER IX   CONCOMITANTS AND IMPLICATIONS (pages 184–200)

91a Bouglé studied the implications of the system in his *Essais*, especially those to do with the law, economics and literature. The aspects considered here are chosen rather arbitrarily, and are no doubt determined more by our standpoint with regard to the caste system than by the system in itself. This viewpoint was brought to the forefront in *La Civilisation indienne et Nous*, in which I insisted on complementarity, as opposed to the modern notion of the individual. For a concrete psychological account, see G. M. Carstairs's monograph, *The Twice Born*, 1961 (valuable even if questionable).

92a It scarcely needs to be recalled that the opposition between worldly and other-worldly (*weltlich/ausserweltlich*) plays a central role in Max Weber's sociology of religion. Here this distinction has simply been made coextensive with two others: Brahman/renouncer, and caste interdependence/the individual. Appendix B, n. 17.

This comparison between the renouncer and the modern individual may be found surprising; for does not the renouncer aim in one way or another to rid himself of self? But this very endeavour gives the self reality, a reality unprecedented in the world of caste. To quote Nehru once again on these questions: 'The mystic tries to rid himself of self, and in the process usually becomes obsessed with it' (*Toward Freedom*, p. 243, quoted by Cox, *Caste*, p. 39). Was the author thinking of his master Gandhi when he wrote this?

In 'Vinaya et droit laïque', Lingat studied in Siamese law the kind of osmosis between the two worlds produced by the fact that a Buddhist monk's vows are not irrevocable, so that he may return to secular life.

93a Hindu-Jain castes in Gujerat, *cf.* Nesfield, *Brief View*, p. 118; Sangave, *Jaina Community*, pp. 72, 315.

93b On the Sadhs, Gosains, etc., of U.P., *cf.* Blunt, *Caste System*, pp. 132–3. Note that the Gosains have two successive initiations, to the sect and to the state of renouncer. *Cf.* also Crooke, *Tribes and Castes, s.vv.*

93c On the Lingayats, for social organization: Enthoven, in *Encyclopaedia of Religion and Ethics*, *s.v.* (following the Bombay Census Report of 1901; likewise Enthoven, *The Tribes and Castes of Bombay*), and also Thurston, *Castes and Tribes*; for the religious aspect, Bhandarkar, *Vaiṣnavism, Śaivism*, pp. 131–40; Farquhar, *An Outline of the Religious Literature of India*, especially pp.

259–65; Dubois, *Hindu Manners*, I, p. 116, etc. Recent note: McCormack, 'Lingayats as a Sect', 1963 (problem of definition; the remarks about Max Weber need to be modified, *cf. Hinduismus und Buddhismus*, p. 20).

93d This is a simplified view. According to Thurston, p. 251, the first level is segmented into seven, with hypergamy and even some possibility of upward movement by initiation. Roughly speaking our résumé should be regarded as provisional. There is still no good intensive description.

93e Most of the priests are celibate in Dubois, *loc. cit.*; they are married in Bhandarkar, §104.

93f *Cf.* McCormack, pp. 63–4, and Farquhar, p. 262.

93g Bhandarkar, §§102, 105; Farquhar, pp. 261–2, etc.

93h According to the Abbé Dubois, only the notion of the equality of men is peculiar to the Lingayats, whilst the rejection of impurity and transmigration, vegetarianism, and remarriage of widows, are common to other Shaivite groups in the south.

93i This hypothesis is confirmed by reading an unpublished monograph by Miss Parvathamma (*Religion and Politics in a Mysore Village*), which gives a precise description of the ceremonies of the ages of life among the Lingayats. The presence of the Jangama priest is indispensable in all these circumstances. Not only does he give the linga to the newborn at birth, but in the cemetery he must place his foot on the head of the dead person; some statements make it quite clear that he transcends impurity. We shall say that it is abolished by his presence. Rather than say that impurity does not exist, it must be said that it does not exist *for the Lingayats*. In this way this feature, very surprising at first sight, can be understood. In short, the men-in-the-world are permanently freed from impurity in virtue of the truth of the renouncer.

94a On toleration, *cf.* J. F. Staal, 'Ueber die Idee der Toleranz im Hinduismus'; many authors have indicated that the norm is a matter of action, not belief, *cf.* O'Malley, *Indian Caste Customs*, pp. 19–20, Bouglé, p. 170 (ref.).

A quotation from François Bernier, *Voyages*, II, p. 125, will show the contrast of attitudes. Concerning the frequency of ablutions, he recounts as follows his discussions with the pandits (learned Brahmans):

> When I told them that in cold countries it would be impossible to observe their law during the winter, which showed that it was nothing but a pure invention of men, they gave me this rather amusing reply: that they were not claiming that their law was universal, but that God had made it for

them alone, which was why they could not receive a foreigner into their religion; that moreover, they were not in the least claiming that our religion was false, but that it might be good for us and that God might have made several different paths to heaven; but they would not agree that as ours was general for the whole world, theirs could be but fable and pure invention.

(*Cf. La civilisation indienne et nous*, pp. 21, 26.)

94b On Sanskritization: M. N. Srinivas, 'Sanskritization and Westernization', 1956, and again in *Caste in Modern India*, pp. 42–62; criticism: J. F. Staal, 'Sanskrit and Sanskritization', 1963.

94c On imitation: *cf.* Dumont, *La civilisation indienne et nous*, pp. 108–10; *Sous-caste*, p. 416; 'A Remarkable Feature of South-Indian Pot-Making' (*Man*, 1952, No. 121), p. 83. Opler noted that borrowing 'is not always directed towards technical progress' ('Selective Culture Change', pp. 126, 130). On the existence of two models, one Brahmanical and the other royal, both imitated by lower castes, *cf. Contributions*, I, p. 33; above §36; one could speak of Brahmanization and also of Kshatriyaization. S. K. Srivastava has even spoken of the Desanskritization and Kshatriyaization of the Brahmans of the Agra region in the present day ('The Process of Desanskritization'). It has also sometimes been suggested that there were as many models of imitation as varnas (Marriott, 'Interactional and Attributional Theories of Caste Ranking', *Man in India*, XXXIX, No. 2, 1959, pp. 99–101).

A good example of imitation of the dominants is provided by Gandhi in his autobiography (*The Story of my Experiments with Truth*, trans. M. Desai, pp. 32–6, 55–6, 64–7, 76–80) in connection with diet. Born in a family of vegetarian Banyas (Vaishyas), he was first as an adolescent tempted to acquire the strength of the English by eating meat like them, despite his repugnance. At his departure for England, his mother made him promise, against his own preference, not to eat any. But it was not until he discovered an English book on vegetarianism and a circle of English vegetarians, and thus that Europe sanctioned his atavism so to speak, that he definitively adopted vegetarianism. The fact is typical and general: the glory and popularity of Tagore and Vivekananda in India sprang from their being recognized by the West; the *satisfecits* granted by Mrs Besant to the Hindu tradition increased its authority in the eyes of many Indians of European culture.

94d Srinivas, *op. cit.*, pp. 51 ff., 60; Aiyappan, *Iravas*, p. 1. For the Untouchables' efforts to 'sanskritize', see §117.

95a Both Srinivas (see *Contributions*, III, p. 42) and Karvé (*Hindu*

*Society*) seem to assume that a tribe becomes a caste without modification of its values. For an example of ideological adaptation to Hindu dominance whilst exterior independence is maintained, see the case of the Saoras (*Contributions*, III, pp. 61, 66, 74).

95b In a remarkable article, Surajit Sinha describes among other things a precise process of Kshatriyaization or 'Rajputization' of dominant lineages in a tribe (Bhumij). It is remarkable that the Rajput model is in this case dictated by the Brahmans (it is a vegetarian model!). Sinha mentions among other things the imitation of the Rajput model by ordinary Bhumijs (p. 55). ('State Formation and Rajput Myth in Tribal Central India', *Man in India*, XLII, No. 1, 1962, pp. 35–80.)

95c For an allied distinction to that between intrinsic and extrinsic borrowing, that between 'progressive' and 'agglutinative cumulation', *cf*. H. C. Moore, 'Cumulation and Cultural Processes', *American Anthropologist*, LVI, No. 3, 1954, pp. 347–57. In a particularly clear case, the beliefs of a carnivorous group in the south appear as a totality based on the opposition between two kinds of spirits: carnivorous spirits, to this extent like the worshippers themselves, and vegetarian gods, borrowed from superior castes. One half expresses the group, the other its submission to the system and its legitimization in it (*cf*. *Sous-caste*, pp. 370–1). This is quite different from a juxtaposition of Aryan and Dravidian elements (*pace* C. Fürer-Haimendorf, review of the book in *Sociologus*, IX, 1959, pp. 79–83). In the opposition between carnivore and vegetarian, each of the supposed elements is transformed by its combination with the other: carnivorous spirits accede to the rank of gods by being made subordinate, a subordination which modifies their being.

95d On the intellectual movement in the nineteenth century see my contribution, 'The British in India', in *The History of Mankind: Cultural and Scientific Development*, vol. 5, *The Nineteenth Century*, ed. Charles Morazé pt. 4 (New York: Harper Row, 1979), pp. 1084–1144.

A movement like the Brahmo Samaj has indeed the character of a sect, and the Arya Samaj has perhaps gone beyond the sect only in an apparent and ephemeral way.

95e On the probable historical origin of vegetarianism, *cf*. above, §65 and n. 25h.

96a *Cf*. the analyses by Robert Lingat ('Time and the Dharma', *Contributions*, VI, and *Les Sources du Droit*), and, especially for *rites de passage*, that by David Pocock, 'The Anthropology of Time-Reckoning', *Contributions*, VII. I cease to follow this author when he introduces dynamics into the account, and speaks of the 'threat' that certain facts of human experience, like the experience of change, level at the society. This is a resurgence of Radcliffe-Brown's attitude. For him, the permanence of a society constituted a kind of miracle and was always in danger, whilst the modern conception of man as an individual, and hence of society as a mere association, is not considered 'threatened' in traditional society where it in fact has no place.

96b Lingat, *Les Sources du Droit*.

96c The quotation is taken from *La civilisation indienne et nous*, p. 111 (see Appendices B and C, *in fine*). Chapter 2 of the same work is devoted to the question, and Biardeau has written a comment ('l'Inde et l'Histoire'). *Cf.* in English 'The Individual as an Impediment to Sociological Comparison and Indian History' (rather more detailed). In a general fashion the ideological implications of the system in relation to us (idea of 'nature', absence of 'the individual') have been indicated in the work cited. A major implication remains to be studied: the concept of space. The place of territory has been mentioned here, and the appropriation of the land. But there is much more. In particular, a clear dichotomy can be seen between cultivated or inhabited space and wild space, 'forest' or jungle, the village and the hermitage (*āśrama*) in which dwells the man who has left society, the renouncer.

97a This fact is mentioned by Cox, *Caste, Class and Race*, p. 8 (references).

97b In connection with hypergamy (§55) it was mentioned that this pattern enables different statuses to be encompassed within the same subcaste, whilst in the isogamous pattern the emergence of differences would lead to scission.

97c Blunt, *op. cit.*, pp. 51 ff., 236–8; Nesfield, *Brief View*, p. 108; Gait, 'Caste' (*Encyclopaedia of Religion and Ethics*, *s.v.*, III), p. 233a; Karvé, *Hindu Society*, pp. 26 ff., etc. In the 1911 Census Report, groups 'obtaining access' to a caste are called 'subcastes of fusion' (Gait).

CHAPTER X   COMPARISON: ARE THERE CASTES AMONG NON-HINDUS? (pages 201–216)

102a J. Bertrand, S.J., *Nouvelle Mission du Maduré*, p. 93. We have already encountered situations in which power becomes the equal of religion, *within certain limits*. Here the limits are transgressed since the person who in fact holds the *kṣatra* has the customs of an Untouchable and does not recognize the Brahman's superiority. From this there results the psychological tension defined by

Father Bertrand, exactly corresponding to that with respect to the Muslim masters indicated by N. C. Chaudhuri (*cf. La civilisation indienne et nous*, p. 85, n. 38). 'In practice the Muslims and the Christian Europeans being conquerors have not been untouchables' (K. K. Thakkar, in *Journal of Social Work*, XVII, No. 1, June 1956, p. 45). A place must be made between the Europeans and the converts for the very special case of the half-breeds and their descendants, 'Eurasians' or 'Anglo-Indians'. On the latter and their adaptation in independent India, see Grimshaw, 'The Anglo-Indian Community' (*Journal of Asian Studies*, XVIII, 1958, pp. 227–40).

102b There seems to be little information on this question. *Cf. Census of India*, 1911, XV, U.P. Part I, Report (E. A. H. Blunt), especially p. 107, also p. 352 and pp. 144–9, and *idem.*, 1931, pp. 547–8. According to R. S. Wilson, *Indirect Effects of Christian Missions*, 1928, converts ceased to be untouchable, in theory if not in practice, thanks to the presence of the European missionary (pp. 21–3). Some precisely dated information for the Andhra country is in Fishman's *Culture Change*, 1941, pp. 140, 146. The situation mentioned by Hutton, *Caste*, p. 147 (non-Hindus treated as superior to the Untouchables in some Hindu temples) is reversed where the Untouchables have been given the right to enter the temples, from which Europeans are excluded: Gandhi's Neo-Hinduism has given the definition of Hinduism a political twist, and has virtually created a category for non-Hindus inferior to that of the Untouchables.

102c In this way, the conversion of Untouchables certainly excited claims for social rights, not only by converts but by their cognates and neighbours who remained Hindus. One thinks for example of the Nadars in the south of the Tamil country, among whom the Protestants were very active in the nineteenth century (see Thurston, *Castes and Tribes*, *s.v.*, Shanar) and of their equivalents in Kerala, the Iravas or Tiyars (Aiyappan, *Iravas*, pp. 151 ff.). This effect was combined with the general impact of democratic ideas and Hindu reform, *cf.* my 'The British in India', *op. cit.* (see note 95d). Conversion was often accompanied by 'modernization' (education, modern profession, spatial mobility) and it may be wondered whether it was not through the latter that conversion sometimes brought about a rise on the social ladder, mainly in a Christian environment, by assimilation to a higher category.

102d On the history of the Syrian Christians, see *Encyclopaedia of Religion and Ethics*, *s.v.*, Syrian (Christians) (McLean); on their organization and on the Christians in Kerala in general, L. K.

Anantakrishna Ayyar, *Anthropology of the Syrian Christians*, p. 60 (the Syrians are also divided into Southerners, superior, and Northerners, inferior, with no intermarriage), pp. 215, 258–9.

102e We cannot here summarize the history of these missions nor the affair of the 'Malabar rites' occasioned by the daring policy, inaugurated by de Nobili, of adapting to local customs. For the 'quarrel of rites' in general (China) reference should be made to: S. Delacroix (Mgr), *Histoire Universelle des Missions catholiques*, 4 vols., Paris, 1956–9, II, and for India to the article 'Malabares (rites)' by Mgr Amman, in the *Dictionnaire de Théologie Catholique*, IX, 2, 1927, pp. 1704–46. The Madura Mission was Jesuit, except between 1774 and 1836; for the first period *cf.* J. Bertrand, S.J., *La Mission du Maduré*, 4 vols., Paris, 1847–54, which will be our main source. The famous *Lettres édifiantes et curieuses* contains letters from French Jesuit Missions set up at the end of the seventeenth century. Once the Jesuits were abolished, the 'Missions Étrangères' moved in: A. Launay, *Histoire des Missions de l'Inde (Pondichéry, Maïssour, Coïmbatour)*, Paris, 1898, 5 vols. The Jesuits returned to Madura in 1836: Bertrand, *Lettres ... de la Nouvelle Mission du Maduré*, two vols., Paris–Lyon, 1865.

102f We alluded at the beginning (Chapter I, §14) to the theory of the social rather than religious nature of caste customs by which de Nobili justified his adoption of certain customs. De Nobili reasoned strictly from his implicit premiss that the religious element among the Hindus is to be defined by analogy with the Christian religion. In particular, religion is concerned with spiritual beings and is a matter of the individual, hence of the sect and not of the caste, *cf.* in Bertrand, II, pp. 151 ff., the extracts from de Nobili's self-justifying memorandum.

102g This terminology carries with it certain difficulties. First of all, de Nobili gave himself out to be not a Brahman but a noble (a Kshatriya by analogy) who had renounced the world (sannyasi). He wore a special belt, analogous to those of the twice-born; he seems to have discovered only later that sannyasis, in most sects, do not wear one, and he then gave it up (Bertrand, II, pp. 3, 20, 102 and especially 110, *cf.* p. 164). Further, *paṇḍāram* (a Tamil word) may be contrasted with sannyasi as a renouncer of lowly origin to a renouncer of exalted or Brahman origin. The difficulty is that the renouncer does not officiate as a priest, he only teaches and instructs. The word *paṇḍāram* also refers to priests, and is then contrasted with Brahman. The missionary is as it were both renouncer and priest, and this is doubtless the reason for the vacillation between the words 'brame' and 'sannyasi' (the first seems to predominate, *cf.* Bertrand, II, pp. 25 n., 236, 284, 394, etc.; see Thurston, *Castes and Tribes, s.v.,* Pandaram).

102h Bertrand, II, pp. 394, 324; III, 190.

102i 'Plan d'une église avec son presbytère, dans l'ancienne mission du Maduré, présenté au Souverain Pontife en 1725 par le Père Brandolin', Bertrand, IV, pp. 434–5 and *id., Mémoires historiques,* pp. 460–1.

102j Pope Gregory XV, while on the whole deciding in favour of de Nobili in his Bull of 1624, added: 'We conjure those who take pride in their nobleness ... to in no way despise, especially in the churches ... persons of low or obscure condition ... (etc.)' (Amman, *loc. cit.,* col. 1715). For the sequel, *cf.* Amman, ccl. 1738, and A. Launay, *Histoire des Missions de l'Inde,* I, pp. 98–101, and II, pp. 290–1 (Christians complain to Rome after the Synod of Pondicherry, 1844). Nearer our own times, Suau, *L'Inde tamoule,* 1907, p. 73 (photo of a church with two diverging naves), Hutton, *Caste,* p. 106. In 1883, the Congregation of the Propagation of the Faith declared separation in the churches to be an abuse whose disappearance it desired, but which it tolerated 'to avoid greater evils'.

102k Bertrand, IV, pp. 437 ff. *Cf.* Amman, *loc. cit.,* for the Decree of the Legate of 1704 and the sequel to the Quarrel of Malabar Rites up to the Bull of Benedict XIV, *Omnium Sollicitudinum,* of 1744.

102l On the mixture of customs among the Christians there is now available a valuable study by Carl G. Diehl of the Lutherans in the south (*Church and Shrine,* Uppsala, 1965). On the hierarchical division into endogamous groups among the Jews who say they have been established on the West coast for two millennia, see Strizower, 'Jews as an Indian Caste', *Jewish Journal of Sociology,* 1959, pp. 43–57; *cf.* Mandelbaum, 'The Jewish Way of Life in Cochin', *Jewish Social Studies,* 1959, pp. 423–60.

103a The following is condensed from Appendix D, 'Nationalism and Communalism'.

103b For example, during the Mutiny of 1857, the Emperor took care that the Muslims did not sacrifice cows for the feast of Id-ul-Zuha (Spear, *Twilight of the Mughuls,* 1951, pp. 195–6, 207).

103c See Appendix D, n. 9 and corresponding text.

103d Concerning Muslims in a Mysore Village, Srinivas (*Village India,* p. 22) writes: 'their membership in another religion raises excessive uncertainties as to their hierarchical position'; he does not include them in his hierarchical order of castes.

103e Uttar Pradesh: *cf.* Nesfield, *Brief View,* pp. 122 ff., and especially Blunt, *op. cit.,* Chapter 10, and Ghaus Ansari, *Muslim Caste in*

*Uttar Pradesh*, 1960; details in Vreede-de-Stuers, 'Le mariage chez les . . . Ashraf', *Orient*, p. 25. The categories are not equivalent in Bengal, *cf*. A. F. A. Husain, 'Pakistan', in Lambert and Hoselitz, *Le Rôle de l'épargne*, p. 305; Gait in *Census*, 1911, Bengal, Report, pp. 238–49; Nazmul Karim, *Changing Society in India and Pakistan*, 1956, pp. 120 ff.

104a Frederik Barth, 'The System of Social Stratification in Swat, North Pakistan' in Leach, ed., *Aspects of Caste*, pp. 113–46; *cf*. the editor's Introduction, especially pp. 4–5. It is possible here to give only a summary of the detailed critique which this remarkable work requires, and which we have carried out in class. See note 104c for some complements.

104b The separation between sociological analysis and cultural history is due to Radcliffe-Brown, but he would probably not have subscribed to the postulate isolated here, for he gave the stability of a social system as a condition for the analysis he recommended (*Structure and Function in Primitive Society*, 1952, pp. 192–3).

It goes without saying that we are not here introducing into our account Radcliffe-Brown's idea of structure, still less that of function, which has been amply criticized. In connection with our present concerns, it will be remembered that some authors have insisted on the existence of 'dysfunctions'.

104c Like us, Barth tried to reduce hierarchical distinctions to a number of criteria, each producing a dichotomy of the social body (p. 141: 'The relative hierarchical positions . . .'). His picture of hierarchy (p. 138) may give the impression that the distinction of purity *encompasses* the others here as elsewhere. In reality this picture requires correction, for the analogy which it suggests between the position of the 'Saints' and that of the Brahmans is without foundation. There is no fundamental distinction between *status* and *power*, the 'priests' are inferior to the dominants; the religious nature of the 'Saints' is expressed in the guise of dominance, whilst among Hindus the dominance of the Kshatriya is forced to find expression in a religious guise. The fundamental opposition is not that of purity, but that between 'patrons' and 'clients' (dominants and dominated). *Within the dominant group* there is a *secondary* distinction between 'Saints' and Pakhtuns. Only in the inferior part of the system (and among the 'clients') does the Hindu distinction of purity operate (superior artisans, inferior artisans, impure specialists): the Hindu system is here *beheaded*, subordinated to a different system.

105a More exactly, one must distinguish between the ideology which we must assume theoretically (in relation to general observation) in order to extract an intelligible model, and that which is actually encountered in specific circumstances: it is not claimed that the total theoretical model is always actually present everywhere. It is not merely a matter of the 'survival' of an institution which has lost its characteristic function or lost the function which brought it into existence; rather, more generally, it is probable that our grasp of the interconnections between social phenomena is still quite inadequate for everything which is not explicitly present to the minds of the people studied.

107a *Cf.* Appendix, 'Caste, Racism and "Stratification"'. It is sometimes said nowadays that anyone may define his terms as he pleases for a specific purpose. Then the tendency in question will be praised for having brought out what is common to caste and racism. But science was not needed for this: modern common sense knew it all along, and sociologists have only afforded a justification. In this matter, science begins once common sense is left behind and the problem raised of the comparison between traditional and modern society. There are good and bad definitions.

Questionable as the expression 'social stratification' is, not all the authors who use it share the tendency criticized. Thus we have quoted a passage from a work by Talcott Parsons who uses the phase but genuinely recognizes hierarchy (p. 19).

107b Many terms have acquired such an 'extension' that their loss in 'comprehension' has discredited them (thus 'totem', 'taboo' and nowadays 'structure'). The terminological alternatives in the case of the word 'caste' contrast two attitudes, call them classifying and typifying. The first relies essentially on dividing social reality in terms of partial viewpoints, often promoted to the rank of 'system' ('political system', etc.), the second on the internal consistency of the overall social fact. The first pays scant attention to extremes, limiting cases, and actual situations in their entirety, in order to construct classes of phenomena. The second on the contrary applies itself to the radical exploitation by monographs of the most systematic and highly developed forms, with the aim of bringing to light each time at least one fundamental aspect of social reality. The first pays scant attention to the facts of consciousness and proceeds after the fashion of the natural sciences. The second tries to introduce scientific rigour to the comprehension of human wholes, each of which is universal yet unique. It moves in the region indicated by many a concept of Mauss, Weber and even Durkheim (total social fact and privileged case, ideal type, merits of the crucial experiment).

108a *Cf.* Bailey, 'Closed Social Stratification in India', *European Journal of Sociology*, 1963, p. 109. Nadel thought he had found more or less developed castes in various regions of Africa: 'Caste and Government in Primitive Society', *Journal of the Anthropological Society of Bombay*, VIII, 8, 1954, pp. 9–22.

108b *Cf.* Robert Lingat, 'L'Influence juridique de l'Inde au Champa et au Cambodge d'après l'épigraphie', *Journal Asiatique*, 1949, pp. 237–2.

108c W. H. Gilbert, 'The Sinhalese Caste System', *Ceylon Historical Journal*, II, 3–4, 1953; Brice Ryan, *Caste in Modern Ceylon*, 1953; Ralph Pieiris, *Sinhalese Social Organization*, 1956.

108d All this naturally in no way diminishes the interest of Sinhalese society, the topic of vast historical literature and, following Hocart, of remarkable contemporary studies (Leach, Tambiah, Yalman). It will be objected that it is convenient to speak of castes in Ceylon, and difficult to do otherwise. But it will doubtless be agreed that difficulties of terminology should not hinder the recognition of fundamental sociological facts.

CHAPTER XI    COMPARISON: THE CONTEMPORARY TREND
(pages 217–238)

111a This question has been touched on in: 'The British in India' *op. cit.* (see note 95d); *La civilisation indienne et nous*, Chapter 3; *Contributions to Indian Sociology*, VII, 1964, p. 13 and pp. 33 ff. Apart from the works quoted below, the following, among others, make profitable reading, and give an idea of the general problem: K.P. Chattopadhyay, ed., *The Study of Changes in Traditional Culture*; *idem.*, *Some Approaches* ...; T. S. Epstein, *Economic Development and Social Change in South India*; N. Karim, *Changing Society* ...; McKim Marriott, 'Technological Change', 'Social Change', *cf. India's Villages*, pp. 96 ff.; M. Orans, 'A Tribal People in an Industrial Setting'; M. S. A. Rao, *Social Change in Malabar*; D. Thorner, 'The Village Panchayat as a Vehicle of Change'; E. Shils, *The Indian Intellectuals*.

111b Quite recently Ramkrishna Mukherjee wondered why two centuries of British domination in India, which 'had cast the death-knell to the previous system of her economy and social life, could not demolish the caste system' (p. 60). The reader is in a position to explain this disappointment: the changes have been confined to the politico-economic 'pocket', as it were, which, as we have described, is both insulated from and contained within the system of values: where one would postulate a direct link as in our own society, there is really complementarity, enabling the system to tolerate novelties, and protecting its essence from them.

111c (Personal observation.) Contrast between the nineteenth-century jewellery in the Lucknow Museum and the contemporary jewellery from the same region (Gorakhpur district).

112a  Ghurye, *Caste and Race*, 1932; *Caste and Class*, 1952, Chapters 7 and 8 (references are to the latter work).

112b  These points have often been recognized. Thus for profession, for example, E. K. Gough, *Aspects*, pp. 32–3 : in Kerala caste has become 'a limiting rather than a determining factor in the choice of occupation' (no one has adopted a profession traditionally associated with an inferior caste). The relaxation of rules about food by contrast to those of endogamy is a commonplace. Ghurye (pp. 202–3) reports a revealing occurrence: reformers are inclined to expect a great deal from the University, which creates an environment in which educated men and women can react against preoccupation with caste. But in Bombay,

> one fairly large caste which is highly educated, whose members are very well placed in life and generally progressive, has been quick enough to sense the danger. . . . Five or six years ago it started a social centre for its youth . . . in short, where young people of both sexes, who are members of the caste, can join in pleasurable activity and form acquaintanceships and friendships which ripen into marriages. . . .

112c  On the association called *sabhā* or *samiti*, 'assembly', *cf.* the *Census of India*, 1911, in the special study on caste government. The authors for Uttar Pradesh and Bengal respectively have subsequently summarized the question, Blunt in *Caste System* (p. 130) and O'Malley in *Indian Caste Customs* (pp. 174–5) (and in *Modern India*, p. 161): they are annual conferences organized like Western associations. The Ahirs publish a monthly journal for the whole of Northern India. The object of these associations is to improve the caste's 'position'; their main concerns are education and social reforms of modern inspiration, like raising the age of marriage, contrary to imitation of high castes. The *Census of India*, 1931, U.P. (*Report*, pp. 544 ff.) notes the developments between 1911 and 1931. See the article by Rudolph and Rudolph, 'Political Role of India's Caste Associations', *Pacific Affairs*, XXXIII, 1960, pp. 5–22, which contains a monograph on the Vanniya caste of the Madras region. *Cf.* Bailey, 'Closed Social Stratification in India' (*European Journal of Sociology*, IV, No. 1, 1963, p. 122), and *Politics and Social Change, Orissa in 1959*, 1963, p. 130 (Orissa oil-pressers).

112d  In this summary I have left on one side the contradictory effects of British policy (pp. 161–72). On the one hand, the British stamped out inequality before the law (except in connection with the temples and with untouchability in general, which was done by Gandhi and the 1951 Constitution), and they also weakened caste by relieving it of its judicial powers (a point which is currently admitted, even if exaggerated). On the other hand Ghurye reproaches the British for having indirectly consolidated caste by the attention they gave it in the decennial census, especially by Risley's effort in 1901 to find an order of precedence for each Province. This measure, dictated by misplaced intellectual curiosity, may have set in motion the status claims and been the origin of the caste associations. In fact the author fails to mention that the British took care not to touch the religious aspect of caste and confined themselves to introducing the minimum of equality which seemed to them indispensable in the field of law and politics. Our analysis shows that this calculation was correct, and it is doubtful whether the equality in question really weakened or threatened caste. It is quite other in the case of the religious measure (giving Untouchables the right to enter the temples) introduced at Gandhi's behest, as we shall see.

Ghurye presents as his conclusion an unhappy comparison between the present and the past, the latter, conjectural and highly idealized, being characterized by the 'village community'. The present situation is taken from a good description which does not establish the fact of change but only the disappointment of the author in finding fact different from fiction. At the end of this comparison, Ghurye concludes that the (mythical) 'village community' was replaced by caste solidarity (p. 193).

112e Most of the changes noted by Ghurye tend in the same direction. The weakening of hierarchy and impurity, and the relaxation of behaviour about food in towns, indicate the decadence of the religious aspect on which the system was founded. The contrast between commensality (relaxed) and connubium (still rigid at the level of the caste, if not the subcaste) may seem to justify those who have considered the second more important than the first, but it is only a question of the modern mentality. The liberties of connubium between different subcastes should be compared to the mixing between different subcastes in the same area following the disintegration of the old territorial units: the change is more to do with territory than with the caste aspect proper. One must also take into account the context of the changes to do with food: in the house, the rules are strict, as in the case of marriage: here as in other cases, more liberal behaviour exists side by side with orthodox behaviour in the lives of the people concerned. All this suggests, finally, that what used to be a caste *system* with a religious basis is tending to become a collection of closed groupings corresponding to modern ideas of social stratification.

112f When Gandhi was assassinated by a Brahman extremist, there was an 'anti-Brahman' reaction among the Marathas which Ghurye deplores as a fanatical caste act. Now, if retaliation can be considered as fanaticism (though was not Ghandhi's assassin the main fanatic?), if it is probable that anti-Brahmanical feelings were expressed in this reaction, then what exactly is the place of caste in the affair? More exactly, was it a manifestation of progress or of reaction? The identification of the Brahmans of Maharashtra, victims of reprisals, with Gandhi's murderer, obviously springs from caste spirit, but it was not absolutely unjustified in this society. Yet the fact that an inferior caste should dare to rise and punish its superiors *par excellence*, deemed guilty, is rather a proof of emancipation, a phenomenon of progress. It would be an illusion to suppose that the castes could be abolished without bringing any affliction on the Brahmans. It is inevitable that they should suffer, perhaps unjustly, in the transformation Gandhi professed to desire, simply because they are at the summit of the hierarchy to be abolished.

112g *Cf.* below n. 114d.

113a A. R. Desai's only addition to Ghurye is a superficial optimistic judgment (*Social Background*, pp. 235–6). I. P. Desai and Y. B. Damle, 'A Note on Change in the Caste', *Ghurye Felicitation Volume*, pp. 268 ff.; K. M. Kapadia, 'Caste in Transition', *Sociological Bulletin*, XI, 1962, pp. 77, 86 ff. Fishman noted (*Culture Change and the Underprivileged*, pp. 147–8) in connection with certain spectacular cases: 'These instances, seen in their true light, then, are cases of only temporary relaxation of caste rules under stress of special circumstances of social coercion rather than instances of permanent weakening of caste prejudice . . .'. On the opinion surveys among students, *cf.* Kapadia, *loc. cit.*; B. V. Shah, *Social Change and College Students of Gujarat*, Baroda, M.S. University, 1964.

113b The case was quite different in for example Bengal at the beginning of the nineteenth century. The attitude was completely reversed, and this explains how an author like N. C. Chaudhuri, brought up on Bengal renaissance sources, can denounce the fall in intellectual level which, according to him, has accompanied the victorious reassertion of traditional values since Gandhi's time (*Autobiography*, *passim.*): the Indian intelligentsia has to some extent shut itself in on itself.

113c K. Chandrashekharaiyah, in *Sociological Bulletin*, IX, 1962, p. 63.

113d Sachin Chaudhuri in R. Turner, ed., *India's Urban Future*, p. 225;

Desai and Damle, *loc. cit.*; R. D. Lambert, 'The Impact of Urban Society upon Village Life', in Turner, pp. 117–40, but *cf.* Ellefsen, 'City-Hinterland Relationships', *ibid.*, pp. 94–116, and, as an example of changes induced in a village by the proximity of a large town (Bombay), N. G. Chapekar, 'Social Change', *Ghurye Felicitation Volume*, pp. 169–82; R. D. Lambert, *Workers, Factories and Social Change in Poona*, Princeton, 1963; *cf.* Pundalik and Patwardhan, in *Sociological Bulletin*, XI, 1962, pp. 68–72 (attitude of castes after the floods in Poona), V. A. Sangave, 'Caste Organization in Kolhapur', *Sociological Bulletin*, XI, 1962; for a critical bibliography on urbanization in India and its characteristics, see B. F. Hoselitz in R. Turner, *op. cit.*, pp. 425–43 and pp. 157–91.

114a M. N. Srinivas: *India's Villages*, Introduction (1954); 'Caste in Modern India' (1957); *cf.* the book of the same title, pp. 15–41; *Report of the Seminar on Casteism* (1955), p. 136. Other authors have expressed analogous views *en passant*. Thus according to Aiyappan (*Sociological Bulletin*, IV, No. 2, p. 179) caste is reinforced in new directions (politics); B. Kuppuswamy (*Journal of Psychology*, XLII, 1956, p. 172): 'Common observation reveals that caste consciousness has increased rather than decreased with education.'

114b According to Miller ('Caste and Territory in Malabar', *American Anthropologist*, LVI, No. 3, 1954, pp. 410–20), the dominant caste has probably always had more extensive external relations than its inferiors. The fact of extending these further would not modify the situation in the village. Srinivas is somewhat uncertain about the relations between the village and the outside world in former times. In *India's Villages*, he admits that the 'village community', as completely independent of environment, is a 'myth' (pp. 9–11); yet in his own article in this collection he adopts Metcalfe's famous statement on the subject (p. 23). In his book *Caste and the Economic Frontier*, 1957, F. G. Bailey is exclusively concerned to discover the impact of the mercantile economy and political administration on a rather particular village. Although there may be some reservations about the method, postulates and extrapolations in his book, it is reasonable to subscribe to the following conclusions. Three categories became rich: the local group of the caste of distillers invested its acquired wealth in land and bettered its hierarchical position (perhaps less than the author would like); merchants from outside (the 'distillers of Ganjam') also bought land, but to a large extent they remained outside the local collectivity; finally, the main caste of Untouchables, thanks to the privileges in recruitment to public employment granted by the Government, managed to acquire a significant amount of land, but their efforts to improve their status came up against the 'untouchability barrier': their superiors retorted by depriving them of their ritual prerogatives, in short the village rejected them as much as it could within the general official system (p. 224: 'They are moving out of the social structure of the village'). Finally, one can recognize here the same tendency to pass from structure to substance that we have already noticed while following Ghurye.

114c Under the label 'tensions', UNESCO had a study made, at the request of the Indian government in about 1953, of some antagonisms, especially those between Hindus and Muslims, but also between Brahmans and non-Brahmans in the south. See especially Gardner Murphy, *In the Minds of Men*. See also the following studies and opinion surveys: R. K. Mukerji, *Inter-Caste Tensions*, 1951; K. Prasad, *Social Integration Research, a Study in Intercaste Relationships*, 1954; B. Kuppuswamy, 'Attitudes to the Caste System', 1956; Vakil and Cabinetmaker, *Government and the Displaced Persons*, 1956; Vakil and Mehta, *Government and the Governed*, 1956; B. S. Guha, ed., *Studies . . . among the Refugees*, 1959.

114d N. K. Bose, in Singer, ed., *Traditional India*, pp. 191–206. Srinivas' attitude to the so-called 'non-Brahman' movement in the former Madras State (Justice Party, Dravidian Association) is reminiscent not just of Ghurye and other authors, but also of the attitude of the liberals of the Congress Party, the 'anti-communalist' attitude of Motilal Nehru, who for example refused the Muslim minority distinct representation in the name of the abstract principles of liberal democracy (cf. *Coll. Pap.*, No. 5 (forthcoming); cf. in a similar vein, Rudolph and Rudolph, 'Political Role', p. 10). For such intellectuals, the recognition of existing antagonisms is not a precondition of emancipation, and the liberal attitude seems on analysis apt to give expression to caste while ignoring it. The anti-Brahman movement is no doubt a caste movement in the broad sense, but one must nevertheless distinguish between a movement's form or mode of expression and its content (as intention and as result): is it directed against the caste system or does it work in its favour? A movement which resulted in sapping the prestige of the Brahmans and depriving them of their actual quasi-monopoly in administration (in Madras State today) represents a weakening of the system, as Ghurye recognized at least in one passage. The role of caste in elections, and in politics in general, while also contrary to the Western model, is at the same time natural and inevitable in the present period (Rudolph, *op. cit.*). Moreover, as compared with the traditional system – if one is willing to abandon the myth of the village community – it represents a development, doubtless a quite remarkable one, rather than a genuine innovation.

114e David F. Pocock, 'Difference in East Africa', *Southwest Journal of Anthropology*, XIII, No. 4, 1957, pp. 289–300; *cf.* recently O. M. Lynch in Balaratnam, ed., *Anthropology on the March*, pp. 198–9 (no caste *system* in the towns). Here the structuralist has the satisfaction of being able to refer to Aristotle:

> Now things are always defined by their function and poten-tiality; so when they are no longer in a state to execute their work, they must not be said to be the same things, but only to have the same name . . . if the whole body is destroyed there would be no foot or hand save by mere homonymy. (*Politics*, 1253a.)

(This translation is made from the French translation of Aristotle by Tricot, which Dumont quotes. The standard English trans-lation of the *Politics* is by Jowett in Ross's edition of *The Works of Aristotle.*—TR.)

115a Leach, ed., *Aspects of Caste*, pp. 6–7; Bailey, 'Closed Social Stratification in India'. D. Mackenzie Brown has clearly isolated competition 'in marked contrast to Indian ideas involving non-competitive castes which recognize a single source of political power and virtue' (Park and Tinker, *Leadership*, p. 13).

115b Srinivas, *India's Villages*, 1955, p. 6: 'strong rivalries which exist between the members of a non-agricultural or servicing caste'; 'this monopoly both unites as well as divides the people enjoying the monopoly'. There was indeed competition between members of different castes in non-specialist situations, for example when it was a question of obtaining a plot to work or agricultural employment from a master of the land, and there was also competition for status between different castes.

116a This is accompanied on occasion by exaggerations and attitudes which show that the imported idea is still quite artificial. Thus the purism of the intellectuals which has been criticized. Here is quite another fact. The delivery of the sugar cane crop to a refinery in the Gangetic plain is regulated by the producers' co-operative in conformity with the strictest equity. Such an organization is useful, for it is to the advantage of the cultivator to deliver early, whereas deliveries have to be spread over several months. The village receives the delivery orders, which are dis-tributed in rotation throughout three categories simultaneously and proportionately (large, middling and small producers). There is an arrangement whereby a person faced with exceptional expenses (marriage, etc.) may be allowed an exceptional delivery. The distribution is regularly recorded in a register containing all the cultivators in each category in alphabetical order, without any fraud. In spite of everything, all the people concerned gather together at six in the morning, even on days when they know the village has received no delivery orders, and engage in lengthy complaints and discussions. Even if one takes into consideration illiteracy, which prevents some of them from checking the records, and the fact that the register is kept by the former Zamindar who has his own interests as a large supplier, the fact remains that the villagers do not adapt to the system because they do not really believe in it: they still think that incessant importunings and more or less skillful pressures will affect the distribution. Hence the recourse to complicated and burdensome rules of equity, which in turn make the working of the co-operative impracticable, and effectively open the door to malpractices (personal inquiry).

116b Dr Béteille of Delhi University has replied to Bailey in correspondence and defended, on the whole, Srinivas' position (*European Journal of Sociology*, 1964, I, pp. 130–4). He is right to remind Bailey of the segmentary nature of the system of groups. Béteille implies that there is no essential difference between the interior and the exterior of a group of the nature of the caste, and he in effect reintroduces the structural view of the traditional caste, but neglects precisely the fact that the structural aspect has diminished in modern times. On close inspection, the two authors are the victims of an inadequate conception of the place of territory in such a system: Bailey in that he shifts the notion of segmentation from the conceptual plane to the material-territorial plane, Béteille in that, following Srinivas, he wrongly equates the spatial extension of a set of castes with structural interdependence as if they were two species of the one genus 'solidarity'.

117a *Cf.* for an important aspect of the Constitution, A. Alexandrovicz, 'La liberté religieuse dans la Constitution de l'Inde', *Revue internationale de Droit comparé*, 1964, pp. 319–30. To quote an exceptional but characteristic judgment, the Supreme Court, against the counsel of its president, 'considered the prohibition on excommunication as an unjustifiable intervention in the autonomy of religious institutions guaranteed by article 26' of the Constitution (p. 8).

In order to facilitate the progress of backward strata, a partial preference in their favour has been shown in recruitment to public service and even to colleges. Ghurye, except with respect to the Untouchables, A. R. Desai, and K. M. Kapadia (*Sociological Bulletin*, XI, 1962, p. 87) all condemn this procedure as promoting caste spirit. (It is also often said that it leads to a lowering of the level of recruitment.) But in default of this corrective measure all civil service posts would be in the hands of the high castes, a situation which would do much more to promote caste spirit.

117b Apart from the general economic loss resulting from this procedure, the Untouchables' resolution no longer to dispose of dead animals or work their hides necessarily miscarried most of the time. The suggestion came from Arya Samaj only in the north; there is ample anthropological literature on this point. *Cf.* after Blunt, pp. 334 ff., Srinivas, 'The Dominant Caste', p. 3; Cohn, 'The Changing Status of a Depressed Caste', etc.

117c Srinivas, *Caste in Modern India*, 1962 (ref.); Park and Tinker, *Leadership and Political Institutions*; Myron Weiner, 'Changing Patterns', *Pacific Affairs*, XXXII, No. 3, 1959, pp. 277–87; Bailey, *Politics and Social Change*, 'Traditional Society and Representation' (*European Journal of Sociology*, I, 1960, pp. 121–41), and 'Politics in Orissa', *Economic Weekly*, Aug.–Nov. 1959.

117d For example, in the case of the temple of Alagar, a centre of pilgrimage frequented by peasants and situated near Madura, people of low and even middle castes habitually sacrificed goats near the outer door of the temple proper, the door they have peopled with 'black gods' (the Karuppu of the eighteen steps, etc.). In 1949, after the introduction of the new law, I observed sacrifices carried out in a slaughterhouse put up nearby, the head of the animal being as usual the perquisite of the temple administration, which made money from it. The reason that the act forbidding all sacrifices in general was passed is simply that, as the representatives of the eaters of meat did not *dare* protest, there was little opposition.

118a One could include the antithesis between *homo major* and *homo minor* in a circular diagram: in the centre of 2 one would put the individual, and around him the appropriate implications. But then, in conformity with what has been learnt, we would have in diagram 1, *homo major*, to place the essentials at the periphery (that which encompasses: whole, hierarchy). The two diagrams would thus have to be read in opposite directions, one from the centre towards the periphery, the other from the peripery towards the centre. It is more convenient to arrange the diagram so that corresponding features occupy corresponding positions.

118b In what follows, I shall refrain from insisting on the strict relation between the procedure employed and the preceding analysis.

Here for example the procedure refers to everything that has been said about the hierarchical opposition both in the varnas and in the castes, about the working of the criteria, etc.

118c In general, the position of the horizontal axis or 'threshold' is arbitrary or relative. It can be placed higher or lower according to the aim, situation or domain in view. Here it has been placed at the highest, but one might choose to introduce the politico-economic domain into $S$, in a subordinate position, in order to bring forth in $a$ the other implications mentioned.

118d The postulate for comparison used here can be expressed as follows: all societies contain the same 'elements', 'features' or 'factors', it being understood that these 'elements' can in each case be located either in $S$ or in $a$ and are profoundly altered by their position. This last condition naturally removes all 'reality' from the 'elements' and on this condition $\Sigma S + \Sigma a =$ Constant. This amounts in practice to saying that in any society there will always be found that which corresponds in a residual way (in $a$) to what another society differentiates, articulates and valorizes (in $S$).

118e An attempt at defining comparatively the nation will be found in Appendix D.

118f See Appendix B, Section 5. There are no doubt traces of the individual elsewhere (place of the woman in marriage and the family according to the Dharmashastras). One must also think of the substantialist logic of the texts (Appendix B, Section 1 and note 14). Heesterman traces the tendency back to an early period ('Brahmin, Ritual and Renouncer', *Wiener Zeitschrift für die Kunde Süd- und Ostasiens*, 8, 1964, pp. 1–31).

118g The preceding consideration, with its mnemonic diagram, may be contrasted with the often alleged impossibility of studying society overall without recourse to an arbitrarily defined viewpoint (e.g., Berreman, *Contributions*, VI, p. 125). We have not laid Indian society on the Procrustean bed of 'social stratification', or of 'social control', or of a political or economic system which exists as such only in the mind of the analyst and for the needs of premature classification. It is true that considerations are always relative to a special viewpoint, even if reference to the whole is maintained. Yet the fundamental opposition, between holism and individualism, is in this case, at least from our viewpoint, an overall one. Does the horizontal axis or 'threshold' occupy a special position in the diagram? The answer is no in the case of India, where it represents the main and primary distinction that is to be made; yes in the case of the West, to the extent that it is determined by the particular comparison.

119a 'The Modern Conception of the Individual, Notes on its Genesis and that of Concomitant Institutions', *Contributions*, VIII, 1965.

POSTFACE (pages 239–245)

1  I shall use a recent article from *L'Homme* 18, Nos. 3–4 (July–December 1978), cited hereafter as 'L'Homme' [English translation in Social Science Information 18, No. 6 (1979)], and I shall refer for some details to an earlier text, 'On Putative Hierarchy and Some Allergies to It,' *Contributions to Indian Sociology* n.s. 5 (December 1971), cited hereafter as 'CIS 1971'.

2  Raymond Apthorpe, 'Social Change: An Empirical and Theoretical Study' (PhD. diss., Oxford University, 1956). According to a communication from the author, a brief presentation has appeared in 'Nsenga Social Ideas', *Mawazo, Journal of Makerere University*, Kampala 1, No. 1, June 1967; errata in No. 2, December 1967.

APPENDIX A (pages 247–266)

1  Raymond Aron, 'Science et conscience de la société', *European Journal of Sociology*, I, 1, 1960, p. 29.

2  The tendency, which its only systematic opponent, O. C. Cox, has called 'the Caste School of Race Relations', seems to have won the day. Another, more moderate, tendency consists in applying the word 'caste' to U.S.A. in a monographic manner, without comparative prejudice (Myrdal, etc., see below). The dictionaries give, besides the proper sense of the word, the extended meaning, e.g., *Shorter Oxford English Dictionary*, *s.v.*: '3. *fig.* A class who keep themselves socially distinct, or inherit exclusive privileges 1807.' [The French text has here a reference to Littré instead of O.S.D.]

3  Yet, among recent authors who are familiar with the Indian system, a sociologist working in Ceylon insists on the fundamental difference between India and U.S. (Bryce Ryan, *Caste in Modern Ceylon*, New Brunswick, N.J., 1953, p. 18, note), while F. G. Bailey asserts *a priori* that this comparison must take place under the word 'caste' (*Contributions*, III, p. 90). Morris Carstairs is less categorical, but he accepts, with Kroeber's definition (below), the American usage, because of its advantages as compared with 'race' (*The Twice-Born*, London, 1957, p. 23). Much earlier an Indian author, Ketkar, insisted on a hierarchical division of American society based on race and occupation, and he enumerated ten groups (based in fact on the country of origin). He did not use

the word 'caste' but he underlined with some relish the features which in his view were reminiscent of the Indian system. (Shridar V. Ketkar, *The History of Caste in India*, I, Ithaca, N.Y., 1909, pp. 100 n., 102 n., 115 n. 5.) The general question has recently been discussed in: E. R. Leach (ed.), *Aspects of Caste in South India, Ceylon and N.-W. Pakistan*, Cambridge, 1960 (Cambridge Papers in Social Anthropology, No. 2), notably p. 5.

4   W. Lloyd Warner (Dir.), *Deep South, A Social Anthropological Study of Caste and Class*, Chicago, c. 1941, ed. 1946, p. 9. B. S. Ghurye's position is close to that of Kroeber: well marked status groups are common in Indo-European cultures; comparatively, the Indian caste system represents only an extreme case (untouchability, etc.), see *Caste and Race in India*, New York, 1932, pp. 140, 142.

5   Max Weber, *Wirtschaft und Gesellschaft*, II, pp. 635–7. Discussed by Cox, *Caste, Class and Race*, p. 287, and: 'Max Weber on Social Stratification', *American Sociological Review*, 11, 1950, pp. 223–7; cf. also Hans Gerth, 'Max Weber vs. Oliver C. Cox', *American Sociological Review, ibid.*, pp. 557–8 (as regards Jews and castes).

6   Pitrim A. Sorokin, *Society, Culture and Personality, Their Structure and Dynamics*, New York, c. 1947, p. 259 (the 'order' or 'estate' as a 'diluted caste', *cf.* what has been said above about class and caste). Max Weber distinguishes between open and closed status groups (*Ges. Aufs. z. Religionssoziologie*, II, ed. 1923, pp. 41–2). It is to be noted that a recent work recognizes two fundamental types of 'social stratification', the caste type which comprises 'orders' or 'estates', and the open class type, related respectively to the poles of Talcott Parsons' alternative of particularism-universalism (Bernard Barber, *Social Stratification, A Comparative Analysis of Structure and Process*, New York, 1957).

7   W. Lloyd Warner, 'American Caste and Class', *American Journal of Sociology*, XLII, 1936, pp. 234–7.

8   Gunnar Myrdal, *An American Dilemma, The Negro Problem and Modern Democracy* (with the assistance of Richard Sterner and Arnold Rose), New York and London, c. 1944, p. 675; also p. 668: 'The scientifically important difference between the terms "caste" and "class" as we are using them is, from this point of view, *a relatively large difference in freedom of movement between groups*' (his italics). Same justification for the use of the term (practical reasons, not indicating identity with the Indian facts), in Westie and Westie, *American Journal of Sociology*, LXIII, 1957–1958, p. 192, n. 5.

9  *Op. cit.*, pp. 667–8. In a footnote, Myrdal takes up an objection made in particular by Charles S. Johnson: the word 'caste' connotes an invariable and stable system in which the tensions and frictions which characterize the relations between Whites and Blacks in the United States are not found; he replies that he does not believe that a caste system having such characteristics exists anywhere (pp. 1374–35, n. 2) and says earlier (p. 668) that Hindu society today does not show that 'stable equilibrium' that American sociologists, observing from a distance, have been inclined to attribute to it. We see here some trace of the egalitarian Creed. The author has, since, had first-hand experience of India and one wonders whether he would maintain this today, whether, even, he would continue to use the word 'caste' for American phenomena.

10  *Ibid.*, pp. 670–1. There is here an interesting judgment on the Lloyd Warner school: according to Myrdal, one must take account of the extreme egalitarianism in the 'popular national theory' in order to understand both the tendency among these authors to exaggerate the rigidity of distinctions of class and caste in America, and the interest aroused by their works, which has been greater than their strictly scientific novelty.

11  It is a little surprising to find, next to the ideas here summarized, a rather narrow idea of the place of concepts in science: 'Concepts are our created instruments and have no other form of reality than in our usage. Their purpose is to help make our thinking clear and our observations accurate' (p. 667).

12  W. Lloyd Warner and Allison Davis, 'A Comparative Study of American Caste', in Edgar T. Thomson, ed., *Race Relations and the Race Problem*, Durham, North Car., 1939, pp. 219–45; for India see pp. 229–32.

13  The operation of this choice is clear in principle: the caste system of India has been characterized by only those of its traits that it is thought may be found in America, where however they do not constitute a complete system but only part of a system which is called a class-and-caste system.

14  Oliver C. Cox, 'Race and Caste, A Distinction', *American Journal of Sociology*, 1944–1945, pp. 306–8, and above all *Caste, Class and Race, A Study in Social Dynamics*, New York, 1918, to which the references in the text relate.

15  Cox's thesis appears to have had little effect. Sorokin however refers to his article and takes a similar position: the relation between Blacks and Whites has some of the elements of relations between castes but it differs fundamentally (*op. cit.*, p. 258, n. 12).

16  John Dollard, *Caste and Class in a Southern Town*, New York,

*c*. 1937, ed. 1940, p. 64; Kingsley Davis, 'Intermarriage in Caste Society', *American Anthropologist*, XLIII, 1941, pp. 376–95.

17 Harold W. Pfautz, 'The Current Literature on Social Stratification, Critique and Bibliography', *American Journal of Sociology*, LVIII, 1953, pp. 391–418. The theory of stratification is approached, not starting from class, but from an absolutely general point of view, by Talcott Parsons in 'A Revised Theoretical Approach to the Theory of Social Stratification' (R. Bendix and S. M. Lipset, ed., *Class, Status and Power, A Reader in Social Stratification*, Blencoe, Ill., 1953). While it adopts the same label, the work is outside the current here criticized; the general conception (*in fine*) removes the habitual implications of the word. The argument proceeds from values and the hierarchy which necessarily results from them. The conceptual framework is that of the general theory.

18 Kingsley Davis, 'A Conceptual Analysis of Stratification', *American Sociological Review*, VII, 1942, pp. 309–21; K. Davis and Wilbert E. Moore, 'Some Principles of Stratification', *A.S.R.*, 10, 1945, pp. 242–9; W. Buckley, 'Social Stratification and Social Differentiation', *A.S.R.*, 23, 1958, pp. 369–75; K. Davis, 'A Reply to Buckley', *A.S.R.*, 24, 1959, p. 82; Dennis H. Wrong, *A.S.R.*, 24, pp. 772–82. Reference will be found in the articles of Buckley and Wrong to other articles not used here.

19 I was unfortunately unable to consult during the preparation of this article Kingsley Davis's book, *Human Society*, New York, 1949, quoted by Wrong, and which would have been of particular interest since the author was concerned with India at that time (*cf. The Population of India and Pakistan*, Princeton, 1951).

20 Nelson N. Foote, 'Destratification and Restratification', Editorial Foreword, *American Journal of Sociology*, LVIII, 1953, pp. 325–6.

21 *European Journal of Sociology*, I, 1, 1960, p. 14.

22 Célestin Bouglé, *Essais sur le régime des castes*, Paris, 1908, p. 4. The English translation of Bouglé's thesis, and a commentary on his book together with that of Hocart, which poses the problem of power, is in *Contributions*, II, 1958.

23 Talcott Parsons, *loc. cit.*

24 What follows is summarized from my chapter on the conception of Kingship in ancient India, to appear in L. Renou and J. Filliozat, *L'Inde Classique*, III.

25 On Hobbes and the artificial society, 'rational' in the sense of being devised according to the reality of man (the individual) and not inspired by an ideal order, *cf.* Léo Strauss, *Natural Right and History*, Chicago, 1953, Chapter 5; Élie Halévy, *La formation du radicalisme philosophique*, 3 vols., Paris, 1901–1904, I, pp. 3, 41, 53, 90; III, pp. 347–8, etc.

26  *Cf.* Gunnar Myrdal, *ibid.*, p. 581 ff., the 'Jim Crow Laws', etc.
The reaction to the abolition of slavery was not immediate but
developed slowly. Discrimination appears as simple separation
under the slogan 'separate but equal'. For the period before the
civil war also, Myrdal gives a succinct history, but the analysis,
apparently, remains to be done. It promises to be fruitful, see for
example the declarations of Jefferson and Lincoln (*cf. Times
Literary Supplement*, July 22, 1960, pp. 457–8, according to J. W.
Schulte-Nordholt, *The People That Walk in Darkness*, London,
Burke 1960). Recent articles by P. L. Van der Berghe partly
satisfy my wish. *Cf.* the last one: 'Apartheid, une interprétation
sociologique de la ségrégation raciale', *Cahiers internationaux de
sociologie*, XXVIII, nouv. sér., 7ᵉ année, 1960, pp. 47–56. According to this author, segregation has replaced etiquette as mode of
social distance. The change would correspond to the movement
from slavery to racism.

27  The fact that the transition from 'equality' to 'identity' operates
chiefly at the level of popular mentality makes it more difficult
to seize on than if it were present in the great authors. I propose
nevertheless to study elsewhere more closely this particular
complementarity between egalitarianism and racism.

28  Gunnar Myrdal, *ibid.*, pp. 83 ff., the quotations are from p. 89.
Myrdal also takes account of the development of the biological
view of man: *Homo sapiens* as a species in the animal world; *cf.* also
p. 591: 'The persistent preoccupation with sex and marriage in
the rationalization . . . is, to this extent, an irrational escape on
the part of the whites from voicing an open demand for difference
in social status . . . for its own sake.'

29  *Cf.* Claude Lévi-Strauss, *Race et histoire*, UNESCO, *c.* 1952.

30  Machiavelli observes that a 'republic' which wishes to extend its
empire and not remain small and stagnant, should like Rome
confide the defence of liberty to the people and not, like Sparta
and Venice, to the great. (*Discourses on the First Decade of T. Livy*,
I, chapters V–VI.)

31  *Cf.* n. 17.

32  E. E. Evans-Pritchard, *Social Anthropology*, London, 1951, p. 129.

APPENDIX B (pages 267–286)

1  This is what Marcel Mauss said as early as the first number of the
*Année Sociologique* (p. 161, his review of Jevon's *Introduction*) and
in 1897: 'To deny the irreductibility of races is to posit the unity
of human kind. To do away with the historical method is to be
left . . . with the anthropological'. (*Revue de l'Histoire des Religions*,
t. 35, review of Steinmetz's *Strafe*, p. 31). See now in M. Mauss,

*Œuvres*, edited by V. Karady, 3 vols., 1968, vol. I, p. 110, vol. II, 'La religion et les origines du droit pénal d'après un livre récent', pp. 651–98 – a methodological beacon for anthropologists today – p. 653.

2   *Cf*. Frazer's 'The Scope of Social Anthropology', *Psyche's Task*, 1913, pp. 159–176. Mauss wrote: 'Intellectualism is only concerned with similarities . . . a scientific picture requires the consideration of differences, and for that purpose a sociological method is necessary.' (*Année Sociologique*, vol. I, *loc. cit.*).

3   For example, Barth wrote in his *Religions de l'Inde* (Œuvres, vol. I pp. 140–41): 'The sectarian or neobrahmanic religions . . . despite many attempts . . . to reduce them to some kind of unity . . . have constantly resisted any such systematisation . . . Diversity is the essence [of Hinduism] and the true expression of it is the sect.

'. . . sectarian unity . . . is the only true one: in order not to get lost in infinite details or insignificant enumerations, we shall be obliged to remain at the level of generalities and to proceed by the use of categories.'

Farquhar wrote (*The Crown of Hinduism*, 1913, p. 216): 'Here then, we have the Hindu world theory in all its permanent essentials: God real, the world worthless; the one God unknowable, the other gods not to be despised; the Brahmans with their Vedas the sole religious authority, caste a divine institution serving as the chief instrument of reward and punishment; man doomed to repeated birth and death, because all actions lead to rebirth; world flight the only noble course for the awakened man and the one hope of escape from the entanglements of sense and transmigration.' (The absence of links between the different features in this inventory will be noted). Risley quotes instructive definitions such as these of Sir Alfred Lyall: 'the religion of all the people who accept the Brahmanic scriptures', 'a tangled jungle of disorderly superstitions' and then goes on to give his own: animism more or less transformed by philosophy, magic tempered by metaphysics. (*People of India*, ed. 1915, p. 233). *Cf*. E. A. H. Blunt, *The Caste System of Northern India*, 1931, pp. 292–93.

4   The dichotomy of Brahmanism and 'demonolatry' was proposed in the middle of the 19th century by the missionary Bishop Caldwell, author of the Comparative Grammar of Dravidian Languages (*cf. Contributions to Indian Sociology*, No. III, p. 57). Nearer to our own time the writer Bankim Chandra Chatterjee proceeds in an analogous manner in an unfinished essay published after his death (*Letters on Hinduism*, Calcutta, M. M. Bose, 1940). The author is concerned with the rehabilitation of Hinduism after it was condemned by certain Occidentals. The first part of the

essay is a brilliant and sustained polemic in the course of which certain popular cults are thrown out of Hinduism: 'the worship of "stocks and stones", of the rude blocks under the umbrageous trees besmeared with yellow ochre ... may be dismissed with a single word. They do not belong to Hinduism ... There is no warranty for them in the Hindu scriptures ... They are not accepted by the Hindu community at large. The local fetish of one village finds no votary outside the local limits of its worship. The better class of Hindus wholly rejects them.' Bankim poses a question which merits attention: he remarks that those Europeans who condemn Hinduism confuse what is truly religious with what is not, while they are quite able to distinguish religion from morality or politics in the Occident. Leaving any value judgment on one side it is certainly true that the terms of a comparison should be treated in parallel fashion. If, as here, we try to take a total view of Hinduism and refuse to separate literary religion and popular 'superstition', we should do the same in the West, and if the sociologist is in favour of this, he must also admit that so far it has not been done. On the other hand, parallel treatment is not identical treatment. Bankim also says that in India religion is not distinct as in the West but is mixed with everything else, which might be said to justify the Occidentals. We should add that for him Hinduism was not one but several religions, having, apart from their source, the fact that they were backed by Sanskrit or other scriptures in common.

5 I employ 'confrontation' here to distinguish it from 'comparison'. By confrontation I mean first the historical fact that brought Hinduism and Christianity together and then the results of this: an attitude of rivalry, particularly on the moral plane, as much as a tendency toward syncretism which insists upon similarities and neglects differences (*cf. Coll. Pap.*, p. 10): both are 'committed' attitudes opposed to scientific comparison.

6 'Hinduism' is used here in the habitual sense to mean the present religion of those Indians who are not Muslims, Christians, Parsis, Jains, Sikhs, and with these exceptions, the religion of the caste society. Only I do not limit Hinduism by excluding so-called 'inferior' practices: Hinduism goes on beyond literary Brahmanism. Hinduism of caste is often opposed to the animism of tribe, but tribal religion often participates to some extent of Hinduism (for an example of this see *Contributions*, No. III, p. 60 sq.). Historically we can say that Hinduism was completely built up in the period which saw the decline of the great heresies. The terms orthodoxy, heresy, etc. are taken in a slightly different sense from the one they have in the West, as this passage itself shows.

Socially, interdiction amounts to degradation, the condemned practice is simply the inferior one. Nevertheless it was in the nature of religion, even here, to adopt a more absolute attitude on occasion. Discussing the process of the aggregation of innovations, Burnouf wrote in the preface to his Bhagavata Purana (p. cxi): 'apart from these innovations introduced by the sectarian [bhakti] spirit, which are always easily recognised, modifications to the old Indian system have been made by way of addition rather than by way of substitution, and they have preserved the ancient elements with a rare fidelity.'

7   If for example it is true – which is not certain – that the founders of the Vira Shaiva or Lingayat sect wished to abolish caste, the history of this sect shows that caste has reintroduced itself. (Farquhar, *Outline*, pp. 262–63; Thurston, *Castes and Tribes*, *s.v.* Lingayat). The biography of a *bhakta* like Chaitanya shows an accommodation to caste rules, particularly in the matter of food. (M. T. Kennedy, *The Chaitanya Movement*, Calcutta, 1925, p. 119; 57, 61, 164).

8   Wherever description only uses what seems to be generally admitted, detailed bibliographic references have not been thought worthwhile. The reader can be referred to: L. Renou and J. Filliozat, *L'Inde Classique*, 2 vols., Paris, 1947, 1953; J. N. Farquhar's *An Outline of the Religious Literature of India* is useful both for its bibliography and its chronological handling. Among attempts at a general survey, I particularly mention a recent synthesis by L. Renou, *Religions of India*, London, 1953 (Jordan Lectures, 1951); I came across this work too late to make full use of it, but I hope that I have not wandered too far from what this great Indianist considers as established. One of the difficulties in description is that Comparative Religion does not, at present, provide any general framework for reference. It would really be necessary to indicate at least the corresponding Christian formula for each Hindu one; in fact I only offer some notes in this direction here.

9   *Coll. Pap.*, pp. 12–13.

10  For fieldwork results see *Contributions*, No. III, 1959, and my monograph, *Une sous-caste de l'Inde du sud*, Paris, 1957, 3rd part, p. 313 sq. (pure and impure, pp. 416–19; pantheon and individual gods, pp. 363–71; priesthood and possession, pp. 339–54; god and goddess, p. 383 sq.).

It has often been said that membership of Hinduism is essentially defined as the observance of caste rules and respect for the Brahman. T. Parsons, following Max Weber, is categoric: 'Hinduism as a religion is but an aspect of this (social) system, with no independent status apart from it.' (*The Structure of Social Action*, p. 557). More subtle is the following judgment: 'In some regards, it [Hinduism] is inseparable from philosophic speculation; in others, it is inseparable from social life.' (L. Renou, *L'Hindouisme*, Paris, 1951, p. 28).

11 An anecdote shows how these relations between village deities escape people of high caste. In North India, in 1954, I tried to find out whether, in the Dasarah festival, the goddess entertained relations similar to those met with in the South. A young college teacher who had come to spend the vacation in his village was with me. He could think of nothing of the sort, and when the enquiries revealed precisely what I was looking for (findings which later were to be confirmed and amplified), it was a small revelation to him, because he was wont to look at each deity in isolation.

It will be noted that the emphasis on marriage which gives the great gods one or two wives is not accompanied by any corresponding accent upon filiation. I have noted briefly (*Sous-caste*, p. 402) the difficulty which those two great lovers, Shiva and his wife Parvati, seem to experience in engendering children in the human way. (It would appear that only the Linga Purana bestows this faculty upon them, *cf.* Gopinatha Rao, *Hindu Iconography*, I, p. 35 sq.; II, p. 415 sq.). Parvati is never, in the iconography, represented as a mother like our own Madonna. The maternity of Mary reflects, as much as the Mystery of the Incarnation, an emphasis upon filiation in accordance with the kinship vocabulary of our countries. It appears that the accent is either on filiation as with us or on marriage as in India, and that one cannot divinize all the elementary kinship relations at the same time. Let us note also that Uma [Parvati], herself sterile, sometimes curses the goddesses who become sterile as a result. It thus appears that the sterility of the goddesses has attracted the attention of the Purana authors. The situation of Shiva and Parvati recalls that of Zeus and Hera. Parvati's anger, in the Skanda Purana, when Shiva gives birth to a son by himself, recalls Hera's rage after the birth of Athena.

12 The identification of the officiant with the god or gods is elaborated in the Agamas, *cf.* C. G. Diehl, *Instrument and Purpose*, Lund, 1956, pp. 100–104, and p. 75 (*nyāsa*); *cf. L'Inde Classique*, I, p. 569 (*nyāsa*); I, p. 575 (*dhyāna*). Similarly the vedic sacrifier 'passes from the world of men to that of the gods' (*Śat. Brāhm.* quoted by Hubert and Mauss in their Essay on Sacrifice, *Mélanges d'Histoire des Religions*, Paris, 1929, p. 26; the priest, p. 29 sq.).

13 To consider not only Brahmanic theory, but also Brahmanic practice is a delicate matter. It would call for great precision, and even perhaps require a monograph. One can always say that the

fact that Brahmans sometimes perform blood sacrifice is an aberration, or better still that such facts are not relevant to the theory. (But here precisely the theory is inconsistent and needs to be completed to be understood; we shall return to this). It is more difficult to ignore clear and widely spread facts of interdependence, as for instance when one sees the Brahman at a certain point in the festival leave the temple of which he is ordinarily the priest to return to it after the bloody sacrifice to the goddess is over (*Contributions*, No. III, p. 34, from Srinivas). In general, during the festival of Navaratri or Dasarah, the Brahman reads the Devi Mahatmya which finishes with the execution by the goddess of the Buffalo Demon (*cf.* the iconographic theme of Mahishasura Mardini so abundantly found). At this time also the people sacrifice a buffalo to the goddess (see Henry Whitehead, *Village Gods*) and the episode in the Mahatmya obviously represents a myth corresponding to this rite. Here, then, the Brahman, if he does not operate, does recite the sacrifice.

The relative inconsistency of Brahmanism has frequently been noted but it has been considered from another angle; it has been taken as the result of the aggregation to Vedic of indigenous or 'Hindu' traits. Masson-Oursel, for example, speaking of religion towards the beginning of the Christian era, wrote: '... to the extent that Brahmanism means, apart from the content of the *brāhmaṇas*, the inclusion of more and more "Hindu" factors, the more it is reduced to a form, we might even say, a label.' (*L'Inde Antique et la Civilisation Indienne*, Paris, 1933, p. 211). This emphasizes that Vedism does not provide the organizing principle of Brahmanism, and it is a confession that Brahmanism is not to be understood in this way. If on the contrary we look at Brahmanism from the point of view of observed Hinduism, which is itself consistent, we can see that, unable to rationalize the presence of complementary opposites, Brahmanism sifts and substantializes Hinduism. Shall we say that the place occupied by the goddess is the result of a 'compromise', that she is 'tolerated'? Is it not better to state that she is present but that the system cannot account for her presence? We shall see later (§3) why it is the goddess that raises this significant contradiction.

14  About 'substantialization' in Brahmanic theory, I have drawn from exchanges with D. Pocock. On the trilogy (*trivarga*) of human ends (*puruṣārtha*), *cf. L'Inde Classique*, I, §1150 sq.; P. V. Kane, *Hist. Dharma.*, II, 1, pp. 8–9, see also III, pp. 8–9; I have benefited greatly, on this point and as regards *dharma* in general, from the as yet unpublished lectures of R. Lingat. See R. Lingat, *Les Sources du Droit* (see Bibliography). Heterodox

movements classify differently. In conformity with an Indian tendency, even *kāma* has been codified.

To say that *artha* corresponds to the royal function should not be taken to mean that the king is not subject to *dharma*: the hierarchy of ends governs all, but *artha* defines the particular sphere of royal activity. The non-differentiation of power and wealth, politics and economics, is important (see for instance Pusalker, *Studies in Epics and Puranas*, Bombay, 1955, p. xlvi). For the Occidental counterpart – how from Hobbes to Marx power has been abstracted in political economy – see Talcott Parsons, *Structure of Social Action*, ed. 1949, p. 93 sq., *cf.* Karl Popper, *The Open Society*, London, 1945, II, p. 120: 'it is only through active state interference, through the protection of property by the laws and the physical power of the state, that wealth can give a man any power at all. Economic power is therefore entirely dependent on political and physical power.'

In such a hierarchy there is no room for a radical principle of evil. As Max Weber says: 'The conception of a "radical Evil" was quite impossible in this world order' (*Hinduismus und Buddhismus*, Tübingen, 1923, p. 143). It is tempting to think that the Indian trilogy on many occasions plays the same role as our distinction between good and evil. This is not to say, of course, that any conception of evil analogous to our own is absent, but where we condemn and exclude, India hierarchizes and includes.

15 To express the lack of conceptual reality of the individual being, one could perhaps employ Hegelian terminology: what is found is the particular (*Besonderheit*), not the individual, i.e. the particular in which the universal is reflected (*Einzelnheit*). This may well seem obscure, and the formulation should certainly be made more specific, but we are dealing with a massive, all-pervading fact which it is difficult for the present to circumscribe more precisely. It is impossible to bring together here all the relevant evidence. A certain amount will be found in *Contributions*. As far as personal observation is concerned, I have concluded my *Sous-caste* with these words: 'Here there is no reality, only appearances, or better, relations.' And the book perhaps contains not one analysis which fails to illustrate this statement. (See also *Contributions*, No. III, p. 84.)

16 In the passage quoted above, Max Weber emphasizes the absence in India of anything that might be called Natural Law. That is true from the point of view of the content of Natural Law. One cannot follow him in making *dharma* appear as positive law: 'There was, in theory at least, only one law, it was holy, particularized according to status class, but positive'. ('*es gab – für die*

431

*Theorie zum mindesten – nur heiliges, ständisch besondertes, aber positives Recht'*). In reality, as the analysis of the *trivarga* has already shown, *dharma*, insofar as it is a law, is an ideal law factually having the same relation with positive law as our Natural Law. Since it is conformity with the order of the world, it is, at its deepest, that which becomes Natural Law when nature and convention are distinguished (*positive Sozialordnung* and '*natürliche' Ordnung* in Weber).

17  The attribution of ultramundaneity to the Brahman is more implicit in Max Weber, more explicit in Schweitzer. Weber has a very apt sense of Brahmanic ritualism and quasi-puritanism, and of the problems involved, when he writes: 'Orthodox Brahmanic Shivaism has, by [a sort of] ritualistic castration, transformed an orgiastic rite into the cult of the lingam' (*ibid.*, p. 336). Schweitzer, rightly on the whole, opposes world and life affirmation and their negation, as dominant in Christianity and Indian religions respectively (*Indian Thought and its Development*, London, 1951). But 'life negation' is not absent from Christianity, and there is a need for a more precise distinction. Schweitzer aptly notes on occasion the blending of the two tendencies, as regarding *bhakti*. About the situation of the Brahman in the world, it is true that while being foremost he has to serve his employers (*Contributions*, No. 11, p. 58), but the fact does not account for more than his relative permeability to the ultramundane tendency.

18  It should be clear that what the sanyasi renounces is the social world (*saṃsāra*) and not the material universe (*jagat*) [remark from J. F. Staal]. At the same time we have to extend the meaning of what we call society in order to include in it, not only the 'world' or society proper, but also the condition of the renouncer. This is so much an integral part of the system that we cannot even surmise that the world of castes would endure without it.

We wrote rather summarily elsewhere that every man has the right to become a sanyasi and at that time dies to his caste [See *Coll. Pap.*, p. 12]. One should be more precise. On the first point it is a matter rather of usage than of the written law: in fact there are renouncers of *śūdra* origin, but English law, following the texts, did not recognize them as sanyasis (Kane, *Hist. Dharma.*, II, pp. 944–45). In fact I have generalized the Brahmanic idea and have called renouncers, or even sanyasis, all those who have left the world in a manner analogous to that of the orthodox sanyasi including, for example, Buddhist monks. (It should be noted, in passing, that heretical monasticism has deeply influenced the institution as we find it in Hinduism, *cf.* amongst others Jawaharlal Nehru, *Discovery of India*, New York, 1946, p. 173).

NOTES TO "APPENDIX B"

As to the sanyasi dying to the world the facts are that he gives away his goods and loses all right to family property, he draws into himself his sacrificial fires and henceforth must light no fire, he completes his own funeral ceremonies (Kane, *op. cit.*, II, p. 958: 'sixteen *śrāddha* of himself and *sapiṇḍikaraṇa*' that is the total number of *śrāddha* called *ekoddiṣṭa* necessary), he is not touched by mourning impurity, over only slightly so (*ibid.*; Dubois, *Manners and Customs*, 3rd ed., p. 540), he is buried in a particular way and not cremated (Kane, *op. cit.*, IV, p. 231, for description see Dubois, *loc. cit.*) and immediately becomes an ancestor and the object of *pārvaṇaśrāddha* (Kane, IV, pp. 518–19). If later he returns to the life of a householder, both he and his children, despite the performance of penances, are treated as untouchables (Kane, IV, p. 113). Opinion is divided as to whether he should abandon his sacred thread and lock of hair on becoming a sanyasi, however Shankara is of the opinion that he should (*ibid.*, II, pp. 963–64). Similarly not all the different sorts of sanyasis are allowed to take food from non-Brahmans or from the four varnas (*ibid.*, p. 934, etc.).

19   On renunciation and the *āśrama* theory, I have indicated the most common view, but there are two others (Kane, II, p. 424). M. Lingat's lectures already mentioned have been of help to me in distinguishing more precisely between the worldly view and that of the sanyasi. *Cf. L'Inde Classique*, I, §1230 sq.; L. Renou, *La Civilisation de l'Inde ancienne*, p. 79. On *vānaprastha*, see Farquhar, *Outline*, p. 29; Kane, II, pp. 927–28.

As regards the aggregation of liberation and renunciation to the worldly view, I may be accused of arbitrarily splitting enumerations which are given as wholes. The reproach has often, and sometimes rightly, been levelled at philologists. It would be the more natural here, as, for the Hindu common sense, *mokṣa* and *dharma* are not felt as heterogeneous. I have given my particular reasons, there is also a general one which involves a point of method: aggregations of the type are a common feature in this field. In all such enumerations it is essential to distinguish the true wholes and the false, whether the latter are factitious collections designed to fill a sacred number, or the results of aggregation. We have to deal here with one of a few fundamental cleavages, which we must recognize in order to consider real wholes systematically [*Coll. Pap.*, pp. 12, 15, 17].

20   L. de La Vallée Poussin, *The Way to Nirvana, Six Lectures on Ancient Buddhism as a Discipline of Salvation*, Cambridge, 1917 (Hibbert Lectures, 1916). The first pages (pp. 1–7) describe the distinction with which we are concerned in all its essential traits. If these 'disciplines of salvation' are so different from religions

proper, it might seem unjustifiable to include them here. But our author himself notes that these 'disciplines' have had a strong influence on the religions and are superimposed on them without at the same time destroying them. This interaction justifies their inclusion here, as we are dealing with two different parts of one whole.

21  The renouncer is often of course of Brahman origin. It is frequently emphasized that the great heretic sanyasis, the Buddha and Jina, were of kshatriya or royal class origin; the fact is of secondary importance to the distinction with which I am concerned here. At the other end of the development, the Brahman absorbs the sanyasi: the great orthodox theorists and founders of orders, Shankara and Ramanuja were sanyasis and, not only by origin but also by their preoccupations, Brahmans. Shankara accepts and defends Hinduism but remains faithful to tradition to the extent that he denies the efficacity of works in the achieving of salvation. Ramanuja effects a synthesis: for him works play their part in salvation, and his sanyasis keep their sacred threads; *bhakti* had prepared the ground (*cf.* §4). The development of Brahmanism is often thought of as the progressive accretion to a vedic base of aboriginal elements; vegetarianism has in this way been considered as a 'primitive' element; one can certainly compare Brahmanism and Vedism but there is a discontinuity between them. The true historical development of Hinduism is in the sanyasic developments on the one hand and in their aggregation to worldly religion on the other. A historical approach like Farquhar's immediately shows the sectarian developments and their successive aggregation. A typical example is that of food in Manu. While flesh is still offered to the manes and to the gods and its consumption is permitted, and even obligatory, in such circumstances, the pressure of the vegetarian ideal, a sanyasic ideal, is so strong that abstention from meat is mentioned as being as meritorious as the regular performance of the horse-sacrifice (*Manu*, V, 53; Kane, *op. cit.*, II, pp. 772–82; IV, p. 422 sq.).

22  Max Weber, *op. cit.*, p. 117 sq., 367; *cf.* Talcott Parsons' summary: *Structure of Social Action*, particularly pp. 558, 574. Weber, following Blunt, notes that inferior status and present misfortunes are explained as the result of sins committed in previous existences (also in *Une Sous-caste*, p. 414). Observation does not seem to confirm that the belief in transmigration is a 'dogmatic belief'. Farquhar noted the absence of these notions and of nirvana or deliverance, both in Ashoka's edicts which are, nevertheless, infused with *ahiṃsā*, and in the Arthashastra which refers to popular religion and to atheistic philosophies. Kane points out the

434

contradiction between orthodox rites addressed to the dead and ideas of *karman* and rebirth, and adopts an historical explanation (IV, p. 335 sq.). One could possibly say that death liberates several different principles, as this is probably implied in popular funeral practices. It is true also that Brahmanic funerary rites have petrified ancient beliefs. But above all transmigration is not a belief, in the sense that there is nothing corresponding to it in the religion of the group, no kind of rite: it is speculative and belongs to that field of religion which is open to individual option, its main relation is with liberation; more than 'a product of Brahmanic intellectualism' as Weber described it, it is a product of the situation and the thought of the sanyasi. Australian transmigration, for example, being related to the totem, is quite different (Durkheim, *Formes élémentaires*, p. 353 sq.).

23 Barth saw rebirth in the Upanishads as 'the very condition of the personal being' (*Rel. Inde*, p. 79). He found in it 'speculative audacity rather than lassitude and sufferance' (*ibid.*, p. 84). If the idea emerged before caste we must be careful not to project into that remote period what we find in modern India; in speaking of 'renouncers' in a slightly later age we must also guard against the same danger. Strictly one should be more precise and speak, to begin with, of Brahmans, Kings, hermits (*vānaprastha*), etc. . . .

24 Lilian Silburn, *Instant et Cause. Le discontinu dans la pensée philosophique de l'Inde*, Paris, Vrin, 1955, who admirably demonstrates the 'theory of action' aspect of Buddhism. La Vallée Poussin has emphasized the rationalistic, quasi-scientific aspect of retribution, and pointed out that it only becomes moral with Buddha (*op. cit.*, p. 58 sq.). Determinism was already present in Vedism where it warranted the efficacy of ritual action, *karman*. In the subsequent development, while knowledge is extolled above action, action is widened and tends to acquire a moral value. Both facts show that we have passed from the priest to the philosopher.

I have employed the terms 'salvation' and 'liberation' indifferently; while the Christian conception of salvation has a moral aspect, the sanyasi's liberation, *mokṣa*, transcends morality, which is limited to the sphere of *karman*. Again, it is not one man with a particular existence who is liberated, a whole string of successive existences comes to an end, having previously become condensed in the renouncing individual: he is not only himself; there is here a necessary link with what has been called Buddhist charity.

25 According to La Vallée Poussin, Buddha judged those who believed in a permanent individual Self – which prevented them from reaching sanctity and nirvana, but not from acquiring merits – quite differently from those who denied both future life

and retribution. Such a negation was adjudged as a sin like murder or theft, a heresy *par excellence*, for 'it is destructive of all morality, and precipitates the unbeliever into hell: "You say that there is no future life. Well, the executioners of Yama, the king and the judge of the dead, will soon change your opinion on the matter"' (*op. cit.*, p. 46). L. Silburn aims to show that there is no contradiction on Buddha's part as has been claimed in denying any principle of permanence in the person and at the same time in holding to the belief in transmigration. Continuity is only the result of the will. La Vallée Poussin had already pointed out that the person born of a death is no more as the one who died than he is different, here is the 'middle way': neither permanence nor complete discontinuity. Buddha took the continuity of the living person and rebirth as two facts on the same level of experience. His anger, noted above, shows the necessity of the attitude: for him there was neither morality nor human liberty without retributive transmigration; this shows that transmigration is not pessimism but the necessary condition of the individual's existence.

26 This summary is inevitably very crude. I wanted simply to point to a general development (*cf.* particularly L. Silburn, *op. laud.*, Chapter III). It seems *a priori* that there are two ways open to the man who leaves the world and finds himself endowed, as a result of his renunciation, with an individuality. He can assume this individuality only to end it by liberation, this is the way of Buddha, who only maintains the liberty of man for this end (with the proviso that the end may be delayed out of compassion). Or he can accept his individuality and settle down with it, such would seem to be the way corresponding to *sāṃkhya* dualism and the monotheism of *bhakti*. In this case, note the parallel with the predominant representations accompanying the assertion of the individual in the West.

27 I take Tantrism here as being essentially the literature of the *śākta*, and secondarily the related texts of other movements. The following may be referred to: *Inde Classique*, I §844 sq., 1181, 1217 sq., 1277 sq., and Farquhar, *Outline*, pp. 150–51, 199 sq., 265 sq. The choice of quotations is taken from Heinrich Zimmer, *Kunstform und Yoga im Indischen Kultbild*, Berlin, 1926, p. 178 sq., *cf. Kulārṇavatantra*, ed. A. Avalon, *Tantrik Texts*, Vol. 5, London, 1917, respectively IX, 57; II, 23; IX, 50 (quoted in *Inde Class.*, I, §1221); II, 24.

28 Quoted by B. K. Majumdar in A. Avalon, *Principles of Tantra*, II, p. cxlix (with the variant *samyak* instead of *sākṣat*) and translated '... and the world becomes the seat of liberation'. The lack of

exactitude is remarkable in a probable Tantrist; the fact that he takes *saṃsāra* to mean 'world' is perhaps characteristic. On the sanyasis, *cf.* note 30; on transmigration, karman: *Mahanirvana Tantra*, trad. Avalon, London, 1913, XIV; p. 10 sq. and *Principles*, I, pp. 203–4.

29   As regards the left-hand forms, it is considered good taste to speak of extreme, excessive or even abominable forms, or to attempt to minimize and excuse them. As if the sacred were a matter of measure! M. Renou, on the contrary, has shown that these are the essential forms (the left-handed *vīra* mode), and that, since it is a sacramental matter, the usual moral condemnation is out of place (*Inde Class.*, pp. 593–96).

Farquhar has offered the historical hypothesis (*op. cit.*, p. 268). The tantra is not only open to all five classes (four *varṇa* plus the *sāmānya* or common people), and to women, but supernatural sanctions threaten anyone refusing to initiate an untouchable, a woman can be a guru, and the sacrifice of widows is forbidden (*Mahanirvana Tantra, ibid.*, V, 12, p. 159; V, 187, 178, 180 p. 357; X, 74). There is even a trace of hostility to the twice-born.

In a reputedly late work like the *Mahanirvana Tantra*, Tantrism emerges as a mixture of heteroclitic conceptions, with Shankarian monism predominant. Nevertheless one finds, even in a modern work like the *Tantratattva*, the profound inspiration which I have noted together with the emphasis on realization (*sādhana*): monism is true but inaccessible, the starting point is in the dualism of the world. Finally the world is rehabilitated in a subordinate position as 'a most spacious and sacred field full of materials for *sādhana*'. Here we are at the opposite remove from renunciation and classical ultramundaneity (including samkhyan dualism), and nearer to Christianity than anywhere else in India (*Principles of Tantra*, p. 82 sq.). It can easily be seen how this attitude is related to the sacramental usage of the things of this world by virtue of reversal.

30   According to the *Mahanirvana Tantra* two conditions (*āśrama*) are distinguished instead of four: that of householder and that of renouncer or *avadhūta*. The initiation of the latter is described; it must always follow upon life in the world and no one is allowed to leave the world who has close relatives to maintain (pp. 158–60; 184 sq.).

In principle four classes of *avadhūta* or *saṃnyāsin* are distinguished (pp. 352–54). In fact it is difficult to escape the impression that this is merely theoretical: the different modes (*ācāra*) marking the progress of the devotee are also mentioned, the highest being the *kula* or *kaula* mode: the *kaula* is the most celebrated of all, and since there is mention of kula-sanyasis, it is clear that there are *kaula*, and even 'imperfect' sanyasis, in the world (*ibid.*, v. 172 sq., v. 150). There are contradictions (pp. xliv, 184 sq., 249 sq., 351 sq.). The same text describes two initiations (pp. 184 sq., 249 sq.). The first, probably *dīkṣā* (lxxiii), is the initiation to *saṃnyāsa*, the candidate leaves the world and receives the brahmamantra, no distinctively *śākta* element is in evidence. The other is an initiation to the *kaula* grade, and conversely there is no reference to renunciation in the ceremony itself, which is truly *śākta* and consists essentially in the initiation to wine (Chapter X, v. 112, p. 249, 'By the mere drinking of wine, without initiation, a man does not become a kaula'), it is not called *dīkṣā* but *pūrṇa-abhiṣeka*, complete (aspersion or) enthronement. It would seem that this last initiation is that of those who are called 'Shaiva renouncers', the first is that of the 'Brāhma renouncers'. Indeed we read in the last chapter (XIV, v. 147, p. 352) '. . . I have already spoken of the . . . Kaulas who are Brahma avadhūtas, and of the Kaulas who have been initiated [by abhisheka].' As far as the first category is concerned, is there anything more here than an attempt to aggregate (in the sense in which I have used the word) non-shakta renouncers? In fact this tantra is concerned, like an orthodox shastra, with the stages of life, the *rites de passage*, and funerary rites. We may conclude, hypothetically, that the renouncer does not play an essential role in Shaktism. The renouncer is celebrated as sacred and as purifying everything he touches (p. 192, v. 289; p. 335, v. 173), but it is a matter of the kula-yogis, i.e. of people who have remained in the world as well, in fact not of yogis but of kaulas (namely, p. 248, v. 105, *cf. Principles*, p. 51).

31 *Cf.* Alexandre Koyré, *From the Closed World to the Infinite Universe*, New York, 1958, Chapter VII. Quotation from Newton, pp. 178–79: 'That gravity be innate, inherent, and essential to matter . . . is to me so great an absurdity that I believe no man who has in philosophical matters a competent faculty of thinking can ever fall into it'. As J. F. Staal recalls, Newton continues a philosophical tradition going back to Aristotle.

32 *Cf.* A. M. Esnoul, 'Le courant affectif à l'intérieur du brahmanisme ancien', *Bulletin de l'École Française d'Extrême-Orient*, vol. XLVIII, 1956, pp. 141–207 (etymology, p. 143). I cannot do better than refer the reader to this excellent work where the sociologist is pleased to see the 'objective side' and the 'subjective side' confronted (pp. 164–65).

33 Burnouf wrote: 'It is the influence of this easy dogma of devotion, which is, I believe, alien to Buddhism, which gives the Puranas that authority they have enjoyed for several centuries in India.'

438

(Preface to the *Bhagavata Purana*, 1840, I, p. cxi). The sectarian aspect generally attributed to the Gita is in agreement with the view proposed here (*cf.* the following section). As regards the coexistence of tendencies, it will be noted that even in the Gita the personal Lord is also the impersonal and universal Being (*cf.* Shankara's commentary, A. Mahadeva Sastri, *The Bhagavad-Gita with the Commentary of Sri Sankaracharya*, Madras, 4th ed., 1947). The god *par excellence* of bhakti is Krishna, incarnation of Vishnu, and the theory of avatars establishes economically the relation between the personal God, almost a hero, and the Supreme identified with Brahman.

It is not possible here to point out the relations between Tantrism and Bhakti. To mention only one, it is remarkable that in the later development, the symbol of the love of the devotee for his god, the love of Radha for Krishna, is (generally) an adulterous love: in this way the transcendance of divine love in a context often tinged with eroticism is marked by the reversal, on the whole infrequent, of worldly values.

34   On possession, for the features mentioned here, *cf.* in particular, *Une Sous-caste*, p. 349 sq. On the circumstances of individuation, *ibidem*, pp. 359, 412–13. The stereotyped cry of the possessed 'Govinda, Govinda' (one of Krishna's names, *ibid.*, p. 351) suggests the influence of bhakti cults on popular religion. It is the common foundation that interests us here. Another feature of the day-to-day is found in bhakti, and is submission in the face of a superior (in religion, *ibid.*, p. 412), but love does not come from the world of caste, and the name 'Lord' is reserved for the divine. Certain bhakta extasies are so close to possession that one wonders whether one could not speak of 'en-stasis' as is proposed, rather more as regards yoga, by the regretted Rev. Gathier (in oral communication).

APPENDIX C (pages 287–31?)

1   Georges Dumézil, *Mitra-Varuna*, Paris, 1940, p. 43 (ed. 1948, p. 76), etc.; A.M. Hocart, *Les Castes*, Paris, 1939, p. 69; both quoted in *Contributions* II, p. 52.

2   The different characteristics I enumerate have been distinguished by Albrecht Weber, *Indische Studien*, X, 1, Leipzig, 1867, p. 1 sq.; the quotations are often in Dumézil (*Jupiter, Mars, Quirinus*, Paris, 1941, p. 44, etc.), *cf.* also *Śat. Br.* V, I, 1, 12 (distinction); the *brahman* produces the *kṣatra Śat. Br.* XII, 7, 3, 12 (*sattra*, it filters milk).

3   The interpretation of this statement has been recently revised by Heesterman (J. C. Heesterman, *The Ancient Indian Royal Consecration*, The Hague, Mouton *c.* 1957, pp. 75–78). This author says that it should not be taken as a juridical statement, he adds much that is relevant for its understanding, but concludes that it consists in an identification, only half-veiled in mystery, of the king with Soma. This is difficult to admit: there seems to be in the statement at least an element of mental reservation. Later in the ritual the king will be straightforwardly identified with *brahman*. The author does not seem to make any difference between the two. One misses here the sense of a progress, a development in the sacrifice as found in Hubert and Mauss's Essay (*Contributions* I, p. 7; *cf.* similarly *Contributions* III, pp. 15–16).

4   W. W. Hunter, *Indian Empire*, 3rd ed., p. 136, quoted, together with James Mill, in: N. N. Law, *Aspects of Ancient Indian Polity*, Oxford, 1921; pp. 44–45. On the dominant caste, *cf. Contributions* II, p. 53; I, pp. 27–34.

5   See mainly J. Muir, *Sanskrit Texts*, 2nd ed., I, p. 287 sq., and Keith and Macdonell, *Vedic Index*, II, pp. 249, 255–56; G. Dumézil, *Jupiter, Mars, Quirinus*, p. 43; for Mill, see note 4 above; E. W. Hopkins, 'Ruling Caste', *Journ. Amer. Or. Soc.*, 13, 1889, pp. 57–376; O. C. Cox, *Caste, Class and Race*, New York, 1948, p. 102 sq.; also C. Bouglé, *Régime des Castes*, p. 181.

6   The texts are brought together in Muir, *Sanskrit Texts*, I, 2nd ed., p. 296 sq., particularly p. 388 sq. for the different versions of the cycle of *Viśvāmitra* and *Paraśurāma*. For *Śunaḥśépa* (parallel between *Ait. Br.* and *Rāmāyana*), R. Roth, in *Indische Studien*, II, pp. 112–23. Excessive kings: Muir, *loc. cit.*, p. 306 sq., *Arthaśāstra*, I, 6. On *Veṇa* and *Pṛthu*, see here §7. F. E. Pargiter on Satyavrata: *Journ. of the Roy. As. Soc.*, 1913, pp. 885–904.

7   Probably all modern Indian authors dealing with ancient Indian polity have a chapter on the question. The most militant views are in K. P. Jayaswal, *Hindu Polity*, [1924], 3rd ed., Bangalore, 1955; it is a characteristic of the period that they intrude even in a work like that of D. R. Bhandarkar, *Some Aspects of Ancient Hindu Polity*, Benares, 1929, see pp. 126–68, but this author has seen that it was difficult to speak of 'divine right' in a polytheistic milieu. In contrast, U. N. Ghoshal, *Hist. of Hindu Political Theories*, London, etc., OUP., 1923 [more recently *History of Indian Political Ideas*, OUP., 1959], sketches the perspective of the 'contract theory' from the Digha Nikaya onwards; he sees in the divine creation of the king in the Mahabharata a reaction against 'the individualist tendencies of the buddhist canon' (*HPT.*,

p. 268). Against the latter statement, P. V. Kane, *History of Dharmaśāstra*, III, pp. 28–37 recalls how old the notion of the divinity of the king is; Ghoshal has rejoined ('Hindu Theories of Social Contract and Divine Right', *Ind. Hist. Quart.*, XXIV, 1948, pp. 68–70). Recently, R. S. Sharma, who recognizes the nationalist inspiration of certain exegeses (*Aspects of Political Ideas and Institutions in Ancient India*, Delhi, etc., M. Banarsidas, 1959, pp. 1–13), examines the 'contract theories' in relation to the 'historical context of their sources', but this is in fact a materialist interpretation of the differences which leaves out, I believe, the essential.

8   Muir, *Sanskrit Texts*, I, 2nd ed. (*Pṛthu*, p. 304 sq., *parivettṛ*, p. 275, n., *Paraśurāma*, p. 455, *cf.* p. 464). On *Pṛthu*, see Georges Dumézil, *Servius et la Fortune*, Paris, 1943, p. 33 sq. On rain in the Jatakas: Ratilal N. Mehta, *Pre-Buddhist India*, Bombay, 1939, pp. 84–85 (also other features: the fruits of the earth lose their taste, etc.). *Cf.* MhBh., XII, 69 (Ghoshal, *HPT.*, p. 98 sq), XII, 141, 9–10; also in Tamil texts (Kural, Manimegalai), see K. A. Nilakantha Sastri, *The Cōḷas*, Madras, 1959, pp. 68–69. The king enjoys the earth as a wife in *Arthaśāstra*, I, 5, end.

9   Digha Nikaya, XXVII, §10 sq., transl. Rhys Davids, III (S.B.E., IV), p. 82 sq. The legend of Manu in the Mahabharata is in XII, Chapter 67. About the favour shown in the Smriti texts to the idea of conventional kingship, see the numerous references in Kane, *Hist. of Dharmaś.*, III, pp. 36–37.

10  On *artha* as means of *dharma*: R. Dikshitar, 'Is Arthashastra secular?', *Report of the Third Orient. Conference*, 1925, p. 624; and *The Mauryan Polity*, Madras, 1932, p. 249; S. K. Aiyangar, *Evolution of Hindu Admin. Institutions in South India*, Madras, 1931, p. 40; even in some measure U. N. Ghoshal, *Hindu Pol. Theories*, p. 74. On the secular inspiration of Arthashastra, *cf.* Jolly's Preface to his edition, Lahore, 1923, pp. 3–5. On the *trivarga* as a structural classification of types of action, *cf.* above, Chapter 3, pp. 43–44; the best Indian authors recognize that *mokṣa* is heterogeneous in the series: Ghoshal, *H. Pol. Th.*, p. 7; Kane, *H. of Dh.*, II, 1, p. 8; III, pp. 204–5. On the 'mutual relations' between Arthashastra and Jaina literature, see Jolly's edition, p. 10.

11  The references to the text of the Arthashastra are to Jolly's edition, Lahore, 1923; *cf.* the translation by Johann Jakob Meyer, *Das Altindische Buch vom Welt- und Staatsleben*, Leipzig, 1926.

12  Jayaswal translates: 'territory with . . . population', but precisely the distinction is not made in that sense (*cf.* §14, *janapada*).

13  It is confirmed from I, 3 (about the occupations of the Shudra)

that *vārtā* does not include handicrafts, etc. (*kārukuśilavakarma*).

14  This was already written when I found that the great historian
Marc Bloch, in a course of lectures given in 1936 but only recently
published, had defined the manor precisely in this fashion, by
'the union, or rather the fusion of an economic concern with what
I shall dare to call a group of sovereignty' ('Il y a lieu d'insister
fortement sur cette union, cette fusion plutôt, d'une entreprise
économique et de ce que j'oserai appeler un groupe de souve-
raineté', *Seigneurie française et Manoir anglais*, Paris, 1960, p. 17).
A passage from Maine is relevant here; it refers to the question
whether the Land Revenue is a tax or a rent. 'We may lay down,
at least provisionally, that in the beginning of the history of
ownership there was no such broad distinction as we now commonly draw between political and proprietary power' (Henry
Sumner Maine, *Village Communities*, ed. 1890, pp. 228–29). For
parallel and pregnant statements by Maitland see *Contributions*,
VII, p. 104.

15  On the enumeration of the seven elements in the Smriti, see Kane,
III, 17, n.: the elements Nos. 1 and 2, 5 and 6 form pairs in
Manu. On the hierarchical aspect: *Arthaś.*, VIII, 1, 5; Manu, IX,
295; other enumerations Manu, VII, 156 (12 elements) and 157
(5 elements). On territory and population: D. R. Bhandarkar,
*Aspects*, pp. 68–69, cf. *Arthaś.*, XII, 4; Pran Nath, *A Study in the
Economic Condition of Ancient India*, London, 1929, *passim*. On
the dimensions of *janapada*, Pran Nath, *op. cit.*, p. 45 sq. Bouglé
notes that in India there is no local usage (*lex loci*): 'each individual, wherever he emigrates, carries with him the law of his
group', the law is 'personal' (*Régime des Castes*, p. 184, with ref.).
A recent and important study of the form of the Arthashastra,
which throws light on its content as well, reminds us that the
discussion of alternatives is not peculiar, but is typical of the
grammarian Patanjali and is found even in philosophical literature
(L. Renou, 'Sur la forme de quelques textes sanskrits', *Journal
Asiatique*, Paris, 1961, No. 2; *Kauṭilya*, pp. 191–92).

16  *Une sous-caste*, respectively pp. 141 sq., 150–52; 12–13; 156, §3.

17  Now see 'The Modern Conception of the Individual', 1965 (see
Bibliography). The main point in this hypothesis is to formulate a
relation between two domains or 'systems' with which the
anthropologist is concerned. One apparent difficulty, cursorily
mentioned here (above, §8 *in fine*) and in another context
(Appendix A, §F), should perhaps be more explicitly discussed.
It can be objected that the very word of polity (politics, political)
comes to us from the Greek *polis*, and that, even if we lay aside its
actual political constitutions, ancient Greece confronts us, in the

thought of its philosophers, with a political domain which is neither opposed to religion as a system of ultimate values nor based on the individual. But precisely Greek speculation is markedly different from that of Machiavelli and Hobbes, it differs from it as political philosophy from political science; the one, essentially normative, starts from the society or state, the other, in principle at any rate empirical, starts from the individual. In philosophy as in religion, everything is governed by ultimate values, and this is why Plato's ideal state is a hierarchical society. In other terms, philosophy belongs, or at any rate begins, within the sphere of religion (or more precisely of ultimate values of the general type), the political domain as the moderns think of it is not yet there. At the same time, philosophy differs from religion in that ultimate values are not given from revelation, tradition or faith, but discovered or established by the sole use of human reason. (There is nothing new here regarding the relation between philosophy and religion, cf. Hegel, *Vorlesungen in die Geschichte der Philosophie*, ed. Michelet, Stuttgart, 1940 [*Sämtliche Werke*, Band 16], I, p. 92). As reason in fact argues through particular men, the recourse to reason could not but lead to the recognition of the individual, as with the Stoics, and with the Moderns reason was to become the weapon of the individual.

It is not passing a value judgment on ancient philosophy, nor denying the part it played in the genesis of the individual in the West, to say that political philosophy, and particularly that of the Greeks, represents on the whole an intermediary stage between the two extremes I have been considering in so far as the yardstick it applies to society and state is not the individual, but is derived from all-embracing ultimate values, as in the religious sphere. It might then be asked whether it is advisable to define the political sphere as narrowly as I have. As this is the (dominant) modern conception of it, within which we live, and which the sociologist or anthropologist consciously or not carries with him, I think it is at any rate necessary to distinguish it, under one name or another, if confusion is to be avoided.

APPENDIX D (pages 314–334)

15 See for instance John Stuart Mill's definition of a 'nationality' in Sir Percival Griffiths, *The British Impact on India*, London, 1952, pp. 237–38. Marcel Mauss was very much concerned with looking comparatively at the nation, and some of his manuscript notes on this theme, dating most probably from 1919–20, have been published posthumously ('La Nation', *L'Année Sociologique*, 3e

série, 1953–54, pp. 7–68, now Marcel Mauss, *Œuvres*, ed. by V. Karady, 1968, Vol. III, pp. 573–625; see also the communication referred to below in note 19). To give a definition of the nation as a type of society, he classified – provisionally he said – societies, and among 'non-segmentary' societies he distinguished two kinds, those with 'diffuse integration and extrinsic central power, which we propose to call peoples or empires . . .' (p. 584), and, contrasted with them, the nations: 'We call nation a society materially and morally integrated, having a stable, permanent central power and determined boundaries, and where there is a relative moral, mental and cultural unity between the inhabitants, who adhere consciously to the State and its laws' (p. 584, literal translation). By this definition, the ancient Greek city-states are nations (p. 581). About 'moral integration' see below, note 4.

16 This is the point of view from which the 'injection of religion into politics' is condemned. Political science being one of the *forts* of Indian universities, this attitude was to be expected of the more enlightened political leaders, and we owe to it the fact that the Constitution of independent India (Bharat) is, rightly, secular. At the same time, these enlightened leaders failed to recognize that the most successful political agitators of their party, like Tilak and Gandhi, had in actual fact most effectively injected religion into politics, and that this could not simply be ignored without damage. That religion permeates everything in India is a commonplace, but it is a merit to recognize it in the present context, as is done, not always in happy terms, in a recent book: 'Muslim and Hindu religions were not religions in the Western sense of the term, for the social and political lives of their followers were intertwined with their religious practices. It was not easy for such cultures to coalesce to produce a united Indian nation' (K. B. Sayeed, *Pakistan, The Formative Phase*, Karachi, 1960, p. 22).

17 The revolution consists in having joined and confused under 'the individual' (man) the empirical agent and the normative subject (see *Coll. Pap.*, p. 9, and' The Modern Conception of the Individual', *passim*). The case of Islam may appear as a difficulty insofar as Islam does not give autonomy to the political domain, although 'the word of God is addressed directly to the individual' (K. Callard, *Pakistan, a Political Study*, London, 1957, p. 196). But Islam has not (prepared and) accepted, as Christianity did, the modern revolution in values; it is not a religion of the individual in the above sense of the term.

18 That the nation is a political group made up of individuals (in the empirical sense of the term) is pointed out by Mauss. This is actually the concrete aspect of what he calls 'moral integration'

(in the definition, above note 15): such a society has abolished 'all segmentation by clans, cities, tribes, kingdoms, feudal domaines'. . . . 'This integration is such in the nations of a naturally achieved type, that there exists so to say no intermediary between the nation and the citizen, . . . that the individual is all-powerful in the society and the society on the individual', and that to moderate this interplay the reconstitution of sub-groups of some kind has to be contemplated [as Durkheim thought] (*Œuvres*, III, p. 588).

19   It may appear that there is a logical inconsistency in the conjunction of the two aspects: how can a collection of individuals be at the same time an individual of a superior order? This is an important issue, the locus in modern opinion of an effective division which sociology alone can probably reconcile, and which can only be mentioned here. The two aspects of the nation are given empirically in different parts of modern ideology, but one tendency refuses the second aspect in the name of the first: the individual is everything, the nation is only a collection of individuals, i.e. a purely empirical datum, with no absolute and normative reality (the State is merely the instrument of the domination of some kind of interests over others). The individual does not find anything ontologically real between himself and mankind as a whole. In a communication of 1920 ('La notion de nation et l'internationalisme', *Proceedings of the Aristotelian Society*, London, N.S., vol. XX, 1920, pp. 242–52, now in *Œuvres*, 1968, vol. III, pp. 634–36) Mauss calls this kind of internationalism the cosmopolitan 'utopia' of a 'sect'. He says that these ideas do not correspond to any actual group and do not express any defined interest: 'they are only the final outcome of pure individualism, religious and Christian or metaphysical'. The notion of 'man as a citizen of the world' is the consequence 'of an abstract theory of man as a monad everywhere identical to itself, and as agent of a morality which transcends the actualities of social life', something that may be true in the limiting case but which cannot be 'the motivation of action either for most men or for any society'. This text is precious for us; it says in substance that this kind of internationalism, which Mauss prefers to call cosmopolitism, is a mistaken development of individualism. But after all, starting from the generally assumed modern, normative idea of the individual as the embodiment of the absolute, the development is logical. It fails because it neglects society in two ways: 1) by taking the modern ideology of man as an individual as being sufficient to account for the actual life of man in society; 2) correlatively, by preferring the immediate consistency of its intel-

lectual scheme to the recognition of the existence of the nation in the very social universe which has given birth to that ideology. For the sociologist, the nation is in the first place the society which *sees itself as* made up of individuals.

20 *Cf.* K. Callard *Pakistan, a Political Study*, London, 1957, pp. 295–96, and 'The Modern Conception of the Individual', §3.

21 Beni Prasad, *India's Hindu-Muslim Questions*, London, 1945. See also N. C. Chaudhuri's indispensable *Autobiography of an Unknown Indian*, New York, 1951, p. 408 sq., and K. M. Panikkar's article 'The Psychology of Hindu-Muslim Riots', *Contemporary Review*, 1927, pp. 230–36. *Cf.* David G. Mandelbaum, 'Hindu-Moslem Conflict in India', *Middle-East Journal*, I-4, 1947, pp. 369–85. See also note 37 below.

22 The distinction generally made between Muslims of the upper category (the four noble 'tribes') and of the lower category, divided into castes or quasi-castes, is socially very clear. The lower category lives in much closer relationships with its Hindu neighbours. The following quotation from an orthodox Muslim leader (quoted in Khalid Bin Sayeed, *Pakistan: The Formative Phase*, Karachi, 1960, p. 38) starts from a correct observation but shows the confusion of levels: 'But even today go to the villages and see for yourself the brotherly feelings that exist between Hindus and Muslims, and how the two communities participate in each other's functions *as if they were related to each other by family ties*' (my italics).

23 *Cf.* N. C. Chaudhuri, *op. cit.*, and S. V. Ketkar, *An Essay on Hinduism* (*History of Caste in India*, vol. II), London, 1911, p. 149, quoted in Narmadeshwar Prasad, *The Myth of the Caste System*, Patna, 1957, p. 27. *Cf.* Ibbetson, *Panjab Castes*, 1916, pp. 15–16, quoted in O'Malley, *Indian Caste Customs*, p. 57 sq.

24 I am thinking of Northern India and especially of Eastern U.P. During a tense period, a Muslim was careful lest a rumour might spread that he had bought a piece of beef (from field notes).

25 For Mughal times: François Bernier, *Voyages*, ed. 1830, vol. I, pp. 49, 222, 311, 319. Regarding Hindu India, the statement in the text is intentionally provoking. Little work has been done on the question. There were no juridical nor moral safeguards for wealth in the face of political power. Factually, at first sight different periods tell different stories.

26 W. W. Hunter, *The Indian Musalmans*, London, 1872. Arnold Toynbee adopts a similar view. He says that the Muslims were 'handicapped by an intellectual inertia that was the legacy of a former military and political ascendency, and demoralized, instead

of being stimulated, by the shock of their military and political debacle' (*A Study of History*, t. VIII, 1954, p. 203).

27    From H. H. Wilson before the Select Committee of 1853. Quoted in the following work, p. 390.

28    Bimanbehari Majumdar, *History of Political Thought from Rammohun to Dayananda (1821–84)*, vol. I, *Bengal*, Calcutta, 1939.

29    W. W. Hunter, *op. cit.*; re. Patna: K. K. Datta, *Biography of Kumar Singh and Amar Singh*, Patna, 1957; H. P. Chattopadhyaha, *The Sepoy Mutiny 1857, A Social Study and Analysis*, Calcutta, 1959.

30    About their precursors, Sisirkumar Ghosh and others, see B. Majumdar, *op. cit.*, Chapter vi, etc.; see also, for Maharashtra, the following (n. 31), p. 121ff.

31    J. E. Sanjana, *Caste and Outcaste*, Bombay, 1946.

32    Of course the hypothesis results from some study, but it cannot be substantiated here.

33    Report of the Indian Statutory Commission (Simon Commission), London, 1930, vol. I, pp. 29–30. The following quotation is *ibid.*, II, p. 12, §19.

34    Henry Summer Maine, *Ancient Law*, London, 1887, p. 103 sq.

35    Jean-Jacques Rousseau, *Contrat Social*, I, IX.

36    K. Callard, *op. cit.*, p. 215.

37    The bibliography of this essay is anything but complete. A number of recent books throw light upon one or the other aspect of the ideological and political development. Among those that I have seen, Ishtiaq Husain Qureshi, *The Muslim Community of the Indo-Pakistan Subcontinent (610–1947), A Brief Historical Analysis*, The Hague, Mouton, 1962, has valuable remarks (notably, p. 280 sq.), and marks the consequences of the change in power (p. 212 sq.). The lasting heterogeneity of the two communities is clearly noticed by F. Rahman, 'Muslim Modernism in the Indo-Pakistan Subcontinent', *Bull. of the School of Or. and Afr. Studies*, XXI, 1958, p. 89 sq. (p. 90: no religious basis for rapprochement; instead, revivalism), and by Percival Spear, *India, a Modern History*, Ann Arbor, Univ. of Michigan Press, 1961: 'There was much give and take, but no fusion or synthesis. In daily life there was much day-to-day tolerance and consideration, but behind it all was a permanent tension between the two ways of life' (p. 101, *cf.* pp. 408–9).

# BIBLIOGRAPHY

The following list is confined to works cited in the text (excluding the Appendix). It has seemed impossible to give a fuller idea of the contemporary literature without excessively extending the list and going beyond the limits of the present work. For further information, and particularly for the study of 'social change', the reader is referred to a series of bibliographies in the following list:

(1) Gilbert's monumental general bibliography; (2) the bibliography in Hutton's book, easily available, stopping effectively at 1940; (3) for recent works, the critical bibliography by Srinivas *et al.*: *Caste, a Trend Report and Bibliography*, 1959 (161 titles); (4) the anthropological bibliography by Mrs E. von Fürer-Haimendorf, which gives all the recent works and should be completed by an index in its third volume; (5) see also: PATTERSON and INDEN, *South Asia, an Introductory Bibliography* (section c); KANITKAR *et al.*, *Bibliography of Indology*, I; J. M. MAHAR, *India, a Critical Bibliography*.

*Order of classification:* for a given author, first books, and then articles, are classified in alphabetical order.

AIYAPPAN, A.: *Iravas and Culture Change*. Madras, 1944 (*Bulletin of the Madras Government Museum*, N. S., General Section, vol. V, no. 1).

—— 'Caste and Joint Family in Tamilnad' (*Sociological Bulletin*, vol. IV, no. 2, 1955, pp. 177–222).

ALEXANDROVICZ, A.: 'La liberté religieuse dans la Constitution de l'Inde' (*Revue internationale de Droit comparé*, no. 2, 1964, pp. 319–30).

ALSDORF, Ludwig: *Beitrage zür Geschichte von Vegetarismus und Rinderverehrung in Indien*. Wiesbaden, F. Steiner Verlag, 1962. (Akademie der Wissenschaften und der Literatur in Mainz—Abhandlungen der Geistes- und Sozialwissenschaftlichen Klasse, Jahrgang 1961, no. 6, pp. 559–625).

AMMAN, Mgr.: 'Rites Malabares' (*Dictionnaire de théologie catholique*, vol. IX-2, 1927, pp. 1704–46).

*Annuaire de l'École pratique des Hautes Études, section des Sciences économiques et sociales*, 1964–5. Paris.

ANSARI, Ghaus: *Muslim Caste in Uttar Pradesh. A Study of Culture Contact.* With a foreword by J. H. HUTTON. Lucknow, The Ethnographic and Folk Culture Society, 1960.

*Anthropology on the March.* See: BALA RATNAM (ed.).

APPADORAI, A.: *Economic Conditions in Southern India* (A.D. 1000–1500). Madras University, 1936, 2 vols. (Madras Univ. Hist. Series, 12, 12*b*).

APTHORPE, Raymond: *Social Change: An Empirical and Theoretical Study*, Unpubl. D.Phil. Thesis, University of Oxford, 1956.

ARISTOTLE: *La Politique.* J. Tricot, Paris, Vrin, 1962. 2 vols. English translation in W. D. Ross, ed., *The Works of Aristotle*, Oxford, 1921.

*Aspects of Caste.* See LEACH, E. R. (ed.).

AYYAR, L. K. Anantakrishna: *Anthropology of the Syrian Christians.* Ernakulam, Govt. Press, 1926.

BADEN-POWELL, B. H.: *The Land Systems of British India.* Oxford, 1892. 3 vols.

BAILEY, F. G.: *Caste and the Economic Frontier. A Village in Highland Orissa.* Manchester Univ. Press, 1957.

—— *Politics and Social Change, Orissa in* 1959. Berkeley, Univ. of California Press; London, Oxford Univ. Press, 1963.

—— 'Closed Social Stratification in India' (*European Journal of Sociology*, vol. IV, no. 1, 1963, pp. 107–24).

—— 'For a Sociology of India?' (*Contributions to Indian Sociology*, III, 1959, pp. 88–101 [*cf.* discussion: 'A Rejoinder to Dr Bailey', *ibidem*, IV, 1960, pp. 82–9].

—— 'Politics in Orissa' (*Economic Weekly*, vol. XI, no. 35, pp. 37–42, Aug.–Nov. 1959).

—— 'Traditional Society and Representation. A Case Study in Orissa' (*European Journal of Sociology*, vol. I, 1960, pp. 121–41).

BAINES, Athelstane: *Ethnography (Castes and Tribes).* Strasbourg, K. J. Trübner, 1912. (Grundriss der Indo-Arischen Philologie und Altertumskunde II, 5.)

BALA RATNAM (Ed.): *Anthropology on the March. Recent Studies of Indian Beliefs, Attitudes and Social Institutions.* Madras, 1963. [Social Sciences Association, for the birth centenary of L. K. Anantaktrishna Iyer, 34 contributions.]

BALES, R. F. and SLATER, Ph. E.: 'Role Differenciation in Small Decision Making Groups' (T. PARSONS and R. F. BALES, *et al.*: *Family, Socialization and Interaction Process*, London, Routledge and Kegan Paul, 1956, pp. 259–306).

BARTH, Fredrik: 'Ecological Relationships of Ethnic Groups in Swat,

North Pakistan' (*American Anthropologist*, vol. LVIII, 1956, pp. 1079–89).

—— 'The System of Social Stratification in Swat, North Pakistan' (E. R. LEACH, Ed., *Aspects of Caste*, 1960, pp. 113–46).

BEALS, Alan R.: 'Interplay among Factors of Change in a Mysore Village' (McKim MARRIOTT, Ed., *Village India*, 1955, pp. 78–101).

—— 'Leadership in a Mysore Village' (PARK and TINKER, Eds., *Leadership*, 1959, pp. 427–37).

BEALS, A. R. and SIEGEL, B. J.: 'Pervasive Factionalism' (*American Anthropologist*, vol. LXII, 1960, pp. 394–417).

BECK, Brenda: *Marriage Ceremonies in South India*. Oxford, Institute of Social Anthropology, 1964. [Unpublished thesis.]

BEIDELMAN, Thomas O.: *A Comparative Analysis of the Jajmani System*. Locust Valley, N.Y., *c.* 1959. (Monographs of the Association for Asian Studies, VIII.)

BERNIER, François: *Voyages de F. Bernier . . . contenant la description des États du Grand Mogol . . . et où l'on voit comment l'or et l'argent après avoir circulé dans le monde, passent dans l'Indoustan d'où ils ne reviennent plus*. Paris, 1830, 2 vols.

BERREMAN, Gerald D.: *Hindus of the Himalayas*. Berkeley, Univ. of California Press, 1963.

BERREMAN, Gerald D. and DUMONT, Louis: [Discussion of] 'Caste, Racism and Stratification' (*Contributions to Indian Sociology*, VI, 1962, pp. 122–4).

BERTRAND, Joseph, s.j. (ed.): *Lettres édifiantes et curieuses de la nouvelle Mission du Maduré*. Paris-Lyon, 1865. 2 vols.

—— *Mémoires historiques sur les ordres religieux et spécialement sur les questions du clergé indigène et des rites Malabares d'après des documents inédits*. Paris, 2ᵉ éd. 1862.

—— *La Mission du Maduré d'après des documents inédits*. Paris, 1847–1854. 4 vols.

BETEILLE, André: *Caste*. See: M. N. SRINIVAS *et al.*

—— 'A Note on the Referents of Caste' (*European Journal of Sociology*, vol. V, 1964, pp. 130–4).

BHANDARKAR, Ramakrishna Gopal: *Vaiṣṇavism, Śaivaism and Minor Religious Systems*. Strasbourg, K. Trübner, 1913. (Grundriss der Indo-Arischen Philologie und Altertumskunde, III, 6.)

BHATT, G. S.: 'The Chamar of Lucknow' (*Eastern Anthropologist*, vol. VIII, no. 1, 1954, pp. 27–41).

BHATTACHARYA, Jogendranath: *Hindu Castes and Sects*. Calcutta, 1896.

BIARDEAU, Madeleine: *Théorie de la connaissance et philosophie de la parole dans le Brahmanisme classique*. Paris, La Haye, Mouton, 1964. (École pratique des Hautes Études, 6ᵉ section: Le Monde d'Outre-Mer Passé et Présent. Première série: Études, XXIII.)

—— 'L'Inde et l'histoire' (*Revue historique*, 475, July–Sept. 1965, pp. 47–58).

BLUNT, E. A. H.: *The Caste System of Northern India with special Reference to the United Provinces of Agra and Oudh*. London, Oxford Univ. Press, 1931.

—— 'United Provinces of Agra and Oudh' (*Census of India*, 1911, vol. XV, Part I, Report. Allahabad, Govt. Press, 1912).

BOSE, Nirmal Kumar (ed.): *Data on Caste, Orissa*. Calcutta, Anthropological Survey, 1960. (Memoir no. 7.)

—— 'Caste in India' (*Man in India*, vol. XXXI, no. 3–4, 1951, pp. 107–23).

—— 'Some Aspects of Caste in Bengal' (M. SINGER, ed.: *Traditional India*, 1959, pp. 191–206).

BOUGLÉ, Célestin: *Essais sur le régime des castes*. Paris, Alcan (1st ed., 1908) 1927 (Travaux de l'Année Sociologique). [The first part of the book was originally published as an article: 'Remarques sur le régime des castes'(*Année sociologique*, t. IV, 1900, pp. 1–64).] English translation with an introduction by D. F. POCOCK, Cambridge, Cambridge University Press, 1971.

—— *Les Idées égalitaires: étude sociologique*. Paris, 1899.

BROGLIE, Louis de: *Continu et discontinu en physique moderne*. Paris, Albin Michel, 1941.

BROWN, D. Mackenzie: 'Traditional Concepts of Indian Leadership' (PARK and TINKER, eds.: *Leadership*, 1959, pp. 3–17).

BROWN, W. Norman: 'The Sanctity of the Cow in Hinduism' (*Journal, of the Madras University*, Section A, vol. XXVIII, no. 2, Jan. 1957, pp. 29–49). In French, with a later appendix: 'La vache sacrée' (*Annales, Économies, Sociétés, Civilisations*, vol. XIX, no. 4, 1964, pp. 643–64).

CAMPBELL, George: *Modern India. A Sketch of the System of Civil Government*. London, 1852.

CARSTAIRS, G. Morris: *The Twice-Born. A Study of a Community of High-Caste Hindus*. Bloomington, Indiana Univ. Press, 1961. [Severe criticism by D. F. POCOCK in *Contrib. to Indian Sociology*, V, 1961, pp. 46 ff.].

—— 'Bhil Villages of Western Udaipur' (M. N. SRINIVAS, ed., *India's Villages*, 2nd ed. 1960, pp. 68–76).

*Caste. A Trend Report and Bibliography*. See: M. N. SRINIVAS *et al*.

*Census of India* [Decennial statistics, for the whole of India by provinces or States, from 1881 to 1961. As far as possible, the texts cited have been brought under the respective authors].

*Census of India* 1881, Punjab. See: D. C. J. IBBETSON.

—— 1901, India. See: H. H. RISLEY.

—— 1911, India. See: E. A. GAIT.

—— 1911, United Provinces. See: E. A. H. BLUNT.

—— 1931, Rajputana. See: B. L. COLE.

CHAMBARD, J.-L.: 'Mariages secondaires et foires aux femmes en Inde Centrale' (*L'Homme*, vol. I, no. 2, May–Aug. 1961, pp. 51–88).

CHANDRASHEKHARAIYAH, K.: 'Mobility Patterns within the Caste' (*Sociological Bulletin*, vol. XI, no. 1–2, 1962, pp. 62–7).

CHAPEKAR, N. G.: 'Social Change in Rural Maharashtra' (K. M. KAPADIA, ed.: *Ghurye Felicit. Vol.*, 1954, pp. 169–82).

CHATTOPADHYAY, K. P. (ed.): *Study of Change in Traditional Culture* (Proceedings of Conferences held by the University of Calcutta in Co-operation with UNESCO). Calcutta, Univ. of Calcutta, 1957.

CHATTOPADHYAY, K. P.: *Some Approaches to Study of Social Change.* Poona, Gokhale Inst. of Politics and Economics, 1959. (R. R. KALE Memorial Lecture, 1959.)

—— 'History of Indian Social Organization' (*Journal of the Asiatic Society of Bengal*, Letters, vol. I, 1935, pp. 377–95).

CHAUDURI, Nirad C.: *The Autobiography of an Unknown Indian.* London, Macmillan, 1951.

CHAUDHURI, Sachin: 'Centralization and the Alternate Forms of Decentralization: A Key Issue' (Roy TURNER, ed.: *India's Urban Future*, 1962, pp. 213–39).

COHN, Bernard S.: 'Chamar Family in a North Indian Village. A Structural Contingent (*Economic Weekly*, Bombay, vol. XIII, Sp. Nr. 27–28–29, July 1961, pp. 1051–5).

—— 'The Changing Status of a Depressed Caste' (McKim MARRIOTT, ed., *Village India*, 1955, pp. 53–77).

—— 'Changing Traditions of a Low Caste' (M. SINGER, ed., *Traditional India*, 1959, pp. 207–15).

—— [review of] 'McKim MARRIOTT: *Caste Ranking* (Poona, 1960)' (*Journal of the American Oriental Society*, vol. 82, no. 3, 1962, pp. 425–30).

—— 'Law and Change (Some Notes on) in North India' (*Economic Development and Cultural Change*, vol. VIII, no. 1, 1959, pp. 79–93).

—— 'Madhopur Revisited' (*Economic Weekly*, Bombay, vol. XI, July 1959, pp. 963–6).

—— 'Political Systems in Eighteenth Century India: The Banaras Region' (*Journal of the American Oriental Society*, vol. 82, no. 3, July–Sept. 1962, pp. 312–20).

COLE, B. L.: 'The Rajput clans of Rajputana' (*Census of India*, 1931, vol. XXVII (App.). Meerut, 1932, pp. 134–41).

*Contributions to Indian Sociology.* Paris, La Haye, Mouton, I–IX, 1957–1966. L. DUMONT and D. F. POCOCK, eds. [and joint authors for nos. I–III.] (École pratique des Hautes Études, 6e section, Paris.)

COUPLAND, Sir Reginald: *India, a Re-statement*. London, Oxford Univ. Press, 1945.

COX, C. Oliver: *Caste, Class and Race: a Study in Social Dynamics*. New York, Doubleday, 1948.

CRAWLEY, Ernest: *The Mystic Rose*. London (1902), 4th ed., Watts, 1932.

CROOKE, W.: *Tribes and Castes of the North-Western Provinces and Oudh*. Calcutta, 1896, 4 vols.

—— 'Hinduism' (*Encyclopaedia of Religion and Ethics*, s.v., vol. VI, pp. 686–715).

—— 'The Veneration of the Cow in India' (*Folklore*, 23, 1912, pp. 275–306).

DALTON, Edward Tuite: *Descriptive Ethnology of Bengal*. Calcutta (1872) 1960.

DAMLE, Y. B.: *Caste*. See: M. N. SRINIVAS *et al.*

DAS, Abinas Chandra: *The Vaisya Caste*. I. *The Gandhavaniks of Bengal*. Calcutta, 1903.

DAVIS, Kingsley: *The Population of India and Pakistan*. Princeton Univ. Press, 1951.

DAVY, Georges: *Éléments de Sociologie*. I. *Sociologie Politique*. Paris, Vrin (1924) 1950.

DELACROIX, Mgr. S. (ed.): *Histoire universelle des missions catholiques*. Paris, Grand, 1956–9, 4 vols.

DESAI, A. R.: *Recent Trends in Indian Nationalism*. Bombay, Popular Book Depot, 1960.

—— *Social Background of Indian Nationalism*. Bombay, Oxford Univ. Press, 1948. [Critical discussion: L. DUMONT: *Contributions to Indian Sociology*, VII, 1964, pp. 32–9.]

DESAI, I. P. and DAMLE, Y. B.: 'A Note on the Change in the Caste' (K. M. KAPADIA, ed., *Ghurye Felicit. Vol.*, 1954, pp. 266–76).

DHILLON, H. S. *et al.*: *Leadership and Groups in a South Indian Village*. New Delhi, Govt. of India Press, 1955. (Planning Commission, Programme Evaluation Organization, Publication 9.)

DIEHL, Carl Gustav: *Church and Shrine. Intermingling Patterns in the Life of some Christian Groups in South India*. Uppsala, 1965 (Acta Universitatis Upsaliensis, Historia Religionum, 2).

DUBE, S. C.: *Indian Village*. London, Routledge and Kegan Paul, 1955. (International Library of Sociology and Social Reconstruction.)

DUBOIS, Abbé J. A.: *Mœurs, institutions et cérémonies des peuples de l'Inde*. Paris, Imprimerie Royale, 1825. 2 vols. An earlier edition appeared in English in 1917. The standard English translation, to which page references are made, is by Henry K. Beauchamp: *Hindu Manners, Customs and Ceremonies*, 3rd ed., Oxford, 1906.

DUMÉZIL, Georges: 'Métiers et classes fonctionnelles chez divers peuples Indo-Européens (*Annales, Économies, Sociétés, Civilisations* 13ᵉ année, no. 4, Oct.–Dec. 1958, pp. 716–24).

DUMONT, Louis: *La civilisation indienne et nous. Equisse de sociologie comparée*. Paris, A. Colin, 1964. 2nd ed., 1975 (coll Uprisme).

—— *Collected Papers*, see *Religion, Politics and History in India*.

—— *Hierarchy and Marriage Alliance in South India Kinship*. London. Royal Anthropological Institute, 1957. (Occasional Papers, no. 12) In French: *Dravidien et Kariera, l'alliance de mariage dans l'Inde du sud et en Australie*. Paris-La Haye, Mouton, 1975.

—— *Religion, Politics and History in India*. Collected Papers in Indian Sociology, The Hague, Mouton, *c*. 1970.

—— *Une Sous-Caste de l'Inde du Sud. Organisation sociale et religion des Pramalai Kallar*. Paris, La Haye, Mouton, 1957. (École pratique des Hautes Études, VIᵉ section. Le Monde d'Outre-Mer Passéet Présent, Iʳᵉ série, Études I.)

—— *La Tarasque*, Paris, Gallimard, 1951.

—— 'The British in India' (*History of Mankind: Cultural and Scientific Development*, vol. V, The 19th Century, ed. by Ch. MORAZÉ, London, Allen A. Unwin, *c*. 1976, Part 4, pp. 1084–1144).

—— 'Caste: a phenomenon of social structure or an aspect of Indian culture?' (in: A. V. S., DE REUCK and Julie KNIGHT, eds., *Ciba Foundation Symposium on Caste and Race: Comparative Approaches*, London, Churchill, 1967).

—— 'La dette vis-à-vis des ancêtres et la catégorie de *sapiṇḍa*'(*Purushartha*, 4, 1980).

—— 'The Individual as an Impediment to Sociological Comparison and Indian History' V. B. SINGH and Baljit SINGH, eds.: *Social and Economic Change Essays in Honour of D. P. Mukerji*. Bombay, Allied Publishers, 1967; repr. in *Coll. Pap.*, no. 7).

—— 'Introductory Note: Change, Interaction, and Comparison' (*Contributions to Indian Sociology*, VII, 1964, pp. 7–17).

—— 'Marriage in India, the Present State of the Question: I. Marriage Alliance in S.E. India and Ceylon; Postscript to Part I, II. Marriage and Status, Nayar and Newar; III. North India in relation to South India' (*Contributions to Indian Sociology*, V, 1961, pp. 75–95; VII, 1964, pp. 77–98; IX, 1966, pp. 90–114).

—— 'Le mariage secondaire dans l'Inde du Nord'. (*VIᵉ Congrès international des Sciences anthropologiques et ethnologiques*, Paris, 1960, I–II, pp. 53–5).

—— 'Les mariages Nayar comme faits indiens' (*L'Homme*, vol. I, no. 1, 1961, pp. 11–36).

—— 'The Modern Conception of the Individual, Notes on its Genesis' (*Contributions to Indian Sociology*, VIII, 1965, pp. 13–61).

—— 'Pour une sociologie de l'Inde' (*La Civilisation indienne et Nous*,

1964, pp. 89–115). English version: 'For a Sociology of India' (*Coll. Pap.*, no. 1).

—— 'A remarkable Feature of South-Indian Pot-Making' (*Man*, 1952, no. 121).

—— 'A structural Definition of a Folk Deity of Tamil Nad' (*Coll. Pap.*, no. 2).

—— 'The Village Community from Munro to Maine' (*Coll. Pap.*, no. 6).

DUMONT, Louis and POCOCK, David F.: 'A. M. Hocart on Caste: Religion and Power' (*Contributions to Indian Sociology*, II, 1958, pp. 45–63).

—— 'Commented Summary of the Ist Part of Bouglé's Essais' (*Contributions to Indian Sociology*, II, 1958, pp. 31–44).

—— 'On the Different Aspects or Levels in Hinduism' (*Contributions to Indian Sociology*, II, 1958, pp. 31–44).

—— 'Possession and Priesthood' (*Contributions to Indian Sociology*, III, 1959, pp. 55–74).

—— 'Pure and Impure' (*Contributions to Indian Sociology*, III, 1959, pp. 9–39).

—— 'Village Studies' (*Contributions to Indian Sociology*, I, 1957, pp. 23–41).

DURKHEIM, Émile: [review of] 'B. H. BADEN-POWELL, *The Indian Village Community* (London, 1896)' (*Année sociologique*, I, 1897, pp. 359–62).

DUTT, N. K.: *Origin and Growth of Caste in India*, vol. I (2000–300 B.C.). London, Trübner, 1931.

DUTT, Romesh Chunder: *The Economic History of India*. London, Routledge and Kegan Paul (1902), 1956. 2 vols.

ELLEFSEN, Richard A.: 'City-Hinterland Relationships in India' (Roy TURNER, ed.: *India's Urban Future*, 1962, pp. 94-116).

ELLIOT, H. M.: *Memoirs on the History, Folklore and Distribution of the Races of the N.W. Provinces of India* (ed. by J. BEANES). London, 1869. 2 vols. [enlarged edition of the following work].

—— *Supplement to the Glossary of Indian Terms*. Agra, 1845.

ELMORE, Wilbur Theodore: *Dravidian Gods in Modern Hinduism. A Study of the Local and Village Deities of Southern India*. New York, Hamilton, 1915.

ELPHINSTONE, Mountstuart: *Report on the Territories conquered from the Paishwa. Submitted to the Supreme Government of British India.* (Calcutta, 1821.) Bombay, Govt. Press, 1838.

ENTHOVEN, R. E.: *The Tribes and Castes of Bombay*. Bombay, Govt Central Press, 1920–22. 3 vols.

—— 'Lingayat' (*Encyclopaedia of Religion and Ethnics, s.v.*, vol. VIII, pp. 69–75).

EPSTEIN, T. Scarlett: *Economic Development and Social Change in South India*. Manchester Univ. Press, 1962.

*Essays on Caste* 1851 [three essays written by missionaries, respectively: H. BOWER, S. C. DATTA and K. M. BANERJEA, published in Calcutta; British Museum, 4505 aaa16].

EVANS-PRITCHARD, E. E. (ed.). See: FORTES, M. and EVANS-PRITCHARD, E. E. (ed.).

EVANS-PRITCHARD, E. E.: *Kinship and Marriage among the Nuer*. Oxford, Clarendon Press, 1951.

—— *The Nuer. A Description of the Modes of Livelihood and Political Institutions of a Nilotic People*. Oxford, Clarendon Press, 1940. French translation, *Les Nuer*, Paris, Gallimard, 1968. Preface by L. DUMONT.

FARQUHAR, J. N.: *An Outline of the Religious Literature of India*. London, Oxford Univ. Press, 1920. (The Religious Quest of India.)

*Fifth Report*. See: FIRMINGER, W. K. (ed.).

FIRMINGER, W. K. (ed.): *The Fifth Report from the Select Committee . . . 28th July* 1812. Calcutta, 1917–18. 3 vols.

FIRTH, Raymond *et al.*: 'Factions in Indian and Overseas Indian Societies' (*British Journal of Sociology*, vol. VIII, 1957).

FISHMAN, Alvin Texas: *Culture Change and the Underprivileged. A Study of Madigas in South India under Christian Guidance*. Madras, The Christian Literary Society, 1941.

FORTES, M. and EVANS-PRITCHARD, E. E. (ed.): *African Political Systems*. London, Oxford Univ. Press (1940), 1961. (International African Institute.)

FUCHS, Stephen: *The Children of Hari: Study of the Nimar Balahis in the Central Provinces of India*. Vienna, Herold, 1950 (Wiener Beiträge zur Kulturgeschichte und Linguistik, vol. 8).

—— 'The Scavengers of Nimar District in Madhya Pradesh' (*Journal of the Bombay Branch of the Royal Asiatic Society*, vol. XXVII, no. 1, 1951, pp. 86–98).

FÜRER-HAIMENDORF, Christoph von: [review of]: 'L. DUMONT, *Une Sous-caste de l'Inde du Sud* (1957)' (*Sociologus*, NF. Jahrgang 9, Heft 1, 1959, pp. 79–83).

FÜRER-HAIMENDORF, Elizabeth von: *An Anthropological Bibliography of South Asia, together with a Directory of Recent Anthropological Field Work*. Paris, La Haye, Mouton, 1958–1964. 2 vols. (I. [up to 1954]; II. 1955–1959). (École pratique des Hautes Études, VIᵉ section. Le Monde d'Outre-Mer, Passé et Présent. 4ᵉ série: Bibliographies, III).

GAIT, E. A.: 'Caste' (*Encyclopaedia of Religion and Ethics*, s.v., vol. III, pp. 230–39).

—— 'India' (*Census of India* 1911, vol. I, Part I, Report. Calcutta, Govt. Printing, 1913).

GANDHI, M. K.: *An Autobiography, or The Story of My Experiments with Truth*, trans. M. DESAI. Ahmedabad, 1948 (1927–1929). French translation: *Expériences de vérité. Autobiographie*. Paris, Pr. Univ. de Fr., 1950.

GEIGER, Wilhelm: *Culture in Mediaeval Ceylon*. Ed. by Heinz BECHERT. Wiesdbaden, Otto Harrassowitz, 1960.

GHURYE, G. S.: *Caste and Race in India*. London, Kegan Paul; New York, 1932. [See also the following work.]

—— *Caste and Class in India*. Bombay, Popular Book Depot, 1950. [Modified re-edition of the previous work.]

*Ghurye Felicitation Volume*. See: KAPADIA, K. M. (ed.).

GILBERT, William H.: *Caste in India. A Bibliography*. Washington, D.C., Library of Congress, 1948 [Roneo, 5340 titles].

—— 'The Sinhalese Caste System of Central and Southern Ceylon' (*The Ceylon Historical Journal*, vol. II, no. 3–4, Jan.–Sept. 1953). [Reprinted from: *Journal of the Washington Academy of Sciences*, vol. XXXV, 1945.]

GIST, Noël P.: 'Occupational Differentiation in South India' (*Social Forces*, Chapel Hill, N.C., 33, 1954, p. 129).

GOLDSTEIN, Kurt: *Der Aufbau des Organismus*. Haag, 1934 [French trans., Paris, Gallimard, 1951].

GOODDINE, R. N.: *Report on the Village Communities of the Deccan*. Bombay, 1852. (Selections from the Records of the Bombay Government, no. IV.)

GOUGH, E. Kathleen: 'Caste in a Tanjore Village' (E. R. LEACH (ed.): *Aspects of Caste*, 1960, pp. 11–60).

—— 'Criteria of Caste Ranking in South India' (*Man in India*, vol. XXXIX, 2, 1959, pp. 115–26).

—— 'The Hindu Jajmani System' (*Economic Development and Cultural Change*, vol. IX, no. 1, Oct. 1960, pp. 83 ff.).

—— 'The Social Structure of a Tanjore Village' (M. N. SRINIVAS (ed.): *India's Villages*, 1955, pp. 82–92).

—— 'The Social Structure of a Tanjore Village' (McKim MARRIOTT (ed.): *Village India*, 1955, pp. 36–52).

GOULD, Harold A.: 'Sanskritization and Westernization: A Dynamic View' (*Economic Weekly*, vol. XIII, 1961, pp. 945–50).

GRIMSHAW, Allen D.: 'The Anglo-Indian Community; the Integration of a Marginal Group' (*Journal of Asian Studies*, vol. 18, 1958–9, pp. 227–40).

GUHA, B. S. (ed.): *Studies in Social Tensions among the Refugees from Eastern Pakistan*. Calcutta, Govt. of India Press, 1959 (Govt. of India, Dpt. of Anthropology, Memoir no. 1, 1954).

GUNE, Vithal Trimbak: *The Judicial System of the Marathas*. Poona, Deccan College Research Institute, 1953.

HALÉVY, Elie: *La formation du radicalisme philosophique*. Paris, Alcan, 1901. 2 vols. English translation by M. MORRIS: *The Growth of Philosophical Radicalism*, London, 1928.

HARPER, Edward B.: 'Two Systems of Economic Exchange in Village India' (*American Anthropologist*, vol. LXI, 1959, pp. 760–78).

HEESTERMAN, J. C.: 'Brahmin, Ritual and Renouncer' (*Wiener Zeitschrift für die Kunde Süd- und Ostasiens*, vol. VIII, 1964, pp. 1–31).

HEGEL, G. W. F.: *Leçons sur la Philosophie de l'Histoire*. French trans. by J. GIBELIN. Paris, Vrin (2 vols., 1937), 1946. English translation from third German edition by J. SIBREE, *Lectures on the Philosophy of History*. London, 1888.

HITCHCOCK, John T.: 'Leadership in a North Indian Village: Two Case Studies' (PARK and TINKER (eds.): *Leadership*, 1959, pp. 395–414).

HOBSON-JOBSON. See: YULE and BURNELL.

HOCART, A. M.: *Caste, A Comparative Study*. London, 1950. French version: *Les Castes*. Paris, Geuthner, 1938. (Annales du Musée Guimet, Bibliothèque de Vulgarisation, v. 54).

—— *Kings and Councillors*. Cairo, 1936.

HOPKINS, Edward Washburn: *India, Old and New, with a Memorial Address*. New York, 1896. [Ancient and Modern Guilds, pp. 169–205.]

HOSELITZ, Bert F. (ed.): *The Progress of Underdeveloped Areas*. Chicago, Univ. of Chicago Press, 1952.

—— 'The Role of Urbanization in Economic Development: Some International Comparisons' (Roy TURNER (ed.): *India's Urban Future*, 1962, pp. 157–81).

—— 'A Survey of the Literature on Urbanization in India' (Roy TURNER (ed.): *India's Urban Future*, 1962, pp. 425–43).

HOSELITZ, Bert F. and LAMBERT, Richard D. ed,: *Le rôle de l'épargne et de la richesse – Asie du Sud et en Accident*. Paris, UNESCO, 1961.

HSU, F. L. K.: *Clan, Caste and Club*. Princeton, New Jersey, D. van Nostrand, 1963.

HUBERT, H. and MAUSS, M.: 'Essai sur la nature et la fonction du sacrifice' (*Mélanges d'Histoire des Religions*. Paris, Alcan, 1929, pp. 1–130). [or: *Année Sociologique*, II, 1899, pp. 29–138.] English translation by W. D. HALLS: *Sacrifice: its Nature and Function*. London, 1964.

HUSAIN, A. F. A.: 'Pakistan' (in LAMBERT and HOSELITZ: *Le Rôle de l'épargne*).

HUTTON, J. H.: *Caste in India, its Nature, Function, and Origins*. Cambridge Univ. Press, 1946. [French trans., Paris, Payot, 1949.]

—— [Review of]:'A. M. HOCART, *Caste, a Comparative Study*' (*Man*, 1951, no. 235).

IBBETSON, Denzil Charles Jelf: *Panjab Castes*. Being a Reprint of the

Chapter on 'The Races, Castes . . .' in . . . the Census of the Punjab (1881). Lahore, Govt. Printing, 1916.

—— 'The Races, Castes and Tribes of the People' (*Report on the Census of the Punjab, taken on the 17th Feb. 1881*. Calcutta, Govt. Printing, 1883. Chapter VI, pp. 172–341).

*Inde Classique*. See: L. RENOU *et al.*

*India's Urban Future*. See: Roy TURNER (ed.).

*India's Villages*. See: M. N. SRINIVAS (ed.).

IRVING, B. A.: *The Theory and Practice of Caste, Being an Inquiry into the Effects of Caste on the Institutions and Probable Destiny of the Anglo-Indian Empire*. London, 1853.

JACKSON, A. M. T.: 'Note on the History of the Caste System' (*Journal of the Asiatic Society of Bengal*, N.S., vol. III, no. 7, July 1907, pp. 509–15).

JOLLY, Julius: *Recht und Sitte*. Strasbourg, 1896. (*Grundriss der Indo-Arischen Phil. u. Altertumskunde*, II, 8). English translation by B. GHOSH: *Hindu Law and Custom* (Greater India Soc., publ. 2). Calcutta, 1928.

JOLLY, J. and SCHMIDT, R. (eds.): *Arthaśāstra of Kauṭilya*. Lahore, 1923–4. 2 vols.

KANE, Pandurang Vaman: *History of Dharmaśāstra* (*Ancient and Mediaeval, Religious and Civil Law*). Poona, Bhandarkar Oriental Research Institute, 1930–1962, 5 vols. (Govt. Or. Series, Class B, no. 6).

KANITKAR, J. M., BANERJEE, D. L. and OHDEKAR, A. K.: *A Bibliography of Indology*. Vol. I. *Indian Anthropology*. Calcutta, National Library, Govt. of India, 1960.

KAPADIA, K. M. (ed.): *Ghurye Felicitation Volume. Issued under the Auspices of Ghurye 60th Birthday Celebration Committee*. Bombay, Popular Book Depot, 1954.

KAPADIA, K. M.: *Hindu Kinship. An Important Chapter in Hindu Social History*. Bombay, Popular Book Depot, 1947.

—— *Marriage and Family in India*. London, Oxford Univ. Press, 1955.

—— 'Caste in Transition' (*Sociological Bulletin*, vol. XI, 1–2, 1962, pp. 73–90).

KARDINER, Abram and LINTON, Ralph: *The Individual and His Society. The Psychodynamics of Primitive Social Organization*. New York (1939), 1947.

KARIM, Nazmul: *Changing Society in India and Pakistan. A Study in Social Change and Social Stratification*. Dacca, Oxford Univ. Press, 1956.

KARVE, Irawati: *Hindu Society. An Interpretation*. Poona, Deccan College, 1961.

—— *Kinship Organisation in India.* Poona, Deccan College, 1953 (Deccan College Monograph Series, 11).

KARVE, I. and DAMLE, Y. B.: *Group Relations in Village Community,* Poona, Deccan College Res. Inst., 1963 (Deccan Coll. Monogr. Ser. no. 24). [144 tables.]

KETKAR, Shridhar V.: *The History of Caste in India; Evidence of the Laws of Manu on the Social Conditions in India during the Third Century A.D., Interpreted and Examined; with an Appendix on Radical Defects of Ethnology,* vol. I. Ithaca, N.Y., 1909.

—— *An Essay on Hinduism, its Formation and Future; illustrating the Laws of Social Evolution as reflected in the History of the Formation of the Hindu Community.* (History of Caste in India, vol. II.) London, Luzac, 1911.

KÖHLER, Wolfgang: *Gestaltpsychology.* London, 1930. [French trans.: *Psychologie de la forme.* Paris, Gallimard (coll. Idées).]

KOSAMBI, D. D.: *An Introduction to the Study of Indian History.* Bombay, Popular Book Depot, 1956.

—— 'Early Stages of the Caste System in Northern India' (*Journal of the Bombay Branch of the Royal Asiatic Society,* 22, 1946, pp. 33–48).

KOYRÉ, Alexandre: *Études d'Histoire de la Pensée Philosophique.* Paris, Armand Colin, 1961. (Cahiers des Annales, 19.)

—— *Introduction à la lecture de Platon. Entretiens sur Descartes,* Paris, Gallimard, 1962. (Collection Les Essais, CVII.) The work on Plato is translated into English by L. C. ROSENFIELD: *Discovering Plato.* New York, 1945.

KROEBER, A. L.: 'Caste' (*Encyclopaedia of Social Sciences,* vol. III, 1930, 254*b*–257*a*).

KUPPUSWAMY, B.: 'A Statistical Study of Attitudes to the Caste System in South India' (*The Journal of Psychology.* Worcester, Mass., vol. XLII, 1956, pp. 169–206).

LAMBERT, Richard D.: *Workers, Factories and Social Change in India.* Princeton, N.J., Princeton Univ. Press, 1963.

—— 'The Impact of Urban Society upon Village Life' (Roy TURNER (ed.): *India's Urban Future,* 1962, pp. 117–40).

LAMBERT, Richard D. and HOSELITZ, Bert F.: *Le rôle de l'épargne* (see HOSELITZ).

LASLETT, Peter (ed.): *Philosophy, Politics and Society.* Oxford, Blackwell, 1956.

—— and RUNCIMAN, W. G. (ed.): *Philosophy, Politics and Society,* 2nd Series. Oxford, Blackwell, 1962.

LAUNAY, Adrien: *Histoire des Missions de l'Inde (Pondichéry, Maïssour, Coïmbatour).* Paris, 1898. 5 vols.

LEACH, E. R. (ed.): *Aspects of Caste in South India, Ceylon and North-*

*West Pakistan*. Cambridge Univ. Press, 1960. (Cambridge Papers in Social Anthropology, 2.)

LEACH, Edmund R.: *Pul Eliya. A Village in Ceylon. A Study of Land Tenure and Kinship*. Cambridge Univ. Press, 1961.

*Lettres édifiantes et curieuses*. . . . Paris, Le Clerc, 1707–1776. 34 vols. [etc.]

[Lettres édifiantes . . .]. *Choix des Lettres édifiantes*. . . . *Missions de l'Inde*. Paris, 3 éd., t. VIII, 1835.

LÉVI-STRAUSS, Claude: *Anthropologie structurale*. Paris, Plon, 1958.

LEWIS, OSCAR: *Village Life in North India*. Urbana, Univ. of Illinois Press, 1958.

—— and DHILLON, Harvant Singh: *Group Dynamics in a North Indian Village. A Study of Factions*. Delhi, Planning Commission, Programme Evaluation Organization, 1954.

LINGAT, Robert: *Les Sources du Droit dans le système traditionnel de l'inde*. Paris, La Haye, Mouton, 1967; trans. by J. D. M. DERRETT, *The Classical Law of India*, Berkeley, University of California Press, 1973.

—— 'L'influence juridique de l'Inde au Champa et au Cambodge d'après l'épigraphie' (*Journal Asiatique*, 237–2, 1949, pp. 273–90).

—— 'Time and the Dharma; on *Manu*', I, 85–6 (*Contributions to Indian Sociology*, VI, 1962, pp. 7–16).

—— 'Vinaya et droit laïque' (*Bulletin de l'École Francaise d'Extrême-Orient*, vol. XXVII, 1937, pp. 415–77).

LYALL, Alfred: *Asiatic Studies*. London, Murray (1849) 1899. 2 vols.

LYNCH, Owen M.: 'Some Aspects of Rural-Urban Continuum in India' (BALA RATNAM (ed.): *Anthropology on the March*, 1963, pp. 178–205).

McCORMACK, William: 'Factionalism in a Mysore Village' (PARK and TINKER (ed.): *Leadership*, 1959, pp. 438–44).

—— 'Lingayats as a Sect' (*Journal of the Royal Anthropological Institute*, vol. XCIII, no. 1, 1963, pp. 59–71).

MACIVER, R. M.: *The Web of Government*. New York, 1947.

MACLEAN: 'Syrian (Christians)' (*Encyclopaedia of Religion and Ethics*, s.v., vol. XII, pp. 167–81).

MAHALINGAM, T. V.: *South Indian Polity*. Madras, Univ. of Madras, 1955. (Madras Univ. Hist. Series, no. 21.)

MAHAR, J. Michael: *India, A Critical Bibliography*. Tucson, Arizona, The Univ. of Arizona Press, 1964.

MAHAR, Pauline M.: 'A Multiple Scaling Technique for Caste Ranking' (*Man In India*, vol. XXXIX, no. 2, 1959, pp. 127–47).

MAINE, H. Sumner: 'India' (Humphrey WARD: *The Reign of Queen Victoria*. London, 1887. 2 vols., vol. I, pp. 460–522).

MAJUMDAR, D. N.: *Caste and Communication in an Indian Village*. Delhi, Asia Publ. House, 1959.

—— *Races and Cultures of India* (Lucknow, 1944). Bombay, Asia Publ. House, 1958.

MALSON, Lucien: *Les enfants sauvages, mythe et réalité*. Paris, Union générale d'Éditions, 1964.

MANDELBAUM, David G.: 'Concepts and Methods in the Study of Caste' (*Economic Weekly*, vol. II, nos. 4–6, 1959, pp. 145–8).

—— 'The Jewish Way of Life in Cochin' (*Jewish Social Studies*, vol. I, no. 4, 1939, pp. 423–60).

—— 'The World and the World View of the Kota' (McKim MARRIOTT (ed.): *Villiage India*, 1955, pp. 233–54).

MARCUSE, Herbert: *Reason and Revolution* (New York, 1941). Boston, Beacon Press, 1960.

MARRIOTT, McKim (ed.): *Village India. Studies in the Little Community*. Chicago, Univ. of Chicago Press, 1955 (Comparative Studies of Cultures and Civilizations. Publ. also as Memoir no. 83 of the Amer. Anthrop. Association).

MARRIOTT, McKim: *Caste Ranking and Community Structure in Five Regions of India and Pakistan*. Poona, 1960 (Deccan Coll. Monogr. Ser., no. 23). [Originally in: *Bull. Decc. Coll. Res. Inst.*, 1958.]

—— 'Caste Ranking and Food Transactions, a Matrix Analysis' (in Milton SINGER and Bernard S. COHN (eds.): *Structure and Change in Indian Society*. Chicago, Aldine, *c*. 1968 [Viking Fund Publications in Anthropology, no. 47]).

—— 'Interactional and Attributional Theories of Caste Ranking' (*Man in India*, vol. XXXIX, no. 2, 1959, pp. 92–107).

—— 'La modernisation de l'agriculture dans les régions rurales surdéveloppées' (*Chronique Sociale de France*. Lyon, Ap. 1954, pp. 123–34) [in English: 'Technological Change in Over-developed Rural Areas' (*Economic Development and Cultural Change*, vol. I, 1952, pp. 261–72)].

—— 'Social Change in an Indian Village' (*Economic Development and Cultural Change*, vol. II, June 1952, pp. 145–55).

—— 'Social Structure and Change in a U.P. Village' (SRINIVAS (ed.): *India's Villages*, 1955, pp. 96–109).

—— 'Village Structure and the Panjab Government. A Restatement' (*American Anthropologist*, vol. LV, no. 1, 1953, pp. 137–43).

MARTIN, Montgomery: *The History, Antiquities, Topography and Statistics of Eastern India*. London, 1838. 3 vols. [Text by Francis BUCHANAN, for years 1807 ff.]

MARX, Karl: *Le Capital*, vol. II. Paris, Éditions Sociales, *c*. 1948 English translation, *Capital*, Moscow, 1954.

MATHUR, K. S.: 'Village Studies in India' (*Man in India*, vol. XXXIX, no. 1, 1959, pp. 45–52).

MATTHAI, John: *Village Government in British India.* London, 1915 (Studies in Economic and Political Science, no. 48).

MAUSS, Marcel: *Manuel d'Ethnographie.* Paris, Payot, 1947 (Bibliothèque scientifique).

―― 'Parentés à plaisanteries' (*Annuaire de l'École pratique des Hautes Études*, Section des Sciences Religieuses, 1927–1928, pp. 3–21).

―― See: HUBERT and MAUSS.

MAX MÜLLER, Friedrich: *Chips from a German Workshop.* London, 1867. 3 vols. ['Caste', vol. II, pp. 297–356.]

MAYER, Adrian C.: *Caste and Kinship in Central India. A Village and its Region.* London, Routledge, 1960.

―― 'Associations in Fiji Indian Rural Society' (*American Anthropologist*, vol. LVIII, 1956, pp. 97–108).

―― 'The Dominant Caste in a Region of Central India' (*Southwestern Journal of Anthropology*, vol. XIV, 1958, pp. 407–27).

―― 'Local Government Election in a Malwa Village' (*Eastern Anthropologist*, vol. XI, 1958, pp. 189–202).

MAZUMDAR, Bhakat Prasad: *Socio-Economic History of Northern India* (A.D. 1030–1194). Calcutta, K. L. Mukhopadhyay, 1960.

MERLEAU-PONTY, Maurice: *La Structure du comportement.* Paris, Pr. Univ. de Fr., 1942 (Bibl. de Philosophie Contemporaine). English translation by A. L. FISHER: *The Structure of Behaviour.* London, 1965.

METCALFE, C.: 'Minute' in *Report from Select Committee*, 1832, Evidence, III, Revenue, App. No. 84, pp. 328 ff.

MILL, James: *The History of British India.* London, 1817. 3 vols. (5th ed. with notes and continuation by Horace Hayman WILSON, 1858, 10 vols).

―― 'Caste' (*Encyclopaedia Britannica*, Edinburgh, Supplement 1824, 6 vols., s.v. [signed 'F.F.']).

MILLER, Eric J.: 'Caste and Territory in Malabar' (*American Anthropologist*, vol. LVI, no. 3, 1954, pp. 410–20).

MOOKERJI, Radha Kumud: *Local Government in Ancient India.* Oxford (1919), 1958 (Mysore Univ. Studies, Hist. Ser. no. 1).

MOORE, Harvey C.: 'Cumulation and Cultural Processes' (*American Antropologist*, vol. LVI, no. 3, 1954, pp. 347–57).

MUIR, J.: *Original Sanskrit Texts on the Origin and History of the People of India, their Religion and their Institutions*, 2nd ed. London, 1868. 5 vols.

MUKERJI, Radha Kamal: *Inter-caste Tensions. Caste Tensions Studies.* Lucknow Univ., 1951.

MUKHERJEE, Bhabananda: 'Caste-Ranking among Rajbanshis in North Bengal' (BALA RATNAM (ed.): *Anthropology on the March*, 1963, pp. 206–12).

MUKHERJEE, Ramkrishna: *The Dynamics of a Rural Society. A Study of the Economic Structure in Bengal Villages.* Berlin, Akademie Verlag, 1957.

MURDOCH, John: *Caste, its supposed Origin; its History; its Effects.* . . . Madras, The Christ. Vernacular Educ. Soc., 1887.

MURPHY, Gardner: *In the Minds of Men. The Study of Human Behaviour and Social Tensions in India.* New York, Basic Books, 1953.

NADEL, S. F.: 'Caste and Government in Primitive Society' (*Journal of the Anthropological Society of Bombay,* vol. VIII, no. 2, 1954, pp. 9–22).

NATH, Y. V. S.: 'The Bhils of Ratanmal' (*Economic Weekly,* Combay, vol. VI, 4–12, 1954, pp. 1355–60).

NEHRU, Jawaharlal: *Toward Freedom. The Autobiography of Jawaharlal Nehru.* Boston, Beacon Press, 1958.

NESFIELD, John C.: *Brief View of the Caste System of the North-Western Provinces and Oudh, together with an Examination of the Names and Figures shown in the Census Report,* 1882. Allahabad, 1885.

*Notes and Queries on Anthropology.* 6th ed. revised and rewritten by a Committee of the Royal Anthropological Institute of Great Britain and Ireland. London, Routledge and Kegan Paul, 1951.

OLDENBERG, H.: 'Zur Geschichte des Indien Kastenwesens' (*Zeitschrift der Deutschen morgenländischen Gesellschaft,* 51, 1897, pp. 267–90).

OLIVIER, Georges: *L'anthropologie des Tamouls du sud de l'Inde.* Preceded by: Les divisions sociales du sud de l'Inde par Jean Filliozat. Paris, Ecole Française d'Extrême-Orient, 1961. (Publ. hors série de l'Ec. fr. d'Extr.-Or.)

O'MALLEY, L. S. S.: *Indian Caste Customs.* Cambridge Univ. Press, 1932.

—— (ed.): *Modern India and the West. A Story of the Interaction of their Civilizations.* London, Oxford Univ. Press, 1941.

OPLER, Morris E. and SINGH, Rudra D.: 'The Division of Labour in an Indian Village' (C. S. COON (ed.): *A Reader in General Anthropology,* New York, 1948, pp. 464–96).

OPLER, Morris E.: 'The Extensions of an Indian Village' (*Journal of Asian Studies,* vol. XVI, 1957, pp. 5–10).

—— 'The Problem of Selective Culture Change' (B. F. HOSELITZ (ed.): *The Progress of Underdeveloped Areas.* Chicago, Univ. of Chicago Press, 1952, pp. 126–34).

ORANS, Martin: 'A Tribal People in an Industrial Setting' (M. SINGER (ed.): *Traditional India,* 1959, pp. 216–39).

ORENSTEIN, Henry: 'Exploitation and Function in the Interpretation of Jajmani' (*South-western Journal of Anthropology,* vol. XVIII, no. 4, 1962, pp. 302–15).

PARK, Richard L. and TINKER, Irene (ed.): *Leadership and Political Institutions*. Princeton, Univ. Press, 1959.

PARSONS, Talcott: 'A Revised Theoretical Approach to the Theory of Social Stratification' (in Reinhard BENDIX and Seymour Martin LIPSET (eds.): *Class, Status and Power: A Reader in Social Stratification*. London, 1954. In French, F. BOURRICAUD, trans.: *Éléments pour une Sociologie de l'Action*. Paris, Plon, 1955 (Recherches en Sciences Humaines).

—— *The Structure of Social Action. A Study in Social Theory with Special Reference to a Group of Recent European Writers*. New York, The Free Press of Glencoe (1949), 1961.

PARVATHAMMA (Miss): *Religion and Politics in a Mysore Village*. University of Manchester [date?; unpublished thesis].

PATNAIK, Nityananda: 'Service Relationship between Barbers and Villagers in a Small Village in Rampur' (*Economic Weekly*, vol. XII, no. 20, 1960, pp. 737–42).

PATTERSON, Maureen L. P. and INDEN, Ronald B. (ed.): *South Asia: An Introductory Bibliography*. Chicago, The University of Chicago Press, Nov. 1962. (Introduction to the Civilization of India) [Section C: 'Social Structure and Organization', pp. 104–70)].

PIEIRIS, Ralph: *Sinhalese Social Organization. The Kandyan Period*. Ceylon Univ. Press Board, 1956.

PIGNEDE, Bernard: *Les Gurungs. Une population himalayenne du Nepal*. Paris, La Haye, Mouton, 1966 (École Pratique des Hautes Études, VIᵉ section. Le Monde d'Outre-Mer Passé et Présent. 1 ᵉ série: Études).

PITT-RIVERS, Julian: *The People of the Sierra*. London, Weidenfeld & Nicolson, 1954.

—— 'On the word caste' (in T. O. Beidelman, ed., *Essays presented to E. E. Evans-Pritchard*, London, Tavistock Pubs., 1970).

POCOCK, David F.: 'The Anthropology of Time-Reckoning' (*Contributions to Indian Sociology*, VII, 1964, pp. 18–29).

—— '"Difference" in East Africa: a Study of Caste and Religion in Modern Indian Society' (*Southwestern Journal of Anthropology* vol. XIII, no. 4, 1957, pp. 289–300).

—— 'The Hypergamy of the Patidars' (K. M. KAPADIA (ed.): *Ghurye Felicit. Vol.*, pp. 195–204).

—— 'Notes on *Jajmāni* Relationships' (*Contributions to Indian Sociology*, VI, 1962, pp. 78–95).

POHLMAN, Edw. W.: 'Evidence of Disparity between the Hindu Practice of Caste and the Ideal Type' (*American Sociological Review*, XVI, 1951, pp. 37–59).

POLANYI, Karl: *Origins of Our Time: The Great Transformation*. London, 1946.

465

PRASAD, Kali: *Social Integration Research. A Study in Intercaste Relationships.* Lucknow Univ., 1954.

PREMCHAND: *Karmbhūmi.* Banaras, Sarasvati Press, *c.* 1946 (in Hindi).

PUNDALIK, V. G. and PATWARDHAN, Sunanda (Smt.): 'A Note on the Behaviour of the Caste in a Crisis-Situation' (*Sociological Bulletin*, vol. XI, no. 1–2, 1962, pp. 68–72).

RADCLIFFE-BROWN, A. R.: *Structure and Function in Primitive Society.* London, Cohen and West, 1952.

RAO, M. S. A.: *Social Change in Malabar.* Bombay, Popular Book Depot, 1957.

—— 'Caste in Kerala' (*Sociological Bulletin*, vol. IV, no. 2, 1955, pp. 122–9).

REDDY, N. S.: 'Functional Relations of Lohars in a North Indian Village' (*Eastern Anthropologist*, vol. VIII, 1955, pp. 129–40).

RENOU, Louis: *L'Hindouisme. Les textes, les doctrines et l'histoire.* Paris, Pr. Univ. de Fr., 1958 (Que Sais-je, no. 475).

—— et FILLIOZAT, Jean: *L'Inde classique. Manuel des études indiennes.* Vol. I. With the collaboration of P. MEILE, A. M. ESNOUL, L. SILBURN. Paris, Payot, 1947. Vol. II. With the collaboration of P. DEMIÉVILLE, Olivier LACOMBE, P. MEILE. Hanoï, École française d'Extrême-Orient, 1953.

*Report from the Select Committee of House of Commons*, 1832, Evidence, vol. III, Revenue.

*Report of the Seminar on Casteism and Removal of Untouchability, Delhi September 26–October 2, 1955.* Bombay, Indian Conference of Social Work, 1955.

*Report of the Study Team on Nyaya Panchayat, April 1962. Government of India, Ministry of Law.* Delhi, Manager of Publications, 1962.

RHYS DAVIDS, T. W.: 'Ahiṃsā' (*Encyclopaedia of Religion and Ethics*, *s.v.*, vol. I, p. 231).

RISLEY, Herbert H.: *Census of India 1901*, vol. I: India, Report I, Report II, Ethnographic Appendices. Calcutta, Govt. Printing, 1903. 2 vols.

—— *The People of India.* London, W. Thacker, 1908.

—— *The Tribes and Castes of Bengal. Ethnographical Glossary.* Calcutta, Bengal Secretariat Press, 1891. 2 vols.

RIVERS, W. H. R.: 'The Origin of Hypergamy' (*Journal of the Bihar and Orissa Research Society*, Patna, vol. VIII, 1921, pp. 9–24).

RONALDSHAY (Earl of): *India, a Bird's-Eye View.* London, 1924.

ROSE, H. A.: 'Caste' (*Encyclopaedia Britannica*, 1945 edition, vol. IV, *s.v.*, pp. 976–86).

ROUSSEAU, Jean-Jacques: *Du Contrat social. Œuvres complètes*, vol. III. Paris, Gallimard, 1964 (Bibliothèque de La Pléiade). English translation by G. D. H. COLE: *The Social Contract.* London, 1913.

ROY, Sarat Chandra: 'Caste, Race and Religion in India' (*Man In India*, vol. XIV, 1934, Parts I–III; vol. XVII, 1937 et XVIII, 1938 Part IV).

RUDOLPH, Lloyd I. and RUDOLPH, Susanne Hoeber: 'The Political Role of India's Caste Associations' (*Pacific Affairs*, vol. XXXIII, no. 1, 1960, pp. 5–22).

RYAN, Brice: *Caste in Modern Ceylon*. New Brunswick, Rutgers Univ. Press, 1953.

SANGAVE, Vilas Adinath: *Jaina Community, a Social Survey*. Bombay, Popular Book Depot, 1959.

—— 'Changing Pattern of Caste Organization in Kolhapur City' (*Sociological Bulletin*, vol. XI, 1962, pp. 36–61).

SARDESAI, Govind Sakharam: *New History of the Marathas*. Bombay, Phoenix Publications, 1946–48. 3 vols.

SASTRI, K. A. Nilakanta: The *Cōlas*. Madras, Univ. of Madras (1935–37, 2 vols.), 1955 (Madras Univ. Hist. Series, no. 9).

—— *Studies in Cōla History and Administration*. Madras, Univ. of Madras, 1932 (Madras Univ. Hist. Series, no. 7).

SENART, Émile: *Les Castes dans l'Inde. Les faits et le système*. Paris, E. Leroux, 1894.

SHAH, A. M.: 'Caste, Economy and Territory in the Central Panchmahals' (*Journal of the M.S. University of Baroda*, vol. IV, no. 1, 1955, pp. 65–95).

—— 'Political System in Eighteenth Century Gujarat' (*Enquiry*, Delhi, vol. I, no. 1, 1964, pp. 83–95).

SHAH, B. V.: *Social Change and College Students of Gujarat*. Baroda, M.S. University, 1964.

SHAHANI, S. See: M. N. SRINIVAS et al., *Caste*.

SHARMA, R. S.: *Śūdras in Ancient India. A Survey of the Position of the Lower Orders down to circa A.D. 500*. Delhi, Motilal Banarsidass, 1958.

SHELVANKAR, K. S.: *The Problem of India*. London, Penguin Books, 1940.

SHILS, Edward: *The Intellectual between Tradition and Modernity: the Indian Situation*. The Hague, Mouton, 1961 (Comparative Studies in Society and History. Supplement, I).

SHORE, Frederick John: *Notes on Indian Affairs*. London, 1837. 2 vols.

SINGER, Milton (ed.): *Traditional India: Structure and Change*. Philadelphia, Am. Folk. Soc., 1939 (Bibliogr. a. Special Series, vol. X).

SINGH, Indera: 'A Sikh Village' (M. SINGER (ed.): *Traditional India*, 1959, pp. 273–97).

SINHA, Surajit: 'State Formation and Rajput Myth in Tribal Central India' (*Man In India*, vol. XLII, no. 1, 1962, pp. 35–80).

SMITH, Marian W.: 'Structured and Unstructured Class Societies' (*American Anthropologist*, vol. LV, no. 2, 1953, pp. 302–5).

SPEAR, Percival: *Twilight of the Mughuls. Studies in the Late Mughul Delhi*. Cambridge Univ. Press, 1951.

SRINIVAS, M. N. (ed.): *India's Villages*. London, Asia Publ. House, (1955), 1960.

SRINIVAS, M. N.: *Caste in Modern India and Other Essays*. Bombay, Asia Publ. House, *c.* 1962.

—— *Religion and Society among the Coorgs of South India*. Oxford, Clarendon Press, 1952.

—— *The Study of Disputes*. University of Delhi, s.d. (Roneo).

—— 'The Case of the Potter and the Priest' (*Man In India*, vol. XXXIX, No. 3, 1959, pp. 190–209).

—— 'A Caste Dispute among Washermen of Mysore' (*Eastern Anthropologist*, vol. VII, no. 3–4, 1954, pp. 149–68).

—— 'Caste in Modern India' (*Journal of Asian Studies*, vol. XVI, no. 4, 1957, pp. 529–48) [et] (*Caste in Mod. India*, pp. 15–41).

—— 'The Dominant Caste in Pampura' (*American Anthropologist*, vol. LXI, 1959, pp. 1–16).

—— 'Introduction' (*India's Villages*, 1955, pp. 1–12) [originally: *Economic Weekly*, vol. VI, 1954, pp. 695–8].

—— 'A Joint Family Dispute in a Mysore Village' (*Journal of the M.S. University of Baroda*, vol. I, 1952, pp. 7–31).

—— 'Sanskritization and Westernization' [AIYAPPAN and BALA RATNAM (ed.): *Society in India*, Madras, 1955, pp. 73–115] (*Far Eastern Quarterly*, vol. XIV, no. 4, 1956, pp. 481–96), [repr.] (*Caste in Mod. India*, pp. 42–62).

—— 'The Social Structure of a Mysore Village' (*India's Villages*, 1955, pp. 19–32), [originally: *Economic Weekly*, vol. III, 1953, pp. 1051–6].

—— 'The Social System of a Mysore Village' (McKim MARRIOTT (ed.): *Village India*, 1955, pp. 1–36).

—— 'Varna and Caste' (*A. R. Wadia: Essays in Philosophy presented in His Honour*, Bangalore, 1954), [repr. in] (*Caste in Modern India*, pp. 63–9).

—— DAMLE, Y. B., SHAHANI, S. and BÉTEILLE, André: *Caste, A Trend Report and Bibliography*. Oxford, Blackwell, 1959 (*Current Sociology*, vol. VIII, no. 3, 1959).

SRIVASTAVA, S. K.: 'The Process of Desanskritization in Village India' (BALA RATNAM (ed.): *Anthropology on the March*, 1963, pp. 263–7).

STAAL, J. F.: 'Sanskrit and Sanskritization' (*Journal of Asian Studies*, vol. XXII, no. 3, 1963, pp. 261–75).

—— 'Über die Idee der Toleranz im Hinduismus' (*Kairos*, Salzburg, 4, 1959, pp. 215–18).

STARK, Werner: *The Sociology of Knowledge. An Essay in Aid of a*

*Deeper Understanding of the History of Ideas.* London, Routledge and Kegan Paul, 1958.

STEVENSON, H. N. C.: 'Caste' (*Encyclopaedia Britannica*, 1961, vol. IV, pp. 973–82).

—— 'Status Evaluation in the Hindu Caste System' (*Journal of the Royal Anthropological Institute*, vol. LXXXIV, no. 1–2, 1954, pp. 45–65).

STOKES, Eric: *The English Utilitarians and India.* Oxford, Clarendon Press, 1959.

STRIZOWER, Schifra: 'Jews as an Indian Caste' (*Jewish Journal of Sociology*, 1959, pp. 43–57).

SUAU, Pierre, s.j.: *L'Inde tamoule.* Paris, 1907.

TAMBIAH, H. W.: *The Laws and Customs of the Tamils of Ceylon.* Colombo, Tamil Cult. Soc. of Ceylon, 1954.

TAMBIAH, S. J.: 'The Structure of Kinship and its Relationship to Land Possession and Residence in Pata Dumbara, Central Ceylon' (*Journal of the Royal Anthropological Institute*, vol. LXXXVIII, Part I, 1958, pp. 21–44).

THAKKAR, K. K.: 'The Problem of Casteism and Untouchability' (*Indian Journal of Social Work*, Bombay, vol. XVII, no. 2, 1956, pp. 44–84).

THOMPSON, Edward: *Suttee. A Historical and Philosophical Enquiry into the Hindu Rite of Widow-burning.* London, Allen and Unwin, 1928.

THORNER, Daniel: 'Marx on India and the Asiatic Mode of Production' (*Contributions to Indian Sociology*, IX, 1966, pp. 33–66).

—— 'The Village Panchayat as a Vehicle of Change' (*Economic Development and Cultural Change*, vol. II, 1953, pp. 209–15).

THORNER, D. and A.: 'Employer–Labourer Relationships in Agriculture' (*Land and Labour in India.* Bombay, etc., Asia Publ. House, c. 1962, pp. 21–38 [from *Indian Journal of Agric. Economics*, vol. XII, 2, 1957, pp. 84–96]).

THURSTON, E. and RANGACHARI, K.: *Castes and Tribes of Southern India.* Madras, 1909. 7 vols.

TINKER, Hugh: *The Foundations of Local Self-Government in India, Pakistan and Burma.* London, The Athlone Press, 1954. (University of London Historical Studies, no. 1.)

TOCQUEVILLE, Alexis de: *L'Ancien Régime et la Révolution.* Paris, Gallimard, 1952–53. 2 vols. (*Œuvres complètes*, vol. II.) English translation by M. W. PATTERSON: *De Tocqueville's L'Ancien Régime.* Oxford, 1933.

—— *La Démocratie en Amérique.* Paris, Gallimard, 1961. 2 vols. (*Œuvres complètes*, t. I.) English translation by Henry REEVE: *Democracy in America.* London, 1875.

TOD, James: *Annals and Antiquities of Rajasthan, or the Central and Western Rajpoot States of India* (1829–32, 2 vols.). London, Routledge and Kegan Paul, 1950.

TROUBETSKOI, Nicolas Serguevitch: *Principes de phonologie*. French translation by Jean CANTINEAU. Paris, C. Klincksieck, 1949.

TURNER, Roy (ed.): *India's Urban Future. Selected Studies from an International Conference.* . . . Berkeley and Los Angeles, Univ. of California Press, 1962.

ULLAH, Inayat: 'Caste, Patti and Factions in the Life of a Punjab Village' (*Sociologus*, vol. VIII, no. 2, 1953, pp. 170–86).

VAKIL, C. N. and CABINETMAKER, P. H.: *Government and the Displaced Persons: a Study in Social Tensions*. Bombay, 1956.

VAKIL, C. N. and MEHTA, U.: *Government and the Governed: a Study in Social Tensions*. Bombay, Vora and Co., 1956.

VIDYARTHI, L. P.: 'The Extensions of an Indian Priestly Class' (*Man In India*, vol. XXXIX, no. 1, 1959, pp. 28–35).

*Village India*. See: MARRIOTT (ed.).

VREEDE-DE-STUERS, Cora: 'Le Mariage chez les Musulmans de condition "Ashraf" dans l'Inde du Nord. Coutumes et cérémonies (*Orient*, vol. 25, 37 pp.).

WEBER, Max: *The Protestant Ethic and the Spirit of Capitalism*. London, 1930 (translated from the German: *Gesammelte Aufsätze zur Religionssoziologie*, Band I).

—— *Gesammelte Aufsätze zur Religionssoziologie*, II. *Hinduismus und Buddhismus*, Tübingen, Mohr, 1920. English translation by Hans H. GERTH and Don MARTINDALE: *The Religion of India. The Sociology of Hinduism and Buddhism*, Glencoe, 1958.

—— *The theory of Social and Economic Organisation*, trans. HENDERSON and Talcott PARSONS. Glencoe, Illinois, s.d. [translated from *Wirtschaft und Gesellschaft*, 1st part].

WEIL, Eric: *Philosophie Politique*. Paris, Vrin, 1956.

WEINER, Myron: 'Changing Patterns of Leadership in West Bengal' (*Pacific Affairs*, vol. XXXII, no. 3, 1959, pp. 277–87).

WHITEHEAD, Henry: *The Village Gods of South India* (London, 1916). Calcutta, Association Press, 1921 (The Religious Life of India Series).

WILLIAMS, J. Charles: *Oudh* [Census of 1869]. Vol. I, *Report*. Lucknow, 1869.

WILSON, John: *Indian Caste*. Bombay; London, 1877. 2 vols.

WILSON, Robert Smith: *The Indirect Effects of Christian Missions.* . . . London, 1928.

WISER, William Henricks: *The Hindu Jajmani System: a Socio-Economic System Interrelating Members of a Hindu Village Community in Services*. Lucknow, Lucknow Publ. House, 1958 (1st ed., 1936).

YALMAN, Nur: 'The Flexibility of Caste Principles in a Kandyan

Community' (E. R. LEACH (ed.): *Aspects of Caste*, 1960, pp. 78–112).
—— 'On the Purity of Women in the Castes of Ceylon and Malabar'
(*Journal of the Royal Anthropological Institute of Great Britain and
Ireland*, vol. XCIII, Part I, Jan. to June 1963, pp. 25–58).
YULE, H. and BURNELL, A. C.: *Hobson-Jobson. A Glossary of Colloquial
Anglo-Indian Words and Phrases*. London (1886), 1903.

# INDEX

Aberle, K. Gough, *see* Gough, E. K.
*ābhira*, 94
accountants, 102
accretion, 280 *see also* aggregation
actors, 94
adultery, 113
  penalties, 110, 296
Africa
  castes in, 330
Agarwals
  caste segmentation, 121–2
  food rules, 304
aggregation, 193–6
agriculture
  changes in, 217–18
  labour force, 100
  and non-agricultural castes, 96
  and subcastes, 94, 197–8
*ahimsā*, 147, 148–51, 306
  and transmigration, 307
  and vegetarianism, 149
*Ahir*, 94
Ahmedabad, 176
Aiyappan, A., 323, 326, 335
alcohol, 141
Alexandrovicz, A., 338
Alsdorf, L., 147, 148, 149, 150, 305, 306, 307
Ambedkar, 223
America, *see* United States
Amman, Monsignor, 327, 328
*Ancien Régime and the Revolution, The*, 13, 15, 16
Andhra Pradesh, 81
Anglo-Indians
  status, 326
Ansari, Ghaus, 328
Anstey, Vera, 170
anti-clericalism, and the caste system, 23
*anuloma* marriages, 126–7, 301
Apthorpe, Raymond, xii, 287
Aristotle, xxix, 337
aristocratic societies, Tocqueville on, 18

Aron, Raymond, 239, 250, 341
*artha*, 49, 165, 273, 314
  definition, 251
  and *dharma*, 196
Arthashastra, 150
artisans, 288, 290
  *see also* professional castes; specialized castes
Arya Samaj, 230, 324, 339
*āśauca*, 49
Ashoka, Emperor, 149
Ashraf, 207–8
authority, and power, 167–8
Ayyar, L. K. Anantakrishna, 327

Babeuf, F. N., 13
Baden-Powell, B. H., 310, 311
Bailey, F. G., 181, 182, 225, 227, 228, 271, 272, 273, 287, 303, 310, 317, 318, 320, 330, 332, 335, 337, 339, 341
Baines, A., 312
Bales R. F., 301
Ballal Sen, 123
*Baniyā*, 94
  *see also* Vaishya
*banjiga*, 189
banquets,
  food rules, 139, 145
  mourning, 305
  and panchayat meetings, 174
Barber, Bernard, 342
barbers, 55, 79, 85, 93, 96, 110, 143
  boycott by, 176
  caste panchayats, 218
  caste variation, 34
  on contractual terms, 294
  functions and fees, 292–3
  as funeral priests, 48, 49, 289–90
  and impurity, 302
  in *jajmāni* system, 110
  locality and rank, 57–8
Barhais (carpenters), 143
Barth, Frederik, 208, 272, 294, 329
Basavi, 98

473

*see also* Sanskritization
implements and weapons, worship of, 290
impurity
 duration of, 70–1, 279
 bathing as remedy, 48
 family, 50
 and food, 139–40
 and Lingayats, 322
 and non-Brahman movement, 221
 personal and caste, 132
 professional, 48–9, 55, 290–1
 social rather than innate, 90
 temporary and permanent, 46–7, 48–9
 weakening, 333
 *see also* pure and impure; pollution
*Indian Caste Customs*, 58
individualism, 4–8
 Tocqueville on, 17–18
individual, society and the, 4–10
inequality, 12
inequality of combination, 12
Indo-European theory of caste, 27–8
infant marriage, 110
infanticide, 118
inheritance
 and hypergamy, 124
 inter-varna marriages, 128
interaction between castes, 289
interdependence, 30
 *jajmāni* system, 103
intermarriage
 and colour question, 245
 as determinant of group status, 123
 students' views on, 223
Iravas, 309, 326
Irving, B. A., 269, 286
isogamy, 116–18
 *see also* primary marriage

Jackson, A. M. T., 154, 308
Jacobi, H. G., 150
Jainism, 56, 58–9, 147, 150, 166, 187, 194, 279, 307
 and *ahimsā*, 149
*jajmāni* system, 36, 92, 99–108, 152–3
 definition, 98
 division of labour, 98–9
 not egalitarian, 102
 misinterpretations, 103
 religious in nature, 106, 107
 relationships under, 99–101
*jangama see* priests; Lingayat
Japan, castes, 215, 240
*Jātaka*, 52, 53
jāti *see* caste
Jats, 136
 panchayats, 175, 182, 318
 villages, 159, 160, 163

Jesuits
 attitude to caste, 25
 missions, 327
jewellery, 331–2
Jews, 242, 328
Johnson, Charles S., 342
Jolly, J., 296, 307
jugglers, 94
jurisdiction, panchayats, 175–7
justice
 classical arrangements for, 167–8
 Marathas, 314
 role of the king, 314
 in territorially segregated castes, 320
 traditional and official, 182
Justice Party, 221

*Kaccā*-food, 84, 85, 86, 88, 142, 304–5
 acceptance of, 133, 143
Kahars (water bearers), 95, 133, 143
Kaibarta, 93
*kalivarjya*, 195
Kallars, 181, 320
Kanaujiya Brahmans, 300
Kane, P. V., 48, 50, 68, 283–4, 296, 297, 301, 304, 305, 306, 307, 315
Kangu country, 288
Kapadia, K. M., 223, 282, 301, 334, 338
Kardiner, A., 282
Karim, Nazmul, 329, 331
Karimpur, *jajmāni* system in, 99–102
Karvé, I., 32, 62, 121, 155, 199, 228, 271, 280, 298, 300, 311, 323, 325
Kashmir, caste government, 169
Kayasthas, food rules, 144–5
Kayré, A., 264, 265
Kerala, 80, 156
 caste ranking, 286
 caste system, 287
 caste unification, 309
 Christians in, 203, 326
 gradations of distance, 134, 136
 *see also* Malabar
Ketkar, Shridhar V., 63, 79, 132, 277, 280, 283, 287, 302, 315, 341
*Khaṭik*, 95
Khattris, 300
kings
 authority over castes, 168–70, 315
 and caste system, 215
 judicial authority, 168, 314
 purity, 51
 religious functions, 284
 status, 77
 traditional role, 157
 *see also* Kshatriyas; Rajputs
kin groupings, used to explain caste, 28